# PUBLIC POLICY
## IN THE
# UNITED STATES

### 3rd Edition

## At the Dawn of the
## Twenty-First Century

# Mark E. Rushefsky

*M.E. Sharpe*
Armonk, New York
London, England

**Library of Congress Cataloging-in-Publication Data**

Rushefsky, Mark E., 1945-
    Public policy in the United States : at the dawn of the twenty-first century / by Mark E.
Rushefsky.—3rd ed.
       p. cm.
    Includes bibliographical references and index.
    ISBN 0-7656-0859-6 (cloth: alk. paper) — ISBN 0-7656-0647-X (pbk.: alk. paper)
       1. Political planning—United States. 2. United States—Politics and government. 3. United
States—Economic policy. 4. United States—Social policy. 5. Policy sciences. I.
Title.

JK468.P64 R87 2002                                2001042661
320′.6′0973—dc21                                   CIP

# PUBLIC POLICY
## IN THE
# UNITED STATES

### 3rd Edition

To the men and women of the New York City police and fire departments, to all of the other rescue workers who risked their lives, and to the victims who died in New York, Washington, DC, and Pennsylvania, during the terrorist attacks of September 11, 2001

# Contents

# List of Tables

# List of Figures

# Preface

I first taught a public policy survey course entitled "Issues in American Politics" at the University of Florida in the summer of 1978. Since that time, I have continued to teach this type of course, and of all the courses I have taught, both graduate and undergraduate, this one is my favorite. Like many who consider writing a textbook, I felt that the available texts were missing something and that I had something to say: *Public Policy in the United States: At the Dawn of the Twenty-First Century* is the result.

## About the Third Edition

*Public Policy in the United States* has been considerably revised for the third edition. All of the material has been updated and in some cases completely rewritten. All of the case studies are new. All of the chapters examine Clinton administration public policy and consider the impact of the 2000 elections: a new, more conservative president combined with Republican control of the presidency and Congress for the first time in four decades (though the Senate became Democratically controlled after Vermont Senator James Jefford's defection from the Republican party).

Many important elements are incorporated into the presentation of the material in this text. First, it presents to the student a set of ideas, or concepts, about how public policy is made and why it takes the form it does. Chapter 1 covers the policy process, certain features of the American political system that affect the making of public policy, and the role of ideology in structuring policy debates. The policy process is then used as an organizing framework for the eight substantive chapters. This format is intended to provide a consistency to the text that seemed to be lacking in other textbooks. Some new material is included in this chapter. Social constructionism, where interpretations of problems and targets of public policy are crucial, is discussed in the section on problem identification. There is a new section on public opinion, the media, and trust. Communitarianism is added to the discussion of ideology. Although some areas (such as transportation and agriculture) are not covered here, a student reading this book should be able to apply the concepts to those policy areas as well.

Second, this text shows the consistency of ideas among different policy areas by exploring ideology as it relates to the early stages of the policy process. The conservative position in one policy area is similar to the conservative position in another policy area; the same is true for liberal policy positions. The similarities are illustrated in examination of policies concerning poverty, education, health care, and the environment. Furthermore, ideology is presented in a way that explains differences among various viewpoints. The emphasis in *Public Policy in the United States* is on the values (order, freedom, and equality) that underlie ideologies.

Another point presented in this book is that there are only a small number of ends or goals that the public sector seeks to achieve and a small number of policy tools with which to achieve them. Deborah Stone's *Policy Paradox* (1997) is an excellent statement of this argument, and the reader is referred to that delightful and insightful book. Many of her ideas have been adapted here.

There is also a demonstration of the interrelationships of public policy issues. Economic problems affect the ability to seek policy solutions, but the links go beyond this. For example, there appears to be a connection between some aspects of homelessness, drug abuse, and AIDS. Attacking each problem separately invites failure, yet our political system has difficulty in responding comprehensively because of fragmentation and incrementalism.

Finally, *Public Policy in the United States* looks both backward and forward. There is a fair amount of policy history in the substantive chapters. I have always felt that we can best understand where we are as a nation, as well as where we are going, only if we understand how we got there. The patterns of the past project into the future. The subtitle of the text, *At the Dawn of the Twenty-First Century*, underscores the book's future orientation.

It is always hazardous to predict the future, especially in a book with a long production schedule. Events may make predictions outdated and ridiculous. As of the writing of this preface (April 2001), the U.S. economy has experienced a record period of economic expansion. But there are signs everywhere of a slowdown and, possibly, a recession. We may enter a recession; then again, we may not. I dare not tread where economists have sometimes gone astray. Whatever direction the economy takes, it will affect public policy in different areas: the future of Social Security, welfare reform, health care, and so forth.

There is also a new administration in power, that of George W. Bush. The early indications are of changes in many policy areas, including foreign and defense policy, education, health care, Social Security, and the environment. But the defection of U.S. Senator Jeffords may have tipped the delicate balance to the Democrats. The 2002 off-year elections could return one or both houses of Congress to Democratic control. But maybe that will not happen.

The first and second edition were influenced by the large and seemingly endless federal budget deficits. Such deficits constrained policy initiatives and expansions. But the deficits turned into surpluses and predictions of continued surpluses. Who could have foreseen that development in 1990, when the first edition of *Public Policy in the United States* was published, or in 1996 when the second edition was published? The twists and turns of developments like this make policy predictions an entertaining exercise.

One other note about this third edition: There is a tone of optimism about the book. I do not argue that everything that government has done has gone perfectly as planned. But government programs emerging from public policy have worked much better than most give them credit for. Improvements can certainly be made, but cynicism and skepticism are overreactions.

***

Sadly, the events of September 11, 2001, when the United States experienced the most serious terrorist attack in its history, also will affect American public policy. As the nation mourns and recovers and rebuilds, the Bush administration promises a war against terrorists (and this war, the president has declared, will be the defining feature of his administration). The economy will be strongly affected, and the country will never be the same. Many of the pressing issues discussed in this text, such as Social Security, the war on drugs, and so forth, have been temporarily pushed aside. The text still discusses them because they remain important. But the attack on the United States means that the loss of a sense of innocence can never be recovered.

Like everyone else, I was stunned by the attack and glued to any available television. On the morning of the attack, I held my public policy class at 9:30 A.M., shortly after it occurred. I could see the sorrow and agony in my students' eyes. We talked about the attack for a few minutes, before we knew the full effects, and then I dismissed the class. Like those who experienced the assassination of President Kennedy in 1963 or the Challenger tragedy in 1986, these students—indeed the whole country—will always remember where they were when they heard about the attacks.

# Acknowledgments

For instructors who have been using this book since it first appeared, there may appear to be a sense of wandering regarding publishers. Without providing the details of the book's odyssey, it has now found a home with M.E. Sharpe. I have coauthored two books with them and found Patricia Kolb, the editor, and her staff to be fully professional and a delight to work with. She has been supportive of this project (as well as the others, including future ones), and I thank her for that. Her staff—including Elizabeth Granda, Irina Belenky, Esther Clark, and Susan Rescigno—have been wonderful to work with.

Over the years, my students have assisted by pointing out what works and what does not work. Thanks also go to my colleagues at universities and colleges who have used the book over the years. Please keep using it and tell all your friends about it!

My thanks also go to the Faculty Leave Committee of Southwest Missouri State University. They awarded me a sabbatical for the fall 2000 semester. That time enabled me to complete this project faster than would otherwise have been possible.

My children are grown and have moved out of the house. Our home would seem empty without them, but for the two dogs, three cats, and a ferret that fill up the available space. The one constant has been my wife, Cynthia. We have been married for over thirty-two years now, and I am thankful for the life we have together. It's nice to have someone your own age to play with.

Mark E. Rushefsky

# PUBLIC POLICY
## IN THE
# UNITED STATES

### 3rd Edition

# 1 Process, Structure, and Ideology

*Our primary thesis is that the American political system, built as it is on a conservative constitutional base designed to limit radical action, is nevertheless continually swept by policy change, change that alternates between incremental drift and rapid alterations of existing arrangements.*
(Baumgartner and Jones 1993, p. 236)

*Politics is how society manages conflicts about values and interests.*
(Brown 1994, p. 175)

Those who have studied public opinion in the United States have come to two important conclusions. First, the public does not know much about government, politics, and public policy. For example, as we shall see in chapter 8, vouchers are one of the most important issues in the educational policy area. Yet according to a report by Public Agenda, very few of the public know anything about vouchers or have heard about them (Public Agenda 1999).

Second, attitudes toward government have deteriorated. Trust in the ability of government, especially at the federal level, to do what is right and what the public wants has declined dramatically since the 1960s (Craig 1993). The title of a book by *Newsweek* and *Washington Post* economics columnist Robert Samuelson (1995), *The Good Life and Its Discontents*, captures the feeling about government. Susan Tolchin (1996), a professor of public administration at George Washington University, wrote about *The Angry American*.

Both of these ideas are important. If the public is ignorant about whether government programs work or even the nature of those programs, it is likely to remain skeptical that anything government does will have a positive effect. Cynicism seems to run rampant. Yet there is much information available about government and public policy. The advent of the Internet has opened up the possibility of discovering more about our society and our government.

To be informed takes time and effort, however, with little apparent reward. Generally, we tend to become concerned only when government personally affects us. If American lives are needlessly lost or the economy is not performing well (the peace and prosperity issues), then we mobilize. Without these and other direct impacts, we go about our own lives. Because the actions that government takes may have important effects on our lives, this text is designed to help explain and evaluate what government does.

**Public policy** is a course of action made up of a series of *decisions*, discrete choices (including the choice not to act), over a period of time. According to David Easton (1965), **politics** involves the "authoritative allocation of values." Lawrence Brown (1994), in the second quote opening this chapter, writes that politics has to do with resolving conflicts over interests and values. Both definitions say basically the same thing. Values are issues that are important to us, and they include money, property, life, and health, and more abstract values such as freedom. **Government** is the set of institutions that make these allocations, that resolve these conflicts. The focus of this text is on what decisions government makes and why (and, to a lesser extent, how), and what the results of those decisions are.

**Inputs** to a political system consist of two types, supports and demands (Easton 1965). **Supports** include the overall support for a political system (its legitimacy), support for its leaders, and the acceptance of specific policies. The actions of political leaders and the outputs and outcomes of the political system feed these supports: Consider the support for President Clinton as a result of the Monica Lewinsky affair and the president's subsequent impeachment, or the loss of support for House Speaker Newt Gingrich (Rep.-GA) after the 1998 elections. The decline in trust, briefly mentioned above, suggests less support, less legitimacy, for the political system (Wills 1999). **Demands** are requests for action on the part of the political system and feed directly into the policy process. Both demands and supports can be seen in public opinion polls (supporting or opposing policies or presidential action) and in the behavior of interest groups.

Two types of policy results can be distinguished: outputs and outcomes (Sharkansky 1970). **Outputs** are the tangible and symbolic results of government decisions. Tax changes are an example of a tangible product; a presidential speech is a symbolic output.[1] The president says something (a policy statement), but government policy may not necessarily change. **Outcomes** are the results of government outputs. If the tax laws are changed, the results of those changes can be evaluated. Are more people satisfied with the new tax system than with the older one? What effect does the tax change have on the level of spending, investment, and savings? What is the result of a presidential speech? Does it satisfy the demands of certain groups? Does the policy have unexpected or unintended repercussions?

Figure 1.1 **The Policy Process**

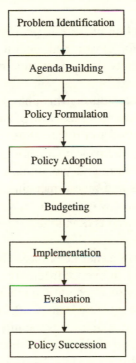

Source: Adapted from Jones (1984).

Policies change can be contradictory (Stone 1997). For example, one portion of the federal government (Department of Agriculture) provides price supports for tobacco farmers. At the same time, another part of the federal government (U.S. Surgeon General) requires warnings that use of tobacco products may result in adverse health consequences. The two policies seem to work at cross-purposes. This frequently occurs in policy making and is due to the different policy dynamics of agencies, legislative committees, programs, goals, and interest groups. Public policy in the United States is rarely cohesive. The reasons for this are the twists and turns of the policy process and the characteristics of the American political system.

## The Policy Process

Public policy is the product of a number of steps or phases (Fig. 1.1). The course of public policy is a tortuous one; policies may be changed at any step or may fail to pass through a step.

To help explain policy making, the process will be presented in a linear fashion, that is, as if a policy starts at the first step and emerges from the last. The reality is much more complex, and some of these complexities are described at the end of this section.[2]

## Problem Identification

The first stage of the policy process is **problem identification**.[3] This stage begins with a demand for government action to resolve a problem or take advantage of an opportunity: it is an attempt to get government to see that a problem or opportunity exists.

Two important processes during this phase are perception and definition. **Perception** is the "registering or receiving of an event" that has consequences for people or groups. **Definition** is the interpretation of those events, giving meaning to them, making them clear (Jones 1984, p. 52). But problems do not define themselves (Lindblom and Woodhouse 1993). Someone has to point out that a problem exists and give it meaning. Different people will register the same events in different ways and give them different definitions, so it is important to understand who is doing the perceiving and how that perception is defined.

The definition/perception that goes on in this stage has another vital aspect. Not only do we look at events differently, but we look at those affected by public policies differently depending on their status and resources. This is one of the key insights of a policy framework known as **social constructionism**. Under social constructionism, it is the *interpretation* of events, policies, and people that we need to understand (Schneider and Ingram 1997, especially chapters 5 and 6; Rochefort and Cobb 1994; Stone 1997). Consider two separate groups affected by social constructionism. In the case of welfare reform, welfare recipients are a very important group of people greatly affected by the changed policy. However, they are poorly organized, have few resources, and do not have high status. Welfare reform was thus punitive in nature (though that is not the only rationale for the change; see chapter 4). Physicians have been greatly affected by the change to managed care. But they are relatively well organized and have a very high status and many resources. While they have lost much of their power and autonomy (see chapter 5), physicians and physician groups have acted to reverse some of the controls placed on them by managed care organizations, with much of that activity applauded by the public (e.g., the patients' bill of rights). A study of the response to acquired immunity deficiency syndrome (AIDS) in the U.S. Senate substantiated much of Schneider and Ingram's theory. Advantaged groups, such as veterans who had contracted AIDS, were treated much differently than deviant groups, such as intravenous drug users. The former group was given benefits or, at most, only symbolic burdens; the latter had burdens imposed upon them (Schroedel and Jordan 1998).

Knowing who does the perceiving and defining offers some understanding of differences in policy proposals. It is also helpful to know what shapes these different perceptions and definitions. Such shaping factors can include the mass media, particularly television;[4] critical life experiences, such as wars and economic hardship (compare the effects of the depression on the generation that came of age in the 1930s with the effects of the economic turmoil of the 1970s on that generation); the process of socialization; values grounded in religious beliefs; and values grounded in ideology. Perhaps more important than these shaping factors is the critical role that the different definitions of policy problems take in structuring the rest of the policy process. Different definitions have different policy implications.

Consider the issue of poverty. There are a number of explanations that can be offered for why poverty exists in the United States. The traditional view is that poverty is the result of moral defects in the individual; the person is too lazy to work. Some have argued that the welfare system has encouraged poverty because it is so much more generous than the low-income jobs available (Murray 1984). Discrimination, lack of job skills, and poor education constitute other possibilities. The breakdown of the traditional two-parent family results in increasing numbers of poor families headed by women, often called the "feminization of poverty." A Marxist might say that poverty is perpetuated by the capitalist system because it provides a "reserve army of the unemployed," which discourages those who do have jobs from upsetting the status quo by strikes or slowdowns.

Thus one problem or issue, poverty, has many definitions or explanations. Each explanation has associated with it a specific policy solution. If poverty is due to moral defects in the individual, then the appropriate policy response might be to do nothing. If the welfare system is viewed as encouraging poverty, then welfare reform of some sort might be justified. If discrimination is the problem, then equal opportunity and affirmative action programs might be useful. If the problem is lack of job skills, then a job-training program should be undertaken. Similar measures could be started to improve educational opportunity. If "feminization of poverty" is the problem, then appropriate policies might focus on child support. If the Marxist explanation is correct, then a replacement of capitalism with socialism should be encouraged. Whoever can define and frame the discussion of an issue will generally prevail in policy disputes.

The fact that problem perception and definition are absolutely vital in understanding American public policy is a dominant theme of this book. Problem definitions can be categorized by ideology, and in each policy area the text examines how issues and problems are identified. As this exploration is conducted, problem definitions tend to fall into a few categories (Stone 1997).

Some problem definitions involve **narratives** that relate stories of decline or loss of control and helplessness (see chapter 8 on education). Other problem definitions rely on **numbers** or statistics to make the case for public action; chapter 4 on poverty is a good example of this.

Still other problem definitions are based on understanding the underlying **causes** of a problem; the chapter on poverty could be included here, as well as discussions on the environment (chapter 6) and crime (chapter 7). Of course, many problems use all three types of explanations.

Figure 1.2    **Agenda Building**

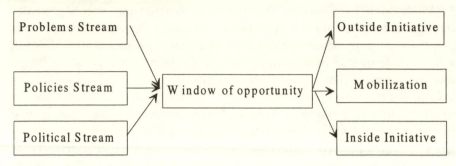

*Source:* Adapted from Kingdon (1984) and Cobb, Keith-Ross, and Ross (1976).

## Agenda Building

The second stage of the policy process is **agenda building**. What is agenda building? We have some idea of what an agenda is. If we go to a meeting, say of a city council or a congressional committee, the agenda is a list of items to be discussed at that meeting. In a similar vein, a policy agenda consists of those items that policy makers are discussing and seriously considering. Not all problems are seriously discussed or considered, so we are interested in understanding how items make it to the government's agenda.

Issues become part of the agenda through the conjunction of three sets of streams (Kingdon 1984; Zahariadis 1999) (Figure 1.2). First, there is the **problems stream**, the problem identification stage discussed previously. Second is the **policies stream**. This stream consists of both a community of policy specialists (such as bureaucrats in evaluation and planning offices, legislative staffers, academics, experts in interest groups) and the proposals this community generates. The third process stream is the **political stream**. It is composed of swings in national mood, changes in public opinion, election results, changes of administration, shifts in partisan or ideological distributions in Congress, and interest-group pressure campaigns. These three streams are largely separate from one another, having different forces, considerations, and styles. The key to agenda and policy change is the coupling of the streams at critical points, or **windows of opportunity**. At these points, profound changes in the governmental agenda may occur (Baumgartner and Jones 1993; True 2000).[5] The following mini case study of health care reform in the 1990s illustrates the importance of these windows of opportunity as well as the workings of each of the three streams.

The problems stream included several of the factors. First there was the problem of ever-increasing health care costs. These costs impacted different sectors of the economy, but especially business and government. Medicare (the federal health care program for the elderly and disabled) and Medicaid (the federal/state health care program for the poor) were taking increasing shares of federal and state (in the case of Medicaid) budgets. Business was facing increasing premiums for their workers. The response of the business sector included trying to shift more of the costs to employees and self-insurance (thus giving business more control over health-care costs). A number of companies initiated *managed care* programs to reduce the use of health resources.[6] The result, for workers, was that fewer of them were covered by employment-based health insurance.

Changes in the economy at large also created problems. First, much of the growth of jobs was in small business, the sector least likely to provide employee health insurance. Second, the recession of 1990–91, though not nearly as deep as the one a decade earlier, also created distress. The number of people without health insurance continued to grow. Third, American companies, in their effort to become more competitive, engaged in downsizing or reengineering: They were cutting the number of employees at the same time that employee productivity was increasing. The number of good-paying blue-collar jobs was decreasing.

Compounding this situation were two other factors. One was an increasing tendency for insurance companies (and self-insured employers) to refuse to cover people at high risks of disease and to cut off those who developed expensive maladies. This policy created the other factor, "job lock," where workers were afraid to leave their jobs because they or a family member had a preexisting medical condition. The combination of all these factors created great distress and the feeling among the people and the business sector (especially large businesses) that something had to be done.

The policies stream consists of proposals to deal with an issue, though not necessarily connected directly to the problems as described above. The idea of national health insurance has been around for some time. So has the example of other Western industrialized nations that have had national health insurance systems (Moore 1993). Canada, perhaps the most cited example, has such a system, what became known in the United States as a *single payer system*. Under such a system, the national government pays the costs, with provinces and territories administering the program. Under the German plan, the oldest in the world, residents join sickness funds either through work or geographical groups. The sickness funds than negotiate with provider organizations to obtain health care for their subscribers. The British national health system is largely rejected in the United States. Under this system, which is properly labeled "socialized medicine," hospitals are owned by the government, and doctors are essentially government employees (though they are allowed to have private practices). The Japanese have a system known as *play-or-pay*. Companies either provide health insurance for their employees or pay into a national fund.[7]

Apart from using plans from other nations as models for health care reform, there were also policy proposals that were unique to the United States based on competition or market reform. We had the growing example of health maintenance organizations (HMOs) and similar organizations, which by 1993 had over 40 million subscribers (Freudenheim 1994). The originator of the concept of health maintenance organizations, Paul Ellwood in the 1990s was promoting a modification of the health maintenance strategy. This newer strategy was *managed competition*. Under managed competition, groups of providers and insurers would form health plans that would compete for subscribers. Subscribers would be grouped together, either through their employers (if large enough), or through *health care alliances* if they were self-employed or in smaller businesses or uninsured. The alliances would negotiate with the health plans, offering a variety or menu of such plans (Enthoven and Kronick 1992). Alain Enthoven, who was prominent in the late 1970s and early 1980s debate over competition in health care (Enthoven 1980), was perhaps the foremost theorist of managed competition. Ellwood brought Enthoven and others (including industry representatives) together at his home in Jackson Hole, Wyoming, to develop and push managed competition principles (Eckholm 1993; Reinhold 1993).

The problems and policies were floating around, waiting, in a sense, for something to happen. That something, the politics stream, began in a totally unanticipated and tragic fashion. In 1991, Senator John Heinz (Rep.-PA) died in a plane crash. Pennsylvania's Democratic governor, Robert Casey, appointed a little-known college professor, Democrat Harris Wofford, to Heinz's seat. There was to be a special election in November 1991 to decide who would serve the three remaining years in Heinz's stead.

The Republican who ran against Wofford was a formidable opponent, Richard Thornburgh. A popular politician, Thornburgh, was the former governor of Pennsylvania and U.S. attorney general in the first Bush administration. Given Thornburgh's popularity and fund-raising ability, the conventional wisdom was that Wofford had no chance. However, Wofford ran a populist campaign pitched to the growing economic insecurity of the times. In particular, Wofford used the lack of national health insurance as his most potent weapon. His most memorable "sound bite" was that if people had the right to an attorney in a criminal case, they should have the right to see a doctor, regardless of ability to pay. To the surprise of nearly everyone, Wofford won.

Wofford's unexpected victory sent a message to the political world in 1992, when President George H.W. Bush would be running for reelection. In early 1992, the president proposed a health-care reform measure that was based on tax incentives to business and individuals to provide and buy health insurance. It did not guarantee health insurance to all; it only made it easier for people to purchase it. The Bush plan also contained some malpractice liability reforms (Wines 1992).

The Democratic challenger, Arkansas Governor Bill Clinton, made health care reform an important part of his campaign. Clinton's victory in November 1992 was widely interpreted as a mandate to focus on domestic problems and to make policy changes.

Given that a critical juncture or a window of opportunity exists, what path does the issue take (Cobb, Keith-Ross, and Ross 1976)? In the most familiar of these paths, outside groups demand the resolution of a problem and petition government to meet those demands—a description of normal interest-group activity, such as lobbying. The issue arises first among some part of the public and then is discussed within governmental circles. The classic example of this **outside initiative** path is the civil rights movement during the 1950s and 1960s. Here was a relatively powerless group with few resources, activating the public through the media and essentially compelling Congress and the president to pass laws ending segregation (Lipsky 1969).

Sometimes there are issues that appeal either to those in government or those close to government officials, and political leaders then attempt to garner public support; this is the **mobilization** path. In 1981, President Reagan made a televised address to Congress, appealing for support of a budget reduction package. The address was to Congress, but the appeal was to the public to support the proposed cuts. The cuts were passed by a coalition of Republicans and conservative Democrats against the Democratic leadership of the House of Representatives. In 2001, President George W. Bush also pushed for tax cuts.

Another example of mobilization is efforts by the Health Insurance Association of America in 1993–94 to block health-care reform and by the pharmaceutical industry in 1999 to block adding a prescription medication benefit to Medicare. In this case, the attempt is to mobilize to keep an issue off the policy agenda.

Finally, there are issues that arise within government, similar to the mobilization path, but whose supporters do not want them expanded to the public. Typically, these issues involve national defense and foreign policy. A powerful example of **inside initiative** concerns what might be called the "Iran-Contra Connection." In 1985 and 1986, the United States, with the assistance of third parties such as Israel and private arms sellers, sent several shipments of arms to the Iranian government. Two reasons were given. First, the shipments were overtures to moderates within the radical, anti-American Khomeini government. Second, it was hoped that American hostages held in Lebanon by Iranian sympathizers (Shiites) would be released. Indeed, three such hostages were released. The other part of the "connection" was a diversion of a portion of the funds from the arms sales to bank accounts in Switzerland, possibly for assistance to the contra rebels in their attempt to overthrow the Sandinista government in Nicaragua. The connection with the contras was apparently only one part of a network of covert activities in support of the "Reagan doctrine."

Both the arms sales and the diversion of funds were kept hidden from Congress, the public, and much of the governmental bureaucracy. The United States officially had taken a position that Iran was a significant source of terrorism (and had funded the 1983 bombing of American Marines in Beirut Airport), and it strongly opposed arms shipments to Iran for its long war with

Iraq. Indeed, during the time the shipments were sent, several U.S. citizens were being prosecuted for selling arms to Iran. Additionally, from 1984 to 1986, Congress outlawed direct or indirect U.S. support to the contras. The government's covert policy was rationalized as necessary because public knowledge of these actions would have led to opposition.

## Policy Formulation

Once the attention of people in government is aroused and they have started to seriously consider an issue, the next step is to develop a plan to remedy the problem. This phase of the policy process is known as **policy formulation**. In one sense, policy formulation is very much like the process of problem solving all of us often face. Consider a married couple who decide to purchase an automobile (Quade 1982); the preferences of both will have to be considered. If there is disagreement between the two, some resolution and compromise will eventually be made. This is typical of the policy process. Of course, defining the problem in the policy process is much more complicated than buying an automobile, if for no other reason than that there are many political actors who try to impose their own definitions. Part of the difficulty, as well as the fun, of policy formulation is first figuring out what it is we are trying to do. If there is just one decision maker, then only that preference counts.

The process of examining and evaluating alternative courses of action is known as **policy analysis** (or problem solving on the individual level). It should quickly become obvious that there are limitations in our ability to evaluate all alternatives (Lindblom 1959; Simon 1985). For the automobile problem, there are many alternatives: three domestic producers (General Motors, Ford, and Daimler/Chrysler) and a variety of foreign producers. Each automobile manufacturer has different product lines, and each product line has different options. Most people do not have the technical competence, the information, or the time to evaluate all the potential alternatives.

Fortunately, the tendency is to limit this search for information and to use various aids (Simon 1985). If financial resources are essentially unlimited, the choice is probably the best car that money can buy. But most of us—even the federal government with its ability to spend more than it makes—have fiscal limitations. So we eliminate cars that we cannot afford. Information can be gathered easily by using guides such as *Consumer Reports* and *Car and Driver*, which provide information about the cost of cars, their driving characteristics, and so forth. The Internet is another source of both good and bad information on cars and much else. We may limit our search by how we define the problem. We might specify a domestic car ("Buy American!") for less than $20,000 that has to be a station wagon (or sports coupe); our search-and-decision problem is greatly reduced. Though this is a commonplace example, the process of analysis at this individual level is very similar to what goes on in government.[8]

At the heart of analysis is a **model**, an abstraction from reality that focuses on only those things (variables) that are important to the particular problem (Stokey and Zeckhauser 1978). Economic models are frequently employed in policy analysis (Stokey and Zeckhauser 1978 and Weimer and Vining 1992). On the individual level (microeconomics), the familiar supply-and-demand curves are an important tool. As the price of a good or service increases, suppliers are more willing to produce and consumers, less willing to buy. Macroeconomic models are used to evaluate, for example, the effect of universal health care coverage on the federal budget as well as its possible effects on job loss. Environmental programs also require considerable modeling. For example, we might be interested in knowing how much reduction in acid rain in the northeast United States (and Canada) would result from a 30 percent reduction of sulfur dioxide emissions in the Ohio Valley. We would develop an air diffusion model that included, for example, how air currents flow from the Ohio Valley to the northeast. The use of models is critical to policy formulation and policy analysis, even if many of the models are not as explicit as the air pollution example.

An important aspect of policy formulation is a **policy goal**—what it is that government is trying to achieve through public policy. Stone (1997) discusses four generic policy goals.[9] Generic means that the policy goals are general and not specific to a particular policy area. We should expect to see one or more generic policy goals in any policy area, in addition to policy goals specific to that area. Each of the policy chapters that follow will discuss policy goals as well as policy tools (see below).

- The first such goal, and probably the most important, is **security**, the protection of a society, both externally and internally. Government has the responsibility to defend society against threats, whether they be from foreign terrorists or domestic terrorists (e.g., the bombing of the federal office building in Oklahoma City in 1995 or the rash of school shootings, such as at Columbine High School in Littleton, CO, in 1995 or Santana High School in Santee, CA, in 2001). Security will also be seen in such areas as environmental protection and health care.
- The second generic goal is **efficiency**. This goal raises the question of how well government programs are working. Are the programs meeting their objectives? Is the money being spent wisely? For example, questions are being asked about whether spending more money on public elementary and secondary schools leads to better educational outcomes ("Does More Money Make Better Schools?" 1999). Are strict rules the best way to achieve environmental goals?
- The third goal is **equity**. This goal looks at the distribution of goods and services in society by both the public and private sectors and asks whether that is a fair distribution. Equity is related to the concept of **equality**. Equality means treating everybody the same, based on the requirements of the occasion. For example, if two people are applying for a job, they

should be judged based on their qualifications for that job and not some other basis, such as friendship, race, or gender. Equity goes further than equality by suggesting that sometimes people and groups have to be treated unequally to create equality. That is a rather paradoxical statement. What it means, for example, is that we as a society might need to devote more resources to a group so that they will be able to compete on an equal basis later on. This is the rationale behind compensatory spending programs in education, such as Head Start, Title I, or even some of the proposed school voucher programs that limit participation to low-income families or families of children in failed schools (see chapter 8).

• The final generic policy goal is **liberty**. This usually means the freedom to do what we want without interference from some outside body, usually government but sometimes the private sector. The whole civil liberties area, with its focus on freedoms of speech, press, assembly, and religion, encompasses this idea. The patients' rights bills involve a similar idea aimed at managed care organizations, in this case, freedom from restrictions that managed care organizations place on access to services (see chapter 5). Liberty as a goal can also be seen in the environmental policy area. Rules of any kind restrict behavior. Environmental rules are perfect examples, and an argument against many environmental rules (apart from the efficiency argument) is that they infringe too much on private property.

The expected result of policy formulation is a solution to the problem. Stone (1997)[10] has identified five types of generic **policy solutions**.

• One set of solutions involves the use of **inducements** to influence behavior. Inducements can be positive, such as tax incentives, or negative, such as a prison term for the commission of a crime. The fundamental premise of building up a defense force is to deter others from attacking (mutual assured destruction)—a negative inducement.

• A second type of solution is **rules**, mandates, or required specific behaviors. Environmental policy is characterized primarily by a reliance on rules, such as meeting sulfur dioxide emission standards. The federal government often requires states to undertake particular actions by attaching rules to grants. Congress passed legislation requiring states to lower the blood-alcohol level for determining whether someone is driving under the influence. This was a combination of rules and negative inducements, what is essentially a mandate.

• The third type of solution is **facts**, informing and persuading targets to behave in a particular way. The "Just Say No" campaign against drug use is a good example. Disclosure requirements, such as the new food-labeling standards, that provide information allowing informed judgment is a variant on this solution.

- The fourth type of solution is **rights**, which give certain people rights or duties. The civil rights and women's movements are examples of interests asserting their rights in society. More recently, there has been much controversy over gay rights, at both the federal (gays in the military) and the state and local levels. In education, new "choice laws" in some states (e.g., Iowa and Minnesota) give parents the right to choose what public school their child will attend. In the late 1990s, Congress and the states considered patients' rights bills, providing protections against managed care organizations.
- The fifth category of solutions is **powers**, which change the way decisions are made. Powers may include changing the size of a decision-making body, changing the membership (including people and groups that have not previously participated in the process), or changing the place where decisions are made: between branches of government (legislative, executive, judicial); between levels of government (national, state, local); or between the public and private sectors.[11] We will see examples of this type of solution in the areas of health, environment, and education.
- There is one other important category of policy tools. Government often provides the services itself. Examples of **direct services** include public education, police, and correctional services. In some cases, say, for veterans, the federal government directly provides health services through the Department of Veterans Affairs.

### Policy Adoption

After formulating a proposal, and perhaps after examining alternatives, one preferred proposal emerges; this is **policy adoption**. That proposal must be accepted by some person or group that has the legitimate power and authority to make decisions. Agencies within the executive branch can adopt policies via **regulations**, often only after considerable bureaucratic infighting. A bureau within the Environmental Protection Agency (EPA), for example, proposes a regulation to reduce sulfur dioxide emissions. Another bureau within the EPA, such as a planning or evaluation bureau, might oppose the proposal because it is economically inefficient, and offer modifications. The agency head will then have to decide among the competing proposals. Usually there is some provision made for public input either through a formal hearing or a comment period. (This process became even more complicated because of new oversight powers granted to the Office of Management and Budget [OMB] during the Reagan and the first Bush administrations. The Clinton administration returned full regulatory authority to the agencies.)

Some policy adoption can be made directly by a chief executive (such as a governor or a president) through **executive orders**. Presidents Reagan and Bush issued an executive order prohibiting family planning clinics receiving federal funds from performing, counseling, or suggesting abortions. The enabling legislation did not call for such a gag order. President Clinton rescinded the order in the first month of his administration. Another example of the use of executive authority came in January 1995. The Mexican peso collapsed in December 1994, which threatened in subtle ways the American and world economy. The Clinton administration sought congressional approval of a $40 billion bailout. Support for the move was lacking among both Republicans and Democrats in Congress. To forestall any further repercussions of the drop in the value of the peso, President Clinton ordered loans and loan guarantees totaling $20 billion in conjunction with loans from the International Monetary Fund (IMF) and the World Bank. Congressional approval was unnecessary (Apple 1995). Presidents (as well as governors) have made substantial use of executive orders over the years (Posner 2000). Affirmative action programs in the state of Florida were ended via a gubernatorial executive order.

On the foreign policy level, agreements between the United States and other nations can be reached through **executive agreements** rather than by following the elaborate and difficult treaty process in the Senate. One example of an executive agreement was the North American Free Trade Agreement (NAFTA). This agreement phased in an open market among the United States, Canada, and Mexico. Executive agreements such as NAFTA may require approval by a majority of the House and Senate.

Policy adoption may also occur through **judicial action**. Desegregation of school systems in the South and the use of busing to promote integration were accomplished largely through court orders backed by congressional action. More recently, the Supreme Court has struck down as discriminatory efforts to create congressional districts with African-American majorities designed to increase minority representation (see chapter 9).

**Legislation** is one of the most important and publicized means of policy adoption.[12] Passage of legislation is a complex process involving the building of a series of majorities at different points in the legislative process. Bills begin in subcommittees in the House and Senate and, if passed, go on to the full committees. From the committees they go to the floor of each house (in the House, they first go through the Rules Committee, which sets limits on debate and amendments), and then they are voted on by each house. If the House and Senate disagree, there is a conference committee to iron out differences; then back to each house for a final vote. This sometimes tortuous process provides legitimacy (acceptance) to legislation because of the need to assemble majorities (build support) at each step (Jones 1984).

For a variety of reasons, what goes in is not necessarily what comes out. The different barriers—or access points, depending on one's perspective—such as subcommittee, committee, floor votes, and conference committees, provide opportunities for delay and change. In addition, the absence of strong political party control in both houses makes it more difficult to direct what goes in. For example, after the 2000 elections, the U.S. Senate was temporarily split evenly between Republicans and Democrats. Not all proposed legislation emerges from this obstacle course (e.g., the Clinton Health Security Act; see chapter 5), and that which does is frequently modified. These changes are due, again, to the need to build majorities by bargaining for support (legitimacy) by members of the legislature, whether city council, state legislature, or Congress. President Clinton's plan to stimulate the economy in 1993, a centerpiece of his presidential campaign in 1992, was defeated in Congress. Instead, budget cutting became the focus. Even then, Congress modified the president's proposals. The North American Free Trade Agreement was passed by Congress after the president made numerous promises to various representatives and senators, not all of which were related to the trade agreement.

More so than with bureaucratic, executive, or judicial adoption, legislative adoption is a public and relatively open process. The result of this openness is that legislative policy adoption requires agreement among two of the following three sets of actors: the executive branch, the legislative branch, and public opinion (Schneider 1988). The absence of consensus can thwart policies, such as attempts to balance the budget in the 1980s and 1990s. President Reagan's support for the contras against the Sandinista government of Nicaragua foundered because of congressional and public opposition. Tax reform was passed in 1986 despite public apathy and skepticism about the impact of reform because both the president and Congress supported it.

Majority building, bargaining, and legitimation grew increasingly difficult as Congress and the president became deadlocked by the enormous deficits of the 1980s and 1990s, and the public refusal to support the remedies required. As a result, Congress did less and less, and to take action at all required unusual mechanisms. Rather than pass appropriations bills, Congress sometimes resorted to large continuing resolutions covering half the federal budget. Similarly, budget cutting occasionally required fast-track vehicles such as omnibus reconciliation acts or debt-ceiling bills that include provisions (riders) circumventing the usual process.[13] John Hoadley writes of the dangers and lack of appropriate input of these streamlined, fast-track procedures:

> The passage of Gramm-Rudman-Hollings [the Balanced Budget Act of 1985 originally designed to reduce the federal budget deficit to zero by fiscal year 1991] marks the approval of major legislation affecting macroeconomic policy, the fate of numerous government programs, and congressional budget procedures, without public hearings, without debate by any standing committee of the House or the Senate, and without any debate on the House floor (other than on motions whether to seek a conference or on a motion to approve the final conference report). (1986, p. 31)

Even when the budget situation changed for the better, as chronic deficits unexpectedly turned into budget surpluses, Congress was unable to agree by itself or come to agreement with President Clinton on how to treat the budget. Passing the budget in 1999 (for fiscal year 2000) turned out to be as difficult with a surplus as it had been previously with a deficit (see chapter 2).

The difficult decisions and the unwillingness to face them led to what one observer called a "no-hands government," one that is unwilling to take responsibility for actions (Broder 1989; Weaver 1988). Decision makers look for impersonal mechanisms, such as automatic cost-of-living adjustments in entitlement programs or commissions, such as the commissions on closing military bases, reforming social security, or increasing pay. These commissions work when a decision is absolutely vital, time is short, and no political advantages can be gained from exploiting the issue. Thus, the Kissinger Commission on Central American policy and the Scowcroft Commission on new strategic nuclear missiles had little impact and did not settle policy. There was no critical element to those issues, no pressure to decide immediately, and partisan gain still had to be achieved (Schneider 1989).

It should be pointed out, however, that the failure by Congress to take positive action, in 1993 with President Clinton's economic stimulus and in 1994 with the Health Security Act, is also an expression of a policy. In the first case, it was felt that the stimulus was perhaps not needed and involved too much in the way of government programs. In the second case, considerable skepticism was expressed about the feasibility of the Health Security Act, coupled with partisan and ideological disagreement about features of the plan.

These problems, related to divided government (see below), were partially remedied by the elections of 1992, which created a unified federal government under the Democrats for the first time since 1980. Even here, as NAFTA and the budgeting mentioned above suggest, Congress was still divided enough to make legislative adoption a problematic activity. The elections of 1994 returned the country to divided government as the Republicans gained control of both the House and the Senate. The 1997 Balanced Budget Act does show that even with divided government, agreement on difficult issues can be reached. The elections of 2000 temporarily returned the federal government to unified party control, this time under the Republicans, though the split in the Senate, the thin margin of control in the House, and the disputed presidential election created their own problems.

The final type of policy adoption is **direct democracy mechanisms**. Here the people themselves, in states or local governments, get to make policy decisions, generally through two types of elections. **Initiatives** are proposals placed on a ballot as a result of petitions. Some group outside of government wants the public to vote directly on a law. Examples of such initiatives include votes decriminalizing marijuana (see chapter 7) and ending affirmative action (see chapter 9). An interesting, though ultimately unsuccessful, initiative in Missouri would have allowed citizens to carry concealed handguns.

The other major type of direct democracy election is the **referendum**. Here government, usually a legislative body such as a city council or state legislature, asks the voters' approval for some policy. Typically, referenda are held, depending on the state, for tax increases and bond issues (say for new school construction).

Figure 1.3 **Changing Budget Priorities**

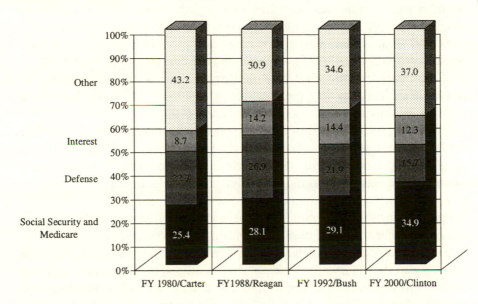

*Source:* Office of Management and Budget (1999).

## *Budgeting*

It is a fact of life that the mere adoption of a solution is seldom sufficient to achieve a goal. To achieve policy goals, programs require funding. As with the other phases of the policy process, **budgeting** is a multifaceted process involving many actors at different levels of government (Rubin 1999).

Budgeting is clearly an important function in the executive branch of government. Under the system of executive budgeting, where the chief executive (president, governor) presents a budget to the legislature (Congress, state legislature), budgeting politics provides an opportunity, perhaps *the* opportunity, to assert priorities. Some programs within an agency or bureau will receive greater increases than others; some agencies may suffer decreases. At higher levels, budgetary politics indicate the priorities of the chief executive and the legislature. The big budget battles between President Clinton and Congress in 1995–96, which led to two government shutdowns, was precisely over spending priorities (Rushefsky and Patel 1998).[14]

Look at Figure 1.3. It shows four categories of spending for four fiscal years of the last four presidencies. While the three bottom spending categories are obvious, the fourth needs a bit of explanation. It represents everything else the federal government does, including Medicaid (itself a sizable program), environmental protection, college student loans, Head Start and Title I funds, foreign assistance, highway trust funds, and so forth. The chart shows differences in priorities among the four administrations. The Reagan administration increased defense spending significantly relative to the Carter administration. Defense spending in the post–Cold War period (George H. W. Bush and Clinton administrations) shrank as a proportion of the budget. As we shall see in chapter 3, defense spending is on the rise again. Interest on the debt increased dramatically during the Reagan administration, reflecting the run-up of the national debt (see chapter 2). Relatively speaking, interest on the debt declined during the Clinton administration.

But chief executives do not adopt a budget; they merely propose one. It is the legislature that passes a budget. Much of the activity of Congress is taken up with budgetary concerns, but the priorities of Congress as an institution often conflict with the priorities of individuals in important positions within Congress (such as Senate majority leader, House speaker, chairmen of the budget committees). And congressional leaders usually have different goals than the president, even if they are members of the same party.

The congressional budgetary process, reformed in 1974 and modified in 1985, is particularly complex and not always followed. The process involves three sets of committees. The House and Senate **budget committees** approve budget resolutions, set overall targets for revenues and expenditures (and, by implication, deficits or surpluses), and can order spending cuts to conform to the budget resolution (called reconciliation). **Legislative (or authorization) committees** set ceilings on how much *may* be spent. Finally, there are two congressional **appropriations committees** (each with thirteen subcommittees) that decide how much *will* be spent. To make things even more complicated, much of government spending does not require annual authorizations or appropriations. Future spending appropriated in the past (known as budget authority) can wreak havoc on budgets. For example, the Defense Department has hundreds of billions of dollars in budget authorizations (future spending) for weapons procurement that will affect the size of future federal budgets.

Apart from that, a significant portion (over half) of the federal budget consists of **entitlements** (Peterson 1993). "Entitlements are legal obligations created through legislation that require the payment of benefits to any person or unit of government that meets the eligibility requirements established by law" (Wildavsky 1988, p. 259). Social Security, food stamps, and student loans are examples of entitlement programs. Entitlements have grown faster than any other part of the budget, and they are relatively uncontrollable. That is, many of these programs do not require annual appropriations or authorizations. Unless Congress deliberately chooses to change an entitlement (something it has hesitated to do), then the growth in entitlements is affected by growth in the number of those eligible and by changes in the cost of living. One successful effort to control and change an entitlement program came in 1996 when Congress enacted, and President Clinton signed, the welfare reform bill (see chapter 4).

Budgeting can affect program development. A recent example of how budgeting can impact programs can be seen in the Balanced Budget Act of 1997 (Palazzolo 1999). One provision of the legislation restored some of the welfare benefits that were removed by the 1996 welfare reform bill (see chapter 4). Another provision made significant changes in Medicare, including limits or caps for spending for therapy ("Patients, Therapists Reel from Medicare Reform" 1999). Obviously budgeting is fundamental.

## Implementation

If budgeting is fundamental, implementation is critical. **Implementation** is the carrying out or execution of a program that has been adopted by legislation or by executive or judicial order. Jones (1984) argues that implementation involves three activities: organization, interpretation, and application.

First, there needs to be an **organization** or set of organizations with appropriate resources (people, funding, facilities, etc.) to carry out the program. Frequently, new programs are assigned to ongoing organizations, and some times new organizations are created to carry out new programs, either to emphasize the importance of the new program or as an indication of dissatisfaction with existing agencies. Organization is important, though not overriding by itself. In studying implementation, the concerns are whether the implementers are favorably or unfavorably disposed to the program, whether resources are adequate to carry out the program, and how easy (tractable) the problem is (Mazmanian and Sabatier 1983).

The second activity of implementation is **interpretation**. Congress passes legislation that frequently requires further explanation. In some areas, Congress cannot anticipate all possibilities, so it delegates authority to agencies to write rules. In other areas, the issues are so technically complex that Congress defers to the expertise of the bureaucracy. Congress sometimes fails to make controversial decisions when writing legislation, forcing administrators to make them when the legislation must be interpreted and implemented. Peter Woll's (1977) description of the creation of the Interstate Commerce Commission, the first independent regulatory agency, makes this point:

> The Interstate Commerce Commission (ICC), for example, was established in 1887 to regulate the railroads because of pressure from agricultural interests that were being subjected to various types of economic coercion by the railroads. Congress was aware of the charges made against the railroads, but could not take the time to investigate them and develop minute regulations to control economic abuses; the subject was too vast, complex, and fraught with political danger. Congress decided to yield to pressures for regulation by creating an independent regulatory agency; at the same time this device prevented Congress from having to make difficult decisions involving regulation that would undoubtedly cause dissatisfaction in many of the groups being regulated. (p. 11)

Sometimes, the wording of a statute is vague. The Toxic Substances Control

Act (TSCA) is designed to protect the public against "unreasonable risks" from exposure to chemicals. What is "unreasonable risk"? It is an agency's task, in this case the Environmental Protection Agency, to decide.

Whatever the reason, interpretation is a vital function. Rules are statements of general applicability that apply to the community and have the effect of law (Woll 1977). It is as if Congress itself had passed the law, only we do not elect the bureaucrats. The way rules are written and the way legislation is interpreted can make for effective implementation of a law, can effectively undermine the intent of the law, or can move the law into areas perhaps unintended by the legislation. As a result of congressional legislation, for example, the Immigration and Naturalization Service (INS) requires that employers verify the citizenship of new employees; thus someone applying for a new job has to prove that he/she is an American citizen. Regulations issued by the Federal Reserve Board require that those endorsing checks sign in a specified area on the back of a check: This regulation helps implement 1988 legislation mandating that checks be cleared by banks within a certain time period. In neither case did the legislation passed by Congress call for those actions.

One particularly intriguing example of how interpretation can lead to new policy issues concerns what has been called the "gag rule," briefly mentioned above.[15] In 1988, the U.S. Department of Health and Human Services (DHHS) issued regulations forbidding family planning clinics receiving federal grants from advising their clients of (or even mentioning) the possibility of abortion as an option to pregnancy. Nothing in the legislation suggested that such a limitation was what Congress had in mind. The issue went to the Supreme Court, and, in *Rust v. Sullivan*, the Court ruled that such action was legal. The gag order was controversial, and the George H. W. Bush administration sought a mild modification by allowing doctors affiliated with federally funded family planning clinics to counsel patients. There were two problems with this change. First, doctors in such situations rarely counseled clients, so the change was symbolic. Second, a federal court ruled that such a change must go through the standard administrative process of rule making. In any event, one of President Clinton's early actions was to rescind the gag order (Weitz 1993).

Once the rules are in place, the last implementation activity is the **application** of the rules. If a program is set up to collect and disburse funds for retired people, the checks should go out to Social Security recipients. If a student loan program is set up, the loan applications should be processed, and the checks should be sent in a timely fashion.[16]

Application can also change programs. According to a report from the Health Care Financing Administration (HCFA), which administers Medicaid, a number of states are seeing declines in their Medicaid enrollment because of welfare reform. Prospective welfare recipients are diverted from the program but not told that they are eligible for Medicaid. Welfare recipients as well are not always informed that they are so eligible. This also appears to be the case for food stamps (see "States Illegally Denying Medicaid, Audit Finds" 1999).

Not all program implementation is successful. Policy goals may not be achieved because implementation was never tried (**program failure**). If insufficient time, staff, or money are allocated or political leadership is unsupportive, then the goals will not be achieved. For example, in 1995 the Republican-controlled Congress launched a major assault on a variety of environmental programs, proposing, among other things, significant reductions in the Environmental Protection Agency staff and budget levels (Cushman 1995). On the other hand, a program may be successfully implemented but policy goals still not achieved (**theory failure**), in which case the appropriate resolution is change, modification, or abandonment of the program (Weiss 1972). Some scholars, for example, have suggested that our welfare programs are counterproductive by encouraging people to go on welfare and should be eliminated (Murray 1984). Peter Peterson (1993) has suggested that many of our entitlement programs, such as Medicare, also tend to encourage behavior that is counterproductive.

There are three final considerations. First, an examination of the literature on implementation shows that most programs are unsuccessful when compared with the originally stated goals. Most government programs therefore seem to have little positive effect and may even have negative impacts. The difficulty is that selling a policy or program may require creating overblown expectations. Federal legislation is often trumpeted as the solution for the crime problem. For example, President Clinton, and others, called for a "three-strikes-and-you're-out" policy. Such a policy (see chapter 7) requires a life sentence with no chance of parole for those convicted of a third violent felony. Some have suggested that it will have little effect on crime. One basis for such an argument is that after age thirty-five, most violent offenders no longer commit crimes, but we would, under this proposal, continue to house them in prisons.

Second, the course of implementation varies over time, something few scholars and political actors note. Mazmanian and Sabatier (1983) propose several paths that implementation might take: effective implementation (relatively simple, noncontroversial problems); gradual erosion (where implementation is initially effective but later worsens); gradual improvements in implementation (cumulative incrementalism); or almost wave-like declines and increases (rejuvenation). Implementation is a complex process of ebb and flow.

Finally, the process of program implementation is itself complex (Pressman and Wildavsky 1984). An important recent analysis of congressional legislation shows that programs are often assigned to more than one agency, at more than one level of government, and include the profit and nonprofit sectors (Hall and O'Toole 2000).

## *Evaluation*

At some point during or after program implementation, judgments are made about how well a program has worked. This stage of the policy process is called **program evaluation**. As with the policy analysis aspect of the policy-formulation stage, program evaluation can be systematic or nonsystematic.

Suppose that you are a college senior who wants to go to law school. A friend of yours is a first-year law student. Her grades were virtually identical to yours, but you have yet to take the law school admission test (LSAT). You know your friend's score was pretty high, and you are uncertain whether you would do as well. Your friend tells you that she took one of the commercial LSAT preparation courses and that it was great. She enthusiastically endorses it, claims that it was the reason she did well, and recommends you take it. But the course costs hundreds of dollars. Paying the money would hurt a bit, but it would be worthwhile if it did help you get into law school. Should you invest in the course?

Maybe! From the information your friend has given, you really cannot tell if the course is a good investment. You do not know how well your friend would have done on the LSAT if she had not taken the course. Maybe she would have done very well anyway. You might also be interested in knowing how well other students who took the course did. You might even try an experiment: Find some students who took the LSAT without the course, then took the course, then retook the LSAT. Is there improvement? If so, is the improvement significant? You could find some other students who took the test twice without ever taking the course and then compare the two groups. (Often we tend to do better the second time around because of our earlier experience.) But what if there were differences between the two groups that could affect or bias the results? Maybe the students taking the course had better (or worse) grades than those not taking the course. Maybe there were socioeconomic differences; low-income students would be less likely to afford the hundreds of dollars in fees. The only way to be sure is to randomly select students for the two different groups (Figure 1.4).

This, in a nutshell, is the essence of systematic evaluation—comparing groups and results and then arriving at a conclusion. You might imagine that in the real world it is difficult to set up these types of experiments, though occasionally it is done. One of the best examples of policy experimentation is the Tennessee STAR program to assess the impact of class size on student achievement (Feldman 1999; see also chapter 8). Where there is evaluation, one or more of the canons of good research (in terms of choosing subjects, making the appropriate comparisons, etc.) are often violated.[17]

Most evaluations are unsystematic or impressionistic. Legislative hearings on the progress of a program are good examples of unsystematic evaluation. Agency officials testify and are questioned by committee and subcommittee members. Congressional staff agencies may investigate how well a program is working.

Figure 1.4 **Random Selection Evaluation Model**

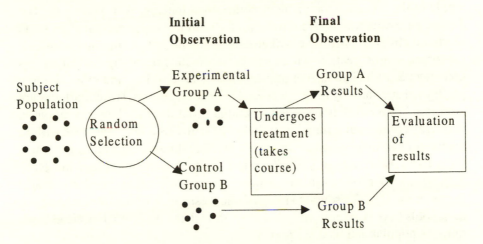

Public policy programs may also have unintended effects and, whether systematic or unsystematic, evaluations must address them. Unintended effects may, in some cases, be more significant than intended ones. Charles Murray (1984) has argued that welfare policies had the unintended effect of increasing dependency and the decline of families. More recently, Murray (1993) asserted that our welfare policies have led to an increase in illegitimacy (out-of-wedlock births), especially among whites.[18]

## Policy Succession

What happens after the evaluation stage? Not all programs are evaluated, though they may be changed. Whatever the case, change after evaluation is part of the phase called **policy succession**. This phase brings us full circle, returning us to other parts of the policy process.

What are the possibilities? First, programs and policies may not be changed. This may be because of favorable evaluations (whether systematic or not), the lack of any evaluation, or in spite of unfavorable evaluations. The first two reasons are obvious, but the third reason requires elucidation. Evaluations by themselves do not determine the future course of a program. Programs and policies may have substantial political support despite negative findings. An example will illuminate the point.

One of the lasting legacies of the War on Poverty and President Johnson's Great Society is the Head Start program. The theory behind Head Start is that children from poor families come from a culturally deprived environment that puts them at a permanent disadvantage when they start school. Head Start was designed to provide these children with preschool preparation, giving them a "head start" toward school. Does Head Start indeed provide a "head start," and, if so, are the impacts lasting?

These are perfect questions for systematic evaluation, similar to the example of the law exam preparatory course mentioned earlier. During the late 1960s, an evaluation was conducted of children who participated in Head Start and children of similar backgrounds who did not, comparing academic outcomes several years down the road. The conclusion of the evaluators was that Head Start had no lasting impact. Head Start children and other children performed similarly by the third grade.[19] For some reason, Head Start was not working, but because it was such a popular program, the clamor went out to save Head Start, and it remains to this day (Williams and Evans 1976). More recent studies of Head Start and other early childhood education programs show more positive results (McKey et al. 1985), but the point remains: Even in the face of negative evaluations, popular programs thrive. Similarly, evaluations of the DARE program (Drug Abuse Resistance Education) in the public schools have been uniformly negative, though the program, like Head Start, remains popular and well supported.

Another possible course after evaluation is some **modification** of the program, returning to earlier stages of the policy process, such as adoption or budgeting. Modifications may be needed because political leaders desire change, whether or not supported by evaluations. As we shall see in chapter 4, the major federal/state cash assistance welfare program, Aid to Families with Dependent Children (AFDC) was transformed into the much more restrictive Temporary Assistance for Needy Families (TANF) program. In 2001, the DARE program began to make changes (Zernike 2001).

The third possibility is **termination**, the killing of a program or policy.[20] There are, again, several reasons why termination might occur. The need for the program might disappear or the political atmosphere may no longer support a government program. The deregulation of the late 1970s and 1980s is an example of policy termination. In just a few years, oil and natural gas prices, transportation, banking, and communications were partially or completely deregulated. The 1980s and 1990s saw deregulation of the telecommunications industries.

Policies or programs might be terminated partially or fully in spite of evaluations or, on the opposite side, in the absence of evaluations. Recall President Clinton's cancellation of the "gag order" placed on family planning clinics, discussed above.

Policy succession is the final stage of the policy process. Not all issues go through the entire cycle (Eyestone 1978). Rather than start from the first stage and move systematically through the remaining stages, policies move in and out and back and forth between stages. Problem definition and formulation, for example, occur throughout all phases of the policy process. Making public policy is a difficult, but not impossible, task.

Many of the issues on the policy agenda are not new but are replays of old battles, and the replays are sometimes over different aspects of policy. One of the underlying themes of this book is the role of government, the

**government issue** (Stone 1997, chapter 15).[21] Should government play a role in a given issue area? In some cases, such as foreign and defense policy, the answer is obviously yes. In other cases, such as poverty or health policy, the role of government is more problematic. In areas where government has a role to play, the subsidiary issue might be the extent of that role. Some scholars have suggested that we rely on market-like mechanisms to achieve public goals in such diverse areas as health care, education, and the environment. There is one further aspect of the government issue: As government moves into a policy area, the role of government in that area tends to become the overriding concern, particularly in periods of fiscal constraint. Recent debates over poverty policy have changed from a focus on the problem of poverty to the problem of welfare, government's solution to the poverty problem. While many do not accept this perspective of public policy, we do have to recognize its existence and its important role in policy debates. It should also be noted that the government issue is strongly related to our historic mistrust of government, especially at the federal level (discussed below; see also Wills 1999).

## Characteristics of the American Political System

The making of public policy is strongly affected by various features of the American political system. Some of these features are constitutional; others are the result of the development of the system itself.

### Separation of Powers/Checks and Balances

The first characteristic of the American political system that affects the making of public policy is **separation of powers** and **checks and balances**. Separation of powers means that the legislative, executive, and judicial powers are constitutionally located in separate and discrete institutions (Congress, the president, and the courts). Checks and balances means that each institution has to share some of those powers with the other institutions and therefore can thwart actions of the other branches. For example, the president can veto legislation, Congress approves presidential appointments, and the courts can declare actions by Congress as unconstitutional. Perhaps the better expression of the combination of the two principles is that the United States has "separate institutions sharing powers" (Neustadt 1960, p. 33).

Consider the alternative to separation of powers or a presidential system of government, such as the parliamentary system found in England. The prime minister of England is a member of Parliament, as are cabinet ministers. All cabinet ministers are from the prime minister's political party, which is the majority party in Parliament. Votes in the House of Commons are virtually all along party lines, because failure to support the party's position (the prime minister is also the head of the party) would lead to elections and possible replacement by the opposition. Further, party members are reluctant to cross the prime minister because of the threat of disciplinary action, such as the loss of one's seat in Parliament.

This is not the case in the United States. Congress and the president are elected separately, and each institution is jealous of its prerogatives and power. Even when the president and Congress are of the same party, as in the Kennedy, Johnson, Carter, Clinton (the first two years), and George W. Bush administrations, a recalcitrant, stubborn Congress may go its own way.[22] This trend is exacerbated when **divided government** exists—the president is of one party and Congress is of the other (Eisenhower, Nixon, Ford, Bush, Clinton's last six years)—and reaches the height of contentiousness when Congress itself is split, as in the first six years of the Reagan administration.[23] Electoral politics is about what separates us, what distinguishes one candidate for office from another. Governance, making decisions, requires that people in institutions work together. When electoral politics and governance collide, say within a legislative branch or between the legislative and executive branches, then policy making becomes more difficult as parties vie for control and hold up legislation as a means of scoring political points. An election year can produce gridlock, though the need to win elections can also lead to productive sessions.[24] Governing is difficult and making coherent public policy is problematic.[25]

There is an argument that the Founding Fathers who wrote the Constitution in 1787 designed government to be less than fully effective. Confronted with the weaknesses readily apparent under the Articles of Confederation and the experience with strong, harsh rule by England after the successful conclusion of the French and Indian War, the founders were faced with the dual task of creating a government that would work, yet not be oppressive. James Madison expressed this most eloquently in *Federalist No. 51*:

> But what is government itself but the greatest of all reflections on human nature? If men were angels, no government would be necessary. If angels were to govern men, neither external nor internal controls on government would be necessary. In framing a government that is to be administered by men over men, the great difficult lies in this: You must first enable the government to control the governed, and in the next place, oblige it to control itself. (quoted in Janda, Berry, and Goldman 1995, p. A20)

Some have suggested that our failure to eliminate the federal budget deficits for so long was due to divided government (Cutler 1987).

The situation is most troublesome in foreign policy, where the necessity of speaking with one voice to other nations is paramount but hard to achieve. Presidents can usually dominate in foreign policy, but only because the Constitution gives some foreign policy powers to Congress (ratifying treaties, making appropriations, setting laws), creating what one scholar called "an invitation to struggle for the control of foreign policy" (Corwin 1940, p. 200).[26] Passage of NAFTA required considerable bargaining with Congress, and U.S. policy toward the war in Bosnia was complicated by the need for congressional backing for a military role in support of the beleaguered Muslims.[27] Perhaps the best, recent example of the difficulties presidents face in dealing with Congress and foreign policy was the NATO war in Kosovo. Consider the behavior of Congress in just a few weeks in 1999:

> In a bewildering series of votes over the past three weeks, the House refused either to declare war in the Balkans or stop it, then refused to authorize a ground war without congressional permission or endorse the current air war. A few days later the Senate defeated a resolution allowing President Clinton to use "all necessary force" in the Balkans.
>
> Then, in a full back-flip May 6, the House approved a $13.1 billion special appropriation so that the U.S. armed forces, among other things, could continue waging war in the Balkans for another five months. The money was twice as much as Clinton requested. (Gugliotta 1999)

This kind of negotiating, much rarer in a parliamentary system, is frustrating to presidents, though applauded by congressional leaders.[28]

There are several counters to this argument, an argument that feeds into the historic mistrust of government. Gary Wills (1999) asserts that the three branches of government were never meant to be coequal, that Congress was given primacy by the Constitution. The same priority appears in the *Federalist Papers*. Wills (1999) and Daniel Palazzolo (1999) also observe that a major purpose of separation of powers was to enhance the efficiency of government, through specialization and division of labor.

Further, it can be argued that even in periods of divided government at the national level, which has characterized the majority of the period since the end of World War II (nearly 62 percent of the time, and nearly 100 percent of the time from 1981 to 2000), government has been able to act. The federal government passed comprehensive tax reform in 1986, health insurance legislation in 1996 and 1997, welfare reform in 1996, and an important budget deal in 1997 (Palazzolo 1999). David Mayhew (1991) argues that the national government accomplished about as much during periods of divided government as it did during unified government (one party controlling Congress and the presidency).

## Federalism

> Federalism in America creates a great number of distinct and partially autonomous venues for policy action. Subnation jurisdictions often are the areas where new ideas are tried out, later to be adopted and mimicked by others if they are successful, or abandoned if they are unworkable. (Baumgartner and Jones 1993, p. 216)

The second characteristic is the seemingly mundane and unexciting one of federalism, or the more modern concept of intergovernmental relations. **Federalism** may be defined simply as the division of power between two or more separate and independent levels of government. Burns and colleagues (1998) write that federalism exists when a constitution distributes power to the different levels of government. In the United States, the federal constitution recognizes the national and state governments. **Intergovernmental relations** refers to relations among governments at all levels. Federalism and intergovernmental relations affect the making of public policy in three major ways.

First, many federal domestic policies are carried out by state and local governments. For example, the major welfare program, Temporary Assistance to Needy Families, formerly Aid to Families with Dependent Children, is a joint federal-state program. The federal government contributes about one-half of the expenditures for each state (sometimes more), with the states contributing the remainder. The states then determine eligibility standards and benefit levels, make payments, and so on. There are advantages to this split responsibility, for example, the increased flexibility of dealing with state-local conditions and the smaller bureaucracy. But there are also problems: getting states to comply with federal policy[29] and inequitable variations in benefit and eligibility standards (e.g., Mississippi's welfare benefit levels are considerably less generous than California's).[30] Federalism makes consistent nationwide policy more difficult.

Second, states and local governments can also act independently. As we shall see in subsequent chapters, there are many areas where states have long had primary or sole jurisdiction, such as education and criminal justice.

Third, as Frank Baumgartner and Bryan Jones (1993) point out, the federal and state governments have had, at least since the 1960s, different functions. Much of the federal budget is spent on consumption and redistribution activities (see also Peterson 1993), whereas state and local governments spend a much larger portion of their budget on investment activities. Consumption activities are those aimed at improving the lives of individuals. Food stamps provide a good example, where the focus is on spending in the immediate period. Progressive income taxes, welfare (prior to 1996), and Social Security are redistributive policies, transferring funds from one group or generation to another or taking more from one (high-income) group than from another (low-income) group in the case of progressive taxation. Investment activities include education (human capital, in economic terms) and construction of roads and bridges (physical capital).

Prior to the New Deal, the federal government was very limited in what it did, with a few exceptions (the Civil War, the Progressive Era), and was particularly constrained by its meager income sources. The passage, in 1913, of the Sixteenth Amendment to the U.S. Constitution eventually provided a more generous revenue source, the income tax. The Great Depression and the federal government's response to it, the New Deal, saw the federal government move into new areas of regulating the economy, such as securities and banks, public works programs, welfare and social security programs, and so forth. The successful conclusion of World War II resulted in a standing military and a national security apparatus (the Central Intelligence Agency was the successor to the World War II Office of Strategic Services). Two decades of continued economic growth following the war created a sense that government could accomplish tasks.

The Kennedy administration, though modest in its actions, created a sense of purpose and mission. The civil rights and women's movements led to legislation that increased the power of the federal government (i.e., the 1964 Civil Rights Act and the 1965 Voting Rights Act). The Johnson administration's War on Poverty/Great Society programs (conceived during the abortive Kennedy administration) also led to new federal programs, many of them bypassing the states. These programs included Medicare and Medicaid, Head Start, the Community Action Program, and the Model Cities program.

These programs were accompanied by powerful tools that the federal government could use to influence the states to move in desired directions. On the fiscal level, the 1960s saw an enormous increase in **fiscal federalism**, the transfer of monies from the federal to the state governments. Most of these were in the form of categorical grants, which specified how the funds were to be used. For example, money allocated to AFDC could be used only for cash payments to welfare recipients. The federal government has given billions of dollars to local governments for the construction of sewage and water treatment plants to help them comply with the provisions of the Federal Water Pollution Control Act.

The other important set of such tools available to the federal government comes under the category of **administrative federalism**, orders or incentives (Advisory Commission on Intergovernmental Relations 1984). Sometimes they were **direct orders** or **mandates**, not always accompanied by funds. For example, public agencies were ordered to retrofit buildings and sidewalks to comply with the 1990 Americans with Disabilities Act. The federal government has also engaged in **preemption**, which includes substituting federal laws and regulations for state laws and regulations.[31] Sometimes the federal government has threatened to withhold funds in one area to obtain results in another (called a **crossover sanction**). For example, the federal government threatened to withhold a state's share of highway trust fund money if it did not raise the alcohol drinking age to twenty-one or lower the blood-alcohol level from .10 to .08. A final example of administrative federalism is **cross-cutting requirements**. For example, recipients of federal assistance are not allowed to discriminate against minorities or women. The result of these activities was a blurring of responsibilities between the states and the federal government (Bowman and Kearney 1986).

Given the historic distrust that Americans have for big government (Wills 1999), it is not surprising that there was a reaction to it. President Nixon sought to reduce controls on state and local government recipients of grants, through programs such as revenue sharing. President Reagan sought to go further.

In his 1982 State of the Union message, President Reagan presented his "new federalism"[32] policy, a sorting out of state and federal functions. He proposed that the states pay for all of AFDC (and take over food stamps), while the federal government would pay for all of Medicaid. The federal government would return some federal tax dollars to the states to pay for the programs, and the federal tax dollars, mostly excise taxes, would be gradually phased out. A formal proposal was never made, and the plan faced considerable opposition, mostly from state governments. They liked the idea in theory but not the specific proposal. In 1992, Alice Rivlin, the first director of the Congressional Budget Office and the head of the Office of Management and Budget under Clinton, wrote a book advocating a similar swap of programs (Rivlin 1992).

In some ways, President Reagan's ideas have gained acceptance. Cutbacks in federal responsibilities during the early years of the Reagan administration created a void in which the states marched in. The fiscal constraint of the budget deficits of the 1980s and 1990s (the deficits ended in the late 1990s) made it difficult for the federal government to enact new programs. Divided government and polarization of the political parties led to deadlocks, again creating a void for states. For example, while Congress and the president debated the issue of patients' rights in managed care organizations, many states took legislative action (Patel and Rushefsky 1999).

Two other set of events signaled **devolution**, the returning of responsibilities to the states. One was the Supreme Court's decisions (as well as some decisions of lower courts) limiting what the federal government could do. In *United States v. Lopez* (1994), the Court overturned a federal law banning firearms within a certain distance of schools. More recent decisions moved in this direction as well (Greenhouse, 1999).

The other was the aftermath of the 1994 congressional elections. House Republican candidates, under the direction of then-minority whip Newt Gingrich (R-GA), ran under a campaign platform known as the Contract with America (Gillespie and Schellas 1994). The Contract promised that if Republicans were given control of the House of Representatives, it would take specific actions, many of them on the first day in the first hundred days (echoing Franklin D. Roosevelt's first one hundred days of his first administration). Many of the provisions of the Contract did indeed become law, and many involved turning power and responsibility back to the states. Two laws in particular stand out. One forbade unfunded mandates, with certain exceptions. The other was the passage, in 1996, of welfare reform (see chapter 4). The welfare reform bill ended the federal entitlement to cash assistance and converted that cash program from a categorical grant to a block grant. Somewhat in the same manner, the Clinton administration used waivers (exceptions) to the Medicaid and welfare laws to give states more responsibility and flexibility in administering those programs.

### Pluralism, Elitism, and the Policy Elite

The next features of the American political system are based less on constitutional structure than on the evolution of our political system. One such feature focuses on one of the enduring questions of politics and policy: Who participates in making and influencing decisions? Several answers have been offered. **Pluralism** means that there are many interests represented by pressure groups; it addresses the question of who governs in our society. Pluralism has a long, though not always honorable, history. Madison, in *Federalist No. 10*, expressed the view that government had to be designed to cure the "mischiefs of faction," largely due to economic differences:

> But the most common and durable source of factions has been the various and unequal distribution of property. Those who hold, and those who are without, property have ever formed distinct interests in society. Those who are creditors, and those who are debtors, fall under a like discrimination. A landed interest, a manufacturing interest, a mercantile interest, a moneyed interest, with many lesser interests, grow up of necessity in civilized nations, and divide them into different classes, actuated by different sentiments and views. (quoted in Ginsberg, Lowi, and Weir 1999, p. A25)

From a policy perspective, the importance of pluralism is that on any given issue, there are competing interests and groups that must be addressed. In most cases, some kind of compromise is necessary; in others, coalitions need to be formed to overcome opposition.

Entrenched interest groups of all persuasions may distort the economy by opposing new technologies and ideas that might threaten them. Further, as resources become scarce (say, because of budget deficits), the conflicts among interest groups make it difficult to assemble majorities in favor of change. As societies mature, more interest groups arise, and the result is the political equivalent of hardening of the arteries. Jonathan Rauch (1999) calls this **demosclerosis** (see also Olson 1982).

When President Clinton, in 1993, proposed to reform the health care system, he faced a rather daunting vista. As we will see in chapter 5, health care is the largest sector of the economy, accounting for 13.7 percent of gross domestic product in 1993 (Levit et al. 2000). Such a large sector is bound to have many interest groups, each with its own interests and concerns. There are interest groups of all kinds of providers (physicians, nurses, hospitals, nursing homes), pharmaceutical companies, insurance companies, various state interest groups (e.g., the National Governors Conference, the National Conference of State Legislatures), various business groups (large, middle-sized, and small), labor groups, consumer groups, and so forth. Most of those interests have divisions within themselves, which complicates matters even more. Any attempt to get a consensus among all these groups would take a heroic, if not impossible, effort.[33] The following quote captures the political atmosphere created by pluralism as Congress began to consider health care reform proposals in March 1994:

> Consider last Tuesday in the nation's capital: 800 doctors were massed at an American Medical Association conference; 210 restaurateurs were trooping to Capitol Hill, ventilating their opposition to the idea of requiring businesses to pay for health insurance; President Clinton was making the case for health care overhaul to the American Society of Association Executives (a kind of trade group for trade groups);

> Ralph Nader was denouncing the A.M.A. at a news conference; former First Ladies Rosalynn Carter and Betty Ford were arguing for mental health coverage before the Senate Labor and Human Resources Committee; and the line of interested parties stretched down a long hall when the House Ways and Means Subcommittee on Health began considering a health care bill.
>     And this was all before noon. (Toner 1994)

There are many examples of pluralism at the administrative level. With the abortion "gag rule" regulation mentioned previously, right-to-life (anti-abortion) groups supported the administrations' actions, whereas pro-choice (pro-abortion) groups opposed it. During the first Bush administration (1989–1992), there was much interest-group activity concerning the proposed definitions and protection of wetlands by the Environmental Protection Agency and changes suggested by Vice President Quayle's Council on Competitiveness (Tiefer 1994). Interest groups may advocate governmental action, propose policies, impede policies, have an impact on implementation, conduct evaluations, and so on. EPA proposed a broad definition of wetlands, and interest groups lobbied both the EPA and the Council (which was given some authority over agencies) for a narrower, more restrictive definition of what would qualify as a wetland and, thus, be subject to federal protections.

Pluralism provides one answer to the question of who participates in politics and government, who influences those who make decisions, who has power. Pluralists maintain that no single elite or set of elites is overwhelmingly influential or participates alone in decision making (see, e.g., Dahl 1967; Polsby 1980). But another view is provided by **elitism,** a belief that power and influence are concentrated in society. Elitist theorists suggest that governmental and private actors in institutional positions of power make or greatly influence most of the policy decisions (Domhoff 1983; Dye 1983; Mills 1956). Both elitist and pluralist schools of power say the same thing. The elitists by definition see only a few exercising power. The pluralists also agree that only a few participate, but they assert that participation is considerably more fluid. In a sense, the pluralists confront what the early twentieth-century French political scientist Robert Michels ([1916] 1962) called the "iron law of oligarchy." Even in those organizations that were committed to democratic procedures and wide participation, such as the European social-democratic parties that Michels studied, only the active minority participated over time.

The elitist model has several variants. The view described above may be labeled as the "ruling elite model." This model is based on overall or societal power structures but does not necessarily identify those who make decisions or are influential in specific policy areas. Other terms have been used to describe a set of elites in policy areas. "Iron triangles," "policy clusters," and "subgovernments" suggest close interaction among congressional committees and subcommittees, executive branch agencies, and relevant interest groups. Policy decisions made by these groupings are often conducted with little publicity (Ripley and Franklin 1984).

Iron triangles are more likely and stable in some policy areas than others. Policies that distribute money, services, contracts, and so forth tend not to be controversial. In more controversial issue areas, as in those involving redistribution of income or regulation of behavior, participation is more open. The term "**issue networks**" describes a more fluid flow of actors in and out of policy issues (Heclo 1978; Van Horn, Baumer, and Gormley 1992); the model of agenda building described above also suggests this fluidity. Perhaps the most useful term is "**policy elite**" (Dietz and Rycroft 1988). Policy elite suggests that participation in policy areas is limited but that the participation differs from issue to issue. We recognize the importance of group activity (pluralism) at the same time that we recognize that only a few actively participate in policy making. The task then becomes one of identifying the participants in and out of government.

A more recent formulation is the vigorous and rigorous research surrounding the concept of **advocacy coalitions**. Within a policy subsystem, such as health care or, even more refined, surrounding Medicare, there are people grouped into coalitions that share beliefs and coordinate action.[34]

Baumgartner and Jones (1993) provide an additional, highly useful perspective on iron triangles and issue networks. They argue that iron triangles predominate during stable periods of policy making, but as a policy area becomes more conflictual and new issues in the area are brought up, the iron triangles are challenged by new groups and new ideas, resulting in new institutions and new policies. During these more turbulent or unstable times, the more fluid types of configurations predominate. In Paul Sabatier and Hank Jenkins-Smith's formulation (1999), the advocacy coalitions would change.

## Fragmentation

Fragmentation is a fourth characteristic of the American political system. It means that no one agency or committee has sole authority or power in a policy area. This circumstance has several impacts. First, because there is overlap, there are generally several access points that interest groups can use. Second, fragmentation creates coordination problems, developing coherent and consistent policy in a given area with many different actors. There are also virtues to fragmentation. Overlap for the system may be functional because if one element fails, then another part of the system may make needed corrections (Landau 1978).

Fragmentation can occur in legislative and executive branches. There are numerous cases of jurisdictional overlap among congressional committees. The fate of President Clinton's Health Security Act was hindered by fragmentation of committee jurisdiction. While there were three important committees in the House of Representatives that claimed some responsibility for health policy, a situation that itself was a sign of fragmentation, the House leadership referred parts of the bill to ten committees altogether. In the Senate, the Finance and Labor and Human Resources committees vied for leadership over the bill. The Senate leadership was unable to resolve the dispute, and they referred the bill to both committees. The leadership in both houses could have used ad hoc committees that would contain members of all appropriate committees as a way of getting around the jurisdictional fragmentation (in administration, this is known as interagency task forces). The fact that they did not contributed to the failure of the proposal (Rushefsky and Patel 1998).

The problems of fragmentation in the executive branch can be seen in employment training programs (General Accounting Office 1994). The federal government has 154 such programs aimed at four different target groups: the economically disadvantaged, older workers, youth, and dislocated workers.

A recent example of fragmentation in the executive branch concerned a listeria contamination of a hot dog plant. One agency with prime responsibility was the Food Safety and Inspection Service in the U.S. Department of Agriculture. The Centers for Disease Control and Prevention (CDC) studies patterns of human disease, and it found the hot dog contamination to be "the most lethal case of food-borne illness in the United States in 15 years" (Perl 2000). The Food and Drug Administration (FDA) regulates the safety of most food products but not meat and poultry. Although the federal government does have the authority to recall unsafe products, such as pesticides or automobiles, the U.S. Department of Agriculture (USDA) does not have such authority over food-processing plants (Perl 2000). Fragmentation permits a situation where no one has responsibility or authority to take action.

A second recent example of administrative fragmentation can be seen in gene therapy (Sung 2000). As the biomedical sciences and biotechnology advance, the possibility for creating flaws in someone's genetic makeup becomes more feasible, and some experimental gene therapy tests have been undertaken. The death of Jesse Gelsinger in 1999 resulted from an experiment to correct a genetic liver disorder. There have apparently been other deaths as well.

Fragmentation comes into play because proposals to undertake genetic therapy tests at one time had to be approved by a National Institutes of Health (NIH) advisory committee on recombinant DNA. That authority was transferred to the FDA in 1997. However, the FDA keeps reports of deaths and other adverse occurrences confidential.

As with many of the other features of the American political system, fragmentation creates multiple access points. If federalism allows those seeking to influence policy making to work at different levels of government, and separation of powers allows working one or another branch of government, fragmentation creates influence points within branches.

## Incrementalism

The fifth feature of the American political system that affects policy is the style of decision making utilized, known as **incrementalism**. Incrementalism means that comprehensive, one-time decisions are rarely made. Rather, small decisions are made and then modified over time as more is learned about the program or problem or as the context changes.[35] One could argue that the nearly two-decade-long effort that eventually resulted in a balanced budget was an example of incrementalism (Palazzolo 1999; see also chapter 2).

Incrementalism reinforces some of the other features discussed earlier. For example, the fact that policy decisions are rarely final means that an interest group that loses today has opportunities tomorrow to achieve its goals.

Secretary of State George P. Schultz captured the spirit of incrementalism in December 1986. Schultz was testifying before a congressional committee about the arms shipments to Iran, a policy he strongly opposed. He lectured the committee about the frustrations of policy making.

> Nothing ever gets settled in this town. It's not like running a company or a university. It's a seething debating society in which the debate never stops, in which people never give up, including me, and that's the atmosphere in which you administer. (quoted in Apple 1986)

This is not to say that innovative measures are never undertaken. The discussion of windows of opportunity and agenda building suggests how such innovation might occur (Kingdon 1984; Baumgartner and Jones 1993; True 2000). One notable example of a nonincremental change was the creation of NASA and the Apollo moon project (Schulman 1975). Another important example is welfare reform in 1996 (see chapter 4). While there are some such examples, most decisions are of the incremental variety.

There are some observers who have looked at the impact of these features, such as incrementalism and separation of powers, and argued that they make policy formulation and execution difficult. Certainly the cumulative impact of these five features creates a **diffusion of power**, where political power is dispersed within institutions such as Congress, among different agencies, across branches of government, and among different levels of government.[36] Pluralism means that there are many groups seeking to influence the course of public policy, and incrementalism implies that decisions will usually be revisited.

These features, and the policy process itself, seem to imply that it is impossible to get anything done and that even when something is accomplished, it is done badly. Certainly, it is difficult to get policies passed, but the American political system was designed to be slow and deliberate in order to prevent tyranny by the majority. But things do get accomplished. Policy making, changing policies, and creating new programs are arduous, time consuming, continuous, but not impossible.

## Public Opinion, the Media, and Trust

One last consideration in our journey through the American political system and its impact on the making of public policy: the interconnected impact of public opinion and the media and its impact on trust in government.

Ultimately, a democratic government rests on popular sovereignty, the consent of the people. Over the last sixty years or so, the science of public opinion has become well developed, and politicians often refer to public opinion polls to get a sense of what the public wants. Some have argued that our political leaders are too tied to public opinion, that we have too much democracy, and our leaders do not exercise their own judgment sufficiently (King 1997).

At the same time, there is some evidence to suggest that the public does not believe it has very much influence over government officials. According to a 1999 survey, the public believes that when public officials refer to public opinion polls, they do so only in a symbolic way, to appear to be listening to the public (Morin 1999).

That survey is only one of the latest in a series of public opinion polls that have documented the decline in the public's view of political (and other institutions) since the 1960s. Public opinion survey polls (such as the American National Election Studies series) have asked a series of questions about whether the respondents trust government to do the right thing most of the time, whether government is responsive to public demands, and whether government listens to people like them. Addressing just the trust question, in 1964 76.4 percent of the respondents answered that they trusted government to do the right thing just about always or most of the time; in 1992 the number had declined to 28.9 percent. Similar results can be seen for questions about efficacy and responsiveness (see Craig 1993; see also general discussion in Nye, Zelikow, and King 1997).

Two important questions to ask are why the decline in trust occurred and why that is important. One answer to the question of why the decline in trust in government is the belief that special-interest groups, the media, elected officials, and political parties are to blame for the poor performance and lack of responsiveness of government. Groups, officials, and parties are seen as concerned only for their self-interest and are not primarily concerned about what is good for the nation. Most people refer to "the government" rather than "our government" as if government (at all levels) were distant from the people. This disconnection from government seems especially pronounced among young people (Council for Excellence in Government 1999).

Robert Samuelson (1995) argues that the inability to fulfill the grand promises of the 1960s Great Society and War on Poverty programs led to perceptions of failure. He notes that while things have gotten better, the public perception remains one of failure and unfulfilled promises.

It was mentioned above that the public blames the media for its lack of trust in government. The public gets virtually all of its information from the media, with television as a major source. The media view of government and politics has likewise declined since the 1960s. According to Larry Sabato (1991), press reporting on politics went through three stages. Up to 1966, members of the press were essentially "lapdogs"—reporters were respectful of public officials, accepted what they said at face value, and protected them. From 1966 to 1974, reporters engaged in "watchdog journalism," character-ized by skepticism and investigations. The fallout from Watergate and the Vietnam War contributed to this result. From 1974 to the present, "junkyard dog journalism" has characterized reporters' attitudes toward politics and government officials. The focus is on being aggressive and intrusive; cyni-cism is the watchword. Patterson (1994) and Kerbel (1995) have a similar analysis of the role of the media.

Cappella and Jamieson (1997) argue that the media tends to focus on the "game" of politics rather than on the substance. In the case of elections, the media look more at the "horse race" aspect (who is winning) and the strate-gies of campaigns rather than what the campaigns stand for. In the case of policy issues, there is a tendency to focus on which elected officials and spe-cial interests benefit from proposals and actions rather than on the substance of the policy and its effects. This focus on the game over substance leads to cynicism on the part of both the media and the public, which depends on the media for its information.

It is not only the news media that create a poor image of government and government officials. Television entertainment also contributes in terms of how it depicts public officials.[37]

According to a careful analysis of television programs going back to the 1950s (Lichter, Lichter, and Amundson 1999), prime-time television is likely to picture politicians as motivated solely by self-interest and greed, not caring much for the needs of their constituents. Television has portrayed civil ser-vants (bureaucrats) as largely, though not entirely, jaded, lazy, self-absorbed, and so forth. Robert Lichter and colleagues (1999, p. 75) conclude:

> In sum, the far-flung administrative apparatus of government has a low profile on prime time. Few memorable characters appear as civil servants, and those who do make a lasting impression often fit the stereotype of the officious, indifferent, or inefficient government bureaucrat. On television in the 1990s, public employees frequently put their own private interests above those of the public whose interests they are sworn to serve.

News and entertainment programs have another important effect on public opinion and thus the policy process. The media programs can give a mislead-ing impression about the problems of society and how well government works. News programs often highlight crimes, especially particularly vicious and shocking crimes. There was tremendous media coverage of the shootings at Columbine High School in Littleton, Colorado, in 1999. Certainly the shootings were a tragedy; certainly there have been shootings at other schools (and workplaces) before Columbine; certainly there are problems in the schools that need to be dealt with. And while statistics are not comforting to those who mourn the loss of loved ones, the fact remains that school violence has decreased over the last decade or two (Egan 1999) and that children are actually safer from crime at school than they are at home.

There are many crime-oriented television shows: *Law and Order*, its offshoot *Special Victims Unit*, *NYPD Blue*, *The Practice*, and so forth. One would not know from watching the news or entertainment programs or reading the papers that crime had gone down. One might expect there to be fewer crime stories if there was less crime. That does not seem to be the case.

Consider the following quote, which deals with the media's portrayal of poverty and race:

> News coverage of the poor has consistently distorted black poverty, portraying it more negatively and less accurately than white poverty. Over the past four decades, the country's elite media organizations have offered a portrait of American poverty that exaggerates the racial differences and unfairly associates blacks with the less attractive subgroups of the poor. And when news stories on poverty do take a more sympathetic turn (as they tend to do during economic downturns), images of the black poor are replaced with images of poor whites. . . .
>
> The news media offers the public a portrait of poverty in which blacks far outnumber non-blacks, while in reality fewer than three out of ten poor Americans are black. (Gilens 1999)[38]

Given what we have said about the connection of the people with politics and government, their disconnection from government, and the media problems, it should not be very surprising that the American public is not well informed about politics and government issues. For example, a public opinion survey asked respondents whether Medicare was larger (in dollar terms) than U.S. foreign aid or vice versa. Sixty-four percent thought that U.S. foreign aid was a larger program than Medicare. The reality is that Medicare costs more than $200 billion, while foreign aid is at less than one-tenth that level. What we find is ignorance about the details of policy (Edwards, Wattenberg, and Lineberry 1996). Another survey questioned Americans about federal entitlement programs, such as Social Security and Medicare, and found similar levels of ignorance. The authors suggest that the gap in public knowledge about entitlement programs makes it difficult to bring about major reforms (Blendon et al. 1997). Yet a third survey documented the public's ignorance (perhaps the better phrase is "ill-informed perceptions") about basic economic facts (such as unemployment and inflation rates) (Morin and Berry 1996).

These results do not mean that there is no role for public opinion in the policy process. While the people may be ignorant of the details of public policy, they seem to be clearer on the general outlines and have firm preferences, have deeply held values, and are rational in their opinions taken as a whole. Further, beliefs and attitudes do change, and politicians and interest groups are both responsive to those changes and try to shape them (Jacobs and Shapiro 2000).

A comparison of changed public attitudes toward policy issues makes the point (Geraghty 2000). The federal deficit is no longer an issue, and the unwillingness to spend because of the fiscal constraint of the deficit remains. Crime remains an issue of concern, followed by education and economic issues (such as the impact of globalization on American workers). The public are concerned about the future of Social Security and look increasingly favorably toward investment. The antipathy toward government has lessened somewhat.

The public also show much ambiguity about government. A majority of the public thinks that government is too big, does too much, and should leave more activities to individuals or the private sector. On the other hand, when asked about specific government programs or policies, there is majority support for those programs (Cantril and Cantril 1999). Those who make public policy or propose public policies or seek to influence the policy process need to keep this ambivalence in mind.

Further, it does appear that public opinion and public policy are reasonably consistent. Scholars who have looked at the issue of **policy congruence** have found that while public opinion and public policy varied over time, agreement between opinion and policy has been mostly over 50 percent but did decline in the 1990s (see Monroe 1979; Jacobs and Shapiro 1997; and Page and Shapiro 1992).

## Is Government a Failure?

One of the important themes of this book, new to this third edition, is a more explicit focus on the success of government programs. What is argued is not that all programs succeed all the time, nor is it argued that there are no failures. What is argued instead is that government programs do experience successes and those successes need to be acknowledged. Gregg Easterbrook (1995) argues that in the environmental policy area, there have been substantial successes. For example, the air is cleaner that it was twenty or thirty years ago, at least in part because of clean air legislation. This is all the more remarkable because of the growth of the economy and of the population. There are more cars on the road, yet the air is cleaner.

Similarly, the Thernstroms (1997) have argued that the status of African Americans in the United States has improved drastically since the 1950s. The same is true about crime rates, teen pregnancy rates, declines in welfare rolls, improvements in real wages, and so forth. By 2000, the economy had experienced its longest period of economic growth in its history combined with relatively low inflation and unemployment. Chronic federal budget deficits have, to the astonishment of virtually everyone, turned into surpluses. In foreign policy, the United States stands as the world's strongest nation both economically and militarily. This view can be seen in such works as John

Schwarz's *America's Hidden Success* (1988) and David Whitman's *The Optimism Gap* (1998). Whitman writes (p. 1):

> Much of what everyone "knows" is wrong. A large majority of Americans now believe that the nation is in decline. The causes of this decline are both familiar and disputed. Conservatives blame family breakdown, crime and spiritual sloth for our national atrophy. Liberals attribute the decline to the forces of modern-day capitalism, racism and greed; the poor and the working-class stiffs in the factories can no longer get ahead the way they once did, or so the argument goes. Yet while liberals and conservatives disagree about first causes, they nonetheless agree that the nation, like Rome before the fall, has already been compromised. The American Dream is now endangered.
>
> Beneath this glum appraisal, however, lies a paradox. While most Americans attest to the country's deterioration, they are equally adamant that they and their families are, on the whole, flourishing. This optimism gap—the gulf between people's upbeat assessment of their personal lives and their downbeat assessment of the country and its public institutions—helps explain much of the country's current political paralysis.[39]

This is not to say that the United States no longer faces problems or that things could not get better. Issues of equality, such as race, remain to be fully dealt with. In late 2000 and early 2001, the economy slowed down. Crime rates, while continuing to decrease, are beginning to plateau. We will examine how well we are doing and how we can improve throughout the remainder of the book. The point is, again, that we must recognize that there have been successes and not ceaselessly downgrade government and society.

Further, if the United States is experiencing good times, then this is perhaps the appropriate time to address programs that need fixing and problems that need remedying. Brownstein (1999a; see also Brownstein 1999b) argues that there are plenty of good ideas out there but also a lack of willingness to compromise. Further, society should be able to undertake new programs as experiments: We should see what works and what does not work. We should tolerate failure and be willing to admit that some programs do not work.[40] As we saw above, the policy process is about not just addressing problems, but taking advantage of opportunities.

## Ideology: From Value Positions to Issue Positions

A concept that strongly affects the policy process is **ideology**. Ideology consists of a set of beliefs about what the world is like, values with which to appraise the state of the world (good/bad, satisfactory/unsatisfactory), and beliefs and attitudes about how to make the world conform to these values (Herson 1984). Ideology includes the idea of a **public philosophy**: what government should and should not do.

The usual discussion of ideology looks at the content of the various ideologies, such as liberalism, neoliberalism, conservatism, neoconservatism, and the New Right. The focus on this text is on how ideology relates to public policy. Ideology affects our perceptions of events and the way we organize and define or give meaning to those perceptions.

This is exactly what happens in that all-important first stage of the policy process, problem identification. To recall, problem identification consists largely of perceiving and defining an event as a problem or opportunity, or absence of a problem or opportunity. Because we are faced with an overload of information, we require some kind of perceptual screen that tells us what is important and what is not. Ideology fulfills that role. We experience events and interpret them according to our ideology.

Going further, recall how problem identification structures the rest of the policy process; different problem definitions are associated with different solutions. Ideology has an action component, so if ideology structures our perceptions and definitions, it also suggests particular solutions (including doing nothing).

In the United States, ideology has generally been limited to the conservative-liberal continuum (Cantril and Cantril 1999; Ginsberg, Lowi and Weir 1999). There are at least two problems with this conceptualization. First, public opinion is not clear about what the terms "liberal" and "conservative" mean. Those identifying themselves as being of one ideology (say conservative) may give answers to specific questions that are liberal and vice versa. A second problem is the finding that many people are not consistently one or the other. They are often called moderates, an unsatisfactory and meaningless category (Ginsberg, Lowi, and Weir 1999). Albert Cantril and Susan Cantril's (1999) research demonstrates these very problems. Their very important study of American public opinion finds the public ambivalent about government. The public states a general distrust of government (see above): it is too big, it does too much, taxes are too high. When questioned about specific government actions, however, there is considerable public support for it. The result is that the public gives off mixed signals.

The resolution is to distinguish between ideological positions on issues based on values rather to focus on ideologies per se.[41] Thus we can talk about a liberal position on a given issue and a conservative position on a particular issue. At its most elemental level, ideological positions are based on three values (Janda, Berry, and Goldman 1995; Maddox and Lilie 1984; Wells and Hamilton 1996).

The first of these values is **order**. Order refers to the protection of society, of life and property, from both external (other countries) and internal (criminal) forces. The value of order also includes the importance of tradition and moral values usually based on religion. This other notion of order, based on social values, has become more prominent in recent years. It has been a major theme of elections (White 1990). It is also, as we shall see, an important component of policy debates. Government is viewed as an important instrument for upholding order in society.[42]

The second of the political values is **freedom** or liberty. Freedom refers to freedom from government restraints, from government tyranny. The provisions of the Bill of Rights are protections from arbitrary government. These

Figure 1.5  **Ideology and Values**

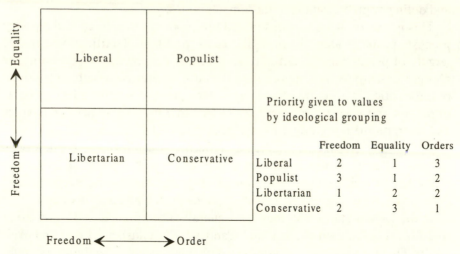

Source: Janda, Berry, and Goldman (1995).

include the rights of those accused of crimes, the right to petition government, and freedoms of speech, press, and religion. Those who hold freedom as a primary value (libertarians) are interested in minimal government. Freedom might also mean freedom from private-sector intrusions. As more and more people use the Internet and look for information, visit websites, or make online purchases, the possibility of gathering data and then selling it to marketing companies increases. So privacy concerns emanating from the private sector would fall under this value. Some of the antagonism toward managed care (see chapter 5) is due to restrictions on patient and provider activities. New developments in understanding our genetic makeup also raise privacy concerns.

The final political value is **equality**. Equality may have three different meanings. **Political equality** refers to voting; each person has one vote. It has also meant equality of representation in state legislatures; the one-person, one-vote decision of *Baker v. Carr* (1962). A second meaning of equality is **equality of opportunity**, giving each person the right to develop to his or her potential. This is a procedural value: As long as no one is discriminated against, then the outcomes of achievement are of little concern. The third meaning of equality is the most controversial, **equality of outcome** or results. Here the emphasis is on social equality through programs such as affirmative action and progressive income taxes. While political equality and equality of opportunity are widely held values in American society, equality of outcome has been contentious.

Ideologies can be constructed on the basis of their preferences among these three values (see Figure 1.5). **Liberals** place greatest preference on equality, followed by freedom and then order. **Conservatives** are the opposite; they prefer order to freedom, then equality. **Libertarians** prefer freedom to both equal-

Figure 1.6    **Ideology and Issue Positions: When Should Government Intervene?**

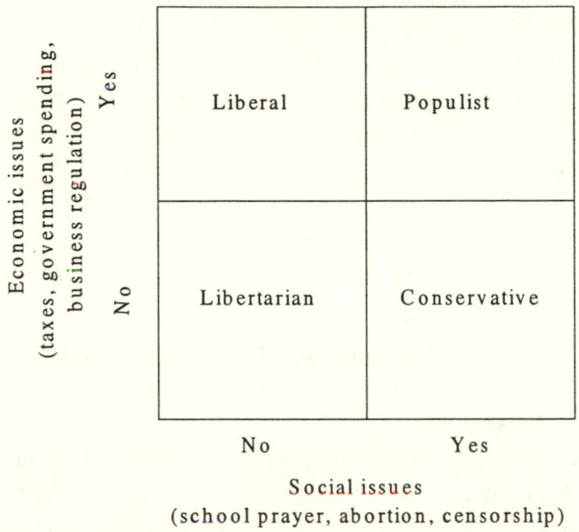

Source: Adapted from Maddox and Lilie (1984). Reprinted with permission.

ity and order, while **populists** prefer equality to freedom and order to freedom. These value priorities are reflected in ideological preferences or positions on policy issues, illustrated in two broad types: economic issues and social issues.

Economic issues relate to spending and taxation, including the budget, taxes, and concerns about the size of government. The liberal position favors government intervention to manage the economy and promote equality through progressive taxation and such policies as raising the minimum wage. Conservatives prefer smaller government, lower taxes, and tax reform (such as a flat tax or national sales tax).

There are two types of social issues. Conservative social issues concern regulation of behavior not involving taxing and spending decisions. These issues include right to life, family planning, gun protection, school prayer, immigration reform, and control of pornography (Schneider 1986). The conservative position, with its emphasis on order over freedom, prefers government action to support traditional values. The liberal position, based on a preference for freedom over order, opposes an active government role on those issues. Figure 1.6 shows how the four ideologies fit these two issue positions. Comparing Figures 1.5 and 1.6 shows the relationship between values and issue positions.

This analysis also helps clear up some confusion about ideologies and government. It has sometimes been said that liberals favor government action and conservatives oppose government intervention. It turns out that this is not necessarily case. It depends upon the issue. For some kinds of social issues, conservatives want government to step in and liberals do not.

To take this idea a little further, consider that there is a set of liberal social issues that reverses the positions of liberals and conservatives. These issues concern the conflict between equality and freedom and include such things as civil rights, sexual discrimination, poverty and health policies, energy, and the environment. The liberal position favors an active government role, whereas the conservative position prefers little or no public-sector involvement. In many of these areas, the conservative position is that if government is to play a role, then it should rely as much as possible on market-like mechanisms, reflecting an emphasis on freedom. Note that while the position of liberals toward government depends on the issue, this is not as true for libertarians and populists. Libertarians seek minimal government, one that does the least amount necessary to keep society and private markets running. Populists, on the other hand, support government action on social (both conservative and liberal) and economic issues.

There is a fifth ideology that should be examined that does not quite fit the conceptual scheme sketched above.[43] This ideology is **communitarianism**. While there does not appear to be a clear definition of this ideology, its outlines can be traced. In essence, communitarianism seeks a balance between the values of order and freedom. In other words, its seeks to reconcile the ideology of **radical individualism** (libertarians, civil libertarians), who seek freedom and the priority placed on the individual person, and **social conservatives**, who seek to use the powers of government to restore what they see as the lost moral order. To put it yet another way, communitarianism searches for a balance between rights and responsibilities. So, for example, communitarians favor character education in schools and colleges, but would encourage rather than require it.

Beginning with economic issues in the next chapter, this ideological view of liberal and conservative positions based on value preferences will be employed to help structure the analysis of problems in each area and to examine proposed solutions. Considering the ideological positions on the issues helps to cut through the myriad studies and proposals and uncover the essentials, leading to a better understanding of policy issues.

---

## Key Concepts

administrative federalism

appropriations committees

advocacy coalition

authorization committees

agenda building

budget committees

application

budgeting

causes

checks and balances

communitarianism

conservatives

crosscutting requirement

crossover sanction

definition

demands

demosclerosis

devolution

diffusion of power

direct democracy mechanisms

direct orders

direct services

divided government

efficiency

elitism

entitlements

equality

equality of opportunity

equality of outcome

equity

executive agreements

executive orders

facts

federalism

fiscal federalism

fragmentation

freedom

government

government issue

ideology

implementation

incrementalism

inducements

initiatives

inputs

inside initiative

intergovernmental relations

interpretation

issue networks

judicial action

legislation

legislative (or authorization)
committees

liberals

libertarians

liberty

mandates

mobilization

model

modification

narratives

numbers

order

organization

outcomes

outputs

outside initiative

perception

pluralism

policies stream

policy adoption

policy analysis

policy congruence

policy elite

policy formulation

policy goal

policy solutions

policy succession

political equality

political stream

politics

populists

powers

preemption

problem identification

problems stream

program evaluation

program failure

public philosophy

public policy

radical individualism

referendum

regulations

rights

rules

security

separation of powers

social conservatives

social constructionism

supports

termination

theory failure

windows of opportunity

# Reflections

1. Some political scientists and other observers have suggested that we need to make changes in the structure of government so that policy can be more coherent and policy changes can be facilitated. The key target for such changes is the separation-of-powers feature. The British political system is often held up as a model to follow. What do you think might be the impact of such a change? Who would benefit and who would gain from such a change? In 2001, the same party controlled both Congress and the presidency. Do you think that will make policy changes easier? Do you think the closeness of the 2001 elections (a disputed presidential election, an even split in the Senate, and decreased majority for the Republicans in the House) will affect policy making and the resulting policies? Is the problem the structure of government or the pain associated with policy cures? What do you think about such changes?

2. There is considerable literature on the controversy over power structures in the United States. As we saw, some analysts see power as fairly diffuse, spread among different interest groups. Others see power as considerably more concentrated among a few people in positions of power. Which do you think better describes your community, your college or university, your state, or the nation as a whole? Does it make a difference in policy outputs, the policies that are adopted, whether the pluralists or elitists are correct?

3. Another feature of the American political system that has been widely criticized is fragmentation. We can see fragmentation most easily in Congress. Why do you think there is so much fragmentation in Congress? What are the implications of diffuse power in Congress? What conditions would be necessary to reduce fragmentation and consolidate power?

4. In the section on ideology, I described four basic types of ideologies: conservatism, liberalism, libertarianism, and populism. Reread that section or the references cited and try to characterize your political beliefs. Which one best describes you? There seemed to be a trend toward libertarianism among students in the 1980s. Does your experience agree with this? Why do you think that is so? What is the significance of this? I also described a fifth ideology, communitarianism, which splits some of the differences among the other ideologies. Does communitarianism seem attractive to you? Do you think the notion of people having rights and responsibilities could help resolve some of the problems facing the United States today? Most Americans have difficulty characterizing their ideology correctly as most do not think in ideological terms. Why do you think this is so? What might be the significance of this for electing leaders and for making public policy? One study discussed in the chapter pointed out that Americans do not like government in general, but do like many of the things government does. Why do you think this is so? What might be the significance of this for electing leaders and for making public policy?

5. One of the themes running through this book is optimism, in the sense that, at least through 2000, there have been government programs that have

worked. As you read the substantive policy chapters, see if you can pick up this theme. I will return to it in the final chapter.

## Notes

1. Murray Edelman (1964) has done some of the best work on symbols and politics.

2. This text uses Jones (1984) as a framework but introduces modifications to it. For a similar exposition to Jones, see Anderson (1997). For an insightful discussion and critique of these types of process models, see Sabatier (1999) and DeLeon (1999).

3. Dery (1984) uses the broader term "opportunity identification." See also Rochefort and Cobb (1994).

4. A number of scholars have suggested that the media has led to public cynicism and mistrust of government. See, for example, Cappella and Jamieson (1997), Kerbel (1995), and Patterson (1994). For a discussion of the role of the media in health policy, see Rushefsky and Patel (1998, chapter 6). For a general discussion of the media, see Kurtz (1996). For an incisive critique of television, see Scheuer (1999).

5. Baumgartner and Jones (1993) argue that, most of the time, the United States experiences stability in its policy making, especially in this agenda-building stage. At times, however, instability and change take place. The result is what they call "punctuated equilibrium" (True, Jones, and Baumgartner 1999). We will have more to say about this in the section on incrementalism.

6. Managed care refers to a set of controls designed to limit the utilization of medical services. These controls include such things as mandatory second opinions and preadmission certifications. A health maintenance organization is often considered a managed care organization. This issue will be discussed in chapter 5.

7. For a discussion of health-care systems in other countries and the lessons they hold for the United States, see Glaser (1993), Graig (1999), and White (1995).

8. A classic formulation of policy analysis is Quade (1982). See also Stokey and Zeckhauser (1978) and Weimer and Vining (1992).

9. The list is from Stone (1997), but her interpretation of policy goals is much more complex than is discussed here.

10. As with policy goals, the list is from Stone (1997), but the interpretation is mine.

11. Baumgartner and Jones (1993) combine the concepts of changing policy images (or definitions/interpretations) with changes in policy venues (what we just called "powers" to explain agenda change).

12. Jones (1984) refers to policy adoption by legislatures as "legitimation."

13. Riders, as in "going along for the ride," are amendments that are added onto bills that are likely to pass without a presidential veto. This practice is much more common in the Senate, which allows unlimited amendments. Riders are also inviting because the president does not have the power to veto specific items or lines in a bill passed by Congress.

14. For a discussion of incrementalism as well as of large policy changes related to budgeting, see True (2000).

15. For a discussion of the Reagan administration's administrative strategy, as well as a similar but less successful attempt during the Nixon administration, see Nathan (1983). For a discussion of specific abortion regulation from 1981 to 1992, see Weitz (1993).

16. For a discussion of other factors affecting implementation, see Mazmanian and Sabatier (1983).

17. For a very readable discussion of why evaluations are often not utilized and what might be done to improve them, see Patton (1978).

18. See chapter 4 for a discussion of these issues.

19. The evaluation of Head Start points to one of the major problems in any program evaluation: The timeline may be either too short or too long between the output and the impact to clearly indicate effectiveness. Moreover, especially with implementations that attempt to change behavior, the human resource variable in terms of administrative personnel is vital. My thanks goes to one of the reviewers for pointing this out.

20. See Brewer and DeLeon (1983) for a guide to literature on termination.

21. Robert Samuelson (1995) argues that debates over the federal budget are about, or should be about, how much government we want.

22. For an analysis of problems that Bill Clinton had in his first year in office with the Democratically controlled Congress, see Cohen (1993). For a more extensive analysis of the first two years of the Clinton presidency, see Stoesz (1996).

23. An argument can be made that government is less divided than is apparent. Frymer (1994) demonstrates that voters are electing candidates who support their political and ideological preferences, whatever the party. Thus, the conservative coalition that ruled Congress in the 1950s and early 1960s and stymied civil rights changes was made up of conservative Democrats and Republicans. The same was true in 1981–82 when Congress approved significant budget and tax cuts. A similar coalition appears to have defeated President Clinton's health care bill in 1994.

24. For a review of recent election-year productivity in Congress, see Cohen (2000).

25. For a discussion of presidential and parliamentary systems, see the special 1994 issue of *Political Science Quarterly*. For an examination of the proposition that changes in the country and the political system since 1969 have made the governing more difficult, see the June 18, 1994, issue of *National Journal*. See also Rauch (1999).

26. Parliamentary government with many parties or that lacks a party with the ability to gain a majority has its own problems. Such systems may be unstable, as in Italy, or may produce extreme policies, as in Israel.

27. There was also the reluctance of the Clinton administration, as well as the Bush administration, to use force, such as air combat missions, and its inability to convince either Congress or the public that there were reasonable grounds for such actions. See chapter 3.

28. For a detailed discussion of presidential congressional relations, see Jones (1994) and LeLoup and Shull (1999).

29. In the wake of welfare reform after 1996, there have been reports of numerous people not being told by state case workers that they are still eligible for Medicaid and food stamps. See Pear (1999) and "States Illegally Denying Medicaid, Audit Finds" (1999).

30. For a discussion of unevenness in state fiscal policy, see Qiao (1999).

31. For a discussion of preemption and the federal government versus states, see Nivola (2000). Pietro Nivola argues that Republican as well as Democratic presidents and Congresses have engaged in this type of activity.

32. President Nixon also used the phrase "new federalism," so the Reagan proposal could be labeled New Federalism II.

33. For a discussion of the role of interest groups in American politics, see Berry (1997) and West and Loomis (1999).

34. For a thorough discussion of the advocacy coalition model, see Sabatier and Jenkins-Smith (1999).

35. For a discussion of incrementalism, see Lindblom (1959), Lindblom and Woodhouse (1993) and Hayes (1992).

36. Diffusion of power is the major theme of Hedrick Smith's *The Power Game* (1988).

37. Part of the problem here may be that there has been a blending of news and entertainment divisions within television.

38. The internet source of the quote and the three articles on the media and the poor are based on Gilens book, *Why Americans Hate Welfare* (Chicago: University of Chicago Press, 1999). A similar phenomenon may occur in the criminal justice area. As one example, a recent article in the local newspaper, *The Springfield News-Leader*, focused on people convicted of crimes who continually violate prohibition and go virtually unpunished. The story included pictures of five such habitual offenders. Two of them, forty percent of the pictures, were of African Americans, three (sixty percent) were of whites. Springfield, MO, is a very white city, with an African-American population of no more than 5 percent. But the impression given by the pictures is that African Americans are responsible for much of the crime, an impression belied by statistics. See Menner (2001).

39. For a similar assessment, see Easterbrook (1999) and Sullivan (1999).

40. The discussion above about incrementalism suggests an experimental view of public policy making.

41. For a review of the ideology literature and an initial use of this values-based ideology, see Glathar and Rushefsky (1999).

42. Some political theorists such as Hobbes have argued that government and society are necessary to protect ourselves from the brutality of the war of all against all that characterizes the state of nature (the absence of government). Other theorists justify the existence of government on the grounds that in its absence we would expend natural resources in a way detrimental to all. Whichever view one takes, the essential purpose of government is the protection of its citizens and the establishment of order.

43. Communitarianism has a journal, *The Responsive Community: Rights and Responsibilities*. The example in this paragraph is from Karp 1996/1997. The founding father of communitarianism is Amitai Etzioni (1993; 1996).

# 2 Economic Policy: To Promote the General Welfare

*Wrong decisions in the 1980s condemned the nation to a decade of high deficits; right ones in the 1990s have liberated it from past budgetary misdeeds* (Schick 2000, p. 36).

One of the criticisms of the Articles of Confederation, our governing document from 1781 to 1788, was that the central government was too weak to allow for the development and expansion of the newly formed nation. The national government could not regulate trade among the states or with foreign countries. Both the states and the national government could issue currency, but soon both sets of currencies became worthless. The national government lacked the power to tax and had to rely on contributions from the states. Economic chaos reigned and debtors were protesting the foreclosure of their farms. The country was in danger of falling apart into thirteen separate political entities.

What a contrast to the United States at the start of the twenty-first century! The Constitution of 1787 gave new powers to the national government that enabled the United States to become, by the 1990s, the sole economic and military superpower. But while the nation developed as an economic power in the late nineteenth and early twentieth centuries, the national government did not have the tools to influence the economy's growth. Presidents and congresses may have been blamed for the state of the economy, but there was little that either could do to stave off a recession or cool off an overheated economy.

That changed as the federal government devised tools that led to a new responsibility for managing the economy. The health of the economy, and therefore economic policy, is vital to the ability of the nation to undertake other policy goals. An economy that is growing at a healthy, moderate rate with low inflation can develop new programs and help those who need assistance. A stagnant economy does not allow for new programs or the expansion of old ones. Even defense policy, vital to a nation's survival, faced the decline of resources due to the end of the Cold War and the need to reduce large federal budget deficits.

The economic policies of the 1980s were a reaction to policies and problems of the 1960s and 1970s and shaped much of the economic policy debates of the 1990s. The economy suffered a mild recession in the early 1990s, ending what Robert Bartley (1992) called the "seven fat years" (1982–89). To the surprise of many, the experience of the 1990s turned out to be much different from what had been expected. The expansion that began haltingly in April 1991 was going strong as the new century rang in. By February 2000, the expansion had reached its 107th month, the longest in the country's 200-plus years of history. Perhaps even more dramatic was that the chronic federal government budget deficits that had exploded in the 1980s seem to magically disappear. Rather than deficits as far as the eye could see, budget officials were projecting decade-long (and perhaps longer) surpluses. There was even talk of eliminating the $3 trillion-plus deficit. The good economic news seems to keep coming: a stock market boom, high increases in productivity, low inflation, low unemployment. Even those at the lower income scale began to see real (inflation-adjusted) increases in their incomes. Perhaps the good news would last forever!

But even as the boom economy continued, problems remained and some signs of a slowdown were on the horizon. Nothing lasts forever. The end of 2000 and the beginning of 2001 saw a slowdown of the economy and a decline in the stock market.

With this as a backdrop, this chapter examines how policy instruments were developed earlier this century and how they have been used. The discussion focuses on the state of the economy by the beginning of the new century, the problems and opportunities that exist, and some proposed solutions. The problems, opportunities, and issues discussed include the federal budget surplus and what to do with it, issues of entitlements such as Social Security, international trade issues, and income and wealth distribution. The case study focuses on Social Security.

The concepts introduced in chapter 1 will guide this exploration of economic policy. Ideology and problem definition play vital roles here. Liberal and conservative positions differ regarding the appropriate role of government in managing the economy (the government issue), preferences among policy tools, what economic problems exist, why they exist, and what ought to be done about them. Indeed, perspectives differ about the success of our economic policies in the 1990s and early 2000s.

Institutional features play a role also. Economic policy relies to a certain extent on policy adoption by Congress, with all that entails, and so separation of powers becomes important. The Federal Reserve Board, an independent regulatory agency, also adopts and implements economic policy. Here separation of powers is not a problem.

The following section, problem identification, examines the available economic policy tools, how they are used, and how they are seen through the perspectives of liberal and conservative ideological positions.

## Problem Identification

### *The Economic Policy Toolbox*

Managing the economy refers to efforts by the federal government to smooth fluctuations of the business cycle, promoting economic growth and stability with low inflation and unemployment rates. From the standpoint of the discipline of economics, this is the area of **macroeconomics**, examining the behavior of the economy as a whole, in particular concentrating on what economists call "large aggregates," such as the inflation rate. (Microeconomics focuses on the behavior of individual and group actors.) The responsibility for managing the economy is largely a post–World War II phenomenon, but the basic tools were in place before then.

In general, there are two broad sets of tools available to the federal government to manage the economy, fiscal and monetary policy. **Fiscal policy** employs taxing and spending powers to influence the business cycle and various measures of the health of the economy: inflation rate, unemployment rate, productivity, and so forth. **Monetary policy** focuses on interest rates and the growth of the nation's money supply. Both sets of policy instruments are based on **inducements**—rewarding desired behavior and punishing or deterring undesired behavior.

### *Fiscal Policy*

In 1913 the **Sixteenth Amendment** to the Constitution was passed, giving Congress the authority to impose an income tax. When the federal income tax became large enough after World War II, it permitted the federal government to expand its domestic, foreign, and defense functions. It could be manipulated to affect decisions by individuals and groups in a wide variety of ways and also could be used to influence overall demand for goods and services in the economy. Taxes could be employed to encourage desired behavior. For example, investment tax credits provide an incentive to undertake new investment by allowing some of the cost of that investment to reduce tax obligations, thereby reducing the total cost of investment. Taxes can also be used as an alternative means to accomplish social purposes. As we will see in chapter 4, the Earned Income Tax Credit is one of the country's major welfare programs, aimed at the working poor. The deduction for employee health insurance payments has been a major inducement for employer-based health insurance. Tax credits are now available to offset the cost of higher education (for those who qualify). Medical savings accounts are an experiment to create a kind of investment retirement account for medical needs (see chapter 5).

The other important fiscal policy development came in 1921 with the passage of the **Legislative Budget and Accounting Act**. The primary accomplishment of the act was the creation of an **executive budget**. Prior to 1921, each federal agency submitted its budget directly to Congress; the president had little say in what these agencies would do. Now agencies submit their budget to the president, who can make changes that conform to his policy preferences. Of course, presidents really do not do this; they have staff assistance. The 1921 legislation also created the Bureau of the Budget (BOB) within the U.S. Department of the Treasury to assist the president in assembling the budget. BOB eventually became a powerful force in the federal government, assuming new powers of not only budget oversight, but also managing the government and overseeing the writing of regulations. In 1939, the bureau was transferred from the Treasury Department to the new Executive Office of the President (EXOP); in 1970 the name of the agency was changed to the **Office of Management and Budget (OMB)**.[1] It was not until after World War II that the federal budget became large enough to have a significant impact on the economy.

Presidents propose budgets; Congress adopts them. The congressional process for budget adoption, briefly described in chapter 1, is complex, involving three sets of committees and elaborate timetables (Rubin 1990 and Wildavsky 1988). The budgeting process is inherently political, involving differing priorities between presidents and Congress and within Congress between the Republicans and Democrats. Budgeting was especially controversial as federal budget deficits dramatically increased during the 1980s and 1990s. When the deficits disappeared (or seemed to disappear, see below) and surpluses returned, the process should have become easier. Disagreements over how to spend project surpluses continue to plague the process.

These two instruments, taxing and spending, form the foundation of fiscal policy. The theoretical basis for the use of these two sets of tools was set forth by British economist John Maynard Keynes in a 1936 book titled *The General Theory of Employment, Interest, and Money*.[2] Keynesian economics suggests the use of these tools to stimulate or discourage the demand for goods and services. Keynesian economics has become very controversial, as it appeared to fail in the 1970s. Not all economists, especially those identified with supply-side economics, agree that fiscal policy has the kinds of impacts described below.

If federal policy makers wish to stimulate the economy, then some combination of increased spending and decreased taxation—lowering rates or allowing additional deductions and tax credits—would be desirable (see Table 2.1). Both of these actions put more money into the hands of consumers. Lower taxes mean that workers and businesses pay less to the government, while increased government spending in public works programs or training programs benefits consumers and producers. An increased demand for goods and services encourages producers to produce more, hire more workers, and use more of their capacity to produce. This is the rationale for budget stimulus programs such as the one President Clinton proposed in early 1993 (but which was defeated by Congress). One implication of increased spending and

Table 2.1

**Fiscal Policy Tools**

|                           | Stimulate | Restrain |
|---------------------------|-----------|----------|
| Revenues (taxes)          | Decrease  | Increase |
| Expenditures (spending)   | Increase  | Decrease |
| Effect on federal budget  | Deficit   | Surplus  |

decreased revenue is budget deficits. Thus budget deficits, up to a certain point, may be seen as stimulating the economy.

The reverse actions could be used to slow an overheated economy. Here a combination of increased taxes and reduced spending takes money out of the hands of consumers, lowering their demand for goods and services. Companies have fewer sales and so greater inventories, workers are laid off, less capacity is used, and so forth. Again, the result of decreased spending and increased revenues may be a smaller deficit or a budget surplus; budget surpluses may be viewed as restraining on the economy. The post–World War II experience is that the United States generally has followed half of Keynes's advice, with budget deficits greatly outweighing budget surpluses.[3] In neither instance, stimulating or restraining the economy, does the federal government directly order the behavior it wants. Rather it puts or takes money out of producers' and consumers' hands hoping to influence their decisions in the desired direction.

Problems with fiscal policy include some dealing with the policy process and characteristics of the American political system and some with conflicting ideologies. The basic problem with fiscal policy is that it generally requires congressional action. The adoption phase becomes critical, and the need to gain a consensus among the executive, the legislature, and the public becomes critical. Because such action may be necessary, the problem of timing appears to be a problem of implementation. Given the lengthy nature of congressional proceedings (the need to build a series of majorities), it may be that by the time the solution is applied—for example, cutting taxes and increasing spending—the need has passed. Indeed, by the time the new programs go into effect, the business cycle may have changed, say from little or no growth to a rapid, inflationary period. Thus measures designed to stimulate the economy may actually overstimulate the economy. On the other hand, measures designed to slow an overheated economy may take effect at the wrong time. In early 1967 President Johnson proposed a 4 percent income tax surcharge (a tax on a tax), and by the middle of 1968 Congress finally passed a one-year 10 percent income tax surcharge. The surcharge was one factor in causing the 1969 recession.

That being said, fiscal policy probably does not have much effect on the course of the economy (Crook 2000; Samuelson 1994a). Monetary policy probably has a larger effect; the largest effects are changes in the domestic and international economy.

A related problem is our limited ability to predict the direction of the economy. The Office of Management and Budget, the Council of Economic Advisors (also in the Executive Office of the President), and the **Congressional Budgeting Office (CBO)** have to make predictions of the likely state of the economy, including whether the federal budget will experience a deficit or a surplus, several years down the road. Although certain statistics such as the composite index of leading indicators seek to predict the future course of the economy, such measures are not perfect. Thus the prolonged nature of the congressional budgeting process combines with a certain amount of fortune telling to create a problematic situation.[4]

Some aspects of fiscal policy—automatic stabilizers—do not require congressional action. For example, the number of people receiving unemployment compensation payments increases as the unemployment rate increases, and it decreases as unemployment decreases. Most policy makers are rarely satisfied with such automatic programs and prefer to add stimulus (or discouragement) of their own.

There is also the ideological aspect surrounding the government issue. Fiscal policy represents a rather direct intervention of the government in the economy. This feature is favored by liberals and opposed by conservatives. That is, as presented in chapter 1, the liberal position on the economy favors government action while the conservative position opposes government intervention.

When Congress increases taxes, paychecks become smaller. The tax changes passed in 1986 now treat tuition assistance as taxable income. Program cuts designed to reduce budget deficits decreased GI benefits, barring some students from obtaining GI Bill educational benefits. When Congress passes or increases an investment tax credit, which occurred during the Kennedy and Reagan administrations, businesses are encouraged to increase their level of investment and improve productivity. In this manner, fiscal policy represents fairly direct, though limited, government intervention in our lives.[5] Conservatives prefer the other major tool of economic policy, monetary policy, in some cases desiring to limit this tool as well (Bartley 1992).

In any case, fiscal policy has lost a great deal of its impact. The economy recovered from the relatively mild 1990–91 recession without any fiscal stimulus. Indeed, the agreement between President George H. W. Bush and Congress in 1990 to reduce the deficit should have intensified the recession, but the effect was small. The similar agreement between President Clinton and Congress (after Clinton abandoned his economic stimulus program) also did not slow down the economy.

### Monetary Policy

When the Federal Reserve was created in 1913, its instructions were to prevent financial panics and bank runs. In the aftermath of the depression, its mandate was extended in the Employment Act of 1946 to include the promotion of "maximum employment, production, and purchasing power." In 1978 the Full Employment and Balanced Growth Act required that the Fed pursue policies to "promote employment . . . and reasonable price stability." (Papadimitriou 2000, p. 6)

Monetary policy—control over interest rates and the supply of money—is conducted by the **Federal Reserve Board**, an independent regulatory agency established by Congress in 1913. The "**Fed**," as it is commonly known, is headed by seven governors, appointed by the president and confirmed by the Senate. The independence of the Fed from presidential and legislative control can be seen in the terms of office of the governors: fourteen-year, overlapping appointments. The chairman of the Fed is appointed every four years. While the president appoints members of the Fed, he cannot remove them from office. The purpose of such provisions is to prevent political manipulation of the money supply and the regulation of banking, in the same sense that the federal judiciary is insulated from the excesses of politics.

Part of the conflict, an important one, between the Federal Reserve Board and whatever administration is in office is based on differences in goals between the two institutions. Administrations put emphasis on economic growth, the Fed fears inflation and the impact of inflation on bond markets (Samuelson 1994b, Uchitelle 1994c).[6] Rapid economic growth tends to put pressure on prices and inflation tends to push down bond prices (Greider 1987; Uchitelle 1994a). By 2000, the Fed has been criticized for maintaining its concern with inflation in the absence of some inflationary pressures; perhaps, some critics have argued, Fed chairman Alan Greenspan did not understand how the economy has changed (see, e.g., Kudlow 2000).

The reality is that both the Fed and the courts read the election returns, and the Fed, through its chairman, has frequently worked with presidential administrations (Woodward 1994). This is not always obvious because there have been frequent complaints that the Fed undermines administration policy.

This cat-and-mouse game could be seen in exhortations by Reagan administration officials that interest rates were too high, retarding economic growth. Additionally, congressional leaders called for greater political control, using such advocacy to influence Fed policy. The Fed was, despite the public arguments, extremely accommodating to Reagan administration economic policy, to the extent that the Fed was largely responsible for continued economic growth in the 1980s and into the 1990s.[7]

This clash came into focus in 1993 when the Clinton administration was pushing its economic program. According to Woodward (1994), Fed chairman Alan Greenspan convinced President Clinton that he should concentrate on long-term interest rates that were most sensitive to federal budget deficits. Thus, the Clinton economic package, which originally emphasized economic stimulus, public investment, and middle-class tax cuts, ended up focusing on deficit reduction. In 1994, the Fed began to raise interest rates to head off possible inflation, resulting in the slowing down of the economy. The result was increasing disagreement over the Fed's course of action as manufacturers

Table 2.2

**Monetary Policy Tools**

|  | Stimulate | Restrain |
| --- | --- | --- |
| Reserve requirements | Lower | Raise |
| Interest rates | Lower | Raise |
| Open market operations (securities) | Buy | Sell |
| Currency transactions | Lower $ value | Raise $ value |

began to resist higher interest rates (Uchitelle 1994b, 1994c) and the Clinton administration claimed that increases were creating havoc in the bond and stock markets. Further, according to one analysis, the Fed has been tightening interest rates in the 1999–2000 election cycle much higher than average, again because of the Fed concerns about the possibility of inflation. The state of the economy usually has an important impact on the outcome of elections at the federal level, especially during presidential elections (Financial Markets Center 2000). The Fed policy during this time did help produce a slowdown in the economy; by 2001, the Fed had reversed course and started raising interest rates again to forestall a recession.

As the quote that opens this "Monetary Policy" section indicates, the Fed has a dual mandate of price stability (keeping inflation under control) and full employment (which does not mean zero unemployment). The discussion above suggests that the Fed under Chair Alan Greenspan has been putting more emphasis on price stability. Thorbecke (2000) presents substantial evidence that the Fed has tried to maneuver between these twin goals.

To meet its statutory mandate, the Fed has four major and one minor monetary policy tools (see Table 2.2). The first is the **reserve requirement**. Banks that are members of the Federal Reserve System (which includes all national banks and many state banks) are required to keep on hand a certain percentage of the bank's deposits. If the reserve requirement is 15 percent and the bank has $100 million in deposits, then the bank must retain $15 million. If the Fed lowers the reserve requirement to, say, 10 percent, then the bank can lend out an extra $5 million. Such additional lending can provide stimulus to the economy through new investments and purchases. Conversely, if the Fed raises the reserve requirement to 20 percent, then the bank either will have to call in $5 million worth of loans or borrow money. This has a contracting effect on the economy; less money is available for investment and purchases.

The second set of monetary tools centers on short-term interest rates; the two major rates that the Fed controls are the discount rate and federal funds rate. The **discount rate** is the interest rate that the Fed charges its member banks for borrowing money from it; interest rates reflect the cost of borrowing funds. The **federal funds rate** is the interest charged when one bank borrows from another to keep its reserves in balance (Greider 1987). Interest rates can exert a strong influence on the economy. Consider the housing market; high mortgage rates can price out some potential homebuyers, whereas low rates permit those who are otherwise unqualified to buy homes. If the Fed lowers interest rates, it provides a stimulus to the economy by lowering the cost of borrowing money, thus allowing more investments and purchases. If the Fed raises the discount rate, then economic activity is retarded by the higher cost of borrowing money. Further, those who have adjustable-rate mortgages or adjustable-rate credit cards can feel the effects of interest increases very directly. For example, a family with a $150,000 home and an adjustable mortgage rate would find their mortgage payment increased by about $250 depending on the size of the interest rate increases. Thus their spendable income would decrease by that amount. While long-term interest rates are not directly affected by the Fed and its use of short-term interest rates, policy changes that are reflected in short-term rates trickle up to the longer-term rates. Further, short-term interest-rate changes seem to have a six-month to one-year lag period before they affect the economy. Additionally, the stock and bond markets anticipate as well as react to Fed policy changes.

The third is perhaps the most difficult tool of monetary policy to understand, **open market operations**, which affect the supply of money that is in circulation. The Fed has a **Federal Open Market Committee** (**FOMC**), consisting of seven members of the Fed and (on a rotating basis) the presidents of five of the twelve federal reserve banks, which meets periodically and makes decisions influencing the supply of money.[8] It does this through the buying and selling of government securities. If the committee wants to stimulate the economy by allowing for growth in the money supply, it will buy government securities from its member banks and other segments of the economy. When it does, the Fed effectively writes a check that is then deposited in the account of the member bank. This action increases the amount of money that the bank can lend (usually to other banks for a higher interest rate), and more money available for loans allows for more purchases and investments. Conversely, when the Fed wants the economy to slow down, perhaps because inflationary pressures are getting out of control, then it will sell government securities. The funds that member banks use to buy securities are no longer available for loans.[9]

There is a linkage between open market operations and interest rates that the Fed can directly influence. The FOMC will select a target federal funds rate and then order the buying or selling of securities that would produce the targeted interest rate (Rowe 1999). So both by directly changing the interest rates and by open market operations, the Fed will signal the direction it would like the economy to go.

The money supply was mentioned frequently above. What exactly does this mean? There are several measures of the money supply that can be used to track Fed policy. The most popular of these measures is known as M-1, which consists of cash in circulation, money deposited in regular checking accounts, traveler's checks, and the like. In other words, M-1 is the most liquid form of money. M-2 consists of M-1 plus some less liquid types of money, such as money in regular savings accounts. There are still other more inclusive measures, but these two are the most frequently referred to when discussing the money supply.

The fourth policy tool available to the Fed is **currency transactions**, the buying and selling of dollars in international markets. The dollar itself can be seen as a good that has value. That value is the rate of exchange with the currencies of other countries. A surplus of dollars drives the value of the dollar down, drives the value of other currencies up, makes American exports cheaper, and makes imports more expensive. Of course, increases in the value of the dollar have the opposite effect. Beginning in 1985, the Fed, in concert with the central banks of other major Western industrial nations, acted to reduce the American trade deficit by reducing the value of the dollar. In 1994, the Fed and other industrialized nations bought dollars, hoping to increase the value of the dollar, which had declined precipitously (Friedman 1994a, 1994b). By 2000, the value of the dollar was relatively high but stable, indicating the significant growth and security of the American economy and weaknesses in other countries' economies (e.g., Japan, which has been mired in stagnation for most of the 1990s). The value of the dollar as well as the strength of the U.S. economy has an important effect on this country's balance of trade with other countries. The year 1999 saw record trade deficits, as the U.S. economy was an important engine of economic growth for the entire world.

There is a fifth tool available to the Fed, though one it rarely uses. The Fed has authority of margin requirements for the stock market. The **margin requirement** is the percentage of a purchase that a buyer actually has to pay. If the margin requirement is 50 percent on a purchase of $100,000, then the buyer has to pay at least $50,000, effectively borrowing the rest. Raising the margin requirement would retard stock purchases because it would take more money. Prior to the Great Depression of 1929, the margin requirement was 10 percent, allowing for considerable speculation and then great distress when the stock market crashed and people not only lost the value of their stock but owed considerable money from the purchases.

The Federal Reserve Board does not have complete control over either the supply of money in the United States or the value of the dollar. Not all banks are members of the Federal Reserve system. There are also sources of money outside of the banking system, such as money market funds, investment instruments that are offered by such companies as Sears, Roebuck and E. F. Hutton. The United States, particularly in the 1980s, attracted foreign investment, an important source of money that greatly assisted American economic growth. Sometimes unique events, such as the maturing of a bond note or the selling of bonds because of changes in the tax laws, may temporarily pump money into the economy despite efforts by the Fed to control it.

From an ideological perspective, monetary policy is the policy instrument of choice for those holding conservative economic positions.[10] Monetary policy is less interventionist than fiscal policy in the sense that its effects are less obvious than those of fiscal policy. That is, the inducements of fiscal policy are less subtle: tax cuts, for example, are noticeable in weekly or monthly paychecks. But if a decrease in the growth of the money supply makes it harder for an individual or business to obtain a loan, it is much more difficult to pinpoint the precise cause. The more extreme conservatives suggest that manipulation of the money supply still represents too large of a government role, still too much influenced by politics. These observers (Wanniski 1978; Bartley 1992) would like to see a return to the gold standard, where the supply of money and interest rates is determined on the international market. The United States has not been on the gold standard since 1971 when President Nixon moved the American economy to floating exchange rates (Silk 1984).

There are also important practical advantages that monetary policy has over fiscal policy. Monetary policy can be implemented more rapidly than can fiscal policy. The various components of the Federal Reserve Board can meet on a weekly basis, decide on policy changes, and then carry them out. Monetary policy avoids many of the pitfalls associated with the policy process and the characteristics of the political system. These advantages, combined with pressure of budget deficits on fiscal policy, resulted in primary reliance during the 1980s and 1990s on monetary policy to influence the economy. This being said, it should be pointed out that it is not clear how Fed policy changes influence the economy (Rowe 1999) and that there is some delay in those changes taking their effect.

## How Have We Done?

Understanding the economic issues and the problems facing the United States requires a review of how we have managed the economy. To explore this economic history briefly, it is helpful to divide the post–World War II period into four parts. The first two will be examined in this final section of problem identification. The latter two are discussed in the section on agenda building, providing the foundation for examining current economic policy issues.

Before considering post–World War II economic management, a brief explanation of what we are looking at is in order. Consider economic growth (recovery, expansion) and decline (recessions). The measure of economic growth or decline is the **gross domestic product** (**GDP**). One definition of GDP uses the following formula (the numbers under the formula are the 1999 dollar figures, in billions of dollars, to give you some idea of the size of the American economy as a whole as well as the size of the components of GDP):

$$GDP = C + I + G + (X - M)$$
$$\$9,248.4 = \$6,254.9 + \$1,621.6 + \$1,628.7 + (-256.8)[11]$$

Figure 2.1    **Gross Domestic Product (GDP) in Constant (1996) Dollars**

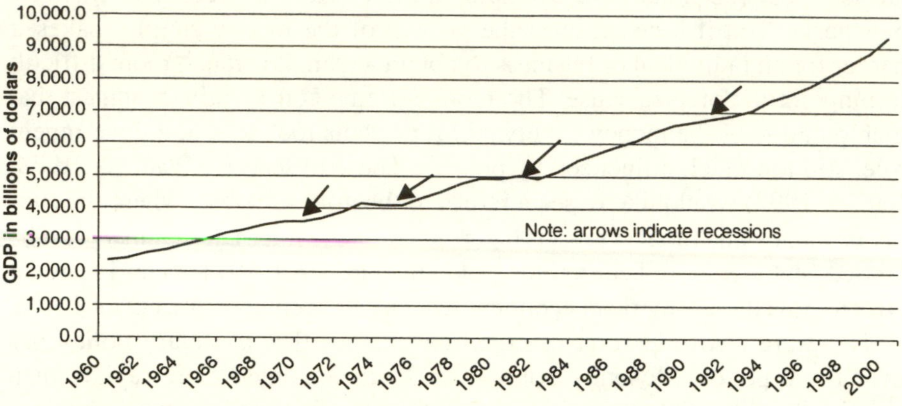

*Source:* Council of Economic Advisers (2001).

where *C* stands for consumer spending, *I* is gross domestic product, *G* is total government expenditures, *X* is exports to other countries, and *M* is imports from other countries (thus *X – M* is net exports).[12] Note that a large trade imbalance (*M* greater than *X*) by definition reduces economic growth. Economic growth is an increase (in real or constant or inflation-adjusted dollars, the three terms mean the same thing) in GDP. A **recession** is at least a two-quarter or six-month (consecutive) period of decline in GDP. Figure 2.1 shows post–World War II recessions.

There are other important measures of economic health that policy makers (and the public) consider. One is increases in the price of goods and services, measured by the **consumer price index (CPI)**.[13] A second indicator is the **unemployment rate** (see Table 2.3), the percentage of people in the labor force who do not have a job and are actively seeking one.[14] A third indicator is interest rates, discussed above, which reflects the cost of borrowing money. A fourth indicator is **productivity**, defined as the amount of output per worker per hour (see Figure 2.2). Economists tell us that productivity increases are the source of real income increases; declines in productivity increases are related to declines in real incomes. We shall address this issue below.

## 1947 to 1960

The first period covers the time from the end of World War II to 1960. In 1946, the Employment Act was passed because policy makers believed there would be a return to the depression conditions of the pre–World War II period. That did not happen, largely because consumer spending had been suppressed by the war effort; after the war, domestic spending soared. The spending surge ended in 1948 and combined with high interest rates to produce a recession. During the 1950s, there were three recessions (1953–54, 1957–58,

Table 2.3

**Inflation and Civilian Unemployment Rates**

|  | Inflation | Unemployment |
|---|---|---|
| 1960 | 1.7 | 5.5 |
| 1961 | 1.0 | 6.7 |
| 1962 | 1.0 | 5.5 |
| 1963 | 1.3 | 5.7 |
| 1964 | 1.3 | 5.2 |
| 1965 | 1.6 | 4.5 |
| 1966 | 2.9 | 3.8 |
| 1967 | 3.1 | 3.8 |
| 1968 | 4.2 | 3.6 |
| 1969 | 5.5 | 3.5 |
| 1970 | 5.7 | 4.9 |
| 1971 | 4.4 | 5.9 |
| 1972 | 3.2 | 5.6 |
| 1973 | 6.2 | 4.9 |
| 1974 | 11.0 | 5.6 |
| 1975 | 9.1 | 8.5 |
| 1976 | 5.8 | 7.7 |
| 1977 | 6.5 | 7.1 |
| 1978 | 7.6 | 6.1 |
| 1979 | 11.3 | 5.8 |
| 1980 | 13.5 | 7.1 |
| 1981 | 10.3 | 7.6 |
| 1982 | 6.2 | 9.7 |
| 1983 | 3.2 | 9.6 |
| 1984 | 4.3 | 7.5 |
| 1985 | 3.6 | 7.2 |
| 1986 | 1.9 | 7.0 |
| 1987 | 3.6 | 6.2 |
| 1988 | 4.1 | 5.5 |
| 1989 | 4.8 | 5.3 |
| 1990 | 5.4 | 5.6 |
| 1991 | 4.2 | 6.8 |
| 1992 | 3.0 | 7.5 |
| 1993 | 3.0 | 6.9 |
| 1994 | 2.6 | 6.1 |
| 1995 | 2.8 | 5.6 |

*Sources:* Council of Economic Advisers (2001); Bureau of Labor Statistics (2001).

1959–1960), caused mainly by tight fiscal and monetary policies, designed to slow inflation. The inflation of the 1950s was relatively small but considered high for its time. An additional factor in the 1953–54 recession was the end of the Korean War and the military build-down. Note that during the 1950s the focus was on keeping inflation in check by relatively restrictive

Figure 2.2    **Yearly Changes in Nonfarm Business-Sector Productivity**

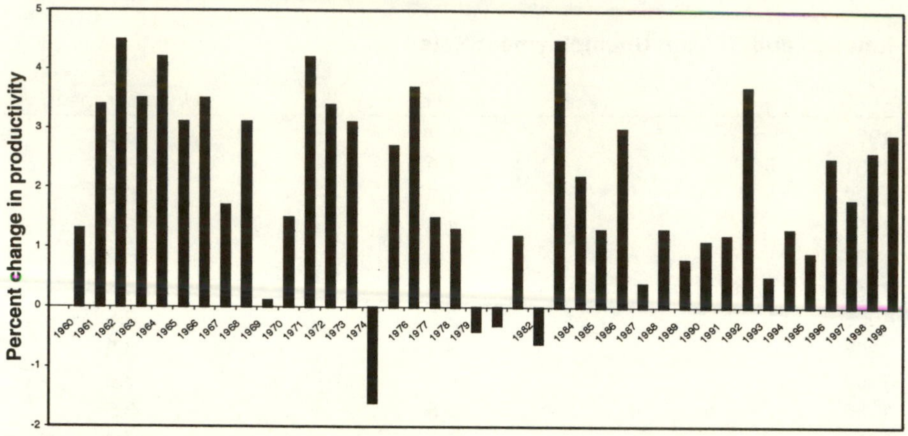

*Source:* Council of Economic Advisers (2001).

monetary policy combined with a restrictive fiscal policy. Productivity increases were strong, and job growth was good.

### 1961 to 1968

These eight years constituted one of the longest periods of sustained economic growth in the postwar era, due to a combination of factors. First, monetary policy was greatly relaxed, particularly during the Johnson years, 1963 to 1968. Second, the Kennedy administration pushed a major tax cut, including tax credits for business investment. The tax cut enacted in 1964 (after Kennedy's assassination) has been pointed to by advocates of supply-side economics as an example of how tax-rate cuts stimulate economic growth without sacrificing government revenues. The final push for economic growth was the Vietnam War, which began to have significant effects on the economy in 1966. Economic growth during the period from 1961 to 1968 averaged 5.8 percent versus only 2.8 percent from 1953 to 1958.

By 1968 the economic expansion had slowed and, more alarmingly, the inflation rate was increasing due to the fiscal push of the Vietnam War, new domestic programs (the Great Society, especially Medicare and Medicaid), and rapid growth in the money supply. President Johnson was finally convinced that some fiscal restrictions were necessary, and in fiscal year (FY) 1969 a one-time surtax was added to the income tax. The result was the last budget surplus the United States experienced for thirty years, a little more than $3 billion.

Some analysts see this period as laying down the foundations for the problems of the 1970s and beyond. David Calleo (1982) argues that the loose fiscal and monetary policies of this period combined with ambitious foreign policy goals (the Vietnam War) to overload the economy.

# Agenda Building and Economic Policy

## *1969 to 1980*

### *The Problems Stream*

The third period began with a recession, from 1969 to 1970, and ended with a short recession in 1980. The early recession was due to tight monetary policy designed to cool inflation brought on by Vietnam War spending and tight monetary policy. But the plan did not work, and inflation remained high.

As a result, the Nixon administration took two measures designed to help the economy. The first was to go off the gold standard and move to floating exchange rates to alleviate the problem that the price of the dollar was much lower than the world market and could not be defended without exhausting our gold supplies (Silk 1984).

The more significant action was the imposition of a peacetime wage and price control program designed to reduce inflation. The program, ordinarily anathema to a conservative administration (headed by a president who had resigned from a similar program during World War II), was on again, off again and suppressed price increases but made no lasting changes. In contrast to most of our experience with economic policy relying on inducements, the Nixon controls were based on rules, stating under what conditions wages and prices could be increased. By 1974, all controls except those on crude oil were removed.

The United States experienced another recession from 1974 to 1975. There were two reasons for this: tightened fiscal and monetary policies in an attempt to lower the inflation rates and the Arab oil boycott of 1973–74. The boycott was in retaliation for U.S. support for Israel during the October 1973 war.

From 1975 to 1980 the United States experienced unprecedented economic problems for which there was no obvious solution, given conventional beliefs. This was a problem known as **stagflation**, a combination of high unemployment and high inflation. The traditional solution to decrease unemployment (or increase employment) was to stimulate the economy through loose fiscal and monetary policies, the choice of the Kennedy administration. The traditional solution for reducing inflation was tight fiscal and monetary policies, the choice of the Eisenhower and Nixon/Ford administrations. But notice the contradiction: The remedy for high unemployment exacerbates inflation, and the remedy for high inflation exacerbates unemployment. Keynesian economics was seemingly discredited because it offered no solution to the problem. The economy was also buffeted by a second oil shock precipitated by the Iranian revolution that overthrew the shah. This began in late 1978 and continued into 1980.

The Carter administration's economic policy vacillated, looking for a solution to this dilemma (Bartley 1992; Greider 1987). It decided on a strategy designed to choke inflation quickly and also to apply a long-term solution. The first part of this strategy was accomplished by the Federal Reserve Board. The Fed, during most of the postwar period, concentrated on interest rates. But in October 1979 the Fed, with its new chairman, Paul Volcker, adopted a new two-part policy. First, it decided to ignore interest rates and concentrate on the supply of money (the open market operations and reserve requirements).[15] Second, it set targets for the different measures of the money supply that were quite low. The purpose of these changes was to choke inflation out of the economy, even at the cost of some short-term pain. Interest rates would increase temporarily and economic growth would be restrained; the solution would take several years.

In addition, President Carter had continually resisted encouraging a recession to cool off the economy until 1980 (an election year). Using presidential powers, he invoked controls on credit that produced a brief (six-month) recession.[16] Finally, the effects of the second oil crisis with its constantly increasing prices also helped bring about a recession. The result was low economic growth in 1980 combined with high inflation and high interest rates. In the 1976 presidential election, challenger Carter had pointed to the informal "misery index" (a combination of inflation and unemployment) under incumbent Ford. In 1980, challenger Reagan had a much higher misery index to use against incumbent Carter.

The years from 1969 to 1980 were critical in terms of economic policy. Perhaps the most critical year was 1973. Paul Krugman (1994a) identifies 1973 as the year that productivity increases declined precipitously, leading to stagnant real (adjusted for inflation) incomes and a relative decline in our economic position in the world economy. Figure 2.2 shows the yearly percentage increases in productivity. Productivity grew about 1.8 percent from the late nineteenth century to World War II. The peak period of productivity increases was from the end of the war to 1973; productivity increases averaged 2.8 percent per year. Since 1973, productivity increases dropped to less than 1 percent per year (Krugman 1994b).[17] Note in Figure 2.2 that there were three significant drops in productivity during the 1973–1980 period. Wages became stagnant, increases in family incomes slowed down, and income inequality grew (see also Peterson 1993).

Why did productivity increases decline? The two energy crises are partly to blame. But there were also demographic changes to consider. There was a substantial increase in the size of the labor force (Schwarz 1988). Two factors were at work: First was the addition of new workers to the work force, the maturing of the baby boomers. Second was a large increase in secondary wage earners, largely women, continuing their movement into the work force.[18] To meet this demand, approximately 12 million new jobs were created. This is a tremendous accomplishment during a period when the perception was that the economy was ailing. New job creation compared quite favorably with preceding and subsequent periods. In fact, new job creation was higher during the Carter years than during the first eight years of the Reagan administra-

Table 2.4

**Job Creation During Presidential Administrations** (in thousands of jobs)

| Year | Total number of jobs | Average number of jobs created | Administration in office |
|------|------|------|------|
| 1960 | 65,778 | N/A | N/A |
| 1968 | 75,920 | 1,268 | Kennedy/Johnson |
| 1976 | 88,752 | 1,604 | Nixon/Ford |
| 1980 | 99,303 | 2,637 | Carter |
| 1988 | 114,968 | 1,958 | Reagan |
| 1992 | 117,598 | 658 | Bush |
| 2000 | 131,425 | 1,728 | Clinton |

*Sources:* Council of Economic Advisers (2001); Bureau of Labor Statistics (2001).

tion and the four years of the first Bush administration (of course, the recessions of 1981–82 and 1990–91 were a factor here) (see Table 2.4).

The unemployment rate rose as a result of the increase in the labor force, but not as much as it might otherwise have. Of course, the private sector was largely responsible for this success, but there were some contributions on the part of the federal government. For example, social security payments increased dramatically, which encouraged people to retire and permitted new workers to enter.

While the increase in the number of jobs indicated a growing economy, it also had an impact on productivity. Newer workers are inexperienced and not as productive as more experienced workers. Further, many of the new jobs were in the service sector. Productivity increases in service industries are much more difficult to achieve than in manufacturing or agriculture.

A final possible explanation is the decline in the savings rate and the associated decline in investment. In 1965 our net national savings rate was 12.7 percent of net national product, while our personal consumption rate was 68.3 percent. By 1991, the savings rate had dropped to 2.4 percent of net national product, and our consumption rate had increased to 76.7 percent (Peterson 1993, Table 3.2). Investment depends on savings and leads to productivity increases. As savings and investment decline, so do productivity and real income increases.

The combination of all these factors overwhelmed the successes of the American economy (especially in job growth); the prevailing perception was that the economy was sick and needed new medicine.

### The Policies Stream: Supply-Side Economics

Economic policy based however loosely on Keynesian economics was discredited by 1980. Its main failing was its inability to resolve the problem of simultaneously high inflation and high unemployment. In response to this perceived failure,[19] a number of conservative economists (with ties to the Republican Party) developed an alternative economic theory that promised to turn the economy around. This alternative theory is known as **supply-side economics**.[20]

Keynesian economics is based on stimulating or discouraging consumer demand for goods and services. The premise is that putting more money in the hands of consumers will lead to more demand, causing producers to produce more goods and services, putting more people to work, and thus having more money to consume, and so on. Supply-side economics starts from what is called Say's Law, which states that supply creates its own demand (Rashid 1986). Rather than trying to stimulate production by manipulating consumer demand, supply-side economics seeks to increase production by creating incentives, positive inducements, to work.

Thus the central focus of supply-side economics was the importance of incentives, and these incentives were based largely (though not entirely) on tax policy. Taxes, it was argued, would have to be cut. Stanford University economist Arthur Laffer, among others, argued that, theoretically, tax cuts, especially for the top marginal tax rates, would prod the economy and might make up for losses of government revenues.

Supply-siders argued that federal tax laws had very high marginal tax rates[21] (the highest rate was 70 percent in 1981) that encouraged businesses and individuals to look for ways to hide or shelter their income. Tax shelters are nonproductive ways of hiding income; the tax laws were replete with deductions and credits that reduce taxable income. If the rates were lowered, then there would be less incentive to hide income and more incentive to search for productive investments. Thus lower rates produce more revenue by inducing individuals and businesses to invest more and work harder. Supply-side economists pointed to the success of the 1964 Kennedy tax cut, which included the investment tax credit, as an indication of what would happen with tax rate cuts. In 1965 and 1966, both government revenue and net domestic investment increased significantly over that of previous years.

Thus, supply-side economists and conservatives (the two are generally synonymous) argued for tax cuts. In the late 1970s, this reasoning became incorporated in the Kemp-Roth tax proposal to cut income taxes by 30 percent over a three-year period. A modified version of Kemp-Roth, along with other tax cuts, was passed in 1981.

This aspect of supply-side economics, which conservatives believe contains a considerable amount of common sense, focused on the economy as a whole—the macroeconomic view. This was also true of Keynesian economics, but supply-side economics also contained a theory of individual and group behavior, lacking in Keynesian economics, that linked up very neatly with the tax incentives argument. This microeconomic theory is known as rational expectations theory and is based on common sense. In its broadest and simplest form, rational expectations theory states that people and groups behave in response to rewards. If people expect taxes to go down, they will behave by increasing their productive investments. If people expect taxes to remain high or increase, they will behave by looking for ways of sheltering income. If the Kennedy tax cut was an example of the benefits of supply-side economics, the depression points to the importance of expectations.

Jude Wanniski (1978) argues that the cause of the Great Depression that began in 1929 was the passage of the Smoot-Hawley tariff, which was to take effect in the spring of 1930. How could a law that would not go into effect for some six months cause a worldwide depression? Wanniski answers that, in anticipation of the imposition of the protective tariff (actually, the rates were so high that punitive or prohibitive describes it better), other countries would impose similarly prohibitive tariffs on the United States and world trade would collapse. Thus, the expectations of the effect of the tariff were sufficient to cause economic dismay. In the same way, Wanniski asserted that a tax cut, such as the Kemp-Roth bill, would work because people and groups would know they would be rewarded for extra work, instead of having most of the extra income taken away in taxes, and would therefore work harder and invest more. One important implication of rational expectations theory is that continuity of government policy is absolutely essential. Adjusting the tax code every few years erodes confidence in the economy and impedes planning; if the environment frequently changes, there can be no rational expectations.[22] Similarly, growth in the money supply should be steady and predictable. It is for this reason that the purists among supply-side economists would like to see us return to the gold standard; the Fed would not be able to make arbitrary changes in monetary policy.

Two other elements made up the Reagan economic program, one possibly essential and the other not necessarily so. The possibly essential portion was the regulatory relief program, consisting of budget and personnel cuts in agencies such as the Environmental Protection Agency and the delaying and withdrawing of regulations. President Reagan's first chairman of the Council of Economic Advisers, Murray Weidenbaum, argued that even if the other elements of the president's program were put into place, economic growth would be retarded by regulations that hurt productivity and investment. The other part of the president's program, consistent with conservative ideology but not necessarily with supply-side economics, was changes in the composition of spending, with cuts in domestic spending and increases in defense spending. The total of these actions made up the Reagan economic program with its basis in supply-side economics.

### Adoption

The politics stream was the election of the Reagan administration and a Republican-controlled Senate in 1981 and the desire on the part of the electorate for a change. The window of opportunity came during the first eight months of 1981. Two pieces of legislation, the Economic Recovery Act of 1981 and the Omnibus Budget and Reconciliation Act of 1981, encompassed the heart of the changes Reagan wanted, set the course for the economy for the 1980s, and outlined the debate over economic policy into the 1990s.

The tax cuts were contained in the Economic Recovery Act of 1981. Consistent with the Kemp-Roth bill, the legislation provided for a 25 percent individual tax cut over a 2½–year period (beginning July 1981 and ending December 1983).[23] The top tax rate was reduced from 70 to 50 percent.[24] In addition, the tax rates, through individual exemptions, were indexed to inflation beginning in 1985.[25] Business tax cuts, which were not originally part of Kemp-Roth, were also included in the package. These included an increase in the investment tax credit, accelerated depreciation, and a rather unusual provision that allowed for the sale of tax credits. In sum, the individual and business tax cuts totaled about $642 billion for fiscal years 1982–86.[26]

The major budget cuts of the Reagan administration also came in 1981 with the passage of the Omnibus Budget and Reconciliation Act.[27] The program cuts targeted domestic spending programs, such as environmental and education programs, dear to the heart of liberals and Democrats (cuts in such programs appear again in the budget battle between President Clinton and Congress, as discussed below). For example, the Environmental Protection Agency budget was cut by over 27 percent between FY 1980 and FY 1984, even though its responsibilities were increasing.[28] Some categorical grant programs were combined into larger block grants, whose budget was then cut by 20 percent (Bartlett 1984). In total, the act cut domestic spending by $263 billion for fiscal years 1982–86.[29]

In addition, and consistent with the president's 1980 campaign platform, there was a massive increase in defense spending, originally budgeted at 8 percent or more per year, after adjusting for inflation. The increase in defense spending (over the Carter defense budget) for the fiscal years 1982–86 was $121 billion.

Because of mounting federal budget deficits, subsequent years of the Reagan administration led to tax increases. In 1982, Congress passed the Tax Equity and Fiscal Responsibility Act (TEFRA), which "enhanced revenues" (in other words, raised taxes) by $146 billion through FY 1986 (Bosworth 1984) and repealed some of the 1981 tax cuts. The Deficit Reduction Act of 1984 raised taxes by $50.8 billion over a three-year period and cut spending by about $100 billion (Congressional Quarterly 1984). After several years of substantial increases, defense spending leveled off. And in 1986, Congress passed what President Reagan called his most important domestic initiative for 1985, tax reform. The business provisions of the Tax Reform Act reduced or eliminated more of the 1981 tax cuts.

Two other economic events of this period are worthy of mention. The first came in 1985 when the major industrial nations agreed on action to reduce the value of the dollar as a means of reducing the U.S. trade deficit. The result was a decline in the value of the dollar by about 40 percent.[30] The second came in October 1987 when the stock market crashed, dropping 508 points in one day. While the crash was huge, comparable in magnitude to the 1929 crash, the economy was not affected very much.

### 1981 to 1992

The recession from 1981 to 1982 was the most severe of the postwar period. For example, at one point, in 1982, the unemployment rate neared 11 percent, the highest rate since the depression (see Table 2.3). The causes of this recession (and perhaps it should be considered a continuation of the brief recession during the Carter administration) were the continued effects of the second oil shock (1978 to 1980) and restrictive monetary policy leading to high interest rates. The restrictive monetary policy stemmed from the October 1979 decision of the Federal Reserve Board to ignore interest rates and concentrate on slowing growth in the money supply. The recession ended when the Fed eased its policy in late 1982 (allowing faster growth in the money supply) combined with the fiscal stimulus of the 1981 tax cuts.

From 1982 to 1989 the United States experienced its third-longest period of sustained economic growth in the postwar period and, up until that time, the longest peacetime expansion—what Bartley (1992) calls the seven fat years. Inflation and nominal interest rates declined dramatically (though real, inflation-adjusted rates, were higher than during the Carter administration), oil prices dropped and remained low until 2000, and new job creation continued at a rapid rate (though not as rapid as during the 1977–1980 period). The unemployment rate fell to 5 percent at the beginning of 1988, a rate not seen since the early 1970s. The peacetime expansion ended with a brief (nine-month) recession in 1990 and 1991, brought about as the Fed raised interest rates (Weisbrot 2000a).

During this period, the United States experienced historically high federal budget and trade deficits, uneven economic growth, recession-like conditions in some industrial and agricultural sectors, and relatively high real (i.e., inflation-adjusted) interest rates (see Figure 2.3). Questions also remained about productivity, investment and savings, and changing income distributions. For example, national savings continued to decline during this period and capital formation was also weaker than in earlier periods. While the tax changes of this period did result in increased work effort, the effect was modest (Akhtar and Harris 1992).

What distinguished the 1981–1992 period from the three previous periods (1945–1960, 1961–68, and 1969–1980) was the unique combination of fiscal and monetary policy that characterized the Reagan administration and continued into the first Bush administration. In the other periods, fiscal and monetary policy were pointed in the same direction. The Eisenhower years frequently combined tight fiscal policy with tight monetary policy. The Kennedy/Johnson years merged loose fiscal and monetary policy. The Reagan administration, on the other hand, joined an exceptionally stimulative fiscal

Figure 2.3    **Prime Interest Rate and Consumer Price Index (CPI) Changes Compared**

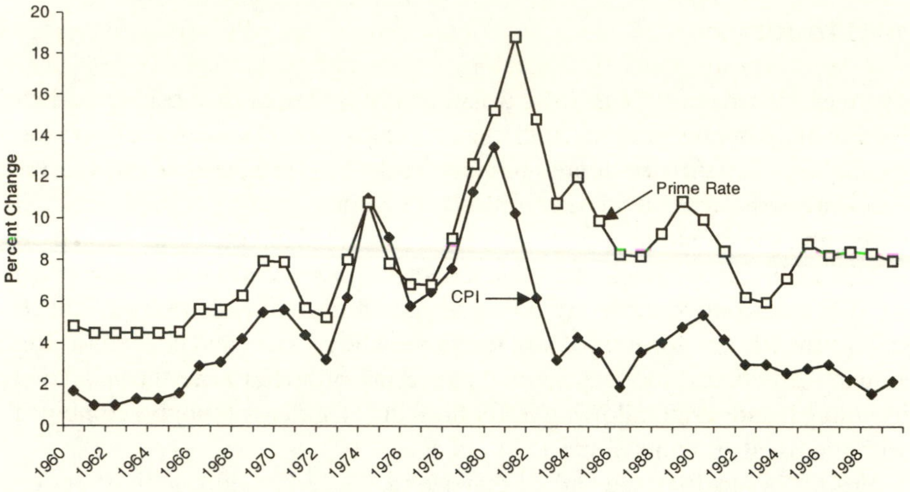

*Source:* Council of Economic Advisers (2000).

policy (as measured by the size of the budget deficits) to a restrictive but accommodating monetary policy. As economic growth resumed in 1983, the Fed kept a sharp lookout on the state of the economy. In 1984 and 1985, the Fed increased the money supply to stimulate a faltering economy. In 1986, the Fed lowered interest rates to produce a monetary stimulus. In 1987, the Fed once again restrained the money supply and raised the discount rates, partially to support the value of the dollar. After the October 1987 stock market crash, the Fed reversed itself, loosening monetary policy to stimulate the economy. Interest rates rose again in the summer of 1988 because of concerns about renewed inflation.

One of the important legacies of the Reagan administration was the undermining (at least temporarily) of tools to manage the economy. The huge deficits already provided a fiscal stimulus. Further fiscal stimulus through increased spending and/or reduced taxes was unacceptable given the size of the deficit, which peaked in fiscal year 1991, and the perceived need to reduce it. The 1990 and 1993 budget agreements (see below) demonstrated the difficulty of creating stimulative fiscal programs. On the other hand, reducing the deficit through a tax increase might retard an economy that has grown at a moderate rate.

This situation was further compounded by political problems. The Reagan administration opposed an increase in taxes and a decrease in defense spending. The Democrat-controlled Congress opposed cuts in domestic spending. Tax indexing, passed as part of the Economic Recovery Act of 1981, eliminated the inflation tax by gearing personal exemptions to increases in the consumer price index. The Tax Reform Act passed in 1986, with its lower and fewer tax rates, eliminated much of the progressiveness of the tax code. While there was virtually no discussion of this point during the two-year tax debate, this result does coincide with the conservative view that the federal government should intervene as little as possible in the economy.[31]

Monetary policy also lost some of its power. The Fed's continued increases in the money supply to stimulate the economy during the 1980s (with a growth rate of 17 percent in M-1 at one point in 1986) diminished its ability to continue the stimulus; indeed, as the supply of money increased, the increase in GDP slowed.[32] Any attempt to decrease growth in the money supply increases the threat of a recession. What remains are interest rates, now the focus of Fed policy. Even then, the attempt by Fed chairman Alan Greenspan in 1999 and 2000 to slow the economy and the stock market boom was slower than hoped for.

On a positive note, the economic legacy of the Reagan and Bush administrations was tax cuts (especially in the high marginal rates) and tax reform, continued deregulation (which had its origins in the Ford and Carter administrations), and wringing persistently high inflation from the economy.

### 1993 to Present

As mentioned, a brief, though unexpectedly deep, recession began in July 1990 and ended in March 1991. The recovery from the recession was agonizingly slow, leading the media to continue to label the U.S. economy as recessionary as late as November 1992, eighteen months after the recession had ended. Articles and books appeared during and after this time expressing the seeming pessimism about the state of the economy.[33]

Arkansas governor Bill Clinton's presidential campaign maintained as its motto "It's the economy, stupid!" This expressed the view that, rightly or wrongly, presidents are given credit for a good economy and blamed for a poor one.[34] Clinton's economic plan, as outlined in his 1993 State of the Union message, promised an economic stimulus for the slowly expanding economy, including increased spending and a middle-class tax cut (Crook 2000). The spending programs included jobs and infrastructure (building or rebuilding roads and bridges) programs, expansion for programs such as Head Start, and so forth. The estimated cost of the stimulus programs was $35 billion. It soon became apparent that there was little political support for an economic stimulus program and much pressure to reduce the deficit. Clinton's plan was defeated in the Senate, and the president turned in the spring of 1993 to deficit reduction. Clinton was also convinced by Fed chairman Alan Greenspan to drop the stimulus package and focus more on deficit reduction. As we will see below, by the end of the decade, the federal deficit disappeared, and the economy continued booming. During this time there were potential economic problems. The Fed eased monetary policy in 1990–92 to help stimulate the economy distressed by the recession. When inflation increased in the middle 1990s, the Fed raised interest rates and then lowered them as the inflationary threat receded (Thorbecke 2000). The Clinton administration along with the

Fed helped the U.S. economy come through the world financial crisis that began in Asia in 1997 and spread to Russia and Brazil. The crisis included the collapse of foreign currencies and the defaulting of Russia's debt. The Dow Jones plunged over 550 points on October 27, 1997, the largest single drop in the history of the Dow. The Fed and the U.S. Treasury Department in conjunction with the International Monetary Fund helped some of those countries by providing analysis to the affected countries, rescheduling loans, and cutting U.S. interest rates.[35] The surging U.S. economy was the engine of economic recovery as its trade deficit continued to increase and many nations (such as Japan) were mired in recession or stagnation for much of the 1990s.

In 1999 and 2000 the Fed again raised interest rates to cool off the economy and the stock market and forestall what it saw as potential inflation. By February 2000, the economy had experienced the longest peacetime expansion in the history of the country. Inflation was under 2 percent, unemployment hovered near the 4 percent mark, economic growth was strong, productivity gains were significant, and incomes at all levels were rising. But by the end of 2000 and into 2001, the booming economy slowed dramatically and the accelerating stock markets reversed course. The Fed began to lower interest rates, and talk of recession increased.

### Comparing the Decades

Table 2.5 compares the decades on a number of economic indicators.[36] As can be seen from the table, the1960s looks very good in comparison, though, as explained above, it led to the problems of the 1970s. On most of the indicators in Table 2.5, the 1960s surpasses the other three decades. The 1970s, commonly thought of as an economic failure, surpasses the 1980s and 1990s in most categories; it surpassed all decades in job creation. Its weaknesses were in the very high inflation rate and the stagnant job market, as measured by the Dow Jones index. The 1980s saw a substantial gain in the stock market and better job creation than in the 1990s. The poverty rate did increase during that time. The 1990s saw low inflation and unemployment, a tremendous increase in the stock market, and a significant increase in productivity gains.

## Policy Issues

### From Budget Deficit to Budget Surplus

> Liquidating the deficit ranks as one of the supreme budgetary accomplishments in American history. (Schick 2000, p. 36)

For much of the 1980s and 1990s, one of the most prominent economic issues was the federal budget deficit. A **budget deficit** occurs when spending ex-

Table 2.5

**Comparing Decades of Economic Gains**

|  | 1960s | 1970s | 1980s | 1990s |
|---|---|---|---|---|
| Economic growth (%) | 52.80 | 38.40 | 34.70 | 36.60 |
| Unemployment average (%) | 4.78 | 6.21 | 7.27 | 5.75 |
| High/Low (%) | 6.70/3.50 | 8.50/4.90 | 9.70/5.30 | 7.50/4.20 |
| Job creation (% decade increase) | 20.50 | 26.90 | 18.70 | 13.80 |
| Productivity gains (%) | 31.80 | 21.70 | 15.60 | 21.00 |
| Inflation (% decade increase) | 28.20 | 103.50 | 64.40 | 33.50 |
| Median family income (% change in real income) | 39.70 | 10.60 | 4.30 | 3.90 |
| Decline in poverty rate (% of poor in total population) | −10.30 | −0.40 | +1.10 | −0.10 |
| Prime rate average (%) | 5.29 | 8.10 | 11.85 | 7.98 |
| High/Low (%) | 7.96/4.50 | 12.67/5.25 | 18.87/5.66 | 10.01/6.00 |
| Dow Jones (decade gain in points) | 244.60 | −32.32 | 1,664.51 | 7,955.97 |

*Source:* U.S. Census Bureau (2000).

ceeds revenues. A **budget surplus** occurs when revenues exceed spending. Table 2.6 presents data for the 1953–2000 period showing the cumulative budget deficit for each presidential administration, starting with the Eisenhower administration. The deficit peaked in absolute numbers in FY 1992. The table also shows the federal budget deficit (surplus) as a percentage of gross domestic product to illustrate the relative size of the deficit (surplus). A large deficit in absolute terms may be easy to handle if the economy is also large. The deficit peaked in relative terms in fiscal year 1983.

We can also look at the cumulative impact of federal deficits. The federal **debt** is the sum of federal deficits and surpluses. Table 2.7 presents data for the federal debt held by the public. By FY 1981, the United States had accumulated about $790 billion worth of debt. Between 1981 and 1989, the debt nearly tripled. Why did the deficit (and the debt) grow so dramatically?

Clearly the financial distresses of the 1970s contributed to the problem. The slowdown of the economy and the relatively high inflation and interest rates of the late 1970s meant that revenues would be coming in more slowly, though spending would be relatively untouched.

A second reason has to do with the policies of the Reagan administration. The 1981 tax cuts, it was argued, would be essentially cost-free. Although tax rates would decrease, government revenues would be pretty much the same or higher because the lower tax rates would encourage new investment and productivity, and the economy would grow faster. While the theory itself may

Table 2.6

## Federal Budget Deficits/Surplus

| Fiscal year | Deficit(–)/Surplus (in billions of $) | % of GDP |
|---|---|---|
| 1953 | –6.5 | –1.8 |
| 1954 | –1.2 | –0.3 |
| 1955 | –3.0 | –0.8 |
| 1956 | 3.9 | 0.9 |
| 1957 | 3.4 | 0.8 |
| 1958 | –2.8 | –0.6 |
| 1959 | –12.8 | –2.6 |
| 1960 | 0.3 | 0.1 |
| Subtotal Eisenhower | –18.7 | |
| | | |
| 1961 | –3.3 | –0.6 |
| 1962 | –7.1 | –1.2 |
| 1963 | –4.8 | –0.8 |
| 1964 | –5.9 | –0.9 |
| 1965 | –1.4 | –0.2 |
| 1966 | –3.7 | –0.5 |
| 1967 | –8.6 | –1.1 |
| Subtotal Kennedy/Johnson | –60.0 | |
| | | |
| 1968 | –25.2 | –2.8 |
| 1969 | 3.2 | 0.3 |
| 1970 | –2.8 | –0.3 |
| 1971 | –23.0 | –2.1 |
| 1972 | –23.4 | –2.0 |
| 1973 | –14.9 | –1.1 |
| 1974 | –6.1 | –0.4 |
| 1975 | –53.2 | –3.4 |
| 1976 | –73.7 | –4.2 |
| Subtotal Nixon/Ford | –208.6 | |
| | | |
| Transitional quarter* | –14.7 | –3.3 |
| 1977 | –53.7 | –2.8 |
| 1978 | –59.2 | –2.7 |
| 1979 | –40.2 | –1.6 |
| 1980 | –73.8 | –2.7 |
| Subtotal Carter | –226.9 | |
| | | |
| 1981 | –79.0 | –2.6 |
| 1982 | –128.0 | –4.1 |
| 1983 | –207.8 | –6.3 |
| 1984 | –185.4 | –5.0 |
| 1985 | –212.3 | –5.3 |
| 1986 | –221.2 | –5.2 |

*(continued)*

Table 2.6 (continued)

| Fiscal year | Deficit(−)/Surplus (in billions of $) | % of GDP |
|---|---|---|
| 1987 | −149.8 | −3.3 |
| 1988 | −155.2 | −3.2 |
| Subtotal Reagan | −1,338.7 | |
| | | |
| 1989 | −152.5 | −2.9 |
| 1990 | −221.4 | −4.0 |
| 1991 | −269.5 | −4.7 |
| 1992 | −290.4 | −4.8 |
| Subtotal Bush | −933.8 | |
| | | |
| 1993 | −255.1 | −4.0 |
| 1994 | −203.3 | −2.8 |
| 1995 | −164.0 | −2.2 |
| 1996 | −107.5 | −1.4 |
| 1997 | −22.0 | −0.3 |
| 1998 | 69.2 | 0.8 |
| 1999 | 124.4 | 1.4 |
| Subtotal Clinton | −751.9 | |
| | | |
| 2000 (est.) | 166.7 | |
| Subtotal | −391.6 | |
| | | |
| 2001 (est.) | 184.0 | |
| 2002 (est.) | 185.9 | |
| 2003 (est.) | 184.6 | |
| 2004 (est.) | 195.0 | |
| 2005 (est.) | 215.5 | |

*Source:* Office of Management and Budget (2000).
*Note:* *Transitional quarter when beginning of federal fiscal year changed from July 1 to October 1.

be debatable, the reality is that for various reasons it did not quite work out that way, at least for the federal deficit. Tax rates were cut, and there were some offshoot spending cuts but not nearly as large as the tax cuts. Further, defense spending increased dramatically, the Reagan administration maintaining that the defense policies of the predecessor Carter administration had created an underfunded defense force. Although the last Carter budget called for increased defense spending (in the wake of the Soviet Union's invasion of Afghanistan in 1979), the Reagan administration increased spending beyond the Carter recommendations. Consider the 1981 tax and spending changes: Taxes were cut by $642 billion, future domestic spending was cut by $263 billion, and defense spending was increased by $121 billion. No wonder the deficit increased so dramatically![37] The 1986 tax reform act also reduced revenues.

Table 2.7

**Real Change in Federal Debt**

| Fiscal year | Public federal debt (in billion $) |
|---|---|
| 1970 | 283.2 |
| 1971 | 303.0 |
| 1972 | 322.4 |
| 1973 | 340.9 |
| 1974 | 343.7 |
| 1975 | 394.7 |
| 1976 | 477.4 |
| Transitional quarter* | 495.5 |
| 1977 | 549.1 |
| 1978 | 607.1 |
| 1979 | 640.3 |
| 1980 | 711.9 |
| 1981 | 789.4 |
| 1982 | 924.6 |
| 1983 | 1,137.3 |
| 1984 | 1,307.0 |
| 1985 | 1,507.4 |
| 1986 | 1,740.8 |
| 1987 | 1,889.9 |
| 1988 | 2,051.8 |
| 1989 | 2,191.0 |
| 1990 | 2,411.8 |
| 1991 | 2,689.3 |
| 1992 | 3,000.1 |
| 1993 | 3,248.8 |
| 1994 | 3,433.4 |
| 1995 | 3,604.8 |
| 1996 | 3,734.5 |
| 1997 | 3,772.8 |
| 1998 | 3,721.6 |
| 1999 | 3,632.9 |
| 2000 (est.) | 3,475.9 |
| 2001 (est.) | 3,305.0 |

*Source:* Council of Economic Advisers (2000).
*Notes:* The table refers to the debt held by the public. There is another measure of the debt, known as gross federal debt, which includes money the federal government owes to trust funds, such as Social Security.
*Transitional quarter when beginning of federal fiscal year changed from July 1 to October 1.

Perhaps the most important factor, unanticipated by the Reagan administration, was inflation. The assumption was made in 1981 that inflation would continue to be high, as it had been in previous years. However, the policies of the Fed under Chairman Paul Volcker helped reduce inflation much faster than anticipated. Without the inflation factor, the effects of supply-side tax cuts were blunted.

Entitlements were often mentioned as a cause of the large budget deficits of the 1980s and 1990s. **Entitlements**, according to Peter Peterson, "are any public-sector payments, received by a person or household, that do not represent contractual compensation for goods or services" (Peterson 1993, pp. 99–100). Entitlements include Medicare, Medicaid, social security, welfare,[38] food stamps, student loans and grants, military and federal civilian employment programs, interest on the debt, and so forth. If one is eligible for the program, one is entitled to the benefits. Entitlements can also include tax expenditures (tax breaks) such as the tax deduction for interest on home mortgages and tax breaks for the business sector, such as the ability to deduct worker health care costs. In FY 1999, mandatory spending (largely entitlements) accounted for 55.1 percent of total federal spending. This portion does not include interest on the debt, another 13.5 percent in FY 1999.

Two other factors are political in nature. First, the political will was not present to make the necessary changes in taxing and spending policies. Tax increases are always unpopular (Makin and Ornstein 1994), and many federal programs, such as Medicare, Medicaid, and Social Security, have significant public support.

A second, somewhat cynical, factor was the political calculations. Having high budget deficits retarded the ability to have expansive and expensive new federal programs. This fiscal constraint, this strategy, had a role in the defeat of the Clinton health care plan in 1994 because at one point the Congressional Budget Office said that, at least in the short run, it would increase the deficit. If raising taxes was unpopular, then the only way to reduce the budget would be to cut spending.

Beginning in the mid-1980s, Congress and the president began to focus on the budget with, in retrospect, rather modest efforts. In December 1985 Congress passed legislation raising the debt ceiling, the amount of money the federal government is allowed to owe. An amendment to the debt ceiling bill was a rider, the Balanced Budget Act of 1985. The act, also known as Gramm-Rudman-Hollings after its sponsors, set specific targets for deficit reductions in succeeding years, with the ultimate goal of reducing the yearly federal deficit to zero by FY 1991. In early 1986, the first round of sequestration cuts were made, totaling about $11 billion in program cuts. If Congress did not act within the set deadlines (the act reformed the Congressional Budget and Impoundment Act of 1974) or was more than $10 billion over the specified targets, then across-the-board cuts were to be made.[39]

A portion of the act was invalidated by the Supreme Court in 1986, and Congress passed a modified version of the Balanced Budget Act in 1987 with a zero-deficit target set for FY 1993. Budget cuts made in late 1987 were relatively mild, designed to keep the deficit from rising again.[40] The pain of much of the automatic cuts was put off until after the 1988 presidential election and put off again during the FY 1990 budget process.

At the Republican national convention in the summer of 1988, Vice President George H. W. Bush, the Republican nominee for president, made a memorable statement. He restated his pledge, originally made during the New Hampshire primary, that he would not raise taxes despite continued pressure from Congress and the Democrats to do so. The vice president led the enthusiastic crowd several times, saying, "No new taxes."

Despite the two balanced budget acts, Congress was still faced with pressure to reduce the deficits. The Republicans, who controlled the presidency but held only a minority in Congress, were adamant that spending cuts were the only acceptable way to reduce the deficit. Democrats were equally adamant that spending cuts had to be accompanied by tax increases. The Democrats, though having a majority in both houses of Congress, would not accept tax cuts without President Bush's endorsement to provide political cover. By June 1990, Bush backed off from his campaign pledge and endorsed higher taxes as a compromise to get spending cuts. Then in the summer of 1990, Iraq invaded Kuwait, and the administration's concentration focused on six months of diplomatic maneuverings and military buildup, resulting in the successful liberation of Kuwait in early 1991. A second factor, unknown at the time, was that the economy had slid into a recession. Recall that a recession is defined as six or more consecutive months of decline in GDP. Thus, if the recession began in July 1990, it would not be clear until early 1991 that this was the case.

Congress was unable to pass all its appropriation bills by the end of the fiscal year (September 1990) and passed a series of continuing resolutions, one of which Bush (who wanted more spending cuts) vetoed. Without such legislation, the federal government could not pay its bills and would have to shut down (as happened in 1995; see below). Thus we have the confluence of various circumstances: war, recession, political differences, and deadlines. After another continuing resolution was passed, Congress and the president finally agreed on a budget by the end of October, and the president signed the bill on November 5—more than a month into the fiscal year.

The budget agreement called for $496.2 billion in deficit reduction over a five-year period, through a combination of spending cuts and tax increases. The tax increases included higher marginal tax rates (31 percent) at the upper bracket (thus reversing the trend of the early and mid-1980s) and a five-cent-a-gallon gasoline tax. Most of the spending cuts came from the defense budget.

The 1990 budget deal had numerous effects and implications. First, it essentially repealed Gramm-Rudman-Hollings. Second, it set budget ceilings for the first three years in three categories (domestic, defense, and foreign aid) and for the total discretionary budget for all five years. The agreement provided that, at least for the first three years, savings in one area could not be transferred to another area (this was to protect foreign aid, always an unpopular program support). The agreement provided that spending increases over the ceiling would have to be accompanied either by reductions in other programs or by new revenues (the "pay-as-you-go" provision). One important effect of the 1990 budget agreement was that having set the federal budget on a course for the next several years, the constant arguing over the budget that had marked Congress disappeared. Budget, authorization, and appropriations committees knew their targets, there was an enforcement mechanism, and the usual budget rancor did not appear.

The 1990 agreement did not end the deficit problem. The 1990–91 recession worsened the situation, and the 1992 presidential campaign of third-party candidate Ross H. Perot particularly focused on the deficit. Although President Bush's public opinion approval rating soared in the wake of the successful conclusion of the Persian Gulf War in 1991 (reaching an unprecedented 91 percent at one point), the perception that the recession was continuing (although the reality was that it had ended eighteen months before the November 1992 election) the slow recovery, the public's desire to deal with domestic problems, and onslaughts from both the Democrats and the Perot campaign all led to Bush's defeat and Bill Clinton's victory.

Clinton, as we saw above, dropped his proposed economic stimulus plan and proposed a deficit reduction plan. The early plans for deficit reduction called for a broad energy tax, known as the "BTU tax." In addition, the Clinton plan called for an increase in income tax rates at the top marginal tax levels (Clinton promised that he would not balance the budget on the backs of the middle class; only those at the upper-income levels would be asked to contribute more money). The BTU tax found little support in Congress and was replaced by a five-cent-a-gallon gasoline tax. The income tax changes remained. The top marginal tax rate was increased to 38 percent. There were additional cuts in the defense budget beyond the Bush cuts, as well as cuts in future spending. The deficit reduction package passed the House by three votes and the Senate by the narrowest of margins: a vote cast by Vice President Al Gore.

The 1993 budget agreement was remarkably similar to the 1990 agreement between President Bush and Congress in terms of the size of reductions (about $500 billion) and in the kinds of reductions made (e.g., raising the gasoline tax). The Congressional Budget Office estimated that the deficit would be reduced through FY 1997 and then begin to rise again (Rauch 1993). Clearly the deficit issue would not go away.

In 1994, Republicans regained control of Congress, the Senate for the first time since 1986 and the House for the first time since 1954. The 1994 victories were enabled by the failure of President Clinton's health care reform plan to pass Congress (see chapter 5). In September 1994, Republican House candidates signed the Contract with America, a document fashioned under the direction of Dick Armey of Texas and Newt Gingrich of Georgia (then the minority whip), which promised, among other things, to downsize the federal government by passing on responsibilities for programs to the states (devolution) and a balanced budget amendment.

The proposed balanced budget amendment failed to get the necessary two-thirds vote, in the Senate. Congress, now in Republican hands (with Bob Dole of Kansas as the Senate majority leader and Gingrich as House Speaker), then turned to reducing the deficit by cutting spending and reducing taxes (a replay of the early Reagan administration years). By June 1995, the House and Senate agreed on a budget resolution that called for $983 billion in deficit reductions through FY 2002. The resolution proposed $245 billion in tax cuts. Deficit reductions would come from a variety of programs: $270 billion from Medicare, $180 billion from Medicaid, $190 billion from discretionary spending, and $174 from other mandatory spending. The defense budget would be increased by about $34 billion (Hager and Rubin 1995). In addition, some of the House appropriations bills contained riders (amendments) that would have made significant changes in environmental policy. The president opposed both the cuts and the riders.

President Clinton vetoed the appropriations bills. Congress passed several continuing resolutions, one of which was also vetoed. In retaliation, Congress refused to pass a new debt ceiling bill, which would have allowed the federal government to borrow more money. This combination led to two government shutdowns. Eventually, in 1996, an omnibus reconciliation bill, which combined the spending appropriations for bills that had not been enacted, was passed.

The 1996 elections came as something of a surprise to the Republicans. Bill Clinton was reelected, and Republican majorities in both houses became slimmer. The big budget deal would come in 1997. By this time, Clinton had signed on to the idea of balancing the budget by fiscal year 2002.

After considerable negotiating between the House and the Senate, Congress and the president, Republicans and Democrats, even the president and Democrats, an agreement was reached in the summer of 1997. The **Balanced Budget Act (1997)** called for spending reductions of $306.3 billion over a five-year period, $31.2 billion in spending increases and $85 billion in net tax savings. The total net deficit reduction over the five-year period was $203.7 billion.

The budget agreement included important program changes. The most important domestic initiatives were the creation of children's health programs to increase the number of children with health insurance (see chapter 5) and the restoration of Medicaid and Supplemental Security Income eligibility for legal immigrants (see chapter 4) (Palazzolo 1999).

Medicare was also targeted for important changes. Reimbursements to providers were cut, and nursing homes and home health care providers were included in the prepayment schedule. Choice of plans was also greatly extended. All told, the reductions in Medicare spending were estimated at $115 billion over the five-year period, more than half of the estimated net savings (Palazzolo 1999).

## The Surplus Appears

A major criticism of the budget deal (and there was plenty of criticism, especially from health-care providers) is that it did not deal with the long-term problem of entitlement spending (see case study below and chapter 5's discussion of
Medicare). Still, a budget surplus did appear. Why after all these years? After
all, some observers thought that deficits would continue. Writing about the FY
1997—ironically the year of the big budget agreement—budget negotiations,
Hager and Pianin (1999) asserted that the budget would not get balanced:

> *Mirage* [the title of their book] is the story of how the nation slid into the deficit
> mess, why it has been impossible to get out, and how wave after wave of confident
> and able politicians has come to Washington with surefire plans for fixing the prob-
> lem only to give up in humiliated defeat. All that was supposed to change in 1995,
> when Republicans seized control of Congress and vowed to live up to promises to
> eradicate the deficit at last. Instead, events merely confirmed past pattens and added
> to the growing sense of hopelessness. (Hager and Pianin 1999, p. 13)

Hager and Pianin's narrative of budget politics is a good example of what
Palazzolo calls the **inevitable gridlock model** of politics. Republicans and
Democrats engage in cycles of revenge politics, divided government leads to
gridlock, interest groups protect their cherished programs, thus creating
demosclerosis (Rauch 1999), entitlements threaten future budgets (Peterson
1993). There is something to all these claims and, as we will see below, the
continuation of budget surpluses is not a foregone conclusion. Yet the surplus
appeared for the first time in FY 1998.

Palazzolo offers an alternative to the inevitable gridlock model. His **realistic model** suggests that the factors mentioned above make it more difficult,
but not impossible, to make significant changes. He points out that the 1997
budget agreement was one of a series of steps that was taken (the incrementalism feature discussed in chapter 1). He also points out that Republicans
and Democrats had an interest in reducing the deficit, partly as a result of the
1996 elections, which were interpreted as meaning the public wanted a reasonable, fair deal. Leadership in both parties and institutions (Congress and
the president) was important. Thus, even in times of divided government,
change can take place.

Certainly the three budget agreements (1990, 1993, and 1997) were important in leading to the surpluses (Schick 2000). Clearly one of the important
areas where savings were made, though not entirely via the three budget agreements, was in military spending. Defense spending peaked in FY 1989 at
$304.1 billion. By FY 1998, defense spending had decreased to $270.2 billion (Office of Management and Budget 2000). If defense spending increases
had continued at the same average rate as they had in the 1980s (approximately 8.6 percent a year), defense spending in FY 1999 would have been
$697.3 billion instead of the $275.5 that it actually was.

Another way of looking at the impact of limiting defense spending is to consider the percentage of gross domestic product that is devoted to defense spending. This number peaked, in recent years, in fiscal year 1986 at 6.2 percent. By FY 1999, that percentage had declined to 3 percent (Office of Management and Budget 2000). If we had the same percentage in FY 1999 as we did in FY 1986, we would be spending about $567.4 billion. Of course, the Cold War ended in the 1989–1991 period and presumably we did not have to spend as much. But the numbers do point up the impact that constraining defense spending had.

Federal government health care programs also played a role. For fiscal year 1998, Medicare spending increased by only 1.5 percent. In FY 1999, Medicare spending actually declined by 1.2 percent. The savings were partly from the extension of managed care to Medicare, but more importantly from changes made by the 1997 budget agreement (Horney and Greenstein 2000; Palazzollo 1999; calculations made from data in Council of Economic Advisers 2000).

Perhaps more critical was the state of the economy. By 1997, the Congressional Budget Office began to predict additional revenues because of economic growth. That made agreement easier. The increased revenues were at least partly a product of the booming stock market. As people realized impressive gains, they sold stock, paid their capital gains tax, and flooded government coffers.

The economy itself was growing strongly, though perhaps too strongly in the eyes of Fed chairman Alan Greenspan. Inflation was low and productivity growth began to improve in 1995 (Uchitelle 2000). Productivity growth is one of the most important economic indicators; it also allows income growth without undue pressure on inflation.

Social Security also played a role here. Changes made in 1983 (see case study below) began to produce considerable surpluses in the Social Security **Trust Fund**. Indeed, much of the decrease in the overall deficit and the appearance of the surplus is due to surpluses in the Social Security Trust Fund. Consider Table 2.8. It has the budget deficit/surplus figures from Table 2.6. Now it adds the surplus/deficit figures for the Social Security Trust Fund. The non–Social Security portion of the budget does not obtain a surplus, and a small one, until FY 1999. The estimated non–Social Security surpluses through FY 2005 are quite small. Over the entire decade, the estimated non–Social Security surplus is $1.9 trillion (though that figure has risen). So clearly, the Social Security trust surplus has played a major role. Nevertheless, the table does show a stronger fiscal balance even in the non–Social Security portion of the budget.

## Budget Surplus Policy Making

Given the above discussion, three important, related questions arise. First, is budget making easier in times of surplus than in times of deficits? Second, is

Table 2.8

**Social Security and Non-Social Security Surplus/Deficits** (in billion dollars)

|  | Social Security | Non–Social Security | Overall surplus/deficit |
|---|---|---|---|
| 1980 | −3.2 | −70.6 | −73.8 |
| 1981 | −0.7 | −78.3 | −79.0 |
| 1982 | −11.3 | −116.7 | −128.0 |
| 1983 | −3.4 | −204.4 | −207.8 |
| 1984 | 0.9 | −186.3 | −185.4 |
| 1985 | 10.7 | −223.0 | −212.3 |
| 1986 | 16.8 | −238.0 | −221.2 |
| 1987 | 20.8 | −170.6 | −149.8 |
| 1988 | 38.7 | −193.9 | −155.2 |
| 1989 | 51.4 | −203.9 | −152.5 |
| 1990 | 55.1 | −276.5 | −221.4 |
| 1991 | 52.0 | −321.5 | −269.5 |
| 1992 | 50.9 | −341.3 | −290.4 |
| 1993 | 49.4 | −304.5 | −255.1 |
| 1994 | 60.7 | −264.0 | −203.3 |
| 1995 | 31.7 | −195.7 | −164.0 |
| 1996 | 51.5 | −159.0 | −107.5 |
| 1997 | 67.9 | −89.9 | −22.0 |
| 1998 | 85.9 | −16.7 | 69.2 |
| 1999 | 109.1 | 15.3 | 124.4 |
| 2000 (est.) | 128.8 | 37.9 | 166.7 |
| 2001 (est.) | 138.3 | 45.7 | 184.0 |
| 2002 (est.) | 151.6 | 34.3 | 185.9 |
| 2003 (est.) | 163.5 | 21.1 | 184.6 |
| 2004 (est.) | 175.2 | 19.8 | 195.0 |
| 2005 (est.) | 194.6 | 20.9 | 215.5 |

*Source:* Office of Management and Budget (2000).

the surplus, especially the non–Social Security Surplus, real? Third, assuming the surpluses are real, how should we spend the extra funds?

The first question asks whether the existence of a surplus makes it easier for Congress to produce a budget. One way we can judge the ease of budgeting is to see whether the process is completed on time, particularly the thirteen appropriations bills. Based on recent history, the FY 2000 budget, the answer must be "no." Ten of the thirteen appropriations bills were not passed by September 1, the start of the fiscal year. Some faced presidential vetoes. President Clinton vetoed the tax-cut bill ($792 billion). Budgeting for FY 2001 was not much better, exacerbated by the 2000 presidential campaign.

We can also examine whether the budget stayed within the limits of the 1997 budget agreement. Again, the answer is no. Congress engaged in "creative" budget accounting to try to stay within the rigid limits. For example, some money was declared "emergency" and therefore not counted as part of the regular budget. One example of so-called emergency spending was the funding for the 2000 census (see, e.g., Weiner 1999). Other techniques include deliberately underfunding some programs and then treating extra expenditures as emergencies; making optimistic revenue projections; and directed scorekeeping (picking between CBO and OMB spending figures to produce low estimates) (Geraghty 2000; Schick 2000).

Given the new fiscal environment (surpluses rather than deficits), one could argue that the budget caps set in 1997 were too rigid and should be eased. Yet those caps make it more likely that surpluses will remain.

The second question asks whether the surpluses are real or, to put it another way, how reliable the projections are. The Congressional Budget Office projections assume that Congress will stay within the 1997 budget agreement guidelines. To stay within those guidelines, Congress would have to make significant cuts in discretionary spending; when inflation is taken into account, the cuts would have to be very large. Defense spending increases, proposed by both Republicans and Democrats, also violate the agreement (Elkin and Greenstein 1999; Horney and Greenstein 2000; OMB Watch 1999). The projections are also based, as are all economic projections, on economic assumptions about GDP growth, inflation, and so forth. Even small changes in those assumptions would greatly change projections. Economist Paul Krugman's analysis of the CBO projections of non–Social Security budget surpluses of $1.9 trillion suggests that about $400 billion is a more realistic figure (Krugman 2000a). Meeting the surplus projections would require a decade-long freeze on domestic spending, which, given inflation, would necessitate cutting discretionary spending by almost $900 billion over this time period (Horney and Greenstein 2000). The Concord Coalition, like Krugman and Greenstein, argued that projected surpluses are much more tentative than is being heralded (Howe and Jackson 2000; see also Greenstein 2001). Further, the Concord Coalition asserted that long-term entitlements problems (see case study below and chapter 5 on Medicare) will cut into if not eliminate surpluses in the future (see also Peterson 1993, 1996).

Now we get to our third question, what to do with the surplus funds, if there is a surplus. This was the subject of some debate during the 2000 presidential elections, and part of the debate was over President George W. Bush's budget and tax proposals. First, we could cut taxes. Republicans and conservatives often suggest this. The Republicans in Congress proposed a $792 billion tax cut, Republican presidential nominee George W. Bush proposed a smaller one (in the $400–500 billion range), and the FY 2001 budget resolution called for an even smaller one ($140 billion range). The Clinton administration proposed targeted tax cuts, as did Democratic presidential nominee Al Gore. President George W. Bush proposed $1.6 trillion in tax cuts over ten years.

But there did not seem to be any takers, at least in 2000. For example, President Clinton vetoed the congressional bill calling for the $742 billion tax cut in 1999. Congress recessed for August and when it came back, made no effort to override the veto. Republican legislators talked with their constituents and found little support for the tax cut. Why? Consider the following quote:

> Each of the studies slices the data in a different way, but the bottom line is the same: Most Americans this year will have to fork over less than 10 percent of their income to the federal government when they file federal income taxes.
>
> The Congressional Budget Office estimates the middle fifth of American families, with an average of $39,100, paid 5.4 percent in income tax, compared with 8.3 percent in 1981. The Treasury Department estimates a four-person family, with the median income of $54,900, paid 7.46 percent of that in income tax, the lowest since 1965. And the conservative Tax Foundation figures that the median two-earner family, making $68,605, paid 8.5 percent in 1998, about the same as 1955. (Kessler 2000, p. 18)[41]

Policy changes, dating back to the 1981 Reagan tax cuts and including the 1986 tax reform bill, lowered taxes for the middle and lower classes. As we shall see below, most of the federal income taxes are paid by the upper classes. Therefore, most tax-cut policies would benefit the upper classes much more than other income segments.

There is another reason for the apathy that greeted tax cut proposals. The economy was doing very well, as of early 2000, and some, such as Alan Greenspan, thought it was growing too quickly. The Fed raised interest rates to slow down the economy. A large tax cut would stimulate an economy that some believed was already overheated. The policy reaction to large tax cuts on the part of the Fed would likely be to raise interest rates even higher. So at best we should expect small cuts. In the changed economic and political atmosphere of 2001, tax cuts garnered more support.

A second proposal for dealing with the surplus is to use it for new spending. For example, during the 2000 presidential campaign, both Governor Bush and Vice President Gore offered new spending programs in health care and education. Others on the liberal side also suggested new spending, suggesting that needed public investments could now be made in housing, sewers, schools, and so forth (Kuttner 2000; Sawicky 2000).

A third possibility, related to the second, is to use the money to reinforce the two large federal entitlement programs, Social Security and Medicare. This choice would forestall the day of reckoning when the trust funds go bankrupt (see case study below).

The fourth possibility, and the simplest, is to do nothing with the surplus. First of all, as discussed above, there are questions about how real and long-lasting the surpluses are. If we commit to new spending or new taxation, the surpluses will obviously shrink, but what if the assumptions behind the projections are wrong? Another advantage of the do-nothing course of action is that not spending the surpluses would reduce the public debt. Both President Clinton and House Speaker Dennis Hastert (R-IL) proposed eliminating the publicly held debt by the middle of the next decade (Jenislawski 2000). Presi-

Table 2.9

**Disposable Income Per Capita** (in constant 1996 dollars)

| Year | Dollar amount | Percentage change |
|------|--------------|-------------------|
| 1959 | 9,167 | N/A |
| 1960 | 9,210 | 0.005 |
| 1961 | 9,361 | 0.016 |
| 1962 | 9,666 | 0.033 |
| 1963 | 9,886 | 0.023 |
| 1964 | 10,456 | 0.058 |
| 1965 | 10,965 | 0.049 |
| 1966 | 11,417 | 0.041 |
| 1967 | 11,776 | 0.031 |
| 1968 | 12,196 | 0.036 |
| 1969 | 12,451 | 0.021 |
| 1970 | 12,823 | 0.030 |
| 1971 | 13,218 | 0.031 |
| 1972 | 13,692 | 0.036 |
| 1973 | 14,496 | 0.059 |
| 1974 | 14,268 | −0.016 |
| 1975 | 14,393 | 0.009 |
| 1976 | 14,873 | 0.033 |
| 1977 | 15,256 | 0.026 |
| 1978 | 15,845 | 0.039 |
| 1979 | 16,120 | 0.017 |
| 1980 | 16,063 | −0.004 |
| 1981 | 16,265 | 0.013 |
| 1982 | 16,328 | 0.004 |
| 1983 | 16,673 | 0.021 |
| 1984 | 17,799 | 0.068 |
| 1985 | 18,229 | 0.024 |
| 1986 | 18,641 | 0.023 |
| 1987 | 18,870 | 0.012 |
| 1988 | 19,522 | 0.035 |
| 1989 | 19,833 | 0.016 |
| 1990 | 20,058 | 0.011 |
| 1991 | 19,919 | −0.007 |
| 1992 | 20,318 | 0.020 |
| 1993 | 20,384 | 0.003 |
| 1994 | 20,709 | 0.016 |
| 1995 | 21,055 | 0.017 |
| 1996 | 21,385 | 0.016 |
| 1997 | 21,838 | 0.021 |
| 1998 | 22,672 | 0.038 |
| 1999 | 23,191 | 0.023 |

*Source:* Council of Economic Advisors (2001).

dent George W. Bush has proposed reducing much of the public debt over the next ten years. Reducing the debt would also reduce the interest payments on the debt, thus increasing the surplus. Lower interest payments would also free up money for the other possible uses.

Perhaps the most difficult task is not to rationally figure out what to do with the surplus, but to make sure that policy makers do not make it disappear. And given the tentativeness of the assumption behind budget surpluses—that Congress will stay within the 1997 caps—permanent additional changes should be made only with great reluctance.[42]

## Economic Inequality

We will directly address equality as a policy issue in chapter 9. But equality as one of our three political values has important dimensions in other policy areas; economic policy is no different. The argument that is made is that on several important indicators there is substantial and growing economic inequality. These include income distribution, wealth distribution, and wage increases (see, in general, Marshall 2000). It also addresses issues of class mobility. So let us first look at what the data shows.

We start with income distribution. Table 2.9 presents data for disposable personal income per capita for the 1959–1999 period. For the entire period, the annual average growth rate was 2.4 percent. To make appropriate comparisons, we will look at a number of smaller periods. As we saw previously, the 1960s was a particularly good period of economic growth. For the 1961–68 period, the second longest economic expansion in American history, the average annual growth rate was 3.6 percent. Some have argued (Krugman 1994a, 1994b) that 1973 was the time that problems hit the economy. For the 1959–1973 period, the average annual growth rate in disposable per capita income was 3.3 percent; for the 1973–1999 period, the growth rate was 2.0 percent. What about the seven fat years (Bartley 1992)? For the 1982–89 period, the average annual growth rate was 2.5 percent, 2.8 percent if we start counting in 1983. For the most recent period of growth, 1991–99, the longest expansion (and without a war stimulus that characterized the 1960s), average annual growth was 1.6 percent, or 1.9 percent if we started counting in 1992.

What can we conclude? First, 1973 does seem to have been a turning or inflection point in terms of income increases; increases have come more slowly since that time. Second, the 1982–89 seven fat years show an increase over previous and subsequent periods. However, the increase is a bit smaller than for the 1959–1973 period. Third, the 1991–99 period saw slower increases than in the previous period. Now let us look at wages.

Table 2.10 presents data on average weekly earnings, adjusted for inflation. Wages peaked in 1972, pretty close to our 1973 turning point, at $315.44 per week. For the entire 1959–1999 period, wages increased by $10.39. How-

Table 2.10

**Average Weekly Earnings** (in 1982 dollars)

| Year | Earnings | % Change |
|------|----------|----------|
| 1959 | $260.86 | N/A |
| 1960 | 261.92 | 0.406 |
| 1961 | 265.59 | 1.401 |
| 1962 | 273.60 | 3.016 |
| 1963 | 278.18 | 1.674 |
| 1964 | 283.18 | 1.797 |
| 1965 | 291.90 | 3.079 |
| 1966 | 294.11 | 0.757 |
| 1967 | 293.49 | (0.211) |
| 1968 | 298.42 | 1.680 |
| 1969 | 300.81 | 0.801 |
| 1970 | 298.08 | (0.908) |
| 1971 | 303.81 | 1.922 |
| 1972 | 315.44 | 3.828 |
| 1973 | 315.38 | (0.019) |
| 1974 | 302.27 | (4.157) |
| 1975 | 293.06 | (3.047) |
| 1976 | 297.37 | 1.471 |
| 1977 | 300.96 | 1.207 |
| 1978 | 300.89 | (0.023) |
| 1979 | 291.66 | (3.068) |
| 1980 | 274.65 | (5.832) |
| 1981 | 270.63 | (1.464) |
| 1982 | 267.26 | (1.245) |
| 1983 | 272.52 | 1.968 |
| 1984 | 274.73 | 0.811 |
| 1985 | 271.16 | (1.299) |
| 1986 | 271.94 | 0.288 |
| 1987 | 269.16 | (1.022) |
| 1988 | 266.79 | (0.881) |
| 1989 | 264.22 | (0.963) |
| 1990 | 259.47 | (1.798) |
| 1991 | 255.4 | (1.569) |
| 1992 | 255.22 | (0.070) |
| 1993 | 254.87 | (0.137) |
| 1994 | 256.73 | 0.730 |
| 1995 | 255.07 | (0.647) |
| 1996 | 255.73 | 0.259 |
| 1997 | 261.31 | 2.182 |
| 1998 | 268.32 | 2.683 |
| 1999 | 271.25 | 1.092 |

*Source:* Council of Economic Advisers (2001).

ever, wages in 1999 were $44.13 lower than in 1972. Indeed, wages did not surpass the 1959 level until 1997. For the most recent expansion (1991–2001), average weekly wages did not begin to increase until 1996. Again, a comparison of the three major post–World War II economic expansions is illuminating. The 1960s expansion (1961–68) saw consistent wage gains, that is, wage gains in every year, something that the 1980s and 1990s did not see. For the 1960s expansion, wages increased by $32.83. In the 1980s expansion, the seven fat years, wages increased from 1982 to 1984, largely as a result of the recovery from the very severe 1981–82 recession. For the 1983–89 period, average weekly wages declined by $8.30. For the entire 1992–99 period, wages increased by $16.03. Stagnant wages begin their recovery only in the latter part of the 1990s economic expansion.[43]

Now we need to look at income distribution itself. Table 2.11 presents the data. The table, based on analysis of Congressional Budget Office data by the Center for Budget and Policy Priorities (Shapiro and Greenstein 1999), shows the after-tax distribution, by quintiles of the population (20 percent of the distribution) and the highest 1 percent. It is important to note that the distribution is in *after-tax income*. Given the somewhat progressive nature of the system and the observation that much of the federal income tax is paid by those at the top of the income distribution, this means that the before-tax income distribution would be even more highly skewed than the after-tax one.

Two important observations can be made from Table 2.11. First, after-tax income is certainly skewed toward the upper-income levels. The highest 20 percent of families in 1999 had more than half of all income. Second, the distribution has become more unequal over time. The highest 20 percent of families had 44.2 percent of after-tax income in 1977. It experienced a 14 percent gain in the ensuing twenty-two years. For the highest 1 percent, the data are even more dramatic. In 1977, the top 1 percent had 7.3 percent of after-tax family income; in 1999 that figure rose to 12.9 percent, a gain of over 76 percent. All the other groups saw losses in income share over the same period; the lower down on the income distribution, the greater the loss.

The increase in maldistribution hit the media in 1995 and 1996. Stories pointed out that inequality was increasing (see, e.g., Greenfield, 1996; Mishel 1995; Passell 1996; Pearlstein 1995a, 1995b).[44] But this is not the whole story. There are two more sets of observations that need to be made.

Distribution of wealth is even more skewed than income distribution. Table 2.12 presents the data. Whereas the top 1 percent of the income distribution had 13 percent of all the income, the top 1 percent had 39 percent of all wealth. The top 20 percent had half of all income but 84 percent of all wealth (Krugman 2000b; Mishel, Bernstein, and Schmitt 2001; Wolff 1995, 1998, 2000).

We also need to look at one other area. Inequality of income, and its richer cousin wealth, would be acceptable if opportunities were open to much of the

Table 2.11

**Income Distribution: Percentage of Shares of National After-Tax Income Held by Various Groups of Families**

|  | 1977 | 1999 (projected) | % change over time period |
|---|---|---|---|
| Lowest fifth | 5.7 | 4.2 | −26.3 |
| Second fifth | 11.5 | 9.7 | −15.7 |
| Middle fifth | 16.4 | 14.7 | −10.4 |
| Fourth fifth | 22.8 | 21.3 | −6.6 |
| Highest fifth | 44.2 | 50.4 | 14.0 |
| Top 1 percent | 7.3 | 12.9 | 76.7 |

*Source:* Shapiro and Greenstein (1999).

population to improve their lot in life, to move up in the distribution. Michael Cox and Richard Alm (2000; see also Cox and Alm 1999) argue:

> America isn't a caste society, and studies that track individuals' incomes over time show that Americans have a remarkable ability to propel themselves upward. A 17-year study of lifetime earnings by the Federal Reserve Bank of Dallas found that only 5 percent of people in the economy's lowest 20 percent failed to move to a higher income group. In a similar study by the Treasury Department covering 1979 to 1988, 86 percent of Americans in the bottom fifth of income earners improved their status.

Yet other analyses suggest that economic mobility is much less than indicated by Cox and Alm. Many of those in the above-mentioned study were young people in college or graduate school from upper-income families. In that sense, there is no economic mobility for that segment of the population (Weinstein 2000). Further, children in families in the lowest-fifth percentile (lowest 20 percent) also found themselves in the lowest percentile as adults or, at best, in the lowest two percentiles (Weinstein 2000; see also the brief discussion in McMurrer and Sawhill 2000).

Another dimension of inequality has to do with the vast chasm in compensation between those at the top of major enterprises and those at the bottom. In April 2000, Los Angeles experienced a strike of janitors who, while making more than the minimum wage, were not making much more. David Broder (2000) cites the *Wall Street Journal*'s analysis of executive compensation. The highest-paid executive received $170 million in compensation, and the average at the surveyed firms was nearly $1.7 million dollars.

Perhaps even more outrageous was the $37 million-plus severance package given to Mattel's chief executive. This was despite the fact that the company's stock had decreased in value by nearly 60 percent at a time when the overall stock market value almost doubled (Montagne 2000).

These disparities are perhaps best captured in Robert Frank and Philip

Table 2.12

**Shares of After-Tax Income vs. Shares of Wealth**

|  | Income (1999 projected) | Wealth (1995) |
|---|---|---|
| Top 1 percent | 13 | 39 |
| Top 20 percent | 50 | 84 |
| Bottom 80 percent | 50 | 16 |

*Source:* Shapiro and Greenstein (1999).

Cook's *The Winner-Take-All Society* (1995). They look at those who are the major victors in various kinds of endeavors, from sports to culture to business, and how just small differences are highly disproportionately rewarded.

While the trends are clear, there is evidence to suggest that in more recent years, since 1995, income inequality has at least not become worse and may have even diminished somewhat. This is because, as the data in Table 2.10 indicate, there has been an increase in real average earnings. Poverty and unemployment rates have decreased as the economy continued its expansion (Lawrence 2000).

So why is there this inequality and should we worry about it? Inequality, first of all, is inherent in a capitalist system. Second, inequality in a capitalist society provides "an incentive for people to invest in self-improvement" (Will 1996, p. 92). Emphasizing equality of outcome over equality of opportunity leads to resentment and class warfare. Third, income inequality, at least, seems related to education and race. Those with more education tend to have more income. Blacks and Latinos as a group have less income and considerably less wealth than whites. The distribution of income among blacks is less skewed than among whites. The top quintile of black families had 23 percent of all black family income in 1996, not much changed from 1949 (Levy 2000; see also Chapa 2000; Holzer 2000; Mishel, Bernstein, and Schmitt 2001). Possession of skills needed for the new technology-based economy is also a factor. Wilson (2000) argues persuasively that one of the problems is the disappearance of good paying jobs for low-skilled people in inner-city neighborhoods. Finally, the ability to invest in the stock markets made a considerable difference (until the markets declined beginning in late 2000). While almost half the country now invests, either directly or through a employer-retirement plan, most of the gains have been made by a relatively small percentage of the population.

Burtless (1999) offers some reasons we should care, acknowledging that public opinion suggests that we, in fact, do not really care. He argues that the gap, and its increases, may lead to decreasing social cohesion and an increasing lack of political efficacy. Spelman (2000) suggests a relationship between inequality (especially due to unemployment) and crime rates.

A further consideration is that the economic expansion that began in 1991 has left a portion of the population behind. Schwarz (1998) notes that official statistics on poverty and unemployment understate those two problems. There are also studies (and the data on wages discussed above) suggesting that working-class families have not gained from the expansion (Mishel et al. 2001; Reich 2000; Rogers and Teixeira 2000; and Skocpol 2000). Thus enhanced earned income tax credits and higher wages would be necessary to help those left behind.

## Globalization and International Trade

By any measure, globalization—the unprecedented rapid flow of private capital, ideas, technology, goods, and services—is a net benefit to all countries. The opening of once-sheltered countries and untapped markets has helped nations and peoples across the globe. Real incomes in developing nations are 50 percent higher than they were fifteen years ago. Over the past twenty years, the poverty rate in Asia has been cut in half.

However, the same global forces also pose and uncover real challenges—the outflow of domestic and foreign capital, excessive short-term borrowing in foreign currencies, cronyism, corruption, and a lack of financial transparency and necessary legal and regulatory frameworks. The political consequences of the crisis have toppled leaders in Indonesia, Thailand, Japan, and Russia. (Eizenstat 1999)

As the new global economy creates growing inequality in the labor market and increasing economic and emotional stresses for ordinary families, including those where the working mother is the only parent, many of the policies and actions of the government do more to aggravate than alleviate their economic woes. I have in mind trade policies that facilitate the pursuit of cheap labor in the global marketplace, monetary policies that elevate real interest rates and thereby lower employment rates, tax policies that favor the truly wealthy, and partisan opposition to programs of public investment and national health insurance. (Wilson 1999)

At the end of World War II, the United States stood as the dominant economic (and military) power in the world. The war had been fought off American soil and we did not experience the devastation of Europe, Russia, and Japan. During the war, the United States and its allies (largely Britain) developed an agreement in 1944 that would effectively be a new international economic order. The agreement created two international economic institutions, the International Bank for Reconstruction and Development, better known as the World Bank, and the International Monetary Fund (IMF). The purpose of the bank was to help in the reconstruction of war-torn countries and to promote international trade and private investment. The IMF focused on currency transactions that support international trade.[45] The United States, through the Marshall Plan, helped rebuild western Europe. Japan, too, with considerable support from the United States, recovered from the war. By the 1970s, the United States was still the largest economy, but not nearly so dominant as it had been. In 1950, the U.S. share of the total economy of Organization for Economic Cooperation and Development (OECD) nations in 1950 was 59.2 percent. By 1975 that number had declined to 38.5 percent (Nau 1990).

In the 1970s, the United States found its economic preeminence challenged on several fronts. Japanese goods began to challenge American products internationally as well as in this country. This situation was typified by the automobile industry as Toyota and Nissan cars began to enter the market in a significant way and were able to compete on both quality and price. The electronics industry was especially hard hit by Asian competitors. The Zenith plant in Springfield, MO, the home of the author, was the last American plant to build televisions. It ceased operations in the 1980s. The fear, one that continued into the 1990s, was that American industry was becoming less competitive on the world markets, and American jobs were being sent overseas.

An even less benign warning of the susceptibility of the American economy to the international economy was the Arab oil embargo of 1973–74 and the Iranian revolution that began in 1978. Both resulted in massive increases in crude oil prices, thus increasing gasoline, heating oil, and jet fuel prices. These moves by the Organization of Petroleum Exporting Countries (OPEC) created inflationary pressures on the United States and slowed economic growth. This was a major reason for the stagflation of the late 1970s. In 2000, new efforts by OPEC to boost flagging crude oil prices again sent gasoline prices to record highs. By 1997, the U.S. economy was 36.6 percent of OECD nations (calculated from the 1999 *Statistical Abstract of the United States*).

Another important aspect is the U.S. trade balance. As Table 2.13 shows, the period of large **trade deficits** (when a country imports more than it exports) began in the 1980s, tapered off by the early 1990s, and then increased dramatically in the late 1990s. By 1999, the trade balance hit a record of over $331 billion. An important reason for the jump in the trade deficit in the late 1990s was the financial crisis that began in Asia in 1997 and the overall stagnation of the world economy during a good portion of the 1990s. Demand for U.S. goods grew, but not nearly by as much as demand for imported goods in the United States because of their low cost. The upside of this is that the flow of low-cost imported goods into the United States helped keep inflation low here. It should also be noted that the trade deficit as a percentage of gross domestic product was about the same in 2000 as it was in the late 1990s (Shaikh 2000).

A third aspect of trade and globalization is capital flows. Consistent with the trade imbalance in goods and services, the United States is a net importer of capital. This factor has helped keep interest rates down. Since the late 1980s, America has become a net debtor nation; that is, we owe more than other countries and investors owe us (Council of Economic Advisers 2000, 2001). This, too, follows from the trade deficit.

Trade between countries is centuries old. **Globalization**, however, is a recent term. It may be defined as "the worldwide integration of national economies through trade, capital flows, and operational linkages among firms" (Council of Economic Advisers 2000, p. 199). The argument made by supporters of globalization is that it increases the prosperity of everyone involved,

Table 2.13

**U.S. Trade Balance on Current Account** (in million dollars)

| Year | Trade deficit balance |
|------|----------------------|
| 1977 | −14,335 |
| 1978 | −15,143 |
| 1979 | −285 |
| 1980 | 2,317 |
| 1981 | 5,030 |
| 1982 | −5,536 |
| 1983 | −38,691 |
| 1984 | −94,344 |
| 1985 | −118,155 |
| 1986 | −147,177 |
| 1987 | −160,655 |
| 1988 | −121,153 |
| 1989 | −96,982 |
| 1990 | −76,961 |
| 1991 | 6,616 |
| 1992 | −47,724 |
| 1993 | −82,681 |
| 1994 | −118,605 |
| 1995 | −109,457 |
| 1996 | −123,318 |
| 1997 | −140,540 |
| 1998 | −217,138 |
| 1999 | −331,479 |

*Source:* Council of Economic Advisers (2001).

due to technology changes and diffusion and openness of economies (Council of Economic Advisers 2000). At the same time, there are losers in globalization, including workers in both developed and developing countries. Overall, advocates say, globalization has a positive influence. What we need is policies that enhance it.

That was the purpose of much of U.S. policy in the period after World War II, coming to its peak with the establishment of the **North American Free Trade Agreement (NAFTA)**, the **General Agreement on Tariffs and Trade (GATT)**, the creation of the **World Trade Organization (WTO)** by GATT, and the normalization of trade relations with the People's Republic of China (PRC) in the spring of 2000, perhaps leading to China's entry into the WTO.

The Clinton administration was a major advocate of globalization. The administration argued that it helped the U.S. economy. For example, corporate interests strongly supported normalization of trade relations with the PRC because they saw considerable potential in a massive market. Equally important, however, was the administration's contention that globalization leads to political reforms in repressive countries, such as the PRC. Sanger (2000) points out how Clinton used this argument to win support for normalization:

> But in the end, Mr. Clinton ultimately prevailed because he was able to sell a long-term vision of how America could use its economic power to change, and perhaps undermine, the nature of one-party rule in China. And his opponents in the floor debate—both those who feared the loss of American jobs and those who fear China's rising power—offered no real alternative, no convincing strategy of how America would expand its presence in China or attempt to open up its political system.

## Problems with Globalization

While increased globalization certainly has its benefits, there have also been problems, and globalization has been challenged by liberals and conservatives. The conservative concern is particularly focused on countries where there have been human rights violations. The key target here is the People's Republic of China (PRC). China is accused of suppressing religious expression and, for that matter, any kind of free expression. It remains a communist country politically, if not economically. The concern is that the desired political changes may not occur.

The liberal/populist view of globalization points to other problems. One is that NAFTA, in particular, has led to the loss of jobs in the United States. An analysis of 1999 data found that the largest growth in the trade deficit was with Canada and Mexico, with Western Europe and Mexico not far behind. Further, according to this same analysis, more than 340,000 jobs were lost in the manufacturing sector (Scott 2000; see also Scott 1999). The argument is that the business sector, free to move its capital and other resources, goes where labor costs are very low, labor conditions are bad (low pay, child labor), and business regulation is minimal.

This last point is another one made by liberals against globalization: the environment. Environmental groups argue that developing countries have little in the way of effective regulations. Further, they fear that the WTO will lead to the decline of environmental regulations in the United States.

These concerns have led some to engage in protest demonstrations in 1999 and 2000. The WTO meeting in Seattle in late 1999 was the site of disruptive demonstrations, as was the World Bank/IMF meeting in Washington, DC, in spring 2000. Even the meeting of the Organization of American States in Toronto in May 2000 saw demonstrations.

## The Bottom Line

The December 1999 WTO meeting saw not only protests, but also the failure to continue reducing trade barriers. Resistance to the complete lowering of barriers can be found on all sides (Pearlstein 1999). Further, by tying nations around the world together, what happens to one or a few affects the rest. This result can be seen in the financial crisis that started in Thailand in July 1997 and then, over the next year-and-a-half, spread to Indonesia, South Korea, Russia, and Brazil. While the United States weathered that storm well and its economy and economic leaders helped stem the crisis, we are not immune from this kind of turmoil (Kristof and WuDunn 1999). It is also true that our trade deficit has worsened.

Yet, as Richard Kristof and Sheryl WuDunn (1999) write, no national economy is an island. The failure of negotiations in 1999 to reduce agricultural subsidies hurt American farmers (Pearlstein 1999). Even the job losses mentioned above, while not unimportant and certainly vital to those who have lost jobs, pale beside the size of the American workforce and the continued increase in jobs with the expanding economy.

Further, despite qualms of environmentalists and consumer advocates, the WTO has limited power and has ruled in favor of the United States on several occasions (see, e.g., Olson 2000).

# Case Study: Social Security in Crisis?

As we have seen, Social Security is the largest federal program. By FY 1999, the Social Security Administration was spending over $387 billion, with spending in FY 2005 estimated at over $516 billion (Office of Management and Budget 2000). Social Security surpluses have made up for deficits in the non–Social Security portion of the federal deficits and enabled the appearance of recent budget surpluses.

But depending on whom one listens to, the future of Social Security is problematic. Some, like the Cato Institute and the Concord Coalition, argue that unless significant changes are made in the program, Social Security will be unable to meet its obligations and will threaten the federal budget. They call for significant change, such as partial or full privatization.

Others, such as FamiliesUSA and the Center on Budget and Policy Priorities, argue that Social Security is sound and needs, at best, minor changes. So what is in store for Social Security?

## *Background*

Social Security was created as part of the **Social Security Act** (**1935**). That legislation created the foundations for social welfare policy for the remainder of the twentieth century. Unemployment insurance and welfare programs (Aid to Families with Dependent Children; see chapter 4) were also part of the program; later additions included Medicare and Medicaid (see chapter 5). But Social Security remains the biggest and most popular federal program.

Social Security represented something of an innovation in American social policy. There were previous attempts and proposals to enact such legislation. One precedent for old-age pensions was pensions for Civil War veterans, many of whom were alive as late as the second decade of the twentieth century

(Skocpol 1995). Others included the state experience in Wisconsin and the Townsend movement for old-age pensions in the 1920s.[46]

The major precipitating factor leading to the creation of Social Security was the Great Depression that began in 1929. While the Franklin D. Roosevelt administration took steps to alleviate the miseries caused by high unemployment (approaching 25 percent at one point), he also sought to create a lasting set of programs that would deal with long-term problems that perhaps could be prevented. A major cause of poverty, beyond the capability of individuals, was old age. While corporations could and did (and still do) offer retirement pension programs, the depression undermined the corporate capacity to do so (Skocpol 1995). Additionally, the states were not able to undertake such a program, nor did states have old-age pension programs.

In response to these considerations, President Roosevelt established several committees to develop a plan that eventually became the Social Security Act of 1935. Its basic elements were that covered workers (coverage was limited in the original legislation, but was extended over the decades) would contribute to a fund that would pay out benefits to retired workers. Social Security made its first payments in 1940, as there needed to be time to build up the trust fund.

The design of the program was based on practical and political considerations. Social Security was deliberately developed as a nonmeans-tested program. That is, although not everyone was covered, those who were covered did not face an income standard as found in traditional welfare programs. Not only were all workers eligible, but they all contributed and developed a stake in the program. Thus, it could not be passed off as a simple welfare program going only to those who had failed to support themselves. Everyone would contribute, everyone would benefit.

Another element of the design was that Social Security was never meant to be the sole source of retirement income. But it would place a foundation for the private pension system of corporations and personal savings.

Yet a third set of elements created the ideology that helped protect (though later weakening support for) the program. This included the notion that people were contributing to accounts that would be for their own retirement. There was supposed to be a fair return on this "investment" and essentially a "social contract" that if you contributed, you would receive benefits. Further, the idea of a trust fund helped insulate Social Security from other programs, and it could be declared as sound from a financial or actuarial standpoint (Skocpol 1995).

Over the years, Social Security has been extended to other sectors of the population. The original legislation applied only to workers and retired workers (and then not even all workers). Amendments in 1939 added two new categories, dependents and survivors. Dependents were the spouses (largely wives at the time) and children of retired workers. Survivors were the widows and dependent children of workers who died prior to retirement. Thus, Social Security became more family- than worker-based (Social Security Administration 2000b).

Congress would periodically increase benefits, with the first such increase coming in 1950. The reason for the increase was changes in the cost of living. Doing so created political difficulties for Congress and the president, and so in 1972 Congress passed legislation providing for automatic **cost-of-living adjustments** (known by the acronym **COLAs**) to depoliticize the program and protect the buying power of Social Security.[47] From 1954 to 1960, amendments were passed that added disabled people to the Social Security roles, regardless of their age. New legislation in 1980 called for periodic reviews of disability status (Social Security Administration 2000b). The Reagan administration removed a significant number of people from the disability roles, requiring them to prove their disability to get back on. Legislation in 1983 and 1984 virtually eliminated the reviews (Social Security Administration 2000b).

In 1977, legislation was passed to shore up the trust fund revenues. In 1983, Congress accepted the recommendations of the Greenspan Commission (named after the current head of the Federal Reserve Board, Alan Greenspan) that gradually raised the retirement age, allowed for taxing Social Security benefits, and, more importantly, raised payroll taxes so that the trust fund would build up reserves for when the baby boomer generation began to retire. That set the ground for the large Social Security trust fund surpluses that appeared in the 1990s and helped offset federal budget deficits. In 1994, the Social Security Administration was removed from the Department of Health and Human Services and became an independent agency.

Legislative changes from 1996 to 2000 made minor changes in the legislation. These included electronic transfer of checks to banking accounts, eliminating substance abuse as grounds for disability payments, and eventually eliminating the limit on earnings before benefits would be reduced for those between sixty-five and sixty-nine (Social Security Administration 2000b).

## Social Security in the Twenty-first Century

The social security payroll tax is 12.4 percent. This portion is split evenly between employee and employer. Those who are self-employed pay the full 12.4 percent.[48] The tax is taken out up to a specified level of income; in 2000, that level was $72,600. That is, any income above $72,600 is not subject to the Social Security payroll tax.[49] This makes the tax mildly regressive. For those whose income is $72,600 or less, the tax is proportional: Everyone pays the same rate or percentage. For those whose income is greater than that amount, the proportion of income taken by the tax is reduced. For example, someone making $100,000 would pay $4,501.20 in Social Security taxes (we are not addressing the question of whether the employee effectively pays the full 12.4 percent), an effective tax rate of 4.5 percent rather than 6.2 percent. The higher the income, the smaller the effective tax rate. Further, because of income tax changes such as the Earned Income Tax Credit, low-income workers may pay more in Social Security payroll taxes than in income taxes.

Table 2.14

**Social Security Beneficiaries and Average Monthly Benefit, 1998**
(in millions of beneficiaries)

|  | Number of beneficiaries | Average monthly benefit |
|---|---|---|
| Total beneficiaries | 44, 246 | N/A |
| Retired workers | 27,511 | 780 |
| Spouses and dependents | 3,303 | 379* |
| Disabled workers | 4,698 | 733 |
| Spouses and dependents | 1,636 | 195* |
| Survivors of deceased workers | 7,097 | 588* |

*Source:* Social Security Administration (2000), p. 15.
*Note:* *This an approximate calculation based on Social Security data.

Having said that the taxing system was mildly regressive, it should also be pointed out that the benefit structure is progressive in nature. That is, those with lower lifetime earnings will receive relatively higher benefits than those at the higher levels. In 2000 low earners received a monthly benefit of $677, while the maximum benefit was $1,378 (Social Security Administration 2000a).

Table 2.14 shows the number of beneficiaries by category and the average monthly benefit. As one can see, these are not very generous numbers. Earlier it was mentioned that Social Security was never meant to be a full replacement of income for retired (or disabled or survivors). Nevertheless, Social Security benefits are critical to beneficiaries.

On average, Social Security provides 40 percent of the income for the elderly. Pensions and annuities account for another 18 percent, income from assets about 20 percent, and income from earnings about 20 percent. Even these figures understate the reliance the elderly have on Social Security: 66 percent of retirees depend on Social Security for 50 percent or more of their income; 16 percent depend entirely on Social Security for their income (Kosterlitz 1999). Further, Social Security keeps a significant number of the retired elderly out of poverty. Nine percent of the elderly are poor; without Social Security, that number would be close to 50 percent (Kosterlitz 1999; Social Security Administriaton 2000a).

## Problem Identification

While Social Security remains one of the most popular federal government programs, it has not been without enemies, even at its inception (Skidmore 1999). Senator Barry Goldwater (R-AZ) suggested during his 1964 presidential campaign that Social Security be made a voluntary program rather than mandatory. He was supported in that position by a rising Republican, Ronald Reagan (see Skidmore 1999, p. 93), who consistently pointed to Social Security as a threat to liberty and a failure. President Reagan's 1981 budget proposal called for massive cuts in Social Security, which, along with the deep recession of 1981–82, led to significant Republican losses in the 1982 election.

The modern critique of Social Security takes a largely different tack. It suggests that while Social Security is currently running a surplus, the long-term outlook is for insolvency. The major reason for this is the coming retirement of the enormous "baby boomer" generation (some 76 million people [Peterson 1993]) and the decline in the number of workers per retiree. And it is not just the size of the baby boomer population that creates the problem, but also that life expectancy has increased—and thus the time a person spends retired.

This situation can be seen most clearly in the work of the Concord Coalition (www.concordcoalition.org) and its major spokesperson, Peter Peterson (Peterson 1993, 1996). In *Facing Up* (Peterson 1993), Peterson notes the large percentage of the federal budget taken up by entitlement programs such as Social Security and Medicare (Peterson also includes tax expenditures in his discussion, such as the tax deduction for interest on home mortgages). He then points to the year 2010 when the baby boomers begin to retire, which he suggests will lead to a quickening of entitlement spending, especially in health care.

Peterson then goes on to attack some of the "myths" of Social Security. For example, he argues that the trust fund surpluses will not pay for the benefits of the baby boomers when they retire. Rather, the surplus is temporary and in fact is being spent rather than saved or invested (more about this below). In his later work, Peterson (1996) repeats the survey result that young people think it is more likely that unidentified flying objects (UFOs) exist than that they will receive Social Security. A final problem that Peterson discusses is that Social Security reduces savings and investments. A full-page ad in the *New York Times* in early 1998 argues that now is the time to reform entitlement programs such as Medicare and Social Security and that the budget surpluses that began to appear are misleading because there are tremendous unfunded liabilities (including Social Security and Medicare and other federal retirement programs, Concord Coalition 1998).

How valid is the critique of Peterson and others (such as the Heritage Foundation, the American Enterprise Institute, and the Cato Institute)? Certainly they have found grounds for their concern in the annual reports of the trust fund trustees.

The trustee reports are required by law to project the solvency of the Social Security Trust Fund. The board typically reports three projections: pessimistic, intermediate, and optimistic. Generally speaking, the policy debates focus on the intermediate projections (see Board of Trustees 2000). The trustees project that expenditures will exceed revenue in 2015, and the trust fund is estimated to be exhausted by the year 2037 (or later by a more recent report).

At that time, revenue would be able to cover 72 percent of benefits. The difference amounts to about 1.89 percent of taxable payroll income (Board of Trustees 2000).

Further, Social Security as an investment program is a poorer deal as time goes on, especially for those above the low-income level (this is the redistributive nature of the benefits). In 1940, the rate of return (in real dollars) on Social Security tax payments was 36.5 percent, a good deal by any reckoning. By 1990, the rate declined to 4.8 percent. By 2035, the number will be 1.9 percent (Kosterlitz 1999).

Some are considerably more critical than the Concord Coalition. Michael Tanner (2000) of the Cato Institute, a libertarian-oriented think tank, argues that Social Security discourages private savings because of the expectation of Social Security benefits upon retirement. So the program's antipoverty effects are overstated. Further, Social Security still leaves a significant portion of the population impoverished, such as retired single women and African Americans. Indeed, Tanner argues that rather than reduce poverty, Social Security contributes to it because the benefits are so small (Tanner 2000, p. 4). Additionally, Social Security benefits are not inheritable beyond the immediate family. That is, if the worker dies without any spouse or appropriate-aged children, the benefits are gone.

Tanner states that Social Security fails as a retirement program as well. The rate of return, as mentioned above, has declined, whereas the rate of return for stock market investments since 1926 has averaged 7.7 percent. Further, Social Security replaces only an inadequate portion of income earned during the working years. Tanner cites studies that say retirement benefits should replace between 60 and 85 percent of wages, but at best Social Security replaces just over 57 percent (for low-income workers, the ones who rely on it the most) and that this amount will decline into the twenty-first century.

A third argument made by Tanner against Social Security is that it is unfair on several dimensions. It is unfair to younger generations who support current and near-retirees but will get low rates of return when they retire. Groups with low life expectancies, such as the poor and minorities, are subject to unfairness because they do not receive benefits for as long a period of time as others. Social Security is also unfair to women, Tanner contends, because married women who work part-time will get only 50 percent of their husband's benefits, which may be larger than their own benefits, and thus lose benefits they paid into the system.

Finally, Tanner contends that Social Security makes retired people dependent upon government, supplicants, subject to the whims of politicians.

## Defending Social Security

The above statements make a strong case that Social Security needs to be either reformed or replaced (we will consider policy proposals below). But are the opponents of Social Security correct? And are some of the arguments philosophical or ideological arguments against Social Security?

Just as Social Security has strong opponents, so too does it have strong defenders. Let us start with the issue that has perhaps received the most publicity, the trust fund. Remember, under the changes made in 1983, those currently working are contributing to those currently retired and to the baby boomer generation, which will begin retiring around 2010. There are two issues here. One is the solvency of the trust fund, and the other is whether the trust fund is a myth.

As we have seen, the trustees are required by law to make long term projections (up to seventy-five years) about the solvency of the trust. The 2000 report tells us two things: First, the surpluses that are now accumulating will disappear by 2015; second, the trust fund will be empty (bankrupt) by 2037.

Defenders of Social Security make several points concerning the trustees' report. The report makes three sets of projections, and most people pay attention to the intermediate one. But defenders argue that even the most optimistic report is very pessimistic in that its projections for economic growth and productivity increases are very low. Dean Baker and Mark Weisbrot (1999) point out that the 1999 report (which uses the same figures for growth and productivity as the 2000 report) assumes an annual growth rate of the economy of 1.7 percent and productivity growth of 1.5 percent a year. These rates are considerably lower than recent years' growth and below historical averages. The same is true for the productivity figures. We can see the impact of this by comparing bankruptcy estimate dates in the yearly trustee reports. The 2000 report added three years to the life of the trust fund. Baker and Weisbrot (2000) argue that if we continue to have growth rates of the past couple of years (well over 3 percent per year), the trust fund would never become bankrupt! In 1997, the trustees projected exhaustion of the Social Security surplus (trust funds) in 2029; three years later, it added eight years to the projection. Another consideration is that seventy-five-year projections are almost always going to be wrong, even if required by law.

What does it mean that the surplus will be exhausted or, to use the more alarming language, the trust fund will be bankrupt? According to the trustees' report, Social Security would still be able to pay about 70 percent of benefits after 2037 (Center on Budget and Policy Priorities 2000). So the program will not collapse (despite the survey mentioned above that seemingly suggests it). But this is a shortfall from 100 percent of benefits

There is a more serious question raised about the trust fund. Those opposed to it argue that the trust fund is fictitious. The money paid by the payroll taxes does not go into a separate fund, marked "trust fund," that would be used when the surpluses end. Rather, by law, the surplus funds go into government securities, earning about 7 percent a year, and that money is then available for use by the federal government.[50] Rather than an asset earning money, the "trust fund" is a liability that grows bigger each year. When it comes time to reach into the surplus, the federal government will either have to raise taxes or cut spending on other programs. To put it another way, the trust fund is a hoax and worthless, an IOU. By December 1999, the trust fund had accumulated $896.1 billion (Board of Trustees 2000).

To a large extent, this conclusion appears correct. Clive Crook (no friend of Social Security) makes the following observation:

> All "bankruptcy" means in this context is that the system's trust fund will eventually (sometime after 2030 under current law) have sold all its bonds, with the result that the Treasury will have to finance benefits through new bond sales, rather than through the fund itself, or through higher taxes. In other words, the limit on the system's ability to pay benefits is not the assets it pretends to own, but the capacity of the government as a whole to collect taxes and borrow from the public. If this seems odd, remember that the trust fund's assets are themselves liabilities of the government— and you cannot create real assets by writing IOUs to yourself. The current "solvency" of the system is itself a bookkeeping illusion. Nothing that matters for the economy changes in 2030, or whenever the bogus IOUs eventually run out.
>
> The fiscal problem is therefore not that the trust fund will ever go bust, but that some future government will quail at the deficits or taxes that will be required to cover the cost of mandated benefits. (Crook 2000, p. 1733)

To put it another way, the threat to Social Security, according to Baker and Weisbrot, is from political attacks on the program itself. The government has not defaulted on its debt.

A second line of attack, as we have seen, is that Social Security is not a good investment for young people still working. Here the defenders argue that the opponents misunderstand what Social Security actually is. It is an insurance program rather than an investment program (Skidmore 1999). Further, defenders of the program point out that it is an insurance program that not only protects the worker when he or she retires, but also provides financial assistance for survivors and disabled people. Skidmore (1999) says that the life insurance provisions of Social Security are worth over $12 trillion.

Defenders also argue that Social Security is administratively efficient. According to the Social Security Administration, the administrative costs to run Social Security are about 1 percent of benefits (Board of Trustees 2000; Social Security Administration 2000a; Century Foundation, "10 Myths About Social Security"). By comparison, private insurers have costs of about 12–14 percent of benefits, and the Chilean mandatory savings program more than 20 percent (Century Foundation, "10 Myths About Social Security").

Related to the nature of the program (insurance versus investment) is the question of returns. It was argued above that the returns on contributions have been decreasing and will continue to decrease. Social Security's defenders make several points about this: The transition costs to a private system lower the rate of return from private accounts. Management fees (the efficiency argument above) will also eat into returns. Private accounts are risky; it depends on how well investments are chosen and how well the market does (and the market in early 2001 was doing very poorly). Social Security provides guarantees against inflation (Century Foundation, "10 Myths About Social Security") with its built-in COLAs.

An important argument made by Social Security's critics is that the program especially hurts minorities and women. The Century Foundation argues that, to the contrary, minorities benefit from the program. This is true first because of the progressive nature of the program. Because minorities on average have lower incomes than whites, Social Security replaces a greater percentage of their income in retirement than for more affluent sectors of society. Further, minorities have lower savings and assets and are more dependent on Social Security.

One of the most powerful arguments about Social Security is the worker/beneficiary ratio. This argument says that as the ratio gets smaller (fewer workers per beneficiary), taxes will have to be significantly increased to maintain benefits (apart from arguments over the nature of the trust fund). Skidmore (1999) asserts that the ratio will decline only a bit over the next thirty years and even then will be greater than in the 1960s because of the entrance of women in the workforce. Baker and Weisbrot (1999) calculate that while the proportion of the population over the age of sixty-five will increase from just under 13 percent in the late 1990s to about 20 percent around 2030, the economy will grow by an estimated 59 percent over the same period. This rise should be more than sufficient to cover the increase in retired beneficiaries. Further, as the baby boomers die off, the proportion of elderly will decline. They continue by noting that productivity of workers will increase so that relatively fewer workers could support a larger population. Their analogy is to agriculture. We can feed ourselves quite well though there are far fewer agricultural workers than in years past.

One final argument that can be made is, in essence, a defense of Social Security. One of the arguments above suggested that Social Security depresses the national savings rate. According to a Brookings Institution study calculations (Rich 2000), when one brings in equity in homes, stocks and gains on stocks, and savings, most people will be able to achieve the goal of replacing their retirement income at the 65–85 percent rate. Further, continued economic and productivity growth will make people better off.

## Policy Proposals

What should be clear is that there is considerable controversy over Social Security, some of it animated by ideological views over the role of government. Given all that has been said and written about the program, what policy proposals are out there? As it turns out, there is a whole range of proposals from very modest to very radical. As discussed in chapter 1, how one defines problems or opportunities goes a long way toward determining what a person's favored policy proposals will be. We will start with the modest proposals.

One policy alternative is always the do-nothing alternative. That is, it can be argued that a particular policy problem is not really a problem and therefore no changes ought to be made. The strongest defenders of Social Security in a sense take this position. If you argue that economic growth will keeping pushing back the dates when the surpluses disappear or the trust fund is emptied, then there is no need to do anything. This is certainly the most optimistic of all proposals. It is somewhat supported by the Brookings Institution study mentioned above.

Moving along our continuum, if we go along with the projections of the Social Security trustees, then there will be a shortfall of about 1.89 percent over the seventy-five years of the projections (Center on Budget and Policy Priorities 2000). This short fall would require some combination of changes to taxes and benefits (Samuelson 2000a). By the accounting of Social Security defenders, such increases in taxes or decreases in benefits would be modest (Baker and Weisbrot 1999; Center on Budget and Policy Priorities 2000; Skidmore 1999). One way of doing this might be to raise the retirement age to seventy, though the public appears strongly opposed to such action (Rich 2000). The benefit of raising the age is that retirees will delay receiving benefits and thus reduce the demand for funds. As life expectancy is increasing and people are healthier at older ages, certainly in their sixties, this move is a possibility. Also, one could reduce the amount of benefits by lowering cost-of-living adjustments, but because they are not overly generous and so many retirees depend on Social Security for such a large proportion of their income, this idea would not be either responsible or politically feasible.

A related possibility is one suggested by Peterson (1996) as part of what he calls the shared sacrifice necessary to rein in the entitlements explosion. He suggests that there be an affluence test for Social Security. An affluence test would gradually phase out benefits at a given income level (perhaps adjusted for inflation); retirees with high incomes would not receive any benefits. Ross Perot also made this suggestion in his 1992 presidential campaign. Perot argued that rich people like him did not need the money. This approach is similar in effect to an increase in the tax on benefits (mentioned below).

A third possibility is to raise taxes or revenue going into Social Security. There are three ways to do this (Rich 2000). One would be to increase the payroll tax above its current rate. Economist Martin Feldstein (2000a) argues that the combined tax would have to increase to 19 percent, an increase of over 50 percent, though defenders argue that the increase would be much smaller and easily covered by economic growth. A second possibility would be to raise or eliminate the ceiling on income subject to the payroll tax (which is already the case for Medicare). If the current ceiling is $76,200 for 2000, that might be raised to $100,000 or eliminated entirely. A third possibility is to fully tax Social Security benefits as opposed to partially taxing them. Not surprisingly, there is strong public support for the second option and opposition to the first and third, particularly the third (Rich 2000).

A fourth type of proposal would use the surplus from the non–Social Security portion of the budget to shore up or reinforce Social Security. A variant on this would be to use both the Social Security and non–Social Security surpluses to reduce or eliminate the public debt and use the savings from interest not paid to feed the trust fund. The major critique of this type of proposal, particularly the use of interest savings, is that it amounts to a bookkeeping operation but does not deal with the long-term problem (Stevenson 2000).

A fifth set of proposals would make partial use of the stock market. Those who support this set of options point to the greater returns from investments than from Social Security. And if the trust fund is a fiction, then those funds are not receiving any return from government securities. President Clinton, in his 2000 state of the union address, proposed taking a portion of the surplus and investing it as a whole in the stock market rather than by individual investors. With the non–Social Security portion of the budget in a surplus, the trust fund surplus would not be needed to fund regular government programs. The return on the investment would then provide additional revenues when the Social Security surpluses disappear, currently estimated at about 2015.

Texas Governor George W. Bush, the successful Republican candidate for president in 2000, proposed the beginning of privatization, what could be called **partial privatization**. This would maintain benefits for the retired and near-retired (though the proposal does not specify what near-retired means) and allow younger workers (again, not specified) to divert 2 percent of the 12.4 percent total payroll tax into private accounts that workers would have control over. Part of the deal is that such workers would get lower Social Security benefits. The plan was attacked as risky because it would reduce the surpluses and trust fund sizes, thus enhancing a problem that critics of Social Security already see (for a critical analysis of the Bush plan, see Aaron et al. 2000).

Feldstein (2000b), on the other hand, strongly defends the plan. His analysis shows that the plan has no risks and would increase national savings. The 2 percent diversion could be paid out from budget surpluses, though the Aaron et al. (2000) analysis takes into account Bush's proposed tax cuts, which would eat into those surpluses. We will consider the question of privatization after describing the final proposal.[51]

On the end of the continuum are proposals for complete **privatization**. Groups such as the Cato Institute are the major advocates of such proposals. Michael Tanner (2000), for example, says that partial privatization proposals such as George W. Bush's do not go far enough. He writes:

> Instead of saving Social Security, we should begin the transition to a new and better retirement system based on individually owned, privately invested accounts. A privatized system would allow workers to accumulate real wealth that would prevent their retiring to poverty. Because a privatized system would provide a far higher rate

of return, it would yield much higher retirement benefits. Because workers would own their accounts, money in them could be passed on to future generations. That would particularly benefit the poor and minorities. Finally, again because workers would own their own retirement accounts, they would no longer be dependent on politicians for their retirement incomes. (p. 3)

Feldstein (2000a) also touts a total privatized system based on mandatory savings. This system would increase national savings and enhance the nation's capital stock by some 34 percent over seventy-five years, resulting in an increase in GDP and average wages of about 7.5 percent. Feldstein also considers the transition costs for a fully funded, privatized system and suggests that they would be relatively small.

There is some experience with privatized systems, most notably in Chile, England, and three counties in Texas. After the overthrow of the Allende government in 1973, the government under Augusto Pinochet, with the advice of University of Chicago economist Milton Friedman, replaced its social security–type system with a privatized one in 1981. According to Jacobo Rodriguez (1999), almost all of the Chilean population is part of the system, giving the people property rights in their pensions and a return in excess of 11 percent. Under the system, which includes voluntary savings as well as mandatory ones, if workers have not been in the system for a sufficiently long enough period (twenty years or more) or their capital accumulation is too low, the government will make a contribution. Further, if a retired worker exhausts his pension funds, then the government provides the guaranteed minimum benefit.

Other countries have also adopted private pension plans. These include Singapore, Britain, other Latin American countries such as Argentina and Mexico, Hungary, Kazakhstan, Australia, Switzerland, and Denmark (James 1998).

In the United States, the primary example of privatizing is three countries in Texas, in which, under the "Galveston plan," the contribution was 13.9 percent of payroll invested in "conservative private investment plans with fixed rates of return" (Weisman 2000). The returns compared to Social Security have been very attractive. So what could be wrong with such privatized plans?

Let us start with the Texas plan. According to a 1999 study by the General Accounting Office (GAO), the returns are best for those who have high incomes and are single. For those who have middle or lower levels of income or families, the returns are not nearly as good. Further, such plans do not have the redistributional aspect of Social Security. That is, under Social Security, lower-income workers receive relatively more than do higher-income workers. Under the Galveston plan, lower-income workers would get lower returns. Further, and this may be a problem with privatization plans in general, the benefits are not indexed to inflation as are Social Security benefits. And there is the possibility of outliving one's pension, which is not possible under Social Security (Weisman 2000).

An important conceptual aspect of pension plans, whether public or private, should be explained at this point. Social Security is what may be called a **defined-benefit plan**. Such a plan promises benefits, which may or may not include indexing for inflation, as long as the pensioner lives. But these can be expensive as retirees live longer during retirement, a problem with Social Security mentioned earlier. Employers and privatized public plans have moved toward **defined-contribution plans**, where the employer or government makes a contribution to an investment account, such as a 401(k) plan, and the retiree's pension comes from the returns and principal of that plan. If the funds run out, there is a problem, though as we have seen, the Chilean model does provide for a minimum benefit in those cases.

The Chilean plan has had its critics, as there has been critiques of privatized plans in general. According to an analysis by the Century Foundation (Century Foundation, "Chile's Experience with Social Security Privatization"), the Chilean plan provided terrific returns until 1994 when the economy cooled. Returns on investments in the late 1990s have been less than 2 percent. Further, the costs of administering the private plans were between 15 and 20 percent of contributions, though Rodriguez (1999) argues that administrative costs are actually about the same as for Social Security. The Century Foundation also argues, as with the Galveston plan, that those who have lower income, especially those who have extended retirement periods, do not save sufficiently under the Chilean system to live comfortably.

Gary Burtless (2000) conducted a study looking at the risks of privatizing Social Security in depending on stock markets for high returns. He notes that private plans based on the Chilean model differ from public pension plans such as Social Security in two important ways. First, the benefits from the private plans depend on the size of the contributions made on workers and on the success of their investing. Second, because the benefits in a private plan are paid for out of previous savings, their accumulation is much more than would be needed in a public system. The question Burtless addresses is the riskiness of depending on private investments.

This means that in a private system, there will be less redistribution than in a public system (see the discussion above) and that outcomes will vary, again, because of the size of the contributions and the luck or wisdom or timing of investments. And the success of investments depends on the state of financial markets. Using historical data on stock markets, bonds, and inflation dating back to 1871, Burtless found that the value of the investments, and therefore of the annuities, depended on when a worker retired. A further possible problem with a privatized system is the administrative costs, which are much higher than under Social Security (see, e.g., the discussion in Century Foundation, "Broken English") Thus, privatization may not, depending on circumstances, provide a better rate of return than a public system.[52]

There is one more set of proposals that in a sense combines the ideas of Social Security and privatization. We might call these **capital accumulation proposals**. These are proposals to build up the capital assets of Americans.

During the 2000 presidential campaign, Democratic candidate Vice President Gore proposed a plan, known as "retirement savings plus," that would focus on low- and middle-income families (Seelye 2000). These would be tax-free accounts that the federal government would match with tax credits. For example, a couple making $30,000 a year would receive a tax credit of $1,500; the maximum amount contributed per year by the individual or couple would be $2,000. The owners of the account would then have set investment options. President Clinton offered a similar plan (Reich 2000). These plans would supplement but not replace Social Security.

Senator Bob Kerry (D-NE) offered a different plan, though with similar ideas (boost the capital assets of families). Under his plan, the federal government would give each newborn $1,000 in an account and then $500 a year through the fifth birthday. This would give each child a stake. Kerry estimates that at age twenty-one, the value of the accounts would be about $25,000 (Reich 2000).

Even more ambitious is the plan outlined in *The Stakeholder Society* (Ackerman and Alstott 1999). This proposal would give all twenty-one-year-olds $80,000 to do with as they pleased. The money would be returned to society through some kind of tax. This would make every person a capitalist, a stakeholder in society.

### Evaluating the Proposals

In the preceding discussion we examined a variety of proposals designed to resolve the problems attributed to Social Security. What we really have is three sets of debates, with a minor theme. One set of debates, typical of many policy areas, might be called "dueling proposals" with dueling think tanks and other policy people making claims. The major issue is the soundness of Social Security over some given time period. Some argue that Social Security is inherently unsound. The demographics of an aging population, the big baby boomer generation starting to get near retirement, and actuarial projections of trust fund insolvency suggest that Social Security is doomed unless some action is taken. That action ranges from tinkering with benefits and revenues to investing surpluses, to partial privatization, to full privatization.

On the other hand, there are those who argue that the projections are, first of all, meaningless over a seventy-five-year period and, second, given continued reasonable growth in the economy, augur well for the future of Social Security. At its most extreme, the defenders argue that no changes are necessary. At most, minimal changes might be needed. The question is which set of assumptions does one believe.

A second theme in the debates over Social Security has to do with the nature of the program. Is it, as defenders claim, simply an insurance program, available to survivors, retirees, and the disabled? Or is it, as Social Security's critics depict it, or rather should it be, an investment program in which one seeks to maximize one's return?

The third theme is the government issue. Should government be in the business of public pensions in the first place? Is the private sector a better place to take care of pensions? Should the program be a public or social one, with everyone contributing and everyone receiving? Or should the program be individualized, every person having their own account, and their retirement depending on how good an investor they are?

Obviously, there are ideological differences here. Conservatives and libertarians generally seek to privatize public programs, while liberals and populists prefer that the public sector maintain its responsibility. Given the somewhat redistributive nature of Social Security, which would disappear in a privatized program, one can see, going back to the discussion in chapter 1, the divide along the government role in economic issues and the equality-versus-freedom distinction.

The subtheme is that investment firms are lobbying for privatizing and subsidizing think tanks, because the new money diverted from Social Security will be a boon to those firms, particularly the commissions generated (Common Cause 2000; Moyers 2000). It should also be pointed out that liberal groups such as labor unions prefer Social Security as it is.

## Conclusion

As the U.S. economy moves into the twenty-first century, the country, and its policy makers are faced with both opportunities and problems. One opportunity has been afforded by the longest sustained economic expansion in the country's history; the country's gross domestic product exceeded $10 trillion. It has led to the end of budget deficits and surpluses predicted over the next decade. Certainly policy decisions had an impact on the deficit. The budget deals of 1990, 1993, and 1997 played a role, as did the relative decrease in defense spending since 1986 (though defense spending is on the rise, as we shall see in the next chapter). The stock market boom also assisted by adding to the wealth, at least on paper, which led to increased government revenues, though the decline of the markets in 2000 and 2001 places budget surpluses in some jeopardy (Redburn 2001). Further, unemployment rates have dropped far below previous expected levels (from above 6 percent to around 4 percent) without threatening the economy.

One issue related to the boom and the surplus is what to do with the surplus, with proposals ranging from tax cuts to paying down the public debt to helping Social Security (and Medicare) to public investment programs. It turns out that the politics and policy making during an era of surpluses is not much easier than during the long era of budget deficits.

Another important change in the economy is growing globalization, part of the Clinton administration's economic and foreign policy. Globalization, the growing interdependence of national economies and the consequent decline in trade barriers such as tariffs, undoubtedly has significant benefits for the United States and other countries. It has helped keep inflation and interest rates down but also exerts restraints on wages. Those who oppose increasing globalization, as reflected in the WTO and the vote over permanent normal trade relations with the PRC, have protested and lobbied against these trends. Some have argued that environmental and working conditions issues are hurt by globalization.

Related to globalization is the trade deficit, which continued to soar in 2000. The increased trade deficit has a number of causes, including the strength of the dollar and the U.S. economy and weaknesses in the economies of other countries, as well as consumer tastes for imported goods.

At some point, the dollar will start losing its value, and the foreign debt will be difficult to sustain (Weisbrot 2000b).

Inequality and those left behind by the economic boom are issues that are not currently on the policy agenda. Yet they remain and can fester. If the slowdown of 2000 and 2001 continues or turns into a recession, economic inequality could widen (Bernstein 2001).

On the other hand, Social Security is at the top of the policy agenda. Debates and political campaigns rage over what the program's problems are and what should be done about them. The government issue underlies this political and policy debate.

Perhaps the chief concern that policy makers, especially at the Federal Reserve Board, were most worried about is whether the economy was growing too quickly, and thus headed for a breakdown (i.e., recession), and whether the stock market was overvalued. A decline in the equity markets and/or a recession will change the nature of our economic policy issues. The decline in the markets has occurred and talk about recession has increased. We have come to depend on monetary policy and the wisdom of Fed chair Alan Greenspan to steer the economy to a "soft landing," slower economic growth but not a recession. Whether Greenspan has the knowledge or the tools to carry off such a feat remains to be seen (see, e.g., Samuelson 2000b).

---

## Key Concepts

Balanced Budget Act (1997)

budget deficit

budget surplus

capital accumulation proposals

Congressional Budgeting Office (CBO)

consumer price index (CPI)

cost-of-living adjustments (COLAs)

currency transactions

debt

defined-benefit plan

defined-contribution plan

discount rate

entitlements

executive budget

federal funds rate

Federal Open Market Committee (FOMC)

Federal Reserve Board ("Fed")

fiscal policy

General Agreement on Tariffs and Trade (GATT)

globalization

gross domestic product (GDP)

inducements

inevitable gridlock model

Legislative Budget and Accounting Act

macroeconomics

margin requirement

monetary policy

North American Free Trade Agreement (NAFTA)

Office of Management and Budget (OMB)

open market operations

partial privatization

privatization

productivity

realistic model

recession

reserve requirement

Sixteenth Amendment

Social Security Act (1935)

stagflation

supply-side economics

trade deficits

Trust Fund

unemployment rate

World Trade Organization (WTO)

---

## Reflections

1. The United States now finds itself in the happier position of having federal budget surpluses rather than deficits. What do you think we should do

with those surpluses: lower taxes, pay down the debt, increase spending in certain areas (say defense or education), bolster Social Security and Medicare, or some combination?

2. Globalization has increasingly characterized the U.S. and world economy. What do you think is the likely effect of globalization? Do you think it will result in more economic growth for the country? What impact is it likely to have on jobs or the environment? Will it help the economic development of other countries?

3. There seems to be a clear linkage between ideology and preferences in economic policy. Where do you stand on the appropriate mix of fiscal and monetary policy?

4. Presidential elections have sometimes turned on the state of the economy. Is the federal government really responsible for economic growth or lack of growth, high or low inflation, high or low interest rates, high or low employment rates? What is, and what should be, the role of the federal government in managing the economy?

5. The case study focused on Social Security. The demographic reality is that there will likely (except under the most optimistic, though not entirely improbable, conditions) be a shortfall in the trust fund. The magnitude of that shortfall is controversial. What do you think we should do about Social Security? Should we raise payroll taxes, lower benefits, devote more general funds to the trust fund, partially or fully privatize it? How does ideology reflect differences of opinion here?

6. Economic policy and the state of the economy have an impact on the other policy areas discussed in the book. As you read the other chapters, examine in what ways this might be so.

## Notes

1. Perhaps the most powerful of BOB/OMB directors was President Reagan's first budget director, David Stockman. Under Stockman, OMB turned the budget process upside down; instead of agencies submitting budgets to OMB under OMB guidelines, OMB informed the agencies what their budgets would be. See Rauch (1985).

2. For a comprehensible discussion of Keynes's work and his life, see the delightful book by Robert Heilbroner (1961). Paul Krugman (1994b) also points out that Keynes emphasized the importance of monetary policy. For a discussion of the conservative attack on Keynesian economics, see Bartley (1992).

3. For a discussion of the history of federal deficits, see Makin and Ornstein (1994). It should be pointed out that until the mid-1970s, large budget deficits or, to put it another way, large increases in the national debt were the product of war. More recent deficits have other causes.

4. Robert Samuelson (1999) argues that the projections of surpluses beginning in FY 1999 surprised economists because they underestimated how the economy would perform. For a discussion of how those projections are made, see Bruni (1999). This is an important part of the issue of the solvency of the Social Security Trust Fund, the subject of this chapter's case study. The Social Security trustees have to project (guess) balances in the trust fund for a seventy-five-year period. As the economy performed better than expected in the late 1990s, the solvency of the trust fund extended further along in time. See Skidmore (1999).

5. Fiscal policy as described does not represent the maximum amount of government intervention. During wartime, direct wage and price control programs were used, and from 1971 to 1974, the conservative Nixon administration imposed the only peacetime wage and price control programs that we have faced.

6. According to James Robinson (1994), the Fed's "obsession" with inflation is misplaced because shortages of goods and workers can be supplied by the new, more open world market. The Fed, Robinson asserts, does not take into consideration the changing nature of the world economy.

7. For a comprehensive discussion of the Federal Reserve Board, see Degen (1987), Greider (1987), Woodward (2000), and Woolley (1984).

8. The Fed prides itself on the secrecy of its open market committee deliberations. Decisions of the committee, in the past, were not revealed until months after they had been made. It came to light, however, that Fed chairman Alan Greenspan had been taping the committee meetings for years. As a result, the committee's decisions are acknowledged much quicker. See Starobin (1991; 1993). Further, the twelve presidents of the Fed's district banks are not appointed by the president or confirmed by the Senate. See Starobin (1994). For a more recent discussion of how the Fed operates, see Rowe (1999) and Woodward (2000).

9. According to Greider (1987, pp. 208–209), the actual process of open market operations is the reverse of that just described:

> The typical sequence went like this: commercial banks initiated the process by making new loans, then scrambled around to find the added reserves required to support their expanded portfolios. The banks could borrow the needed reserve funds in the money market, or if excess reserves were scarce, the banks would be compelled to turn to the Discount window at the Fed and get the funds there.

10. Keynes's theory put most of the emphasis for managing the economy on monetary policy. Fiscal policy was only to be used as a last resort in times of deep recessions. See Krugman 1994b.

11. The source for the gross domestic product numbers is the Bureau of Economic Analysis (2000).

12. For a discussion of the meaning of gross domestic product and other economic measures, see Eisner 1994.

13. There are other measures of price changes that may be used, for example, the GNP implicit price deflator and the producer price index. There is an argument in favor of using the GNP price deflator because until the 1980s, the CPI overestimated the impact of housing costs. However, most of us are more familiar with the CPI. In 1995, Federal Reserve Board Chairman Alan Greenspan called for a revision of the consumer price index, arguing that it overstated inflation. See Berry 1995.

14. The official unemployment rate understates actual unemployment. It counts as unemployed those who are not working but are seeking jobs. Those who have given up and are not seeking work are considered out of the workforce. Further, there are people working part-time who would like to work full-time; these are known as the underemployed.

15. In 1994, after fifteen years of focusing on the money supply and letting interest rates float, the Fed under Chairman Alan Greenspan reversed policy, focusing on interest rates and concerning itself less with the money supply.

16. Some of the effects of the credit controls remain to this day, such as annual fees on credit cards and the high interest rates associated with those credit cards.

17. Productivity increases gained dramatically in the mid-1990s. But for various reasons, discussed below, they had little impact on real income increases. It should also be noted that while other countries, such as Japan and Germany, made significant productivity increases during this time, the United States still has the highest productivity rate of any country.

18. It was the growth in secondary wage earners, many for economic reasons, that was responsible for the large increase in the middle class. If you take away the second wage earner, then family income would be considerably lower.

19. It may be argued that events such as the two oil shocks and the increase in the labor supply explain much of the problem. If this is correct, then placing the blame on Keynesian-like economic policy is misplaced. In addition, if one accepts the thesis that the new monetary

policy of October 1979 was also partially responsible for some of these economic turns, such as the severe 1981–82 recession, and the return to economic growth, then the Reagan administration is neither largely responsible for the recession nor for the recovery and expansion that followed it.

20. Reagan administration economic policy, dubbed Reaganomics, included more than the pure supply-side strain, but was consistent with it. For a discussion of supply-side economics, see Bartlett (1981), Bartley (1992), Fischer (1980), Joint Economic Committee (1981), Krugman (1994b), Meyer (1981), Silk (1984), Thurow (1983), and Wanniski (1978).

21. A marginal tax rate is the tax rate in effect at a certain level of income. Let's say that the top marginal tax rate (70 percent in 1981) took effect with incomes over $100,000. This means that any income earned over $100,000 would be taxed at 70 percent. Obviously, those at that level either would be discouraged from earning more money or would look for ways to hide it from their taxable income. Actual tax rates (average tax rate) are, of course, lower than the marginal tax rate.

22. The 1986 tax reform bill violated this principle in two ways. First, it eliminated many of the beneficial tax incentives of the 1981 tax bill. Second, the law's provisions regarding the investment tax credit were made retroactive to the beginning of 1986. Thus, businesses planning new investments under rules in effect at the time of the new investment found the rules changed after the fact.

23. This was actually less than a 25 percent tax cut. The first round was 5 percent in 1981 and the two 10 percent increments were calculated from the new rather than the old levels.

24. David Stockman, director of OMB from 1981 to 1985, maintained in his conversations with William Greider that this was the real rationale of the individual tax cuts. See Greider 1981. Indeed, the tax cuts were skewed toward the upper-income classes, on the grounds that they were most likely to invest their extra income.

25. This was suggested by the Senate Finance Committee chairman, Robert Dole (R-KS).

26. This conclusion is based on Bosworth (1984). See especially the table on p. 31.

27. Reconciliation is the part of the congressional budget process that orders cuts in spending. Reconciliation normally comes at the end of the budget process. However, in 1980, the Carter administration and the Democratically controlled Congress used early reconciliation to make some small budget cuts. The Reagan administration expanded on this precedent in 1981.

28. For a discussion of the Reagan administration and budgets for environmental programs, see Bartlett (1984).

29. This figure is calculated from Table 4.1, Office of Management and Budget (1986). See also Bartlett (1984). Many, but not all, of the cuts consisted of cuts in increased (future) spending, a trend that continued in budget agreements between Congress and presidents Bush and Carter. This meant that they would be cut in constant (inflation-adjusted) dollars. Other programs experienced actual budget cuts.

30. As mentioned earlier, in 1994 the Federal Reserve Board and other industrialized nations intervened in foreign currency markets to bolster the value of the dollar.

31. Indeed, as we shall see below, there are those who credit President Clinton's handling of the economy with what amounted to basically leaving it alone.

32. Part of the explanation for the increase in growth of the money supply is factors outside the purview of the Fed. Because of banking deregulation and lower interest and inflation rates, more money was kept in cash and in savings accounts. In technical economic terms, the *velocity* of money declined. Despite this technical factor, the growth of M-1 is highly stimulative. See Clark (1987) and Greider (1987).

33. See, for example, Bartlett and Steele (1992, 1996), Hershey (1992), *New York Times* (1996), Samuelson (1995).

34. Morris (1993) argues persuasively that this is an invalid premise. By 2000, Clinton was given credit for the continued booming economy but mainly for staying out of the way. See, for example, Crook (2000).

35. For a description of the financial crises and the U.S. role in stabilizing the situation, see Hirsh (1997), Powell (1997), and Ramo (1999).

36. Republicans and Democrats argue over which decade, the 1980s or the 1990s, was the better one. For an analysis of the argument and a comparison of the decades, see Cannon (2000).

37. There are two additional perspectives on the huge budget deficits of the 1980s. David

Stockman (1987) argues that the reduction of inflation was an unintentional contributor to the large deficits. Kemp-Roth would work only with the assumption of continued high inflation, which itself was a tax increase as discussed earlier. This was why Stockman placed such great emphasis on raising taxes and cutting budgets. He writes that a projection of the Carter budget with high inflation into the 1980s would have produced a surplus, rather than a large deficit. His analysis is consistent with that of Eisner (1986). In addition, some have asserted that the large budget deficits were deliberately crafted to create pressure for budget cuts and to make it virtually impossible for new programs to be passed. It is irrelevant whether this notion of "strategic deficits" is correct because the impact of the deficit is the same anyway. See Ornstein (1985) and Moynihan (1985). Stockman (1987) denies the charges, insisting instead that the large deficits were a product of misunderstanding and an unwillingness to face reality.

38. The old welfare program, Aid to Families with Dependent Children, was an entitlement. As a result of legislation passed in 1996, its entitlement status has diminished (legally it has been eliminated). See chapter 4.

39. For a discussion of Gramm-Rudman-Hollings, see Makin and Ornstein 1994; Rauch 1986; and Rubin 1990.

40. Gramm-Rudman-Hollings' major effect was to restrain spending increases, an effect that remains to this day. However, its failure to eliminate the federal deficit was due to a fatal flaw: The legislation did not require actually meeting statutory deficit reduction targets, it only required that the targets be met (within $10 billion) on paper. While missing the targets meant that increased pressure was put on subsequent-year budgeting, the overall outcome was that none of the targets were actually met. However, Sung-Deuk Hahm et al. (1992) argue that one important impact of the Balanced Budget Acts was to return federal priorities (based on budget figures) to those in effect prior to 1981.

41. See also Lav (2000).

42. This is an argument that the economic journalist and professional pessimist Robert Samuelson has been making for several years. See, for example, Samuelson 1998.

43. Cox and Alm (1999) argue that income is not a good indicator of how well people or the country are doing. Rather, they suggest we look at consumption, what people are buying and how well off they are. Using these alternative indicators, they find that the country as a whole and people in all economic classes are doing better than they were in the 1970s.

44. For more detailed analysis of income inequality in the United States, see Burtless 1999; Danziger and Gottschalk 1995; Danziger and Reed 1995; Galbraith 1998; Levy 2000; and Mishel, Bernstein, and Schmitt 2001.

45. The original Bretton Woods agreement can be found at the following Internet website: www.yale.edu/lawweb/avalon/decade/decad047.htm. For a thorough discussion of the Bretton Woods agreement and the new post–World War II economic order, see Nau (1990).

46. For a discussion of the history of Social Security, see Skidmore 1999; Skocpol 1995.

47. One can see the difference between Social Security and AFDC, the welfare program created by the 1935 legislation. Over the years, welfare payments lost much of their buying power, particularly in the 1980–1996 period. During the same time, Social Security payments lost none of their buying power. For a discussion of COLAs in Social Security and elsewhere, see Weaver 1988.

48. Another 2.9 percent, split the same way as the Social Security payroll tax, goes into the Hospital Insurance (HI) Trust Fund.

49. In the case of the HI tax, there is no such income limit.

50. The calculations of the viability of the trust fund include the interest from the government securities.

51. An interesting irony of Governor George W. Bush's 2000 proposal is that his economic advisor, Lawrence Lindsay, got out of the stock market in 1998 because he thinks it is overvalued (Herbert 2000). Further, *Fortune* magazine printed its annual list of richest people in 2000. Microsoft founder Bill Gates still headed the list. But the $90 billion he was worth in 1999 had shrunk to $67 billion in 2000. That is still a sizable fortune and some of the loss is clearly attributable to the federal antitrust case against Microsoft. Still, it raises a caution flag about depending too much on the markets.

52. For an argument that privatization would work no better than, and perhaps even poorer than, diversified Social Security trust fund surpluses, see Weinstein (1999).

# 3   Foreign and Defense Policy: To Provide for the Common Defense

*"American foreign policy" is not an abstraction. It is what the governed and their government do from day to day about world security and international relations. "Policy" is driven by what happens. What happens is seldom initiated by the President of the United States. So U.S. policy is mostly and necessarily reactive. But in reacting, the President and his advisors are guided by some general ideas, articulated or not, about where they want to go, what they are trying to do. And this frame of reference is heavily influenced in turn by the leaders' perceptions of what actions will elicit "the consent of the governed" (on TV tonight, in Congress next month, at the polls next year).* (Cleveland 1986, p. 97)

*The Cold War was a period of certainty and stability. The United States, with its huge markets and productive capacity, controlled the international economy. The East-West conflict was the dominant security issue. It gave order to the world. . . . The end of the Cold War will make things more difficult for the United States. We will have to adjust to a world of complex situations, shifting allegiances and diplomatic surprises.*
(Schneider 1989, p. 1670)

Until the post–World War II period, the United States was not a major actor in world affairs. The nation heeded, for the most part, Washington's farewell address warning to have as little to do with other countries, especially Europe, as possible. Thomas Jefferson warned the nation against engaging in "entangling alliances" (Solomon 1999, p. 1006). This is not to say that the United States was totally isolated from the world. During the colonial period, the French and Indian War was the American theater (to use modern terminology) of the Seven Years' War between Britain and France. The Mexican War in the 1840s helped fulfill our "Manifest Destiny" to expand to the Pacific. The Spanish-American War made America a colonial and Pacific power ("winning" the Philippines). The United States reluctantly entered World War I, and President Franklin D.

Roosevelt prepared the country to enter World War II on the side of the Allies. Even then, it took the Japanese attack on the naval base at Pearl Harbor to shake off isolationist tendencies. But all of these conflicts were aberrations.[1] Blessed with abundant resources, relatively benign neighbors to the north and south, and large oceans to the east and west, the United States could develop into a world-class economic and military power.

The post–World War II period ended this picture of happy innocence. Exhausted by the war, Britain and France abandoned their traditional role as major players, and a new challenge appeared, primarily from the Soviet Union. The United States was forced to fill the void and address this threat, real and perceived.

Although accepting this new responsibility, the United States faced internal disagreement as to how it should be met. In some ways, foreign policy offers the president more freedom of movement than does domestic policy, where many interests and groups have to be considered during the policy process. In foreign policy, those interests and groups are fewer in number. Further, foreign policy, including defense policy, arises from the sovereignty of the United States irrespective of the Constitution. The Constitution establishes the presidency in the strongest position with respect to the exercise of policy positions, including the use of executive agreements. And in the period just after World War II, the beginning of the Cold War, the United States had a bipartisan foreign policy where politics, in the words of the chairman of the Senate Foreign Relations Committee, Arthur Vandenberg, stopped at the waters' edge (Crabb and Holt 1984; see also Neustadt and May 1986). That freedom of movement led one observer to distinguish between two presidencies, one foreign and one domestic (Wildavsky 1975). Presidents, Wildavsky argued, usually began their terms with an emphasis on domestic policy but eventually turned to the greater freedom permitted in foreign policy.

That bipartisanship, and the felicitous distinction of the two presidencies, ended in the 1960s and 1970s because of the lengthy and unsatisfactory war in Vietnam, the Watergate affair, and revelations of covert activity by the Central Intelligence Agency (CIA). Congressional mistrust led to reassertion of congressional prerogatives, such as the War Powers Act of 1973, which attempted (not very successfully) to limit presidents' discretion in sending American forces into combat (Smyrl 1988). The conflict inherent in the ambiguity of the constitutional division of foreign and defense powers between the president and Congress created what Edwin Corwin (1940) called "an invitation to struggle" and made foreign policy formulation and implementation more difficult. Separation of powers combined with both old and new challenges to complicate our ability to achieve our foreign as well as domestic policy goals (see Spanier and Nogee 1981; Ladd 1987, especially chapter 10).

In addition, new interrelationships tied American domestic policy to foreign and defense policy, leading to what might be called **intermestic policy** (Spanier and Uslaner 1994). Two examples demonstrate this interconnection. As the United States became ever more dependent on oil imported from the Middle East in the 1970s, events in that region affected the U.S. economy. The Arab oil embargo, begun in November 1973, was precipitated by U.S. military shipments to Israel during the October war. Consumer oil prices increased, and the United States began a seven-year odyssey to develop an energy policy. The Iranian revolution (which replaced the pro-U.S. shah with the anti-U.S. Ayatollah Khomeini) produced a second oil crisis from 1978 to 1981. In 2000, increases in gasoline prices were blamed at least partially on restrictive oil production practices of Organization of Petroleum Exporting Countries (OPEC). The Clinton administration had as part of its foreign policy globalization (discussed in the previous chapter), which clearly unites domestic economic and foreign policy considerations.

## Problem Identification

### Goals of American Foreign Policy

In some ways, there is more certainty of what is desired in foreign policy than in domestic policy. While there is agreement on goals, there is controversy over what those goals mean and how to achieve them. The major responsibility placed on any nation is protection from foreign powers. Thus **national security** emerges as the primary goal of American foreign policy. A country that cannot defend itself from external threat or internal discord will not survive.

National security is a goal that all nations must have. A related goal that only some nations have is responsibility for the **security of allies**. This responsibility is the unique feature of post–World War II American foreign policy, representing "entangling alliances" with other countries. Thus, American troops today are stationed overseas, mainly in Western Europe, Korea, and Japan.

The last goal of American foreign policy is to **support U.S. economic interests**. American businesses have made considerable investments in other countries and established substantial trade with other nations. Globalization is designed to open foreign markets to U.S. corporations as well as open our markets to foreign businesses.

### Tools of American Foreign Policy

Given these three rather broad goals—national security, security of allies, and protecting economic interests—what tools are available to achieve them? Traditionally, nations have utilized three sets of tools.

The first and most common of these tools is **diplomacy**—the range of contacts between nations. The major form of contact is political, such as exchanges of ambassadors and formal and informal negotiations. The development of nuclear nonproliferation treaties among the various nations is one prominent example of the use of diplomacy to achieve a national security goal, in this case to reduce the spread of nuclear weapons. Cultural and scientific interchanges are also included in this category.

The second major tool that nations have is **economic relations**, involving both positive and negative inducements. Normal economic relations involve trade among nations, and part of the normalization of U.S. relations with China beginning in 1979 included increasing trade. Indeed, an important component of the Clinton administration foreign policy was to expand trade, opening other countries to U.S. markets. Part of the rationale was that, for example, with China, it would lead to changes in the economic system (such as greater transparency of financial transactions and greater openness in general), which might lead to changes in the political system. Thus, the United States pushed for the NAFTA, the GATT (and its replacement by the WTO), permanent normal trade relations with the PRC, and opening trade relation with African countries.

The economic tools range from economic assistance (positive inducement) to economic embargo (negative inducement). The bulk of U.S. economic assistance goes to just two countries, Egypt and Israel. While the United States has been a strong supporter of the Jewish state since its founding in 1948, substantial aid to Egypt is more recent. The assistance to Egypt was a reward for its participation in and maintenance of the Camp David Accords with Israel, sponsored by President Carter. Of the approximately $13.8 billion in U.S. government foreign assistance, $2.8 billion went to Israel and $2 billion went to Egypt, about 35 percent of total foreign assistance (U.S. Census Bureau 1999). The United States and other nations promised assistance to Russia for its difficult transition to a capitalist society. Similar promises were made to the Palestinians to help assist in the development of what may become their own country.

Economic tools can also be used to punish countries. President Carter ordered a grain embargo in partial retaliation for the Soviet invasion of Afghanistan. (The United States also withdrew its participation in the 1980 Summer Olympic Games in Moscow.) In 1986, the United States imposed a partial embargo on South Africa because of its racial-separation policies (apartheid). The Arab oil embargo mentioned earlier is another example. President Clinton issued sanctions on China in 1995 because of disputes over copyright protections. An embargo was placed on Iraq after its invasion of Kuwait, and it remains somewhat in place (as of early 2001) because of Iraq's refusal to allow weapons inspectors into the country. Embargoes have also been placed on Serbia because of its support of Bosnian Serbs and of Haiti after the overthrow of its democratically elected president, Jean-Bertrand Aristide. Embargoes generally do not work if other nations do not follow suit. In the early days of the Haitian embargo, the border with the Dominican Republic was essentially a sieve, allowing fuel and other needed supplies to cross. Further, while embargoes do cause pain, they work slowly; Haitian military leaders refused for a while to allow Aristide's return, and Iraqi's Saddam Hussein remains in power.

Hendrickson (1992) argues that economic sanctions for human rights purposes have several dangers: they inflict widespread suffering on the less privileged in target states; they do not promote, indeed they obstruct, the building of civic institutions; they can produce a flood of refugees (e.g., Haiti); and they may lead to war if the imposed standards of democracy and decency are not met (for other critiques of the use of sanctions as a tool of foreign policy, see Amuzegar 1997 and Haass 1997b).

Despite Hendrickson's concern, the United States has increasingly resorted to economic sanctions as a tool of foreign policy (Hufbauer 1998), especially during the Clinton administration.

> The National Association of Manufacturers (NAM) in 1997 estimated that the U.S. has applied sanctions for foreign policy purposes a total of 115 times since World War I, 104 times since World War II, and according to the count of the President's Export Council, 61 times since 1993. (Flatin 2000)

By the summer of 1998, the administration, under some pressure from American business and questioning of their effectiveness, was rethinking its use of sanctions (Schmitt 1998).

The final policy tool is the threat and use of **military power**. Karl Von Clausewitz ([1833] 1976, p. 87) in the nineteenth century stated: "War is the continuation of diplomacy by other means." One could argue that war signifies the failure of diplomacy. And while there have been a considerable number of wars in our century, war is still unusual.

Military power, as with the economic tool, can be employed in a variety of ways. War is the most obvious: We build strong defenses in hopes of avoiding war. Indeed, one should look at the ultimate weapon of war, nuclear explosives, as having a largely deterrent effect. Their chief value is that they need never be used.

Military power also includes arms sales, training of other troops, and covert assistance. The United States has sold military equipment to moderate Arab nations such as Saudi Arabia as a means of retaining influence among those countries. U.S. advisors in Honduras helped train contra troops. In 1984 the Central Intelligence Agency (CIA) mined Managua harbor in an attempt to stop the flow of arms shipments into Nicaragua destined for communist guerrillas in El Salvador.

Thus, any country has three sets of tools with which to meet its foreign policy goals. The question is, as with economic policy, how successful has past performance been?

## Formulation, Adoption, and Implementation: Changing Direction

### Postwar Priorities

U.S. foreign policy after World War II retained a remarkable degree of consistency in viewing the major threat to national security, the security of U.S. allies, and American economic interests, until 1989. That threat was perceived to be communism, especially as embodied in the Soviet Union. The notion that we faced a challenge from communism and had to resist, roll back, or contain it provided the major thread of continuity to American foreign policy. Not only did the communist threat provide coherence for U.S. foreign policy and necessitate America's "rise to globalism" (Ambrose 1985), but it also affected policy in other areas. For example, the Reagan administration resisted pressuring South Africa to change its racial policies because the major black opposition group, the African National Congress, was considered to be under communist influence. Similarly, the United States resisted an international conference to discuss the Arab-Israeli dispute because it would legitimize a role for the Soviet Union.

The origins of the anticommunism policy lay in the aftermath of World War II. Soviet troops occupied the eastern half of Europe and posed a threat to the western half. Relations between the Soviet Union and the United States deteriorated and set in motion the course of American foreign policy. British Prime Minister Winston Churchill provided the rhetoric when he stated that the Soviet Union had in effect dropped an iron curtain over Eastern Europe. Further, in 1949, communist forces under Mao Tse-tung were victorious over the Chinese nationalist government, led by Chiang Kai-shek.

In 1950, **National Security Council Directive 68** set forth objectives that guided American foreign policy for the next forty years (Allison 1989). The directive had three objectives: (1) to thwart Soviet attempts to control Europe and Asia; (2) to build up the material and moral strength of the free world; and (3) to allow internal contradictions to emerge within the Soviet Union. The purpose of these objectives was to induce Russia to accept peaceful coexistence on reasonable terms with the West. The directive also stated that surrender or subjugation of the Soviet Union was an unacceptable policy goal.

### Changes in Europe

The events of the mid-1980s and 1990s saw the fruition of the policy first enunciated in 1950. Despite the large defense buildup from 1981 to 1986 and President Reagan's depiction of the Soviet Union as the "evil empire" (Fitzgerald 2000), by 1984 the administration was seeking a rapprochement, or better relations with the Soviet Union (Fischer 1997). Mikhail Gorbachev came to power in the Soviet Union in 1985. He began a new policy course, trying to defuse the

Cold War, restructure the Soviet economy and society (perestroika and glasnost), and save the Communist Party. Arms control treaties were signed with the United States, such as the 1987 Intermediate Nuclear Force Treaty that led to the removal of intermediate-range nuclear weapons from Europe. Gorbachev and his foreign minister, Eduard Shevardnadze, ended the Soviet invasion of Afghanistan, which began in 1979. Support for other countries was either eliminated or decreased; Cuba, Angola, and Iraq are cases in point.

Equally as important were changes that took place in Europe. When the Eastern European nations that were part of the Warsaw Pact under Soviet domination broke away, Gorbachev's Soviet Union did nothing to stop the changes. Some of the changes in Eastern Europe were peaceful, such as in Poland, Hungary, and Czechoslovakia (the latter through what was called the "velvet revolution" [Kopecky 1994]). Other Eastern European countries experienced violent change, such as Albania and Romania (with the execution of Romania's leader Ceausescu).

Perhaps the most symbolic event of this period was the Berlin wall. Erected in 1961, it became the embodiment of Churchill's iron curtain. Its destruction in 1989 and the reunification of Germany symbolized the end of an era.

Other countries sought freedom from communism with much less success. The freedom movement in China was epitomized by the rally in Tiananmen Square and its brutal suppression by tanks.

The Soviet Union, too, became the victim of these changes. Its breakup, envisioned by National Security Directive 68, began with the flight by the Baltic republics of Latvia, Lithuania, and Estonia. Other republics also left the union, primarily the resource-rich Ukraine. In response, Gorbachev and the remaining republics formed the Commonwealth of Independent Nations (CIS), led by the Russian republic and its leader, Boris Yeltsin.

Gorbachev himself became the final victim of the reforms he had started. In August 1991, hard-liners staged a coup against Gorbachev. The coup, in its immediate goal, failed. Thanks to spontaneous demonstrations in Moscow and the courageous stand by Yeltsin, the army refused to fire on the people (unlike China in 1989). Gorbachev remained in power. But only four months later, with his power continually decreasing and republics continuing to flee, Gorbachev resigned and the Soviet Union ceased to exist (Rubenstein 1991).[2]

With the end of the Soviet Union, the primary threat to the United States ceased. And with the end of that threat, the foundation of post war U.S. foreign policy also crumbled (Haass 1995). The United States became the world's sole superpower, in terms of economic and military might. But how we were to use that power in what was originally called "the new world order" was difficult to see. In some respects, the end of the Cold War created a safer but more complex world. The United States was now headed into uncharted waters.

A further complication came after the November 1994 elections, when the Republicans captured control of both houses of Congress. The new Republican leaders began criticizing President Clinton's foreign policies, such as the use of U.S. troops and the role of the United States in United Nations peace-keeping operations. In Richard Haass's framework, the Republicans (and per-haps the nation as a whole) were seeking a "minimalist" foreign policy (Haass 1995). Divided control of government exacerbated the continuing conflict for dominance over the course of U.S. foreign policy (Greenhouse 1994; Sciolino 1995a, 1995b).

## The Persian Gulf War

It was hoped that the **Persian Gulf War** might shape what would come to be called a **new world order**.[3] To help understand the potential importance of the war, some background is in order.

In 1978, the shah of Iran, a close ally of the United States, was overthrown and eventually replaced by an Islamic republic under the direction of the Aya-tollah Ruhollah Khomeini. The Shiites, the Islamic sect that predominates in Iran, were a minority in Iran's neighbor, Iraq. The Iranian revolution threat-ened to spill over to other nations, and in 1980 Iraqi forces invaded Iran. The war between the two nations continued until 1988. Iran, the more populous country, had the larger army (mostly conscripts); Iraq had more sophisticated weaponry. The slaughter on both sides, particularly of Iranians, was immense. To help finance the war, Iraq borrowed money from Persian Gulf nations, such as Kuwait. U.S. policy, while ostensibly neutral, tilted toward Iraq.[4]

The war ended in 1988 with neither country the victor. But Iraq was left with heavy debts. Kuwait, a small desert but oil-rich country bordering Iraq, refused to forgive the debt, which added to other grievances that Iraq had. Iraq and Kuwait shared a large oil field. Iraq claimed that Kuwait was mining the field too rapidly, depleting the resource and depriving Iraq of much needed revenue. Further, Iraq had always claimed that Kuwait was a province of Iraq and existed only because of boundaries set during colonial rule. Finally, Iraq and Kuwait had disputed claims over two islands in the Persian Gulf.

Tensions mounted in the summer of 1990 as Iraqi forces moved toward the Kuwaiti border. Iraq invaded Kuwait on August 2. The crisis had begun.

The question arose: What should be the response of the United States? The invasion of Kuwait was clear aggression by a large country against a much smaller one. Kuwait, along with the other conservative Persian Gulf coun-tries, was allied with the United States. Oil was an important factor. Iraq has a modest amount of oil, but Kuwait has very large oil resources. Iraqi troops threatened Saudi Arabia, a country with one of the world's largest oil re-serves. The United States (and its European and Japanese allies) relied heavily on those resources. If Iraqi leader Saddam Hussein's effort was successful, he could control some 40 percent of the world's oil reserves.

With Saudi approval, the United States began to move air, sea, and ground forces into the area.[5] President George H. W. Bush began mobilizing interna-tional support for what was first called Desert Shield (to prevent further Iraqi invasions) and then later Desert Storm (to repel Iraqi forces from Kuwait). The UN Security Council approved efforts to repulse Iraqi forces. This, too, was important. The Soviet Union, as one of the other permanent members of the Security Council, had a veto power over the council's actions. Gorbachev sought to delay U.S. action against its former ally,[6] but the effort failed. President Bush's courting of Gorbachev (and other foreign leaders) paid off handsomely. An international force, mostly American but including other countries such as Saudi Arabia, Britain, and France, and remnants of Kuwait's army, joined together. A number of countries, although not contributing militarily, helped offset the costs of the war (Germany and Japan are examples). While there remained some domestic opposition to the war, Congress, after long debate, approved the war effort (though a majority of Democrats voted against it).

By early 1991, sufficient forces were in place to begin Desert Storm. For some 100 days, Iraqi forces in Kuwait and Iraqi were subject to air attacks. By March, the land invasion began and with breathtaking speed overwhelmed the demoralized Iraqi forces. After 100 hours, Desert Storm was halted and the Kuwaiti government returned to power.[7]

The significance of the Persian Gulf War was immense. First, the war demonstrated the military power of the United States (confirming the role of America as the world's only superpower) and the willingness to use it to repel aggression. During the crisis, President Bush and Secretary of State James A. Baker showed their expertise in foreign affairs, lining up support and organizing the effort (Woodward 1991).

Second, the Persian Gulf crisis united two contradictory analogies that affected the use of American military power. The first of these was the **Munich analogy**. In 1938, European leaders met in Munich with German Chancellor Adolph Hitler, attempting to head off the impending war. Hitler promised that if he were allowed to keep the Sudetenland territory of Czechoslovakia (which contained a sizable population of ethnic Germans), he would make no further demands. The leaders agreed and British Prime Minister Neville Chamberlain returned home declaring that he had achieved "peace in our time." Shortly thereafter, Germany invaded Poland, and World War II began. The moral of this story is that appeasing aggressors and tyrants does not work, only the use of force does.

Opposing the lesson of Munich was the **Vietnam analogy**. Though the United States was not militarily defeated in Vietnam, it was unwilling to pay the price to continue the war effort.[8] The lessons of Vietnam were several. First, do not get bogged down in a long effort with little expectation of a quick and satisfying end. Second, do not fight a protracted conflict without public support. Finally, use sufficient military force to accomplish the goal in the shortest possible time.

The Vietnam analogy affected the willingness of the military to use its forces. Rigid conditions were set down. Some efforts met those conditions:

Panama and Grenada. Others did not. The Reagan administration sent troops to Lebanon during that country's civil war. The mission of the troops was ill-defined (protect Beirut airport) and ended after the Marine barracks at the airport was bombed, resulting in some 250 casualties. One could argue that the U.S. effort to help alleviate hunger and then end the civil war was similar to the Somalian effort, when eighteen U.S. soldiers died and one was dragged through the streets of the Somalian capital, Mogadishu.

But the Persian Gulf War met the conditions of the Vietnam and Munich analogies. There was a clear aggressor; the objectives were limited; sufficient military force was available; and public support was forthcoming.[9]

A third important implication of the Persian Gulf War was its impact on the Middle East. Much of the Arab world recoiled with horror that one Arab country had invaded another. The Iraqi invasion showed that Arab unity and brotherhood was an illusion (Ibrahim 1992). Not all Arabs opposed Iraq. Most prominent among Iraqi supporters were Palestinians and Jordan. Iraq furthered the divisions by sending Scud missiles into Saudi Arabia and Israel (having to fly over Jordan). The pictures of Palestinians cheering the Scud attacks led to the loss of support by conservative Arab countries such as Saudi Arabia.

The war also had an effect on Israeli-Arab relations. Israel, of course, supported the allies against Iraq. Indeed, Israel had attacked Iraqi nuclear facilities in 1982, greatly delaying Iraqi efforts to develop a nuclear capability. For the first time, Israel and the Arabs were on the same side. A twist on this situation came when Israel became subject to Scud attacks. Traditionally, Israel responds with great force when attacked; would it enter the fray now? The United States did not want it to respond.[10] To keep Israel from entering and complicating the war, the United States sent Patriot antimissile batteries to Israel. Though there was minor damage from the Scud attacks, Israel stayed out.[11] The Palestinians and their major organization, the Palestinian Liberation Organization (PLO), found themselves without their important sponsors (Soviets and Arabs). The end of the war led to negotiations between the PLO and Israel, resulting in a peace agreement in 1993 (the Oslo accords) and the creation of autonomous territories in the Gaza strip and the West Bank town of Jericho. Israel and Jordan concluded a peace treaty in the fall of 1994 (Haberman 1994).[12] By 2000, the Palestinians and Israel were preparing for final negotiations, but an agreement could not be reached, and sporadic violence broke out along the Israeli-Palestinian border.

## A New World Order?

We have spent considerable time discussing the Persian Gulf War and its implications. The war along with the breakup of the Soviet empire, appears to have created the conditions for this new world order, with the United States in the lead. However, the Bush administration was never able to articulate a vision for this new world order.[13] Further, the Persian Gulf War as a model or analogy, so far at least, has proven to be exceptionally unusual (Stedman 1992–1993). Subsequent crises and problems have not been so clear-cut; rather, they have been fraught with difficulties and no clear endings.

Further, the Bush administration, so skillful in Desert Storm and in helping to guide the breakup of the Soviet empire, reaped few domestic rewards from its efforts. By the end of the Persian Gulf War in March 1991, President Bush's approval ratings were at a historic 91 percent. After the war, however, the country turned inward, focusing on domestic problems, particularly the sluggish economy, for which the Bush administration seemed to have no apparent remedies. The Democratic challenger, Arkansas Governor Bill Clinton, had no foreign policy experience but was able to focus the election on the economy.[14] The motto of the campaign was, "It's the economy, stupid" (Woodward 1994).

After Clinton took office, however, foreign policy in many areas became prominent. But without vision or experience, American foreign policy seemed to lurch from one problem and solution to another. Further, the world was not cooperating with our aspirations for order; far from being orderly, the world, in some respects became disorderly. It is to this more complex world that we turn next.

## Problem Identification: Current Foreign Policy Issues

### Resolving an Identity Crisis

> This summit [between Israel and the Palestinian Authority in July 2000 at Camp David, MD] raises anew the overarching question dogging Bill Clinton, his would-be successors and the Congress. Toward what ends should America harness—not for a few days in July, but day in and day out—the astounding economic, military, political and cultural power it has.
>
> Put another way, why is the country having so much trouble establishing its international priorities? The truth is, hegemony's not all it's cracked up to be. It seemed easier in the early 1990's, after the Cold War had been won, but before the American economy began its flight into the stratosphere. Twenty million new jobs ago, making the world safe for American exports, for freer and fairer trade, was a rallying call that resounded far beyond the Chamber of Commerce.
>
> Since then, as American economic might has soared, the confusion about how to wield it has deepened. One day American power is about expanding democracy, the next it is about a (short-lived) "Clinton Doctrine" of humanitarian intervention, even in places where America's national interests are remote. In the last two years the emphasis has turned to new initiatives to combat old threats, from nuclear proliferation to narco-terrorism, and to bestowing national security threat status on new issues, such as cyber-crime, global economic meltdown and AIDS. (Sanger 2000)

One way of understanding the problems the United States faces now and well into the twenty-first century is to consider the argument made by Samuel Huntington (1993a) in an article entitled "**The Clash of Civilizations**?" (see also Huntington 1993b and 1996). He argues that cultural differences divide groups and nations and that these "fault lines between civilizations will be the battle lines of the future" (Huntington 1993a, p. 33). To Huntington, a civilization "is thus the highest cultural grouping of people and the broadest level of cultural identity people have short of that which distinguishes humans from other species. It is defined both by common objective elements, such as language, history, religion, customs, and institutions, and by the subjective self-identification of people" (Huntington 1993a, p. 24).

Civilizations, Huntington continues, usually cross national boundaries and have subvariants. He identifies the following as the major civilizations: "Western, Confucian, Japanese, Islamic, Hindu, Slavic-Orthodox, Latin American and possibly African civilization" (Huntington 1993a, p. 25).

Using this conceptual framework, the Persian Gulf War can be seen as the fruition of the conflict between Western and Islamic civilizations. Further, Huntington notes that one of the major problems facing the west is the Confucian-Islamic connection. While Western countries are slimming their defense capabilities with the end of the Cold War, Iran, Iraq, China, and North Korea are expanding theirs.

Most interesting is the application of Huntington's framework to the Bosnian situation. Huntington shows a map of Central Europe with a "fault line" right in the middle of the former Yugoslavia. Here the clash of civilizations is between Western, Orthodox, and Muslim. No wonder the fighting is so bitter and ending the conflict so difficult.

Although Huntington's analysis has been critiqued,[15] it does provide some organizing framework for understanding the outbreak of ethnic conflict. In this sense, one can almost sense nostalgia for the good old days of the Cold War. Communism had many failings, but it did suppress ethnic conflict, perhaps causing it to break out with greater viciousness than in the absence of suppression. This was true in Yugoslavia, Eastern Europe, and the Soviet Union. Without the guiding force of communism, countries and ethnic groups feel freer to seek military means to objectives.

Max Singer and Aaron Wildavsky (1993) provide a second framework. They argue that there is a **real world order**, if we just understand it correctly. They distinguish between two zones: the **zone of order** (Western, democratic, market-oriented countries) and the **zone of disorder** (basically everyone else). The West is now free of a military threat to its survival. The major competition is economic rather than military. Democracies do not fight democracies. Based on this principle, an important goal of the Clinton administration was to support democratization in previously authoritarian or communist countries.[16]

Similarly, Jonathan Clarke (1993) notes that while there are real dangers out there (his list includes "Nuclear proliferation, anti-democratic movements, Islamic fundamentalism, narcotics, ethnic tumult, international terrorism" [Clarke 1993, p. 56]), none of them poses a threat to the security of the United States, nor do they represent systematic challenges to us.* He also notes that

---

*Of course, all of this changed with the terrorist attack against the United States on September 11, 2001.

the period of the Cold War was a period of global instability[17] and its disappearance has provided a sense of stability.

However, Clarke argues that we remain in much of a Cold War posture further complicated by the idea that we are the sole remaining superpower and are somehow responsible for all the world's problems. This "conceptual poverty" in foreign policy leads us to decisions that overextend ourselves with a reliance on military intervention.

A number of analysts have tried to fill in this conceptual poverty by offering guidelines for American foreign policy, essentially trying to resolve the U.S. foreign policy identity crisis. David Sanger (2000), in the article from which the opening quote of this section was taken, offers several suggestions. The first thing our policy makers should do is to understand that while American power, especially military power, is substantial, that same power makes it difficult for us to act unilaterally. Resistance to our hegemony or dominance on the part of countries such as China and Russia is growing, and our power is applied inconsistently. Second is the need to focus on what we do. We have limited resources and cannot solve the entire world's problems. Third is to accept the interrelationship of foreign and economic policy, globalization. Sanger writes that President Clinton's most significant and lasting contribution in foreign policy may be drawing a connection between a stable, growing world economy and peace. The final recommendation is that we (i.e., the United States) and other countries recognize that national sovereignty is eroding (more about this below). Sanger ends his article by suggesting that American power can be sustained if we are seen as sharing power with other countries and institutions, rather than trying to maintain our dominance.

Joseph Nye argues that the post–Cold War period looks like a "three-dimensional chess game" (Nye 1999, p. 24). At the highest level is military power, and the world is unipolar. The United States far outdistances other countries, even American military allies, as was shown in the Kosovo war. The middle level is economic, which is multipolar—Japan, Europe, and the United States The bottom level is "transnational relations" (Nye 2000, p. 24) such as information flows, in which power is dispersed. Thus the United States is not the dominant power, the hegemon. Rather, it is the major power.

Nye also distinguishes between hard and soft power. **Hard power** refers to military and economic capability. **Soft power** refers to ideology and culture. He argues that soft power is becoming more important than hard.

He then looks at what American priorities should be. The "A" list is composed of countries that can threaten the survival of the United States. In the aftermath of the Cold War, only Russia has such power, and that threat has greatly diminished. The "B" lists consists of countries that pose threats to U.S. interests, such as North Korea or Iraq. Other terms for such countries include "rogue nations" and "nations of concern," a recent addition to the list (Marquis 2000). The "C" list of priorities consists of problems that do not directly threaten U.S. interests, but may pose humanitarian concerns or indirectly affect the United States through military alliances. These include countries such as Haiti, Rwanda, Kosovo, Bosnia, and Somalia. Nye points out that the "C" list nations have dominated the foreign policy agenda because the humanitarian crises in those countries led to coverage by the media, what some call the **CNN effect**. These visuals stimulate the public and put pressure on the government to act. On the other hand, Nye points out that Americans are not willing to accept casualties if the only goal of the intervention is humanitarian and the United States acts alone, unilaterally.

The United States, Nye writes, must be concerned about maintaining international order because disorder can hurt us and because we want to influence others on issues that are important to us. Thus the country has to make the necessary investments in military power and foreign assistance[18] and has to be willing to take casualties (see conclusion). Further, Nye argues that because the United States gains the most from maintenance of international order, we must be prepared to do the most, including engaging in efforts to end conflict, as the United States has attempted in Northern Ireland and the Middle East.

Haass (1997a), a foreign policy analyst with the Brookings Institution who worked in the first Bush administration, argues that what has replaced the Cold War as a way of structuring the international arena and providing a unifying framework for American foreign policy is "international deregulation" (Haass 1997a, p. 25). This less structured international arena is safer for the United States in the sense that the possibility of world war has decreased but is less stable at the same time. There are no set rules, and conflicts still occur.

He then reviews six frameworks or doctrines for structuring American foreign policy. The first is **hegemony**, in which the United States attempts to maintain its place as the most powerful nation. The second is **isolationism**, the United States's original foreign policy doctrine, which states that America should have as little to do as possible with the outside world. The third is **Wilsonianism**, where the United States seeks to get other nations to follow the American model of democracy and civil society. **Economism** is the fourth doctrine. This one states that the major goal of American foreign policy is to meet the economic needs of the United States. **Humanitarianism** is the fifth framework. It argues that foreign policy should focus on what affects people, as opposed to nations, such as human rights abuses, poverty, overpopulation, and the environment. The sixth and final framework is **realism**, which is an attempt to maintain order among nations by balancing power (Haass 1997a). Haass finds all six of these doctrines to have weaknesses. Instead, he offers what he calls a "doctrine of regulation" (Haass 1997a, p. 68).

Haass writes that the appropriate goal for the United States in the post–Cold War period "is to encourage a multipolarity characterized by cooperation and concert rather than competition and conflict" (Haass 1999a, p. 38). What does this mean?

Haass argues that American primacy or predominance in the political and economic arenas is not likely to last. What the United States should be doing is moving to a world where there are multiple centers of power (multipolarity), but these multiple centers of powers will interact peacefully and cooperatively rather than competitively. A consensus on important issues will underlay this international arena, and Haass points out the progress that has been made in the economic field and even in the political and military arenas.

According to Haass, this new international order will rest on four building blocks, the fourth of which is perhaps the most controversial and requires the most explanation. The building blocks are lessening the use of military force, decreasing the amount of weapons of mass destruction (nuclear, chemical, and biological) and countries and others that possess them, economic openness, and "a limited doctrine of humanitarian intervention based on a recognition that people—and not just states—enjoy rights" (Haass 1999a, p. 39).

The issue of intervention for humanitarian reasons is one of the most troubling questions in American foreign policy. During the Cold War, the United States intervened in a number of conflicts—some between countries, some within—if it met the goal of containing communism.[19] Such interventions, overt as in Korea and Vietnam, covert as in Nicaragua and Afghanistan, were justified by national security and national interest considerations.[20] Humanitarian interventions, where it was not clear who the enemy was or what the purpose was or how to get out, were more controversial. Haass offers an analytical framework to help decision makers and policy elites (and the public) decide when and how to intervene.

Haass argues that to make the right decision concerning humanitarian intervention, one must ask three sets of questions. The first question is whether to intervene. To answer this question, a number of others should be asked: How serious is the repression? Are there economic, political, or military interests apart from the humanitarian concern? Will other countries go along with us? What are the benefits, costs, and consequences of intervening? Will intervention reduce or eliminate the problem? What would be the benefits, costs, and consequences of alternatives apart from intervening, including doing nothing (see also Haass 1999b)?

The second set of questions Haass asks us to consider is how to intervene. What tools or instruments are available to us and to our partners (if we have any), and what are the consequences and costs of using them? The available policy tools range from diplomacy to economics to military. Related to this, Haass asks about the length of the intervention, noting the limits of resources for long-term interventions.

The third and final set of questions focuses us to consider the purpose of intervention. Is it to prevent starvation? Is it to prevent genocide? Is it to support a government or perhaps help forge a new one?

Haass concludes this section of his article by noting that humanitarian problems do not cause global problems. Therefore, they take fourth or last place in the building blocks mentioned above. To quote Haass:

> At the end of the day, order is more fundamental than justice; one can have the former without the latter, but not vice versa. Adhering to this precept will take discipline, but discipline is essential in foreign policy if the urgent is not to crowd out the important. (Haass 1999a, p. 48)

Haass offers the above guidelines as a way to keep the United States from trying to dominate the world, which would fail anyway. However, he also argues that a problem the United States faces is doing too little rather than doing too much. The United States must be willing to take risks, such as committing ground troops and possible casualties, to give presidents the authority to negotiate trade deals, to explain U.S. purposes with other countries and the U.S. public. He ends his article with a call for a "national dialogue on this country's role in the world" (Haass 1999a, p. 49).

If Haass argues for an active U.S. role in creating this new world order, including limited humanitarian intervention, others have been more cautious in urging such a strong role. Two analysts suggest that foreign policy under Republican leadership would be quite different from what it was during the Clinton administration. With George W. Bush's ascension to the presidency in 2001, these views should be carefully considered.

Condoleezza Rice (2000), the major foreign policy advisor to Texas governor George W. Bush during the 2000 campaign and his national security advisor after the election, argues that the post–Cold War period is a propitious time for the United States to reconsider its foreign policy. The United States is in an enviable position where its major enemy has disappeared, and it has benefited from economic changes more than any other country. International trends are moving countries toward economic openness, democracy, and individual liberty (much faster and more surely in the first trend than in the second two).

American foreign policy, she writes, should focus on the national interest, with the following key tasks:

- To ensure that America's military can deter war, project power, and fight in defense of its interests if deterrence fails;
- To promote economic growth and political openness by extending free trade and a stable international monetary system to all committed to these principles, including in the western hemisphere, which has too often been neglected as a vital area of U.S. national interest;
- To renew strong and intimate relationships with allies who share American values and can thus share the burden of promoting peace, prosperity, and freedom;
- To focus U.S. energies on comprehensive relationships with the big powers, particularly Russia and China, that can and will mold the character of the international system; and
- To deal decisively with the threat of rogue regimes and hostile powers, which is increasingly taking the forms of the potential for terrorism and the development of weapons of mass destructions (WMD). (Rice 2000, pp. 46–47)

While Rice considers humanitarian interventions, it is clear that such interventions are best if they serve American national interests. The Kosovo intervention was justified, she argues, because of strategic interests in the Balkan regions; she argues that the intervention was not well handled. Other possible humanitarian interventions are not mentioned. The United States, she asserts, cannot be the world's "911" because we do not have the resources to respond to every emergency (Rice 2000, p. 54).

Robert Zoellick (2000, pp. 68–70) argues that a proper foreign policy (i.e., Republican) would be based on the following five principles: (1)respect for military power and using it to meet American interests; (2) nurturing coalitions and alliances especially with Europe and Japan; (3) viewing international institutions and agreements as a means of meeting foreign policy objectives and not an end in and of itself; (4) embracing changes in economics, communications, and technology; and (5) recognition of evil in the world. This last refers to countries and other organizations that have access to weapons of mass destruction and hate the United States. It also means building American military forces in an intelligent way to meet the challenges.

Zoellick concludes:

> A new generation must chart a course for America amid revolutionary changes in technologies, economies, societies, and weaponry. It is a mistake for the United States simply to react to events. America needs a strategy that blends traditional truths with the opportunities of a networked marketplace and a modernized army. It must be realistic about human nature and conflicting interests while being optimistic about the world's potential. America must deploy its power wisely, selectively, and consistently to mold an international system that will enhance its influence in future events. (p. 78)

## Europe

The United States's major focus remains the European continent (Sullivan 1992). A number of important challenges face us in the post–Cold War period. First, given the demise of the communist threat, what is the future of the collective security arrangement known as the **North Atlantic Treaty Organization** (**NATO**)? Who should be included in NATO? In 1998, NATO expanded by including three former Soviet satellite countries: Hungary, Poland, and the Czech Republic. Because Russia saw this action as a threat to its national interests, NATO included an associate status for Russia. Should NATO expansion continue? Does Russia see this as threatening its security?

A second problem is one that became apparent during the Persian Gulf and Kosovo wars. While the United States is part of NATO, the United States clearly demonstrated its military superiority over its allies, such as Britain and France. To what extent should NATO European countries develop their military capability apart from the United States? There are serious discussions under way for a European quick-response force.

Another problem has to do with economic assistance. Both Russia and its former Eastern European allies are attempting, to various degrees, to make the transition from a centrally controlled economy to a free market in a very short time. Some of the Eastern European countries (Poland, Hungary, Slovakia, and the Czech Republic) have made considerable progress toward a free market economy. Russia is experiencing more difficulty, though making more progress than most realize (Aslund 1994). Further, political turmoil within the republics of the Commonwealth of Independent States (including Russia), as well as between them, create great uncertainties. Additionally, Russia has used a combination of weapons sales and peacekeeping missions (in republics such as Georgia and Tajikistan) to, in a sense, reconstruct the old Soviet Union (Banerjee 1994). Further, the bloody Russian effort to subdue the attempt of the Chechnya Republic to leave the federation has created tensions between Russia and the West and influenced some of the former Soviet Republics to seek NATO protection (Erlanger 1995). The transition to a new Russian government under the presidency of Vladmir Putin, a hard-line former head of the Soviet spy agency, the KGB, has exacerbated concerns about the future direction of Russia. These developments have made it politically difficult to extend aid to Russia.

There are several goals here. First, the Central European nations need to be reassured about possible threats from Russia (Brzeziński 1994). Second, we want to assist the economic development of all the new countries. While Central Europe is perhaps the most attractive place for aid and investment, there is hesitation when it comes to Russia. It may be that the transition to a market economy is so difficult and the resistance to change among the population and the bureaucrats so strong that assistance or investments might be the equivalent of throwing money down the drain. On the other hand, such economic aid is likely necessary to ease the transition. The question, and no one really knows the answer to it, is how much aid to give?

## Case Study: The New World Order and the Balkans

The most difficult and tragic of foreign policy problems in Europe is in the Balkans region. It was also the place where NATO engaged in military activity for the first time, first in Bosnia, then in Kosovo. Yugoslavia was a federation of a seven republics (Bosnia-Herzegovina, Croatia, Kosovo, Macedonia, Montenegro, Serbia, and Slovenia) born in the heart of Europe after World War I and, using Samuel Huntington's (1993a) framework, at the fault line of clashing civilizations. A long history of enmity exists among the different groups, dating back to the 1400s and the Turkish conquest. Under the rule of the fading Austrian-Hungarian Empire in the early part of the twentieth century, this enmity provided the spark that began World War I when a Serb assassinated Archduke Francis Ferdinand in Sarajevo. During World War II, casualties were higher from Serb and Croat conflicts than from German rule (Hartmann and Wendzel 1994).[21] Under independent Communist rule, beginning in 1948, the various ethnic groups were intermixed in the different republics. When longtime leader Marshall Tito died in 1980, the federation remained together until 1991 (Omicinski 1992; Sloan 1998).

## *Bosnia*

In the aftermath of the demise of communism, noncommunist leaders were elected in Croatia and Slovenia who then sought to leave the Serbian-dominated Yugoslav federation. Britain opposed the move, and Germany supported it. The U.S. position was that some sort of confederation was preferable to breakup (Gompert 1994). A deal between Britain and Germany led to recognition of Slovenia and Croatia. Bosnia and Macedonia then also sought independence. A referendum in Bosnia, boycotted by Bosnia Serbs, ratified separation. Serbia sought to prevent the secession, and armed conflict broke out, first in Croatia. A 1992 cease-fire ended the Serbian-Croatian phase. The Serbs then moved their forces to Bosnia, and a new phase began. Bosnian Serb forces, backed by Serbia, took over much of Bosnia territory against a virtually defenseless Bosnian army. For a while Croatia also tried to take Bosnia territory. A mortar attack in a market square in Sarajevo, widely televised, led to a NATO air attack against Serbian mortar positions. This attack led to the withdrawal of the Serbs and an attempt to regain normalcy in Sarajevo. The UN Security Council, which ordered the economic embargo, also sought to protect several enclaves in Bosnia.

Why did the conflict turn so bitter that terms such as "ethnic cleansing" and "holocaust" to describe the actions of the Serbs began to be heard? The main distinction between the major combatants is religious: Serbs are Orthodox, Croats are Catholic, and Bosnians are Muslim. Apart from this, ethnic differences are minimal. History is important.

From the standpoint of the Serbs (the dominant group in what is left of the Yugoslav federation), their fellow Serbs in the other republics would now be dominated by the hated ethnic groups. The Serbian leader, Slobodan Milosevic, talked of a Great Serbia and sought to assist Bosnian Serbs in carving up Bosnia. Europe, through NATO, imposed an arms embargo on all sides, but it worked to the advantage of the Bosnian Serbs who could get arms from Serbia. Bosnia, at least at first, could not defend itself from either Serbia or Croatia. An economic embargo was placed on Serbia, and some European ground troops were brought into the area. Further, NATO threatened, and occasionally carried out, air strikes against Serb positions, particularly around Sarajevo and the Gorazde enclave.

The United States took ambivalent positions during both the Bush and Clinton administrations. The two administrations were afraid of getting caught up in quagmires from which they could not successfully extricate. In the case of the Bush administration, the quagmire was Vietnam. In the case of the Clinton administration, it was Somalia (see below). Both administrations sought U.S. involvement, but were told by NATO allies that it was a European matter (Gompert 1994). A peacekeeping force made up of French, British, and Spanish troops was sent to Croatia to enforce the cease-fire. When the United States urged air strikes, the Europeans refused, citing the risk of reprisal against the ground forces. On the other hand, the United States did not want to send any of its troops there until an acceptable cease-fire could be arranged. An additional concern was that the war not spread to the other former Yugoslavian republics, such as Macedonia and Kosovo, which might eventually also involve Greece and Albania.

During the 1992 president elections, Democratic candidate Bill Clinton attacked the Bush administration for its failure to aid Bosnia. Further, television coverage from Sarajevo showed the American public the devastation that was going on, the ethnic cleansing, and concentration camps (Omicinski 1992).[22] The Clinton administration was no more willing to take action than the Bush administration, except for the occasional air attack (Gordon 1994). Although options were available, short of introducing ground troops,[23] lack of unity among the European nations made any concerted action difficult. Further, Germany supported the Croats, Russia, the Serbs, Arab nations, and the Bosnians. In 1994, a peace plan written by the Americans, the Russians, and the Western Europeans proposed dividing Bosnia essentially in half but ensuring that Bosnia had sea access. The allies put pressure on the combatants to accept the plan, though the Bosnian Serbs rejected it. As a result of this rejection, Serbia stopped supplying arms and fuel to their fellow Bosnians. The Bosnian government began a counterattack (aided by the Croatians) and regained some of its lost territory. When Croatia turned on Serbia, and with Bosnian Muslims and Croatia being supplied with arms by outside parties despite the embargo (see Pomfret and Ottaway 1996), NATO forces went after the Serbs, both in Bosnia and Serbia (Dobbs 1999). This move led to a ceasefire, an agreement brokered by the United States known as the **Dayton Accords**, and the de facto partition of Bosnia into three parts: Serbian, Croatian, and Muslim. Efforts to piece back the republic have faltered. President Clinton sent American troops to Bosnia as part of the international peacekeeping force. While the original promise of American ground troops was for one year only, the absence of a permanent settlement meant that American troops remained there, though in smaller numbers. While no permanent solution is on the near horizon and ethnic enmity remains, the violence has ended. No exit strategy for NATO peacekeeping forces exists at present.[24]

## Kosovo

The U.S. intervention in Kosovo[25] raised all kinds of questions. Kosovo is largely inhabited by ethnic Albanians (Muslims) and by Serbs. In a 1974 revision to the Yugoslavian constitution, Kosovo and the other provinces were given autonomy. In 1989, that autonomy and other privileges were taken away by the central government under the rule of Slobodan Milosevic ("Kosovo: The Jerusalem of Serbia" 1999). From 1992 to the beginning of the war, the U.S. position was that threats to the province would be met by force. In a letter to Serbian president Slobodan Milosevic, President Bush wrote in late 1992: "In the event of conflict in Kosovo caused by Serbian action, the United States will be prepared to employ military force against the Serbians in Kosovo and in Serbia proper" (quoted in Gellman 1999b).

In 1998, Serbia began a campaign to put down resistance from ethnic Albanians, particularly by the Kosovo Liberation Army (KLA), which had begun attacks on Serbian troops in Kosovo as early as 1996 ("Kosovo: The Jerusalem of Serbia" 1999). In doing so, it sought to move the Albanians out of Kosovo. This created refugee problems in Albania itself and in Montenegro, another Yugoslav republic. The campaign continued into 1999. The Serbian forces included the regular army, Serb police, and warlords who had been involved in the previous conflicts in Croatia and Bosnia (Kifner 1999; Smith and Drozdiak 1999). Thus, Serbs planned the ethnic cleansing before the war began in March 1999. It enhanced its efforts as negotiations failed and the war began.

The United States sought to impose a solution during negotiations in Rambouillet, France. But the Serbs never attended and Kosovo Albanians were upset that the proposed solution did not provide for complete independence for Kosovo (Sciolino and Bronner 1999).

The U.S. response to the failure of negotiations was the NATO air war that lasted a little more than seventy days. The air attacks against Serb positions in Kosovo and against Serbia were limited so that no casualties would occur. This is one of the lessons the Clinton administration seemingly learned from Somalia: that Americans will not put up with casualties unless it clearly is in the national interest. This makes the United States, again, the sole remaining military and economic superpower, reluctant to undertake interventions because of a perceived lack of support (Haass 1997a, Wheatcroft 1999). On the other hand, a strict adherence to the Powell doctrine (named after the Colin Powell, former chairman of the Joint Chiefs of Staff and the secretary of state in the George W. Bush administration), stemming from the Vietnam analogy, would have precluded intervention in Bosnia, Kosovo, and Haiti (Harden and Broder 1999).

Another impact of the war is the question of sovereignty. In the Kosovo air war, NATO (and some of the NATO members such as Germany, Greece, and Italy who were not very supportive of the effort [Safire 1999]) engaged in its first attack against a nation. In the Bosnian situation, Bosnia had declared its independence from the Yugoslav federation and that led to the ethnic cleansings and war. Kosovo, despite the desire of the KLA, was, and remains, a province of Yugoslavia. Thus, we were bombing a country, Serbia, with which we were not at war.

Thus is created, essentially, a new doctrine: States that violate the human rights of their citizens violate the implied social contract that governments will protect their citizens. Therefore, other countries may intervene. This was the case in Kosovo and, as we shall see below, was also the case in Rwanda, though the United States did not act (Kitfield 1999b; Miller 1999).[26]

One of the questions about the war in Kosovo was what impact it had on relations with other countries. Certainly, Russia opposed the war and tried to intervene diplomatically to forestall the NATO attack. Russia participated in the negotiations to arrive at a settlement to end the war (Harden 1999). After the end of the air war, a small contingent of Russian troops entered Kosovo, ostensibly as part of the peacekeeping force but aimed at protecting the Serbs. In the case of China, the fallout was more dramatic. China, like Russia, opposed the war. More importantly, it became a victim of the war when U.S. war planes mistakenly bombed the Chinese embassy in Belgrade. This clearly hurt U.S.-Chinese relations (Kissinger 1999; Rodman 1999).

One of the major criticisms of the Kosovo war was the administration's constant refrain that to avoid casualties, it would not send in ground troops. Given the limitations of fighting a war solely from the air, this may actually have prolonged the effort (Gellman 1999a; Safire 1999). Further, there is evidence that the Serbs stepped up the ethnic cleansing in Kosovo (Harris 1999; Whitney and Schmitt 1999). Negotiations plus KLA counterattacks and the threat of ground troops (who were being assembled for the peacekeeping force) led to the climax of the war.[27] The agreement was less strict than the one demanded of the Serbs in Rambouillet. For example, the Serbs did not agree to a referendum in Kosovo to determine its future status (Odom 1999).

At present, the cease-fire is holding and foreign troops remain in Kosovo, as they do in Bosnia. However, Albanian ethnic forces in Kosovo are still trying to secede from the Yugoslav republic.

## Lessons Learned?

Since the end of the war in Kosovo, there have been attempts to draw lessons and to declare winners and losers (see, e.g., Cordesman 1999; Daalder and O'Hanlon 1999; and Safire 1999). Clearly, this was not the massive victory achieved in the Persian Gulf War. The interventions in Bosnia and especially in Kosovo were for humanitarian reasons. In the case of Kosovo, NATO attacked a sovereign nation for the first time. The danger in Kosovo especially, apart from the humanitarian interest, was the possibility of the conflict's spreading to other countries. As we shall see below, the doctrine of humanitarian intervention was limited.

Questions have been raised about the efficacy of an air-war-only strategy (Kitfield 1999a; Cordesman 1999). For example, assessments of how effective the air war was suggested that it was considerably less than first appeared (Kitfield 1999a).

Another set of issues stemming from both Bosnia and Kosovo is peace-keeping and nation building. The ethnic animosities that led to the Balkan conflicts are long-lived and remain. Bosnia faces effective partition. Kosovo has seen ethnic Albanians attack the Serbs. Refugees from both areas remain a problem. The successful conclusion of the wars in Kosovo and Bosnia has ended the humanitarian crisis. The conflicts may be over, but the underlying problems remain (Daalder and Froman 1999; Rohde 2000).

One of the more intriguing moments came when the U.S. House of Representatives was asked to support the Kosovo air war. The dislike of President Clinton on the part of most House Republicans (who had majority control) and the fact that the impeachment process had just concluded led to a bizarre outcome. The House refused to authorize the mission and then appropriated more than twice what the Clinton administration had requested (Kitfield 1999a).

## The Middle East

It is the birthplace of three of the world's great religions—Christianity, Islam, and Judaism—and called the cradle of civilization. It is the largest source of one of the earth's most important resources, petroleum. And it has been the site of armed conflicts for millennia. It also is a place of great hope and important challenges.

In some ways, tensions have dramatically eased. The end of the Cold War and the traumatic effects of the Persian Gulf War created new opportunities for defusing or decreasing tensions between Arab nations and the state of Israel. But opportunities have been missed.

Much of the Middle East was under colonial rule through the first half of the twentieth century. Prior to World War I, the Turkish Empire included the land of Palestine, which encompassed what is now Israel and Jordan. After the war (Turkey having fought on the losing side), Britain took over the mandate under the auspices of the League of Nations. Although Jews had lived in the area since biblical times, Palestine was predominantly Arab. Anti-Semitism in Europe, culminating in the Nazi holocaust of World War II, led to Jewish migration to Palestine despite Arab opposition. Pressure by Jews convinced Britain to give up its mandate after World War II, and the United Nations voted in 1947 to create two nations out of Palestine, Israel and Trans-Jordan (now Jordan). Arab nations bordering Israel refused to accept the UN vote and attacked Israel after it declared its independence in 1948. The infant nation won.

There were three other open conflicts between Israel and its Arab neighbors. In 1957, a crisis arose when Egyptian president Abdul Nasser seized the Suez Canal, then still under British control, and closed it to Israeli traffic. Britain, France, and Israel attacked Egypt, but pressure from the United States brought a halt to the military offensive.

In 1967, Egypt and other Arab nations again threatened Israel. In response, Israel undertook a preemptive attack and won a dramatic victory in what was known as the Six-Day War. Israel captured territory in the Gaza Strip with Egypt and the West Bank territory with Jordan (including East Jerusalem).

Six years later, in 1973, Israel's Arab neighbors (Egypt, Jordan, and Syria) attacked in what may be called, depending on one's perspective, the October War or the Yom Kippur War. The initial attack led to the first Arab victories over Israel. Israel's counterattack, aided by American resupply efforts, brought the war to a stalemate and marked the end of that conflict. However, the Arab members of OPEC organized a six-month boycott against the United States, leading to massive oil price increases.

There have also been unofficial conflicts. The civil war in Jordan in 1976, when the forces of King Hussein drove the Palestine Liberation Organization (PLO) out, is one example. The Israeli invasion of Lebanon in 1982 is another. In December 1987, Palestinian residents of the occupied territories (West Bank and Gaza) began an uprising known as the **intifada** against Israeli rule. Additionally, Arab countries have engaged for years in a secondary boycott against Israel, officially refusing to deal with companies or people who have relations with Israel.

Not all the relations between Israel and its Arab nations were warlike. Most importantly, in 1977, Egyptian President Anwar Sadat offered to go to Israel and speak to the Israeli parliament (the Knesset). This dramatic opening led to an invitation by President Jimmy Carter to Sadat and Israeli Prime Minister Menachem Begin to come to the United States and negotiate a peace treaty. The **Camp David Accords** constituted the first official peace agreement between Israel and an Arab country. In 1988, Jordan announced that it would no longer administer Palestinian areas. PLO chairman Yasir Arafat declared that a Palestinian state existed in the occupied territories, but also renounced terrorism and recognized the state of Israel. The United States then began meetings with the PLO.

As discussed above, the Persian Gulf war precipitated negotiations between Israel and the PLO. The PLO supported Iraq and then found that its Persian Gulf supporters (Kuwait, Saudi Arabia, and Oman) would no longer support the PLO. At the same time, the idea of Arab unity was also broken. Israel and most of the Arab world were on the same side against Iraq. Negotiations between the two parties began in 1991, culminating, after many stops and starts, in a peace agreement allowing self-rule in the Gaza Strip and the West Bank town of Jericho ("Framework for Peace" 1994). While opposition to the agreement remains (in Israel, primarily among settlers in the Gaza Strip and right-wingers, including the conservative Likud Party and in Gaza by radical Arab groups such as Hamas), the agreement represented a sea change in the politics of the area. In July 1994, Israel and Jordan signed an agreement ending the forty-six-year state of war between the two countries (Jehl 1994; Sciolino 1994b).[28]

Israel and its Arab neighbors undertook a series of meetings to resolve their differences and end the tension and threat of war in the Middle East. As we have seen, Egypt and Jordan signed peace agreements with Israel. The Egyptian agreement eventually led to the assassination of President Sadat. Negotiations with Syria have been unproductive and were interrupted by the death in 2000 of Syrian president Haffiz al-Assad and the succession by his son Bashar. Complicating the Syrian negotiations as well as Israel-Arab negotiations in general was the invasion of Lebanon by Israel in 1982 and the occupation of the southern portion of Lebanon by Israel. Israel wanted to protect its allies in the Christian militias in southern Lebanon and also provide a buffer zone between Israel and terrorist groups, such as Hezbollah. In the spring of 2000, after years of trying to tame the area, Israel unilaterally pulled out.

Most of the negotiations, brokered by the United States, have been between Israel and the Palestinian National Authority. The big breakthrough came in October 1993 when Israel and the PLO officially recognized each other. Under the Oslo Accords, the two would continue negotiations to settle the issues. Additionally, the accords allowed the PLO to declare Palestinian statehood by September 13, 2000, which it did not do.

Another agreement was reached a year later, in September 1995, dealing with a whole range of issues. In November 1995, an Israeli fundamentalist assassinated Israeli Prime Minister Yitzhak Rabin, and in May 1996, Benjamin Netanyahu became Israeli prime minister, promising a tougher stance toward the Palestianians. In October 1998, with the intervention of Jordanian King Hussein (who would die of cancer early in 1999), the Palestinian Authority and Israel agreed to the Wye River Memorandum. In May 1999, Ehud Barak became prime minister, with a platform to achieve a lasting peace with the Palestinians. In July 2000, President Clinton brought Barak and PLO leader Yasir Arafat together at Camp David to try to reach a final settlement. While progress on some important issues was made, the meeting did not reach an agreement. Barak lost in elections in 2000 to hard-liner Ariel Sharon. Negotiations between the Palestinians and the Israelis continue sporadically. The failure to reach a final settlement led to a resumption of violence along the border.

Why have the negotiations not reached a final settlement? One reason is the city of Jerusalem, a holy city to the three religions. The PLO has declared that Jerusalem should be the capital of a Palestinian state. Israel, too, would like Jerusalem to be its capital. Both claim sovereignty over the city, or at least parts of it. A second important issue is refugees. The camps created in the aftermath of the 1948 war remain. Palestinian refugees and their descendants would like to return to what were their homes in what is now Israel. To allow all of them to return would change the essential nature of the Jewish state. So it is a question of how many, in what way, and perhaps what reparations might be made to those who cannot return. A third related issue is Jewish settlements in lands captured during the 1967 war.

Apart from the Arab-Israeli tensions, two other countries are cause for concern. Relations between the United States and Iran have been distant since the Iranian revolution of 1979 and the embassy hostage crisis. Iranian fundamentalists still retain power, though the political leadership has become somewhat more moderate. Iran is suspected of housing and fostering terrorist activities and has also sought to upgrade its military capabilities.

The other country is Iraq. In the wake of its defeat in the Persian Gulf War, Iraq remains isolated (though less so than after the war), subject to a (leaky) embargo and in some senses a divided country. In the north, the allies enforce a "no-fly zone" over areas populated by Kurds. In the south, Shiite Muslims are separated from the rest of the country. British and American planes have been engaged in an undeclared war with Iraqi ground batteries.

The major problem that the United States faces concerns inspections. After the Persian Gulf, an inspection team, under United Nations auspices, was in Iraq to make sure that Saddam Hussein was not hiding facilities for the manufacture of chemical and biological (and nuclear) weapons. Hussein resisted at every stage, and by 1998 the inspection teams were forbidden to enter Iraq, despite some air attacks on retaliation. There are indications that Hussein is rebuilding Iraq's military capability (Myers 2000a). While the United States would like to see Saddam Hussein replaced, it is not clear who would replace him and whether conditions would change. It remains a pariah state. The enthusiasm for maintaining the embargo (except for food and medical supplies and oil exports to pay for them) has waned among the U.S. allies such as Germany and France.

## Asia

U.S. foreign policy has traditionally been tilted toward Europe. The United States, however, has long been a Pacific power and there are important developments going on there as well. Much of Asia has been rapidly developing, and some Asian countries, such as the PRC, have been growing at an astounding rate. Paul Krugman (1994), though, argues that rapid growth in East Asia is due to governmental mobilization of resources and that, in the absence of a strong private sector, growth in that region would significantly diminish. Krugman's observation seemed to be cogent as the late 1990s saw economic and other problems in the region. The financial crisis that began in 1997 in Thailand spread to other countries, such as Indonesia (and Brazil and Russia). The Japanese economy has been stagnant for much of the 1990s. The Asian miracle and ideas about the economic decline of the United States were not borne out by the events of the 1990s. Also, developments with India and Pakistan, the Koreas, and China made Asia an area of much concern for the United States.

China looms ever larger on the international scene as an economic engine, a political force, a military power, and an environmental bombshell (Gill 1999). Perhaps no country in Asia, maybe not even the world, has raised more issues and concern than China. While the PRC has changed dramatically in the economic sphere, political change has been much slower. The United States is troubled by human rights abuses. This was evident in 1989 with the suppression of political demonstrations symbolized by Tiananmen Square in 1989. In 2000, the ruling Communist Party continued to suppress all political dissent.

Human rights violations have become entwined with economic considerations, as mentioned in chapter 2. Under U.S. law, the PRC has been granted most-favored-nation status (trading without restrictions) on an annual basis, with the administration certifying China's improvement in human rights. In 2000, the administration requested permanent normal trade relations, which would be a precursor to China's entry into the WTO. Congress granted the request. The Clinton administration believed that bringing the PRC more closely into the international economic arena, having to obey new rules, would open up the Chinese economy, would make it more transparent, and might also effect political change.

Another issue is the status of Taiwan. Both the PRC and the Republic of China (Taiwan) agree that Taiwan and China should be the same country; the question is when. Taiwanese elections in 2000 brought a new president who supported an independent status for Taiwan. The PRC threatened military action should such status be declared (and has on several occasions engaged in near-military action, such as the Taiwan Strait Crisis of 1995–96; see Scobell 2000). The United States holds to this one-China policy, but also has seen Taiwan as an ally, with an obligation to prevent it from being overrun by the PRC. The U.S. position, as stated in the Taiwan Relations Act of 1979, is that the future of the island should be determined by peaceful means. The United States has supported Taiwan in several different ways, such as arms sales, sharing of intelligence, and so forth (see Hickey 1999 for a full discussion of these issues).

A third issue is the PRC's attempt to reach a more powerful status in the world, or at least in Asia, both politically and militarily. China has a small nuclear force and a large army. It has also traded weapons technology to nations the United States is concerned about, such as North Korea, Iran, and Iraq. The ongoing debate in the United States over a limited missile shield has alarmed the Chinese because they feel the shield is aimed at them (see case study below).

And, of course, the accidental bombing of the Chinese embassy in Belgrade during the Kosovo war exacerbated all the tensions that were already there in the military and political arenas. The PRC has never fully accepted the U.S. explanation that it was an accident. China is not a U.S. ally, in the sense that England, France, Germany, and Japan are. It has its own perceptions of its national interests. Also hurting the relationship were allegations that elements within China had funneled funds to the 1996 Clinton reelection campaign and charges that ethnic Chinese working at the Los Alamos weapons laboratory were spying for China.

China is a permanent member of the UN Security Council, so the UN's ability to do things in ways that support U.S. foreign policy objectives depends to a certain extent on its relationship with China (and Russia).

A second critical area is the Korean peninsula. The two Koreas, an aftermath of World War II and the Cold War (including the Korean War from 1950 to 1953) are separated by an ironically named "demilitarized zone." The United States has formed an alliance with the Republic of Korea (South Korea) and maintains a force of about 37,000 troops ("Global Hot Spots: Korea" 2000). The Democratic People's Republic of Korea (North Korea) remains heavily armed, with its ground troops within twenty-five miles of the capital of South Korea, Seoul. North Korea is very isolated from the rest of the world and has also recently experience massive crop failures. The country has also developed or threatened to develop a nuclear capability and has been testing missiles. The United States has reacted to some of these developments by arranging for food assistance and by trying to divert North Korea's nuclear program in a peaceful direction.

In 2000, a potential breakthrough in relations between the two Koreas took place. A summit between the two leaders, North Korea's Kim Jong Il and South Korea's Kim Dae Jung, was the first meeting between the leaders of the two countries in half a century. Kim Dae Jung visited North Korea, and that led to the beginning of some exchanges. The United States, in response, has lifted many of its economic sanctions. While many of these are positive developments, North Korean remains a country of concern. The George W. Bush administration has indicated some backing away from the Clinton policy (Sanger 2001).

Another highly inflammatory area is the Indian subcontinent. India and Pakistan were created as a result of the partition ending British colonial rule in 1947. The animosity between the two ethnically diverse nations has led to several wars between the two countries and continued strife over the conflicted territory of Kashmir, controlled by India but claimed by Pakistan. India is the world's largest democracy, with a rapidly growing population, expected to overtake the PRC in the early part of the twenty-first century. India also has had tense relations with the PRC, and in reaction to Chinese buildup, especially of its nuclear arms capability, India has developed a nuclear capability. Pakistan, reacting to the Indian buildup, also showed that it had such a capability. Both countries conducted nuclear tests in 1998, though both promised not to use the weapons. The tests by the two countries have set back U.S. efforts to limit the proliferation of nuclear arms (Cohen 1998).

The relationship between the United States and the two giants of South Asia were based on the Cold War (Cohen 1998). Pakistan was a strong U.S. ally. Pakistan became a base for one of the covert activities supported by the Reagan administration in Afghanistan. Since the end of that conflict in 1988, Pakistan has faced continuing political turmoil, especially along its border with Afghanistan. Robert Kaplan (2000) argues that the country is falling apart because of ethnic/religious divisions. He warns that the danger is compounded by the country's possession of nuclear weapons. James Clad and Michael Rabjohns (2000) argue, especially in the wake of President Clinton's visit to India, Pakistan, and Bangladesh, that U.S. strategic interests are much closer with India than they are with China and should move in that direction.

Steven Cohen (1998) suggests a strategy that combines incentives with sanctions. This would include bringing the two countries in as members of the nuclear club, part of a series of international agreements. The United States should also help both countries develop civilian nuclear power capabilities to meet their growing needs for energy.

Kashmir remains an area of great concern and the cause of several wars. According to Cohen (1998), it is perhaps the place most likely to see a war with nuclear weapons. The United States should encourage talks between Pakistan and India, as it has brokered peace agreements between the two countries in the 1990s. The United States should see India as an emerging power and work toward helping it develop. For Pakistan, the United States should encourage the development of civilian institutions and democracy (though Kaplan [2000] is very pessimistic about how likely that is to occur).

## Africa

> Throw a dart at a map of sub-Saharan Africa. Assuming you don't hit a remote wilderness, you will doubtless hit an area of the world where: AIDS is rampant, extreme hunger prevalent, corruption endemic, animal species endangered, and so on. . . .
>
> In nation after nation, warlords and rebel generals harass and murder by the thousands—motivated by no discernible ideology except clannish ambition, cruelty, and greed. There has been a holocaust rolling across Africa for decades, and nobody cares. (Goldberg 2000)

Africa presents perhaps the most stark contrasts of problems and opportunities of any continent. It is the poorest continent, long subject to Western colonial rule, and many of its countries the last to emerge from colonialism. There is wealth and an abundance of resources in places, and drought, war, and abject poverty in many others. Some countries have tried and are succeeding with democracy and market economies. Others are mired in civil war and military dictatorships (Darnton 1994; see also Fatton 1990).

A number of countries are engaged in either civil war or external conflict. The Democratic Republic of the Congo (Zaire at one point) is experiencing both. The origins of the wars in the Congo are with the ethnic conflict in Rwanda. Three countries—Angola, Zimbabwe, and Namibia—support the current regime, which took power in 1997. Three others—Rwanda, Uganda, and Burundi—support the rebels ("Global Hot Spots: Congo" 2000). The result has been what the United States has called "Africa's first world war" (Brown 2000). Other trouble spots include the Angolan civil war (and its skirmishes with neighboring Zambia), periodic border fighting between Ethiopia and Eritrea, a nine-year brutal civil war in Sierra Leone (which has involved

UN peacekeeping troops), continued factional fighting in Somalia, civil war in Sudan between Christian and Muslim factions, and racial antagonisms in Zimbabwe (related to land distribution).

Nigeria is a country that has both great promise and great problems. It is rich in oil, one of the United States's major oil suppliers. But little of the oil revenue has gone to help the Nigerian people. Nigeria is also the most populous country in Africa but has many ethnic and religious divisions. Politically, the country has suffered from military dictatorships. In 1999, the military ruler died in a plane crash and the Nigerian military allowed democratic elections to be held. The ethnic strife remains, however, as militant Islamic fundamentalists have tried to impose Islamic law on some of the Nigeria states, causing unrest within the nation.

One area that has absolutely devastated the continent is HIV/AIDS. Of the total of 33.6 million people infected with HIV/AIDS worldwide, 23.3 million are in sub-Saharan Africa (almost 70 percent of the infected population). This represented about 8 percent of the adult working population in 1997, the majority of whom are women (International Labour Office 2000). In a few countries, the infection rate is as high as 20 percent of the adult population (International Labour Office 2000). Infected people are often stigmatized, forcing children to work to support the family. There are both human rights and economic development implications to the continued spread of HIV/AIDS in the subcontinent. For example, the high infection rate leads to a shortage of workers. It also necessitates spending resources to help those infected, resources that are scarce in the countries (International Labour Office 2000).

Two African countries illustrate some of the problems of American intervention. Somalia has been the site of tribal conflict and civil war for more than a decade, and there is no effective government. The result has been death due to war and drought. Somalia has the resources to feed itself, but the civil war and possible partition prevent that possibility.

Television carried the Somalian story back to the United States, and pictures of starvation moved many in this country. In December 1992, after the presidential elections, President Bush sent U.S. troops, under United Nations auspices, to Somalia on a rescue mission to intercede to feed the people. The mission was originally difficult but successful. The Clinton administration changed the mission from alleviating starvation to engaging in nation building, a much more problematic objective. UN troops were fired upon and killed by a tribal clan under the leadership of Mohammed Aidid. UN Secretary-General Boutros Boutros-Ghali ordered UN troops, which were primarily American, to capture Aidid. On the verge of capturing Aidid, U.S. troops found themselves in a fight with Aidid's troops, and some eighteen Americans died, one of whom was dragged through the streets of Mogadishu. The Clinton administration then began to pull U.S. troops out, and by spring of 1994 all U.S. troops had been withdrawn (Sloyan 1994). The Somalia situation, like the one in Bosnia, presented the problems of when to get in, what to do, and, and, most importantly, how to get out. By 1995, United Nations peace-keeping forces had ended its mission, but the chaotic political situation that led to the initial intervention remained (Richburg 1994). Looking at the American experience in Somalia, columnist George Will wrote:

> U.S. intervention in Somalia may prove to be, on balance, beneficial because it will be so discouraging. Perhaps, given the intermittent learning processes of our forgetful society, we now need a prophylactic failure to prevent a spate of similar episodes.
>
> A medical analogy is apposite. Public health owes much to immunology, the science which sometimes uses small doses of diseases to stimulate resistance to diseases. The Somalia experience may inoculate America's body politic against the temptations of humanitarian intervention. If so, Operation Restore Hope, as it was called at the outset, may one day be remembered as a constructive failure. The dialectic of political life is like that. (Will 1993, p. 62)

Crocker (1995) offered a somewhat more hopeful view of the U.S. experience in Somalia. He argued that U.S. and UN intervention, at least at first, was successful. It had limited goals: Stop the civil war and provide assistance to the population. Lives were saved and politics within Somalia, at least for a while, were improved. The problems arose when the mission changed and the United States and the United Nations attempted to create a political order. The lesson for Crocker, as opposed to Will, is that under certain limited circumstances, foreign intervention can be successful.

The American experience in Somalia had an impact on how we would respond to the catastrophe in Rwanda. In early 1994, a plane carrying the presidents of Rwanda and neighboring Burundi crashed, killing all survivors. Rwanda, during and since Belgian colonial rule, had been governed by the minority Tutsi tribe (Sadowski 1998; Schmidt 1994). The more numerous Hutus, with long-held grievances, began to slaughter Tutsis in April. The estimate is that between 200,000 and 500,000 people died during the rampage, mostly at the hands of the military, though some of the killings were also by Tutsis of Hutus (Gourevitch 1998). The Rwandan Patriotic Front (RPF) began to seize territory and by July 1994 had established a provisional government, with a Hutu as president. Hutus, encouraged by the provisional government fled before the oncoming RPF, though it promised no reprisal. Over 1 million Hutus fled to neighboring Zaire (now the Democratic Republic of Congo), staying in refugee camps that lacked food, water, and shelter. France sent a contingent of troops for humanitarian purposes. After the Somalia debacle, the United States and the West in general were reluctant to get involved and, when involved, to get out quickly (Sciolino 1994b; Smith 1994).[29] Indeed, the Clinton administration discounted reports of genocide (Crossette 1999). However, the massive deaths in the refugee camps and the cholera epidemic led to a major relief effort in July 1994 (Cushman 1994; Thomas 1994). The Hutu/Tutsi conflicts spilled over into neighboring Burundi and the Democratic Republic of Congo. By 1999, a brittle peace was holding in Rwanda, but tensions remain (Fisher 1999; see also Power 2001).

A 1999 report by a three-person panel appointed by UN Secretary-General Kofi Annan concluded that both the United Nations and the United States failed to act to stop the genocide in Rwanda, despite early warnings of the impending massacre (Crossette 1999; see also Power 2001). During his 1998 trip to Africa, President Clinton apologized for the United States's failure to intervene (Crossette 1999; Gourevitch 1998). Alan Kuperman (2000), on the other hand, argues that while military intervention to end genocide may be justified, the United States could not have intervened in time to save many of the Tutsi lives. Samantha Power (2001) argues that even a minimal effort would have saved lives.

Given the conflict, starvation, disease, and other problems afflicting Africa, is there an appropriate role for the United States and the Western nations, including the United Nations? Johathan Goldberg (2000), writing from a conservative/libertarian point of view, argues that the United States should try to use any method to help Africa become "civilized," including spending money and sending troops. Goldberg understands that this looks like a new form of colonialism or white man's burden, but the alternative, for him, is to let Africa continue sinking.

Stremlau (2000) contends that the United States should try to prevent conflicts from arising. He says we should do this through South Africa, which has made the transition to democracy, to help distribute assistance and inculcate liberal values. Democratic governments exist in South Africa, Nigeria, Botswana, Senegal, Mauritius, and Gambia (Stremlau 2000). Stremlau also calls for greater American investment and trade with African countries. Only 1 percent of U.S. trade is with Africa, and most of that with oil-rich countries and South Africa. After a contentious year-long debate, Congress passed the African Growth and Opportunity Act in 1999. And, despite all the ethnic wars going on in Africa and elsewhere, Ted Gurr (2000) argues that there is a decline in ethnic wars since the early part of the 1990s and greater recognition of group rights.

## Problem Identification: National Defense

Apart from the disorder and confusion that plagues a good portion of the world, the end of the Cold War also brought changes to defense policy. Containment required a large defense establishment, capable of fighting a major war in Europe, deterring nuclear attacks, and acting in parts of the world for which, apart from containment, we would have little interest. But the end of the Cold War changed the mission and, therefore, the size of the American military forces. Much of the debate can be put under the label of **defense build-down**. Whereas the defense buildup began during the later years of the Carter administration and continued through much of the Reagan administration, the build-down began during the first Bush administration and continued into the Clinton administration.[30] The major questions that the end of the Cold War and the build-down raise are what is the appropriate size of the military and what are its missions.[31] There are also issues related to the arms trade and stopping the proliferation of weapons of mass destruction. Lawrence Korb (2000), writing an issue brief for the presidential candidates during the 2000 elections, says there are four issues to consider: how much should be spent on defense, what is the appropriate military strategy, when to use our military forces, and whether to deploy a missile defense system.

The United States underwent a number of demobilizations during the twentieth century. Demobilizations occurred after World War I and World War II, after the Korean War, and after the Vietnam War. In each case, demobilization left the United States militarily at risk for the next conflict. After World War I, the United States negotiated a number of treaties aimed at reducing the armies and navies of the world's major powers. When World War II began in 1939, the United States was militarily unprepared for conflict, a situation that did not change much until the attack on Pearl Harbor. The demobilization after World War II was rapid; it reversed with the communist movement into Eastern Europe aided by the Soviet army, the fall of China to the forces of Mao Tse-tung, and particularly the Korean War.

The demobilization after Korea ended in the 1960s as the Vietnam War heated up. When the American role in the war ended in 1973, the last of the Cold War build-downs occurred. Some charged that the military became "hollow," just a shell with insufficient power to cope with renewed challenges from the Soviet Union. The last buildup began in 1979 and greatly accelerated during the first part of the Reagan administration.

By 1985–86, the build-up, epitomized by the strategic defense initiative popularly known as the "Star Wars" program (see case study below), had peaked for two reasons. First, the large budget deficits forced the federal government to trim, and the defense budget (see Table 3.1) was an easy place to cut. Indeed, much of the budget reduction took place via the defense budget. Second, Mikhail Gorbachev became the head of the Soviet Union, and tensions began easing, resulting ultimately in the demise of the Soviet Union. After the Persian Gulf War, which provided a temporary respite from budget declines, the build-down continued. Military spending began to rise again in FY 1999.

Table 3.1 presents several measures of building up and building down of the defense budget. The third column shows military spending as a percentage of the federal budget. In FY 1960, that figure stood at 52.2 percent, reflecting spending on the Cold War and the relatively limited programs of the federal government. By FY 1999, that number had declined to 16.1 percent, reflecting both the relative decline in military spending and the increase in spending for other programs, especially entitlements (see chapter 2). Even with the increases scheduled for the early years of the twenty-first century, the percentage of the federal budget spent on defense will likely continue to decline. The fourth column shows defense spending as a percentage of gross domestic product (GDP). This figure went from a high of 9.3 percent in FY 1960 to 3 percent by FY 1999.

While there have been significant declines in defense spending, the United

Table 3.1

**Defense Expenditures, 1960–2005**

| Fiscal year | Actual outlays (in billion $) | As % of total federal outlays | As % of GDP |
|---|---|---|---|
| 1960 | 48,130 | 52.2 | 9.3 |
| 1961 | 49,601 | 50.8 | 9.3 |
| 1962 | 52,345 | 49.0 | 9.2 |
| 1963 | 53,400 | 48.0 | 8.9 |
| 1964 | 54,757 | 46.2 | 8.5 |
| 1965 | 50,620 | 42.8 | 7.4 |
| 1966 | 58,111 | 43.2 | 7.7 |
| 1967 | 71,417 | 45.4 | 8.8 |
| 1968 | 81,926 | 46.0 | 9.4 |
| 1969 | 82,497 | 44.9 | 8.7 |
| 1970 | 81,692 | 41.8 | 8.1 |
| 1971 | 78,872 | 37.5 | 7.3 |
| 1972 | 79,174 | 34.3 | 6.7 |
| 1973 | 76,681 | 31.2 | 5.8 |
| 1974 | 79,347 | 29.5 | 5.5 |
| 1975 | 86,509 | 26.0 | 5.5 |
| 1976 | 89,619 | 24.1 | 5.2 |
| TQ* | 22,269 | 23.2 | 4.8 |
| 1977 | 97,241 | 23.8 | 4.9 |
| 1978 | 104,495 | 22.8 | 4.7 |
| 1979 | 116,342 | 23.1 | 4.6 |
| 1980 | 133,995 | 22.7 | 4.9 |
| 1981 | 157,513 | 23.2 | 5.1 |

States still spends more on defense than any other country. Indeed, U.S. military spending as a percentage of total world spending on defense increased from 27.4 percent in 1987 to 32.1 percent in 1995 (U.S. Census Bureau 1999).

The important question is whether what we are spending is the right amount. And that depends on what we wish to accomplish. This is the second question mentioned by Korb. One way to get at it is to look at the American military force structure. Table 3.2 presents military force trends from the Clinton administration's FY 2001 budget proposal. One can see from this table that the military has shrunk. Active duty military personnel was to shrink by about 700,000 people from the 1990 level, a decrease of almost 34 percent. The Reagan administration plan for a 600-ship navy has been long discarded, with the target number of ships projected to be 306.

The question behind these numbers and criticisms about downsizing the military or a hollow military is, again, what the potential uses of the military are. Several major analyses of the U.S. military situation and potential threats were made in the 1990s. In 1991, the first Bush administration completed a base force assessment. In 1993, the Department of Defense undertook the "Bottom-Up Review." It called for spending at about 85 percent of Cold War

| | | | |
|---|---|---|---|
| 1982 | 185,309 | 24.8 | 5.7 |
| 1983 | 209,903 | 26.0 | 6.1 |
| 1984 | 227,413 | 26.7 | 5.9 |
| 1985 | 252,748 | 26.7 | 6.1 |
| 1986 | 273,375 | 27.6 | 6.2 |
| 1987 | 281,999 | 28.1 | 6.1 |
| 1988 | 290,361 | 27.3 | 5.8 |
| 1989 | 303,559 | 26.5 | 5.6 |
| 1990 | 299,331 | 23.9 | 5.2 |
| 1991 | 273,292 | 20.6 | 4.6 |
| 1992 | 298,350 | 21.8 | 4.8 |
| 1993 | 291,086 | 20.7 | 4.4 |
| 1994 | 281,642 | 19.3 | 4.1 |
| 1995 | 272,066 | 17.9 | 3.7 |
| 1996 | 265,753 | 17.0 | 3.5 |
| 1997 | 270,505 | 16.9 | 3.3 |
| 1998 | 268,456 | 16.2 | 3.1 |
| 1999 | 274,873 | 16.1 | 3.0 |
| 2000 (est.) | 290,636 | 16.2 | 3.0 |
| 2001 (est.) | 291,202 | 15.9 | 2.9 |
| 2002 (est.) | 298,390 | 15.7 | 2.8 |
| 2003 (est.) | 307,363 | 15.7 | 2.8 |
| 2004 (est.) | 316,517 | 15.5 | 2.8 |
| 2005 (est.) | 330,742 | 15.6 | 2.7 |

*Source:* Office of Management and Budget (2000).

*Note:* *TQ = transitional quarter when beginning of federal fiscal year moved from July 1 to October 1.

levels and discussed the possibility that the United States might have to fight two regional wars simultaneously. The Clinton budget, critics suggested, was not sufficient to meet that goal. Nor did all agree that the world was still as dangerous as the report indicated (see Center for Strategic and Budgetary Assessmen n.d.; Isenberg 1994). A third report, the Commission on Roles and Missions of the Armed Forces, came out in 1995.

In 1996, Congress included in the Defense Authorization Act a provision calling for an outside review of strategic issues, known as the **Quadrennial Defense Review** (**QDR**). The QDR is supposed to be conducted at the beginning of each new administration. Thus, the first one appeared in 1997 and the next one was due in 2001. A National Defense Panel, made up of outside experts, is to assist in making the QDR as well as its own recommendations. In addition, a Task Force on Defense Reform was created to deal with management issues. We shall look at the 1997 QDR.[32]

Looking at the world from 1997 to 2015, the report first identifies a variety of regional threats: Iran and Iraq, the possibility of a Middle Eastern War, the Korean peninsula. Another set of issues involves what the report calls "failed states," including the former Yugoslavia and African nations. A second problem is the spread of biological, chemical, and nuclear weapons to rogue states and South

Table 3.2

**Military Force Trends**

|  | 1990 | 2001 | QDR* Target |
|---|---|---|---|
| Army | | | |
| Divisions (active/ | | | |
| National Guard) | 18/20 | 10/8 | 10/8 |
| Air Force | | | |
| Fighter wings | | | |
| (active/reserve) | 24/12 | 12+/7+ | 12+/8 |
| Navy | | | |
| Aircraft carriers | | | |
| (active/reserve) | 15/1 | 12/0 | 11/1 |
| Air wings | | | |
| (active/reserve) | 13/2 | 10/1 | 10/1 |
| Total battle force ships | 546 | 316 | 306 |
| Marine Corps | | | |
| Divisions (active/reserve) | 3/1 | 3/1 | 3/1 |
| Wings (active/reserve) | 3/1 | 3/1 | 3/1 |
| Strategic Nuclear Forces | | | |
| Intercontinental ballistic | | | |
| missiles/warheads | 1,000/2,450 | 550/2,000 | 500/500 |
| Ballistic missile | | | |
| submarines | 31 | not over 18 | 14 |
| Sea-launched ballistic | | | |
| missiles/warheads | 568/4,864 | 432/3,456 | 336/not over 1,750 |
| Military personnel | | | |
| Active | 2,069,000 | 1,381,600 | 1,367,600 |
| Selected reserve | 1,128,000 | 865,700 | 837,200 |

*Source:* Office of Management and Budget (2000).
*Note:* *QDR = Quadrenniel Defense Review.

Asian countries (India and Pakistan). Third, the report discusses the threat from terrorist organizations, the international drug trade, and organized crime. The fourth threat is from the spread of nuclear weapons and delivery technology that might menace the United States itself. The report notes that the United States is likely to remain the world's sole superpower until at least 2015 but after that might be challenged, say by Russia or China (Department of Defense 1997).

The report then articulates what it calls a "national security strategy of engagement":

> A strategy of engagement presumes the United States will continue to exercise strong leadership in the international community, using all dimensions of its influence to shape the international security environment. This is particularly important to ensuring peace and stability in regions where the United States has vital or important interests and to broadening the community of free-market democracies. Strengthening and adapting alliances and coalitions that serve to protect shared interests and values are the most effective ways to accomplish these ends. (Department of Defense 1997)

Such a strategy requires a strong defense capability and the selective use of force. Force should be used to protect American national interests, and the report lists what those interests are. For humanitarian tragedies, the report argues that military force is not the best way to deal with the situation. If force is used, then a careful analysis perhaps should be used along the lines suggested by Haass (1997a, 1999a, 1999b). The report then goes into detail as to how the Department of Defense can shape the international environment in a manner favorable to the United States. The report, as the Bottom-Up Review did, argues that the United States should be able to fight two regional wars at the same time. The report anticipated that the defense budget would remain at the $250 billion in constant dollars during the time period under consideration.[33] Procurement of military technology and development of new technology was underfunded, according to the report. Table 3.2 shows the military force goals of the QDR.

As with the Bottom-Up Review, the QDR has been criticized. The easy criticism is that the stated goals do not match the resources. The Army, in particular, makes use of the Reserves and in 2000 considered expanding to the National Guard (Myers 2000b). While the armed forces have succeeded in meeting their recruiting targets for active duty service, the targets for reserve recruiting have been missed, possibly because of the increased use of American troops for humanitarian rescue and peacekeeping missions (Myers 2000c).

Isenberg (1998) argues that the QDR is yet another assertion of the status quo. More particularly, Isenberg writes that the QDR assumes a much more hostile environment than is the case and therefore calls for a larger military and defense budget than necessary. For example, Isenberg cites a report of the National Defense University's Institute for National Strategic Studies that the likelihood of having to fight two regional wars simultaneously is decreasing. Isenberg also discounts the possibility that China or Russia, especially Russia, will emerge as a new challenger to the United States.

Isenberg's study, published by the libertarian Cato Institute, is an attack on our defense posture from the right. The left also has attacked U.S. defense policies. Robert Dreyfuss (2000), writing in *Mother Jones*, argues that the threat to the United States from terrorism is highly overstated, yet we are spending about $11 billion on counterterrorism activities. He argues that the State Department and the FBI use worst-case scenarios to depict a possible threat. In a sense, this is what Isenberg is saying about the QDR and its predecessors. Dreyfuss contends that weapons of mass destruction are much more difficult to obtain and use than is commonly thought.

Vickers and Kosiak (1997), in an assessment of the QDR for the Center for Strategic and Budgetary Analysis, found the report to be unimaginative and outdated. They suggested that there were trends in technology that could change the course of war and defense in ways not envisioned by the QDR.

There are some who have argued that the defense budget ought be cut, in line with the decline in threats to the United States. Korb, a former Reagan administration defense official, argues that the United States can meet its needs as a great power with a smaller military and budget (Korb n.d.).

Korb's (and others') assertions that the United States faces a much diminished threat was captured by the tragedy of the Russian nuclear submarine *Kursk* in the summer of 2000. Perhaps from an accident or explosions, the submarine sank to the bottom of the Barents Sea, where all died. The Russians, in the aftermath of the end of the Cold War and the economic distress hurting the country, has been unable to maintain its previous strong military. The Russian defense budget in 2000 was $5 billion compared to about $290 billion for the United States in the same year (Hoagland 2000). In 2001, President George W. Bush ordered Secretary of Defense Donald Rumsfeld to undertake a review of U.S. capabilities and future needs before the defense budget is increased (Myers and Dao 2001).

## Case Study: Missile Defense

In a sense, the age of missiles began when the first rocks and spears were thrown. It enabled warfare from a distance. More contemporaneously, the end of World War II saw the beginning of the missile age. Nazi Germany, near defeat, launched the V-1 rocket and had plans for developing intercontinental ballistic missiles (Baucom, n.d.). Both the Soviet Union and the United States developed a ballistic missile capability in the 1950s on land and in submarines. The Eisenhower administration relied on the United States's nuclear capability (the Air Force was the third leg of the American strategic triad) as a relatively cheap way to deter attack from the Soviet Union. Robert McNamara, secretary of defense during the Kennedy/Johnson years, developed the strategic doctrine of **mutual assured destruction (MAD)**. The basis for this doctrine was that both the United States and the Soviet Union had sufficient nuclear forces to survive an attack and then inflict unacceptable losses on the adversary. Knowing that neither side could win a nuclear war would deter either side from using its nuclear strength. This deterrent seemed to have worked reasonably well.

But there were, and are, at least two grounds for considering defense against ballistic missiles. One way to reduce the threat would be to reduce the number of such missiles, perhaps to zero. Thus the United States and the Soviet Union engaged in a number of treaty negotiations to reduce both countries' nuclear capacities. The Nixon/Ford/Carter administrations engaged in such negotiations under the label of **Strategic Arms Limitation Talks (SALT)**. The Reagan administration substituted the **Strategic Arms Reductions Treaty (START)**, with a START I treaty that has gone into effect. START II has been agreed to but not ratified. START III negotiations are in the works.

In the absence of complete reductions and in the presence of the proliferation of missile technology to other countries, the notion of missile defense has some logic to it. First, MAD can be criticized as essentially holding populations hostage. What if a madman takes control over a rogue nation? The other problem is that there is no defense against ballistic missiles. The United States is thus defenseless and can be blackmailed by some rogue nation.

In 1972, the United States and the Soviet Union approved the **Anti-Ballistic Missile (ABM) Treaty**. It resticted testing and development of ballistic missile defense technology and limited the United States and the Soviet Union to one ballistic missile defense installation, either a missile base or a city. The Soviet Union constructed an interceptor system around Moscow. The United States tried two systems, the Sentinel system to protect a city and the Safeguard system to protect a missile base. Both systems were eventually abandoned as too costly and because of technological problems (Fitzgerald 2000; Kitfield 2000).

These were some of the considerations that animated President Reagan to announce the **Strategic Defense Initiative (SDI)**. His vision, dubbed by his critics as "Star Wars" after the hugely popular science fiction movie series, would create both a land- and spaced-based umbrella that would protect the United States. SDI would have multiple capabilities for destroying missiles, just after launch, during space flight, and during reentry. A think tank headed by former Lt. Gen. Dan Graham, who had persuaded Ronald Reagan in 1980 about the importance of strategic defense, was formed to advocate the development of missile defense technologies (Underwood 2000). The think tank included the eminent, though very controversial, physicist Edward S. Teller. Teller, considered the "father" of the hydrogen bomb, is a long-time advocate of strategic defense (Fitzgerald 2000). Teller pushed such technologies as the X-ray laser and brilliant pebbles. The Strategic Defense Initiative Organization was created within the Defense Department to develop such systems. Congress, controlled by Democrats, funded SDI technologies at a much lower rate than the administration requested (see O'Hanlon 1999 for a discussion of missile defense technologies).

The first Bush administration undertook a review of strategic missile defense. The 1989 report noted that the threat of a massive attack from the Soviet Union had greatly diminished, but the threat of short-range, theater missile attacks would become more important. The program was redirected toward this type of threat (Baucom n.d.).

Missile defense became important, though not critical, during the Persian Gulf War. As the United States and its allies were preparing to repel Iraq's invasion of Kuwait, and during the war, Iraq launched a number of Scud missiles against Saudi Arabia and Israel. The Scud was a Soviet missile (Iraq bought its weapons from the Soviet Union and used Soviet military strategy), but not a particularly accurate one. One of the purposes for firing Scuds at Israel, who, though supporting the U.S. effort, was not participating, was to incite some type of Israeli reaction to the missile attacks that would break the unity of the Arab states aligned against Iraq. To forestall Israeli entry into the war, the United States sent Patriot missile batteries, tactical or theater anti-missile missiles, to both countries.

The Patriot missiles were greeted with great acclaim, and President Bush, military officials, and the media described the Patriots' defense very favorably. The claims were that the Patriots were successful 50 (Israel) to 80 (Saudi Arabia) percent of the time (Hildreth 1992). In congressional testimony in 1992, Steven A. Hildreth of the Congressional Research Service stated that there was insufficient evidence to substantiate the claims made for the Patriot missile. Analysis by a Massachusetts Institute of Technology arms expert, Theodore Postol, stated that the Patriot missile had in fact not destroyed any Scud missiles (Broad 2000). Nevertheless, Patriot missiles have become the most developed of the antimissile technologies (O'Hanlon 1999).

The Clinton administration drastically reduced funding for strategic defense. The 1993 Bottom-Up Review put priority on theater missile defense (TMD), and SDIO was transformed into the Ballistic Missile Defense Organization.

In 1994, the Contract with America, the House Republican platform, called for the development of missile defense. The Contract stated:

> The Defense Department is directed to (1) develop for deployment at the earliest pos-
> sible date a cost-effective, operational antiballistic missile defense system to protect
> the United States against ballistic missile threats (e.g., accidental or unauthorized
> launches or Third World attacks); (2) implement as quickly as possible advanced the-
> ater missile defense systems: and (3) report to Congress within sixty days of enact-
> ment with a plan for both missile defense systems. (Gillespie and Schellhas 1994)

In 1996, under congressional prodding, the administration agreed to what became known as the "three-plus-three program" (Baucom, n.d.; Fitzgerald 2000). The plan was to work on the development of a theater missile defense system by 1999 and then, if testing proved the feasibility of the system, it would be deployed in three years.

One of the key considerations in deciding whether to develop and deploy such a system is the extent to which threats from other countries appeared. In 1995, a national intelligence estimate suggested that it would be at least fif-teen years before a threat to the U.S. mainland would appear. This did not appeal to congressional critics of the Clinton administration, and Congress created a bipartisan commission to assess potential missile threats.

Known as the **Rumsfeld Commission**, after the commission's head, Donald Rumsfeld, former congressman and Secretary of Defense in the Ford and second Bush administrations, the report gave a much more chilling assess-ment of the threat to the United States than the 1995 CIA national intelligence estimate. The Commission, appointed by congressional leaders of both par-ties, concluded that:

> Concerted efforts by a number of overtly or potentially hostile nations to acquire
> ballistic missiles with biological or nuclear payloads pose a growing threat to the
> United States, its deployed forces and its friends and allies. These newer, develop-
> ing threats in North Korea, Iran and Iraq are in addition to those still posed by the
> existing ballistic missile arsenals of Russia and China, nations with which we are
> not now in conflict but which remain in uncertain transitions. The newer ballistic
> missile-equipped nations' capabilities will not match those of U.S. systems for ac-
> curacy or reliability. However, they would be able to inflict major destruction on the

U.S. within about five years of a decision to acquire such a capability (10 years in the case of Iraq). During several of those years, the U.S. might not be aware that such a decision had been made. (Commission to Assess the Ballistic Missile Threat to the United States 1998).

The commission argued that though the threat from Russia had changed, it had not disappeared. It discussed the possibility of accidental or unauthorized launches and the selling of missile technology to other countries. The People's Republic of China, the commission stated, is modernizing its capacity and also sells missile technology (see also Roberts et al. 2000). The commission pointed to the Taiwan Straits crisis of 1995–96 when the PRC tested missiles that flew over the contested island as a possible flashpoint.

The commission was also concerned about other countries. Many of those were developing missiles based on Scud technology. The commission pointed to developments in North Korea and Iran, both of whom were devoting considerable resources to expanding their missile capability. Iraq, India, and Pakistan were also mentioned. In August 1998, North Korea tested a sophisticated ballistic missile. While the test failed, it indicated North Korea's focus on developing missile technology and supported the commission report (Fitzgerald 2000; O'Hanlon 1999). In July 1999, President Clinton signed the National Missile Defense Act, which committed the United States to finding a defense against a missile attack (Spencer and Dougherty 2000).

Deployment of a **theater missile defense** (**TMD**) system in Alaska based on interceptor missiles would be aimed at North Korea (and, some suspected, the PRC). Tests of components of the system have largely been failures (Kitfield 2000; Sciolino 2000). On September 1, 2000, President Clinton deferred the decision on deployment to the next administration. If a subsequent administration decided to deploy such a system, the earliest the first stages of such a system could be in place would be 2006 (Suro 2000). President George W. Bush indicated during the 2000 presidential campaign and after his inauguration that a missile shield was a top priority.

### Controversy over Missile Defense

Development and plans for missile defense, whether theater or national, have been plagued by controversy from all sides of the political spectrum. The Clinton plan that was ultimately postponed was criticized for a number of reasons. First, the plan was expensive. The Congressional Budget Office estimated that the first phase of the limited plan would cost about $30 billion, about $4 billion more than the administration estimate. The full-blown plan would cost in excess of $49 billion. Indeed the cost problems have been an issue since the beginning of the missile defense debate in the 1960s.

A second issue is whether the Clinton plan or any other plan would violate the provisions of the 1972 ABM treaty. Supporters of missile defense, such as High Frontier, the Heritage Institute, and the Cato Institute, are willing to abrogate the treaty. Russia has resisted such efforts even to bend the treaty to accommodate new testing (see the article in *Foreign Affairs* by Russia's foreign minister, Ivanov 2000). Russian President Vladimir Putin has asserted that Russia might reject the START II agreement, which Russia has ratified, if a missile defense is deployed (Congressional Budget Office 2000). China, too, has been hostile to possible deployment of missile defense, charging that the proposed plan was aimed at it rather than North Korea. It has threatened to enhance its missile capability if the United States takes this step (Shuster 2000; Smith 2000). Even America's European allies expressed concern about missile defense, fearing that it might lead the United States to make decisions that would leave Europe in a precarious position (Perlez 2000).

A third issue is how real the threats to U.S. security interests are. The Rumsfeld commission suggested that the threats are serious and closer than realized. Others have suggested that the potential of countries such as Iran, Iraq, and North Korea to develop missile capable of threatening the United States is much less (see Sciolino and Myers 2000).

A fourth issue has to do with feasibility, in many directions (see, e.g., O'Hanlon 1999). Some have argued that the Clinton plan would not work. A report by a DOD-appointed panel, the Welch report, explored the technical difficulties with the Clinton administration plan (see Suro and Ricks 2000). Others have asserted that a sea-based system would be the appropriate direction to start such a system (Spencer and Dougherty 2000).

The overall feasibility issue is whether a defensive shield can ever be successfully mounted. Enemy countries can increase the number of missiles, as China may do. Or they can use decoys. Or the complicated systems may not work as anticipated. Or enemies may use other means to deliver weapons of mass destruction. *Star Wars*, the movie, shows a highly developed technological capability. But it is only a movie. On the other hand, for millennia it was said that man would never fly.[34]

## Conclusion

> No other nation on earth has the power we possess. More important, no other nation on earth has the trust power that we possess. We are obligated to lead. If the free world is to harvest the hope and fulfill the promise that our great victory in the Cold War has offered us, America must shoulder the responsibility of its power. The last best hope of earth has no other choice. We must lead. (Powell 1992/1993, p. 33)

> These, then, are the likely purposes of American military power: defense, insurance, the maintenance of world order, and the maintenance of coalitions. (Cohen 1994, p. 27)

The United States finds itself in a very fortunate situation. While it is not unchallenged, the United States remains the world's remaining superpower. The question that faces the country and its leaders are what to do with that power. The Cold War provided a framework for U.S. policy that lasted unchallenged until the Vietnam War. Even then, while there was a partisan split over how to face the Soviet Union and others, the goal of constraining the Soviet Union was pretty well accepted. With the disappearance of the Soviet Union, the major threat to U.S. national security has evaporated.

As the dominant power, the United States faces an identity crisis. What do we want a world to look like? How can we shape a world that best suits our needs and interests? Some goals are easy to accept. Most people would accept the spread of democracy to other countries.[35] Fostering economic growth in developing countries and integrating them into a seamless world economy is a goal that the Clinton administration sought.

The United States has also, especially in the latter half of the 1990s, sought to bring peace to troubled areas, sometimes through diplomacy, sometimes through the use of military force. The United States has been a major player in trying to end the Arab-Israeli conflict. The United States has also interposed itself into the Northern Ireland peace process. The United States has taken military action in Bosnia and Kosovo, where peacekeeping troops remain, and in Haiti and Somalia. But other areas of strife have been neglected: much of Africa, especially Rwanda and East Timor, where other countries intervened. The United States, at least through 2000, was continuing a low-level air war over Iraq.

One controversy that has marked U.S. foreign and defense policy is whether to intervene militarily. Should we employ our military only when it serves our national interest, or should other goals, such as humanitarian factors, play a role? No solid conceptual framework exists that helps us decide what to do, when to do it, and how. A number of people, such as Richard Haass, have attempted an approach, really a series of questions that our leaders should ask ourselves. Haass's (1997a) memorable phrase is that the United States is a "reluctant sheriff," helping to maintain the peace but not forcing it on anyone. A sheriff does not try to dominate but sets up temporary posses to deal with problems.

One way that the United States can reinforce its role is in the foreign assistance category. We spend proportionately less than other countries on foreign assistance. Related to this is the United States's reluctance to pay its dues to the United Nations.

Another area that may need some reconsideration is the use of economic sanctions. As mentioned during the first part of this chapter, we have made increasing use of this tool. While there have been some successes—the sanctions against South Africa for its policy of racial segregation being perhaps the most notable (though its impact was limited)—there have also been important failures. Cuba is perhaps the best example. The United States would like Castro and the economy he has erected to be replaced; it appears that only illness or death will produce that result. Economic sanctions are used to express U.S. disapproval of a country's policies, but a realistic appraisal suggests that this issue ought to be revisited.

Another important aspect of foreign and defense policy is how our leaders perceive public opinion. For example, the war in Kosovo was fought almost entirely in the air so as to minimize American casualties. The feeling behind this decision was that the American people would not stand for casualties in areas that do not threaten American national interests. This is, presumably, one of the lessons of the American intervention in Somalia. It also partly explains the unwillingness to intervene during the genocide in Rwanda. Are leaders reading American public opinion correctly?

Consider the following quote:

> Americans and their leaders disagree on foreign policy. Polls show that 80 percent of Americans support the Comprehensive Test Ban Treaty (CTBT), but the Senate overwhelmingly rejected it. Two-thirds of Americans want to pay their country's back dues to the United Nations, but Congress took three years to appropriate the money and then demanded that the UN write off more than $400 million in bad debt. Nearly half of all Americans supported using ground troops in Kosovo, but the Clinton administration resisted admitting that it was even considering the options. (Lindsay 2000)

This view of public opinion is supported by others. Steven Kull (1995–1996) argues that the public does not want the United States to be a policeman but also does not want the United States to disengage from world affairs. Indeed, he argues that America should be more supportive of the United Nations, including UN peacekeeping (Hirsh 1999). This would keep the United States from bearing a disproportionate responsibility, but still being an active, important participant in the world arena. James Burk (1999), looking at Lebanon and Somalia, two interventions that led to American casualties, argues that the public does support U.S. peacekeeping operations even if it might result in some American casualties (remember that one motivation behind the air war in Kosovo was to prevent casualties).

Lindsay (2000) argues that our leaders are not necessarily misreading public opinion, that is, thinking the public believes differently than what it does. Rather, politicians do not think that many Americans are very interested in foreign policy. It is an issue of intensity. Thus, the 2000 presidential elections featured debates over Social Security, health care issues (patients' bill of rights, prescription drug benefit for Medicare), and education, but very little, apart from military readiness, about foreign policy.

Lindsay's argument is supported by the 1992 presidential elections. In the aftermath of the successful conclusion of the Persian Gulf War in 1991, President George Bush's approval ratings hovered at over 90 percent, about the highest ever recorded. Eighteen months later, he was defeated by a candidate who had little experience with foreign policy and whose campaign motto was "It's the economy, stupid!"

The result is what Lindsay calls "apathetic internationalism" (Lindsay 2000, p. 4). Lindsay writes that such apathy among the public has three important implications. The first is that politicians neglect the area. This is, Lindsay continues, especially true in Congress (see also Greenberger 1995–1996). The second implication is that because many are not interested in foreign policy, politicians listen to the few who have intense preferences. The final implication Lindsay discusses is that public apathy makes it harder for presidents to lead. Presidents, as we saw earlier, have the primary position in conducting American foreign policy. Congress also has a role and has played that role from time to time (e.g., during the Vietnam War or when Republican Senator Richard Lugar challenged the Reagan administration's perspective on the 1986 elections in the Philippines). But in the absence of the Cold War and a common, agreed-upon enemy, Congress is more willing to challenge the president. The refusal of the House to support the air war in Kosovo is a good example of this (though the impeachment process and the dislike of congressional Republicans for President Clinton also contributed to it).

In sum, America's leaders and policy thinkers need to create some kind of framework for addressing America's role in the post–Cold War period. The United States also needs to devote sufficient resources to the effort. This includes foreign aid, but also an appropriate level of defense and intelligence resources (Haass 1997a). If we are to be the "reluctant sheriff," then a dialogue among the leaders and thinkers and with the American people is imperative.

---

## Key Concepts

Anti-Ballistic Missile (ABM) Treaty

Camp David Accords

"The Clash of Civilizations?"

CNN effect

Dayton Accords

defense build-down

diplomacy

economic relations

economism

hard power

hegemony

humanitarianism

intermestic policy

intifada

isolationism

military power

Munich analogy

mutual assured destruction (MAD)

national security

National Security Council Directive 68

new world order

North Atlantic Treaty Organization (NATO)

Persian Gulf War

Quadrennial Defense Review (QDR)

real world order

realism

Rumsfeld Commission

security of allies

soft power

Strategic Arms Limitation Talks (SALT)

Strategic Arms Reductions Treaty (START)

Strategic Defense Initiative (SDI)

support U.S. economic interests

theater missile defense (TMD)

Vietnam analogy

Wilsonianism

zone of disorder

zone of order

---

## Reflections

1. One of the pressing issues for the United States is whether to take some action to stop the slaughter of human life or to provide assistance to those in great need. The United States faces, in other words, an identity crisis. What should be our role in the world? Where do you stand on this issue? Consider our experience in Haiti, the Balkans (Bosnia and Kosovo), Somalia, and Rwanda. Do you think we took the right actions? What do you think we should have done instead? The Bush administration seems to be moving away from a humanitarian focus. Do you agree or disagree with this trend? Why?

2. One of the pillars of the Clinton administration's foreign policy is increasing economic ties around the world, the globalization that was described in the last chapter. One premise was that economic ties and economic development would lead to political change, particularly in countries such as the PRC. Do you think this premise is correct? Should the Bush administration continue this effort?

3. As the defense case study indicates, President Reagan and others pushed for a missile defense shield, known as the Strategic Defense Initiative or Star Wars. The Clinton administration made a half-hearted effort to develop a much more limited shield, directed at rogue nations or nations of concern such as North Korea, Iran, Iraq, and perhaps the People's Republic of China. The Bush administration intends to develop such as missile defense, despite skeptics who do not think it could ever work or allies such as England and France who do not want to see the United States do it alone. Do you think we should develop a missile defense? Do those nations of concern pose a legitimate threat? Skeptics are not always right. Where do you stand?

## Notes

1. For a discussion of the philosophical basis for American foreign policy from the founders to the present day, see Hendrickson 1992. Solomon (1999) also provides a brief discussion of isolationism and internationalism in American foreign policy.

2. For a discussion of the end of the Cold War, see Beschloss and Talbott 1993 and Gaddis 1992.

3. John Ruggie (1994) argues that the events beginning in 1991 were really the third try by the United States for a "world order."

4. The Iran-Contra scandal that broke out in 1986 had at least part of its origin from Iran, which desperately needed military arms in its battle with Iraq.

5. It was a measure of the depths of the crisis that Saudi Arabia allowed U.S. troops to be stationed on its soil. While Saudi Arabia depended on U.S. support and bought U.S. military equipment, both it and other Arab countries were extremely reluctant to station foreign troops.

6. The Iraqi armed forces were supplied by the Soviet Union and employed Soviet military strategy.

7. The cease-fire left much of Iraq's military capability intact, more than had been thought in 1991. As a result, Iraq had sufficient forces to move troops near the Kuwaiti border in the fall of 1994, resulting in a near crisis and the sending of thousands of U.S. troops to Kuwait. See Gordon and Trainor (1994).

8. Similar lessons can be drawn from the French withdrawal from Vietnam in 1954 and Algeria in 1959, the Soviet withdrawal from Afghanistan in 1988, and even the British withdrawal from colonial America. None of these countries was defeated, but they suffered significant losses and ended the conflicts (Lipsitz 1986).

9. The author very clearly remembers turning on the television in January 1991, flipping through the channels, and coming across the opening ceremonies of the National Hockey League All-Star Game. The national anthem was played and then the crowd erupted for what seemed like hours in a chant of "USA! USA!" There was opposition to the war, but it was clearly muted, and Americans were primed for a victory.

10. While Arab countries were historically opposed to Israel's presence, some said publicly that Israel had the right to defend itself, most prominently Syrian President Assad, a bitter enemy of Iraq's Hussein.

11. There is some controversy over how well the Patriot missiles worked. Studies after the war indicated the Patriot missiles had very limited effectiveness. What was important was not the actual effectiveness but the symbolic meaning of the protection.

12. In 1978, Egypt and Israel signed the Camp David Accords, negotiated by President Carter, effectively ending war between the two countries.

13. David Hendrickson (1992) argues that the Bush administration did have a foreign policy vision, though not well articulated, embodied in the Persian Gulf War. This vision was that the values of "order, freedom and security" (p. 55) were still important. Aggression anyplace ultimately threatened the United States. However, meeting aggression would be done, to the extent possible, through collective security, such as the U.S.-led alliance against Iraq. Joseph Nye (1992), on the other hand, argues that the Bush administration combined elements of different visions in an incoherent manner. In Nye's words (p. 84): "The problem for the Bush administration was that it thought and acted like Nixon, but borrowed the rhetoric of [Woodrow] Wilson and [Jimmy] Carter."

14. For a discussion of the 1992 presidential elections and foreign policy, see Sorenson (1992) and Yankelovich (1992).

15. James Kurth (1994) presents a conservative view, arguing that the real conflict is within the United States between Western civilization and the challenges of the multicultural and feminist movements. Richard Rubenstein and Jarle Crocker (1994) contend that the clashes of civilization that Huntington describes are caused by inequalities, and they suggest that only by lessening those inequalities can the clashes be avoided.

16. On why democracies do not fight other democracies, see Dixon (1994). Edward D. Mansfield and Jack Snyder (1995) argue, on the other hand, that there is a high likelihood that countries making the transition to democracy will engage in war with democratic states.

17. Clarke's list includes the following:

> The Soviet Union really did try to blockade Berlin and draw Greece behind the Iron Curtain; children really did hide under their desks during the Cuban missile crisis; Soviet tanks really did roll into Prague, Budapest, and Kabul; on Soviet orders, refugees really were shot and allowed to bleed to death under the Berlin Wall; dictatorships in Cuba, Ethiopia, Angola, and Mozambique really did rise on the backs of Soviet-equipped and -trained security services; state sponsors of anti-American ter-

rorism really were feted in Moscow; the Soviet Union really did bankroll the Communist parties of Western Europe and Latin America. None of this was a dream. To combat all this, the West really did live on the nuclear high wire. And as for conventional war during the Cold War, the history books burgeon with the records of major conflagrations: Vietnam, Biafra, Chad, the Iran-Iraq War, successive Arab-Israel wars, the India-Pakistan war, Nicaragua, El Salvador, the Indonesian confrontation, the Chinese annexation of Tibet, the ethnic massacres in Sri Lanka, the Turkish invasion of Cyprus. (Clarke 1993, p. 58)

Nye (1992) agrees with Clarke's list, but argues that the wars were brief, some were aborted, and ethnic conflicts were kept under control.

18. Richard Gardner (2000) argues that if the United States is to have a successful foreign policy, it is going to have to devote more than 1 percent of its budget on foreign affairs.

19. U.S. intervention was limited. For example, the United States took no action during revolts against communist rule in Eastern Europe.

20. Not everyone, obviously, agreed with that statement, particularly regarding Vietnam and some of the covert activities of the Reagan administration.

21. The Serbs were politically associated with communists and were the ethnic group that dominated during Yugoslavia's communist years. The Croats allied with Nazi Germany.

22. For a discussion of the media's role in foreign policy crises, see Hoge 1994.

23. These options included air strikes and lifting of the arms embargo. See Gordon 1992.

24. For a discussion of the Bosnia situation and the continuation of American forces there, see Ryan 1998 and Smith 1998. For a discussion of how to get a permanent settlement and peace, see Boyd 1998.

25. For a history of the Balkans, see Hagen (1999).

26. National sovereignty, while it has certainly not died, has faded in the face of globalization, communications technology (i.e., the Internet), environmental concerns, and war crimes trials. For discussion of these factors, see *National Journal*, November 20, 1999.

27. For a discussion of the negotiations leading to the end of the war, see Elliott 1999.

28. Unofficial talks between Israel and Jordan (as well as other Arab nations) have gone on for years (Sciolino 1994a).

29. Some have argued that race also plays a role. Because Rwanda and other African nations are mostly black, Americans are concerned about what goes on there, but certainly not sufficiently concerned to risk American lives. On the other hand, the Black Caucus in Congress pushed for U.S. action in Haiti, also predominantly black. See Alter (1994).

30. The extent of the build-down and the need for increasing defense expenditures became one of the issues of the 2000 presidential campaign. Republican presidential candidate Texas governor George W. Bush charged that the military lacked the readiness that it needed. His vice presidential running mate, Dick Cheney, accused the Clinton administration essentially of starving the military. Cheney was forced to admit, however, that the build-down began while he was secretary of defense in the Bush administration.

31. For a thorough discussion of defense issues in the post–Cold War period, see Cohen (1994).

32. Michael Vickers and Steven Kosiak (1997) provide a readable summary and critique of the QDR.

33. This was before the budget deficits turned into surpluses and before the budget increases during the Clinton administration and the debate during the 2000 election about the readiness of the military.

34. I would like to thank my colleague, Dennis Hickey, for pointing this out to me.

35. There are some exceptions, largely in Muslim majority states, such as Turkey, Egypt, and Algeria. Algeria is probably the best case. In the mid-1990s, it became clear that democratic elections would have brought militant Muslims to power, and the fear was that they would have undermined democracy. The Algerian military canceled the elections, using perhaps the guidance of the American military commander in South Vietnam, who commented that it was necessary to destroy a village to save it.

# 4 Poverty and Welfare: The Poor Ye Always Have With You?

*America's antipoverty policy is posed between a past that has been abandoned and a future that is still unformed. With the demise of AFDC, the decades-old federal guarantee of cash support for poor children is gone. Welfare has been cut back, time limits have been imposed, and states have been freed to impose a variety of restrictions on welfare receipt. For now, our economy is performing well and unemployment is at historic lows. But what will happen when unemployment rises (as it inevitably will) and suffering among the poor increases? How will the public and political leaders respond?* (Gilens 1999, p. 216)

*If previous history is any guide, the latest attempt at welfare reform will only spawn new attempts to change the system. The United States has moved from an individual interpretation of poverty to a structural interpretation and then back again. Welfare has evolved from a local to a state and then to a federal-state and federal-local function, and now it is devolving back to a state function. As long as there are poor people in this country (and there is no reason to expect that we can make poverty disappear), the United States will always have a difficult time determining what to do about them. We are torn between our desire to help the poor, out of a feeling of community with them, and our faith in individualism, capitalism, and hard work as the keys for people helping themselves. We are not sure whether the poor are worthy or unworthy of our assistance, and we have a great deal of difficulty determining the difference.* (Cammisa 1998, p. 137)

The issue of poverty and government's response to this issue, welfare, invokes many of the features of the policy process and the political system discussed in chapter 1. There is disagreement about the causes of poverty—the problem identification stage of the policy process—and therefore disagreement about appropriate solutions. There is disagreement over whether government should be involved in this area and, if so, *how* it should be involved (the government issue). Many welfare programs have shared fiscal and administrative responsibility between the federal government and the states, so federalism becomes a concern. Also, authority for welfare programs is split among a number of different agencies at the federal level and different committees in Congress, so fragmentation is a consideration. Because adoption of policy requires congressional and presidential assent, separation of powers is important. Incrementalism has been a key feature of poverty policy making. New programs and ideas have been added to old ones. But in 1996 significant changes to the nation's welfare system were made. Finally, welfare policy and poverty bring into sharp focus the issue of values. As we shall see, the most recent concern related to poverty and welfare has to do with family structure, the increase in out-of-wedlock births, and dependency. In short, many of the features that were examined in chapter 1 come into full play in poverty policy.

This chapter begins by addressing the question of what poverty is and what its causes are. A statistical profile of those experiencing poverty is then presented. Of particular interest is how the profile of poverty has changed over the past twenty years. A portion of the chapter explores how the United States has responded to the problem over the years. Much of the focus centers on fundamental changes in the nature of the poverty debate since 1969. Beginning in 1969, the heart of the debate shifted from the problem of poverty and what to do about it to welfare as the problem and, in some eyes, the cause of the poverty problem. By 1995, that perspective, welfare as a cause of poverty, dominated the policy agenda.

## Problem Identification

### Policy Goals

A major goal of welfare policy is, in its broadest sense, **security** (Stone 1997). It is an attempt to provide—temporarily or permanently—a minimal level of assistance to those deemed worthy. Included in the category of "worthy" are the elderly (permanent assistance) and the young (temporary assistance). Another term used for this policy area is **income security**; the federal government uses this category in its budget documents. If we employ this broader term, then Social Security would also be included, as we shall see below.

A second goal is to assist those capable of working to become fully supportive of themselves. Thus some programs provide cash and in-kind (noncash) assistance, while others provide job training and educational assistance. A related goal of welfare policy is the desire to discourage dependence on the part of those who should be self-supporting. The tug of war between these two major goals (security/assistance and fostering independence) has affected the makeup of welfare policy over the years, with first one and then the other dominating.

Francis Fox Piven and Richard Cloward (1971) have argued that there is in fact a much more important goal of welfare policy. They assert that the minimal level of assistance provided in the United States is designed not to help poor people, but to maintain the legitimacy and support for the political system. In the absence of aid, the poor, so their argument goes, would become politically activated and radical. Welfare policy creates a quiescence among the poor, and therefore the poor do not threaten the political system. There is something to this argument. The radicalism of the 1930s can be partly attributed to the depressed economic conditions. On the other hand, the poor have shown little political participation since then.

## Policy Solutions

Welfare policy solutions may be categorized into three types: rights, rules, and inducements. In this sense, **rights** are something to which one is entitled; they work closely with rules. One has a right to Social Security if one has made contributions. Similarly, one used to have a right to welfare assistance if one met eligibility requirements (see case study below). The **rules** state who is eligible for what kind of assistance under what conditions. For example, under current welfare laws, unmarried teenage mothers must live at home to receive assistance. A number of states have enacted **family caps**, stating that having additional children on welfare will not result in higher welfare benefits. Rules limit how much in assets or income a family can have and still be eligible for assistance. Once those eligibility rules are met, then one has a right to benefits: Social Security, medical care (Medicare or Medicaid), food stamps, or housing.

The other policy tool or solution, the major one, is **inducements**. Inducements can take two forms, positive or negative. One of the great debates in welfare policy is over what the inducement effects of public assistance are. The original welfare strategy, the punitive strategy, had a negative viewpoint: that public assistance promoted dependence. **Aid to Families with Dependent Children (AFDC)** was widely criticized for its negative effects: It encouraged recipients to stay on welfare and discouraged fathers from staying with their families. The debate over features of the negative income tax partly concerned how high the tax and benefit levels should be set. A high tax level (percentage of benefits decreased for every additional dollar of income earned) would discourage recipients from working. High benefit levels would have a similar effect. The 1988 welfare reform bill contained a provision allowing families to stay on Medicaid for a year after they have gone off AFDC and into the job force. Thus the heart of welfare policy surrounds the kinds of inducements contained in public-sector programs. As we shall see, in the 1990s, the issue of inducements formed the core of the debate over welfare reform.

## Defining Poverty

There are many ways of defining a poverty-stricken population. We could look in an absolute sense at the amenities, housing, and so on, of a group of

Table 4.1

**Number of People Below Poverty Level and Poverty Rate, 1960–1999**

|  | Poverty level (for family of four) | Number of people (in millions) | Poverty rate (% of general population) |
|---|---|---|---|
| 1960 | 3,022 | 39,851 | 22.2 |
| 1965 | 3,223 | 33,185 | 17.3 |
| 1970 | 3,968 | 25,420 | 12.6 |
| 1975 | 5,500 | 25,077 | 12.3 |
| 1980 | 8,414 | 29,272 | 13.0 |
| 1985 | 10,989 | 33,064 | 14.0 |
| 1990 | 13,359 | 33,585 | 13.5 |
| 1991 | 13,924 | 35,708 | 14.2 |
| 1992 | 14,335 | 38,014 | 14.8 |
| 1993 | 14,763 | 39,265 | 15.1 |
| 1994 | 15,141 | 38,059 | 14.5 |
| 1995 | 15,569 | 36,425 | 13.8 |
| 1996 | 16,036 | 36,529 | 13.7 |
| 1997 | 16,400 | 35,574 | 13.3 |
| 1998 | 16,660 | 34,476 | 12.7 |
| 1999 | 16,954 | 32,258 | 11.8 |

*Source:* U.S. Census Bureau (2000).

people. We could define poverty in a relative sense, say those at one-half the median income in the United States (which would imply by definition that there will always be poor people). We could compare those who are poor in America to those in other countries and see that, relatively speaking, the poor in America are not so badly off. We could look at how "poor" people in the United States live now with how they lived twenty years ago.

For this discussion, the federal government's definition of **poverty** will be used. Individuals or families are poor if their money income is below a certain level.[1] The poverty level is adjusted for the size of the family and for changes in prices each year. While there are problems with the poverty-line measure, it is generally recognized for policy purposes.[2]

For 1999, the poverty line for a family of three (a parent and two children) was $13,423; for a family of four (a parent with three children), the poverty line was $16,954 (Dalaker and Proctor 2000). Given this definition, there were over 32 million people living in poverty-stricken households in 1999. Table 4.1 shows the number of people living in poverty from 1960 to 1999.

## Who Are the Poor?

Table 4.2 presents a comparative profile of the poverty population at four times: 1978, 1986, 1992, and 1998. Several features stand out. First, the inci-

Table 4.2

**Profile of Persons and Families Below Poverty Line** (percentage)

|  | 1978 | 1986 | 1992 | 1998 |
|---|---|---|---|---|
| All persons | 14.6 | 13.6 | 14.8 | 12.7 |
| White persons | 8.7 | 11.0 | 11.9 | 10.5 |
| African-American persons | 30.6 | 31.3 | 33.4 | 26.1 |
| Hispanic-American persons | 21.6 | 27.3 | 29.6 | 25.6 |
| | | | | |
| Persons under 18 | 15.9 | 20.5 | 22.3 | 18.9 |
| Persons 65 and older | 15.7 | 12.4 | 12.9 | 10.5 |
| | | | | |
| All related children under 18 in families | 15.7 | 19.8 | 21.6 | 18.3 |
| White related children under 18 in families | 11.0 | 15.3 | 16.5 | 14.4 |
| African-American related children under 18 in families | 41.2 | 42.7 | 46.3 | 36.4 |
| Hispanic-American related children under 18 in families | 27.2 | 37.1 | 39.0 | 33.6 |
| | | | | |
| All families | 9.1 | 10.9 | 11.9 | 11.2 |
| All families with children | 12.8 | 16.3 | 18.0 | 15.1 |
| White families | 6.9 | 8.6 | 9.1 | 8.0 |
| African-American families | 27.5 | 28.0 | 31.1 | 23.4 |
| Hispanic-American families | 20.4 | 24.7 | 26.7 | 22.7 |
| | | | | |
| Married-couple families | 5.2 | 5.6 | 6.4 | 5.3 |
| Male householder/no female | 9.2 | 11.4 | 15.8 | 12.0 |
| Female householder/no male | 31.4 | 34.6 | 35.4 | 29.9 |

*Source:* U.S. Census Bureau (1999).

dence of poverty among the elderly (sixty-five and older) has dropped, while the incidence of poverty among children (18 and under) has increased. Consider the data from 1966: The poverty rate for children was 17.6 percent; the poverty rate for the elderly was 28.5 percent. As we shall see, the two major programs aimed at the elderly, Social Security and Medicare, are largely though not entirely responsible for this.

A second important observation has to do with the structure of the family and what has been called the **feminization of poverty**. Female-headed families, of whatever race, are more likely to experience poverty and for longer periods of time than male-headed or two-parent families (Rank 1994). Women as a group make less than men do, and unmarried teenage mothers tend to be at the lower end of the income scale. African-American children are more likely than whites to be in female-headed families. African-American mother-only families are likely to have more children and stay on welfare longer than white mother-only families (Rank 1994). Those with less education are more likely to be poor than those with higher education (Schwarz and Volgy 1992).

It should be noted that not all poor people receive government assistance. States set eligibility requirements (within federal guidelines) and, depending on the state, these levels are usually well below the federally defined poverty level. For example, the average monthly number of recipients receiving AFDC payments in 1996 was approximately 12.5 million people (U.S. Census Bureau 1999) compared to the approximately 36.5 million people with incomes under the poverty line (see Table 4.1). To put it another way, only about one-third of the people who are considered poor were receiving anything from the major federal cash assistance program. And, as we shall see below, what they received was not especially generous.

## Formulation, Adoption, and Implementation: Antipoverty Strategies

This section examines how the issue of poverty in the United States has been addressed over the years. In doing so, it is helpful to look at government policies in terms of **antipoverty strategies**. The notion of strategy suggests a perspective of what the problem of poverty is (the problem-identification stage). The concept of strategy is also useful because the different problem perspectives inherent in a strategy structure the rest of the policy process, as discussed in chapter 1.[3] At the end of this historical journey, it will become clear that poverty programs are a crazy quilt of much that came before. Elements of all the previous strategies were kept as another strategy was tried. This is incrementalism at its finest (or worst?). To further support this point, the Reagan administration policies had much in common with the first strategy and the welfare reform bill passed in 1996. Thus, if the first strategy is labeled the punitive strategy, policies in the 1980s and 1990s may appropriately be labeled "the return of the punitive strategy."

### Punitive Strategy: The Poor Laws

The first and oldest of public policies directed at the problem of poverty date to Elizabethan times and are exemplified by the Poor Laws of 1601.[4] The underlying assumptions of the Poor Laws were adopted with some modifications in the United States. The rationale of the policy was that poverty was the product of moral or character deficiencies in the individual. If people were poor, it was their own fault. This is an individual-level explanation for the causes of poverty. Given this identification of the problem, the appropriate solution was to try to dissuade people from the indolence (laziness) that kept them poor. To accomplish this, policies were designed to make it as difficult as possible to obtain public assistance, and then provide only a minimal amount of relief. This combination of rationale and solution justifies labeling the strategy the **punitive strategy**.

The features of the punitive strategy can be seen in later poverty policies. Public assistance was primarily a local affair. This meant that state and local governments were responsible for the indigent, with the federal government having little role. The important function that states have in modern welfare policies is thus historically based. Because assistance was a state and local responsibility, residence requirements were established to discourage the poor from migrating to more generous states.

Much of the assistance was institutionally based, such as orphanages and work houses, but noninstitutional care was also provided. Attempts were made to find relatives to provide some support for the poor person. Any care given was minimal—less than what a family could obtain by working.

Perhaps the most interesting feature of the poor laws was the distinction between the worthy and nonworthy poor. The **worthy poor** were those, such as widows, orphans, children, the elderly, and the handicapped, who were poor through no fault of their own. The **unworthy poor** were those able to work and thus provide for themselves. These distinctions underlie differences in antipoverty programs in the 1930s and the 1990s.

### Preventive Strategies: Social Insurance

The Great Depression, beginning in 1929, changed American attitudes about poverty and the response to poverty in two ways. In the period prior to the 1930s, most people believed that the federal government had no role to play in the poverty area. The depression convinced the new Democratic leadership (the Franklin D. Roosevelt administration) that the federal government had to take action to address the problem of widespread poverty. Equally as important, the depression changed many perspectives about the causes of poverty. Where people once thought that poverty was due to individual character defects, they now saw more systemic causes beyond the ability of individuals to cope: unemployment because of economic conditions, retirement, death of a breadwinner, and so forth.

These two changes laid the foundation for the most important piece of social welfare legislation in the United States, the Social Security Act (1935). The act embodied two different sets of strategies, preventive and alleviative, that provided the framework for welfare policies for most of the rest of the century. The **preventive strategy** was designed to ensure that certain groups of people would not enter poverty. A system of social insurance, of income security, was developed—in essence to insure against the causes of poverty.

The major program was **Social Security** (see the chapter 2 case study for a thorough discussion of Social Security). Under this program, employees and employers contribute equally to a retirement system through payroll taxes. Beneficiaries are then entitled to benefits upon reaching retirement age. Social Security covered not just retirement but also those who were disabled, widowed, or orphaned. It was not intended to be the sole retirement pension for a worker, though that has often been the case. Social Security, it was hoped, would be supplemented by private pensions and savings.

Social Security has been successful in moving many of the aged out of poverty, particularly after increases and indexing (cost-of-living adjustments) in the 1970s. But there have been problems and criticisms of Social Security (as discussed in chapter 2). The major problem is the aging of the population: the increasing number of retired people with the relative declining number of workers. Because Social Security originally paid out about as much as it collected, this would imply that workers would be taxed more and more to support the program. Changes enacted in 1983 to place Social Security on a much sounder financial footing included an increase in the retirement age, increases in Social Security taxes (so that those now working are contributing to their own retirement payments), and a tax on half the Social Security payments of upper-income people. The estimate is that the Social Security Trust Fund is now financially secure well into the twenty-first century.

Another criticism is that taxes contributed to the Social Security Trust Fund could be used more effectively in private and individual pensions and thus be available for investment. A related point is that workers, knowing that they have Social Security to rely on, decrease their savings and consume more. Thus the savings rate in the United States dropped significantly, especially as compared to other industrialized nations that rely less on public pensions (Peterson 1993).

The second program that was part of the original act is **unemployment compensation**, which is financed by employer taxes to compensate (for a limited period of time) those who lost their jobs. The belief was that such loss of jobs and income was temporary and only interim replacement of income was necessary.

Additions to the preventive strategy in later years included, in 1965, **Medicare**, a program of health insurance for the elderly. When the original Social Security Act was considered, during the Franklin D. Roosevelt administration, there was some discussion of adding a provision for national health insurance (NHI), but it was felt that the controversy over NHI would doom the entire proposal. The Truman administration's NHI plan was defeated. The political strategy then changed to push for health insurance for groups that could not afford it, in this case the elderly. Medicare will be discussed at greater length in chapter 5, but notice how it fits into the preventive strategy. One reason that people could become poor is because of high medical bills. By thus assisting in the payment of medical bills, we prevent people from entering poverty.

The final addition to the preventive strategy, also medically related, came in 1972. This expansion provided for full payment for the medical expenses of anyone suffering from end-stage renal disease, or kidney failure. There is no cure for kidney failure, but the treatment, dialysis, keeps alive those who suffer from the disease. It is an expensive treatment and time-consuming, thus preventing the sufferer from holding a full-time job. Congress decided that no one should die because of an inability to afford the treatment.

How has the preventive strategy worked? In general, for the elderly population, the strategy has been a success. Although those who live solely on Social Security have some difficulty, one should recognize that these programs have led to a decline in poverty among the elderly, as can be seen in Table 4.2. Because of the personal contributions made to them, most Americans view Social Security and Medicare as insurance programs. Therefore, preventive programs have considerable popular support, though the future prospects of both programs have been the source of some contention (see chapters 2 and 5).

### Alleviative Strategy: Welfare

The second strategy incorporated into the Social Security Act is the **alleviative strategy**. Alleviate means to ease something, in this case the burden of poverty. No attempt is made to attack the causes of poverty, as was true with the preventive strategy, but merely to provide some assistance to those suffering from it. It is these programs that are understood to be welfare, transfer payments from government to a specified population. Further, all of these programs are **means-tested**; that is, eligibility depends on one's income as opposed to entitlements based on previous contributions. Furthermore, while preventive programs were designed to be permanent, alleviative programs were originally intended to be temporary until the economy recovered and Social Security payments began (the first Social Security payments were made in 1940).

The major alleviative program in the original act was AFDC, originally Aid to Dependent Children. This was, as are most of the alleviative programs, a federal/state program. The federal government contributed between 50 and 90 percent of the costs of the program depending on the state, and the states contributed the remainder. The federal government set overall standards, but eligibility standards and payment levels were set entirely by the states. People applied for AFDC and were accepted if they met income and wealth requirements.[5] For example, after changes made by Congress in 1981, families with less than $1,000 worth of assets and no income were eligible for assistance. The Social Security Act also included adult welfare categories: aid to the aged, aid to the blind, and aid to the disabled. These were replaced in 1974 by **Supplemental Security Income (SSI)**.

Other programs have been added that fit the alleviative strategy. In a parallel move with Medicare, Congress created a health insurance program for the poor in 1965 called **Medicaid**. Medicaid is financed out of federal and state general tax revenues and, unlike with Medicare, Medicaid recipients do not contribute financially to the program. Again, the states set eligibility and benefit levels. From an antipoverty standpoint, Medicaid has been successful in

Table 4.3

**Cost of Major Preventive and Alleviative Social Welfare Programs**
(in thousand dollars)

|  | 1970 | 1975 | 1980 | 1985 | 1990 | 1995 | 2000 (est.) |
|---|---|---|---|---|---|---|---|
| **Alleviative programs** | | | | | | | |
| Family and other support assistance (federal) | 4,142 | 5,423 | 7,308 | 9,224 | 12,246 | 17,133 | 20,691 |
| Family and other support assistance (state) | 1,629 | 4,316 | 6,237 | 7,652 | 9,693 | 11,765 | |
| Medicaid (federal) | 2,900 | 7,600 | 13,957 | 21,900 | 40,700 | 82,034 | 114,660 |
| Medicaid (state)* | 2,400 | 6,000 | 11,100 | 17,800 | 31,100 | 55,200 | 83,813 |
| Supplemental Security Income | | 4,320 | 5,716 | 8,654 | 11,493 | 24,510 | 31,494 |
| Food and nutrition assistance | 960 | 6,643 | 13,114 | 16,683 | 21,338 | 33,515 | 29,597 |
| Earned Income Tax Credit | | | | 1,100 | 04,354 | 15,244 | 25,676 |
| Total | 12,031 | 34,302 | 57,432 | 83,013 | 130,924 | 239,401 | 305,931 |
| **Preventive programs** | | | | | | | |
| Social Security | 30,270 | 64,658 | 118,547 | 188,623 | 147,076 | 335,846 | 408,575 |
| Medicare | 6,213 | 12,875 | 32,090 | 65,822 | 98,102 | 159,855 | 216,599 |
| Total | 36,483 | 77,533 | 150,637 | 254,445 | 245,178 | 495,701 | 625,174 |

*Sources:* Office of Management and Budget (2000); Health Care Financing Administration; Patel and Rushefsky (1995).

*Note:* *The data in this line are estimated by the author from data available on the Health Care Financing Administration website.

improving the health of the poor as measured by life expectancy at birth, infant mortality rates, and overall mortality rates (Davis and Schoen 1978; Patel and Rushefsky 1999; Starr 1986).

The third major alleviative program has a different origin. The **food stamps** program is administered by the U.S. Department of Agriculture and started as a means to distribute surplus farm products. As it exists now, the program is designed to provide support for the purchase of food by allowing recipients to purchase stamps at less than face value, the amount depending on the income of the recipient. It is financed entirely by the federal government but administered by the states.

Other alleviative programs include housing subsidies, school feeding programs, special health and feeding programs for pregnant women, and prenatal care. Table 4.3 presents the cost of the major preventive and alleviative programs.

## Evaluation: Comparing the Preventive and Alleviative Strategies

With the development of preventive and alleviative programs, antipoverty policy crossed a divide. From the late 1960s to the present, these two strategies formed the basis of government policy. Policy changes took these programs as their starting point and the problem of poverty has been redefined as the problem of welfare. Given these developments, what follows is an evaluation of how well these programs have worked and what problems they have had.

There are a number of ways to compare the programs of the two strategies. Table 4.3 shows that the preventive strategies are much more costly than the alleviative ones. There is considerably more support for the preventive programs than for the alleviative ones. For one thing, the two strategies largely embody the distinction made between the worthy and the unworthy poor (Cammisa 1998).[6] Schneider and Ingram (1997) argue that welfare recipients were socially constructed in such a way that made them the subject of punitive public policies.

The alleviative programs (welfare) have been attacked as inefficient and costly, providing disincentives for work and for the maintenance of the family. The work disincentives criticism comes about because the benefits of the welfare programs, especially Medicaid, are competitive with low-paying jobs (which rarely offer fringe benefits such as health insurance). Child-care costs are also a problem for welfare mothers seeking to move into the workforce. In addition, there is a very high tax associated with welfare. Once you are ineligible for welfare, you not only lose welfare cash payments, you could also lose Medicaid and food stamps, a problem that has occurred in welfare reform (see case study below). Thus, it is argued, the programs encourage people to remain on welfare and induce dependency. The number of AFDC recipients decreased through the 1950s but increased during the 1960s, which was, paradoxically, the second-longest sustained period of economic growth since World War II. In addition, the 1981 changes removed most of the working poor from the welfare rolls. Nevertheless, the number of AFDC recipients increased through the 1980s and into much of the 1990s (see Table 4.4).

The family disincentive came about because, prior to 1989, having an adult male present generally disqualified a family from receiving benefits (though states could, at their option, provide assistance to such families and the 1988 welfare legislation also made assisting employed parents easier). Given the low-income status of men in this group, welfare, as George Gilder (1981) has pointed out, makes the male provider an option.

The ways the programs are financed and administered also affect how the programs are run and the kinds of political support they have. Recipients of preventive program benefits financially contributed to the programs and thus have a legitimate claim as beneficiaries. Welfare recipients make no financial contributions and are seen as failures. Because alleviative programs are financed from general tax revenues, they become targets of cutbacks when fis-

Table 4.4

**Number of AFDC/TANF Recipients** (in thousands)

| Year | Number |
|---|---|
| 1950 | 2,233 |
| 1955 | 2,192 |
| 1960 | 3,073 |
| 1965 | 4,396 |
| 1970 | 7,429 |
| 1975 | 11,404 |
| 1980 | 10,597 |
| 1985 | 10,813 |
| 1990 | 11,460 |
| 1991 | 12,592 |
| 1992 | 13,625 |
| 1993 | 14,143 |
| 1994 | 14,226 |
| 1995 | 13,652 |
| 1996 | 12,649 |
| 1997* | 10,936 |
| 1998 | 8,770 |
| 1999 | 7,203 |

*Sources:* U.S. Census Bureau, *Statistical Abstract of the United States* (various years). Administration for Children and Families (2000).
*Note:* *After 1996, recipients are in TANF rather than AFDC.

cal distress or constraint occurs (though preventive entitlement programs such as Social Security and Medicare have not been exempt from budget-cutting pressures).

Alleviative programs are administered by the states; the preventive programs are generally administered by the federal government. This administrative federalism has several implications. For the federal government, it means that a portion of its budget is controlled by the states; it depends on state generosity. It also means that we cannot talk about a single welfare program or a single Medicaid program, as we can about Social Security or Medicare. Rather, each state has designed its own programs, depending upon its political culture (generosity) and financial ability. For example, the federal government requires that the states offer a minimum package of services under Medicaid. There is also a series of options that states can add and that the federal government would help finance. New York and California have more comprehensive Medicaid programs than do Mississippi or Alabama.

Finally, unlike Social Security, AFDC was not keyed to inflation but required explicit congressional action to raise benefit levels. The result is that the value of benefits going to AFDC recipients declined, whereas those receiving Social Security have been largely protected against inflation (see Table 4.5)

Table 4.5

**Average Monthly Benefit for AFDC Recipients**

|      | In current dollars | In 1996 dollars |
|------|--------------------|-----------------|
| 1960 | 106                | 559             |
| 1970 | 178                | 734             |
| 1980 | 269                | 523             |
| 1990 | 389                | 470             |
| 1996 | 374                | 374             |

*Source:* U.S. House of Representatives Committee on Ways and Means (1998).

## Curative Strategy: The War on Poverty

The original conception of the New Deal–based strategies was that the preventive programs (income maintenance) would completely take over from the alleviative programs (welfare). Through the 1950s the poverty rolls did indeed decrease (see Table 4.4), but during the Kennedy and Johnson years (1961 to 1968), the problem of poverty regained its place on the policy agenda. Here we can look at our model of agenda building to see how this change took place.

Two important sources pointed out that poverty still existed in the United States. The first was the publication in 1957 of John Kenneth Galbraith's *The Affluent Society*. Galbraith called attention to poverty amidst plenty (the irony of the affluent society) and distinguished between two types of poverty: case poverty, which was a product of personal characteristics, and area poverty, a product of economic deficiencies relating to a particular sector of the nation. The immediate impact of Galbraith's work was limited, because the public view was that America was a rich country.

The other important source was Michael Harrington's *The Other America* (1962), in which he called attention to poverty that existed among blacks in the urban north and rural south, among whites in Appalachia, and among the aged. Harrington's work came at a time when the administration in office, the Kennedy administration, was sensitive to its message.

The 1960 presidential election had an unintentional role in developing the new strategy (White 1962). One of the potentially critical issues of the campaign was the religion (Catholicism) of the Democratic candidate, John Kennedy.[7] The Kennedy forces faced the issue directly in several ways, one of which was to pick a state with a predominantly Protestant electorate and enter its primary to show that a Catholic could win Protestant votes. The Kennedy campaign chose West Virginia and ran against Hubert Humphrey. As Kennedy campaigned through the poverty belt of the Appalachians in West Virginia, he saw hunger at first hand and decided to do something about it.

The early programs, based on Kennedy's experience, were regional development programs; later programs had a wider scope. The most important program was the **Economic Opportunity Act (1964)**. The proposal was prepared during the Kennedy administration but was enthusiastically endorsed by President Johnson shortly after he took office. The aim of the Economic Opportunity Act was to break the cycle of poverty at an early age by providing a wide range of programs (such as Head Start, literacy training, and manpower training) that would attack the causes of poverty (such as poor education and lack of job skills), thus earning the label of **curative strategy**.

**Head Start** is the prototype of curative strategy programs. The basic premise of Head Start is that poor children lack an enriching home and community environment and thus start school at a disadvantage. The program is designed to give students an early start on their education. In addition, the longer students stay at Head Start centers during the day, the less time they spend in their own environments. Head Start also provides nutritional and health programs to the students.

One interesting feature of the **War on Poverty** programs was its federalist nature. The federal government provided money directly to local community groups and local governments and bypassed the states, believing that states were unresponsive to the needs of their poverty-stricken residents.

The Nixon administration dismantled most of the War on Poverty programs, but some, such as Head Start and Meals on Wheels, remain.

## Political Strategy: The Community Action Program

In connection with the curative strategy, a **political strategy** was implemented. The basic premise of this strategy was that poor people and poor communities lacked control or political power over institutions that affected their lives. The 1964 Economic Opportunity Act established the **Community Action Program (CAP)** to set up local community action agencies (CAAs) with board members from the target communities. In the words of the act, the boards were to have the "maximum feasible participation" from the community. Community action agencies received direct funding from the Office of Economic Opportunity and developed a mix of programs depending on their needs. CAP soon became controversial because big-city mayors felt that they should have control over the distribution of funds and in some cases felt they were being politically undermined. The CAP program was reined in, with the mayors gaining control. The Nixon administration dismantled the program, but a few CAAs remain around the country.

## Incomes Strategy: The Negative Income Tax

The War on Poverty was seen as a failure and the new Republican (Nixon) administration was philosophically opposed to it. The alleviative strategy was also discredited because, critics said, it created work and family disincentives and because it increased welfare dependency.

The Nixon administration was looking for positive, uniquely Republican programs that could inexpensively solve social problems. In 1962, University of Chicago economist Milton Friedman (a libertarian) published *Capitalism and Freedom*, in which he argued that government was a major source of coercion (threat to liberty) and suggested alternative programs that would create choice with less government. One of his suggestions was for a negative income tax as a replacement for the welfare system that virtually everybody agreed was a failure. James Tobin, a liberal economist, also supported a negative income tax. Such proposals embody an **incomes strategy**.

The Nixon administration was interested in this new strategy as a possible solution to the welfare problem. Note that the policy problem had been redefined: Beginning with the Nixon administration, the major focus was no longer poverty but welfare, the program originally designed to alleviate it. This frequently happens; government programs themselves become problems that need to be addressed.

The idea behind a **negative income tax** is that the recipient receives a cash benefit (similar to the former AFDC program) while working, but the benefit is reduced as the income increases. At some income level, depending upon the features of such a program, the benefit becomes zero. Up to that level, the recipient is always better off working than not working. Thus the problem of the work disincentive of AFDC appears to be eliminated.

In 1970 and again in 1971, the Nixon administration proposed a family assistance plan, including a **workfare** provision stipulating that able-bodied adults would have to look for work or lose their share of the benefit. The program passed the House but not the Senate. Liberals felt the program was insufficiently generous, and conservatives did not like the idea of a guaranteed income. After 1971, the administration dropped the proposal. While Congress did not pass the Nixon family assistance plan, it did enact a version of the negative income tax in 1974 called Supplemental Security Income (SSI), replacing the adult categories of public assistance (aid to the aged, blind, and disabled). Another version of the negative income tax is the **Earned Income Tax Credit** or **EITC**. It is a form of negative income tax because after a specified income level, it begins to decline and is payable even if no tax is withheld. While SSI has been somewhat controversial (see case study below), the EITC has generally had substantial political support.

### The Return of the Punitive Strategy: The Reagan Administration

Welfare policy in the 1980s was the product of considerable agenda change. Welfare was seen as a failure, costing too much and, perversely, hurting those it was intended to help by discouraging work. This was the government issue: the notion that government was the problem rather than the solution. A related aspect was the economic strain the country was experiencing at this time. Theodore Marmor and colleagues (1990) argue that the economy and particularly incomes stagnated beginning about 1973 (as mentioned in chapter 2). They further note that the Great Society and War on Poverty programs were accused of being responsible for a substantial portion of the economic slowdown. The philosophy or strategy that formed the basis of the original punitive strategy—that individuals, rather than more systematic features, were at fault for poverty—was also revived (Corbett 1993).[8] The successful presidential candidate in the 1980 elections, Ronald Reagan, pointed to increases in social spending as one of the culprits.

Reagan entered the White House having campaigned on a platform proclaiming that government was too expensive and was trying to do too many things. The welfare system (AFDC, food stamps, Medicaid, etc.) was widely criticized by conservatives, and the earlier Republican alternative of a negative income tax was discredited.

Martin Anderson (1978) pointed out that if you counted cash and in-kind assistance (such as Medicaid), then the War on Poverty had virtually eliminated poverty—in short, the War on Poverty had been won. He was very specific in terms of how we should reform welfare and offered a number of "guiding points" for incremental change: assistance only for the needy; increased emphasis on eliminating fraud; fair and clear work requirement (workfare); vigorous child-support enforcement; improved administration; and shifting of more responsibility to state and local governments and the private sector. Welfare policy in the 1980s (and the 1990s) generally followed these guidelines.

George Gilder (1981), in a book cited admiringly by President Reagan, maintained that poor people remained poor because they were paid to do so by welfare programs. He further asserted that the welfare programs were so generous, especially if the cash equivalent value of Medicaid was counted, that it created resentment among the working class. What the poor needed, Gilder argued, were not handouts but jobs and incentives to look for jobs, even if the jobs themselves were not prestigious or well paying. "The only dependable route from poverty is always work, family, and faith" (Gilder 1981, p. 68). He further maintained that welfare denigrates the role of the male provider by making him optional. He suggested replacing welfare with a system of child allowances, as is common in Europe. The allowances would be for all families, would not be means-tested (no eligibility criteria), but would be taxable:

> A disciplined combination of emergency aid, austere in-kind benefits [such as Medicaid for catastrophic needs only], and child allowances—all at levels well below the returns of hard work [thus classifying the strategy as punitive]—offers some promise of relieving poverty without creating a welfare culture that perpetuates it. That is the best that any welfare system can be expected to achieve. (Gilder 1981, p. 256)

Charles Murray's *Losing Ground* (1984) argued the same point. His conclusion, like Gilder's, was that welfare was counterproductive. Unlike Anderson or Gilder, however, Murray suggested that all the welfare programs be
eliminated.[9] As we shall see below, Murray has continued this line of thought,
but focusing on the problem of illegitimacy.

The Reagan administration, armed with arguments by Gilder and Anderson and a philosophical resistance to active government, added an additional
factor: the need to cut the growth of government to reduce the federal budget
deficit. The administration, using a 1980 precedent of the Carter administration and a strategy crafted by Office of Management and Budget director
David Stockman, packaged a series of budget cuts into a single piece of legislation—the **Omnibus Budget Reconciliation Act (OBRA) (1981)**.[10] The act
reduced AFDC benefits for working recipients, virtually eliminating them
from the rolls. This is consistent with the punitive strategy of distinguishing
between the worthy and nonworthy poor: those who were capable of work
should not receive assistance. Again, as we shall see below, this idea underlies much of welfare reform in the 1990s. It also allowed the states to establish "workfare" programs, requiring that welfare recipients work as a condition
of receiving assistance. For Medicaid, the largest of the welfare programs, the
law reduced federal payments to the states. It also provided states with some
flexibility, for example, insisting that recipients obtain services from specified providers such as health maintenance organizations. For food stamps,
income eligibility was reduced, inflation adjustments were delayed, and benefits to the working poor were reduced (Rich 1988). Other programs aimed at
the poor were either reduced or eliminated. For example, assistance for construction of low-income housing was virtually eliminated, which contributed
to the problem of the homeless in the 1980s, even among those who worked
(Rich 1988; Schmalz 1988). The Comprehensive Employment and Training
Act, the public-sector jobs block grant program, was eliminated and replaced
in 1982 with the Job Partnership Training Act, which relied heavily on the
private sector. The Women, Infants, and Children (WIC) supplemental nutritional program and federal subsidies for school lunches were cut and income
eligibility was reduced.

The above-mentioned actions of the Reagan administration and Congress
allowed a test of Murray's thesis about the poor. Murray (1984) argued that
the rational person, given the choice between a low-paying, dead-end job
with few benefits and public assistance that includes health insurance, would
choose the latter. There have been a number of studies suggesting that people
with low incomes share the same values as the rest of the population (Beeghley
1983; Rank 1994).

Recall that the OBRA of 1981 virtually eliminated the working poor from
the welfare rolls, based on the distinction between the worthy poor (those
who could not provide for themselves) and the unworthy poor (those who
could provide for themselves).

Although poor people reported working longer hours at higher wages than they had before benefits were cut, the study said, the increase in earnings was offset by the loss of welfare and food stamps, so there was a net reduction in income. (Pear 1984)

The working poor had problems acquiring food for the entire month and paying rent. In addition, they faced considerable difficulty obtaining medical and dental insurance and thus purchasing the care they and their children needed. Yet they did not quit their jobs to go back on welfare. The economic reasoning that Gilder and Murray use just does not apply.

### Evaluation of the Reagan Program

It is clear that the poverty rate increased after 1980 (see Table 4.1), but the Reagan programs were only partially responsible for this (Bawden and Palmer 1984). In the early years of the Reagan administration, the country experienced its most severe recession since the end of World War II. The unemployment rate, at one point, exceeded 10 percent. Thus, the poverty rate increase is a function of both the Reagan cuts, which pushed substantial numbers of people off the welfare rolls, and unemployment. The recovery began in late 1982, and the unemployment rate fell to below 5 percent by early 1989, but the poverty rate was still higher than it had been during the 1970s. According to the Congressional Research Service (CRS), both the program cuts and recession contributed to the increase in poverty after 1981, with the recession the larger factor: 1.6 million additional people became poor because of the recession; about 557,000 because of the program cuts ("Study Says Budget Made 557,000 Poor" 1984).

The administration claimed that it did have policies to reduce poverty. First, the chief priority of the administration was economic recovery, and it claimed that economic growth would create new jobs. The stimulus for economic growth was to be budget and tax cuts, hence the name of the 1981 tax cut bill: the Economic Recovery Act. Secondly, the administration supported **urban enterprise zones**, tax relief in poor areas in return for which employers (especially small businesses) would employ workers from the area.

Third, included in the 1981 budget cuts were provisions allowing states to institute workfare programs for AFDC. New York and California began workfare programs in 1985. The programs varied dramatically (Kosterlitz 1985). Evaluations of the work-related programs indicated that they have increased "average earnings of economically disadvantaged female participants, especially those who lack recent work experience" (Congressional Budget Office 1987, p. 43).

One other program had a significant effect on working poor. The Tax Reform Act of 1986 contained a provision raising the individual deduction to $2,000 per person. This removed many of the working poor from the federal tax rolls, and in that sense should be considered a major antipoverty program. In addition, the poverty programs were exempted from the automatic cuts of the Balanced Budget Acts of 1985 and 1987.

### The Family Support Act of 1988

The last year of the Reagan administration (1988) saw a major change in the alleviative programs: the passage of a major welfare reform bill. In his January 1986 State of the Union message, President Reagan vowed to make welfare reform one of his major domestic priorities. Research helped develop new understandings about the problems of welfare dependency. Congressional advocates of reform such as newly named chairman of the Senate Finance Committee subcommittee on Social Security and Family Policy Daniel Patrick Moynihan[11] (D-NY) pushed the process. It was signed into law in September 1988.

The **Family Support Act (1988)** required all states to extend AFDC benefits to two-parent families (AFDC-UP [Unemployed Parents]). However, one of the adults must look for work or participate in a workfare program for sixteen hours a week; this provision builds on earlier experience in the states with workfare programs (such as New Jersey). It required single parents with children over three years of age to enroll in a job training and education program, with welfare benefits paying transportation and child care, including the transitional period from welfare to employment (the Job Opportunities and Basic Skills Training [JOBS] program). Child support collections were strengthened (e.g., improved monitoring). And at least 55 percent of welfare benefits was targeted to the chronically poor—those who have been on welfare for thirty of the last sixty months. It is this group that constitutes about one-half of the welfare caseload.

Although the new law represented something of a break from the past,[12] the expectation was that its impact would be gradual (Coughlin 1989; Stevens 1988). First, the additional money ($3.34 billion) was too little. State experience shows that low funding levels lead to modest movement from dependency to work. Second, while some states had implementation regulations ready shortly after the Department of Health and Human Services issued its regulations (April 1989), other states were not ready to begin their programs until the mandated date of October 1, 1990. The legislation called for gradual implementation. For example, the fiscal year 1990 and 1991 requirements were that states had to enroll at least 7 percent of eligible parents in the Job Opportunities and Basic Skills program, increasing to at least 20 percent by fiscal year 1995. Similarly, the work requirement for AFDC for Unemployed Parents was not to begin until fiscal year 1994, when 40 percent of eligible families must participate, increasing to 75 percent by fiscal 1997 (Sottile 1988; see also Cammisa 1998).

## Case Study: The End of Welfare as We Know It

### Problem Identification and Agenda Building

During the early and mid-1990s, several things happened that greatly changed the course of welfare policy in the United States. Implementation of the Family Support Act was slow, largely for fiscal reasons. Further, impatience with

Table 4.6

**Births to Unmarried Women as Percentage of Total Births**

| Year | All women | White | Black | Hispanic |
|------|-----------|-------|-------|----------|
| 1970 | 10.7 | 5.5 | 37.5 | N/A |
| 1975 | 14.2 | 7.1 | 49.5 | N/A |
| 1980 | 18.4 | 11.2 | 56.1 | 23.6 |
| 1985 | 22.0 | 14.7 | 61.2 | 29.5 |
| 1990 | 28.0 | 20.4 | 66.5 | 36.7 |
| 1992 | 32.6 | 22.6 | 68.1 | 39.1 |
| 1993 | 32.4 | 23.6 | 68.7 | 40.0 |
| 1994 | 32.8 | 25.4 | 70.4 | 43.1 |
| 1995 | 23.2 | 25.3 | 69.9 | 40.8 |
| 1996 | 32.4 | 25.7 | 69.8 | 40.7 |
| 1997 | 32.4 | 25.8 | 69.2 | 40.9 |
| 1998 | 32.8 | 26.3 | 69.1 | 41.6 |

*Source:* National Center for Health Statistics (2000).

the welfare program and welfare recipients increased, due to mounting fiscal stress (the 1990–91 recession) and record welfare enrollments (Pear 1993) (see Table 4.4). With the federal government having taken its steps, much of the action in the early years of the decade took place at the state level. And to a large extent, such action fit the views of the punitive strategy.

A number of states, such as California, New York, Tennessee, Minnesota, Virginia, and Kansas, cut welfare benefits in 1991. California, one of the most generous states in terms of welfare benefits and eligibility standards, proposed eliminating additional AFDC benefits for mothers who bore children after going on welfare (DeParle 1991). New Jersey enacted such a plan in 1992 (King 1992). The cuts in the early 1990s were, in some respects, more severe than the Reagan cuts of 1981.

> But they differed in two ways. The 1991 state cuts were targeted at the poorest of the poor whereas the federal cuts in 1981 were aimed at the working poor who had some income. Also the 1991 cuts have hit during a recession . . . The 1981 Reagan budget cuts were enacted before a recession; a second round was proposed in 1982 but killed by Congress, in part because of the recession then. (Taylor 1991, p. 32)

In the most radical action among the states, Wisconsin proposed to withdraw from the AFDC program by 1998 (DeParle 1993), which, as we shall see below, it did as part of welfare reform.

One of the reasons states enacted cuts and restrictions was a new emphasis on out-of-wedlock births, or **illegitimacy**; this would also affect the debate over federal welfare programs. Table 4.6 shows the rate of illegitimacy over time for the entire population and by ethnicity. As we can see, out-of-wedlock births increased dramatically, though they began to drop or slow down in the late 1990s. Related to this development is the birthrate among teenagers. Births among teenagers have declined since 1990. The largest dip is among African-American and Hispanic teens, though the numbers are still high. The out-of-wedlock birthrate for teenagers is much higher than among the general population, about 78 percent in 1997 (Alan Guttmacher Institute 1999; Bennett 1999; Stolberg 1999; Ventura et al. 1998).

Why is increasing illegitimacy a problem? First, it certainly is one indicator of changing family dynamics. As we have seen before, female-headed families are much more likely to be poor (and on welfare) than two-parent families. Further, children born to mothers who have never married are also more likely to be on welfare. These same children are also at a higher risk of showing other troublesome behaviors: dropping out of school, using drugs, committing crime. Thus this increase in out-of-wedlock births among all groups is of great concern.

But concern is not enough. The question raised in the 1990s was why such increases were occurring. To some, the answer was our welfare programs. This argument is made most prominently by Charles Murray. In reacting to a New Jersey plan to end additional AFDC payments for additional children, Murray wrote:

> The New Jersey plan, like similar carrot-and-stick packages proposed in California and other states that offer incentives for job training and education, does not go far enough or address the right problems. Our social tragedy has nothing to do with the money we spend on welfare and little to do with "welfare dependency." The problem is not that single mothers are on welfare, but that there are so many single mothers concentrated in poor communities. (Murray 1992)

To Murray and others, welfare was not necessarily the problem in and of itself; rather, our values had changed so that having children outside of marriage no longer carried the stigma that it previously had. Children, Murray believed, should be raised in families with both parents.

In 1993, Murray took his argument one step further. He noted the increase in the white illegitimacy rate and maintained that we were beginning to develop a white underclass (see also Whitman and Friedman 1994). He pointed out that white illegitimacy rates were much higher for women with a high school education or less than for college-educated women, and for low-income as opposed to higher-income women. Murray observed:

> In raw numbers, European-American whites are the ethnic group with the most people in poverty, most illegitimate children, most women on welfare, most unemployed men, and most arrests for serious crime. . . .
> But now the overall white illegitimacy rate is 22%. The figure in low-income working-class communities may be twice that. How much illegitimacy can a community tolerate? No one knows, but the historical fact is that the trendlines on black crime, dropout from the labor force and illegitimacy all shifted sharply upward as the overall black illegitimacy rate passed 25%. (Murray 1993)

Murray then recommended a set of policies familiar from his 1984 work, *Losing Ground*. We should not, he asserted, make it easy for women to have babies out of wedlock. Thus, he continued to call for the elimination of welfare for single mothers (though he would maintain medical coverage for children). From this, he argued, several things would happen. Poor mothers would have to turn to their families, friend, charities, etc., for support. Second, adoption, if made easier, would also prevent the formation of female-headed families. Third, the stigma of illegitimacy would return because young mothers would not be able to support themselves, and their families would more likely to discourage such behaviors. To put it another way, we are seeing the return of shame concerning illegitimacy and other behaviors (Alter and Wingert 1995).[13]

Murray's argument was echoed during the 1992 presidential campaign when, as part of a speech on values and families, Vice President Dan Quayle attacked the television character Murphy Brown. Brown, played by Candace Bergen, decided not to marry the father of her child. Quayle argued that this legitimized out-of-wedlock births and that teenage girls do not have the financial resources of Murphy Brown. While Quayle was widely ridiculed for criticizing a fictional character, he did make an important point about values and social changes in American life.[14]

Quayle's controversial comment (as well as Murray's focus on illegitimacy) raised important questions about the changing American family structure, its impact, and policy implications. One question is whether Murray's and Quayle's analysis is correct. It is true that social pathologies are more likely to be seen in female-headed families than in two-parent families. But Sara McLanahan and Irwin Garfinkel (1994) note that the overall high school dropout rate in the United States is 19 percent and for children from two-parent families is 13 percent. Thus, they argue, the dropout rate is high whatever the family structure. Further, they observed that AFDC benefits have declined in real (inflation-adjusted) dollars by 26 percent from 1972 to 1992 (see also Table 4.5). Welfare was not much of an incentive for teenage out-of-wedlock births. Additionally, AFDC was less generous than benefits in European countries where the illegitimacy rate is much lower. Finally, they noted that illegitimacy rates are growing the fastest among educated women (though in absolute terms, the numbers remain small).

McLanahan (1994) suggests three reasons for the increase in the illegitimacy rate: the increasing economic independence of women, the relative decline in the ratios men-to-women's earnings since the early 1970s,[15] and changes in values about marriage, divorce, and out-of-wedlock births.[16] Arlene Skolnick and Stacy Rosencrantz (1994) add that it may be that poverty and dropping out of school causes early childbirth, rather than the other way around. Further, Rank (1994) found that the birthrate of women on welfare is *lower* than the national birthrate.

Murray (1994) argued that while the evidence for the impact of welfare payments on illegitimacy is not settled, it is better than McLanahan and others would argue. He makes two adjustments in the data. First, rather than looking at just AFDC payments, he also included other major welfare programs (food stamps, Medicaid, and public housing subsidies) in what he called a "welfare package" (p. 23). Second, he distinguished between *proportion* ("illegitimate births per 100 black live births") from incidence. *Incidence* is usually defined as "illegitimate births per 1,000 single women." However, he argues that it is more properly "illegitimate births per 1,000 population." Charting black incidence against the welfare package (which peaked about 1970) makes a stronger case, Murray asserts, for the impact of welfare on illegitimacy.

To this we should add that the family structure is changing. The classic "Ozzie and Harriet" family is a minority among American families ("No Such Thing as Typical American Family Anymore" 1994; Stanfield 1992). Finally, the changing dynamics of the American family is a long-term process. The increasing numbers of out-of-wedlock births can be traced to the 1950s (and earlier). The problem is less likely the presence of welfare than, as Murray and others pronounce, changing values.

One other element ought to be added to this discussion of the factors leading up to welfare reform. Martin Gilens (1999) argues first that Americans have never liked welfare policies. While Americans support increased spending for a variety of social welfare programs, they strongly favor decreasing spending for welfare or people on welfare (Gilens 1999, Table 2.1). Gilens then looks at four possible explanations for the dislike of welfare among the population: that it violates America's individualist orientation, that middle-class Americans oppose programs that do not directly benefit them, that many of the poor are undeserving and do not need assistance, and negative attitudes toward blacks from whites. To summarize, Gilens finds the last two explanations as the most successful in explaining American attitudes about welfare; indeed, he finds that the undeserving-poor view and the racial view are very much connected.

But Gilens goes further in his analysis. He first makes the following point (also made by Murray in the quote on p. 189):

> After all, it is a simple fact that poor people in this country are disproportionately black. Yet African Americans constitute a small percentage of all Americans, and even though they are more likely to be poor than are whites, they nevertheless constitute a minority of both poor people (of whom 27 percent are black) and welfare recipients (of whom 36 percent are black). . . . however, the public exaggerates the extent to which African Americans compose the poor. On average, Americans believe that blacks make up not 27 percent, but 50 percent of all poor people. (Gilens 1999, p. 102)

Why do Americans overestimate the percentage of poor blacks and black welfare recipients? Gilens demonstrates that the portrayal of poor people in the news media is largely responsible for this perception. For example, he examined the percent of African Americans in pictures in news magazines (*Time*, *Newsweek*, and *U.S. News and World Report*) and found that there was a much higher percentage of blacks portrayed in stories about the poor than the black poverty rate would suggest. Further, when there was discussion of whites who were poor, the whites were portrayed in a sympathetic manner (that is poor because of economic conditions such as a recession). To add just one more piece of evidence, Gilens presents survey data that strongly suggests that people who thought that most of the people on welfare were black had a very strongly negative toward welfare recipients, and those who thought most of the people on welfare were white had a much more sympathetic view of welfare recipients (Gilens 1999).

We will see in other chapters (those on education and crime) that there is a strong racial component. We also know that from the 1968 to the 1988 presidential campaigns, there were strong racial components to elections (Edsall and Edsall 1991).

## Policy Formulation and Adoption

As we have seen, states sought changes in welfare policies to stem the tide of illegitimacy, or at least not to continue to financially support it with scarce tax dollars. Conservatives such as Murray recommend the harsher step of doing away with the entire welfare system (with the partial exception of Medicaid).

The Clinton administration also sought to change welfare, with some focus on the illegitimacy problem. During the 1992 presidential campaign, Bill Clinton promised to "end welfare as we know it" and to set up a two-year time limit for those on welfare (Kosterlitz 1992). In 1993, President Clinton formed a task force to put together a welfare policy proposal. The initiative was to have four main features: to make sure that those who worked had a sufficient income to do better than those who were on welfare, to improve enforcement of child support, to provide services to help those making the transition from work to welfare, and to impose a two-year time limit on welfare once the other three parts were enacted (Stoesz 1996). While the task force was working out the details of the program, the Clinton administration was granting states waivers from federal regulations to enact programs including learnfare, workfare, and time limits (Cammisa 1998; Stoesz 1996).

The administration also made a fateful decision that, in retrospect, affected the welfare reform bill that was eventually enacted. As we shall see in the next chapter, the Clinton administration had a number of policy goals it wanted to achieve during its first two years (1993–94). These included the economic program (originally a stimulus and then more focused on reducing the budget deficit), approval of trade bills (the North American Free Trade Agreement in 1993 and the General Agreement on Tariffs and Trade in 1994), and crime bills (such as the Brady Bill). In addition, a major promise of the campaign was legislation to overhaul the nation's health care system. The administration felt that it could not propose to Congress's both a comprehensive health reform bill and a comprehensive welfare reform. This would overload Congress' capacity. So the administration postponed welfare reform until 1994. But by that time, it had lost on health care, it had lost control of the policy agenda, and its party had lost control of Congress.

But the administration finally did submit a bill in 1994. The bill sought to move teenage mothers from the welfare rolls to employment. It imposed a two-year limit after which recipients would have to work. It mandated that young mothers living at home seek job training or education. It required that AFDC mothers identify the fathers and that more vigorous child support collections from fathers be undertaken. It expanded training and child-care programs. But it also had some sticks to go along with the carrots. The bill proposed eliminating AFDC payments for mothers who, after the two-year AFDC limit, fail to find work and allowing states to deny additional AFDC benefits for children born while the mother was on AFDC (DeParle 1994c, 1994d). One intriguing part of the welfare reform plan was that it focused on the fathers as well as the mothers (Chira 1994; Waldman 1994). The plan would spend $10–13 billion (on child care, job training, and so on) over a five-year period (DeParle 1994a), which was a problem because of the large deficit and requirements that new spending be accompanied either by cuts elsewhere or new revenues.

Congress never considered the bill in 1994, but congressional Republicans did make a proposal that would greatly shape the welfare reform bill that was eventually passed in 1996. In September 1994, House Republicans, under the leadership of minority whip Newt Gingrich (R-GA) agreed upon what was essentially a campaign platform known as the **Contract with America** (Gillespie and Schellhas 1994). The book version of the Contract contained a chapter on welfare reform, which began:

> Isn't it time for the government to encourage work rather than rewarding dependency? The Great Society has had the unintended consequence of snaring millions of Americans into the welfare trap. Government programs designed to give a helping hand to the neediest of Americans have instead bred illegitimacy, crime, illiteracy, and more poverty. Our *Contract with America* will change this destructive social behavior by requiring welfare recipients to take personal responsibility for the decisions they make. Our *Contract* will achieve what some thirty years of massive welfare spending has not been able to accomplish: reduce illegitimacy, require work, and save taxpayers money. (Gillespie and Schellhas 1994, p. 65)

The Contract called for the passage of a "Personal Responsibility Act" that would, among other things, end welfare payments to teenage mothers, require identification of fathers as a condition of receiving AFDC, have a consecutive-two-year time limit and a five-year lifetime limit on receiving assistance, consolidate many of the welfare programs, and convert the AFDC categorical grant into a block grant to give states flexibility in achieving the legislation's goals. The final welfare reform bill reflects most of these provisions. In the 1994 midterm elections, Republicans gained control of both the Senate (for the first time since 1986) and the House (for the first time since 1954). They would set the policy agenda.

In 1995, Congress passed welfare reform legislation, which was vetoed by the president as was a second effort in 1996. The president (and Democrats) had two major objections. First, the legislation combined Medicaid with welfare reform, turning Medicaid into a block grant program. Second, the legislation ended the entitlement status of welfare.

In early 1996, the nation's governors, very much responsible for the implementation and financing of welfare, attempted to influence the debate. The National Governors Association approved a proposal that was somewhat less restrictive than the Republican congressional bills. Some elements of the reform, such as a family cap and work rules, would be made more flexible and more would be spent on child care (Cammissa 1998).

With presidential elections looming in 1996, stalemates over the budget that led to two government shutdowns in 1995, and the governors pushing for reform, the administration and congressional Republicans and Democrats were ready to compromise. In the summer of 1996, Congress passed and President Clinton signed the **Personal Responsibility and Work Opportunity Reconciliation Act (PRWORA) (1996)**.

Not everyone within the Clinton administration was pleased with the president's approval of the legislation. Four top officials in the Department of Health and Human Services (DHHS), the federal department with responsibility for the cash assistance program, resigned (DeParle 1996; Dionne 1996). One of them, Peter Edelman, was a close friend of the president and, along with Mary Jo Bane and David Ellwood, had helped put together the Clinton proposal. Edelman wrote an article in 1997 arguing that signing the welfare reform bill was the "worst mistake" Clinton had made (Edelman 1997). Edelman and Ellwood both asserted that the welfare reform was too harsh. Other groups, such as the nation's Roman Catholic bishops, also denounced the bill. Even as he was signing it, President Clinton vowed to remedy some of the harsher parts of the bill. The president admitted that he signed the bill at least partly to remove welfare as a political issue during the 1996 elections (Clines 1996).

### Provisions of PRWORA

So what did the bill actually do? [17] As will become readily apparent, welfare reform was not incremental change, but comprehensive changing, transforming the nature of America's welfare system.

One important provision affects the notion of entitlements. The law reads as follows:

> (c) TERMINATION OF ENTITLEMENT UNDER AFDC PROGRAM—Effective October 1, 1996, no individual or family shall be entitled to any benefits or services

under any State plan approved under part A or F of title IV of the Social Security Act (as in effect on September 30, 1995). (H.R. 3474, Personal Responsibility and Work Opportunity Reconciliation Act of 1996, ftp://ftp.loc.gov/pub/thomas/c104/h3734.enr.txt).

Thus, AFDC is terminated and there is no longer an entitlement to federal assistance.

A related feature of the law was the replacement of the categorical AFDC program with a new block grant program, **Temporary Assistance for Needy Families** (**TANF**). There are two elements to this change. First is the word "temporary." This word is related to the end of the entitlement status of federal welfare programs and to time limits (discussed below).

Second is the block grant. A **block grant** is a sum of money given, in this case to the states, that can be used by the states in any way it wants to meet the objectives of the law. Under AFDC, the money could only be used for cash assistance. Under the block grant, states could use the funds for cash assistance (while a recipient is still eligible), but could also be used to help the welfare recipient get off welfare and into the work force. Examples of programs to do this include child care, job training, and transportation.

The block grant has another feature that is very attractive to the federal government. Under a categorical program such as AFDC, the amount of money the federal government must spend is uncontrollable. That is, it depends on the level of benefits offered by the states and the size of the welfare rolls. If the rolls go up, say because of a recession, then spending goes up. Under a block grant, the spending is limited to the size of the grant. Further, under the premise that the welfare rolls would decrease (which they were doing anyway and which was a major objective of the legislation), the assumption was made that less money would be needed in future years. And the law specified the size of the block grants in future years. In the event of an economic recession, there is a small contingency fund that states can draw upon.

This arrangement might have caused a hardship for the states, except that Congress was very generous in the early allocations. The size of the block grant for the first year started with the size of the welfare rolls in 1995. But even before the law took effect, the size of the rolls had declined. In subsequent years, the two-year lag remained. The purpose of this provision was to give states extra money to help move recipients off the rolls and into the workplace.

A third feature was the time limits, called for by both Clinton during his 1992 campaign and the Contract with America. Though allowing some exceptions (below), the limits were two consecutive years and a five-year time limit. The law also allows states to set more stringent time limits. States can also exempt up to 20 percent of their caseload from the time limit if those cases are declared as hardships.

Related to time limits are targeted requirements for work participation. The law distinguishes between participation for all families and for two-parent families. For two-parent families, the targeted participation rate was 75 percent by 1997 and 90 percent by 1999. Thirty-five hours a week was required to count toward the participation rate. For all welfare families, the 1997 target was 25 percent participation rate, rising to 50 percent by 2002. There were exceptions made for states that experienced caseload reductions before 1997.

The law also requires that states maintain at least 80 percent of their previous level of funding (known as maintenance of effort), though high-performing states (those that meet the goals of TANF) can reduce their effort to 75 percent.

The law also seeks, though separate from the welfare provisions, to reduce out-of-wedlock births. States that do so will receive a bonus of $4–5 million. In a similar vein, the law prohibits the use of federal funds for unmarried teenaged mothers if the mother is not in school or living with adult supervision (though there are some exceptions).

The law also contains an interesting provision related to private providers of services to the poor. The bill allows states to contract with religious and other private providers, not just public providers. This feature has raised questions about the First Amendment's establishment clause. But supporters of the program argue that religious organizations have a fine track record of working for the poor and should not be excluded from the program. In 2001, the second Bush administration created an office within the White House, headed by John DiIulio, to encourage the participation of faith-based and community-based organizations in social policy.

The welfare reform law also had an impact on other social policies, Medicaid, food stamps, and SSI. Recall that Medicaid reforms were included in the first two welfare reform bills that President Clinton vetoed, but not in the one that was eventually signed. Prior to July 1996, those who were eligible for AFDC were automatically eligible for Medicaid. But the law abolished AFDC. It provided that states use whatever eligibility standard they had as of July 16, 1996. Further, states could allow welfare recipients to continue receiving Medicaid for up to one year after they had left welfare for work. As we will see below in the section on implementation and evaluation, there have been problems of Medicaid eligibility associated with the implementation of welfare reform.

Food stamps and SSI did not fare nearly so well as Medicaid (which remained basically unchanged). The major savings in PRWORA came not from welfare reform (and the concomittant reduction in the welfare roles) but from changes in food stamps and SSI. While the structure of the two programs was left unchanged, eligibility was greatly reduced. In particular, legal aliens who had been in the United States for less than ten years were removed from the programs; new legal aliens were not allowed in the two programs for five years. These provisions were among the major objections that President Clinton had when he signed the bill (see, e.g, "The Depths of the Food Stamp Cuts in the Final Welfare Bill" 1996). In the 1997 Balanced Budget Act (see chapter 2), some of the cuts to legal immigrants were restored (Palazzolo 1999).

One other element must be added to this discussion. Certainly one of the goals of PRWRO and welfare reform in general was to reduce the welfare caseload. An important related goal was to reduce dependency on government assistance, which meant that former welfare recipients should be able to support themselves in the workplace. PRWRO contains some stipulations for states and private/religious providers to furnish services to help make the transition. President Clinton went further and proposed a **welfare-to-work partnership** with the private sector. Such a program began in May 1997. The 1997 Balanced Budget Act contained $3 billion for the program (Greenberg 1997; Palazzolo 1999).

### Implementation of Welfare Reform

Implementation of welfare reform involved a number of steps at the federal level, though, given the nature of the program, most of the focus was on the state level. Indeed, one should see welfare reform as moving more authority from the federal government to the states, a process known as **devolution**. Implementation issues at the federal level included the issuing of regulations and the approval of state implementation plans. States needed to develop those plans and then put them into effect. Implementation issues even went so far down the line as to change the job of the caseworker or, as it is known in the public administration literature, **street-level bureaucrat** (Lipsky 1980). We will briefly consider each of these levels.

On November 20, 1997, the Clinton administration issued a notice of proposed rulemaking for TANF. It then asked for comments allowing a ninety-day period for submissions. On April 12, 1999, the final regulations were published.[18] The rules became effective October 1, 1999, more than three years after PRWORA was passed. These rules governed state activity, that is, for example, how and when penalties would be attached to states that did not meet deadlines for work requirements or how much flexibility states would be given (Administration for Children and Families 1999). The regulations also specified state reporting requirements so that the states could get credit for welfare caseload reductions and exceptional performance. The regulations, as well as the law itself, allowed states to be exempt from TANF requirements if they were working under previously granted waivers. When the waivers ran out, TANF regulations would apply. The other major task for the Department of Health and Human Services and its Administration for Children and the Family (ACF) was to approve state implementation plans. This was done on a timely basis as the states submitted their plans. Other regulations dealt with the bonus contest for reducing the out-of-wedlock birthrate and the welfare-to-work initiative, which is centered in the Department of Labor.

The states, obviously had a major role in welfare room. They had to develop plans, subject to federal approval, to meet the goals of the new law. The federalist nature of the United States assured that there would be no one program for all states. States would vary in the timeliness with which they submitted their plans, the programs that would be developed, and the reductions that would be made. This nonuniformity created all kinds of problems for those trying to understand the implementation and impact of welfare reform (Bell 1999).

By October 1997, all state plans had been approved by DHHS, and most states had passed implementation legislation (Gallagher et al. 1998). As with AFDC, TANF programs varied by state. Differences among the state programs included eligibility, time limits on TANF, earnings disregards (how much income a recipient could earn before TANF benefits were reduced), work requirements, work sanctions, benefit levels, and family caps.

While space precludes a thorough discussion of TANF programs,[19] some variations should be noted. As noted above, the PRWORA provided for time limits, a two-year consecutive period, and a five-year lifetime limit. It also allowed states to have shorter time limits. Michigan's law did not specify any time limits and allowed the state to determine on a case-by-case basis whether to continue its solely state programs. Texas kept the five-year lifetime limit but imposed shorter limits for when openings in a jobs program became available.

Another element of the program is sanctions, that is, what happens to recipients who do not comply with the requirements of the program, generally to seek work or training. In Alabama, there is a 25 percent reduction in benefits that continues until compliance is reached for up to a six-month period, then all benefits are cut off. In California, noncompliance results in loss of benefit and continued noncompliance results in longer losses of benefits. In Florida, any noncompliance results in termination of benefits.

A third element is diversions. The purpose of diversions is to keep new people from going onto the welfare rolls. Sometimes the diversion programs consists of helping the applicant find work. Sometimes the program consists of providing help other than cash assistance, say child care or transportation. Others involve giving a possible applicant a sum of money while extracting a promise not to apply for assistance for a period of time.

A final element to be noted here is the family cap provision. This provision prohibits increasing a family's benefit if additional children are born after the family moves onto the roles. Some states had implemented family caps under waivers granted by the administration. The 1996 welfare legislation does not address this issue; states are therefore free to implement family caps. Twenty-two states had implementation waivers, fifteen states had prior waivers. Most states have a kind of grace period, saying children born ten months after a family is on welfare will not increase benefits.

While there are clearly punitive aspects to the welfare reform law and state implementation, states are allowed to give exemptions from the work requirements or time limits. Exemptions include age, disability, caring for a disabled person or very young child, being victim of domestic violence, and, perhaps the most important category, personal barriers to employment. Again, some states allow for time extension, others do not.

Perhaps the most interesting and innovative program was Wisconsin's. Recall that even prior to the 1996 legislation, Wisconsin's governor, Tommy Thompson, sought to end the welfare program. Under welfare reform, this goal was essentially accomplished. The new program is **Wisconsin Works**, abbreviated as **W-2** (a nice play on the Internal Revenue Service form that employees fill out when hired so their taxes can be withheld). The overall emphasis of the program is on work and personal responsibility. This can be seen symbolically not only in the name of the program, W-2, but in the name of the state department that runs the program, the Department of Workforce Development. Other welfare-related services are housed in the state's Department of Health and Family Services. Two important principles of the program are privatization and managed competition. Counties compete with the private sector for contracts to deliver services, and most counties in Wisconsin deliver the services. In some counties, including Milwaukee, private-sector agencies have been awarded contracts (Nightingale and Mikelson 2000).

The idea behind W-2 is to place recipients in some kind of work assistance, rather than just give cash assistance. Recipients are placed in one of four job categories:

- Unsubsidized employment (for those who are "job ready")
- Trial jobs (subsidized employment for individuals unable to locate unsubsidized work)
- Community service jobs (for those who need to practice the work habits and skills necessary to be hired by a regular employer)
- W-2 transition (for those who, because of severe barriers, are unable to perform independent, self-sustaining work) (Nightingale and Mikelson 2000, p. 4)

Wisconsin also provides considerable support, such as training, child care, transportation, and transitional Medicaid, for those making the move from welfare to work.

One other element of welfare reform merits some discussion, Welfare-to-Work. As can be seen by the title of the act, the act's provisions, and the brief discussion of implementation, PRWORA's emphasis is on reducing the welfare rolls, reducing dependency, and moving recipients into the workforce. One of the problems with PRWORA was that it was somewhat limited in making job opportunities available to the former recipients. The 1997 Balanced Budget Act contained, at the request of the Clinton administration, funds to begin a new program called Welfare-to-Work. This program is administered by the U.S. Department of Labor and by private industry councils (Nightingale and Brennan 1998). States already had many work-related training programs at the time welfare reform was passed (Bell and Douglas 2000).

The focus of the Welfare-to-Work federal grants was on those who were the most difficult to move to the workforce and would need additional services. Typically these would be recipients who had been on welfare for long periods of time and who had one or more serious barriers to employment, such as less than a high school education (Nightingale and Brennan 1998). Unlike TANF, which is a block grant, Welfare-to-Work is a categorical grant; funds are given to states based on a formula or are competitive and can only be used for this purpose. An early study of implementation of this program shows that states have targeted the appropriate population but implementation has been slow (Trutko et al. 1999). All the states have components that include post employment services; that is, the purpose of the program is not just to find jobs for former welfare recipients, but also to help them keep those jobs. Coordination with TANF programs seems to be good, but there are implementation problems. The decline in the TANF caseload makes it harder to find eligible people. Particularly difficult are noncustodial parents (usually fathers not living with the mother and not paying child support). Setting up the appropriate procedures has taken a while (Trutko et al. 1999).

### Evaluation

Evaluation is an important component of welfare reform. The act itself has a number of evaluation components. Further, the act authorizes TANF through FY 2002. That means it is supposed to be preauthorized by the end of that fiscal year, or theoretically the program cannot operate.[20] Reauthorization provides an opportunity for evaluation.

One important measure of how well welfare reform is working is to look at the caseloads. After all, at least half the purpose of welfare reform was to reduce the caseloads. Table 4.4 shows a decline in that measure. According to the Administration for Children and Families within the U.S. Department of Health and Human Services, the number of welfare recipients has declined by 49 percent since August 1996 when the welfare reform was signed into law (Administration for Children and Families 2000). There is considerable variation in caseload reductions by state, from 17 percent in Rhode Island to 89 percent in Wyoming. Wisconsin saw a 70 percent reduction. It would seem that welfare reform is working.

Possibly, but there are other factors to consider. First, as Table 4.4 indicates, the welfare rolls have been declining steadily since 1994. We can ask whether the decline was larger before or after welfare reform. My calculations show the caseloads declined by 11.1 percent in the 1994–96 period and by 43.1 percent in the 1999–96 period.[21] So it certainly seems as if welfare reform had a major impact.

But there is one other possibility we must consider. During this period,

1994–99 and especially 1996–99, the economy grew rapidly, and unemployment declined significantly. Is it possible that the expanding economy had something to do with caseload declines? Certainly some portion of the declines ought to be attributed to the economy. Indeed, at least some of the decline is based on the favorable economic conditions (Danziger 1999). According to a Council of Economic Advisers report, about 26–36 percent of the decline in 1993–96 and 8–10 percent in 1996–98 was due to improved economic conditions (Council of Economic Advisers 1999). On a related matter, the economy of the late 1990s with its low unemployment rate and low inflation has helped reduce poverty, especially among young black men (Dionne 1999).

Another antipoverty measure that was not part of welfare reform, the Earned Income Tax Credit (EITC), has an important impact on the welfare rolls and poverty generally. The EITC, a form of a negative income tax, was greatly expanded by the Clinton administration in 1993. The tax credit is aimed, as the name says, at working families. As welfare families move from welfare to work, the EITC supplements the newly working family's income (DeLong 2000).

Another aspect is that the welfare law was very generous to the states. In 1994, Wisconsin received $317 million from the federal government; in 1998 it received the same amount. However, as we have seen, Wisconsin's caseload has declined significantly. So the money per welfare family has gone up. Wisconsin has used its extra funds to help welfare recipients by raising benefits, subsidizing jobs, and so forth. It also managed to use the money to cut taxes. Other states have also used some of their money to increase help for recipients, but most states have not used all of their money (DeParle 1999b).

As important as the decline in caseloads is the experience of those who have left TANF. Studies have shown variations in outcomes. The most favorably evaluated program is Minnesota's, which began in 1994 and became the state's program after PRWORA was passed. According to an evaluation of the program by the Manpower Development Research Corporation (MDRC), the program resulted in higher incomes for long-term recipients (largely female-headed families), more employment, reduced poverty, reduced domestic abuse, some increase in marital rates, and increased performance of children in schools (Knox et al. 2000; see also Pear 2000).

The Welfare-to-Work program has also been evaluated. A study of the first two years of eleven state programs found that regardless of approach (employment or education focused), all programs resulted in more involvement in job-related activities. The employment-focused programs produced better employment and earnings gains than the education-based programs, though the researchers exhibited some skepticism about how long those gains would last. Welfare dependency was reduced in all programs. Perhaps most interestingly, while earnings were increased, net family income generally was not, even including the EITC (Freedman et al. 2000).

Not all studies have been positive. There are important questions about what happens to families who leave welfare. We also want to know whether there are important differences between those who left the welfare rolls and those who remained on. Further, welfare reforms seems to have had an impact on caseloads in Medicaid and food stamps.

To take the first questions first, studies show that former recipients are working but not making enough to take them out of poverty without some assistance (Loprest 1999; Parrott 1998). Further, some 20 percent of former recipients are not working, and it is not clear how they are being supported (Loprest 1999). A significant number of welfare leavers go back on. A related concern is that there are differences between leavers and stayers. The stayers, as mentioned above, tend to have multiple employment barriers (Loprest and Zedlewski 1999; Zedlewski 1999).

A related consideration is to look at those who leave welfare. Many are leaving because they have found employment. We are also starting to bump into time limits, and some states have been requesting exemptions from the two-year time limits. And some people have been removed from the welfare rolls because they have failed to follow all the rules. In 1997, some 38 percent of those who left the rolls did so because of sanctions (Toy 1998; Vobejda and Havemann 1998a). Some of those cut off from welfare do have some sources of income, just as do some of those who remain on welfare (DeParle 1997; Vobejda and Havemann 1997).

Perhaps the most troubling of welfare trends related to leavers versus stayers is the demographic issue. A much higher percentage of whites are leaving the welfare rolls than either African Americans or Hispanics (Allen and Kirby 2000; DeParle 1998; Swarns 1998; "Whites Leaving Welfare Faster" 1999). If race was an underlying issue in the passage of welfare reform, as Gilens (1999) powerfully demonstrates, then that underlying issue will remain.

There is one other aspect that needs to be mentioned. Two important social programs aimed at the poor are food stamps and Medicaid. The welfare law does not directly affect Medicaid, though it did create restrictions on food stamp eligibility, largely on legal immigrants. But the implementation of welfare reform has affected those two programs. The new focus of welfare programs is to reduce the rolls. This is done, as we have seen, through time limits, various kinds of assistance (training, child care, etc.), and sanctions for failure to comply with requirements. Another way to keep the rolls down is to make it more difficult to get on welfare. This is done through diversion programs, as discussed above (Vobejda and Havemann 1998c). The impact of doing this is that applicants are diverted not only from welfare, but from the other two programs as well. This outcome seems particularly clear in the case of food stamps. Additionally, in the case of food stamps and Medicaid, studies indicate that families who left welfare were still eligible for the two programs but did not retain those benefits (FamiliesUSA 1999; Garrett and Holahan 2000; Zedlewski and Brauner 1999).

## Conclusion

The course of welfare reform in the late 1990s and early 2000 has clearly seen both good and not so good results. The welfare rolls are down significantly, some of it due to economic conditions, but certainly a substantial portion due to the implementation of the Personal Responsibility and Work Opportunity Reconciliation Act of 1996. There are at least two other good pieces of news. The overall poverty rate and the rate among minority groups has decreased. This is most likely due more to the expanding economy than to welfare reform. A third piece of good news relates to teen pregnancy and out-of-wedlock births. While a number of states instituted family caps, it is not clear that the decline in the birthrate among welfare mothers is due to that policy (Lewin 2000; Vobejda and Havemann 1997). In 2000, the federal government gave its second round of awards to states that decreased out-of-wedlock births the most with the condition that those states see no increase in the rate of abortion (Lewin 2000). There is also a decline in teen pregnancies among the entire population, though again the reasons for the decline are not clear (Dionne 1998; Wingert 1998). Teen pregnancy and out-of-wedlock births are related to other social dysfunctions, such as drug use, problems in school, poverty, child abuse, and so forth (Dionne 1998).

While the successes are there, problems remain (for a major critique of welfare reform, see Collins 2000; DeParle 1999a). For example, while the rolls have declined, the lot of those who have left the rolls (whether because of having found employment, because of sanctions, or because of expiration of time limits) has not improved. Many still have incomes below the poverty level. Many did not have access to food stamps and, especially, Medicaid when they left welfare. Child-care availability and employment training also remain difficult to get. Further, availability of employment in urban areas, particularly in large central cities, is below the demand for those jobs (Allen and Kirby 2000; Collins 2000).

Perhaps the most disheartening part of welfare reform is that those who have left welfare (the leavers) are the people with the fewest barriers. Those remaining on welfare will be the hardest to deal with. And an increasing number of the stayers are members of minority groups. Additionally, many of those who left the welfare rolls did so not because they found jobs or even because their time limits ran out, but because they violated one or more of the strict rules imposed by the states. This group of people have experienced hardships (Bernstein 2000; Meckler 2001).

So what can be done? What should be done? First, we must recognize that the best antipoverty program is continued economic growth. Only in the last few years has the expansion of the economy produced lower levels of poverty and increases of income for those at the lowest range. Second, the most important public program for the working poor, something that welfare reform ignores entirely, is the Earned Income Tax Credit. Raising the minimum wage might also help. Third, support services for those below or near the poverty level need to be enhanced. This route includes increasing access to food stamps and Medicaid, as well as assistance with transportation, child care, and training.

The National Jobs for All Coalition (Collins 2000) recommends a number of changes when PRWORA is due for reauthorization in 2002. These include making sure that jobs are available for those leaving welfare. If jobs are not available, then time limits should be extended. There is some $7 billion in TANF grants to states that has not been spent and which could be used for training and education programs.

Some of the questions facing lawmakers as they consider reauthorization of PRWORA include:

- Should the five-year time limit be loosened?
- Should Washington cut the welfare budget since the caseloads have fallen so much?
- How can the government get people leaving welfare to remain on food stamps, which help to supplement low-wage jobs?
- What can be done to help people who leave the rolls advance up the economic ladder and get better-paying work?
- Should the program do more to encourage people on welfare to get married, or to avoid having children out-of-wedlock? (Bernstein 2000)

Despite criticisms of PRWORA, the welfare policy has been changed, moving toward a punitive strategy (work requirements, sanctions, time limits, family caps). While some states have tried to modify some of the harsher aspects of the law, the comprehensive change will lead at best to incremental change. Perhaps the major question facing the federal government and the states in considering reauthorization is what happens if, and when, the economy moves into a recession. Will there be enough resilience in the law to deal with an increase in unemployment and poverty?

---

## Key Concepts

Aid to Families with Dependent Children (AFDC)

alleviative strategy

antipoverty strategies

block grant

Community Action Program (CAP)

Contract with America

curative strategy

devolution

Earned Income Tax Credit (EITC)

Economic Opportunity Act (1964)

family caps

Family Support Act (1988)

feminization of poverty

food stamps

Head Start

illegitimacy

income security

incomes strategy

inducements

means-tested

Medicaid

Medicare

negative income tax

Omnibus Budget Reconciliation Act (OBRA) (1981)

Personal Responsibility and Work Opportunity Reconciliation Act (PRWORA) (1996)

political strategy

poverty

preventive strategy

punitive strategy

rights

rules

security

Social Security

street-level bureaucrat

Supplemental Security Income (SSI)

Temporary Assistance for Needy Families (TANF)

unemployment compensation

unworthy poor

urban enterprise zones

War on Poverty

welfare-to-work partnership

Wisconsin Works (W-2)

workfare

worthy poor

---

## Reflections

1. This chapter has discussed different approaches to remedying the problem of poverty through the concept of strategies. Each strategy implies unique as-

sumptions about the causes of poverty. Which of the various strategies, or combinations of strategies, do you think best describes the causes of poverty? Why?

2. The alleviative programs (welfare programs) present a good example of what some observers call the "government issue," where government programs themselves cause problems. Do you agree that the alleviative programs have hurt the poor and increased dependency?

3. There are a small number of scholars who see poverty as embedded in capitalist society and call for significant changes, such as income redistribution. Is that a good idea? What barriers might exist to such redistribution?

4. While much of antipoverty policy in the United States is incremental, the welfare reform of 1996 was most certainly not. Why do you think comprehensive or nonincremental change was possible in 1996? Notice that it happened during a time of divided government. What does that tell us about separation of powers/checks and balances? What lessons does welfare reform offer to those seeking comprehensive change in other policy areas?

5. In 2002, the PRWORA is up for reauthorization. Based on what you have read in this chapter and elsewhere, what changes, if any, would you make in the legislation?

## Notes

1. Some, such as Martin Anderson (1978), have argued that we should look at the monetary equivalent of in-kind benefits to determine the true poverty rate. If one adds in all these benefits, then the poverty rate would decrease by approximately 5 percent in 1982 (from 11.2 percent to 6.4 percent of the population). By this reasoning Anderson argues that the war on poverty has been won. There are several implications of a different measure of poverty. The number of poor would, as mentioned, be reduced. The composition of the poverty population would change. The distribution of benefits would also be changed (General Accounting Office 1994). However, to do justice to this argument, one should add in equivalent considerations for families that work and have employee benefits. Doing this would cancel out the in-kind benefits and leave us where we are. For a discussion of the poverty line, including background and criticisms, see Beeghley (1983) and Butler and Kondratas (1987). For a history of the federal poverty line, see Stone (1994).

2. John Schwarz and Thomas Volgy (1992) argue that the official poverty line understates actual poverty. If the original conception of poverty was used, income below that necessary to live on a frugal budget, then the number of people below poverty would double.

3. The discussion of strategies is partially based on Dye (1987) and Moynihan (1973). See also Berkowitz (1991). For a discussion of models of why people are poor, see Ellwood (1989) and Rank (1994).

4. For a history of the Poor Laws, see Cammisa (1998), Ierley (1984), and Katz (1989).

5. Rank (1994) contains a detailed description of the process of applying for and receiving assistance.

6. The major important exception to this statement is the Earned Income Tax Credit. As explained below, this tax credit goes only to families that work and thus would be considered worthy.

7. By contrast, the nomination of Connecticut Senator Joseph Lieberman, an orthodox Jew, as the Democratic vice presidential candidate in 2000 was widely applauded as a major breakthrough.

8. For a discussion of different models or explanations of poverty and related phenomenon such as changes in family structure, see Ellwood (1989) and Rank (1994).

9. For a critique of Murray, see Dolbeare and Lidman (1985); Harpham and Scotch (1989); Kuttner (1984); Marmor et al. (1990); and Rank (1994).

10. For a discussion of these developments, see Stockman (1987).

11. Moynihan is a social scientist who specialized in social policy and worked in the Kennedy, Johnson, and Nixon administrations.

12. Marmor et al. (1990, p. 231) claim that the Family Support Act is really "an excellent example of incrementalism packaged as comprehensive redirection." Their point is that the major impact of the act was to increase benefits and the number covered under government assistance.

13. The idea of shame as a community tool to stir values in a particular direction can be found in communitarian writing. See, for example, Etzioni 1996.

14. For an argument that Quayle was correct, see Whitehead (1993).

15. Recall that in chapter 2 we identified the early 1970s, especially 1973, as the point at which the economy and earnings stagnated.

16. Recall that Murray also attributes the dramatic increase in illegitimacy rates to changing social values and the decline of the stigma against out-of-wedlock births.

17. The following paragraphs are based on the text of the law, which can be found at the following website: ftp://ftp.loc.gov/pub/thomas/c104/h3734.enr.txt. Other sources for this section are based on Cammisa 1998; Greenberg and Savner 1996; and Savner 1996.

18. The process of writing regulations is a very lengthy one, involving notices of proposed rule, the proposal itself, inviting comments from interested parties, considering those comments and revising the rule, and then proposing the final rule. For a description of the rule-making process, see Kerwin (1994).

19. The best analysis of state TANF programs is the Urban Institute's "Assessing the New Federalism Project." The Internet site is http://newfederalism.urban.org.

20. In recent years, Congress has had problems in reauthorizing programs, sometimes because they are very controversial. In those cases, Congress allows the program to continue without the reauthorization. See Baumann 1999.

21. The 1996–99 figure differs from the one provided by the Administration for Children and Families. Table 4.4 reflects the average monthly number of recipients for the entire year. The ACF calculation compares August 1996 to December 1999.

# 5   Health Policy: The Problems of Cost and Access

*Over the last decade or so health has moved from a policy area constrained,
indeed often paralyzed, by professional dominance (Friedson's term),
monopoly (Alford's), and beset by "dynamics without change," to one
exhibiting both colorful dynamics and genuine change. . . . One wonders
whether any policy field in the United States has ever sustained a transition
as compressed and far-reaching as that of the last decade in the health field.*
(Brown 1986, p. 571)

*Virtually everyone has heard by now that the American health care system is
in a state of crisis. But what, specifically, is wrong with it? Why is it plagued
by many problems? And why, after twenty years of tinkering, have our
"experts" been unable to fix it? The list of problems is familiar: We pay more
for health care than any other country in the world, and yet our citizens are
not as healthy as those in other industrialized nations. Millions of Americans
have no health insurance, while millions more are underinsured. Those who
are medically affluent receive expensive treatment even when these treatments
offer little chance of success or prolong lives with relentless misery, while the
poor are denied far less expensive services that might actually save and
enhance their lives. The health care system itself is hamstrung by private and
government bureaucratic controls that hinder medical workers and confuse
and infuriate the public. And, we waste huge sums of money on medically
unnecessary administrative costs.* (Leyerle 1994, p. 10)

Brown's quote opening this chapter suggests that the 1980s saw tremendous
change in the health policy area. The 1990s saw even more dramatic change.
A president proposed a national health insurance program that went down to
defeat. The two large federal programs, Medicare and Medicaid, were objects
of budgeting cutting. The continued increase in health care costs diminished
for a while, only to come roaring back. Much of the insured were enrolled in
managed care organizations, and a backlash to managed care followed. Some
expansion in health insurance coverage took place, largely for children. Mod-

cst protections were put in place for those changing jobs. The number of uninsured continued to increase, though 2000 saw the first decrease in that number in a long time. Welfare reform inadvertently resulted in fewer families covered by Medicaid. The fiscal constraint of large budget deficits that made it acceptable to cut or restrain health care programs was replaced by large budget surpluses. And health care became an important policy issue in the 2000 presidential and congressional elections.

The United States spends proportionately more on health care than any other country. In 1965, 5.9 percent of the gross domestic product (GDP) was devoted to health care. By 1986, that number had risen to 10.6 percent. The percent of GDP devoted to health care spending peaked in 1995 at 13.7 percent and then saw a modest decline through 1998. The United States has the best developed technology and more skilled manpower of any health care system. But it is also the most complicated system. It is a mosaic of public and private medical insurance. Some hospitals are publicly owned, some are nonprofit, and some are managed on a for-profit basis. While doctors used to practice as solo practitioners, many if not most are in some kind of organized group, such as a health maintenance organization or a hybrid such as a preferred provider organization. It is a system with the smallest amount of public insurance or public provision of health services of any of the Western democracies, yet it is the most regulated. It is a system of tremendous complexity, paradox, and change. Underlying all the issues and problems associated with health care is the trade-off between access to insurance and care and the cost of that care.

## Problem Identification

### *Policy Goals*

There are three generic goals that are the focus of health care policy: security, equity, and efficiency (Stone 1997).[1] **Security** in this context refers to needs, providing a minimal or baseline of service. In the United States, as mentioned in the last chapter, those whose income falls below a given standard (the poverty line) may be eligible for publicly financed health services such as Medicaid. Even for those whose income exceeds the poverty line, some states provide Medicaid services if their medical bills would impoverish them—the medically indigent. Within the security goal, health care has both direct and instrumental dimensions. The direct dimension is that people should be healthy. The instrumental dimension is that healthy people are more productive and better able to take care of themselves.

The second generic goal, **equity,** is directly related to security. In the United States, equity has often meant access to health services. Access can mean several things. It means, for example, the ability to pay for medical services. Providing access to all economic groups is one of the oldest of health care concerns. As early as the 1930s, the Committee on the Cost of Medical Care focused on the problem of financial access. The development of medical insurance, first through Blue Cross and Blue Shield, later through private insurers, and finally through public insurance programs (Medicare and Medicaid), addressed the issue of financial access.

However, the ability to afford medical care is only one dimension of access. Availability of services is also an access problem. Rural areas, by definition, have fewer doctors and hospitals than urban areas. Inner-city communities may also lack sufficient doctors and hospitals. Thus some public policy has been aimed at increasing the supply of services and practitioners in underserved areas.

The final health care goal is **efficiency**, which again has several dimensions. Efficiency refers to "getting the most out of something" (Stone 1997, pp. 61–62). It is an instrumental goal because "it helps us obtain more of the things we value" (Stone 1997, p. 61). One might, therefore, inquire whether the benefits of an action, whether public or private, exceed its costs.

Given this goal, it is understandable why the control of health care costs has dominated the political agenda. The United States has experienced relative increases in health care expenditures. That is, health care price increases exceed overall price increases, and growth of health care expenditures exceeds growth in GDP. Health care thus consumes an ever increasing portion of the output each year. This was true before Medicare and Medicaid were established in 1965, and it accelerated after those programs were adopted.

The cost of medical care led to restraints and cutbacks in the provision of health care. As we shall see below, the federal government reduced Medicaid payments to the states and instituted new cost-control systems for Medicare. Private employers, the major source of health benefits to the population, have also taken action to reduce their costs of health care. Thus, there has been conflict between efficiency and equity/security.

## Policy Tools

Five policy tools are available to meet the health care goals. Government can **directly provide services**, as, for example, the Indian health care service. A second tool is to pay others to provide services while issuing rules as to who may provide such services, how they may be provided, what services will be provided, how they shall be financed, and who is eligible. Thus, those who have contributed to Social Security are automatically eligible for Part A of Medicare, which pays for covered hospital visits. Physicians providing services to Medicaid recipients (themselves defined by state and federal rules) must accept what Medicaid is willing to pay.

A third set of policy tools is positive and negative **inducements** or incentives. One example of a positive incentive was the National Health Services Corps. New doctors could have a portion of their student loans forgiven by spending a year in an area (rural or urban) where there were limited medical services. An example of a negative inducement is the prospective payment system for Medicare, adopted in 1983. Under this system, hospitals are paid a preset amount for a given diagnosis (say, coronary bypass surgery or the angioplasty that Dick Cheney had in November 2000) regardless of how long the patient is treated. Thus the incentive is to cut down on the length of hospital stays and costs by not paying for extended visits.

A fourth policy tool in health care is **facts** or persuasion. For example, information may be provided to the public to encourage changing unhealthy behavior. There are many examples of the use of persuasion: the surgeon general's reports about the effects of smoking and the warning labels on cigarette packages; the surgeon general's report on acquired immune deficiency syndrome (AIDS); and reports by the American Cancer Society and the National Academy of Sciences on the relationship between diet and cancer.

The final policy tool is **powers**. Powers, as we saw in chapter 1, relate to who makes decisions. There are two arenas of dispute in health care. One is whether the federal government or the states should take the lead. As discussed in the first chapter, the states became significant policy innovators in the 1980s. The other arena is the government issue itself: to what extent government or private markets should provide health care services. This last dispute relates directly to the efficiency goal. Advocates of markets argue that government is inherently inefficient and that health care goals could be better met with less government involvement. These issues will be considered subsequently in more detail.

## Medical Care in the United States

As we entered the twentieth century, medical care in the United States did not have nearly the impact that it does now. The medical profession had little control over the practice of medicine, and hospitals were places to die rather than to recover from illness. In 1911, the Flexner Report (Brown 1979; Starr 1982) began to change the philosophy of the profession. The report recommended that America adopt the German model of medicine, with scientifically based training. Medical schools changed their curricula and, with the advent of effective drugs such as antibiotics, doctors and hospitals began to have genuine impact.

An important development in the history of the U.S. medical care system came in the 1930s. At the time of the depression, medical insurance did not exist in the United States, and many people could not afford to pay physicians or hospitals. The American Medical Association and the American Hospital Association developed insurance plans, Blue Shield and Blue Cross respectively, to assist patients in paying their bills and, of course, to ensure steady payments to providers. During World War II, wages were frozen and employers could offer only few fringe benefits to their employees. One of those was health insurance, where employers would pay part or all of the cost of the premiums. In 1951, the Internal Revenue Service ruled that employers' cost of premiums was a tax-deductible expense, paving the way for the large-scale development of private insurance. Public insurance began with the Kerr-Mills bill in 1960 to help the poor and developed further with the passage of Medicare and Medicaid in 1965.

## The Federal Role in Medical Care

The role of the federal government in health care originates in the eighteenth century with the establishment of the public health service to provide medical care for members of the U.S. Merchant Marine. From the standpoint of coherent health care policy, one can distinguish among three periods of post–World War II federal policy development in health care: capacity development, expansion of financial access, and cost control. As with poverty policy, there are significant elements of all three periods in present-day policy.

### *Capacity Development*

The first period, which began shortly after World War II, was devoted to capacity development: increasing the supply of providers (largely doctors) and medical care facilities (hospitals). One path of capacity development was public funding of biomedical research through the National Institutes of Health (as early as the 1930s) and the National Science Foundation, beginning in the 1950s. Not only did this research help promote new developments in health care, but it also assisted in the financing of medical schools, since much of the research would be undertaken by the faculty of those schools. A related effort was to assist medical school students by offering relatively low-cost loans. Initially, the idea was to ensure an adequate supply of physicians in all areas of medicine. Later, these loans were used to affect the types of doctors who graduated, directing money and hence students to needed areas. At first, specialists in different areas were emphasized in the 1960s and 1970s. Then, as shortages in general practice began to appear, the emphasis shifted to family practitioners. The federal government also attempted to influence location decisions of physicians. The National Health Services Corps was created to induce doctors to locate for several years in underserved areas in return for a salary and some forgiveness of their medical school loans.[2]

The financial problems caused by the depression and the total mobilization needed to win World War II led to little if any new hospital construction. After the war, the federal government provided financial assistance for the construction of new hospitals, particularly in rural areas, through the Hospital Survey and Construction Act of 1946, better known as the Hill-Burton Act, after its sponsors.

## Expanding Financial Access

The second development period has its domestic origins early in the twentieth century, with foreign roots dating to the 1880s, and concerns the finan-
cial-access problem mentioned earlier. Beginning with Bismarck's Germany
in the nineteenth century, virtually every Western industrialized nation enacted some form of **national health insurance** (**NHI**). The one exception
was, and remains, the United States. There were attempts during the twentieth century to pass NHI legislation, but all were defeated. In the early years,
the American Medical Association (AMA) voted in favor of NHI but then
changed its mind. Recall from chapter 4 that there was some discussion of
including NHI in the Social Security Act of 1935. However, the sponsors of
the act felt that, because of strong AMA opposition, an NHI provision would
endanger the entire bill. The Truman administration made NHI part of the
Democratic Party platform of 1948, but its bills, too, were defeated in the
Congress. NHI supporters continued to press for legislation in the late 1960s
and throughout most of the 1970s. Even the Nixon administration offered a
plan, though its effort was half-hearted. The Carter administration offered an
NHI plan contingent on balancing the budget. There were no serious proposals during the 1980s. Most recently, the Clinton administration proposed comprehensive national health insurance legislation, the **Health Security Act**.
For a variety of reasons, many related to previous attempts at enacting NHI
legislation, the effort failed without a single vote in the House or Senate.[3]

The United States instead relied on the private market and employers to
offer health insurance.[4] Private health insurers sprang up during and after
World War II, and the professionally sponsored Blue Cross/Blue Shield programs developed in the 1930s. It was only after World War II that employer
health insurance became a staple of American society, when the Internal Revenue Service allowed the practice to continue. For most Americans, health
care today is covered by some form of employment-based medical insurance.
Problems remain with this system of health insurance. Those without group
insurance have had to purchase individual medical insurance at high rates.
There are also those who do not have any medical insurance at all. Finally,
there are gaps in the insurance coverage, such as for long-term care.

Having failed to achieve an overall national health insurance plan, public
health insurance advocates turned to a more incremental path—obtaining
coverage for needy groups that were unable to get it for themselves. The particular needy groups were the aged and the poor. A small federal-state program for the poor was passed in 1960, the Kerr-Mills Act, but the major
breakthrough came in 1965.

The Democrats did very well in the 1964 elections. They won the presidency (Johnson defeated Goldwater by the largest popular-vote margin in
history) and gained overwhelming control of Congress. Dozens of new liberals were elected to the House of Representatives. The time was ripe and the

focus was on medical insurance for the aged. Congress passed **Medicare** in 1965 as an amendment to the Social Security Act of 1935 and tagged on a **Medicaid** program targeted for the poor.[5] Legislation in the 1980s expanded access to Medicaid. Two programs enacted during the 1990s increased the ability of workers to carry their insurance coverage to new jobs and to ensure more poor children.

### Cost Control

The third period of federal health policy focused on cost control. It has its origins in the 1965 policy changes and can be dated from about 1970 to the present. To understand the emphasis on cost control, we must first examine two programs, Medicare and Medicaid, in detail. As we shall see later in this chapter, those two programs have become the focus of much concern, especially about costs.

# Medicare

Medicare has become more complicated in recent years. The following paragraphs describe the basic, original Medicare program. Recent options will also be described.

Medicare is a federal health insurance program for people in three categories. The largest group eligible for Medicare is those sixty-five years of age and older. Medicare also covers some people with permanent disabilities who are less than sixty-five and all those who have end-stage renal failure (kidney failure).

The basic Medicare program consists of two parts. The larger part is hospital insurance (HI), known as Part A. This part pays for hospital visits out of Medicare trust funds (the payroll tax similar to the tax for Social Security) and through beneficiary contributions. For example, for each hospital visit, beneficiaries have to pay the cost of the first hospital day (known as a deductible) and some co-insurance (out-of-pocket costs). There is other institutional coverage under Part A: limited skilled nursing care following a hospital visit, hospice services, and some home health care services. Part A is compulsory; a person eligible for Social Security is automatically eligible for Part A.

The second part of Medicare is supplementary medical insurance (SMI), known as Part B, which pays for many nonhospital-related items. These include doctor bills (including those incurred as part of a hospital visit), diagnostic services, and hospital outpatient services. SMI, which is voluntary, is financed by a combination of monthly premiums by beneficiaries and general government revenues. As with HI, SMI provides for deductibles and copayments.

Recent changes in Medicare, from the Balanced Budget Act (BBA) of 1997, included more covered services for Medicare, primarily preventive diagnostic screenings for health problems such as diabetes, osteoporosis, breast cancer, and colon cancer (Century Foundation 2000).

There are limits to Medicare coverage. For example, there is a fee schedule for what Medicare thinks physician visits should cost. Medicare then pays 80 percent of that cost. Doctors do not have to accept that schedule (known as full assignment) and can charge the patient more. Patients are then responsible for paying the difference between what the doctor charges and what Medicare pays. There are also fee schedules for hospitals, nursing homes, and home health care services.

In addition, there are a number of services that Medicare does not cover. These include drugs (issued outside of hospitals), eyeglasses, and dental care. Medicare also pays for only a limited amount of nursing home care that is the follow-up to a hospital visit, amounting to only about $1 billion a year. Medicare does not contain a catastrophic disease clause: Medicare finances only the first ninety days of hospital care (though there is a sixty-nine-day lifetime reserve).

As a result of copayments and coverage gaps, Medicare now pays about two-thirds of health care costs for the elderly. The elderly either pay the rest out of pocket or buy additional private insurance to cover the holes in Medicare coverage. The elderly pay, on the average, about 21 percent of their income on health care (Century Foundation 2000). A growing number of Medicare recipients have switched from the traditional fee-for-service Medicare program to health maintenance organizations (HMOs), which cover many of the uncovered parts of Medicare (such as prescription drug coverage). The traditional way of making up these holes in Medicare is to purchase separate private health insurance, known as **medigap** policies. A third way is that Medicare does have provisions to help pay for those who have low income. A fourth possibility, if the recipient has sufficiently low income, is to be enrolled in state Medicaid programs. Medicaid then, in effect, becomes a medigap policy for those recipients.

Medicare expenditures quickly exceeded initial expectations, and policy makers sought ways to stem the rising cost of the program. This was done by adopting a series of fee schedules for providers, first in 1983 for hospitals and then in 1990 for physicians. Fee schedules were adopted for nursing homes, hospices, and home health care agencies as a result of the 1997 Balanced Budget Act. The future solvency of Medicare raises many of the same issues, as does Social Security. These problems include the solvency of the Part A program, the growing number of people on Medicare, and pressures on Medicare for continued expenditure growth. The program became the subject of congressional attention and presidential politics in 1996 and 2000. These events will be discussed in more detail below.

An example of how the political problems play out in health care came in 1988 and 1989. In 1988, Congress passed the **Medicare Catastrophic Coverage Act (1988)**. The act reduced cost-sharing for hospital stays in excess of sixty days, provided that the hospital deductible be paid only once each year no matter how many hospital stays occurred during the year, and placed a ceiling on Part B (physician) copayments. Secondly, it provided for coverage for prescription medications outside of the hospital. It did not, however, extend Medicare coverage for long-term care (Moon 1996; Rice et al. 1990).

However, because of fiscal constraints—both the budget deficits and concern about the solvency of Medicare—the revenue provisions were unusual. The act provided that recipients pay an additional tax, with much of the tax placed on higher-income Medicare recipients. However, those are the recipients most likely to have medigap policies, which give them coverage similar to that provided for in the new legislation. They were being asked to pay, therefore, for new services that they were already paying for privately. Although the major interest group of the elderly, the American Association of Retired People (AARP), strongly supported the legislation, the wealthier membership did not. They, as well as interest groups such as the National Committee to Protect Social Security and Medicare and the Pharmaceutical Manufacturers Association, campaigned against the act, and in an almost unprecedented fashion, Congress repealed the law in 1989 (Moon 1996).

In 1999 and 2000, the lack of prescription-drug coverage in Medicare resurfaced on the policy agenda. The large increase in the price of prescription medication combined with the heavy reliance of many Medicare recipients on medication, the fixed incomes that many of them live on, and the fact that those without prescription drug coverage often pay full retail price created a problem that policy makers discussed. During the 2000 presidential elections, Democratic candidate Al Gore and Republican candidate George W. Bush offered what were essentially dueling prescription drug plans.

One very important, though not fully realized, change relating to Medicare must be mentioned. This is the availability of alternative plans. One has already been mentioned. Since 1985, Medicare has allowed, though it does not require, recipients to enroll in managed care organizations, such as health maintenance organizations. While enrollment in managed care organizations has increased, by 1999 it still represented only 16 percent of Medicare's 39 million recipients (Kaiser Family Foundation 1999). The Balanced Budget Act (BBA) (1997) included provisions creating the Medicare + Choice program, giving Medicare recipients more choices of plans to enroll in. The choices include medical savings accounts, preferred provider organizations (PPOs), HMOs, point-of-service organizations, and even private fee-for-service contracts (Serafini 1997).

Medicare and managed care have not been an entirely happy experience. The Health Care Financing Administration, the federal agency that administers Medicare (and Medicaid and the state child health insurance program) claims that it has overpaid HMOs. On the other hand, HMOs and other managed care plans insist that they are losing money providing services for Medicare recipients. Forty-five HMOs have pulled out of Medicare, leaving more than 400,000 Medicare recipients scrambling for a new health coverage (General Accounting Office 2000; Century Foundation 2000).

Another important provision of the BBA of 1997, in addition to adopting fee scales for nursing homes and home health care agencies, was to cut payments to hospitals. The combination of fee scales, payment reductions, and premium increases, all found in the 1997 BBA, were designed to alleviate fiscal pressure on Medicare. Early indications are that the provider provisions (fee schedules and provider payment reductions) did in fact result in expenditure control. In fiscal year 1999, Medicare expenditures declined for the first time in the program's history, though some have argued that the BBA cut Medicare expenditures by more than Congress intended (Goldstein 1999; Pear 1999e). Most worrisome is that spending for home health care declined dramatically in the wake of the implementation of the BBA provisions. This means that fewer recipients would be taken care of at home and more in costly nursing homes or hospitals (Pear 2000a).

A related Medicare issue is the solvency of the Medicare Part A trust fund, which is funded by payroll taxes similar to Social Security. The solvency issue became important during the 1995–96 budget battles, as reports by the Social Security trustees said that the fund would go bankrupt by 2000 (Marmor 2000; Rushefsky and Patel 1998). Because of the changes made by the BBA of 1997 and the booming economy, as of early 2001, the insolvency date is now estimated to be 2025 (FamiliesUSA 2001).[6]

## Medicaid

Medicaid, as mentioned in chapter 4, is a federal-state program of medical insurance for the poor. The federal government sets overall standards, such as required services—hospital services, outpatient hospital services, laboratory and X-ray services, skilled nursing home services, and physician services—and pays one-half or more of the expense of the program. States pay the remainder and set eligibility standards and benefit levels (mandatory plus optional services). Medicaid is more comprehensive than Medicare, paying for medication, dental care, and nursing homes. Indeed, Medicaid pays for approximately one-half of nursing home expenses. Medicaid is also an expensive program, though not nearly as expensive as Medicare. As with Medicare at the federal level, Medicaid is taking increasingly larger pieces of state budgets. In 1970, Medicaid accounted for 3 percent of state budgets. That figure rose to 7.2 percent of state budgets by 1996.[7]

Medicaid, like Medicare, has been subject to changes. One important change is that states are allowed to require Medicaid recipients to enroll in managed care organizations as a way of saving money. By 1997, almost 48 percent of Medicare recipients were so enrolled, ranging from 100 percent of enrollees in Tennessee and Washington state to a low of 3.6 percent in South Carolina (U.S. Census Bureau 1999).

During the middle and late 1980s, Congress made incremental changes to Medicaid. While the Reagan administration sought to cut back eligibility for the program, Congress was expanding it, particularly to cover very young children and low-income mothers. Under Medicaid law, states are required to cover all children under the age of eighteen in families with income less than the poverty line by the year 2002 (General Accounting Office 1999; Patel and Rushefsky 1999). In 1997, the BBA created a new program designed to cover

Table 5.1

**National Health Care Expenditures** (in billions of dollars)

|  | 1980 | 1990 | 1993 | 1994 |
|---|---|---|---|---|
| Expenditures |  |  |  |  |
|   Hospitals | 102.7 | 256.4 | 320.0 | 335.7 |
|   Physicians | 45.2 | 146.3 | 201.2 | 193.0 |
|   Nursing homes | 17.6 | 50.9 | 65.7 | 71.1 |
|   Home health care | 2.4 | 13.1 | 21.9 | 26.2 |
|   Prescription drugs | 12.0 | 37.7 | 51.3 | 55.2 |
|   Other | 67.4 | 195.0 | 227.5 | 266.5 |
| Total expenditures | 247.3 | 699.4 | 887.6 | 947.7 |
| Percent of GDP | 8.9 | 12.2 | 13.4 | 13.6 |

*Source:* Levit et al. (2000); Heffler et al. (2001).

uninsured children (see below). As mentioned in the previous chapter, welfare reform has had an impact on Medicaid. Because of state diversion programs, a significant number of families who would be eligible for Medicaid are not covered, and many who leave welfare are still eligible for Medicaid but are not covered (see FamiliesUSA 2000a).

An important access issue related to Medicaid is that while the program was designed to provide health care for poor people, it misses many. If we define poor people as those with income less than the federal poverty line, then Medicaid covered only 43.2 percent in 1997 (U.S. Census Bureau 1999). This is because states set the eligibility criteria, and no state's general eligibility criteria is as high as the poverty line.

## Formulation, Adoption, and Implementation: Cost Control

Shortly after the enactment of Medicare and Medicaid, a number of criticisms arose, including accusations of fraud in both programs and claims of poor administration. However, the major source of concern was the expense of the two programs. Indeed, the entire medical industry has been plagued by cost increases. This is the major issue underlying all others—access, the aging of the population, the quality of care, and the availability of "heroic" measures to keep people alive—in health care.

First the dimensions of the problem need to be examined. Table 5.1 presents data showing changes in the cost of health care. A notable feature of the table is the ever-increasing share of the economy devoted to health care (at least through 1993). Increases in health care spending exceeded increases in gross domestic product. To provide more historical perspective, health care spending as a percent of gross domestic product was 5.3 percent in 1960 and 7.4 percent in 1970. The United States spends more on health care than any other country (Graig 1999).

Table 5.2

**Medicare and Medicaid Program Benefits Expenditures** (in billion dollars)

|      | Medicare | Annual % change | Medicaid* | Annual % change |
|------|----------|-----------------|-----------|-----------------|
| 1980 | 33.9     | N/A             | 24.0      | N/A             |
| 1985 | 69.5     | 21.0            | 39.3      | 12.8            |
| 1990 | 107.2    | 10.8            | 68.7      | 15.0            |
| 1991 | 113.9    | 6.3             | 90.5      | 31.7            |
| 1992 | 129.2    | 13.4            | 115.9     | 28.1            |
| 1993 | 148.3    | 10.8            | 121.6     | 4.9             |
| 1994 | 159.3    | 7.4             | 137.6     | 13.2            |
| 1995 | 176.9    | 11.0            | 152.0     | 10.5            |
| 1996 | 191.1    | 8.0             | 153.2     | 0.8             |
| 1997 | 211.2    | 9.2             | 159.8     | 4.3             |
| 1998 | 211.4    | 0.1             | 172.0     | 7.6             |
| 1999 | 213.6    | 1.0             | 187.7     | 9.1             |
| 2000 | 227.0    | 6.3             | 201.8     | 7.5             |
| 2010 | 441.4    | 6.9             | 446.0     | 8.5             |

*Sources:* Health Care Financing Administration (1998); Levit et al. (2000); Pear (1999); Heffler et al. (2001).
*Note:* *Medicaid includes federal, state, and local share.

The slowdown in costs in the latter part of the 1990s has several explanations. One factor is that the economy began growing at a rapid rate. Another is that the managed care revolution, designed to control the costs of health care, seems to have met its goal (though not without problems of its own, see below). A third reason is our old friend the 1997 BBA.

Another aspect of the cost issue is the two large public programs, Medicare and Medicaid. Table 5.2 presents expenditure data for those two programs. Until the mid-1990s, both programs expanded at double-digit rates. The slowdown and dramatic reduction in expenditures in Medicaid in fiscal year 1999 were the result of state efforts to control costs, largely through enrolling Medicaid recipients in managed care organizations, and the BBA. Another factor for slower growth in Medicaid was the implementation of welfare reform (which had the effect of lowering the number of Medicaid beneficiaries) and the strong job growth that was part of the economic boom of the late 1990s. In the case of Medicare, efforts to decrease fraud and abuse also played a role (Levit et al. 2000).

One important area where the news was not so good, and was reflected in overall health expenditures, was in private health insurance. Again, the move to managed care had an impact on private health insurance. From 1990 to 1994, private health insurance spending increased by an average of 6.3 percent a year. From 1995 to 1997, the increases dropped to a little more than 3 percent a year. In 1998, they increased by 8.2 percent (Levit et al. 2000) and continued that high increase in 2000 (Duggan and Levine 2000; Kaiser Family Foundation 2000). Note that the increases in these years exceeded the overall rate of inflation. There appear to be two reasons for these sharp increases. One is the increases in the cost of prescription drugs. A second factor is that insurance companies kept their premiums low in the early 1990s to expand their markets. They took losses and now were making up for them (Duggan and Levine 2000; Levit et al. 2000; Kaiser Family Foundation 2000).

In some ways, these numbers are very good news. Increases in health care costs in prior years were significantly higher than in the 1990s. A variety of techniques were used to control these costs with limited success (see below). While we have clearly not mastered the cost problem and there does seem to be some acceleration in health care costs as we enter the twenty-first century, a certain amount of optimism, even if limited, is justified. Of course, the trade-off of getting some handle on costs is that it exacted pain among both providers and patients of health care.

Whatever the case, the problem of costs led the states and the federal government to take action to limit the impact on their budgets. Eventually, private actors such as insurers and employers also began to take steps.

## Regulatory Response

The early responses to the cost problem were regulatory in nature and were aimed at capacity development and hospital rates. Typically, the states began the programs that were later adopted by the federal government.

### Capacity Controls

Capacity development centered on limiting expansion of medical services, such as nursing homes and hospitals, through certificate-of-need (CON) programs. Under CON programs, providers of new or expanded services needed permission, a license from the state, for that service. Because such a large part of medical care costs was attributable to hospitals, they were the primary focus. Empty hospital beds cost about two-thirds as much as occupied beds. The incentive, therefore, is to fill beds. CAT scanners become profitable only when used at high levels. It follows that if capacity is restrained, costs are held down. In 1972, the federal government added the Section 1122 amendments to the Social Security Act that would limit Medicare/Medicaid reimbursements to approved expenses.[8] In 1974, Congress passed the National Health Planning and Resources Development Act, establishing CON on a nationwide basis under national guidelines. States were to establish health systems agencies (HSAs) to administer the guidelines, with state agencies having the final responsibility.

The CON programs were controversial, particularly the national health guidelines. The idea that the federal government would establish national guidelines in a sector that was predominantly private (though with consider-able government regulation) was anathema to many. Evaluations of the state CON programs, the 1122 program, and HSAs were generally negative. There is no question that fewer facilities were built than otherwise would have been, yet there was little to show for it in terms of decreased health costs. By the 1980s, HSAs had little support, and Congress eliminated their funding, leav-ing states the option to maintain the program; most states eliminated the agen-cies. This type of heavy-handed regulation was seen as a failure.

## Utilization Review

The federal government also tried to stem costs through utilization review, in which medical regional areas established review committees, known as Profes-sional Standards Review Organizations (PSROs), to review hospital admis-sions in a geographical area (hospitals have their own review boards for individual admissions) and create profiles of geographical areas. This information could be used to limit inappropriate use of hospital facilities and to highlight areas of high use. Evaluations of the PSRO program showed that it barely paid for itself. The program was phased out and replaced by Peer Review Organizations (PROs) without the federal mandate attached. Utilization review made a dramatic come-back with the managed care revolution (see below).

### Rate Regulation

The other major type of regulatory response was rate control. CON regula-tion was indirect; the hope was that by limiting supply, demand would also be limited. Rate regulation addressed the problem directly. Again, the states took the lead in this area.

The idea behind rate regulation is that a government agency would ap-prove either specific rates or hospital budgets. (Note again that hospitals were the major target.) Evaluations of state rate-regulatory programs were mixed (Fossett 1994). The larger states with older programs were successful in mod-erating cost increases. The smaller states were less successful (Sloan 1983). Of course, most states did not undertake such a program.

The federal government attempted to control rates in two ways. In 1971, President Nixon, under authority granted to him the previous year by Con-gress, imposed a wage-and-price-control program on the entire economy. The program went through several phases and lasted until the spring of 1974. During this time medical care price increases were restrained, though medi-cal care expenditures continued to climb. Near the end of the program, there was some discussion of keeping hospital controls. The industry maintained that it would restrain costs. Controls were lifted, and costs skyrocketed.

The Carter administration proposed a hospital cost-control program, but it never passed Congress. One reason is that the industry—hospitals and insurers

—promised to make an effort on their own to limit cost increases. This attempt, known as the Voluntary Effort, had some early success in the late 1970s, but with the defeat of the bill and the coming of the antiregulatory Reagan administration, the Voluntary Effort folded.[9]

Much of the regulatory efforts of this period (such as the CON and PSRO programs) were disliked because they shared three basic properties. First, programs were behavioral regulation in the sense that they scrutinized individual decisions in a detailed way and tried to block those that were inappropriate. Second, they worked within the traditional cost-based reimbursement system and tried to modify around the edges. Finally, they were federally mandated (Brown 1986).

During the Reagan period, an ambitious program of rate control was installed. New Jersey established a program of rate regulation for all hospital payers, known as **diagnostic-related groups** (**DRGs**).[10] When a patient entered a hospital, his or her treatment was placed in one of a number of diagnostic categories. The amount of payment for treatment in each of the categories was predetermined; this constituted a **prospective payment system** (**PPS**). The patient was treated and then released. If the cost of treatment was less than the payment schedule, the hospital kept the difference. If the treatment cost more than the schedule calls for, the hospital suffered the loss. The incentive is placed on the hospital as to how the patient will be treated. Of course, the doctor is the major determinant of hospital treatment (and his expenses are not covered by DRGs even if they occurred in the hospital), and so hospitals placed pressure on the doctors for efficient treatment.

In 1982, Congress passed a tax increase law known as the Tax Equity and Fiscal Recovery Act (TEFRA). Part of that law mandated that the Department of Health and Human Services (DHHS) prepare a proposal for the prospective payment of Medicare hospital costs. The next year, DHHS proposed a DRG system, and Congress enacted it into law. Congress wanted to alleviate the impact of Medicare hospital costs on the federal budget deficit. But in so doing, it changed a fundamental deal made back in 1965.

Both the Medicare and Medicaid legislation, as well as other federal legislation passed in the mid-1960s, contained provisions that forbade the federal government to interfere with the practice of medicine. This meant that the federal insurance programs would pay doctors on the basis of "usual, customary, and reasonable fees," and hospitals on the basis of their costs. These are the features that contributed to the explosion of medical care costs.

Theodore Marmor and colleagues (1983) employ a theory of imbalanced political interests to explain "The Politics of Medical Inflation."[11] They argue that physicians and hospitals are faced with the concentrated benefits and costs of payment and regulatory policies and therefore have an incentive to play an active role in determining the features of reimbursement and regulation. Consumers (patients) have little incentive (because they experience diffuse benefits and costs) to participate because most of their costs of medical care are paid by third parties. Marmor and his colleagues maintain, following from this theory, that only when government becomes so involved in paying for medical care that budgetary pressures are created will government act to restrain costs in a meaningful way. Some of the opposition on the part of medical and hospital groups to national health insurance and to Medicare/ Medicaid was precisely on this basis (as was the opposition of the pharmaceutical industry in 1999 and 2000 to including a prescription drug benefit in Medicare). It was not until the 1980s that increasing medical care costs came up against the realities of fiscal constraint. The DRG system was the first incarnation of the government interference that Marmor and his colleagues predicted. Physician payments under Medicare were frozen during the late 1980s as a reaction to overall fiscal stress (large budget deficits) and the particular concerns of Medicare costs on the federal budget. A similar program to restrain physician fees began in 1990. In 1997, prospective payment controls were placed on nursing homes and home health care agencies.

As Lawrence Brown (1986) has pointed out, the DRG system and state rate-regulatory programs embody a different regulatory theory than either CON or PSRO. First, they represented budgetary rather than behavioral regulation: The idea was to set a limit on budgets and then let managers decide how to live within it. Second, rate setting is based on prospective payment and thus breaks with traditional programs.

How well has the prospective payment systems worked? From the standpoint of federal budgets, it has undoubtedly caused slower growth in Medicare expenditures. Because Medicare is such a significant portion of most short-term hospital budgets, hospitals too have been affected. Utilization review committees examine admissions and treatment practices. There is encouragement to release patients sooner than before. Despite some complaints that hospitals had been affected adversely, most seem to have survived the transition. The major exceptions are public hospitals that have been left with an enhanced role in caring for the uninsured. Cross-subsidization of services, where profitable services help fund unprofitable ones, has declined because slack has been taken out of the system. Thus, one impact may be to reduce access of medically indigent people, those without either public or private health insurance. Overall health expenditures and hospital expenditures in particular showed some slowdown in increases. Physicians saw reduced payments and thus some affect on their income. Nursing homes and home health care agencies saw significant cuts in their reimbursements, and that may have hurt the availability of services, particularly home health care services (Pear 2000a).

## Market Alternatives

If regulatory programs are only modestly successful or are successful but cause considerable pain, then perhaps relying on market alternatives would help. In health care, as in other policy areas, conservatives have touted markets or market-like systems as alternatives to regulation. This follows from the belief in the essential superiority of markets over command-and-control systems such as regulation, a belief dating to the 1776 publication of Adam Smith's *The Wealth of Nations*. It also is a fundamental premise of economically based analysis.

Economists argue, and can mathematically demonstrate, that under conditions of perfect competition, the price mechanism can produce the most efficient outcomes. These requirements include perfect information and perfect mobility of resources. But in health care (and in environmental policy discussed in chapter 6), perfect competition may not be in evidence. In health care, where there is considerable discrepancy (asymmetry) in information between doctor and patient, perfect information does not exist. Nor is there interchangeability of units of production. Some doctors or nurses or hospitals are better than others. When the conditions of perfect competition are missing, we have what economists call **market failure**. Market failure is one of the major justifications for government intervention, at least by economic reasoning.

It does not necessarily follow that government regulation is the best cure for market failure (Wolf 1979). Creating conditions that approximate competition may be the route to take—an idea advocated as far back as the 1960s. The attempt to create markets in health care (and in other policy areas) is known as **market reform**, and is a good example of attempting to effect change by altering power relationships (Stone 1997).

Market reform in health care went through two stages, based on the same analysis of the ills of the health care system. The major problem was that the presence of insurance, whether private or public, distorted medical markets by reducing or removing price considerations from decisions about medical care.

The first stage took a supply-side stance by attempting to create new forms of medical care organizations that would compete with more conventional forms and would also remedy some of the problems of insurance. This new form, with an old origin, is the **health maintenance organization (HMO)**.[12] For a set premium, HMOs offer a comprehensive set of services to its subscribers, usually with limited or no additional payments. While this seems as if it goes against the market reformers' analysis that too much insurance is the problem, the incentives are for the suppliers, the HMO. An HMO receives no additional money for providing services, so its incentive is to question unnecessary services and attempt to maintain the well-being of its subscribers.

The strategy was embodied in the Health Maintenance Organization Act of 1973, which provided subsidies to HMOs meeting federal standards. HMO membership grew substantially during the 1970s and 1980s, though much of the growth came in HMOs that did not get federal funds. The Reagan administration, though sympathetic to the market reform strategy, phased out HMO subsidies as no longer necessary.

How well did the HMO strategy work? Health care costs continued their increases, but market penetration on the part of HMOs was too small to make a dent on the national level. There has been considerable research on the impact of HMOs, showing mixed results (Luft 1981). Hospital admissions are fewer for HMO subscribers than for those enrolled in private or public insurance plans, but hospital stays are a little longer. The cost of HMOs is lower than for people enrolled in conventional insurance plans, but cost increases paralleled overall increases. In the 1980s, cost increases associated with HMOs were sufficient to cause businesses to cut back on their employer contributions (Kramon 1987). HMOs also met resistance from the medical profession (though this has diminished considerably), which has a long-standing abhorrence for organized practice. But HMO growth continued in the 1990s, and by the mid-1990s over 40 million Americans were members of HMOs or variants of HMOs (Freudenheim 1994). The health maintenance strategy eventually evolved into a managed care strategy, which had much stronger impacts (see below).

By the late 1970s, the supply-side market reform strategy had established itself but with little effect on the cost problem. The second phase of market reform was the demand-side strategy. Here the idea was to restore the price mechanism by making the patient, the consumer of medical services, more aware of the cost of medical care. This could occur in two ways. The more primitive manner, as described by Feldstein (1977) and others, is to provide insurance only for catastrophic care, defining catastrophe as a certain percentage of income or a certain dollar amount, say $4,000 a year. This means that for the first set of dollars—the small medical needs that result in a doctor visit—patients have to consider whether they really need the service. Further, it is the high-cost care that financially hurts families, not the first or early dollars. This strategy has little support, and analysis suggests that it would have little impact on health care costs. A major portion of health care costs consists of catastrophic care for only a small sector of the population, particularly those in the last year of life (Berk and Monheit 2001). Thus, while there is some sense to the primitive solution, it does not solve the problem of ever-increasing costs.

The sophisticated strategy does not suffer from these problems. It had two variants, one resembling national health insurance and a more modest version using employer-based insurance. Let us start with the modest version. Many employees have no choice among insurers. Suppose they are given a choice of several different plans. One might be an HMO. A second might be traditional indemnity insurance, with deductibles and co-insurance. The third might be a catastrophic-based plan. It would stand to reason that the three plans would cost different amounts for the employee and his or her family. Now suppose that the employer contributes an equal amount to the cost of the plan no matter which plan is chosen, and that the contribution is less than the cost of the cheapest plan—the catastrophic one. (It is the cheapest because the employee would pay higher deductibles, say $4,000.) Then the appropriate decision situation comes when deciding which plan to choose, not whether a particular service is needed.

Through this mechanism, a market is created in health insurance plans. If some features are added, such as the ability to periodically change plans when dissatisfied, then unsatisfactory or costly plans will lose subscribers or will have to change to meet the competition. This is, in essence, what markets are all about. In markets, consumers are sovereign, and producers respond to consumer demand (understanding that in reality producers go a long way toward shaping that demand). The NHI version of such would issue vouchers for a portion of the cost of health plans (Enthoven 1980). The health insurance program for federal employees (Federal Employees Health Benefits Program or FEHBP) and California state and local employees (CalPERS) is based on this idea. The NHI version of it came to be known as **managed competition**, health plans competing for subscribers, and became the basis for the Clinton Health Security Act, proposed in 1993.

While managed competition was the hot policy concept in health care during the late 1980s and early 1990s, managed care became the choice of public (especially Medicaid) and private employers. More than 50 percent of Medicaid recipients are enrolled in managed care organizations, and more than 90 percent of those with employment-based insurance are enrolled in such plans (Walsh 2000).

## Policy Succession

The federal government and the states were successful in passing health-related legislation in the 1990s. At the federal level, 1996 and 1997 were important years. In 1996, the federal government passed the **Health Insurance and Portability Accountability Act (HIPAA)**. This act addressed a problem that was placed on the policy agenda in the early 1990s. This problem, known as **joblock**, came about because workers who had employment-based health insurance would change jobs and find that they were no longer covered, even if the new job had such a benefit. Further, people with preexisting conditions were fearful of changing jobs because insurance companies might deny them coverage. HIPAA provided protections for people switching jobs (this is the portability portion), although it did not limit the costs of new insurance policies. HIPAA represented the first regulation of insurance companies by the federal government (insurance regulation has been a state prerogative), and the law called for implementation by the states (unless they defaulted and then the federal government would take over) (Polzer 1999).

Legislation passed around the same time addressed an issue related to managed care. As we shall see below, the incentives of managed care may lead to providing less rather than more services (as is the case with the traditional indemnity insurance, third party, fee-for-service system). One place where this issue arose was in childbirth. The media carried stories that women who had just given birth in a hospital were released a day after delivery (what was called "drive-through" deliveries and sometimes "drive-by" deliveries). Federal legislation required at least a forty-eight-hour stay for women who had a normal birth, and ninety-six hours for women who had a cesarean section birth.

As mentioned above, 1997 was an important year for health policy. The primary legislation here was the Balanced Budget Act. It affected Medicare in a number of ways. It reduced provider payments and imposed a prospective payment system for nursing homes and home heath care agencies. It created the Medicare + Choice program.

But the BBA contained another important feature, in this case an expansion of insurance coverage. The BBA amended the Social Security Act, adding a new title, XXI, for a **state children's health insurance program**, known as **S-CHIP** or **CHIP**. While previous legislation had as a goal that Medicaid should cover all children living in poverty-stricken families by 2002, it was clear that this goal was not going to be met (though more children were being covered under Medicaid). Under the CHIP program, the federal government would provide $24 billion over a five-year period and $40 billion over a ten-year period to the states, a portion of which the states would have to match. The states then had some choices as to how to cover its eligible children (which could, under state discretion, be in families at up to 200 percent of the poverty line). States could use Medicaid as its primary program. Or they could create a separate program to meet this need (Patel and Rushefsky 1999).

Under the program some 2 million children have been covered who were not eligible for Medicaid (Health Care Financing Administration 2000). Using a somewhat different methodology, the Kaiser Commission found that a little less than a million additional children have been covered (Kaiser Commission on Medicaid and the Uninsured 2000).[13] Some states were quicker than others in implementing CHIP (Pear 1999b; Steinhauer 2000), and this even got caught up in the 2000 presidential elections. Democratic candidate Vice President Al Gore's campaign charged that Texas, the home of his Republican opponent Gov. George W. Bush, was slow to enroll children in the program (Pear 2000b)

During the late 1990, Congress deliberated on and President Clinton called for a patients' bill of rights. Such a bill would give subscribers (and providers) in managed care organizations a set of rights against the organization's attempt to restrict or deny services. This might even include the right to sue a managed care organization. Congress, embroiled in the 2000 elections and with many Republicans opposed to such legislation, passed separate bills in the House and the Senate. No conference meeting was held in 2000, and so the bill languished. President Clinton then issued an executive order providing for patients' rights for employees in private employee plans under the authority of the Employment Retirement Income Security Act (ERISA). Congress continued to consider this legislation in 2001, and President Bush supported a version of it (Pear 2001).

Additionally, most of the states passed legislation providing for patients' rights. The legislation varied in scope, with a few states providing for enter-

Table 5.3

**Number and Percentage of Uninsured People**

|        | Total number of uninsured (in thousands) | % of population uninsured |
|--------|------------------------------------------|---------------------------|
| 1987   | 31,026                                   | 12.9                      |
| 1988   | 32,680                                   | 13.4                      |
| 1989   | 33,385                                   | 13.6                      |
| 1990   | 34,719                                   | 13.9                      |
| 1991   | 35,445                                   | 14.1                      |
| 1992   | 38,641                                   | 15.0                      |
| 1993   | 39,713                                   | 15.3                      |
| 1994   | 39,718                                   | 15.2                      |
| 1995   | 40,582                                   | 15.4                      |
| 1996   | 41,716                                   | 15.6                      |
| 1997   | 43,448                                   | 16.1                      |
| 1998   | 44,281                                   | 16.3                      |
| 1999   | 42,554                                   | 15.5                      |

*Source:* Mills (2000).

prise liability. This brief review of late 1990s actions shows the importance of the states in the health policy arena. The states are responsible for implementing HIPAA and CHIP and their own patients' rights laws.

# Problem Identification

## *The Uninsured*

A number of health issues were featured during the 2000 elections. Ads from candidates at the federal level, including at the presidential level, mentioned the patients' bill of rights and a prescription drug benefit for Medicare. Starkly absent from political discussion was any mention of the problem of those who are uninsured.

Table 5.3 presents data concerning the uninsured in the United States. The data show a clear increase in the number and percent of the population from 1987 through 1999. In tune with a theme of this book, optimism, 1999 saw the first decline in the number and percentage of those not covered. There are two likely reasons for this shift. First, and probably most important, is the continued economic expansion and low unemployment rate. As workers become harder to find, employers have to offer more in the way of salary and benefits. A second possible factor is the implementation of S-CHIP, though this is somewhat offset by people losing Medicaid coverage because of the welfare reform (Holahan and Kim 2000; Mills 2000). Even though there is some good news, the overall problem remains that a sizable portion of the population does not have health insurance, and the economy started faltering at the end of 2000.

One sees gaps in the coverage. For example, some 10 million people who live in families under the poverty level are not covered by Medicaid (Mills 2000). As with poverty, there is a racial dimension to the uninsured. Eleven percent of whites were uninsured in 1999 compared to 21.2 percent for blacks, 20.8 percent for Asians/Pacific Islanders, and 33.4 percent for Hispanics. In terms of age, the group with the highest uninsurance rate is eighteen-to twenty-four-year-olds. A good portion of the uninsured work (Mills 2000; see also Schroeder 2001). While employment-based health insurance coverage did increase in 1999 (Mills 2000), the offsetting problem is the increased cost of health insurance premiums and the shifting of health insurance costs to employees (Miller 2000). Cost shifting and premium increases price workers out of the market, and they turn down health insurance (Findlay and Miller 1999). Further, small employers are less likely to offer health insurance than larger employers.

So a good portion of the population is without health insurance. Does that mean that they cannot get care? The answer is that care is available to all, but at a price. If you cannot afford to see a doctor, you put off taking care of health problems. When the health problem becomes serious enough, you go to a hospital emergency room. This is the most expensive type of care for nonthreatening health that you can find. It is also time consuming. The literature is very clear that those who do not have health care generally speaking have poorer health than those who do (Patel and Rushefsky 1999, chapter 5).

The question then is what should be done. This is a particularly cogent question because the chances of enacting some kind of NHI program are close to zero, especially given the demise of the Clinton plan. Nevertheless, there are several incremental ways the uninsured could be covered.

One way to do this is to take existing programs and expand them. Medicaid could cover a larger proportion of the impoverished population, particularly parents (see Guyer and Mann 1998; Ku and Broaddus 2000). There have been proposals for a Part C of Medicare that would allow families to buy into the program. Another suggestion is to create more community health centers, what is called a Federally Qualified Health Center (Helerman 2000). What all these programs have in common is that they would call for an extension of government programs and heavy state and local government involvement.

Another government-type program occurs at the state level. A number of states have created risk-pools, especially for those who can afford to buy some insurance but are priced out of the market by high premiums. These are generally for individuals and particularly for those who have preexisting medical conditions that preclude the purchase of medical care (Stearns and Slifkin 1997). States can also bring together small employees in alliances that purchase health care for their employees.

As opposed to positive government action, public programs can be designed to subsidize the purchase of health insurance through tax deductions or tax credits. A certain portion, decreasing as income increases, can be taken off an individual or family's income tax obligation. The Heritage Foundation has supported such a plan, arguing that a tax-credit-based program would improve equity in the tax system (tax credits and deductions for health currently in the system benefit higher-income families), allow choice of plan, and turn control over to the consumer (Frogue 2000). Though generally conservative in nature, such plans have had some bipartisan support from people like former New Jersey senator Bill Bradley, who made a brief run in 1999–2000 for the Democratic nomination for president.

In October 2000, House Speaker Dennis Hastert (R-IL) proposed a tax deduction for those paying at least 50 percent of their health insurance costs. According to one analysis, the proposal is poorly targeted because the people who would benefit the most are those who need it the least. Further, the tax deduction is worth more to people at the higher income scale than at the lower income scale. At best, only 6 percent of the benefit would go to low-income families. Further, this analysis suggests that small business employers might drop their coverage altogether (Friedman and Lav 2000). Another analysis of using tax subsidies to help the uninsured suggests that only about 30 percent of the insured would be covered and that such a program would likely cost about $40 billion a year. The authors conclude that tax subsidies would help, but other programs would be necessary as well (Gruber and Levitt 2000).

One of the more interesting sets of proposals came from the insurance industry itself, and it combines the proposals just discussed. The Health Insurance Association of America (HIAA) proposed a four-step program to cover those currently without coverage. The first step would be an expansion of the CHIP to cover everyone with income under the poverty line. Second, those with income of 100–200 percent below the poverty line would be given a voucher worth $2,000. Third, for those who are unable to buy private health insurance because their health is poor, HIAA proposes federal subsidies for state insurance risk pools. The final proposal is a series of tax credits for those buying individual health insurance plans (which are much more costly than purchasing through a group), including those who are self-employed, and for small employers to help defray the cost of health insurance (which is much more expensive for small employers than for large employers). HIAA estimates that such a plan would cost about $60 billion a year but could be adopted incrementally (Pear 1999c).

Most interesting is that the president of HIAA, Charles N. Kahn III, and the executive director of the consumer group FamiliesUSA, Ron Pollack, came out with a joint proposal, or at least the beginning of a proposal, in 2001. Described as a second choice or compromise position, it calls for building on existing structures (such as employment-based insurance and Medicaid and S-CHIP) and focusing on the most needy first. Thus they propose expanding Medicaid eligibility to all those living in households with incomes under 133 percent of the poverty line (remember that Medicaid tends to cover only those with incomes considerably less than the poverty line); establishing a program either through Medicaid or S-CHIP for people living in households between 133 and 200 percent of the poverty line; and, finally, giving a tax credit for businesses to encourage them to offer health insurance to their employees (Kahn and Pollack 2001).

## Long-Term Care and an Aging Population

> In 1900, life expectancy for Americans was 47 years of age. By 1935, when President Franklin D. Roosevelt and Congress enacted the Social Security program, establishing eligibility at age 65, life expectancy had risen to age 62. By 1998, life expectancy had risen to 76.6 years, and it is projected to rise to age 81 in 2030, according to recent estimates by the Social Security Administration's Advisory Board. (Moffit et al. 2000)

The United States faces a problem of an increasingly aging population. It affects public programs such as Medicare, Medicaid, and Social Security. Table 5.4 presents the data. Note that the percent of children is projected to decline as is the percent of those in the prime working years, twenty-five to sixty-four. The segment of the population projected to increase as a proportion of the total population is the elderly, those sixty-five and older. Notice also that the largest increase is among the oldest elderly, those eighty-four and older. That segment is expected to triple in size, relatively speaking, by the year 2050. By 2040, the elderly population will be over 20 percent of the total population. This older population will need more health services, such as nursing homes, assisted-living services, and home health care services. However, the United States has no long-term health care policy.

Medicare pays for a very small portion of nursing home expenditures, about 11 percent (see Table 5.5). Medicaid pays about 47 percent but is means-tested; one has to be impoverished to be covered. Table 5.5 also shows that private long-term care insurance pays for a small portion of nursing home care, though the percentage of such care paid for has grown to 8.3 percent in 1999.

The problem is that while much of the elderly population will not spend any time in a nursing home (though the proportion will likely increase as the 85+ group increases in size), for those who do have to spend time in a nursing home, the costs are very high. In 1985, the average monthly charge for a nursing home was $1,456, or $17,472 a year. By 1997, that figure had increased to $3,609 a month, or $43,308 a year (National Center for Health Statistics 2000). Few people have the assets to cover these kinds of costs, and at this rate it does not take long to become impoverished. Some people engage in early estate planning, the transferring of assets to family members, to get down to the Medicaid-eligible levels and keep the estate for their heirs (Moffit et al. 2000).

Further, home-health and assisted-living services are not cheap either. In 1998, home-health services could cost as much as $36,000 a year, assisted-

Table 5.4

**Population Projections by Age**

|      | Total population | Under 5 to 18 | % of total population | 25 to 64 | % of total population |
|------|------------------|---------------|-----------------------|----------|-----------------------|
| 1999 | 272,330 | 70,548 | 25.9 | 141,632 | 52.0 |
| 2000 | 274,634 | 70,782 | 25.8 | 142,884 | 52.0 |
| 2005 | 285,981 | 71,963 | 25.2 | 149,584 | 52.3 |
| 2010 | 297,716 | 72,511 | 24.4 | 155,660 | 52.3 |
| 2015 | 310,134 | 74,523 | 24.0 | 159,528 | 51.4 |
| 2020 | 322,742 | 77,604 | 24.0 | 162,000 | 50.2 |
| 2025 | 335,050 | 80,783 | 24.1 | 161,942 | 48.3 |
| 2030 | 346,899 | 83,443 | 24.1 | 162,252 | 46.8 |
| 2040 | 369,980 | 88,817 | 24.0 | 171,360 | 46.3 |
| 2050 | 393,931 | 96,117 | 24.4 | 182,620 | 46.4 |

*Source:* U.S. Census Bureau (1999), 17 and ff. of population abstract.

living services as much as $26,000 a year (Moffit et al. 2000; see also Goldstein 2001b). Projections by the Congressional Budget Office (1999) show that by the year 2010, $108 billion will be spent on institutional long-term care and another $52.2 billion on services delivered in the home.

States are also concerned about the impact of long-term care on their budgets, primarily through Medicaid. Some states are considering encouraging the purchase of long-term care insurance policies. Many states (and the federal government) would like to reduce estate planning that protects assets from the cost of long-term care. Some states have sought to get Medicare (a solely federally funded program) to pay more for long-term care. Another policy being looked at is to integrate long-term care services and acute-care services via managed care. Expanding community and home-based services is another option being looked at. And, of course, there are the more traditional regulatory approaches, such as limiting supply and cutting reimbursements. States also have the primary role for ensuring the quality of care by long-term care agencies (Wiener and Stevenson 1998), though assisted-living services face less regulation than nursing homes (Goldstein 2001a).

So what can or should be done about this problem? The cost of long-term care played no role in the 2000 presidential campaign. Further, we should note that much of the care for elderly payment is given privately by families, though there is a considerable cost for this kind of private care (see Rimer 1999). One possible policy alternative is to allow more flexibility in work schedules for those employees (mostly women) taking care of their parents. Such policies are more available through large private-sector employers and public-sector employers (Patel and Rushefsky 1999). One proposal that has been made is tax

| Over 64 | % of total population | 65 to 84 | % of total population | Over 84 | % of total population |
|---|---|---|---|---|---|
| 34,439 | 12.6 | 30,315 | 11.1 | 4,124 | 1.5 |
| 34,710 | 12.6 | 30,451 | 11.1 | 4,259 | 1.6 |
| 36,166 | 12.6 | 31,267 | 10.9 | 4,899 | 1.7 |
| 39,408 | 13.2 | 31,267 | 10.5 | 5,671 | 1.9 |
| 45,566 | 14.7 | 39,373 | 12.7 | 6,193 | 2.0 |
| 53,220 | 16.5 | 46,760 | 14.5 | 6,460 | 2.0 |
| 61,952 | 18.5 | 54,906 | 16.4 | 7,046 | 2.1 |
| 69,378 | 20.0 | 60,923 | 17.6 | 8,455 | 2.4 |
| 75,233 | 20.3 | 61,681 | 16.7 | 13,552 | 3.7 |
| 78,859 | 20.0 | 60,636 | 15.4 | 18,223 | 4.6 |

credits for those who take care of an elderly parent ("Republicans Backing Tax Break for Care of Elderly Relatives" 1999). There are other policy alternatives.

One such alternative would be to rely more on home health care. As Table 5.1 indicates, spending on home health care services increased dramatically in the early 1990s as Medicare allowed coverage of home health care beginning in 1989 (Feder et al. 2000). By 2001, spending on home health care is projected to be $38.3 billion, with Medicare paying $13.1 billion and Medicaid paying about 52 percent of that amount (Health Care Financing Administration website). Private insurance will pay about $4.6 billion, and recipients and their families will pay about $8.7 billion. The advantage of home health care services is that they are considerably less expensive than nursing homes (Patel and Rushefsky 1999). Further, the elderly person remains in a home environment rather than in the much more sterile and depressing nursing home environment.

There have been problems with the quality of care with both nursing homes and home health (and hospice and assisted-living) agencies, so that fraud has taken place in some of these institutions. The BBA of 1997 increased the penalties for fraud and the resources for detecting fraud. In addition, payments to nursing home and home health providers were reduced.

A second alternative would be to expand coverage through Medicare and/ or Medicaid. Given the financial implications of doing so and the debate surrounding Medicare in particular (see next section), this would be a very difficult course of action to take.

A third alternative would be to just let consumers pay more. Given the high price of long-term care, whether institutional or at home, this also seems a difficult way to go.

A fourth alternative, and somewhat related to the above, is for consumers to

Table 5.5

**Personal Health Expenditures Percentage Distribution by Source of Funds, 1999**

|  | Direct consumer | Private insurance | Medicare | Medicaid | Other |
|---|---|---|---|---|---|
| Total personal expenditures | 7.6 | 33.6 | 19.5 | 16.5 | 12.8 |
| Hospital care | 3.2 | 31.2 | 31.1 | 17.1 | 17.4 |
| Physician services | 11.4 | 47.7 | 20.3 | 6.6 | 14.0 |
| Nursing home care | 26.6 | 8.3 | 10.9 | 47.1 | 7.1 |
| Home health care | 27.2 | 19.0 | 26.3 | 16.9 | 10.6 |
| Prescription drugs | 35.0 | 43.2 | 2.0 | 17.3 | 2.5 |

*Source:* Calculated from Heffler et al. (2001).

purchase long-term care insurance. This could even be part of an employee benefit package. Thus the contingency would be taken care of. But given the problems of employer-based health insurance, this also faces some difficulties. First, it would increase the cost of health insurance. For smaller employers, already loath to offer health insurance benefits at all, this result would make it even more unlikely. Further, there is, as we have noted, a sizable portion of the population currently without insurance. An employment-based program would not help them at all. A third consideration is that people are not likely to want to purchase such a plan until the need becomes more evident. Even a tax subsidy, through a credit or deduction, might not have much impact on the long-term care insurance market.

Richard Teske (Moffit et al. 2000) offers a consumer-choice plan. The federal government would provide a refundable tax credit for the purchase of a long-term care policy from a choice of plans. States would pay any copayments and deductibles for those who are poor. And, perhaps the most problematical of this proposal, those middle-aged and elderly people who refused to purchase insurance would have to promise to use up their assets before relying on government programs.

But tax subsidy programs for long-term care insurance have their own problems.

> Observed inadequacies are numerous: market practices that make policies unavailable to those most likely to need long-term care; benefits that cover only a portion of the costs of care and are not guaranteed to keep with rising costs or changing practices of care; and the possibility of unanticipated premium increases (even with policies that promise the same premium for the life of the policy). These features of private insurance, which reflect insurers' incentives to limit risk, create a barrier to spreading risk that is also apparent in the private individual health insurance market. The nation's continued dissatisfaction with this market should generate skepticism about the wisdom of following a similar path for long-term care. (Feder et al. 2000, p. 52)

Another problem with the tax subsidy/private insurance plan is that it benefits most those at the upper-income level (Feder et al. 2000).

# Reforming Medicare

In a sense, Medicare faces two problems that are contradictory. There are some things that it does not cover and perhaps should, and the program faces increasing costs and an expanding eligible population. Medicare is the closest the United States has come to a universal health care program. It is open to virtually the entire elderly population on an entitlement basis. Reform of Medicare is a major public policy task for the twenty-first century.

## Prescription Drug Benefit

As we have seen, Medicare was created in 1965, modeled after private health insurance policies of its time (Marmor 2000). Few, if any, private health insurance policies contained a benefit for prescription medication outside of the hospital. As medical research continued, new drugs were developed to treat a wide range of health-threatening conditions. Further, in the late 1990s, the pharmaceutical industry began a campaign of heavy media advertisement for their new drugs (Wilkes et al. 2000). The basic message to would-be users was the same: "We have a medication that can help you. Ask your doctor about it." Sometimes, the ads just mentioned the drug without mentioning the target health condition.

Thus the amount of money spent on prescription medication increased dramatically, from $37.7 billion in 1990 to over $90 billion in 1999 (see Table 5.1). Private, employment-based health insurance policies increasingly included a prescription drug benefit. But Medicare did not change its basic structure, and older people are more likely than younger people to need prescription medications. Many of these older people found the cost of ever-increasing medication too difficult to keep up with. Further, unlike private insurance policies, particularly those based on managed care, Medicare does not negotiate prices with pharmaceutical companies, nor does it control drug prices as it does provider care (Branigin 1998).

Data shows the importance of prescription medication for the elderly. This is particularly true for the elderly suffering from chronic diseases such as heart problems, osteoporosis, and diabetes (Steinberg et al. 2000). According to a FamiliesUSA study, the elderly make up 13 percent of the population, but they account for 34 percent of prescription drugs dispensed and 42 percent of health care expenditures on prescription drugs. Annual prescription drug spending per senior increased from $559 a year in 1990 to $1,205 in 2000, well above the rate of inflation. The projection for 2010 is that annual spending on prescription medication by seniors will rise to $2,810. The average number of prescriptions per senior grew from 19.6 in 1992 to 28.5 in 2000. The average price rose from $28.50 in 1992 to $42.30 in 2000. Of total out-of-pocket expenditures paid by seniors, 18 percent in 1996 was for medication. On average, seniors paid out of pocket for 47.3 percent for their medication, about $364 per year (FamiliesUSA 2000b).[14]

What kind of coverage do the elderly have for prescription medication? One source is employment-based insurance for retirees (about 30 percent of the elderly), but this coverage is declining largely because of expenditure increases brought about by both increased use and increased prices.

Another 13 percent have coverage from managed care plans. But such coverage is deteriorating and variable. It is variable in the sense that there are managed care plans offering a prescription drug benefit in eleven states. Further, those seniors with such coverage in managed care plans are finding it less helpful. Some managed care plans have dropped out of the Medicare market entirely while others have dropped the drug coverage. Perhaps more importantly, those Medicare managed care plans that retain the prescription medication benefit have reduced its value by imposing deductibles and premiums (FamiliesUSA 2000b).

Another 8 percent of seniors have a prescription drug benefit through a privately purchased medigap policy.[15] The three types of medigap policies with such coverage are fairly expensive (FamiliesUSA 2000b).

A fourth way that seniors can get prescription drug coverage is through Medicaid. The poorest of Medicare recipients are eligible for Medicaid, which then acts as a medigap policy but without the premium and with excellent coverage. Nearly 14 percent of the elderly have drug coverage in this manner.

The rest of the elderly, some 38 percent, have no such coverage at all. And for them, usually in the group just above the poverty level, prescription medication becomes a burden. It is here that we find stories of the elderly having to decide between needed prescriptions and food, or rationing the medication to make it last longer.

Another way of looking at the impact of prescription medication costs on the elderly is to survey them, as AARP has done (Barry 2000). AARP's somewhat unscientific survey of 2,090 people developed two interesting points. One point was that the cost of prescription medication affected both those who had no insurance coverage and those who did. This was true of the latter group because the coverage was becoming more expensive, as were the drugs themselves. The other point, somewhat contradictory to the first one, is that a sizable number of Medicare beneficiaries do like their coverage, and they are concerned that policy changes might disadvantage them (Barry 2000). The following quote illustrates the impact of prescription drug prices and use on the elderly:

> Among those without drug coverage (whom for clarity we will call the uninsured), 57 percent stretch medications, 52 percent sometimes skip filling prescriptions, and 50 percent spend less on food.
> Those with drug coverage do the same to a lesser, but still marked, degree: 30 percent, 24 percent and 23 percent, respectively. More than one in four (27 percent) of the uninsured and one in ten (11 percent) of those with coverage said "yes" to all of these three deprivations. (Barry 2000, p. 22)

A prescription drug benefit was one of the more important issues during the 2000 presidential campaign. Part of this focus was due to the problems, as described above. Part of this focus was due to the belief that Medicare should be changed. And part of it was for partisan political advantage (Serafini 1999).

So what, if anything, should be done about adding a prescription drug benefit to Medicare? The opening shot came from the Clinton administration in 1999. It proposed a Part "D" of Medicare[16] as part of a larger plan to reform Medicare. The program, if started in 2002 as proposed, would pay 50 percent of costs up to $2,000 (i.e., Medicare would pay up to $1,000). By 2008, that number would increase to $5,000 (Medicare would pay up to $2,500) and then be indexed for inflation. The program would be adjusted for inflation, with Medicaid helping low-income beneficiaries. The program would be voluntary and have a monthly premium of $24, rising to $44 by 2008. The Clinton administration estimated that the program would cost $118 billion over a ten-year period (MedicareWatch 1999; Toner 1999). As is typical of such proposals, other analysis suggested it would cost more than suggested (see Congressional Budget Office's analysis in Christensen and Wagner 2000).

Five other plans were offered in Congress, one of which passed the House in 2000 (Gluck 2000; McClellan et al. 2000). In addition, both Governor George W. Bush and Vice President Al Gore offered plans during the 2000 elections. All the plans would include a Medicare prescription drug benefit on a voluntary basis and provide subsidies for lower-income recipients. Most include premiums and cost-sharing for higher-income recipients. The plans also place limits on how much will be paid for the new benefit. Some plans would use contractors for the new benefits; all would utilize formularies (lists of approved drugs). All call for some kind of price negotiation. Estimated costs of the new benefit vary from $146 billion to $338 billion over a ten-year period (Gluck 2000). The major problem that any prescription drug benefit addition faces is to reconcile the desire to cover those with no or inadequate coverage, limit the costs of the new feature, and not disadvantage those who are already covered. This resembles the circus performer balancing three dishes on three poles.

Perhaps the greatest opposition to the Clinton administration's proposal (and similar ones) comes from the pharmaceutical industry and its association, the Pharmaceutical Research and Manufacturers Association (PRMA). The greatest fear of the industry is that including a prescription drug benefit in Medicare would ultimately result in price controls, as happened with providers, most recently nursing home and home health care agencies (Pear 1999d). The industry is undoubtedly correct (see Marmor et al. 1983). PRMA began an ad campaign reminiscent of the one run against the Clinton Health Security Act in 1993–94. To the extent that it supports any of the proposals, it supports the Breaux-Frist bill that would overhaul Medicare (see next section).

Some of the proposals would stay within the traditional Medicare structure. Others seek to address not only the prescription drug gap, but also overall problems affecting Medicare.

## Reforming Medicare

Medicare has evolved considerably since its enactment in 1965. In the 1980s, first hospitals and then physicians were placed within a prospective payment system (DRGs or fee schedule). A second change was opening up Medicare to health maintenance organizations. This change has been relatively slow; as mentioned above, a smaller proportion of Medicare recipients are enrolled in HMOs than in either the private sector or in Medicaid. The third major change came in 1997 with the BBA of 1997. It made a number of changes to the program. These included bringing nursing homes and home health care agencies into a prospective payment system, adding some diagnostic screening, lowering provider payments, and opening up Medicare to more alternatives to traditional Medicare (the Medicare + Choice program), though implementation of the latter feature has been slow.

The overall issue is that Medicare is facing a cost problem. By 2010 (and perhaps earlier for early retirees), the large baby boomer generation will begin retiring and moving onto Medicare. By 2017, the Medicare beneficiary problem will grow from 39 million in 1999 to some 56 million (Century Foundation 2000). It is not just that there will be more people in the eligible population, but that people are living longer (Phillips n.d.). This is the same problem facing Social Security. But in many ways Medicare is a much more difficult program than Social Security.

Social Security payments are based on income earned during the working years. Apart from cost-of-living adjustments, the payments do not change with age. Medicare spending per person depends on the health of the person. As people age, their health needs increase. Further, inflation in this area is generally higher than overall inflation. The estimate is that under current law, spending on Medicare will grow from 2.6 percent of gross domestic product in 1995 to 6.3 percent over the next thirty years (Century Foundation 2000). Another way of putting this is that the costs are going to exceed revenues (Phillips n.d.; see also Penner et al. 2000). This projection is before there is any consideration of extending Medicare to cover some of its gaps, such as prescription drug benefit.

Medicare became part of the policy and political clashes between President Clinton and Congress, especially in the 1995–96 period. Estimates at that time suggested that the Part A Trust Fund (hospital insurance) might be exhausted by as early as 2000 (Marmor 2000; Rushefsky and Patel 1998).[17] More recent estimates put the date of bankruptcy back to at least 2037 (Board of Trustees 2001; for a cautious or pessimistic view of the viability of the trust, see Health Leadership Council 2001). This is because of both the growing economy's producing unexpected revenue (a factor in Social Security as well) and the changes made by the BBA of 1997.

In any event, there are a number of ways to address the cost and reform issues. To address the cost issue first, one could address the revenue or expenditure side. For the revenue side, this would mean tax increases for Part A

(Part B, the supplemental plan, does not have a trust fund and therefore does not need dedicated tax revenues). The elderly might be asked to pay more in terms of monthly premiums (for Part B), copayments, and deductibles. This approach has proven to be politically difficult. On the expenditure side, one could continue or enhance controls on provider payments. Generally speaking, this has been the course of public policy since 1983. The changes made in provider payments to hospitals, nursing homes, and home health care centers have raised calls for reducing the constraints.

Another possibility, though politically difficult, would be to raise the eligibility age to sixty-seven (as is being done with Social Security) or perhaps to seventy. The problem with this proposal is, first, it would not save much money because the sixty-five to seventy age group has fewer heath problems than the older groups. A second problem is that this group would need to find health care coverage from someplace, at a time when employers are reducing coverage to early retirees.

The above proposals employ a regulatory approach. It has clearly not gone away. The alternative is to employ incentives to slow down if not reduce costs. One way this could be done is to enroll more Medicare beneficiaries in managed care programs. As mentioned before, this move to managed care has been slow compared to Medicaid or the private sector, and not without pain (see case study below). Moving more people into managed care would likely result in some cost savings.

The most radical proposal would to be to revamp Medicare entirely. The BBA of 1997 called for the creation of a National Bipartisan Commission on the Future of Medicare. The commission, chaired by U.S. Senator John Breaux (D-LA) and U.S. Representative Bill Thomas (R-CA), issued its final report in March 1999. Though the commission did not get the necessary majority to approve its major proposal, the commission did publish its proposal, much of which was incorporated in a Senate bill offered by Breaux and Tennessee Republican Bill Frist (a doctor).

The commission proposal consisted of three parts. One part addressed the issue of solvency. The commission recommended that there be a single trust fund combining the trust funds for Part A and Part B. The recommendation is that at any time general revenues for the trust fund exceed 40 percent of total Medicare costs, the Social Security trustees should notify Congress of impending insolvency.

The second part of the proposal called for immediate, incremental improvements to Medicare. These included combining Parts A and B, providing prescription drug coverage for low-income beneficiaries, requiring that all medigap policies contain a prescription drug benefit, combining the Part A and Part B deductibles into a single deductible of $400, and then indexing that deductible to the growth in Medicare costs (this would save a Medicare beneficiary needing hospital and physician services $468 in 1999). Finally, in this category, the commission recommended raising the eligibility age to that of Social Security (sixty-seven), but allowing those over sixty-five and not yet eligible to buy into the program.

The third and most significant change would be to move Medicare to what the commission calls a **premium support** system. This proposal would require that Medicare beneficiaries choose from a menu of plans, each of which would charge a premium. Medicare would then pay a portion of that premium, thus the phrase "premium support."

To understand this proposal, it might be useful to look at the language employed in private pension plans. The traditional private pension plan, like the traditional Medicare fee-for-service program, is what has been called a **defined-benefit plan**. In a defined-benefit retirement plan, the employer provides a pension to retirees, perhaps indexed to inflation, that the retiree gets until death (such a plan could cover spouses as well). The longer one lives, the more benefits are paid. Social Security and Medicare are defined-benefit programs. In the case of Medicare, there is a defined set of benefits, with some contributions by recipients, as long as the recipient lives. The benefits depend on how sick or healthy the recipient is.

The private sector has been moving away from a defined benefit plan to a **defined-contribution plan**. With such plans, employees and employers make contributions to private accounts and then the employee draws upon them when retired. The employer makes no further contributions after the employee retires. This is comparable to privatization plans in Social Security.

The premium support plan is similar, though not identical, to a defined contribution plan. Here is one description of how a premium support plan in Medicare would work:

> The government would specify a minimum benefit package, though health plans could offer more services. The government would divide the country into market areas and take bids from health plans that wanted to serve Medicare beneficiaries in each area.
> From those bids, the government would decide on an amount of money that it would pay in premiums for each individual in the area. The idea is that the government payment would cover most of the premium in a basic plan. Beneficiaries who opted for health plans with richer benefits would have to pay more. Each area would have government administrators to provide participants with information about the health plans, collect premiums, enroll participants and distribute payments to the plans. Once the government had paid its share of a beneficiary's premium, the health plan and the covered individual would pay for anything else. (Serafini 1998)

The Bipartisan Commission plan resembles the Federal Employees Health Benefits Program (FEHBP) and the program established for California public employees (CalPERS).

There is another term for the premium support proposal, a **voucher**. As described, recipients would not get a piece of paper worth so much money and then shop around. But the essence is the same. As mentioned, there were insufficient votes to get the required majority, and President Clinton opposed the premium support plan. Clinton's opposition was that the proposal did not contain a prescription drug benefit (though it could be an option for some plans). Further, the president opposed raising the eligibility age; it might cause premium increases for those staying in the traditional program and did not earmark additional revenues from projected budget surpluses for Medicare (Pear 1999a).

Apart from President Clinton's objections, others chimed in as well. A major concern is whether such a market-type approach would generate the savings necessary to keep Medicare going. The Bipartisan Commission plan said that it would extend solvency four to five years. An analysis by the Urban Institute suggests that savings from premium support and the decisions that seniors make may be quite limited. One reason for this is that seniors are not as sensitive to differences and changes in plan prices as are younger people. This is especially true of the sickest beneficiaries. A second reason has to do with continuity of care. Changing plans may require changing providers (this is a problem with managed care organizations). But keeping the same provider may save money over constantly switching. A third factor, one not often thought of by those critical of public-sector programs, is that the traditional Medicare program (fee-for-service) is fairly efficient. Comparing growth in health costs between Medicare and the private sector, one finds that Medicare for much of its time has had slower or equal cost increases compared to the private sector. Finally, and related, Medicare has low administrative costs, much lower than private plans (this is similar to arguments made about Social Security compared to privatization plans) (Urban Institute 1999).

FamiliesUSA, a consumer health group, strongly opposed the Bipartisan Commission proposal. It argued that beneficiaries are likely to find that their benefits are eroding, that they are likely to pay more over time, that it does not ensure the long-term financial stability of the program, and that their benefits and providers change from year to year (again, similar to managed care) (FamiliesUSA 1999a).

One very interesting aspect of the Bipartisan Commission proposal and critiques of it is that the premium support proposal is based on the idea of managed competition that was the heart of the Clinton Health Security Act.[18] Why would such an idea be acceptable in 1999 (and 2001) when it was not acceptable in 1994? Marmor (2000) offers two reasons. First, managed competition (premium support) would only apply to Medicare, and not as much of the health care system as the Clinton Heath Security Act would. The view is that premium support would limit Medicare spending. The second reason offered by Marmor is that this would be a way for providers to escape government regulation and fee schedules (though not necessarily private regulation).

Perhaps the most significant criticism of premium-support-type programs is that they would break the "social contract" that was made with the nation's seniors. Moving toward a premium-support program endangers that contract (Study Panel on Medicare's Larger Role 1999).

## Case Study: Managed Care—Revolution and Reaction

### Problem Identification

The quote that opened this chapter suggests that the 1980s saw a great deal of change in the health care area. The 1990s saw even more change and none more important than the managed care revolution. By 2000, most people with health insurance received it through some kind of managed care organization. But that revolution has caused considerable dissatisfaction among patients and providers. The result has been stories about the quality of care delivered by managed care organizations and legislation proposed and approved (at the state level).

First we need a definition of managed care. **Managed care** refers to restraints placed by health plans on the use of services. Such a restraint can be as simple as authorization before a doctor admits a patient to a hospital. A **managed care organization** (**MCO**) is an organized form of delivery of health care services. The classic example of a managed care organization is a health maintenance organization, which was described above. Another type of managed care organization is a **preferred provider organization** or **PPO**. Here the health insurance plan signs up providers who agree to serve the plan's customers for discount prices. Providers can belong to more than one managed care organization.

The importance of managed care is the notion of restraint or rationing. Rationing is a term that is not often used in discussing managed care organizations, but it is the essence of such care. In a U.S. Supreme Court case in 2000, Justice David Souter wrote: "No H.M.O. organization could survive without some incentive connecting physician reward with treatment rationing" (Greenhouse 2000).

What kind of rationing is involved? Managed care organizations may limit the providers that a patient sees (one hospital rather than another), limit the number of physical therapy sessions someone receives, establish a list of approved prescription drugs (known as a formulary), and so forth. It is this restraint or rationing aspect of managed care that has led to the reaction to it.

Managed care was adopted by the private sector and the public sector (Medicaid and, to a lesser extent, Medicare) to control costs. Large employers and states (under waivers granted by the federal government) led the managed care revolution beginning in the late 1980s. By 2000, most workers with employment-based health insurance (92 percent) were in some kind of managed care program, up from 73 percent in 1995 (Gabel et al. 2000). By 1999, over 55 percent of Medicaid recipients were in some kind of managed care plan

(Health Care Financing Administration n.d.). For Medicare, as mentioned earlier, only about 16 percent of Medicare recipients were in managed care organizations as of 1999 (Kaiser Family Foundation 1999).

For a while, at least, managed care seemed to do its intended job, as health care cost increases moderated. In 1990, private-sector health insurance premiums increased by 15 percent; by 1996, premiums actually declined (Congressional Budgeting Office 1997).

While the cost successes of managed care were apparent by the mid-1990s, by the end of the century costs became a problem again, largely though not entirely due to increased spending on prescription medication. Further, dissatisfaction on the part of patients and providers produced a backlash. The cost and dissatisfaction issues are related.

The fundamental problem with managed care organizations, especially HMOs, resides in the rationing aspect. MCOs save money by not providing services. This is most clearly seen in HMOs. A pure HMO obtains its revenue solely from subscriber premiums. Any money that has to be spent on medication, hospitalization, or treatment comes out of the subscriber premiums. Thus the incentive, unlike the fee-for-service system, is to underserve. To save money, MCOs have to limit service, limit what providers can do, and so forth. This restriction causes dissatisfaction and quality concerns among patients and providers. Patients feel deprived of needed services, and providers feel that their autonomy has been diminished.[19]

Another problem related to managed care concerns Medicare. As we have seen, Medicare managed care enrollment trails Medicaid and private-sector managed care enrollment. When Medicare opened up to HMOs, it decided to pay them 95 percent of average expenditures on Medicare recipients. Even then, the HCFA, the agency in charge of Medicare (and Medicaid), found itself losing rather than saving money. This was because healthier Medicare recipients tended to enroll in HMOs and the sicker ones stayed with traditional Medicare. Even then, Medicare HMOs found that it was difficult to make a profit from what Medicare paid them.

HMOs resorted to two tactics to support their revenue. One was to increase premiums beyond what Medicare paid and to start charging copayments and deductibles. A second tactic was to get out of Medicare entirely, disenrolling. Though the numbers were relatively small as a percent of the Medicare population, with some 1 million recipients becoming disenrolled in the 1998–2000 period, it was a substantial amount of those enrolled in Medicare's managed care plan, about 17 percent. While most of those disenrolled found new coverage, they also found the new coverage more expensive and narrower. To quote from the abstract of a study of HMO disenrollment:

> Two-thirds [of the study sample] subsequently enrolled in another Medicare HMO; one-third experienced a decline in benefits, and 39 percent reported higher monthly premi-

ums. One in seven lost prescription drug coverage; about one in five had to switch to a new primary care doctor or specialists. Those with traditional Medicare by itself or with Medigap, the disabled under age sixty-five, the oldest old, and the near-poor experienced the greatest hardship after their HMO withdrew. (Laschober et al. 1999, p. 150)

## Agenda Building

By the mid-1990s, stories of poor quality of care and denial of service hit the media. HMOs, doctors claimed, issued "gag orders," requirements by the plan not to inform patients about financial incentives they faced (such as bonuses for keeping expenditures down or penalties for ordering too many prescription drugs). A book devoted to showing the abuses of HMOs and other MCOs appeared in 1996 (Anders). The stories have not ended.

Thomas Bodenheimer (2000) describes his internist practice where he was a member of three different independent practice associations (IPA). Each IPA had a different set of specialists that patients could be referred to and different laboratories that could be used. The same was true of hospitals and pharmacies. Trying to keep track of which patients belonged to which IPA led to tremendous frustration and typified the fragmenting of the American health care system.

Sara Singer (2000) relates a more interesting story. Singer, who works at Stanford University as a researcher and a director of a health policy center, is a strong advocate of managed care. Unlike many, she would be expected to understand how to navigate the managed care system. However, when she became pregnant and gave birth to a daughter, she found herself another victim of managed care. She had to choose a pediatrician in an HMO that was different from her HMO. After thirty days, the child would be a dependent and come on Singer's HMO, disrupting continuity of care. While still in the hospital, her medical group refused to pay pediatric expenses for her daughter. While she eventually got the situation straightened out, it took a number of calls and filling out much paperwork. While Singer remains a strong advocate of HMOs, she also said that treatment of customers has to improve.

Stories like this made news. HMOs and MCOs in general became fodder for editorial cartoonists.[20] HMOs were denounced in television programs and movies; one notable example is the movie *As Good as It Gets*, where the mother of a sickly child curses HMOs to a doctor. She then apologizes, but the doctor said he thought the curse words were the HMOs official name.

One important critique of managed care questions whether they are truly efficient, in the sense that they save money for the overall health system and not just for a specific managed care plan. Kip Sullivan (2000) argues while MCOs, such as HMOs, reduce utilization, they do not reduce system costs because of the kind of administrative expenses Bodenheimer discusses above. Sullivan further argues that lower premiums for HMOs do not mean they are more efficient than fee-for-service plans. This may be so because HMOs may try to enroll healthy people and shift costs.

## Policy Formulation

To address issues raised by managed care, real or alleged, a number of policy alternatives are possible. Most of these come under the rubric of **patients' bill of rights**. Such laws or actions provide a variety of protections against action by MCOs. It should also be noted that not only do consumer-type groups support such legislation, but often providers do. This is so because, as we saw above, providers, particularly physicians, found their autonomy (and sometimes income) restrained by MCOs. The opposition for such a bill of rights usually comes from industry, insurance companies, and MCOs. The policy tool being used here is **rights**.

Possible protections under a patients' bill of rights law include access to emergency care, access to providers (including specialists), continuity of care (what happens when a provider leaves or is removed from a plan), prescription drug access, appeals procedures, consumer assistance, patient-provider relationships, access to clinical trials, and enterprise liability (the ability to sue a managed care organization) (FamiliesUSA 1998; see also FamiliesUSA 1999b).

## Policy Adoption

As we saw in chapter 1, there are a number of venues by which policy can be adopted. Five such venues have been used or attempted: state legislatures, Congress, the chief executive, courts, and initiative.

Most of the action has taken place at the state level. By September 1999, all states had passed some type of patients' bill of rights protection, led by Vermont and California. Other states, such as Massachusetts and Wyoming, had adopted very little in the way of patient protections. The most controversial of all protections is the ability to sue a health plan, known as enterprise liability. As of 1999, a small number of states (including California, Georgia, Missouri, and Texas) had passed such legislation (FamiliesUSA 1999b).

A second legislative venue is Congress. As with much of the nation, Congress began addressing this issue in 1996. By the end of 1996, it had passed only one piece of legislation, mandating minimum stays for childbirth deliveries. More ambitious bills were offered in later years, some by Republicans in the House who challenged the leadership on this issue. Those Republicans were often medical providers (doctors or dentists) who had a feel for the issue. Both the House and the Senate passed patients' rights protection legislation. But the House bill was considerably stronger than the Senate bill, and the conference committee (members of both houses appointed to reconcile differences) was unable to put together a compromise.[21] New bills were introduced in 2001, and President George W. Bush has come out in favor of a modest version of such a bill.

A third venue is the chief executive, in this case the president of the United

States. In March 1997, President Clinton appointed an advisory commission on consumer protection and quality in the health care industry. In November 1997, the commission recommended a set of consumer or patient protections. President Clinton then asked private health plans to adopt the recommendations, asked Congress to pass consumer protection, and ordered relevant federal agencies to adopt the proposals ("President Clinton Endorses Consumer Bill of Rights and Calls for Immediate Action to Implement" 1997).

In November 1999, President Clinton ordered the U.S. Department of Labor to publish regulations giving patients the right to an appeals process for those insured in employer self-insurance plans, under the Employment Retirement Income Security Act (ERISA) of 1974 ("Clinton Seeks New Rules to Expand Patient Rights" 1999). Following up the president's action, the HCFA issued regulations modifying what is known as "conditions of participation" for hospitals in the Medicare and Medicaid programs.

A fourth venue is the courts. At the federal level, the most important case dealing with patients' rights was *Pegram v. Herdrich*, decided by the U.S. Supreme Court in 2000. The facts of the case were that the plaintiff, Cynthia Herdrich, complained about abdominal pains. Her HMO refused to diagnose her for eight days, at which point her appendix burst, endangering her life. She sued in federal court, under ERISA. The Court decided to dismiss the suit, arguing that she did not have grounds to sue under ERISA. Justice David Souter wrote that Congress had "sanctioned" MCOs, and it was up to Congress to include protections if it wanted them. Thus, the states, state courts, and Congress have the prime responsibility (Greenhouse 2000).

The final venue is direct democracy. This refers to initiatives and referenda in state elections. In the November 2000 elections, there was a proposition in Massachusetts that would have dramatically changed health care in the state. The proposition, known as Question 5, would have adopted universal health care for all residents, ended managed care in the state, and provided freedoms and protections to patients and consumers. It was the subject of much television advertising, with the opponents outspending the proponents by about 25 to 1 (Mooney 2000). The measure lost.

## Conclusion

Health care has played a role in American politics in the late twentieth century. Medicare and Medicaid were the centerpiece of budget battles between President Clinton and the Republican-controlled Congress. Democrats used proposed Republican cuts to hang on to the presidency and decrease Republican majorities in Congress. In 2000, both George W. Bush and Al Gore offered proposals directed at prescription drugs, patient protections, and Medicare. They were also the subjects of congressional activity, though not passage, in 2000.

What lies ahead? First, it is clear that the managed care revolution will continue, in some form, to affect public and private health insurance. Even if the federal government does not enact patient protection legislation, many states have moved vigorously (a federalism issue).

A second concern is the future of the two giant public programs, Medicaid and Medicare. Medicaid was affected by the welfare reform legislation in 1996 as well as efforts by states to restrain cost increases. Medicare is subject to many of the same forces as Social Security. Demography (population changes) presents a major challenge to the program, but so does technological improvements (including prescription drugs and genetic advances) that will increase cost pressures. Medicare is, in some ways, an old-fashioned program, given its benefit structure and still large reliance on fee-for-service. The 1997 BBA, mentioned often in this chapter, made significant changes in Medicare. More are forthcoming.

And then there are the uninsured. For the most part, policy debates at the government level have ignored this segment of the population since the demise of the Clinton health plan in 1994. States have taken some action to help the uninsured (such as risk pooling) and the expanding economy has finally produced a decrease in the number of uninsured. But the problem remains.

Thus, the future of health care is in flux. The two goals of cost containment and increased access are somewhat contradictory. Changes to meet one or both of these problems are driven from the bottom up.

Again, the existence of budget surpluses allows the political system to reexamine public policy. Whether the surpluses remain as predicted over the next decade or whether we can make necessary changes remains questionable. The proposals are there.

---

## Key Concepts

| | |
|---|---|
| defined-benefit plan | Health Insurance and Portability Accountability Act (HIPAA) |
| defined-contribution plan | |
| diagnostic-related groups (DRGs) | health maintenance organization (HMO) |
| directly provide services | Health Security Act |
| efficiency | inducements |
| equity | joblock |
| facts | managed care |

managed care organization (MCO)

managed competition

market failure

market reform

Medicaid

Medicare

Medicare Catastrophic Coverage Act (1988)

medigap

national health insurance (NHI)

patients' bill of rights

powers

preferred provider organization (PPO)

premium support

prospective payment system (PPS)

rights

security

state children's health insurance program (S-CHIP)

voucher

---

## Reflections

1. As with poverty and welfare, one of the underlying concerns in health policy is the "government issue." In particular, some analysts point to Medicare and Medicaid as major contributors to the health-cost problem. Do you agree or disagree with this viewpoint?

2. A related issue is national health insurance. There are a considerable number of people with no health insurance or with inadequate coverage. 1993 and 1994 was the greatest effort toward national health insurance in a generation. Do you think, given the failure in 1994, that comprehensive national health insurance will be on the policy agenda again? If not, what, if any, incremental changes would you prefer? Several health issues were prominent during the 2000 presidential elections, but the problem of the uninsured was not one of them. Why do you think this was so? What is the significance of neglect for dealing with the problem?

3. The conclusion to the chapter suggested that considerable change in the health care system has taken place even in the absence of federal initiatives. What kinds of changes do you see taking place in your community? What impact do you think those changes will have? One particular change, as the case study indicates, has been the managed care revolution. Are you or anyone you know covered by a managed care organization? What has been your or their experience? Should patients be able to sue a managed care organization?

4. To what extent has your state undertaken health care reform in the last few years? What changes have been made? Why were those changes undertaken? If your state is one where little or no reform has occurred, why do you think that is the case?

## Notes

1. For an analysis of health care goals, see Ginzberg (1977).

2. For a delightful description of the events leading to the formation of the National Health Services Corps, see Redman (1973).

3. There have been a number of books written about the 1993–94 episode. See, among others, Johnson and Broder (1996); Rushefsky and Patel (1998); and Skocpol (1996).

4. Leyerle (1994) argues that much regulation of health care in the United States occurs through the private sector and that managed care will enhance this tendency.

5. For a discussion of the passage of Medicare (and Medicaid), see Marmor (2000).

6. In one sense, the solvency issue is overstated. The trust fund is an accounting device. If insolvency actually looms, legislative changes could be made to divert other tax revenues to the fund.

7. The 1970 figure is calculated from from the U.S. Census Bureau (1994, p. 308). The latter figure is calculated from the U.S. Census Bureau (1999) and Levit et al. 2000.

8. Early federal planning efforts took place under the Hill-Burton, Regional Medical Program, and Community Health Program Acts. See Krause (1977).

9. One could argue that this scenario of real or threatened regulation leading to temporary restraints on increases by industry was replayed in the 1990s. Insurance premium increases were restrained in the mid-1990s, when the debate over the Clinton Health Security Act was taking place (which included, as a backup measure, caps on insurance premium increases). After the demise of the Clinton plan and any type of national health insurance, premiums increased beginning in 1998.

10. For an analysis of the New Jersey "all-payer" system, see Volpp and Siegel (1993).

11. See also Wilson (1980).

12. HMOs are a type of prepaid organization. For background on the health maintenance strategy, see Brown (1983), Falkson (1980), and Thompson (1981).

13. HCFA counted children who were covered by CHIP at any time during the year. So if a child was on one month, she was counted as being on for a year. The Kaiser Commission, on the other hand, counted children covered by CHIP at specific points during the year. The HCFA methodology will produce a higher count.

14. These last figures on out-of-pocket expenditures are average for the country. There is considerable variation among the states. See FamiliesUSA (2000b).

15. Medigap refers to regulated private insurance policies that offer a range of supplemental benefits to Medicare recipients. For a discussion of medigap policies, see Moon (1996) and Patel and Rushefsky (1999).

16. Part A is the hospital insurance portion, Part B is the supplemental medical insurance, and Part C is the CHIP program.

17. There is a sense in which the trust fund issue, a recurring one in Medicare and Social Security, is not as real as it seems. The trust fund is an accounting tool. One could transfer general revenues to the fund or do away with the fund entirely.

18. For a discussion of managed competition, see Patel and Rushefsky 1999.

19. For a detailed, historical discussion of physician autonomy, see Starr (1982).

20. A *Wizard of Id* cartoon has a doctor going into a hospital patient's room announcing that the patient has a rare disease; the HMO will cover it. A *Frank and Earnest* cartoon has the doctor telling the patient that an HMO wants the patient to be discharged, so he must be cured.

21. House Speaker Dennis Hastert (R-IL) appointed House conferees who had, with one exception, voted against the House bill.

# 6 Environmental Policy: Challenges and Opportunities

*Environmental issues soared to a prominent place on the political agenda in the United States and other industrial nations in the early 1990s. The new visibility was accompanied by abundant evidence domestically and internationally of heightened public concern over environmental problems. Reflecting such worries, policymakers around the world pledged to deal with a range of important environmental challenges, from protection of biological diversity to air and water pollution control. . . .*

*Equally evident throughout the 1990s, however, were rising criticism of environmental programs and a multiplicity of efforts to chart new policy directions. Intense opposition to environmental and natural resource policies arose in the 104th Congress (1995–1996). The Republican Party took control of both the House and the Senate for the first time in forty years and mounted a concerted campaign to reduce the scope of governmental activities, including environmental regulation. It was the most direct and forceful attack on environmental policies since the early 1980s during Ronald Reagan's presidency, although like the effort by the Reagan administration, ultimately it failed to gain public support. Nonetheless, increasing dissatisfaction with the effectiveness, efficiency and equity of environmental policies could be found among a much broader range of interests, including the business community, environmental policy analysts, environmental justice groups, and state and local officials.* (Kraft and Vig 2000, p. 1)

*In effect, environmental values (among others) have been added to, and complicate, the old debates between left and right, rich and poor.* (Paehlke 2000, p. 77)

*Yet our political and cultural institutions continue to read from a script of instant doomsday. Environmentalists, who are surely on the right side of history, are increasingly on the wrong side of the present, risking their credibility by proclaiming emergencies that do not exist. What some doctrinaire environmentalists wish were true for reasons of ideology has begun to*

*obscure the view of what is actually true in "the laboratory of nature." It's time we began reading from a new script, one that reconciles the ideals of environmentalism with the observed facts of the natural world.*
(Easterbrook 1995, p. xvi)

The United States has experienced several episodes of intense concern about our environment. The late 1960s and early 1970s was one such period. But the energy and economic problems of the middle and late 1970s moved environmental matters to a corner of the policy agenda and threaten to do so again in the first years of the twenty-first century. Environmental protection may conflict with energy development and use, and environmental regulations impose a costly burden on the economy. By the late 1980s, the environment was once again the center of a prominent set of issues. Public support for environmental protection always existed, though other problems may have been given priority. Perhaps it was the transition from the Reagan administration to the elder Bush administration that effected this change. After all, Bush castigated Democratic opponent Massachusetts Governor Michael Dukakis for impeding efforts to clean up Boston Harbor. Bush appointed the first environmentalist to head the Environmental Protection Agency. Perhaps it was the combination of events and changes in political mood. The Democratic candidate for vice president in the 1992 presidential election, Tennessee Senator Al Gore, wrote an environmental book, *Earth in the Balance.* His Republican opponent, Vice President Dan Quayle, accused Gore of being an environmental radical. The Clinton/Gore team won with the promise, though not necessarily the realization, of increased emphasis on environmental protection. During the 2000 presidential elections, the Democrats attacked Republican candidate Governor George W. Bush for his poor environmental record in Texas. In the early days of his administration, policies were announced that both supported environmental protection and rolled them back.

This chapter has one major theme: Policy implementation is absolutely vital because of scientific uncertainty. That uncertainty lends itself to differing interpretations of evidence and of regulations. The politics of the environment revolves, in many respects, around judgment, evidence, and uncertainty. Additionally, in keeping with the optimism theme mentioned in other chapters, we will note the successes of environmental policy as well as problems.

## Problem Identification

### *Policy Goals*

The major policy goal in the environmental area is **security**. Security in this sense refers to safety, defined as "the prevention of future needs" (Stone 1997, p. 94). People protect the environment partially because a clean environment with a diversity of flora and fauna is a value in and of itself. More importantly, people fear that environmental deterioration will adversely affect the present or future generations. Thus, reducing pollution will, it is hoped, reduce future illnesses and deaths.

> Future needs often have a political potency far greater than actual needs, because fear of the unknown plays a bigger part. The human imagination is capable of creating infinite terrors, and terror explains why there is often an emotional fervor to arguments about this type of need, even when the risks are described in passionless statistics. (Stone 1997, p. 95)

The heated controversy that marks environmental protection concerns, in part, the degree of future risk of a particular action or enterprise. Equally as contentious is the conflict between the goal of security and the goal of **efficiency**, particularly concerning economic and energy policy. To the extent that industry is regulated and certain economic activities are restricted or prohibited, extra costs are incurred and the production of goods and services is limited. Energy production and use pollute the environment, evidenced by the oil spill off Alaska in March 1989. If there are ample oil reserves in, say, Alaska, can they be recovered while at the same time protecting a fragile environment? If burning fossil fuels (primarily coal and oil) leads to a warming of the atmosphere, then perhaps nonfossil fuels should be used. Efficiency, as a goal, also relates to the kinds of regulatory strategy used (see discussion below).

The security-efficiency tradeoff works itself into the environmental area in another way. Environmental protection is expensive, involving (1) administration of public programs at all levels of government, and (2) compliance costs within the private sector. What is needed is environmental protection that is efficient and cost-effective (Field 1994; Stavins 1989).

Our other two policy goals play a role in environmental policy as well. Because environmental regulations, whether coastal zoning, wetlands, or clean air, require that some person or entity undertake some action or be restricted from taking action, environmental policy inherently intrudes upon that person's or entity's **liberty** or freedom of action. The property rights challenge to environmental policy is a good example of the clash between a liberty interest and environmental values.

The final policy goal is **equity**. As we shall see, there is an argument to be made that poor people and minorities are disproportionately the subjects of environmental insults, including the location of facilities designed to clean the environment. The equivalent of the property-rights movement is the environmental-justice movement.

## Policy Tools

In this section, we look first at a major rationale for government intervention in the environmental policy: market failure. Following that, we will look at what policy tools are available for such intervention, given the previous analysis.

Environmental policy, like health policy, addresses one of the underlying themes of public policy, the government issue, which raises two questions: First, should government be involved in a given area? Second, if government gets involved, what should be the nature of that intervention?

In answer to the first question, some economists argue that the free market rather than a centrally planned economy is the most efficient means of allocating resources. However, there are certain conditions under which a free market does not work. This was seen earlier in chapter 5 on health care and is confronted again here in a different form. The rationale for government involvement in the environment is **market failure**. There are three types of market failure that might justify government action (Siebert 1981).

The first is a **negative externality,** which may be defined as the harmful "effect on one or more persons that emanates from the action of a different person or firm" (Samuelson 1964, p. 465). Free markets work as long as resources have prices attached to them. When there are no prices, resources may be strained. Consider a factory located on a river. The river supplies water for the factory's manufacturing processes and, in the course of those processes, the water is returned to the river, but now it is polluted. If there is no charge for the water, there is no concern about how much is used. If there are no requirements that the water be cleaned, say to the level it was when entering the factory, then there is no economic reason for the factory to clean the water. Now suppose that a city is downstream from the factory. It must clean the water so that its citizens, who may include workers and owners of the factory, can drink it. The **private costs** of manufacturing the product include the value of all resources—such as labor, energy, and materials—that the factory has to pay. The price of the product to the consumer includes all these considerations. But the impact on society, the **social costs**, include not only the private costs of manufacturing the product, but also the city's expenditures to clean up the water used in the process. This expense is not included in the market price, but somebody pays. This constitutes a negative externality.

Air pollution—say the emissions of sulfur dioxide from coal-burning power plants—has similar dynamics. The power plant does not have to pay for depositing the sulfur dioxide in the air nor for the damage it might cause, such as acid rain. Thus, in this case of negative externalities, government action would be necessary to bring private costs—the cost of producing electricity—in line with social costs—the cost of damages caused by acid rain.

A second type of market failure is the **free rider** problem. An action that a single actor makes, whether protecting or harming the environment, may be so small by itself that it has no apparent effect. The collective cost of such action, however, may be comparatively high. Consider automobiles and air pollution: There are millions of vehicles on the road; the contribution of each vehicle to air pollution is very small. Voluntarily installing an antipollution device on a car might cost several hundreds of dollars and reduce air pollution only a little. Few rational people, in an economic sense, would be willing to bear the full costs of installing the device for such a small effect. The result is that very few people freely take action to protect the environment. If you install an antipollution device and I do not, then I benefit from the cleaner air that you and other responsible citizens produce without having to pay for it. I am a free rider, a phenomenon that will often occur when individual benefits are far below individual costs. This produces a paradoxical result: Individual (economic) rationality produces collective (environmental) irrationality. No one purchases the air pollution device, the air gets dirtier and dirtier, and all suffer. Consequently, government action might be necessary to require that antipollution devices be installed.

The final type of market failure is the **tragedy of the commons**. This is a phrase made popular in an article by Garrett Hardin (1968). Hardin used the example of the commons, public grazing lands, in nineteenth-century England. The problem, as Hardin explained it, was that if the commons were overgrazed, they would be unable to sustain the various privately owned herds. What was needed was a system for allocating grazing rights. Without the system, each herder had an incentive to graze as much of his cattle as possible before others did. The result, as Hardin pointed out, was that the commons were ruined. Miller (1985, p. 9) summarizes the application of the tragedy of the commons to environmental protection:

> Unless the same degree of pollution control is required for these companies, the *common* resources of air, water, and soil used by everyone will continue to be degraded. In addition, the products of the company whose officials voluntarily acted to help protect the environment will cost more than those of their polluting competitors —driving the company that acted responsibly out of business.

As with the free rider problem, individual rationality leads to collective irrationality, requiring government action to ensure long-term stability of resources. These three versions of market failure suggest that corrective action by government, the agent for society, might be necessary.[1]

## Regulatory Strategy

> The Congress adopted regulatory strategies basically centered around the standard setting-monitoring-enforcement regulatory process coupled with uniform effluent and emission limitation requirements. This process is carried out through a complicated interactive process involving (1) the Congress which establishes policies, goals, objectives, requirements, and the basic structure of the regulatory processes; (2) Federal agencies, which define and implement the regulatory processes; (3) various State and local agencies which also implement the processes; and (4) the Federal and State courts, which review the administration and implementation of the environmental protection laws at the request of opponents and proponents of the various regulatory decisions being made. (General Accounting Office 1980, p. 9)

Thus the next question comes into play: granted that government should take action, what should be the nature of that action? The two major sets of policy tools for protecting the environment are rules and **inducements** (Stone 1997). The United States has chosen to use rules, primarily through regulation.

The **regulatory strategy** is known as **command-and-control**. An agency sets standards for emissions of or exposure to a given pollutant, such as sulfur dioxide, and commands that those standards be met. Within this strategy there are choices involving more or less government.

**Design standards** state not only what the standard should be, but also how they will be met. In the sulfur dioxide example, a design standard would state specific methods, such as a flue gas scrubber, to reduce sulfur dioxide emissions. **Performance standards** set emission levels but permit those covered by the rules to decide how they will be met. Thus a utility might choose to use low-sulfur coal rather than a scrubber. This leaves a greater role for private markets.

Of course, there may be occasions when design standards might be preferred over performance standards. One way of potentially reducing workplace exposure to asbestos is to have workers wear protective mouth and nose masks. However, knowing that those masks are uncomfortable and workers will not wear them, a government agency (in this case the Occupational Safety and Health Administration) might be justified in insisting on alternative ways of reducing exposure.

## Market Reform

The major alternative to rules is inducements or **market reform** (Anderson and Leal 1991; Davis and Webber 1995; Field 1994; Portney 1990; and Stavins 1989). Inducements are rewards and punishments used to influence people and groups (see chapter 1). Economists have suggested several inducement systems for achieving environmental protection. The two major types are **charge systems** and **tradable permit systems** (Field 1994; Stavins 1989). An example of the former is the **effluent** (or **emissions**) **tax**. A tax is levied on a polluter according to the amount of emissions. This internalizes the externality by imposing a tax equal to the cost of cleaning up the environment. The revenues from the tax could be used to compensate the victims of pollution (the downstream city in the earlier example) or to develop new pollution-control technologies. The tax could be varied to achieve a given level of protection. Companies that efficiently reduce pollution would pay a lower tax and have a price advantage over competitors. President Nixon proposed such a tax in 1970 for sulfur emissions (Field 1994).

There are several types of tradable permit systems. With this category of incentives, the amount of permissible pollution is set and then permission to pollute up to that level is granted. One way to do this is through **auction of pollution rights**, as called for under the 1990 Clean Air Act. After the amount of emissions of a given pollutant for a given area is set, the total amount is divided into units. An auction is then held for each of the units. Environmental organizations could compete in the auction, save the pollution rights, and the result would be a cleaner environment than originally planned: auctioning would create the missing market for a clean environment. There are similar market reform proposals in other policy areas such as welfare (negative income tax, housing vouchers), health care (insurance vouchers), and education (tuition vouchers).

The United States has limited experience with quasi-market policy instruments (Lotspeich 1998). To the extent that emission charges or taxes have been used, they have been limited to local governments and cleaning up wastewater. Tradable permit systems have been adopted in some cases for air pollutants and, again at the local level, for water pollution (two municipalities). The Environmental Protection Agency began using market-like incentives, again on a small scale, in the late 1970s. On the international level, the tradable permit system was incorporated in the Kyoto Protocol on global warming (see case study).

In 1995, as part of the Clinton administration's reinventing government movement, President Clinton and Vice President Al Gore issued a statement calling for the reinvention of environmental regulation (Clinton and Gore 1995). The statement was an attempt to bring new flexibility to environmental rules without rolling back environmental protections. One of the ten principles of the statement called for minimizing costs on businesses and governments. A second called for performance-based regulations allowing considerable flexibility. A third principle called for the use of economic incentives where appropriate. Effluent trading and open-market air emissions were two of the actions called for by the statement (Anderson and Carlin 1997).

A study prepared for the Environmental Protection Agency discussed eight types of economic instruments employed in environmental policy making, both in the United States and abroad. The survey found that while considerable use was made of these policy instruments, the savings or efficiency gains from using them were considerably below what might be projected based on economic theory. The authors suggested that implementation issues were the major cause of this less-than-hoped-for policy gain (Anderson and Carlin 1997).

## Adoption and Implementation

### The Rise of the Environmental Movement

The early twentieth century saw the precursor to the modern environmental movement in the conservation movement, associated with President Theodore Roosevelt and Gifford Pinchot. The U.S. Forest Service was created at this time, with Pinchot as its first director and a mandate to focus on preservation of natural resources so they could be safely used for the nation's benefit. This period also marked the beginning of concern for consumer protection, epitomized by the publication of *The Jungle*, Upton Sinclair's exposé of the meat-packing industry, which eventually led to the creation of the Food and Drug Administration.

The modern environmental movement has its origins in 1962, with the publication of Rachel Carson's controversial *Silent Spring* (Caulfield 1989). Carson dramatically pointed out the perils of pesticide use. While the United States had pesticide legislation dating to the late 1940s, there was little concern about their harmful effects on the environment. The power of Carson's attack can be seen in her closing paragraph:

> The "control of nature" is a phrase conceived in arrogance, born of the Neanderthal age of biology and philosophy, when it was supposed that nature exists for the convenience of man. The concepts and practices of applied entomology for the most part date from the Stone Age of science. It is our alarming misfortune that so primitive a science has armed itself with the most modern and terrible weapons, and that in turning them against the insects it has also turned them against the earth. (Carson 1962, p. 297)

The agrichemical industry attacked *Silent Spring* for what it saw as hysteria and misinformation, and others defended Carson's work (Graham 1970). The environmental movement was also aided by the growing affluence of the country, the growing impact of science and technology (and the questioning of technology), and a critique that was inherent in environmental concern. William Ophuls (1977; Ophuls and Boyan 1992; see also Eckersley 1992) suggested that we needed new institutions to save the earth. Barry Commoner's influential *The Closing Circle* (1971) combined critiques of science, technology, and capitalism. He saw new technologies as the primary source of environmental pollution (as well as the massive increase in energy use) and advocated a more socialistic system as a remedy. Garrett Hardin's (1968) article, "The Tragedy of the Commons," pointed up problems with a common resource pool (discussed above as one of the three types of market failure).[2]

An additional factor was evaluations of the mild environmental legislation passed in the 1960s. The Clean Air and Clean Water acts involved a cumbersome process of conferences and consultation with little enforcement mechanisms. The basic design of the legislation guaranteed its ineffectiveness, and criticism stung the major supporter of that legislation, Senator Edmund Muskie (D-ME). The combination of past evaluations and new lobbying by key participants created an opportunity for elected officials to compete in producing newer and stronger environmental legislation (Bosso 1987; see also Whitaker 1976).

Structural changes also created new opportunities for access to policy makers (Bosso 1987), including reforms in Congress and new access to the courts, which environmentalists exploited with great skill. Public support, as measured by public opinion polls, was also strong (Dunlap 1989, 1992; Mitchell 1984). As explained in chapter 1, policy adoption in legislatures often requires the support of two of the following sectors: the public, the president, and the Congress. These requirements were met in the early 1970s. Thus the combination of these factors opened a window of opportunity for change (Kingdon 1984). The result was an outpouring of environmental, health, and safety legislation.

The wave of concern created new interest groups, new agencies, and new

Table 6.1

**Major Environmental Legislation**

| Year | Law |
| --- | --- |
| 1969 | National Environmental Policy Act |
| 1970 | Clean Air Act Amendments |
| | Occupational Safety and Health Act |
| 1972 | Consumer Product Safety Act |
| | Federal Insecticide, Fungicide, and Rodenticide Act |
| | Federal Water Pollution Control Act (Clean Water Act) |
| | Noise Control Act |
| 1973 | Endangered Species Act |
| 1974 | Safe Drinking Water Act |
| | Clean Air Act Amendments |
| 1975 | Hazardous Materials Transportation Act |
| 1976 | Resource Conservation and Recovery Act |
| | Solid Waste Disposal Act |
| | Toxic Substances Control Act |
| 1977 | Clean Air Act Amendments |
| | Surface Mining Control and Reclamation Act |
| 1980 | Comprehensive Environmental Response,Compensation and Liability Act ("Superfund") |
| 1984 | Hazardous Materials and Solid Waste Amendments |
| 1986 | Safe Drinking Water Act Amendments |
| | Superfund Amendments and Reauthorization Act |
| 1987 | Clean Water Act Reauthorization |
| 1990 | Clean Air Act Amendments |

laws. Older environmental groups, such as the Sierra Club, the John Muir Society, and the National Wildlife Federation, were soon joined by more activist groups, such as the Friends of the Earth, the Natural Resources Defense Council, and the National Coalition Against the Misuse of Pesticides (Bosso 2000; Ingram and Mann 1989; McCloskey 1992; Mitchell et al. 1992). New agencies were established, such as the Environmental Protection Agency, the Consumer Product Safety Commission, and the Occupational Safety and Health Administration. The period from approximately 1969 to 1976 saw the passage of far-reaching environmental legislation (see Table 6.1).

In addition to policy and institutional changes, the environmental movement embodied a new set of values that it sought to get society to accept and incorporate into public policy. Robert Paehlke argues that there are three fundamental components to this value set. The first value is **ecology**. At its simplest, this value echoes one of Commoner's (1971) laws, that all things are related to everything else. Paehlke writes (2000, p. 79):

> All life forms are bound up each with the other in a complex, and frequently little understood, web of life. Fruit bats are essential to the propagation of many tropic

trees and numerous other plant species in other climate zones. Forests, in turn, help to determine the climate of the planet as a whole. The transformation of forest to agriculture in Latin America can dramatically affect migratory songbird populations in North America. The web of life ties all species together inextricably.

Human well-being, and indeed human survival, depends on the success of an almost endless list of plant and animal species, often in ways we barely understand. Our global food reserves would endure but for a matter of months should our food production capabilities suddenly decline. That capability is determined in turn by rainfall and temperature, by the activities of many insect species such as bees, and by microbiological life within the soils of the planet. All of these in turn are affected by both plants and animals. Our well-being is determined by other species in other ways as well, not the least of which is our deep need for contact with, or awareness of the existence of, wild nature.

A second core value is **health**. Here the emphasis is on the effect of environmental insults on human health. For example, some have argued that exposure to toxic substances causes health problems. The movie *Erin Brockovich* portrays the true story of a woman working in a law firm who helps residents win a massive lawsuit against a nearby utility company for water contamination that led to health problems in the community. Similarly, the book and movie *A Civil Action* is based on a leukemia outbreak that some thought was due to toxic waste pollution in Woburn, Massachusetts, though the company involved, W.R. Grace and Company, has argued that it did not pollute the drinking water of the town.[3] Of the three core environmental values, health may be the most controversial (see the section on risk control policy below).

The third core value is **sustainability**. Sustainability as a value suggests that the country reduce its dependence on nonrenewable resources, use but not deplete natural resources, and try to limit the impact of human activity on the earth (Paehlke 2000, p. 82). This is, perhaps, the most radical of ecological values because it places ecology and economics on a level plane.

### The Environmental Decade

On January 1, 1970, President Nixon signed the **National Environmental Protection Act (NEPA)**, symbolizing the 1970s as the environmental decade. NEPA created a new organization within the Executive Office of the White House, the Council on Environmental Quality, whose responsibilities included overseeing environmental impact statements (EISs) of proposed federal actions and the writing of an annual report to assess the progress of environmental programs. Later in the year, the president created by executive order the Environmental Protection Agency (EPA), consolidating programs from other agencies. For example, authority over pesticides was transferred from the Department of Agriculture, which had what its critics called a producers' bias, to the EPA, which had an expressly environmental concern.

The legislation of this early period concerned "traditional" or "first-generation" pollutants (Conservation Foundation 1987; Kraft and Vig 2000). One goal was clean air, with a focus on five major pollutants: particulates (small particles in the air), sulfur dioxide, nitrogen dioxide, carbon monoxide, and ozone. There was also concern about acid rain (discussed in more detail below), visibility, and the heating of the atmosphere due to burning of carbon-based fuels (the greenhouse effect) (see case study). The focus on water was divided between surface water (streams, rivers, and lakes) and groundwater. For surface water, the contaminants of concern were dissolved oxygen, bacteria, suspended and dissolved solids, nutrients, and toxic substances such as metals. For groundwater, the pollutants included biological contaminants, inorganic and organic substances, and radionuclides. The third major area within traditional contaminants is solid waste disposal from agriculture, industry, mining, municipalities, and as offshoots of control in other areas.

The Clean Air Act amendments of 1970 and the Federal Water Pollution Control Act (now Clean Water Act) amendments of 1972 moved environmental concerns in a new direction. Both acts provided for standards that were unattainable with current technology—they were "technology forcing" (Rosenbaum 1977; see also 1998).

With one major exception, the legislation required that the EPA set standards in the various areas. Those standards would then be enforced in a variety of ways. For air pollution, the act called for the states to be the implementers. They had to prepare state implementation plans (SIPs), subject to EPA approval. Thus, it was the states that were the subject of EPA action as much as the specific polluters. In the case of the Clean Water Act, the EPA had to approve permits to emit pollution into surface water. The permits specified how much of a specific pollutant could be emitted over a given period and what cleanup efforts had to be made and by when. Congress also provided for a massive public works program to assist in the construction of water and waste treatment plants for municipalities.

The one exception to bureaucratically based environmental standards concerned motor vehicles. The 1970 Clean Air Act contained air pollution standards for the three main automotive pollutants—nitrogen oxides, carbon dioxide, and hydrocarbons—for new cars. The act contained deadlines and penalties. The current emission-control devices date to this time. While those standards have been eased in subsequent legislation, and the EPA has granted compliance delays (Rosenbaum 1998), there is little question that new cars pollute less than older cars.

### Evaluation

What has been the impact of all this activity? Here, again, a certain amount of good news and optimism is warranted (Easterbrook 1995, 1999; Whitman 1998). In the easier, "first-generation" pollutants, progress has certainly been made. On the more difficult problems of toxic pollutants, nonpoint sources of water pollution, and global warming, much less has been done.

On the six major-criteria air pollutants, the quality of air has improved over the 1988–1997 period. Most cities experienced at least some improvement in air quality. The EPA is conducting an inventory of air toxics and has gathered a limited amount of monitoring information. There have also been decreases in acid raid deposition (Office of Air Quality Planning and Standards 1997).

Controlling water pollution, particularly from point (identifiable) sources, has also seen successes, though measurement in this area is less well developed than in the air pollution area (Kraft and Vig 2000; Rosenbaum 1998; see also Office of Wastewater Management 1998). The successes have been primarily in wastewater treatment from industrial plants and municipalities. Groundwater contamination remains a difficult problem (Kraft and Vig 2000).

The EPA's programs on toxic and hazardous wastes have proceeded slowly. Reregistration of pesticides often takes a decade or more. The Superfund program was plagued from the beginning with controversy and poor administration, though it has improved in recent years (Kraft and Vig 2000). One of the EPA's programs involves **brownfields**, abandoned industrial sites, many of them in urban areas. There are an estimated 450,000 such sites across the country (Bruni 2000). The EPA and communities are exploring ways to reclaim the brownfields for community purposes (Bartsch and Collaton 1997; General Accounting Office 1999).

Environmental protection is not cheap. In 1994, the last year for which data are available, almost $122 billion was spent on pollution abatement and control (Blodgett 1997). Government at all levels spent almost $35 billion in 1994, business spent almost $65 billion, and personal consumption (motor vehicles, sewage treatment) was a little more than $22 billion. The EPA estimates that meeting the requirements of the Safe Drinking Water Act Amendments of 1996 will cost municipalities $126.3 billion over the next twenty years (Arrandale 1997).

Another way of evaluating environmental programs is through some of the structural features of the political system. For example, **fragmentation** of government authority is of critical concern, and it shows up in many ways. While the Environmental Protection Agency is the most comprehensive federal agency in this area, it does not have a monopoly on authority. There is overlap with the Occupational Safety and Health Administration, the Food and Drug Administration, the Consumer Product Safety Commission, and the Department of Agriculture (for pesticides). Strip mining is under the jurisdiction of the Office of Surface Mining within the Department of the Interior. The Nuclear Regulatory Commission also has some environmental concerns, such as the disposal of radioactive wastes (see Table 6.2).

Even within a single environmental area, there may be overlapping legislation. For example, at least eleven separate statutes cover the disposal of hazardous wastes (Conservation Foundation 1987). While Rosenbaum (2000) correctly states that there are three major pieces of legislation that provide the

---

Table 6.2

**Major Executive Branch Agencies with Environmental Responsibilities**

White House Office
Office of Management and Budget
Council on Environmental Quality
Department of Health and Human Services
Environmental Protection Agency
Department of Justice
Department of the Interior
Department of Agriculture
Department of Defense
Nuclear Regulatory Commission
Department of State
Department of Commerce
Department of Labor
Department of Housing and Urban Development
Department of Transportation
Department of Energy
Tennessee Valley Authority

*Source:* Kraft and Vig (2000).

---

overall framework for regulating hazardous wastes—Resource Conservation and Recovery Act (RCRA), 1976; Toxic Substances Control Act (TSCA), 1976; and Superfund—the following characterization still applies:

> These laws (a) protect a particular part of the environment from being used for unlimited waste disposal, (b) relate to a specific type or source of waste, (c) specify procedures for management, and (d) provide for cleanup. (Conservation Foundation 1987, p. 425)

Fragmentation within the executive branch is duplicated in Congress and within the states. The EPA is the concern of almost two-thirds of the House of Representatives' standing committees and a similar percentage in the Senate. Some seventy committees and subcommittees control water quality policy (Rosenbaum 2000).

Fragmentation creates both opportunities and problems. The opportunities are there for access. If there are different laws, different agencies, different houses of Congress, and different levels of government, the occasions for environmental and industry groups to lobby are enormous. Losing at one place does not end the debate. The major problem is that no one committee or agency looks at environmental problems as a whole, but each is concerned with only the small piece that it has.

**Federalism** is also vitally important in environmental policy. Both the states and the federal government are involved in five areas of program responsibility: "setting goals and standards, designing and implementing programs, monitoring and enforcement, research and development, and funding" (Ringquist 1993, p. 67). The Reagan and first Bush administrations gave greater responsibilities to the states (devolution) (Lester 1994; see also Rabe 2000).

## Policy Succession: The Reagan, Bush, and Clinton Administrations

### The Reagan Administration

Ronald Reagan entered office more openly hostile to environmental protection than any other president since the beginning of the modern environmental movement. When Reagan campaigned against harsh government regulation and its adverse impacts on the economy, he had in mind the environmental area.

After the election in 1980, two transition reports submitted to the president-elect called for reexamination of environmental programs. One was a massive report by the Heritage Foundation, titled *Mandate for Leadership*, which asserted that the EPA needed redirection, largely achievable through administrative changes. The other report was by conservative Congressman David Stockman (R-MI) and endorsed by Congressman Jack Kemp (R-NY). Entitled "Avoiding a GOP Economic Dunkirk," it warned of a "ticking regulatory time bomb" that would explode in the 1980s.

> Similarly, a cradle-to-grave hazardous waste control system will take effect in 1981 at an annual cost of up to $2 billion. Multi-billion-dollar overkill has bloomed in the regulatory embellishment of the Toxic Substances Control Act. Three thousand pages of appliance efficiency standards scheduled for implementation in 1981 threaten to wreak multi-billion-dollar havoc in the appliance industry. All told, there are easily in excess of $100 billion in new environmental safety and energy compliance costs scheduled for the early 1980s. (Stockman 1980)

Stockman recommended a program of regulatory relief, two parts of which were adopted. The first part was to defer or rescind regulations left over from the Carter administration. The second part was to insert benefit-cost analysis into the regulatory process.

The Reagan administration implemented its agenda through a combination of budgeting, personnel, and administrative changes. The budget decreases came primarily through the Omnibus Budget Reconciliation Act (OBRA) of 1981.The EPA budget was reduced by almost 20 percent, even more if adjustment for inflation is made. Reagan's 1984 budget proposal represented a 30 percent cut from 1981 levels. The number of employees in 1984 was 18 percent less than in 1981. This was at a time when the EPA's responsibilities were increased. Virtually the entire staff at the Council on Environmental Quality (CEQ) was fired; when an uproar ensued, new staff were hired, but only at half the previous level. As a result, one of CEQ's major tasks, the publication of an annual report on the state of the environment, was not completed until 1982. Some of these budget and personnel cuts were partially restored later in the Reagan administration.

The administration also made careful use of presidential power to appoint people at key agency positions who would enthusiastically follow the administration line. The early leadership, such as Anne Burford at the EPA and James Watt at the Department of the Interior, were overtly hostile to environmental protection. Appointees at lower levels were sympathetic to industry interests and less friendly to environmental interest groups, a shift labeled by one scholar (Olson 1984) as "cooperative regulation."

## An Administrative Strategy

The Reagan administration had an opportunity to seek needed reforms in both the governing and legislation of environmental programs. For example, the Clean Air Act was due for reauthorization in 1981. Instead of submitting reform legislation, the administration opted for a list of governing principles for change. It then used an **administrative strategy** (Nathan 1983) of regulatory relief, focusing on the writing and interpretation of regulations, to undercut the legislation. Why is the writing and interpretation of regulations so vital?

The major reason is that environmental standards should be scientifically based. That is, there should be some link between a contaminant and some harm, whether to humans or to the environment. The standard should reduce harm by reducing exposure, and scientific studies are needed to document this connection.[4] This is a daunting enterprise, one that strains the resources of regulatory agencies. Much of the best data resides with users and producers who are understandably reluctant to provide this information. Developing the information also takes time. The data is often controversial, and thus information-based disputes need to be resolved in some manner.

The vagueness of legislation allows administrations to interpret and redefine the legislation to suit their own needs. As mentioned in chapter 1, the 1976 Toxic Substances Control Act (TSCA) states that the EPA administrator will regulate chemicals that cause "unreasonable risk." What constitutes unreasonable risk, however, is not defined in the legislation.[5] The Carter administration tended to see more risk than the Reagan administration.

How agencies handle interpretation problems varies. For example, the Occupational Safety and Health Administration attempted to shortcut the process of developing workplace standards by the not unreasonable strategy of adopting voluntary industry safety standards. Lacking a priority ranking system for the standards, OSHA sought to enforce them all, the important and the trivial, with equal vigor. The result was a severe backlash and ridicule of OSHA, one from which it never fully recovered.

During the Reagan administration, reinterpretations of existing rules were used to allow less regulation. For example, the scientific evidence concerning the cancer-causing properties of formaldehyde was reinterpreted by an EPA official in 1981, making it unlikely that restrictions on formaldehyde use would be imposed (Ashford et al. 1983). There were also charges that the Superfund cleanup program of abandoned hazardous waste sites was being administered in a way that was very favorable to industry (Rosenbaum 1985). Efforts to weaken environmental legislation met with congressional resistance in 1982 and 1983, resulting in a series of scandals focusing on the EPA.

Additionally, the Office of Management and Budget (OMB) was given new powers (based on precedents of the Nixon, Ford, and Carter administrations) that affected the writing of regulations. In February 1981, Reagan issued Executive Order 12291, mandating that executive branch agencies undertake benefit-cost analyses of proposed major regulations (defined as having over $100 million impact). The decision criteria were that benefits should exceed costs. Agencies had to adopt the least costly rule or justify why another alternative was chosen. The OMB had to approve the analysis before the regulation could be published. The OMB also had the authority to waive the benefit-cost analysis requirement.

In practice, the OMB used this requirement to delay new regulations. Dale Whittington and Norton Grubb (1984) point out that the OMB waived the requirement only in cases of deregulation or regulatory relief. Martin Belsky (1984) notes that the effect of the executive order in the environmental policy area was to shift the burden of proof of the need for environmental protection to the EPA.

At the beginning of the second Reagan administration in early 1985, the OMB's powers were further expanded. Executive Order 12498 established a regulatory planning process, again based on a precedent of the Carter administration. Each year, regulatory agencies were to submit to OMB a draft program of all major regulations that would be considered in the coming year. OMB was directed to consider the program's consistency with the regulatory principles of the administration and with other agencies, and to identify efforts that may be necessary to obtain consistency. What this executive order did, even more than the previous one, was to involve OMB in the regulatory process before such proposed regulations became public. Criticism by congressional committees in 1985 and 1986, including Senate committees when the Senate was controlled by the Republicans, led to some restraint on the part of the OMB in the exercise of its new authority over regulations.

## Federalism

One other element affected by the Reagan environmental program was federalism. States were required to develop air pollution implementation plans and perform much of the monitoring. In the water pollution area, congressional legislation allowed states to decide how a body of water would be used

(Rosenbaum 1985). The EPA could turn over the management of hazardous waste control programs to the states if they had an approved plan (Rosenbaum 1985). The Reagan administration, as part of its new federalism program, approved many state plans in this area as well as in the air toxics program (General Accounting Office 1987).

Some states demonstrated a greater concern for the environment than others (Davis and Lester 1989; Lester 1986, 1994). For example, when the Reagan administration reduced environmental funding for states, some states replaced the funds while other did not. Also, industry can play off one state against another. States are allowed to impose standards that are more restrictive (protective of the environment and human health) than the federal government, thus imposing differential costs on industry.

Yet, as with other public policies, states may be very vigorous actors in areas the federal government prefers to avoid. For example, California (and other states) enacted right-to-know legislation to inform workers and the community about the potential hazards of chemicals used in their community. There have been attempts to get Congress to pass a similar national legislation, but none has succeeded. This creates problems for the manufacturing sector; instead of operating under a single law and a uniform set of regulations that apply throughout the country, businesses are faced with a crazy quilt of legislation with different requirements and priorities. Occasionally, this has led to a call for national legislation to preempt what was seen as overly aggressive states. California also enacted automobile pollution laws stricter than those contained in the Clean Air Act. Because the California market is so large, manufacturers often produce cars to meet the more stringent California standard.

## The Bush Administration

Environmental policy during the first Bush administration contained a mixture of innovation and restriction. George Bush had campaigned for the presidency in 1988 as "the environmental president." Upon gaining office, he appointed the first environmentalist, William K. Reilly, as the director of the EPA. Others appointed to policy positions in the EPA also had strong environmental inclinations. However, appointees in other departments with environmental responsibilities, such as Agriculture, Energy, and Interior, had a more developmental orientation. The EPA soon came into conflict with these other departments as well as White House officials who were antagonistic to environmental regulation. These included John Sununu, the White House chief of staff; Richard Darman, the director of the OMB; and Vice President Dan Quayle. As vice president, George Bush had headed up the Task Force on Regulatory Relief. As president, Bush appointed his vice president to head the Council on Competitiveness (Vig 2000), whose goals were similar.

Although considerable regulation was passed during the first two years of the Bush administration, by the last two years a clamp had been put on. At the beginning of 1992, Bush ordered a freeze on new regulations. More importantly, the administration took actions that furthered the administrative strategy begun during the Reagan administration (Tiefer 1994). The OMB review of the writing of regulations came under attack, but the policy remained. The Council on Competitiveness, created by executive order rather than the statutory authority surrounding OMB, intervened in a number of cases. The controversies over wetlands and toxic air emissions illustrate much of what happened during the Bush administration (Tiefer 1994).

Wetlands are lands that are underwater for at least part of the year. They can vary from swamps to more prairie-like conditions. During the 1988 campaign, Vice President Bush promised that there would be no net loss of wetlands. The key here was how wetlands were defined. In 1989, an EPA task force produced a manual defining wetlands as an area saturated for seven days. The Council on Competitiveness intervened and started bargaining with EPA Director Reilly. The Council wanted a twenty-one day definition; Reilly was willing to go along with a ten-day definition. After some deliberations and pressure, Reilly agreed to a more stringent definition (fifteen to twenty-one). The decision was criticized in the press; the administration retreated and never implemented the proposed guidelines.

The administration, through the Council on Competitiveness, also attempted to get a rule passed that would allow businesses to include untreated toxic chemicals in local landfills, rather than detoxify them and dispose of them in either special dumps or in special incinerators. The proposal would have allowed manufacturers to decide on their own what could be included in public landfills. The proposal was dropped in 1992 because of fears it would hurt the president's chances of reelection (Schneider 1992a).

These two examples raise several important points. First, the ultimate regulatory authority resides in the head of the designated agency (in this case, the EPA), not the president. But the president has the power to fire the agency head, a formidable power. Further, the Clean Air Act (and other legislation) and Supreme Court decisions allow review of EPA decisions by the White House and other executive branch agencies (General Accounting Office 1993). Second, unlike some of the earlier efforts during the Reagan administration involving the OMB, Congress had no authority over the Competitiveness Council. Further, the Council kept no records of its proceedings or contacts; it was difficult, therefore, to trace its impact. Finally, these incidents demonstrate the importance of the implementation phase of the policy process, especially the writing of regulations. Had the Council's compromise definition of wetlands been enacted, about half of the nation's wetlands would have lost protection (Tiefer 1994). The devil, it is often said, is in the details.

The Bush administration was faced with another environmental issue, the 1992 Earth Summit Conference in Rio de Janeiro, Brazil. The president refused to attend the conference, a meeting of over 100 nations. He refused to have the United States sign the biodiversity treaty, and he had the U.S. delegation lobby the proposed treaty on limiting global emissions of carbon dioxide (see below) until it contained virtually no binding targets, overruling the head of the U.S. delegation, EPA administrator William K. Reilly (Soroos 1994; Vig and Kraft 1994).

## The Clinton Administration

As Vig (2000) observes, the key issue of the 1992 presidential election campaign was the economy, not the environment. Nevertheless, the Clinton administration seemed to promise a change in the direction of environmental policy. Al Gore, the vice president, had written a well-received book on the environment. Clinton appointees, such as Carol Browner in EPA and Bruce Babbitt in the Interior Department, were also encouraging from an environmental standpoint. By executive order, Clinton eliminated the Council on Competitiveness and returned regulatory authority to agency heads (Kriz 1993b). Another executive order required appropriate federal agencies to consider the impact of environmental decisions on minority and low-income communities (see below). Further, Clinton and Gore argued that environmental protection and economic growth were not incompatible; rather, the one could assist the other.

However, Clinton's record as governor of Arkansas suggested that there would be balance. Governor Clinton worked closely with industry, especially with chicken-industry leader Tyson Foods; that same tendency showed up when he became president. Clinton also showed a strong inclination to compromise. Thus some of the early decisions, on not raising grazing fees on public lands in the West or cleanup of the Everglades, suggested a middle-of-the-road position that would likely satisfy neither environmental nor industry interests (Glick 1993; Kriz 1994a). Environmentalists were also unhappy when Clinton pushed the North American Free Trade Agreement in 1993 and the General Agreement on Tariffs and Trade in 1994. While mainstream environmentalist groups supported the administration, more grass-roots-based groups opposed the agreements (Vig 2000). Demonstrations in 1999 and 2000 against the World Trade Organization (WTO) by, among others, the more radical environmentalists, were based on the notion that the WTO and the free trade agreements would undermine environmental protections in both the United States and abroad. Further, while the Green Party and its presidential candidate, consumer activist Ralph Nader, did not gain an impressive number of votes in the 2000 election (about 3 percent of the vote, insufficient to qualify for federal funding in the 2004 elections), Nader's vote in Florida, some 2 percent of the vote or over 97,000 votes cast, was sufficient to keep Vice President Al Gore from winning Florida and the presidency. Nader, as did some other environmentalists, criticized the Clinton environmental record.

Regardless of the purists' view of the administration, there were notable successes. Clinton created the Council on Sustainable Development and signed the Kyoto Protocol on greenhouse emissions, though he did not submit the treaty to the Senate. The administration also stood firm against attempts after the 1994 elections, by the Republican-controlled Congress, to cut back on environmental laws and regulations through the appropriations process. During the Clinton administration, environmental enforcement was strengthened, as were regulations, and the EPA's budget was increased. The administration also, either through executive order or legislation, moved to protect much of the country's natural resources. For example, Clinton and Congress obtained funding to restore the Everglades; Clinton also added to the size of the Everglades National Park (Alvarez 2000).

## Environmental Issues

Since the early 1970s, the nature of environmental issues has changed. As we have seen, the early environmental emphasis was on conventional pollutants, largely air and water pollutants, which were the most obvious and easily measurable problems. The newer problems that attained awareness and the policy agenda were more problematic. They were longer-term problems, not easily discernible, based on controversy over scientific evidence and marked by great uncertainty. This section considers some of these kinds of problems.

### Acid Deposition

Acid rain, or, more accurately, **acid deposition**, is the result of sulfur and nitrogen oxide being emitted into the air and traveling to a different part of the country and land, changing the acidity of the water or land on which the chemicals fall. Acid deposition in the northeastern United States and southeastern Canada appears to be linked to the burning of coal and the sulfur dioxide emissions that result from it. In the West, acid deposition is more likely to result from nitrogen oxide emissions from utilities and motor vehicles (Conservation Foundation 1987, p. 75).

Much of the concern focused on the eastern United States (and Canada, creating a foreign policy problem). The presumed suspects are coal-fired utilities, many of them in the Ohio Valley region. Acid rain is, to a certain extent, the product of previous efforts to meet the requirements of the Clean Air Act. One way that manufacturers and utilities could meet local emission requirements was to build taller smokestacks, which dispersed pollutants in the immediate air shed, and also sent them into air streams to travel hundreds—or thousands—of miles before finally landing. This is an excellent example of an attempt to address one problem creating or exacerbating another.

Acid rain can have serious environmental and health impacts. G. Tyler Miller (1994, p. 578) lists a number of those impacts: damaging buildings, statues, and metals; contaminating fish in lakes; damaging flora (plants and trees); making trees more susceptible to other kinds of stresses (weather, disease); inhibiting the ability of soil to absorb metals; and contributing to respiratory problems in humans.

There are a number of remedies for acid deposition. Miller (1985) distinguishes between input approaches, which reduce the amount of sulfur dioxide that is burned, and output approaches, which reduce emissions after burning. Examples of input approaches include conservation of energy, shifting from fossil fuels to other sources, converting coal to gases or liquid forms (synthetics fuel), and using low-sulfur coal. A familiar output approach would place scrubbers on the smokestacks to remove sulfur oxides.

The Carter administration opted for a **risk averse** policy. Risk averse means that a decision maker is not willing to take chances, and so acts to limit threats. The Carter EPA and CEQ felt that acid rain was a problem, and an active research program was undertaken. The National Commission on Air Quality argued that the Clean Air Act requires that action be taken to control harmful pollutants even in the face of scientific uncertainty (McNeil 1981). In 1980, Congress created the National Acid Precipitation Assessment Program (NAPAP) to set out the impacts of acid deposition.

The position of the Reagan administration was **risk tolerant**. That is, it was more willing to take chances and less willing to act against threats unless absolute scientific certainty could be established. The Reagan CEQ, in its first annual report, and the Department of Energy, in its 1987 *Energy Security* report, both argued that, given the scientific uncertainties about harm and exposure levels, new expenditures should not be undertaken that would curtail energy security and economic growth (Department of Energy 1987).

The policy deadlock over acid deposition was broken in 1990, with the passage of the Clean Air Act Amendments. Despite heading the Task Force on Regulatory Relief, Vice President George Bush was concerned about pollution and particularly the Clean Air Act. In 1986, he told two close advisors that pollution was his primary concern. During the 1988 presidential election, Bush called for new Clean Air Act legislation, specifically stating that the nation should act to reduce sulfur dioxide and nitrogen oxide emissions that were implicated in acid deposition. He also stated during the campaign that market reform solutions should be investigated (Cohen 1992).

Bush was true to his word. Working with the EPA, the Office of Management and Budget, White House officials, and, to a lesser extent, the Department of Energy, the president presented an outline for a revised Clean Air Act in June 1989. The outline called for reductions of sulfur dioxide emissions utilizing a tradable-allowance system, development of alternative fuels, and a strengthened air toxics program (Bryner 1993; Cohen 1992).

Title IV of the 1990 amendments addressed for the first time the issue of acid deposition. It called for power plants to reduce sulfur dioxide emissions by 10 million tons per year and nitrogen oxides by 2 million tons per year. It set a cap or ceiling on sulfur dioxide emissions for the year 2000. The innovative portion of Title IV was the creation of a market-like system of emission allowances. The emissions trading program began in 1995. The act also required that NAPAP assess the progress of the acid deposition control program.

Implementation of the trading programs differed. In the case of sulfur dioxides, an overall emissions cap was set; for nitrogen oxides, each source has an allowable emissions rate (Environmental Protection Agency 1999a).

What has been the effect of the effort to reduce acid deposition? Clearly, significant reductions in sulfur dioxide emissions have been achieved and they have contributed to cleaner air (Environmental Protection Agency 1999a). According to Munton (1998), all of the first-phase reductions were achieved by 1995. Phase II reductions for sulfur dioxides began in 2000. There have been reductions in nitrogen oxides as well, but the absence of a ceiling or a cap on emissions will likely lead to increases there.

The actual effect on the environment, especially lakes, is much less apparent. A comprehensive study of lakes and streams in the United States and Europe found that most lakes and streams in the United States and Canada affected by acid deposition have not recovered (Roberts 1999).

One interesting aspect has to do with the cost of the projected reductions to meet the 2010 goals. In 1990, the estimate was that the costs for utilities (the major target of the sulfur dioxide reductions) would be $4.6 billion. The most recent estimates suggest costs of around $1 billion (Environmental Protection Agency 1999a; Munton 1998). Further, the impact of the reductions on electricity rates has been increases of 2–4 percent, instead of the 40 percent and upwards predicted when the legislation passed. An important reason for the relatively low costs is that many utilities switched to low-sulfur coal (Munton 1998; see also Kerr 1998).

It appears that further reductions in sulfur dioxide and nitrogen oxides may be necessary for the country's affected surface waters to recover (Carson and Munton 2000). Further, the emissions trading system has had less impact on the reductions than the fact that the law provided for performance standards, allowing the utilities to decide how to meet the required reductions (Munton 1998; for an alternative view of emissions savings, see Burtraw 2000).

### Ozone Depletion

Ozone is a three-oxygen molecule found in the earth's atmosphere. Although breathing ozone would be extremely dangerous, ozone in the atmosphere blocks out much of the ultraviolet radiation from the sun (Miller 1985). Loss of ozone in the stratosphere would lead to an increase in skin cancer and a decline in marine and agricultural productivity (Conservation Foundation 1987; Miller 1994).

Chlorofluorocarbons (CFCs) were discovered in 1930, and their chemical properties made them applicable in a number of important areas, such as air conditioning, plastic foam packing, foam furniture cushions, and personal computers (Shea 1989). CFCs, it turned out, posed a threat to the ozone layer.

In 1974, F. Sherwood Rowland and Mario Molina developed models and conducted laboratory experiments that predicted ozone depletion due to CFC emissions. These results led both the EPA and the FDA, four years later, to ban the use of CFCs as propellants in aerosal cans (Browne 1989).

In the mid-1980s, evidence confirmed the Rowland and Molina predictions; indeed, the scientific evidence suggested that the two scientists underestimated ozone depletion. In 1985, a team of British scientists documented massive ozone loss over Antarctica, and retrospective analysis of remote sensory satellite data showed a "previously undetected hole . . . larger than the United States and taller than Mount Everest" (Shea 1989, p. 78). A 1988 study by the National Aeronautics and Space Administration (NASA) indicated the seriousness of the problem. The study found that the ozone layer had decreased by 1.7 to 3 percent from 1969 to 1986 and that the hole over Antarctica had spread (Shabecoff 1988). Measurements in 2000 found a record hole over the Antarctic. A smaller hole has been seen over the Arctic Circle as well (Revkin 2000a). Again, there were uncertainties about the seriousness of these findings. For example, the ozone layer over the southern hemisphere, and especially over Antarctica, varies significantly on a seasonal basis. Global warming may be a factor here also.

Three international agreements exist for reducing or eliminating substances that deplete the ozone layer (Soroos 1994). The first was the Vienna Convention for the Protection of the Ozone Layer, which called for voluntary measures to reduce emissions of chemicals such as CFCs. The major policy initiative was the 1987 Montreal Protocol on Substances that Deplete the Ozone Layer, which calls for a freeze on CFC production at 1986 levels by 1989 and phased 50 percent reductions in production by 1998. A freeze in production by 1992 of another chemical (halons, used in fire extinguishers) that adversely affects the ozone layer is also part of the treaty. The treaty allowed increased CFC production in Third World countries (Doniger 1988). The third agreement came in 1990 in London. CFCs were to be phased out earlier than called for in the Montreal Protocol, and a fund was established to help developing nations make the transition to alternative chemicals. There have been other international meetings since then to make further adjustments in CFC and other ozone-depleting chemical emissions. In the United States, Title VI of the 1990 Clean Air Act Amendments phased out production of the harmful chlorofluorocarbons and required recycling of CFC products.

How effective have these efforts been? At one level, the record size of the Antarctic hole, mentioned above, suggests that problems remain. The major difficulty is that CFCs are persistent chemicals and remain in the stratosphere for decades. Therefore, the major impact will likely be seen sometime further in the twenty-first century. On the other hand, measurements of atmospheric zone-depleting chemicals have shown a decline (Monastersky 1999; World Meteorological Association 1998).

There is, thus, a general consensus as to the nature of the problem and proposed remedies. Indeed, compared to most environmental problems, including related ones such as the greenhouse effect and acid rain, as well as others such as hazardous wastes, the ozone layer problem is almost a model of policy making in the face of a potential crisis. The scientific consensus is so strong that the political system has been forced to act. If there is a problem, it is that science has outpaced the political system. Of course, the transition to non-ozone-depleting substances (such as more benign CFCs) is not costless. The substitute chemicals are more expensive and less efficient than those they are replacing (Lieberman 1994).

As with many public policy problems, stratospheric ozone depletion and its remedies (the phaseout of targeted chemicals) have been criticized. Fred Singer (1996) argues that the problem has been overly hyped and that the remedies are too costly, especially for developing countries.

Nevertheless, the problem of stratospheric ozone depletion has been addressed in a relatively nonconfrontational way, even though development of the issue has taken almost two decades (Roan 1989; see also Ungar 1998).

### Hazardous Wastes

> The crucial issue of achieving safer overall use and management of hazardous wastes and hazardous materials is an issue for which the most attractive approaches simply do not lend themselves to regulatory postures. Instead, the needed changes go to the heart of industrial production practices and thence to the consumption choices of individual Americans in the 1990s and beyond. They therefore require a mix of publicly set goals, market-based incentives for action, minimal administrative interference, and the rapid introduction of new hazardous waste management technologies and of production technologies that are less waste generating and polluting to begin with. (Mazmanian and Morell 1992, p. 243)

The burden of this section is that the focus of environmental policy concern has shifted to long-term threats. This is seen nowhere better than in the area of hazardous waste. In 1976, Congress passed two major pieces of legislation: the Resource Conservation and Recovery Act (RCRA) to govern hazardous waste from its initial generation to final disposition (what is called from-cradle-to-grave regulation); and the Toxic Substances Control Act (TSCA) to anticipate the possible hazards from chemicals. In reaction to the events at Love Canal (see below), the Comprehensive Environmental Response, Compensation, and Liability Act (CERCLA)—better known as **Superfund**—was enacted in 1980 to assist in the cleanup of abandoned hazardous-waste-disposal sites. In the mid-1980s, strong amendments to RCRA and CERCLA were passed: the Hazardous and Solid Waste Amendments (HSWA) in 1984, and the Superfund Amendments and Reauthorization Act (SARA) in 1986.

Hazardous substances are a perfect miniature of environmental problems. They arise because of externalities; that is, if businesses and individuals can dump the wastes, they do not need to pay the expense of proper disposal or cleanup. Any harm from hazardous waste will be felt in the future. The effect of hazardous-waste dumping on water, land, and human health is difficult to detect and controversial (Verjheid 2000). The **Love Canal** incident illustrates these problems.

William Love attempted to build a canal in the upstate New York community of Niagara; the canal was a failure and subsequently was abandoned. It was later bought by the Hooker Chemical Company, which "dumped 21,800 tons of pesticides, cleaning solution and other toxic wastes into the canal between 1947 and 1952" (McNeil 1981, p. 35). In 1953, the local school board purchased the land for a modest sum and constructed a school on it. Private homes were soon constructed near the school.

By the middle 1970s, the wastes had overflowed the canal and leaked into neighboring soil, including the basements of nearby residents. Eventually, after considerable agonizing and debates over the health impacts of the leaky dumpsite, the state bought the homes of the nearest residents (the "inner ring" houses). The reaction to the Love Canal incident led to the passage of Superfund.

Other incidents that caught public attention included the discovery of dioxin in the soil of Times Beach, Missouri, years after the soil had been spread with waste material. The pesticide kepone was dumped in the James River in Virginia. Other parts of the country, from Massachusetts to Louisiana, could offer their own horror stories.

Another problem associated with hazardous waste is the extent of the problem. EPA's Office of Solid Waste provides the following data for 1995–1996: 214 million tons of hazardous waste were generated, most of which (202 million tons) was wastewater. There were nearly 2,000 RCRA-approved facilities for treating most of the wastes (others were approved under a different program) (Office of Solid Waste, n.d.). Much of the waste (64 percent) was disposed in deep wells, landfills, pits, or ponds. Some 22 percent was discharged into streams, 7 percent was incinerated, and another 7 percent was recycled (Miller 1994). By 1996, there were over 1,200 sites on EPA's priority list targeted for Superfund cleanup (Rosenbaum 1998). Further, the federal government, particularly the Defense Department, produces a sizable portion of the nation's hazardous wastes (Davis 1993; Funke 1994).

There have been political problems associated with the hazardous waste program. Implementation has been difficult, with years passing between legislation and initial regulations. The money appropriated for Superfund is clearly inadequate, and there have been political scandals surrounding implementation of Superfund. Superfund was passed in December 1980, just before the Reagan administration took office. The first administrator of Superfund was Rita Lavelle, an attorney who had worked for a major hazardous-waste generator. The result was predictable:

> The basic implementation approach taken by the agency was first to negotiate with the relevant industries about recovering the costs of cleaning up abandoned hazardous sites and only after that to begin the actual cleanup.[6] Thus, implementation was designed to delay the start of action to remove hazards, an approach that was

> compounded by internal dissension about the program, possibly politically moti-
> vated delays in cleaning up particular sites, and general administrative inefficiency.
> (Vig and Kraft 1984, p. 154)

The consequence of all this was political scandal, congressional investigations, the firing of Lavelle, the resignation of EPA administrator Anne Burford,
and the replacement of other top EPA personnel. The political problems exacerbated a technically complex situation that required considerably more resources than had been allocated. In 1986, Congress passed the Superfund
Amendments and Reauthorization Act, providing for studies and the use of
new technologies. Despite the increased funding ($9 billion), the magnitude
of the problem still dwarfs available resources. The attempt to reauthorize
Superfund, backed by both industry and environmental interests, failed to
pass Congress in 1994, getting caught up in partisan politics as Republicans
sought to deny President Clinton a legislative victory on the eve of the 1994
midterm elections.

Superfund, in particular, is a very difficult program to administer. By 1995, it
took EPA an average of twelve years to clean up a Superfund site (Probst 1995).
As an example of the difficulties in implementing Superfund, consider the town
of Ava, Missouri (near where the author lives). During a twenty-year period
from 1958 to 1978, Sentinel Wood Treating Company dumped toxic wastes
into a lagoon. In 1993, the Missouri Department of Natural Resources found
that there had been no migration of the toxic substances from the lagoon. In
2000, the EPA decided that cleanup was necessary. The company has been cooperative with the EPA (story on KY3 television, November 25, 2000).[7]
Superfund, while showing improvements (Rosenbaum 1998), has been probably the most criticized of environmental programs based on costs of remediation,
implementation problems, and the questionable seriousness of the problems it
addresses (see Mazmanian and Morell 1992; Wilson and Anderson 1997).

## Risk Control Policy

Underlying many of these and other issues is the concept of **risk**, which may
be broadly defined as the threat to health and life as a result of some activity
or exposure to some substance (Fischhoff et al. 1981). Many environmental
programs invoke risks: pesticides, air pollution (air toxics), water pollution,
hazardous waste, toxic substances, food safety, worker safety, and indoor air
pollution (radon). Over the last several decades, more and more federal (and
some state) programs have focused on risk. Many of these threats have come
about because of science and technology (Commoner 1971), but advances in
science and technology also enable discovery of these threats at smaller and
smaller levels.

The process of addressing these issues may be labeled **risk control**
and, conceptually, consists of two parts: **risk assessment** is the determi-
nation of the existence and extent of risk; **risk management** is the actions

based on risk assessment. How acceptable is the risk? Should government undertake such action? If so, how? Risk control is seen in the papers all the time: Love Canal and Times Beach are two examples. The banning of pesticides such as DDT in the early 1970s and Alar in the 1980s are other examples.

Risk-control policy raises a number of questions.[8] As we have seen in other environmental areas such as acid rain, ozone depletion, and hazardous waste, the scientific basis for regulatory decisions is controversial. We can test substances but, for obvious reasons, only on animals. Are animal tests appropriate for making determinations about impacts on humans? In some ways yes and other ways no. Animals are given much larger doses of the substance than humans normally consume. Can we make appropriate judgments based on those large doses? In testing cyclamates (a sugar substitute), the equivalent dosage for humans might require drinking twenty to thirty (or more) cups of a soft drink a day. Assumptions about dosage, exposure, and so forth are made all the time and are necessary if we are to engage in risk-control activities. As James Wilson and J. W. Anderson (1997) point out, much of the scientific controversy revolves around two scientific disciplines, toxicology and epidemiology. Toxicology tries to understand the mechanisms that work at the molecular level and thus rely on animal studies. Epidemiology explores disease patterns within and among human populations. Having data from both disciplines that are reinforcing provides more satisfactory scientific evidence. But much uncertainty remains from both, and controversies continue.[9]

The politics of risk control thus frequently focuses on the adequacy of the scientific evidence. That scientific basis can be thought of as a kind of problem definition. Science determines that some threat or hazard exists, but because the scientific basis is so open to divergent interpretations, there is controversy over the interpretations. This is what problem definition is all about. Defining the problem helps determine the rest of the policy process. If a substance poses little or no risk, then policy action is unnecessary. Some observers (e.g., Epstein 1978) see many threats from chemicals that need to be addressed. Others (e.g., Efron 1984; Whelan 1985) see little threat from chemicals; instead, they see scare tactics and fundamental attacks on society.[10]

A second set of issues concerns the contribution these substances make to human health. The major concern has been cancer. Part of the problem is that cancer usually appears decades after first exposure to a potentially cancer-causing substance (or carcinogen). Also, cancer is not a single disease with a single cause, so attributing cause and effect is difficult—with the major exception of smoking. But studies have shown that lifestyle factors including smoking, diet (consumption of fat and calories), and sexual behavior are frequently more important in causing cancer than exposure to chemicals. While these also are controversial (think of the controversy over smoking), they require different responses from government. Lifestyle factors are mostly voluntarily engaged in and require changes in behavior. Exposure to chemicals is not voluntary, and lifestyle changes are ineffective.

Another good example is the controversy over so-called endocrine disrupters, chemicals that we are exposed to that adversely affect humans' hormonal system (Gist 1998; Kolata 1999). Given the involuntary nature of exposure, there is an argument that can be made for government action.

A third, related set of issues concerns how these and other potential threats are presented to the public and policy makers. The threat of nuclear power or of pesticides has been overstated in the press, some have claimed. We go through a "carcinogen of the month" phase, without a coherent plan.

Finally, given the variety of risks that are faced, are those that pose the greatest risk being addressed? The Environmental Protection Agency issued a report in 1987, known as the Relative Risk Report, in which senior personnel argued that the agency was devoting too many resources to small but publicized threats, and too few to more serious unpublicized threats.

> The rankings by risk also do not correspond well with EPA's current program priorities. Areas of relatively high risk but low EPA effort include: indoor radon; indoor air pollution; stratospheric ozone depletion; global warming; non-point sources; discharges to estuaries, coastal waters, and oceans; other pesticide risks; accidental release of toxics; consumer products; and worker exposures. Areas of high EPA effort but relatively medium or low risks include: RCRA sites; Superfund; underground storage tanks; and municipal non-hazardous waste sites. (Environmental Protection Agency 1987, p. xv)

However, the report makes two additional points. First, the low-risk, high-priority items may be low because of EPA effort. Second, EPA's agenda fits well with what the public is concerned about.

A follow-up report by the Relative Risk Reduction Strategies Committee (1990) suggested that EPA should move away from a reactive posture—acting when a new threat appears on the scene—to a proactive posture. Such a posture would involve basing decisions on high-risk threats and working with the public to educate them about those threats. Budget priorities, the committee wrote, should reflect those threats. One way to address some of these issues, which agencies are doing, would be to conduct comparative risk assessment as a way of rating the relative risks to humans (Konisky 1999).

Industry groups tend to take a risk-tolerant position. Partly because of the costs and the presence of scientific uncertainty, they argue that little or nothing should be done unless sufficient scientific evidence of harm to the environment or human health develops that would justify taking costly action. Environmentalists, on the other hand, tend to take a risk-averse position, also known as following the **precautionary principle**. To quote Montague (2000), "The precautionary principle says that decision-makers have a general duty to take preventive action to avoid harm before scientific certainty has been established." This leads us to our case study, on global climate warming.

## Case Study: Global Climate Warming

### Problem Identification and Agenda Building

**Global climate warming**, or the **greenhouse effect**, is the warming of the earth's atmosphere due to the heightened emissions of certain gases. These gases include carbon dioxide, methane, and chlorofluorocarbons. Increased concentrations of these gases in the atmosphere may retain heat, similar to the way a greenhouse does, raising the atmospheric temperature and potentially causing major disruptions. Another contributor to a possible greenhouse effect is deforestation, particularly in the tropical jungles in Brazil.

The first person to start thinking about the impact of greenhouse gases such as carbon dioxide was Svante Arrhenius in the late nineteenth century. Studies of the greenhouse effect commenced in the 1950s and warnings appeared in the 1960s (Hempel 2000). In the 1980s, the warnings became sharper, as did the denials. Before we get to that, some questions need to be addressed.

As with any policy area, the first question to be asked is, how do we know? What data exists relevant to our problem? In the case of the global climate warming, there are several types of data that are available. One way is to look at the historical record. That is, has earth's surface temperature increased? From 1860 to 1990, the average annual global temperature has increased by about 0.5 to 1.1°F (Miller 1994; see www.epa.gov/globalwarming/climate/). So there clearly has been some increase in temperature.

A second type of historical data relies on looking at earth's geological past. Miller (1994, p. 291) describes this task:

> Analysis of ocean and lake sediments, fossils of climate-sensitive organisms, rock strata, and air bubbles trapped in different levels of glacial ice indicates that Earth's average surface temperature has fluctuated considerably over geological time, with several ice ages covering much of the planet with thick ice during the past 800,000 years. Each glacial period lasted about 100,000 years and was followed by a warmer interglacial period of 10,000–12,500 years. As the ice melted at the end of the last ice age, average sea levels rose about 100 meters (300 feet), changing the face of the earth.

We can look at much more recent data to see if something is going on. According to the EPA (www.epa.gov/globalwarming/climate/), the warmest years of the twentieth century have occurred during the last fifteen years, and 1998 was especially warm. There is some evidence of melting in the Arctic, and sea levels have risen slightly. There has been an increase in precipitation and extreme weather events.

The next piece in the puzzle is, if we accept this and other data, to find the causes of this apparent warming. After all, as the quote above suggests, there has been considerable variation in the earth's weather over the eons. Those who suspect a greenhouse effect present several pieces of evidence. The major one is the increase in atmospheric concentrations of greenhouse gases,

Table 6.3

**1997 Energy-Related Carbon Emissions**

|  | Total carbon emissions (in metric tons) | % of world emissions |
| --- | --- | --- |
| Russia | 421.8 | 6.8 |
| United States | 1,488.5 | 23.9 |
| Japan | 296.7 | 4.8 |
| Germany | 234.4 | 3.8 |
| United Kingdom | 156.9 | 2.5 |
| Brazil | 77.3 | 1.2 |
| India | 237.3 | 3.8 |
| China (PRC) | 821.8 | 13.2 |
| Total |  | 60.0 |

*Source:* Energy Information Administration (1999).

which have also increased over the last several decades (Miller 1994). Again, according to the EPA, concentrations of carbon dioxide have increased by almost 30 percent since the start of the industrial revolution, methane has doubled, and nitrous oxides have risen by about 15 percent. Atmospheric concentrations of CFCs doubled between 1976 and 1992 (Miller 1994). Much of the emissions of greenhouse gases is from natural sources and heavily outweighs manmade sources (EPA 1999b; Easterbrook 1995).

The major source of global warming from human activities is carbon dioxide. It accounts for about 55 percent of total greenhouse emissions worldwide (Miller 1994) and about 82 percent of U.S. greenhouse gas emissions (Environmental Protection Agency 1999b). The bulk of those emissions comes from fossil fuel combustion. Another 18 percent of world greenhouse gas emissions comes from methane (Miller 1994) and the U.S. portion is nearly 10 percent (Environmental Protection Agency 1999b). Chlorofluorocarbons, which were discussed in connection with ozone depletion, accounted for about 24 percent of worldwide emissions (Miller 1994) and about 2 percent of U.S. emissions (Environmental Protection Agency 1999b). The last major greenhouse gas is nitrous oxide, which contributes about 6 percent of both worldwide emissions and U.S. emissions (Miller 1994; Environmental Protection Agency 1999b).

The developed world is by far the largest emitter of greenhouse gases, and the United States is the single largest emitter (Framework Convention on Climate Change 1998; Miller 1994). And much of the emissions relates to energy use (fossil fuel combustion) (Hempel 2000). Table 6.3 presents data on carbon emissions from the largest emitters. Note how the United States stands out.

The consequences of global climate warming are considerable, if the greenhouse effect is real (see below). The major change in rising temperatures is increases in the sea level (as the polar caps melt) and changed weather patterns. The impact of these possible changes is complicated. For example, for food production, we could find decreases and increases. Increases might occur because of drier weather. But increases (or at least smaller decreases) might occur because of increased levels of carbon dioxide and modifications made to adapt to climate change. There might be decreases in world forests, leading to increased carbon dioxide levels. Rising sea levels would lead to some coastal flooding (depending on the severity of temperature increases). Food- and water-supply disruptions might cause human migration and increases in infectious human diseases (Miller 1994).

As is obvious, we are dealing with the future; we are making predictions. Such predictions about future weather patterns are fraught with a great deal of uncertainty. Think of how much trouble meteorologists have predicting the weather over the period of a week. Now, multiply that uncertainty by decades, because that is when temperature increases, if they occur, would happen. So on what basis are warnings about global warming made?

The answer is computer models, known generically as global climate models. Based on data put into the computer, the models generate predictions of future weather. The most comprehensive analysis of models is the product of the United Nations Environment Program and the World Meteorological Organization. Together they established the Intergovernmental Panel on Climate Change (IPCC). Among its tasks is to periodically assess the scientific basis for global climate warming. The first assessment, in 1990, led to the United Nations Framework Convention on Climate Change. The second assessment, in 1995, led to the Kyoto Protocol (see below). The most recent assessment came in 2000. The 2000 assessment stated that global warming was a more serious problem than depicted in the earlier reports (Revkin 2000b).

Of course, not all agree that the computer models or the projections based on them are accurate. There are many factors that are difficult to put into computer models. For example, weather is affected by periodic solar flares and ocean current phenomena such as El Niño. The capacity of the oceans to absorb carbon dioxide is also difficult to model, as are cloud patterns.

The use of computer models has been attacked because they have overestimated temperature increases since the 1940s (see, e.g., Burnett 1999; Michaels 1998a; Shanahan 1992). Further, changes made because of the possibility of climate change would likely be very costly. If unnecessary, as critics believe, then those changes would be even more costly. Those most affected by policy changes, largely industry groups, seek either to prevent policy change or to minimize impacts (Hempel 2000).

Those who support policy changes to prevent global warming have the opposite fear. By the time the greenhouse effect occurs, if it does, it would be too late to do anything about it. The precautionary principle comes into play.

## Policy Formulation

Assuming that we have identified the problem correctly, that is, global warming is occurring and will worsen over the next 50–100 years, what remedial action should be taken? This is the course of policy formation, as we have seen in other chapters. Miller (1994) suggests a number of ways to reduce greenhouse gas emissions, some at low cost and some at somewhat higher costs. The prevention strategies include cutting fossil fuel use, the major target of international agreements (see policy adoption below). This approach includes using fuel more efficiently, as with more gas-efficient automobiles, shifting to more renewable sources of energy, shifting to less-carbon-emitting fossil fuels (e.g., from coal to natural gas). Other preventive measures include halting deforestation and switching to more sustainable modes of farming. To reduce deforestation (largely a function of developing nations), the more developed nations might offer a trade. For example, in exchange for slowing or halting deforestation, the more developed countries might offer to help fund energy efficiencies and forgive foreign debt.

A second set of strategies involves cleanup efforts. This would include planting more trees and recovering more carbon dioxide from fossil fuels. The final strategy Miller discusses revolves around adjusting to the greenhouse effect. This includes breeding plants that are more adaptable to the climate changes, stockpiling food in the event of disruptions (the biblical Joseph and the seven lean years), protecting coastal areas, and so forth.

## Policy Adoption

Although there was little controversy over the fact of increased emissions, the significance of this was uncertain. The first Bush administration position was antagonistic to the environmentalist position, represented by the EPA. The administration argued that the computer simulations were too unreliable, that the cost of alleviating the problem would be very high, especially if the greenhouse effect did not occur, and that some actions were being taken (banning of chlorofluorocarbons). As a result, the administration refused to sign a global warming treaty containing strict deadlines.

The Clinton administration reversed this position. It promised to produce a plan, based on voluntary reductions, to reduce greenhouse gas emissions in line with what other countries wanted (Berke 1993). Some nine agencies were involved in putting together the president's plan, based on such policy tools as a gasoline tax, business tax credits for planting of vegetation (to absorb carbon dioxide), and the easing of regulations on companies that help developing Third World nations reduce greenhouse gas emissions. Environmentalists attacked the plan as unlikely to meet even the modest goals set by the administration. However, opposition from automobile and utility companies made a stronger policy unlikely (Kriz 1993b).

Because of the international nature of the problem, global warming has been addressed largely by international agreements. There are two major international agreements. The first came in 1992: the United Nations Framework Convention on Climate Change signed in Rio de Janeiro. The agreement contained no mandated reductions. Rather, signatories agreed to nonbinding targets, the major one of which was to reduce emissions in 2000 to levels existing in 1990 (Hempel 2000). No country met those targets, but they have met annually to work out agreements to reduce emissions.

The other major agreement came in 1997. This is the **Kyoto Protocol**. The protocol called for 5 percent reductions in emissions, with specific targets for developed nations; the protocol has no such targets for developing nations. Those nations have argued that limiting greenhouse emissions would hurt economic development. This has been one of the major sore points for opponents of the protocol. They have argued, particularly in the U.S. Senate, that the protocol will not be approved until the developing nations have reduction targets as well. President Clinton, while continuing the research program into global warming, never submitted the protocol to the Senate for approval. Other industrial countries, those with the mandated targets, failed to ratify the protocol either (Revkin 2000c). But in July 2001, 178 nations reached an agreement requiring the industrialized nations to reduce greenhouse gas emissions by 2012. The agreement, while mandatory on the signatory relations, met a few of the objections of the United States, although it did not participate (Revkin 2001).

The Kyoto Protocol contained some mechanisms (or escapes, as some critics of the protocol have maintained) for achieving the reductions. These include emissions trading among nations and the "clean development mechanism," by which firms could invest in developing countries and help them reduce emissions (Victor 2000).

Critics dismiss both the problem of global warming and the Kyoto Protocol. Michaels (1998b) is especially critical of the modeling of the IPCC. He argues that over the last eighteen years or so, temperatures have been declining, not rising. Further, his analysis of the protocol is that it would reduce average global temperatures by less than .2°C and would cost the U.S. economy 2–3 percent of gross domestic product. The problem, if it is a problem, is clearly not worth the costs. Even those who support efforts to reduce greenhouse emissions argue that the protocol will likely have little effect. The major reason is that the collapse of the Soviet Union resulted in nearly all the reductions in greenhouse emissions called for by the protocol (Smeloff and Branfman 1998).

The Hague meeting in November 2000 sought to reach new agreements. But the U.S. position, that it should be given credit for American forests' acting as carbon dioxide sinks and paying other countries to plant forests, did not sit well with other conferees, and the conference failed to reach an agreement (Revkin 2000d).

While not submitting the Kyoto Protocol to the Senate, the Clinton administration was supportive of efforts to reduce greenhouse gas emissions. The Clinton program consisted of three parts. The first was an effort to continue research into global climate warming. The research effort, the U.S. Global Climate Change Research Program, coordinated research in different areas, such as the impact of global warming on climate and mitigation efforts. The second part of the Clinton administration program consisted of partnership programs with state and local governments, business, and the nonprofit sector to reduce greenhouse emissions. The Climate Change Action Plan, adopted in 1993, has worked, for example, with utilities around the country to get voluntary reductions and voluntary release of information about greenhouse gas emissions. The third prong of the Clinton program was to work on the international level to obtain reductions.[11] In November 2000, President Clinton proposed that there be new federal rules regulating carbon dioxide emissions, based on market-like ideas incorporated in the 1990 Clean Air Act Amendments (Wald 2000).

The corporate sector has also begun to consider the impacts of global warming (Revkin 2000e). Utility companies have been investing in clean coal technologies (which also reduce air pollution). Some twenty-one businesses have grouped together to support the Pew Center on Global Climate Change (www.pewclimate.org). Automobile manufacturers have been investing in clean fuel technologies. Ford announced in 2000 that its sports utility vehicles were important contributors to global climate warming (Gelbspan 2000).

As with many other issues we have discussed in this book, the results of the 2000 election have had an impact on environmental policy, especially relating to global warming. During the campaign, Texas governor George W. Bush, the Republican nominee, promised to seek reductions in carbon dioxide emissions. After the inauguration, the new EPA director, Christine Todd Whitman, announced that the federal government would live up to the pledge, only to see a reversal of course based on lobbying by industry and Republicans in Congress (Goldstein and Pianin 2001). Part of the reason for the change was the new focus on increases in energy prices and the lack of sufficient electricity capacity within the United States.

So where do we stand? Scientific uncertainty clearly marks debates over global warming. One could take a risk-tolerant position and say there is nothing to worry about. Whatever actions might be needed will be taken by the private sector. Or one could take the risk-averse position, following the precautionary principle that global warming is indeed real and that remediation needs to be done now before it is too late. The second Bush administration, like the first one, takes the risk-tolerant position.

## Challenges

Environmental policy faces several challenges from both the conservative and liberal ends of the political spectrum.

## The Conservative Challenge

### The Property Rights Movement

One of the most fundamental challenges to environmental policy comes from what may be called the **property rights movement**, which is based on portions of the Fifth and Fourteenth Amendments to the U.S. Constitution. The Fifth Amendment reads in part: "No person shall . . . be deprived of life, liberty, or property, without due process of law, nor shall private property be taken for public use, without just compensation." The Fourteenth Amendment extends this protection to the states: "nor shall any State deprive any person of life, liberty, or property, without due process of law. . . ." This clearly fits conservative ideology, which is partly based on the sanctity of property rights.

So how are these constitutional prohibitions applicable to environmental policy? One can conceive of environmental laws and regulations as a restriction on the use of private property or as a "taking," a seizure of private property. For example, zoning regulations may forbid certain uses of property. There are state regulations that restrict development in fragile coastal areas. The wetlands regulations mentioned above restrict certain uses of lands designated as wetlands. It has been argued that such restrictions are effectively depriving property (or the use of property) without just compensation. Consider the following case:

> When he bought 56 acres in Commerce City, Colo., in the 1970's to make room for his expanding business, Kenneth S. Valis believed he was investing in the future of the Colorado Paint Company. But in the 1980's, when a landfill that bordered on his property was found to be an abandoned toxic waste dump, Mr. Valis's purchase suddenly turned into a nightmare caused not by pollutants, but by the Government's environmental protectors.
>
> Under provisions of the 1980 Superfund law giving the Environmental Protection Agency broad powers to clean up toxic dumps, the agency put a lien on Mr. Valis's property, erected a fence around it, dotted the landscape with monitoring wells, pumps and piping and then barred any other use of the ground while the dump was being cleaned up, a process that could last 30 years.
>
> Last November [1991], Mr. Valis filed suit in the United States Claims Court in Washington, charging that the Government's cleanup work was tantamount to seizing his property and demanding just compensation. (Schneider 1992b)

Two court cases reinforced the property rights movement. In the 1992 *Lucas v. South Carolina Coastal Council* case, the U.S. Supreme Court said that, under some situations, it may be a requirement that landowners be compensated for restrictions on use of their land (Bosso 1994; Downey 1992; and McSpadden 2000). In a 1994 case, *Dolan v. City of Tigard*, the U.S. Supreme Court held that local governments had the burden of proof in justifying restrictions on private property use (Greenhouse 1994). A 1987 executive order by President Reagan required "federal agencies to consider potential takings claims before implementating regulations" (Arrandale 1994b).

Some property-rights advocates maintain that it is unreasonable governmental regulations that are at fault and that property rights can lead to better stewardship of the land (think of the "commons" problem mentioned above). Nancie Marzulla (1995), for example, argues that there is nothing incompatible between environmental protection and property rights, if the environmental protection is done right.

The problem these cases and other activities pose to environmental policy is that the potential requirement to compensate for "takings" would be so costly that environmental regulations would be economically unfeasible. This would stop the environmental movement in its tracks. An opposing view is that if real cleanup costs were added to the prices of gas, coal, and oil, their resulting high prices would stop polluters in their tracks.

One observer of the state and local environmental scene brings some needed perspective (a communitarian perspective) to the property rights movement:

> Although real estate markets give land a price, that doesn't make private property worth more to a community's life than clean air, good water and ecologically functioning landscapes. That's even less sensible when influential developers profit because local governments foot the bill for the roads, bridges and sewers that make their properties valuable.
>
> For too long, governments have subsidized the very uses of land that they then must regulate to preserve environmental quality. If the public treasury is at risk in "takings" judgments, governments should rethink the "givings" they bestow that enrich special interests but damage the large community. Some property owners may feel they're entitled to have it both ways, but they aren't. (Arrandale 1994b, p. 82)

## The Conservative Legislative Challenge

The 103d Congress (1993–94), the last Congress controlled by the Democrats, produced little in the way of new environmental legislation, even though some laws, such as Superfund, needed revision (Cushman 1994b). There are several reasons for this. First, the congressional agenda was crowded; there were important bills dealing with the budget, health care, crime, and trade. A second reason was partisanship (gridlock), especially near the end of 1994 as Republicans felt that the November elections would produce either a smaller Democratic majority or potentially Republican victories in one or both houses of Congress (Cushman 1994b).

The third reason for the failure to pass environmental laws was the conservative challenges. Conservative members of both houses of Congress offered three amendments to all environmental bills. One amendment would enact into law the arguments of the property rights movement: that private landowners should be compensated because of environmental restrictions. A second type of amendment would require that cost-benefit analyses or risk assessments be made for all environmental regulations. These amendments also stated that the analyses must demonstrate that the regulatory costs are justified. The third type of amendment would limit "unfunded mandates" on the part of the federal government. A mandate is a requirement that, in these cases, states and local governments undertake action to meet federal environmental laws. The unfunded aspect comes in because the mandates are often costly, and the federal government does not provide funds to meet them (Cushman 1994a).[12]

The legislative challenge emerged more forcefully following the capture of the Congress in 1994 by the Republican Party. The Republican Contract with America (Gillespie and Schellhas 1994) called for significant changes that would affect environmental laws and regulations. The proposed bills would require risk, assessment and cost-benefit analyses, a regulatory budget (and capping that budget at a low percentage to force changes), a limitation on unfunded mandates, limitation on regulatory paperwork requirements, protection against federal regulatory abuse, regulatory impact analyses, and compensation for private property (Gillespie and Schellhas 1994, pp. 131–134; see also Cushman 1995 and Kriz 1994c; for a critique of the Contract, see Portney 1995).

Congress, especially the House, tried a different tactic. It attempted to include many of the environmental changes in appropriations legislation, especially for the EPA. Seventeen riders or amendments were added to the bills, including provisions that:

- Prohibit the EPA from enforcing any rules about wetlands.
- Ban the system used by the EPA to limit the amounts of untreated sewage and storm-water overflows that can be released into bodies of water. (These overflows are the major cause of dangerous conditions that force the closing of beaches.)
- Bar the EPA from implementing standards for water quality in the Great Lakes—standards agreed to after six years of negotiation with the Great Lakes states—or even giving the states technical assistance for their antipollution programs.
- Forbid new rules to control toxic air pollution by oil refiners.
- Provide that when a company using the EPA's self-audit program admits violating pollution standards, the EPA may do nothing about it[13] (Lewis 1995).

None of the riders made it through Congress. Some were eliminated in the Senate; others were vetoed. The environmental riders became part of the budget battles with President Clinton in 1995 that led to the two government shutdowns. Though the rider strategy failed in the 104th Congress, it was repeated in the 105th (1997–98) and 106th (1999–2000) Congresses. Each met a similar fate. With both houses of Congress under Republican control and a conservative Republican president, the chances of such provisions surviving have increased.

One aspect of this change-through-appropriations approach is that, although it may be politically expedient, it does not lend itself to careful deliberation of what changes are needed. None of the riders or amendments was subject to committee hearings or much debate on the floor of the House. The point was to try to get the changes passed, whatever their merits.

## The Liberal Challenge

In the early years of the modern environmental movement, environmentalism was labeled a concern of affluent whites. It was "white" in the sense that the overwhelming majority of members of environmental groups were white and that those participating in the movement were middle- and upper-class people who did not have to worry about earning a living. Minority communities, facing problems such as poverty and racism, were not nearly as concerned about environmental problems.

Beginning in the 1980s, however, a new grassroots movement began calling for **environmental justice**.[14] This movement, with its basis in the civil rights movement, argued that poor and minority communities are more likely than middle- and upper-class communities to suffer environmental insults. These insults range from greater exposure to air pollution to greater likelihood of having hazardous-waste-disposal sites located in minority communities. Consider the following:

- When well-connected Manhattan residents objected to proposals to put the North River sewage treatment plant at West 72nd Street, obliging city officials moved the facility to Harlem. The chronic stench of the poorly designed plant is one more demoralizing obstacle to revitalization of the neighborhood. . . .
- The Environmental Protection Agency said in a report this spring that three of every four toxic-waste dumps that fail to comply with the agency's regulations are in black or Hispanic neighborhoods.
- The nation's largest toxic-waste dump is in Emelle, Ala., an utterly impoverished city that is 80 percent black. The highest concentration of such dumps is on Chicago's South Side. Half of the country's blacks and Hispanics live in neighborhoods with hazardous dumps.
- Two million tons of radioactive uranium have been dumped on Native American lands. Navajo teen-agers have sexual-organ cancer at 17 times the national average. . . .
- Inner-city children in Los Angeles have 10 to 15 percent less lung efficiency than those in less smoggy cities. Pollution-related asthma is killing African Americans at five times the rate it kills whites. (Kennedy and Rivera 1992)

The result is that environmental justice groups (including civil rights, environmental, and labor groups) have begun opposing the siting of hazardous-waste facilities and working toward correcting the inequities.

Although most of the actions that produce this pollution are at the state level (Arrandale 1993), the federal government has begun to be involved. In 1992, Representative John Lewis (D-GA) and Senator Al Gore (D-TN) introduced the Environmental Justice Act (Bullard 1994). It was reintroduced in 1993, though it did not pass the 103d Congress. However, on February 11, 1994, President Clinton issued Executive Order 12898 calling for federal agencies to consider the impact of environmental actions on minority and poor communities. The executive order created an Interagency Working Group on Environmental Justice, composed of representatives from some seventeen federal agencies to provide guidance for achieving environmental justice. Environmental justice groups would like to see the executive order codified in legislation.

Such a task is likely to prove very difficult in practice. It adds another layer of review of environmental regulations and is another mandate placed on state and local governments (Schneider 1993). Further, it will make the siting of waste facilities more difficult (Arrandale 1993). Nevertheless, the environmental justice movement is an important corrective to local, state, and federal environmental policies.

One additional aspect is the "brownfields" initiative. To the extent that brownfields, abandoned contaminated industrial facilities in urban areas, are restored or cleaned up, environmental impacts on poor and minority communities will be lessened.

As with the property rights movement and conservatives, the environmental justice movement fits the ideology of liberalism. The movement is based on inequities and calls for greater participation by poor communities in decision making. As we have seen, the value of equality is an important component of liberalism.

## Environmental Moderation

There is an alternative perspective to both the liberal and conservative views on environmental policy called **environmental moderation**. Conservatives argue that environmental laws are inefficient, do not work, represent government intrusion, and hurt the economy. Liberals say that environmental problems are getting worse and that more stringent legislation is necessary.

Environmental moderates assert that, in fact, environmental laws have worked, that environmental quality has improved since 1970. So we should first recognize the environmental gains in air and water pollution and in other areas. Refusing to acknowledge progress likely hurts environmental advocates more than environmental opponents (who claim that factors other than environmental laws and regulations are responsible for the gains). This attitude contributes to the belief that government frequently fails in what it attempts to do. Environmental moderates, or **ecorealists**, to use Gregg Easterbrook's (1995) term, and conservatives should both recognize these improvements (Easterbrook 1999 and Whitman 1998). That would begin to change the debate over reform of environmental laws.

Environmentalists should also recognize, according to this line of reasoning, that changes are necessary. Easterbrook, the chief spokesman of this view, supports some of the changes proposed in Congress in 1995. For example, Easterbrook supports some of the revisions of the Clean Water Act but also points out that the proposed bill would allow some increase in pollution. Easterbrook also supports regulatory reform.

Environmental moderation or ecorealism does have its critics, mostly among environmentalists (Raven 1995). They argue that environmental problems are real and that no simple solutions or technological fixes are available to alleviate them (McKibben 1995).

## Conclusion: Opportunities

> Our challenge is to create a future in which prosperity and opportunity increase while life flourishes and pressures on oceans, earth, and atmosphere—the biosphere—diminish; to create, as the Council's vision suggests, "a life-sustaining Earth" that supports "a dignified, peaceful, and equitable existence." (President's Council on Sustainable Development 1999, p. i)

Although environmental legislation faces many challenges, policy makers at all levels of government also face some opportunities to make significant changes in environmental policy. Other chances have been squandered. The Reagan administration should have been an appropriate time to reform environmental policy. However, its obvious antagonism to environmental (and similar) legislation produced great distrust. The first Bush administration sought changes in environmental policy, but did it administratively through the Council on Competitiveness and in a way that also cast great suspicion. Congressional Republicans, controlling Congress since 1995, sought considerable reforms in environmental laws and regulations but, like the Reagan administration, were largely antagonistic to environmental programs.

The Clinton administration was better situated to make needed changes. It came into office with a strong environmental bent, primarily through Vice President Al Gore. It named a number of environmentally sensitive people to key administrative positions. It disbanded the Council on Competitiveness and established a Council on Sustainable Development. Further, the administration demonstrated that it could work with business interests; in other words, the Clinton administration sought a middle ground in environmental policy. That may not please extremists on either side, but it may be the more productive path.

One important area where the Clinton administration sought change is in the overall tenor of environmental regulations. The problem is that the regulations have been very inflexible, not allowing for different circumstances (Schneider 1993). This is a product of years of suspicion between a Democratic-controlled Congress and a Republican-controlled presidency (Reagan and the elder Bush). Congress wrote laws with clear but difficult deadlines (Rosenbaum 2000). The result is almost a prescription for failure. The Council on Sustainable Development began some studies to make the regulations more flexible, working with appropriate cabinet officers and environmental and business groups. The Clinton administration's "reinventing government" project was another effort in this direction.

It is this working together on revisions of laws or regulations that is most promising. It replaces the confrontational, legalistic approach typical of regulation with a more consensual one. This was the approach employed in attempting to rewrite the Superfund law. The result of negotiations was a proposal, which, however, fell to congressional gridlock (Cushman 1994c; see also Kraft 2000). Nevertheless, such an approach is necessary to revise other environmental laws.

The advent of the second Bush administration has raised fears among environmentalists. President Clinton issued a number of executive orders, and agencies issued regulations in the waning days (and sometimes hours) of the administration to protect the environment. For example, Clinton approved regulations calling for decreased emissions from buses and tractor-trailers (Jehl 2000). Some early actions of the second Bush administration support these efforts, particularly related to diesel emissions from trucks (Marquis 2001). On the other hand, early appointments to positions in the Energy and Interior Departments have been filled with industry representatives. And other early decisions suggest a less friendly environmental administration (see, e.g., Jehl 2001).

Rosenbaum (1994) has argued persuasively that environmental laws and regulations, especially those that are the responsibility of the EPA, need change (see also Portney 1988). One such change is to employ relative-risk and comparative-risk techniques as means of planning the mission of EPA (and other environmentally related agencies). The *Reducing Risk* report is clearly a start in the right direction, with the goal of concentrating on those risks that are the most pressing, not necessarily those that the public or the media are most concerned about.

A second change Rosenbaum suggests is to rely more on market-reform strategies, such as the tradable permit system of the 1990 Clean Air Act amendments. There are many possibilities for harnessing the power of markets toward environmental protection (see, e.g., Anderson and Leal 1991).

A third suggestion is to improve the scientific basis for environmental decisions. This view has often been the focus of those who oppose environmental laws and regulations. One way of dealing with this problem might be the creation of a National Institute of the Environment, a research institute that could help resolve science-based controversies and promote environmental research. Although there are jurisdictional problems in both the executive branch and in Congress, such an institution might also go a long way toward defusing some of the conflict (Kriz 1994b).

A final suggestion, related to the flexibility concern mentioned above, focuses on mandates placed upon state and local governments by the federal government. The idea is first to allow states more freedom to use their resources for those environmental problems that are most pressing (Arrandale 1993). Another way of reducing the mandates problem is to work from the bottom up. This would involve a process, labeled **civic environmentalism**, that would start with forums at the grass roots, involve industrial, environmental, and community interests, and work up to the federal level (John 1994 and Peirce 1994). Such forums would work within the framework of federal laws and regulations but have more flexibility. The federal role would change:

> The role of the federal government in this new approach is to put its regulatory guns behind the door and leave them there as long as there's hope for reaching environmental goals through community-devised plans. Federal regulators can help by convening groups across state lines, possibly providing matching grants to get the local talks rolling. They can provide technical information and backup. Then they can readjust their resources to help make the locally devised solutions work. (Peirce 1994, p. 136)

---

## Key Concepts

| | |
|---|---|
| acid deposition | environmental moderation |
| administrative strategy | equity |
| auction of pollution rights | federalism |
| brownfields | fragmentation |
| charge systems | free rider |
| civic environmentalism | global climate warming |
| command-and-control | greenhouse effect |
| design standards | health |
| ecology | inducements |
| ecorealists | Kyoto Protocol |
| efficiency | liberty |
| effluent (or emissions) tax | Love Canal |
| environmental justice | market failure |

market reform

National Environmental
Protection Act (NEPA)

negative externality

performance standards

precautionary principle

private costs

property rights movement

regulatory strategy

risk

risk assessment

risk averse

risk control

risk management

risk tolerant

security

social costs

Superfund

sustainability

tradable permit systems

tragedy of the commons

---

## Reflections

1. Perhaps the underlying dilemma of environmental policy is scientific uncertainty. There are few issues in which the scientific evidence can conclusively demonstrate that a particular policy position is absolutely the best one. Given this dilemma, some administrations, as we have seen, have chosen a risk-averse course (deciding to take action to lessen the potential harm despite the absence of conclusive evidence) while other administrations have been more risk tolerant (unwilling to take action until scientific evidence is more conclusive). Where do you stand on this question? Are you willing to take chances and await the results of further research, or are you unwilling to take chances and seek corrective action now? Why? Why do you think that some administrations are more risk averse while others are more risk tolerant?

2. Another issue of environmental policy making is the use of cost-benefit analysis to decide whether to take action (e.g., regulate or prohibit the use of a pesticide). One of the problems with cost-benefit analysis is that it requires us to place an economic value on human life. How do you feel about this? What problems might there be in attempting to place a dollar value on human life? Because environmental regulations have costs, how should we make comparisons between threats to human health and the economic costs of new regulations? Are you comfortable with this kind of analysis?

3. The property rights movement supports the value of liberty. It urges compensation for limitations on the use of private property for environmental protection. This route might very well impede further protection of the environment. Where do you stand in the conflict of values between liberty and environmental protection? At the same time, the environmental justice movement is based on the value of equality. To what extent do you think equity concerns should be a consideration in making environmental policy? If you were a policy maker dealing with the environment, how would you resolve these conflicts?

## Notes

1. Not all agree that such is the case. Some have argued that there is an analogous theory of nonmarket or government failure (Wolf 1979). Government does not always succeed in its programs, incentives exist for perverse outcomes, and so forth. Despite this argument, the United States has sought government solutions in the environmental area.

2. For an analysis of environmental problems based on Commoner's (1971) four laws of ecology and Hardin's "commons" problem, see Smith (2000).

3. W.R. Grace and Company's counterarguments can be found at the following website: www.civil-action.com/civilaction.

4. When the evidence became overwhelming, as in the case of the ozone layer and chlorofluorocarbon emissions, policy action may come rapidly. This is, however, a rare exception.

5. For an analysis of the meaning of "unreasonable risk" in TSCA, see Davies et al. (1979).

6. This made some sense given the inadequacy of funding Superfund and the desire within the Reagan administration to reduce the regulatory burden.

7. For a critique of Superfund based on cost considerations and risk assessment, see Hamilton and Viscusi 1999.

8. For a discussion of risk-control policy, see Andrews (2000), Kraft (1988), and Rosenbaum (1998).

9. For a thorough discussion of scientific uncertainty and risk assessment, see Lemons (1996).

10. For a general discussion of these issues, see Rushefsky (1986).

11. Information in this paragraph was obtained from the EPA's Global Warming Action page at www.epa.gov/globalwarming/actions/index.html.

12. For a discussion of the problem of environmental mandates, see Arrandale (1994a).

13. To put a humorous bent on what this means, there was an episode during *Sesame Street*, which I remember watching when my children were young, about the mythical story of George Washington and the cherry tree. Young George, the story goes, chopped down a cherry tree (violated a pollution standard). His father (the EPA) was angry and asked who had done the dastardly deed. George said he could not tell a lie and admitted he had done it. His father said because he told the truth, George would not be punished (fined). On *Sesame Street*, George, played by Kermit the Frog, then chops down another tree. His father gets upset and the cycle continues until all the trees have been chopped down, but George is not punished. This also reminds me of the Mark Twain comment that he was a better person than George Washington. Washington, he said, could not tell a lie. Twain says that he could but didn't want to!

14. For a general discussion of the environmental justice movement, see Bullard (1994).

# 7 Criminal Justice: To Ensure Domestic Tranquility

*What sets the United States apart from other developed countries is not our high crime rates. What sets the United States apart is our distinctively high rates of lethal violence.* (Zimring and Hawkins 1997, p. 59)

*We suggest that long-term trends in crime rates can be accounted for primarily by three factors. First, shifts in the age structure of the population will increase or decrease the proportion of persons—young males—in the population who are likely to be temperamentally aggressive and to have short time horizons. Second, changes in the benefits of crime (the accessibility, density, and the value of criminal opportunities) and in the cost of crime (the risk of punishment and the cost of being both out of school and out of work) will change the rate at which crimes occur, especially property crimes. . . . Third, broad social and cultural changes in the level and intensity of society's investment (via families, schools, churches, and the mass media) in inculcating an internalized commitment to self-control will affect the extent to which individuals at risk are willing to postpone gratification, accept as equitable the outcomes of others, and conform to rules.* (Wilson and Herrnstein 1985, p. 437)

*The most optimistic view after looking at this is that we are in roughly the same ballpark now in the late 1990s as we were in the late 1960s, when everyone said crime is so bad we need a national commission to study it.* (Lynn A. Curtis, president of the Milton S. Eisenhower Foundation, quoted in Vise and Adams 1999)

*We need to regain a sense of community, to realize that it takes a village—or neighborhood—to raise a child.*

*A city or a nation doesn't fall at once. It goes one family, one neighborhood, one inner city at a time, until a nation of bountiful opportunity, the United States, imprisons more people than any other industrialized country—and needs to build still more prisons.*

*Despite our many divisions, real and imagined, we are one people. We have a responsibility to each other and to all of our children. When one teen or adult goes bad, it diminishes his family, his friends, his neighborhood, his community.*

*Poet John Donne had it right: Ask not for whom the bell tolls, it tolls for thee.*
("Our View: Involvement in Mankind Foils Crime" 1994)

Judging by newspapers, television, and movies, Americans have a fascination with crime and violence. Newspapers feature stories about multiple murders with all their lurid details. Television has a sizable number of series with crime as a theme. Consider the following list of "prime time" programs on ABC, CBS, and NBC: *The Practice, Law & Order, Law & Order: Special Victims Unit, CSI* [Crime Scene Investigations], *NYPD Blue.* Cable channels show reruns of *Homicide: Life on the Streets, The Profiler, Law and Order, Matlock,* and so forth.

Television news also seems preoccupied with crime. From 1993 to 1996, network news increased its coverage of homicides by 700 percent; during this same time period, there was a 20 percent decrease in the homicide rate. Most people get their news from television, and many people, according to surveys, do not think the crime rate has gone down (Morin 1997). A sizable majority (81percent) of the people, according to an ABC News poll, base their perceptions about crime on the print and electronic media (Publicagenda.com [www.publicagenda.com/issues/pcc_detail.cfm?issue_type'crime&list'5]). The crime issue has been an important consideration in many recent presidential elections (though not the 2000 elections).

Apart from the numbers related to crime, specific incidents stand out and affect perceptions and (to a lesser extent) public policy. From October 1997 to August 1999, a period of nearly two years, twelve incidents of violence captured the nation's attention. Five of them were school violence, the most tragic at Columbine High School in Littleton, CO, where thirteen people were killed and another twenty-three wounded. While schools remain a safe place for the nation's children, the concern fueled debates over guns and led to increased security in the schools.

But the facts are that there is much cause for optimism about crime. As will be shown below, crime rates across the board are down and have been declining since the early 1990s (Easterbrook 1999; Whitman 1998).

The overall level of crime remains high, and there are important policy issues. In this chapter, we will examine policy goals and policy tools, sketch out the dimensions of crime in America, and then evaluate efforts to reduce crime. These aspects are followed by a discussion of three important criminal justice issues: police and minorities, capital punishment, and gun control. The case study looks at the war on drugs.

# Problem Identification

## *Policy Goals*

The most essential function of government is the protection of its citizens, or, to put it in the language of political values, government's major concern is **order**. In many respects, the goal of order is the same in foreign and domestic policy. When faced with real and potential threats to the nation's **security**, its citizens rely on government for protection. All three aspects of order (life, property, social order) that were examined in chapter 1 are included as goals in this policy area. Crimes against persons and property are the major categories of criminal activity and are recorded in the Federal Bureau of Investigation's (FBI) **Uniform Crime Reports** (**UCR**), also known as the **crime index**.

Though crime statistics do not relate directly to social order as it is discussed here, the effects of crime can be indirectly felt. One could argue that the prevalence of crime and the disparity in crime rates among countries rest on differences in social order, traditions, and values. For example, the increase in divorce rates and the decline of the traditional family may be related to the disproportionate amount of crime committed by young, single men (Gilder 1986). The increased use of drugs and the amount of drug-related crime also indicate a breakdown in social institutions.

John Lewis, an African American, a veteran of the civil rights movement, and a Democratic congressman from Georgia, argues in a similar vein that crime, poverty, and the breakdown of social institutions in the African-American community are linked:

> The causes of the deterioration, the roots of our present crisis, are many. But surely the most immediate and the most powerful is the fact of the violence itself. Increasingly over the past thirty years, crime and violence have been allowed to run virtually unchecked through poor black communities. This widening gyre of destruction first stripped communities of businesses and jobs. It broke down housing. It made schools places of fear, where a quarter of the students might carry weapons for self-defense, and learning was always a casualty. For as life becomes more dangerous, more subject to hazardous fate, so it becomes progressively difficult to raise children in the settled peace they require. And more and more the most conspicuous models of success were the racketeer, the pimp, and the insidious drug dealer. So more and more children, deprived of reasonable nurture, were sucked into the vortex, to become in their turn the abusers and the destroyers of the children who came after them.
>
> It is not only poverty that has caused crime. In a very real sense it is crime that has caused poverty, and is the most powerful cause of poverty today. (Lewis 1995, p. 49)

As in other policy areas, there is often a conflict between political values and goals. In the case of criminal justice policy, the conflict is between the values of order and **freedom**. The freer a society, from governmental as well as social restrictions, the more difficult it is to impose order and protect life and property. The U.S. Supreme Court, during Earl Warren's tenure as chief justice (1953–1969), delivered a number of decisions protecting those accused of crimes.

These decisions upheld an accused person's right to an attorney, to be informed of his or her rights, and to be protected against the use of illegally obtained evidence. Underlying the Warren Court's decisions extending the application of federal constitutional guarantees to the states was the belief that a person is most vulnerable to government coercion when accused of a crime. The penalties may be awesome, including confinement in prison and death. Public opinion polls continually show that the public favors a tough line on criminals over protecting the rights of criminals (Public Agenda–www.public agenda.com). Putting it in our language of policy goals, the public prefers order to freedom.

**Equity** is a third goal in criminal justice policy. The equity concern is that members of ethnic minorities and low-income groups (the two strongly overlap) are disproportionately more frequent criminal offenders as well as victims. This idea suggests that crime is related to socioeconomic factors and that appropriate anticrime policies should address problems such as poverty. But it also addresses issues such as racial profiling by police agencies that target minority members for careful scrutiny.

### Policy Tools

The major policy tool in the fight against crime is **direct services**: police, prosecutors, courts, and prisons. These tools work by direct punishment and by deterring some from committing crime, **negative inducements**. Another policy tool is **persuasion**. One example of the use of persuasion is the "Just Say No" campaign, which attempts to keep children from starting drug use.

The other set of policy tools is **positive inducements**. Positive inducements do not directly address crime. However, if there is a strong relationship between crime and socioeconomic status, then policies aimed at changing that status are warranted. Antipoverty, health, education, and job training programs might offer an alternative, at least for some, to the benefits of crime.

### A Statistical Portrait of Crime

There are two major sources of data on crime (Maier 1991). The FBI's Uniform Crime Reports are commonly used. The UCR numbers are based on crimes reported to the police. If, however, as the data shows, a considerable amount of crime is committed but not reported, then the amount of actual crime is understated. Further, if you look at how individuals accused of crimes are treated by the criminal justice system and then observe only reported crime, you may get a distorted view of the disposition of suspects. The UCR is, however, reasonably reliable for homicide statistics.

An alternative method of measuring the amount of crime is to survey the population and ask who has experienced crime (been victims) and whether they have reported it. These studies (**National Crime Victimization Survey** or **NCVS**) are known as **victimization surveys** and give a different picture of crime in America from that based on the UCR. This section will rely largely on victimization surveys with the understanding that the numbers from the NCVS are estimates. Further, NCVS data were revised in 1993 and the following paragraphs reflect the new numbers.[1]

The Bureau of Justice Statistics distinguishes between personal victimization (rape, robbery, assault, and larceny) and household victimization (burglary, larceny, and vehicle theft). The victimization surveys do not cover kidnapping and murder, nor do they survey "victimless crimes" such as drug abuse, drunkenness, and prostitution. White-collar crime (such as stock fraud) is not surveyed either.[2]

The first observation to make is that much crime is not reported (see Tables 7.1 and 7.2). Table 7.1 presents four different measures of crime from 1973 to 1999: total violent crime (as measured by NCVS surveys), the number of victimizations reported to the police, the number of crimes reported to the police (as measured by the UCR), and the number of arrests. There are more victimizations than crimes reported to police each year. The numbers do tend to track each other. And the proportion of arrests to total victimizations and reported crimes has increased, providing one possible explanation for the reduction in crime.

Table 7.2 presents data for 1999 on the percent of specific crimes reported to the police. The table tells us that about 36 percent of all victimizations are reported to the police, almost 44 percent of violent crimes, and nearly 34 percent of property crimes. An appallingly low percentage of rape and sexual assaults are reported to the police. Motor vehicle theft has the highest percentage of reporting to the police.

Table 7.1 also provides data about trends. The peak year for crime was 1993, and the number of crimes has declined since then. Table 7.3 presents data about homicides. While there are some peaks and valleys, 1993 again shows up as the peak year, followed by steady declines. In terms of the murder rate (homicides per 100,000), we again see the decline from the early 1990s. The homicide rate in 1998 was only about two-thirds of the 1991 rate. Of course, 14,000 homicides are still too many.

Data from both the NCVS and UCR surveys indicate that crime rates are highest in large, central cities and lowest in rural areas. In 1998, 65 percent of homicides involved firearms. A little over 40 percent of the homicides are committed by someone who knew the victim (13.5 percent by a family member, 26.8 percent by an acquaintance). Among all violent criminalization incidents in 1998, 52.6 percent were committed by someone the victim knew (Pastore and Maguire 2000).

The data show those most likely to be the victims of crime. According to the National Crime Victimization Survey, higher victimization rates are experienced by the following groups: males, blacks, young people between the ages of sixteen and twenty-four, those with lower income, those who were unmarried (with the never married having the highest rate of victimizations),

Table 7.1

**Measuring Crime: Serious Violent Crimes**
(homicide, rape, robbery, aggravated assault)

| | Total violent crimes | Victimizations reported to the police | Crimes reported to the police | Arrests | % of total arrested | % of reported arrested |
|---|---|---|---|---|---|---|
| 1973 | 3,590,500 | 1,861,000 | 715,900 | 392,700 | 10.94 | 21.10 |
| 1974 | 3,800,000 | 2,030,000 | 791,000 | 462,900 | 12.18 | 22.80 |
| 1975 | 3,594,700 | 1,976,100 | 844,100 | 441,100 | 12.27 | 22.32 |
| 1976 | 3,613,300 | 2,039,600 | 822,800 | 414,600 | 11.47 | 20.33 |
| 1977 | 3,662,500 | 1,966,800 | 845,700 | 438,500 | 11.97 | 22.30 |
| 1978 | 3,626,100 | 1,879,800 | 894,100 | 469,900 | 12.96 | 25.00 |
| 1979 | 3,834,800 | 2,020,500 | 998,700 | 467,700 | 12.20 | 23.15 |
| 1980 | 3,794,400 | 2,037,500 | 1,108,300 | 482,900 | 12.73 | 23.70 |
| 1981 | 4,101,700 | 2,217,900 | 1,125,000 | 496,600 | 12.11 | 22.39 |
| 1982 | 3,926,200 | 2,232,700 | 1,108,300 | 547,400 | 13.94 | 24.52 |
| 1983 | 3,455,500 | 1,877,400 | 1,064,900 | 516,600 | 14.95 | 27.52 |
| 1984 | 3,683,300 | 2,003,500 | 1,081,800 | 501,600 | 13.62 | 25.04 |
| 1985 | 3,358,400 | 1,926,500 | 1,126,700 | 506,800 | 15.09 | 26.31 |
| 1986 | 3,284,700 | 1,900,200 | 1,268,800 | 565,000 | 17.20 | 29.73 |
| 1987 | 3,424,900 | 1,987,800 | 1,265,300 | 568,100 | 16.59 | 28.58 |
| 1988 | 3,563,000 | 1,942,000 | 1,336,700 | 600,000 | 16.84 | 30.90 |
| 1989 | 3,533,700 | 1,847,800 | 1,405,000 | 666,100 | 18.85 | 36.05 |
| 1990 | 3,500,600 | 1,949,200 | 1,556,800 | 722,400 | 20.64 | 37.06 |
| 1991 | 3,712,000 | 2,133,000 | 1,632,700 | 738,200 | 19.89 | 34.61 |
| 1992 | 3,987,000 | 2,161,000 | 1,657,300 | 722,700 | 18.13 | 33.44 |
| 1993 | 4,191,000 | 2,218,500 | 1,648,100 | 716,100 | 17.09 | 32.28 |
| 1994 | 4,116,000 | 2,110,800 | 1,605,600 | 778,800 | 18.92 | 36.90 |
| 1995 | 3,493,500 | 1,848,600 | 1,549,900 | 796,200 | 22.79 | 43.07 |
| 1996 | 3,260,000 | 1,740,400 | 1,444,600 | 729,600 | 22.38 | 41.92 |
| 1997 | 3,039,000 | 1,741,800 | 1,405,200 | 717,800 | 23.62 | 41.21 |
| 1998 | 2,776,800 | 1,587,900 | 1,319,800 | 675,900 | 24.34 | 42.57 |
| 1999 | 2,530,000 | 1,408,500 | 1,130,700 | 636,000 | 25.14 | 45.15 |

*Source:* Pastore and Maguire (2000).

those living in the western portion of the United States, and those living in urban areas (Rennison 1999).

The related question is, who are the offenders? Again, the National Crime Victimization Survey sheds light on this question. Victims and offenders share many of the same characteristics (Pastore and Maguire 2000). Offenders (as judged by arrest records) are predominantly male (78.2 percent are male); disproportionately African-American (29.7 percent of all arrests, although only a little more than 12 percent of the population; 68 percent of offenders were white); disproportionately young (e.g., while fifteen-to-nineteen-year-

Table 7.2

**Percent of Crimes Reported to Police, 1999**

| | |
|---|---|
| All victimizations | 36.3 |
| Violent crime | 43.9 |
| Rape/sexual assault | 28.3 |
| Robbery | 61.2 |
| Aggravated assault | 55.3 |
| Simple assault | 38.5 |
| Personal theft | 25.9 |
| Property crime | 33.8 |
| Burglary | 49.3 |
| Motor vehicle theft | 83.7 |
| Theft | 27.1 |

*Source:* Pastore and Maguire (2000).

olds made up just 7.2 percent of the population in 1998, 22.3 percent of those arrested that same year were in that age group). Participation in crime declines with age (Pastore and Maguire 2000).

Marital status and education are two other demographic variables that describe offenders. Looking just at prisoners in state prisons in 1997, only 16.6 percent of prisoners were married at the time of imprisonment and 57.1 percent had never been married; 43.1 percent had less than a high school education and another 25.1 percent had a GED (Pastore and Maguire 2000).

**Recidivists**, those offenders who have already been convicted of at least one crime, commit a considerable amount of crime. Again, looking at prisoners in state prisons in 1997, 18 percent had six or more prior convictions, 42.7 percent had three or more prior convictions; 45.4 percent were on parole or probation at the time of their arrest (Pastore and Maguire 2000). In California, a sizable number of people sent to prison (68 percent) were on parole at the time of their arrest (Butterfield 2000b). We will address prison issues below.

Family background is important in examining who offenders are. To use the language of the Bureau of Justice Statistics, "many offenders have backgrounds that include a turbulent home life, lack of family ties, and poor education" (Bureau of Justice Statistics 1983, p. 37). These are what Lisbeth Schorr (1988) refers to as "rotten outcomes." Offenders are more likely to come from broken homes, to have been abused, and to have relatives who have been imprisoned (see also Widom and Maxfield 2001; Wilson 1994). A high proportion of offenders never married, though many did have children. The report emphasizes that the data is somewhat misleading. Most people who are black or who come from broken homes do not commit crimes. Rather, these characteristics are associated with those who *do* commit crimes and provide a foundation, perhaps, for exploring appropriate solutions to the crime problem.

Table 7.3

**Number of Homicide and Rate per 100,000 People**

| Year | Number | Rate |
|------|--------|------|
| 1964 | 7,990 | N/A |
| 1965 | 8,773 | N/A |
| 1966 | 9,552 | N/A |
| 1967 | 11,114 | N/A |
| 1968 | 12,503 | N/A |
| 1969 | 13,575 | N/A |
| 1970 | 13,649 | N/A |
| 1971 | 16,183 | N/A |
| 1972 | 15,832 | N/A |
| 1973 | 17,123 | N/A |
| 1974 | 18,632 | N/A |
| 1975 | 18,642 | N/A |
| 1976 | 16,605 | 8.8 |
| 1977 | 18,033 | 8.8 |
| 1978 | 18,714 | 9.0 |
| 1979 | 20,591 | 9.7 |
| 1980 | 21,860 | 10.2 |
| 1981 | 20,053 | 9.8 |
| 1982 | 19,485 | 9.1 |
| 1983 | 18,673 | 8.3 |
| 1984 | 16,689 | 7.9 |
| 1985 | 17,545 | 7.9 |
| 1986 | 19,257 | 8.6 |
| 1987 | 17,859 | 8.3 |
| 1988 | 18,269 | 8.4 |
| 1989 | 18,954 | 8.7 |
| 1990 | 20,045 | 9.4 |
| 1991 | 21,505 | 9.8 |
| 1992 | 22,540 | 9.3 |
| 1993 | 23,271 | 9.5 |
| 1994 | 22,076 | 9.0 |
| 1995 | 20,043 | 8.2 |
| 1996 | 15,848 | 7.4 |
| 1997 | 15,289 | 6.8 |
| 1998 | 14,088 | 6.3 |

*Source:* Pastore and Maguire (2000).

James Wilson and Richard Herrnstein (1985) assert that it is not divorce or the single-parent family per se that is the problem. Rather, it is the abusive family that may contribute to criminal behavior, and that could be true of two-parent as well as one-parent families. They state that warm, restrictive parents are more likely to produce a child who "will value adult approval, readily internalizes rules, and be rule abiding" (p. 238). Cold, permissive parents, on the other hand, are more likely to produce children who will have a high rate of delinquency: "cold and permissive parents will not encourage bonds of attachment, will leave the child with a foreshortened time horizon that makes him intensely present-oriented, and will generate little or no capacity for feeling guilt" (p. 239).

Another consideration is juvenile crime, sparked by the killings in schools in the 1997 and 1998 period (and their return in 2001) and the concomitant fear of superpredator youths (Bennett et al. 1996). In recent years, beginning about 1995, crime among juveniles has dropped, though still disproportionate to their numbers in the population (Blumstein 2000; Justice Research and Statistics Association 2000).

The data also show that many of those were using drugs. In thirty-four U.S. cities in 1999, 64 percent of males and 63.1 percent of females arrested tested positive for drugs (calculated from Pastore and Maguire 2000). Drug use was also related to property crime as a means of supporting a habit.[3]

This examination of the statistics relating to victimization and offenders gives some idea of how much and what kinds of crime there are. The final area that the data can help with is in the response to crime. How are suspected offenders treated by the criminal justice system? What are the components of the system? Given the amount of crime, what is the likelihood that someone committing a criminal act will be arrested, brought to trial, convicted, and punished?

The criminal justice system is complex. There are four main stages in the criminal justice process: entry into the system, which focuses on police; prosecution and pretrial services, which center on decisions made by prosecutors; adjudication, which refers to the courts; and sentencing and corrections, which concern punishment for those found guilty.

We start by looking at Tables 7.1 and 7.2. Table 7.1 shows that the number of arrests is considerably smaller than the number of crimes committed. Reported crimes, understandably, show higher arrest statistics. Table 7.2 tells us that only about 36 percent of all victimizations are reported, almost 44 percent of violent victimizations. Thus, much crime is committed that does not result in an arrest.

Second, we can ask what percent of felony arrests result in convictions. This rate differs by the type of felony. Homicide has the highest rate of convictions, 70 percent in 1996; drug offenses also have a high rate of convictions, 66 percent. The lowest rate of convictions was for aggravated assault, about 18 percent (Justice Research and Statistics Association 2000).

Most convictions are obtained by plea bargain, though again this varies by offense. Over 90 percent of drug offenses (possession and trafficking) and 81 percent of sexual assaults, but only 54 percent of murders and manslaughters, are decided by pleas (Justice Research and Statistics Association 2000).

Why is there such heavy reliance on **plea bargaining** (when the defendant admits guilt in return for a lighter sentence)? Because it is useful for both prosecutors and the defense. For the prosecutors, it means that the courts and their schedules will be less crowded. To insist that everyone receive a trial would require greatly increasing the number of courts, judges, and prosecutors. That would obviously be very costly, so plea bargaining reduces prosecutorial workload.

But plea bargaining is also functional for the defense. A suspect will plead (usually on the advice of his or her lawyer) to get a lesser penalty. One takes a chance with a trial: A person might be declared innocent, but the chances are against that outcome. While plea bargaining has been criticized for denying the right to trial by one's peers and for "railroading" or coercing suspects to plead guilty, its functionality guarantees that it will continue.

What do the data show about punishment for those found guilty, either by a trial or by plea bargaining? In 1996, 69 percent of all felony convictions resulted in a prison sentence. The proportions varied by offense: 79 percent of violent convictions resulted in a prison sentence versus 62 percent of property offenses, 72 percent of drug offenses, and 67 percent of weapons offenses (Pastore and Maguire 2000).

A couple more pieces of information are in order. First, the justice system does not work in a very speedy fashion. That is, there is a time delay between arrest and sentencing, which also varies by offense. Homicides have the longest period between arrest and sentencing, followed by sexual assault. Fraud has the shortest period (Justice Research and Statistics Association 2000).

Second, while sentences have gotten longer, there is still a considerable difference between sentence imposed and time served; this, too, varies by offense. For homicides, the average length of sentence in 1996 was 21.7 years (the longest of all crimes), but the time served, on average, was only half the sentence. This outcome is true for other violent crimes. For drug offenses (trafficking and possession), 41 percent of the imposed sentence was served (Justice Research and Statistics Association 2000).

What has been learned from this statistical journey? First, crime rates are down across the board. That is the good news. Second—the bad news—that victimization studies indicate that considerably more crime occurs than is reported to the police. Third, we have a statistical portrait of offenders. The typical offender is young, male, a member of a minority group, and poorly educated, has low income, and is from a troubled family background. Victims have a similar portrait. Fourth, much crime is committed by repeat offenders and is often related to drugs. Finally, once a crime is reported, and especially once an indictment is handed down, the chances of getting a conviction are excellent. But prison time served is almost always less than the sentence imposed.

One last important point: It was noted above that minorities commit a disproportionate amount of crime. Further, most crime is intra-racial; that is, the victim and the offender are likely of the same race. To this we add one additional piece of information: the higher rates of crime are in cities, where minority populations are highest. What are the implications of this?

Young black males are killing each other at a high rate. The Rev. Jesse Jackson is leading a campaign to stop "the wholesale destruction of a generation of black youngsters" (quoted in Herbert 1993; see also Cohen 1993 and Cose 1994), a phenomenon he says is more deadly than segregation, lynching, or slavery. President Clinton made similar remarks. Minority communities are as much, perhaps even more, victims of crime. DiIullio (1994a, 1994b) asserts that crime in the inner-city communities is *the* major crime problem and needs to be addressed.[4]

This statistical summary presents ammunition for people with differing views. For those who focus on the individual offenders (the conservative perspective), the best strategy would be to increase the odds of getting caught, convicted, and spending time in jail. For those who focus on background conditions (the liberal perspective), the strategy of choice would be to reduce those conditions that lead to crime.[5]

## Ideological Perspectives

Given these clashes of values and the statistical portrait, how do liberal and conservative positions on crime compare? Both conservatives and liberals see crime as an important problem. The difference in the two perspectives is in what each views as the causes and therefore the appropriate solutions (Currie 1986; Henig 1985; Scheingold 1984). Again, discussion will show how problem identification—the causes of crime—structures solutions.

From the **conservative perspective**, crime is partly due to a rational calculus that crime pays, viewing the decision to engage in crime as little different from any other decision. With this economic view, the actor compares the costs and benefits of crime versus other ways of making money: crime is committed because crime pays. Other conservative aspects, based on biological and psychological perspectives, focus on the individual criminal.

Wilson and Herrnstein (1985) posit that genetic factors underlie some of the other causes considered related to criminal behavior. These correlated factors include poverty, race, poor education, disruptive family life, and unemployment (sociological factors). In other words, the genetic factors precede and affect these sociological factors.[6]

The genetic traits include impulsiveness, aggressiveness, psychopathology, and low intelligence. Wilson and Herrnstein argue that there appear to be some inheritable genetic traits that predispose individuals to crime. For example, they cite studies of adopted children showing that children whose biological parents had criminal convictions were more likely to have criminal convictions themselves as adults than were children whose biological parents had no criminal convictions. This perspective certainly has some appeal because while crime is committed disproportionately by young, black, single

males, it is also true that only a small minority of this group exhibits antiso-
cial behavior. In other words, given similar life situations, a few turn to crime
but most do not. Wilson and Herrnstein offer some explanations of why this is
the case.[7]

The **liberal perspective** acknowledges individual responsibility for crime,
but searches for societal level explanations as well. The liberal examines the
type of person who commits crimes—lower-class, young, and a member of a
racial minority—sees that discrimination, unemployment, poor schooling, and
blocked opportunities all create a syndrome in which crime pays. William
Julius Wilson (1980, 1987) argues that it is not race that is responsible for
criminal behavior and other social problems but the existence of an underclass.
Thus, although a disproportionate amount of crime is committed by blacks,
race is not the explanation. Rather, it is the poverty of this group that is the
cause (see also Mead 1992). This liberal, sociologically based perspective is
caricatured in the song "Officer Krupke" from *West Side Story*, in which one
of the gang members declares: "I'm depraved on account of I'm deprived!"
Thus, while seeing the need for crime prevention, punishment, and detection,
liberals also advocate solutions to the "blocked opportunity" problem (Henig
1985) and greater emphasis on the rights of the accused.

As we shall see in this chapter's conclusion, the two perspectives are
converging.

### The Federal Government's Role in Criminal Justice

Criminal justice policy is affected by the primary locus of public policy.
Whereas some policy areas are dominated by the federal government (economics and foreign and defense policy) and others involve a complex mixture
of federal, state, and local governments (poverty and health), criminal justice
policy is dominated by state and local governments (Henig 1985; Jacob 1984).
The federal role grew beginning in the 1960s ("The Federal Role in Crime
Control" 1994).

The federal government plays an important role in criminal justice policy.
There are federal crimes and federal prisons: robbing a bank and kidnapping
across state lines are examples of federal crimes. Federal courts play a dual
role in criminal justice policy. They hear cases involving federal crimes and
they also hear appeals from state courts, such as death penalty cases. The
federal judiciary and the federal Department of Justice can strongly influence
how police conduct their activities and protect those accused of crimes.

The federal government also provides data and information to state and
local agencies. The data might be statistical or information relating to specific investigations. The federal government has also supplied technical and
financial assistance to state and local agencies. For example, the computer-
ization of records and the 911 emergency telephone system were developed
with the assistance of federal aid programs. The old Law Enforcement Assis-

tance Administration (LEAA) provided substantial amounts of financial assistance to help local police agencies upgrade the quality of their equipment.
One of President Clinton's proposals, enacted in 1994, provides federal funding for hiring of 100,000 new police officers by police departments.

Presidents can have an effect by their appointments to the federal judiciary. The Nixon and Reagan administrations appointed judges and justices
who had orientations away from the strong civil liberties focus of the Warren
court. For example, the Burger (1969–1987) and Rehnquist (1987–present)
courts relaxed the exclusionary rule, which bars use of any illegally obtained
information or evidence. In 2000, it did, however, uphold the Miranda warnings requiring police to inform those they arrest of their rights.

Finally, the federal government may act as a model for states and local
governments through the conduct of its own police, prison, and court systems. Presidents may also use their positions to focus concern on the crime
problem as a whole or on a portion of that problem. Richard Nixon campaigned on a law-and-order platform, encouraging conviction of criminals
and reversing of court decisions that unduly protect suspects. The Reagan
administration focused on the role of drugs and its impact on crime. Bill Clinton
made crime an important priority of his administration, for example, advocating the "three strikes and you're out" policy (see below).[8]

## Local Governments and the Problem of Fragmentation

**Fragmentation** is a problem at all levels of government. For example, a number of federal, state, and local agencies are involved in attempts to interdict
the entrance of drugs into this country. At the federal level, there are the Coast
Guard (Department of Transportation); the Justice Department and some of
its components, such as the Drug Enforcement Administration (DEA); and
the State Department. As in other policy areas, congressional structure parallels bureaucratic fragmentation (Moore 1988). Drug testing of federal employees, or, at a minimum, of employees in sensitive positions would include
virtually all federal agencies. State highway patrols and other state-level as
well as county and municipal police agencies also play critical roles in trying
to stem the drug problem.

Cities, the major locus of the crime problem, face considerable fragmentation problems (Jacob 1984). There are multiple law enforcement agencies
(city, county) with overlapping jurisdictions, and there frequently are courts
at the county and city level. Prosecutors' offices are separate from both police
and courts. In the case of juveniles, whether delinquents or victims of abuse,
other agencies play a role. For example, in Missouri, the state Division of
Family Services has the mandate to protect victims of abuse. There are also
separate courts for juveniles and a separate juvenile office. In addition, county
prosecutors prosecute perpetrators of child abuse. The coordination problems
of such fragmentation are formidable.

It is not exaggeration to describe these jurisdictional complexities as a three-dimensional tic-tac-toe game. No hierarchy has organized these overlapping authorities. What one agency does can affect many other agencies but does not compel them to cooperate. Establishing a common policy [or even an agreement to work together] is not easier than negotiating a multilateral trade agreement between Europe, Africa and the United States. (Jacob 1984, pp. 11–12)

# Evaluating Criminal Justice Policy: Why Has the Crime Rate Dropped?

The happy news is that crime has decreased over the last seven years or so. As can be seen from Table 7.1, total violent crimes and total victimizations in 1999 were lower than in 1973. This is good news indeed. The big question is why. This question asks whether public policy has an impact on the crime rate and, if so, which policies. That is the subject of this section.

## *Imprisonment*

Over the past twenty years, the fifty American states have engaged in one of the great policy experiments of modern times. In an attempt to reduce intolerably high levels of reported crime, the states doubled their prison populations, then doubled them again, increasing their costs by more than $20 billion per year. (Spelman 2000, p. 97)

At least some public policies have had an impact in reducing crime. One such policy that is pointed to is imprisonment. Indeed, some have argued, as we shall see below, that imprisonment or incarceration has had a major impact on reducing the crime rate.

First, let us look at some of the numbers. Table 7.4 presents data on imprisonment.[9] The first thing we notice is that there are many more prisoners in state and local facilities than in federal facilities. This result reinforces the idea that crime is primarily a state and local government issue. Second, there has been a dramatic increase in the number of prisoners at all three levels, though more at the federal level.

There is also considerable variation in imprisonment by state. Louisiana leads the nation as measured by incarceration rate, with 776 per 100,000 residents, with Texas close behind at 762. The lowest rate is Minnesota, at 125 per 100,000 residents (Beck 2000). Nor, despite the dropping crime rate, has the prison construction boom seemed to decline. A survey in 1999 showed that the states and the federal government were constructing 148 new facilities, with a total of over 55,000 new beds at a cost of more than $2.7 billion ("Prison Construction—Part 2" 2000). Of course, the question is whether this massive project has had an impact on the crime rate, more specifically, the declines since the early 1990s.

To give you some idea of what this means, consider the following: for every 147 people in the United States, one is in prison. This is a rate higher than the People's Republic of China and almost as large as Russia. Additionally, another

Table 7.4

**Number of Prisoners in 1990 and 1999 and Imprisonment Rate per 100,000 People**

|                | 1990      | 1999      |
|----------------|-----------|-----------|
| Federal*       | 65,526    | 135,246   |
| State*         | 708,393   | 1,231,475 |
| Local†         | 406,320   | 605,943   |
| Total number   | 1,180,239 | 1,972,664 |
| Total rate     | 458       | 690       |

*Source:* Beck (2000).
*Notes:* *Prisoners in custody on December 31. †Inmates in local jails on June 30.

4 million or so people are under some kind of correctional supervision (McCormick 2000). Housing prisoners and building prisons is not cheap. It costs between $25,000 and $70,000 a year to house a prisoner, and each new cell costs some $100,000 to construct (McCormick 2000).

As the figures show, blacks make up a disproportionately high number of prisoners and people under correctional supervision. For 1995, statistics show that one-third of young African-American males were under correctional supervision (including prison) (McCormick 2000).

Of course, imprisonment does not stand by itself. Sentencing practices have changed as well. Those convicted of crimes have been given longer sentences and served increasing portions of those sentences (National Center for Policy Analysis 1999). These would, by themselves, increase the prison population, even if the crime rate were stagnant or perhaps dropping. Further, state and federal legislation have moved the country toward longer sentences. This includes "three-strikes" legislation by Congress and some states and mandatory minimum standards at the federal and some state levels.

The strongest evidence for the impact of incarceration on crime rates comes from the National Center for Policy Analysis (NCPA) (1999a; Reynolds 1998). The NCPA studies show that crime rates for specific crimes have decreased at about the same time that the probability of imprisonment has increased. For example, there was a 34 percent decline in the murder rate and a 54 percent increase in the probability of imprisonment for that crime. The numbers for robbery are a 35 percent decrease and a 24 percent increase in probability of imprisonment (National Center for Policy Analysis 1999a).

Similarly, the length of expected sentence increased during the 1980–1997 period. For example, the expected punishment for murder increased from fourteen months to forty-one months during this period (National Center for Policy Analysis 1999a).

There are at least two reasons these correlations might hold, corresponding to two theories of punishment. One is **incapacitation**, which suggests that those in prison cannot commit street crimes while they are in prison. So if we put more people in prison and keep them there longer, crime should go down. A related theory is **deterrence**, which suggests that prospective criminals will refrain from illegal activity because of fear of punishment. As the likelihood of punishment increases, the deterrent effect should get stronger.

Deterrence is based on the notion that for many criminals (with the possible exception of juveniles), the decision to commit a crime is a rational act. This sounds kind of funny, but it means that criminals or prospective criminals are affected by incentives that they face. This is the argument that Morgan Reynolds (1998) makes. Criminals look at the risks and rewards of illegal behavior and will avoid situations that are more risky.[10] Thus, as both the certainty (increasing probability) of imprisonment and severity (increasing length of sentences) have increased, crime has decreased.

William Spelman (2000) makes two important points in his careful analysis of the question of the effectiveness of imprisonment. First, crime rates would have declined even in the absence of increased imprisonment, for factors to be discussed below. Second, increased incarceration accounts for a little over one-quarter of the crime drop.

But some people believe that this incarceration "experiment" did not work nearly as well as it seems. Certainly the national trend is that as the United States continued to put more people in prison, the crime rate dropped. However, if we disaggregated the data, looking at variations among the states, we will see that the relationship is not so simple. States that experienced the largest increases in prison population saw, on average, smaller declines in the crime rates than states that experienced smaller increases in the prison population (Gainsborough and Mauer 2000).

### The Drug Cycle

We will spend some time looking at the war on drugs (see case study below). But relevant to our question of why crime rates have dropped is the cycle of drug use, particularly in the inner cities. Drug use is also related to why crime rates, especially homicide rates, increased in the mid-1980s.

The argument goes as follows: In the mid-1980s crack cocaine emerged as the drug of choice in inner cities, particularly among minority groups. Because of the physical nature of this form of cocaine, much of the selling of the drug took place on the streets, in open markets. This sales venue led to a tremendous increase in violence, as the "subculture of crack" (Johnson et al. 2000) involved assaults, robberies, and homicides against competitors. Wintemute (2000) argues that at the beginning of the crack era, the types of handguns available changed from revolvers to the more potent semi-automatic pistols.

Why did the crack crisis end? Part of it is the imprisonment factor discussed above. Another part is demographics (see below). Crack users became older and their younger siblings saw the consequences of using crack and the violence it engendered (Johnson et al. 2000; Witkin 1998). This is underscored by the drop in crime rates, particularly homicide, among young people and in large urban areas.

### Was It the Police?

This is an intriguing question. There is no question that police have an impact on crime. As Table 7.3 shows, arrests as a percentage of reported crime have increased dramatically since 1973. That obviously has an impact on imprisonment.

One way this might occur is if we put more police out on the streets. To some extent, this has happened, aided by President Clinton's program to put 100,000 more police in communities. While that goal has not been met (up to 70,000 is a closer figure; see Witkin 1998), there was a 19 percent increase in the number of police between 1992 and 1996 ("Crime Drop Linked to More Police" 1998). But the evidence that more police led to a declining crime rate is weak (see the discussion in Eck and Maguire 2000).

But more interesting is the question of whether changes in police strategy and tactics had an impact on crime rates. Changes in policy strategy and tactics include community-oriented policy, "zero-tolerance" policies, focusing on places where crime frequently occurs, and so forth (Eck and Maguire 2000).

New York City made the most use of zero-tolerance and focusing policies. Zero-tolerance applies the ideas behind the "broken windows" thesis, that maintaining order is more important than trying to prevent crime. Thus, any signs of disorder, such as broken windows in buildings or automobiles or graffiti on walls indicate disorder. Thus, if one could limit these minor problems, the major ones would take care of themselves. John Eck and Edward Maguire (2000, p. 225) describe the New York City effort:

> The crux of this strategy was a campaign to restore order in New York by making arrests for minor offenses, such as approaching a vehicle in traffic to wash its windows (the infamous "squeegee men"), littering, panhandling, prostitution, public intoxication, urinating in public, vandalism, and a variety of other misdemeanor public-order offenses.

The number of misdemeanor (minor crimes) arrests increased in New York after 1993, and the more serious crime rates declined. In the latter case, crime rates were going down prior to the institution of the zero-tolerance policy. The policy likely worked in conjunction with other factors. Further, some saw the policy as harassment, particularly of minorities (Eck and Maguire 2000). Focusing police on recidivists and on places where much crime is committed also has worked toward lowering crimes rates, but, again, likely in conjunction with other policies.[11]

There is some evidence that gun patrols have a limited impact on reducing crimes. Gun patrols are police looking for people illegally carrying guns. Trying to cut back on the drug retail market also seems to have had some limited effect (Eck and Maguire 2000).

## It's the Economy, Stupid!

"It's the economy, stupid!" was the internal campaign theme of Bill Clinton's successful 1992 presidential campaign. The economy might also have an effect on the crime rate. This analysis goes in several directions. William Julius Wilson (1987) argues that the collapse of industry in urban areas led to poverty in the inner cities. Economic opportunities for young people, especially young African-American males, were limited. Here we go back to our rational model that suggests, given the incentives and alternatives facing someone living in the inner cities, a life of crime looked pretty lucrative. As the economy recovered and grew following the 1990–1991 recession, opportunities for young people improved.

One could perhaps see this result by correlating crime rates and unemployment rates. As unemployment rates decrease, so do crime rates. In statistical terminology, there appears to be a positive correlation between the two.

But it appears that it is not the unemployment rate by itself that has an impact on crime rates. Rather it is changes in hourly wages that appear to make the difference. Real hourly wages fell between 1979 and 1993 and then began to rise. But as Jeff Grogger (2000) points out, the increase in wages was too small have an appreciable effect by itself. At best, it reinforced the changes that came with the decline of the crack market.

## Demography

One of the most powerful concepts related to crime is demography. **Demography** is the statistical study of populations in a given community. We have used some demographic information when sketching a statistical portrait of criminal offenders and victims. Here we look at demography as an explanation for the falling crime rates.

We know that the most serious of crimes, homicide, is particularly noticeable in the eighteen-to twenty-four-year-old age group and the fourteen-to seventeen-year-old group (Blumstein 2000; Fox 2000). In the 1993–2000 period, the decline in homicides is due to a continuing decline in the number of people under the age of twenty-four and a more recent decline in juveniles (Fox 2000). According to Blumstein (2000), the age-cohort explanation does not explain much of the decline in crime, especially homicides and robberies since 1993. The age-cohort explanation is that as the size of the group most likely to commit crimes (eighteen to twenty-four) varies, so does the overall crime rate. We would, therefore, expect crime rates to increase as the large baby-boom generation entered this period and then decrease as they left this age group. Both of these trends are found (Blumstein 2000; Fox 2000). Fox suggests that the demographic explanation accounts for between 10 and 15 percent of the decline in homicide rates since 1993. But homicide rates among young people remain high, and as the cohort expands, we would expect overall homicide rates to go up. Violence among young people remains a critical public policy concern.

### Abortion and Crime

One interesting, if bizarre, demographic explanation was made in 1999. Two academics, Steve Levitt and John J. Donohue, passed around an unpublished paper arguing that the greater availability of abortion beginning in the 1970s after the landmark U.S. Supreme Court decision in *Roe v. Wade* resulted in a lowered birth rate and thus a smaller population of eighteen-to twenty-four-year-olds, the most vulnerable age group for crime, than would otherwise have been. Crime rates dropped earlier in states in which abortion was available before 1973 than in the other states. Further, states with higher abortion rates in the 1970s saw greater drops in crime rates two decades later ("Abortion Has Cut Crime" 1999; Ebinger 2000; Fox 2000). This is not to suggest that abortion is an appropriate solution to the crime problem, nor is it to suggest that abortion is good or bad. Some who have looked at the paper found it reasonable, while others rejected the findings because of the abortion implications ("Abortion Has Cut Crime" 1999). Fox (2000) argues that the analysis is intriguing but has methodological flaws. Perhaps the major one he mentions is that "so much of the drop [in crime] was among age groups born before 1973" (Fox 2000, p. 304).

## Criminal Justice Issues

Apart from the consideration of why the crime has gone down, a number of issues have marked criminal justice policy in the United States in recent years. Three of them are discussed in this section.

### Guns

One of the most incendiary issues related to crime in the United States is the widespread availability of guns and their use in criminal activity. According to the *Sourcebook of Criminal Justice Statistics*, firearms were used in 24.4 percent of all violent crimes and 64.9 percent of all murders and nonnegligent manslaughters in 1998. Guns were also used in 38.2 percent of robberies and 18.8 percent of aggravated assaults (Pastore and Maguire 2000). Table 7.5 presents the trend of homicides by weapon used. As can be seen, the decline in use of weapons, especially handguns, parallels the decline in overall crime rates and homicide rates. Table 7.6 presents data on homicides by type of weapon and age of offender. As the table shows, the eighteen-to twenty-four-year-olds are a group with a relatively high rate of gun homicides.

Table 7.5

**Homicides by Weapons Type**

|  | Handgun | Other gun | Knife | Blunt object | Other weapon |
|---|---|---|---|---|---|
| 1976 | 8,681 | 3,328 | 3,343 | 912 | 2,546 |
| 1977 | 8,563 | 3,391 | 3,648 | 900 | 2,618 |
| 1978 | 8,879 | 3,569 | 3,685 | 937 | 2,490 |
| 1979 | 9,858 | 3,732 | 4,121 | 1,039 | 2,710 |
| 1980 | 10,552 | 3,834 | 4,439 | 1,153 | 3,061 |
| 1981 | 10,324 | 3,740 | 4,364 | 1,166 | 2,927 |
| 1982 | 9,138 | 3,501 | 4,381 | 1,032 | 2,957 |
| 1983 | 8,473 | 2,794 | 4,214 | 1,098 | 2,730 |
| 1984 | 8,183 | 2,835 | 3,956 | 1,090 | 2,626 |
| 1985 | 8,164 | 2,973 | 3,997 | 1,052 | 2,795 |
| 1986 | 9,054 | 3,126 | 4,235 | 1,176 | 3,018 |
| 1987 | 8,781 | 3,094 | 4,076 | 1,169 | 2,980 |
| 1988 | 9,375 | 3,162 | 3,978 | 1,296 | 2,869 |
| 1989 | 10,225 | 3,197 | 3,923 | 1,279 | 2,877 |
| 1990 | 11,677 | 3,395 | 4,077 | 1,254 | 3,037 |
| 1991 | 13,101 | 3,277 | 3,909 | 1,252 | 3,161 |
| 1992 | 13,158 | 3,043 | 3,447 | 1,088 | 3,024 |
| 1993 | 13,981 | 3,094 | 3,140 | 1,082 | 3,233 |
| 1994 | 13,496 | 2,840 | 2,960 | 963 | 3,071 |
| 1995 | 12,069 | 2,671 | 2,735 | 974 | 3,162 |
| 1996 | 10,731 | 2,531 | 2,692 | 917 | 2,778 |
| 1997 | 9,706 | 2,631 | 2,323 | 832 | 2,678 |
| 1998 | 8,816 | 2,160 | 2,252 | 892 | 2,791 |

*Source:* Bureau of Justice Statistics (2000).

Data also show that gun homicides are largely an urban, especially large urban, phenomenon. Further, within the large cities were a small number of neighborhoods where homicides were especially concentrated. Members of gangs were at unusually high risk of being victims of gun homicides. As mentioned earlier, the types of guns available changed in the mid-1980s, from revolvers to more lethal pistols (Wintemute 2000).

Table 7.7 presents data about the shootings that occurred from 1997 to 1999 that received considerable publicity. These events are relatively rare, partly because of the places where they occurred, partly because of the media publicity surrounding them, and partly because the offenders were, largely, middle-class white people. The publicity of high-profile school shootings leads schools to take measures to prevent them from happening.

Another way of looking at the problem of guns and murder is to compare the United States with other countries. Table 7.8 presents data about murder and murder rates for selected countries. The data are not entirely compat-

Table 7.6

**Homicides by Weapon Type and Age of Offender**

| Year | Under 14 | | 14–17 | | 18–24 | | 25+ | |
|------|----------|--------|-------|--------|-------|--------|--------|--------|
|      | Gun | Nongun | Gun | Nongun | Gun | Nongun | Gun | Nongun |
| 1976 | 53  | 50 | 965   | 809 | 3,586 | 2,658 | 8,413  | 3,817 |
| 1977 | 49  | 51 | 991   | 669 | 3,489 | 2,776 | 8,144  | 4,219 |
| 1978 | 77  | 43 | 885   | 760 | 3,931 | 2,699 | 8,513  | 4,075 |
| 1979 | 49  | 49 | 1,032 | 862 | 4,506 | 3,072 | 9,232  | 4,383 |
| 1980 | 59  | 53 | 1,185 | 898 | 5,085 | 3,620 | 10,131 | 5,169 |
| 1981 | 45  | 32 | 1,034 | 759 | 4,321 | 3,353 | 9,911  | 5,020 |
| 1982 | 42  | 56 | 863   | 753 | 3,820 | 3,359 | 8,927  | 5,061 |
| 1983 | 35  | 43 | 746   | 690 | 3,363 | 3,149 | 8,051  | 4,930 |
| 1984 | 35  | 37 | 711   | 555 | 3,335 | 2,933 | 7,805  | 4,925 |
| 1985 | 54  | 39 | 855   | 581 | 3,374 | 2,788 | 7,864  | 4,816 |
| 1986 | 60  | 34 | 1,004 | 713 | 3,752 | 2,882 | 8,376  | 5,357 |
| 1987 | 53  | 58 | 1,118 | 675 | 3,846 | 2,850 | 7,802  | 5,301 |
| 1988 | 54  | 47 | 1,507 | 733 | 4,477 | 2,849 | 7,858  | 5,308 |
| 1989 | 86  | 43 | 1,963 | 631 | 5,309 | 2,745 | 7,658  | 5,269 |
| 1990 | 58  | 45 | 2,325 | 817 | 6,181 | 3,007 | 8,397  | 5,634 |
| 1991 | 95  | 37 | 2,737 | 839 | 7,676 | 3,058 | 8,165  | 5,662 |
| 1992 | 91  | 49 | 2,869 | 727 | 7,492 | 2,472 | 7,792  | 5,056 |
| 1993 | 115 | 43 | 3,371 | 801 | 8,171 | 2,627 | 7,500  | 5,009 |
| 1994 | 131 | 49 | 3,337 | 778 | 7,824 | 2,403 | 7,147  | 4,820 |
| 1995 | 98  | 40 | 2,692 | 741 | 7,049 | 2,269 | 6,657  | 4,643 |
| 1996 | 60  | 37 | 2,135 | 779 | 6,656 | 2,273 | 5,998  | 4,475 |
| 1997 | 44  | 48 | 1,985 | 563 | 6,048 | 2,127 | 5,767  | 4,020 |
| 1998 | 54  | 44 | 1,433 | 571 | 5,376 | 2,310 | 5,269  | 4,196 |

*Source:* Bureau of Justice Statistics (2000).

ible with the much more carefully drawn U.S. data (i.e., the U.S. data is more reliable than in some of these countries), and the data are a bit old. But the data are instructive nevertheless. First, only Russia comes close to the United States in number of murders (and probably murder rate, though that information was not available). Compare the murder rate in 1998 in the United States, the fifth consecutive year of decline, found in Table 7.3 with the murder rates in the selected countries. Only Denmark in 1993 comes close.

Another way of getting a handle on the violence and gun problem in the United States on a comparative basis is to look at homicides against children. The number of homicides of young people, under the age of fifteen, in twenty-six countries was 1,995 deaths in 1995. Seventy-three percent of those homicides occurred in the United States and the homicide rate for U.S. children was 2.57 per 100,000 population, compared to 0.51 per 100,000 in the other twenty-five countries. Further, the rate of firearm-

Table 7.7

**Highly Publicized Shootings, 1997–1999**

| Date | Place | Location | Age of offender | Number killed | Number wounded |
|------|-------|----------|-----------------|---------------|----------------|
| October 1, 1997 | Pear, MS | Home/School | 16 | 3 | 7 |
| December 1, 1997 | Paducah, KY | School | 14 | 3 | 5 |
| March 24, 1998 | Jonesboro, AR | School | 13,11 | 5 | 10 |
| May 21, 1998 | Springfield, OR | Home/School | 15 | 4 | 22 |
| July 24, 1998 | Washington, DC | Building | 41 | 2 | 1 |
| April 15, 1999 | Salt Lake City, UT | Building | 70 | 2 | 4 |
| April 20, 1999 | Littleton, CO | School | 18,17 | 13 | 23 |
| May 2 and 4, 1999 | Illinois and Indiana | Various | 21 | 2 | 9 |
| May 20, 1999 | Conyers, GA | School | 15 | 0 | 6 |
| July 29, 1999 | Atlanta, GA | Various | 44 | 12 | 13 |
| August 5, 1999 | Pelham, AL | Work | 34 | 3 | 0 |
| August 10, 1999 | Los Angeles, CA | Building | 37 | 1 | 5 |

*Source:* Adapted from "In the Line of Fire," *Newsweek*, August 23, 1999, pp. 20–25.

related homicides for children in the United States was almost sixteen times that of the other twenty-five countries (Centers for Disease Control and Prevention 1997).

On the other hand, Iain Murray (2000) argues that firearms-related homicides are overstated. First, such homicides are more prevalent among the thirteen-to-nineteen-year-olds; among the younger cohort, homicides are largely via other means. He further notes that child murders are very geographically concentrated, with 85 percent of America's counties not experiencing any child murders in 1997.

Firearms are involved in more than homicides; they are also implicated in suicides and accidental deaths. The National Center for Injury Prevention and Control (part of the Centers for Disease Control and Prevention) presents the following data for 1994:

- 38,505 firearm-related deaths
- >17,800 firearm-related homicides
- >18,700 firearm-related suicides
- >1,300 accidental firearm-related suicides
- an estimated three times as many firearm-related injuries as deaths
- >$20.4 billion (in 1990), in hospital and other costs (www.cdc.gov/ncipc/factsheets/fafacts.htm).

Additionally, firearms are used in approximately 440,000 violent crimes each year (Senate Committee on the Judiciary 1999).

So one (perhaps) obvious solution would be to restrict the availability of guns,

Table 7.8

**Comparative Murder Statistics**

| Country | Year | Murder rate | Number |
|---|---|---|---|
| Australia | 1991–92 | 2/100,000 | 356 |
| Canada | 1990 | 2/100,000 | 589 |
| PRC | 1990 | N/A | 23,119 |
| Denmark | 1992 | 6/100,000 | 237 |
| England/Wales | 1994 | N/A | 729 |
| France (convictions) | 1990 | N/A | 624 |
| Germany (murder and manslaughter) | 1991 | 3.4/100,000 | 2,708 |
| Italy | 1992 | 3.31/100,000 | 1,461 |
| Japan | 1990 | N/A | 1,238 |
| Netherlands | 1991 | 1/100,000 | 2,16 |
| Russia | 1993 | N/A | 29,213 |
| Singapore | 1990 | 1.5/100,000 | 44 |
| Sweden | 1993 | N/A | 120 |

*Source:* U.S. Department of Justice, n.d., *World Factbook of Criminal Justice Systems,* www.ojp.usdoj.gov/bjs/abstract/wfcj.htm.

certainly from those who are most dangerous. (We will see below that there is an argument suggesting that the problem is not too many guns, but too few.)

Both states and the federal government have laws banning or restricting guns. The federal government has passed a few pieces of federal legislation. The first major federal law concerning guns was the **Gun Control Act (1968)**. It was passed in the aftermath of the assassinations of Martin Luther King Jr. and Senator Robert Kennedy (D-NY), then challenging for the Democratic nomination for president. The law called for limiting who could not possess and purchase firearms (felons, minors, illegal drug users, the mentally ill, and so forth), required serial numbers on guns and licenses for gun dealers, prohibited the mail-ordering of guns and ammunition, prohibited the interstate sale of guns (now limited to pistols and revolvers), set age limits for purchase of a gun through licensed dealers, prohibited importing certain guns (such as so-called Saturday Night Specials) and tried to limit the purchasing of automatic weapons and semi-automatic weapons conversion kits (Handgun Control Inc., www.handguncontrol.org/stateleg/sixtyeight.asp).

The bans on automatic weapons in particular led the National Rifle Association (NRA) to try to reverse some of the 1968 law's provisions. It finally succeeded in 1986, when Congress passed the **McClure-Volkmer Act**, which:

- Allowed federal firearms license holders to sell guns at gun shows located in their home state.

- Allowed individuals not federally licensed as gun dealers to sell their personal firearms as a "hobby."
- Restricted the ability of the Bureau of Alcohol, Tobacco, and Firearms (ATF) to conduct inspections of the business premises of federally licensed firearms dealers.
- Reduced the recordkeeping required of federally licensed firearms dealers, specifically eliminating recordkeeping of ammunition sales.
- Raised the burden of proof for violations of federal gun laws.
- Expanded a federal program that restored the ability of convicted felons to possess firearms (Violence Policy Center 1998).

One of the most important pieces of federal legislation regarding guns was the **Brady Bill**. James Brady was President Reagan's press secretary when he accompanied him to an appearance at the Washington Hilton Hotel. An attempted assassination of the president by John Hinckley resulted in the president being wounded and Brady being shot in the head. He has since been confined to a wheelchair. His wife, Sarah, then led a campaign to provide for a federal waiting period for the purchase of handguns, becoming the president of Handgun Control Inc.

Although gun control legislation has long had public support (88 percent of the public supported a seven-day waiting period for handgun purchases [Maguire et al. 1993]), getting such a bill passed in Congress has been difficult. A majority of the public opposes banning handguns, and the NRA has long opposed any restrictions on guns. With a Democratic Congress and a Democratic president in power as a result of the 1992 election, the Brady Bill (officially known as the Brady Handgun Violence Prevention Act) was finally passed.

The Brady Bill requires a five-day waiting period for the purchase of a handgun (in states where either no waiting period exists or where the waiting period is less than five days) so that a background check of the purchaser *can* be made. The law does not *require* that the background check be made,[12] and the waiting period can be shortened if the background check is made within five days.

In federal court, two sheriffs challenged the portion of the Brady Bill that requires background checks. In *Printz v. United States* (1997), the U.S. Supreme Court voided that portion of the bill. The background checks (National Instant Criminal Background Checks or NICS) were supposed to be replaced in 1998 by a national system.

According to one early study, within the first month after the Brady Bill went into effect, some 1,600 people were prevented from purchasing a handgun. Many of them were convicted felons and fugitives from the law (Thomas 1994). Under the new instant background checks, which began in 1998, some 13,000 people were denied guns, but none of those people were arrested (National Center for Policy Analysis 1999b). For the entire 1994–1999 period, some 536,000 applications for handguns were rejected, about 2.4 percent of all applications (Gifford et al. 2000).

Assault weapons were banned by Presidents Bush and Clinton, the latter via the Violent Crime Control and Law Enforcement Act of 1994.

In addition to federal legislation, many states have passed legislation limiting or banning guns or those purchasing or possessing them. For example, five states (California, New Jersey, Hawaii, Connecticut, and Maryland) have some form of an assault weapons ban. States vary in the stringency of its laws. Alabama, for example, has one of the least restrictive laws, requiring not much more than a forty-eight-hour waiting period for the purchase of a gun. Texas has similar laws. New York, on the other hand, has more stringent laws, with New York City having one of the nation's most severe gun laws. California and Virginia enacted laws limiting gun purchases to one per month.[13]

Other attempts at controlling guns in communities include the sweeps of public housing that occurred in 1994. The tenants favored the sweeps, because it makes the housing developments safer. Groups such as the American Civil Liberties Union (ACLU) argue that the sweeps do not make the projects safer and are unconstitutional (Springen 1994).

Guns have also become an increasing problem in the nation's schools, including the school shooting incidents that shocked the nation in 1997 and 1998, leading schools to implement tough regulations that include suspending students who bring guns to school and the use of metal detectors, dogs, and locker searches. Eliminating guns in schools is also a goal of the Goals 2000: Educate America Act, passed during the Clinton administration (Celis 1994).

The question to be raised is: Are gun control laws effective in reducing crime? We have seen that crime rates in general, homicides and gun-related offenses in particular, have decreased in recent years, though the numbers remain high. The answer is mixed. There is some evidence that screening gun applicants has an effect. Denying guns to felons or misdemeanants (those convicted of misdemeanors or lesser offenses) reduces the likelihood that they will commit a crime with a firearm (see Wintemute 2000).

Another policy focuses not on buyers, as does the Brady and similar state legislation, but dealers or suppliers of firearms. At the federal level, the number of licensed dealers has declined, which also appears to be the case for state licensed dealers. This is important because a significant portion of guns used in crimes were new purchases rather than from the secondary market (used) or stolen (though this remains an important source of guns) (see the discussion in Wintemute 2000). Further, traces of guns used in crimes find that a relatively small number of dealers are involved. According to a report by the Bureau of Alcohol, Tobacco, and Firearms (BATF), the federal agency with responsibility for overseeing federal gun laws (though its powers and resources are limited), 0.4 percent of federally licensed dealers sold about half the guns used in crimes in the 1996 and 1997 period (for guns that could be traced) (Butterfield 1999).

Sometimes, this is done through what are called "straw purchases," legal purchases made for people who would otherwise not pass the screens. Attempts to limit such straw purchases have had some success. In particular, states that limit the number of gun purchases, say to one a month, can stem the flow of guns used in crimes.

Perhaps the most impressive effort to stem firearms-related crime came in Boston beginning in the mid-1990s. The Boston Gun Project involved enforcing minor ordinances (as did New York City), and intervening especially with gangs and firearms marketing. The focus was on confiscating guns. While Garen Wintemute (2000) notes that no comprehensive evaluations have been made of the Boston effort, the decline in the number of firearm-related youth homicides has been dramatic: In 1992, there were forty-three such incidents; by the second year of the program's implementation, 1997, there were ten. In 1999 and 2000, only one handgun-related youth homicide occurred (see also Prothrow-Stith 1998).[14]

Of course, the gun laws have not been completely effective. Despite the strict laws in places like New York City, guns appear and are used on the streets. The problem is that they are imported from southern states where the gun laws are much more lax; this accounts for a significant portion of guns that appear in those cities (Butterfield 1999; Wintemute 2000).

Another problem in controlling the sale of firearms is gun shows. Some, but not all, of the dealers at these shows are licensed. The Violence Policy Center describes gun shows as essentially "Tupperware parties" where there are no limits on what is bought and sold. According to the center, illegal guns are bought at such shows through "(1) straw purchases; (2) out-of-state sales; and (3) sales from 'personal' collections" (Violence Policy Center 1998). People and groups who have purchased guns from such shows include Timothy McVeigh (found guilty of bombing the federal office building in Oklahoma City in 1995), David Koresh of the Branch Davidians, and antigovernment militia groups (Violence Policy Center 1998).

In addition, gun exchange programs, where local governments offer to buy guns as a way of reducing the supply of guns, do not appear to work very well. Additionally, laws that permit prosecution of adults for allowing children access to guns that result in injury or death also do not appear to be effective.

Gun advocates argue that the federal, state, and local attempts at restricting access to guns, whether through demand via licensing, registration, and background checks on purchasers, or supply, via licensing dealers or programs like the Boston Gun Project, have had limited impact. They argue that the country does not need new laws and regulations, but should more forcefully enforce the laws on the books. Note the report mentioned above from the National Center for Policy Analysis that the background checks found some 13,000 with denied gun applications but no arrests.

For example, the National Rifle Association argues that only law-abiding citizens would register guns and thus more registration laws would affect them but not criminals (Institute for Legislative Action 2000a). The NRA also argues that tracing firearms rarely involves weapons used in crimes (Overstreet 2000).

A third argument made by the NRA and others concerns the Brady law. The NRA argues that the law is much less effective than its proponents depict. This is for several reasons. First, there are "Brady exempt" states that had background checks at the time the law was passed. Those states accounted for 57 percent of murders and 63 percent of violent crimes in 1993, the year the law was passed. Second, the NRA argues that waiting periods have no effect on crime, based on previous state experience. Third, states that were subject to Brady provisions were low-crime states. Fourth, there are avenues for criminals to obtain guns other than through licensed dealers (Institute for Legislative Action 1999).

There are two other important arguments against gun control laws; one is political/ideological, the other is empirical, though with a strong ideological component.

The political/ideological argument revolves around the Second Amendment to the U.S. Constitution, which reads: "A well-regulated Militia, being necessary to the security of a free State, the right of the people to keep and bear Arms, shall not be infringed."

From an ideological standpoint, debates over the Second Amendment and its meaning involve the values of order and freedom and the tradeoff between them. A literal reading of the amendment would focus on the question of order: militia, security, and free State. The literal meaning is that states have the right to protect themselves, and a militia (what might in modern terms be called a National Guard) is required to maintain it. It does not necessarily mean that anybody can have a gun, but having a gun under certain conditions is acceptable.

So few words, but so many arguments! Gun control advocates argue that the availability of guns should be limited *because* of security concerns. That is, guns are used in crimes and can inflict serious damage or death; the fewer guns, the less damage. Thus, for example, gun control advocates favor sweeps of public housing as a means to protect residents. Further, federal courts have ruled that the Second Amendment does not prohibit regulation by states and that individuals do not have a right to own guns under the Second Amendment (see the discussion of court cases in the Policy Violence Center website: www.vpc.org/fact_sht/secondfs.htm).

Those opposed to gun control regulations argue on the basis of individual liberty. The NRA cites U.S. Supreme Court cases that assert that owning a gun is an individual rather than a collective right (Institute for Legislative Action 2000b). Further, the NRA and others argue that the right to own guns is an individual liberty and provides a guarantee against a possibly tyrannical government. Both sides also look at the history of the amendment to bolster their arguments.

The empirical argument (also ideologically related) suggests a rather counterintuitive line of reasoning. Gun control advocates (or prohibitionists, as the NRA would say) argue that if we remove or limit guns, there will be less violence, certainly less lethal violence. Gun advocates argue that only law-abiding citizens would obey the laws and therefore they would be placed in danger.

The empirical argument says the problem is not that there are too many guns, but that there are not enough guns. This theme is presented most strongly by economist John Lott (2000). Lott first applies economic reasoning to the problem of crime. He states that if more people carried guns and criminals knew that, they would avoid people who might carry guns. Even if only a few people carried guns, as long as would-be criminals did not know who, they would be hesitant to engage in violence. Lott is arguing that allowing people to carry guns, which means concealed-weapons laws, creates an **incentive** for criminals to go elsewhere or do something else, such as larceny rather than robbery or rape. Carrying guns also gives people a feeling of security.

Lott's analysis is based on more than just economic or logical reasoning; it employs statistics to test theories. A number of states have concealed-weapons or right-to-carry laws. Lott compares those states with states that do not have such laws. He also compares states that enacted such laws before and after such laws were implemented. Lott goes even further and does his analysis on a county rather than state basis.

The results support his hypotheses. Crime rates, especially personal-violence type crimes such as murder and rape, go down more in concealed-weapons states than in those that do not have such laws, and in concealed-weapons states after the laws were implemented. Further, the declines in the crime rate are largest for counties that have had the most crime and have the largest population density. Blacks in inner cities, Lott finds, would especially benefit from such laws.

Lott's work has been criticized.[15] Wintemute's (2000) review of the literature on concealed-weapons laws (or "shall carry" laws) finds that they had little impact on crime rates. One study that Wintemute cites suggests that the declines in murder rates were entirely accounted for by decreases in juvenile homicides, the least likely to be affected by concealed-weapons laws. That same study found that only a very small percentage of the population requested permits after such laws were enacted. The conclusion Wintemute draws is that this is too small to have been much of a factor.

The Violence Policy Center did an analysis of the Texas experience with a concealed-weapons law. They found that a sizable number, over 3,000, of people issued permits in Texas were later arrested: "From the law's enactment to the end of 1999, the weapon-related arrest rate among Texas concealed handgun license holders was *66 percent higher than that of the general population of Texas aged 21 and over*" (Violence Policy Center 2000; emphasis in original).

## Crime and Equality

Here's a riddle: Why was the internationally known Princeton professor stopped for driving too slowly on a street where the speed limit was 25 miles per hour? How

> come a Maryland state trooper demanded to search the car of a lawyer who graduated from Harvard? And why were an accomplished actor, a Columbia administrator, a graduate student, and a merchandiser for Donna Karan arrested together in New York although none of them had done anything wrong?
>
> The answer is elementary: All of the men were black. (Quindlan 2000)

> Our analysis of race and crime in the United States suggests that those who conclude that "the criminal justice system is not racist" are misinformed. Although reforms have made systematic racial discrimination—discrimination in all stages, at all places, at all times—unlikely, the American criminal justice system has never been, and is not now, color-blind. (Walker et al. 1996, p. 232)

Criminal justice typically involves conflicts or tradeoffs between order and freedom. When one brings in issues of race and ethnicity (which will be discussed at more length in chapter 9), equality comes in as well. More specifically, order is contrasted with both equality and liberty.

The basic argument by those who suggest that there is inequality in the criminal justice is that certain groups, such as African Americans or Hispanics, are more likely to be in contact with the criminal justice system beyond their numbers in the population. In other words, there is a question of disproportionality here. Let us begin by looking at some numbers, starting with overall population figures.[16]

In 1998, according to the *Statistical Abstract of the United States*, whites made up 82.5 percent of the population in the United States, blacks made up 12.7 percent, Asians 3.9 percent, and Hispanics 11.2 percent. (Hispanics can be white, black, or Native American; therefore, there is an overlap.) Table 7.9 presents data about minority populations in the United States and the relative numbers in regard to the criminal justice system. While we will consider the war on drugs more thoroughly in the case study, the impact of the war on drugs and equality can be seen in the numbers: According to Mauer and Huling (1995), "While African Americans constitute 13% of all monthly drug users, they represent 35% of arrests for drug possession, 55% of convictions and 74% of prison sentences." As Walker et al. (1999) argue, the numbers show a disparity between whites and African Americans. They do not by themselves prove discrimination. They argue that racial minorities are treated differently by some parts of the criminal justice system.

The other aspect of equality (and liberty) that has been emphasized has to do with police and minorities. This area gets particularly into the issue of **racial profiling**, where police agents target members of minority groups, sometimes for arrest and sometimes just for stops. There is considerable anecdotal evidence suggesting this occurs. Here is one example:

A black married couple, Janis F. Kearney and Bob J. Nash, were, at the time of the incident, top aides in the Clinton White House. On their way home driving their sport utility vehicle (SUV), they were stopped by Montgomery County, MD, police at gunpoint and handcuffed. The police were looking for a stolen black SUV. After the officers saw Nash's driver's li-

Table 7.9

**Comparing Whites and Blacks in the Criminal Justice System**

|  | White | Black |
|---|---|---|
| Percent of total population in the United States | 82.5 | 12.7 |
| Estimated percent distribution of violent victimization by lone offenders | 66.8 | 22.5 |
| Percent of total offenses charged | 67.3 | 30.5 |
| Percent charged with murder/manslaughter | 44.2 | 54.1 |
| Percent charged with violent crime | 58.2 | 39.8 |
| Percent of felony offenders convicted in state courts (total offenses) | 54.0 | 44.0 |
| Violent offenses | 52.0 | 46.0 |
| Murder/manslaughter | 44.0 | 54.0 |
| Robbery | 32.0 | 66.0 |
| Drug possession | 49.0 | 49.0 |
| Drug trafficking | 43.0 | 56.0 |
| Rate per 100,000 of male adults held in prisons or jails (1997) | 990 | 6,838 |
| Estimated percent of population of adults under correctional supervision (1997) | 2.0 | 9.0 |

*Source:* Pastore and Maguire (2000).

cense, they let him go. Nash got a copy of the incident report and found the following:

1. We did not violate any traffic laws that would justify us being stopped.
2. The incident report indicated that the suspect was a 5-foot, light skinned Black male. I am 5′11,″ and dark-skinned.
3. My vehicle is blue, not black. The street was well-lit and there were numerous spotlights on me, my wife, and the vehicle.
4. My tag number is registered to my wife and I, not to the owner of the stolen vehicle. ("Cops Terrify President's Top Black Aides" 2000, p. 7)

Other labels have been attached to racial profiling, such as "**driving while black**" (**DWB**). An American Civil Liberties Union (ACLU) report details a number of such incidents similar to the one described above (Harris 1999). But such profiling goes on in other places, from swimming pools to airports (see, e.g., Cole 1999 and Stout 1999).

One way of getting a handle on racial profiling is to look at public opinion data. In December 1999, the Gallup organization released the results of a poll it had taken on the issue. While a majority of both whites and African Americans agreed that racial profiling by police was fairly widespread, a greater portion of African Americans (77 percent) than whites (56 percent) believed this was the case. Some 40 percent of African Americans said they were stopped by police solely because of race, compared to 6 percent of whites; 72 percent of young African-American men (ages eighteen-to-thirty-four) report being stopped by police because of race; 30 percent of African Americans of all ages report being stopped by police because of race six or more times (Gallup Poll 1999).[17]

Racial profiling occurs in lots of different places and ways. New York City's policy to reduce crime, discussed above, involved a quality-of-life focus and concentrated on people in particular neighborhoods. According to the New York City Police Department, its Street Crime Unit stopped at least 45,000 people in the 1997–1998 period, though it arrested less than 10,000; virtually all of these people were non white (Herbert 1999c; see also Cole 1999).

Broadway actor Alton Fitzgerald White was in the lobby of his New York City apartment building when he was arrested by police looking for armed drug dealers. White was not armed nor did he have any drugs on him (Herbert 1999b). In 1992, in the town of Oneonta, NY, a woman told police she was robbed by an African-American man. The police stopped and questioned every African-American man (and one African-American woman) in the town, including all the African-American students at the nearby university. A federal appeals court upheld the police (Herbert 1999c).

Brooke Gladstone, a reporter for National Public Radio, began the November 30, 1999, *Talk of the Nation* show with the following words:

> There's a traffic violation all too familiar to African-Americans of which the white majority may be serenely unaware. It's called DWB, driving while black. Of course, DWB is not the only infraction. There's SWB, shopping while black, prompting a number of lawsuits in recent years, brought, for example, by a young black man forced to take the shirt off his back in Eddie Bauer's because he couldn't produce a receipt. And then there's the infamous WWB, walking while black, when you are stopped because you, quote, "fit the description." To that list you could add HCWB, hailing a cab while black, which, though not strictly speaking a violation, is certainly an exercise in futility and the cause of a crackdown on cabbies lately in New York after actor Danny Glover called a press conference to complain. (Gladstone 1999)

New York is hardly the only place where racial profiling exists. New Jersey, Maryland, and California are other states where the practice occurs.

Racial profiling can prove deadly, as in the case of Amadou Diallo, who was killed by four New York City policemen in the vestibule of his apartment. While the officers were later found not guilty in the subsequent trial, it was clear that Diallo, an immigrant from western Africa who was reaching for his wallet, was shot because he was black.

The rationale by police for stopping African Americans and Hispanics at a very high rate is that the officers are often in high-crime neighborhoods and African Americans and Hispanics cause a disproportionate amount of crime (see, e.g., Taylor and Whitney 1999). This mind-set is captured by Rev. Jesse Jackson in 1993:

> There is nothing more painful to me at this stage in my life than to walk down the street and hear footsteps and start thinking about robbery—then look around and see somebody white and feel relieved. (quoted in Cole 1999, p. 40)

However, a study of racial profiling by the New York State Attorney General's Office found that, controlling for the higher crime rates among African Americans and Hispanics, the police still stopped and questioned disproportionately more minorities than whites (Flynn 1999).

Part of the emphasis on racial profiling may have come from the federal government. As part of the war on drugs, the Drug Enforcement Administration has suggested possible profiles for police agencies to use in interdicting drug traffic (Kocieniewski 2000).

The organization Building Blocks for Youth found that minority and white teenagers were treated differently by the juvenile justice system, through disparities in arrests, convictions, and sentencing (Poe-Yamagata and Jones 2000; see also Cole 1999; Office of Juvenile Justice and Delinquency Prevention 1999).

Stuart Taylor (2000a, 2000b) argues that racial profiling by police is wrong, at least not worth the costs. But Taylor (2000a) also notes that racial profiling by cab drivers and delivery drivers may make some sense, even when a sizable number of these drivers are African Americans. He mentions an op-ed piece by Steven A. Holmes of the *New York Times* (Holmes 1999a), who was stopped by a police officer in Washington, DC, for no apparent reason other than he was black. He was very upset about this and then recalled that when he was working as a cab driver while going to college in New York City, he was robbed twice by young black men. From that point on, he was very careful about whom he picked up. Taylor's remedies (2000a) are more sensitivity on the part of the police and the hiring of more minorities.[18]

In June 1999, President Clinton issued an executive order requiring federal enforcement agencies to gather data on the racial composition of people stopped by federal law enforcement officials (Holmes 1999b). In early 2001, President Bush asked Attorney General John Ashcroft to investigate the issue.

## The New Debate over the Death Penalty

> We are the only country in the West to employ capital punishment and to use the death penalty against teenagers. (Donziger 1996, p. 1)

> To say that society should refrain from executing murderers for fear of making a mistake is not noble. It is a cop-out. . . .
> Granted, it is not easy to condemn someone to death, still less to carry out the sentence. Executions are irrevocable and irreversible; to take away anyone's life—even a brutal criminal's—involves an assertion of moral certainty that might make many of us tremble.
> But trembling or not, we have a duty to carry out. A duty to proclaim that murder is evil and will not be tolerated. That it is the worst of all crimes and deserves the worst of all punishments. And that while we will bend over backward not to hurt the innocent, we will not let that paralyze us from punishing the guilty. (Jacoby 2000)

The death penalty is one of the most contentious issues in the criminal justice area. There are those who support the death penalty because it expresses society's outrage at the actions of a murderer (**retribution**). Others suggest that the death penalty has a deterrent effect, while still others point out capital punishment's incapacitation impact. Incapacitation means that someone is placed in a situation where he or she cannot harm anyone else. The death penalty is the ultimate in incapacitation: we know that if someone is executed, that person will not commit more crimes. Because the death penalty is the ultimate sanction, it is applied only in the most severe cases (although those against the death penalty argue against this assertion).

Before examining the debate over the death penalty and how it has changed in recent years, let us look at some statistics. Table 7.10 presents data on number of murders/manslaughters, people on death row, and number of executions from 1972 to 1998. To update the table a bit, there were ninety-six executions in 1999 (Duggan 1999). As the table shows, not many people were given the death sentence, and almost no one was executed during the 1970s. This is because of two important U.S. Supreme Court cases.

In the first case, *Furman v. Georgia* (**1972**), the Court ruled that the death penalty, as currently practiced, was "cruel and unusual" under the language of the Eighth Amendment. The Court held that the penalty was used for too many kinds of crimes and in an arbitrary and capricious manner. In response, states revised their death penalty statutes, and four years later (1976) the Court reexamined the validity of the death penalty. In this case, *Gregg v. Georgia* (**1976**), the Court held that the new state laws were acceptable and the death penalty was not unconstitutional (though two justices, Brennan and Marshall, dissented) (Death Penalty Information Center). States are required to have a separate trial to impose the death penalty after the first trial finds a person guilty of a capital offense. To provide some historical perspective, since 1972 (and counting 1999), there have been a total of 599 executions. In the period from 1930 to 1967, there were 3,857 executions (calculated from Pastore and Maguire 2000).[19]

The bulk of the executions are conducted by just a few states, mostly in the southeastern portion of the country. Table 7.11 presents the data of the states with the highest number of executions from 1977 to 1997. As the table shows, Texas by itself accounted for one-third of all executions, and the thirteen states listed in the table accounted for nearly 88 percent of all executions. According to the Death Penalty Information Center website (www.deathpenaltyinfo.org), thirty-eight states have death penalty statutes, though seven of those states have not executed anyone since the death penalty was reinstated in 1976.

There is also data about the racial and ethnic composition of those who have been given the death sentence or executed. Of those given the death sentence in 1998, 55.2 percent were white, 43 percent were African American, and 10 percent were Hispanic (Pastore and Maguire 2000). Of those

Table 7.10

**Executions in the United States**

| | Murders and nonnegligent manslaughters | Persons under death sentence | Executions |
|---|---|---|---|
| 1998 | 16,910 | 3,452 | 68 |
| 1997 | 18,210 | 3,335 | 74 |
| 1996 | 19,650 | 3,219 | 45 |
| 1995 | 21,610 | 3,054 | 56 |
| 1994 | 23,330 | 2,890 | 31 |
| 1993 | 24,530 | 2,716 | 38 |
| 1992 | 23,760 | 2,575 | 31 |
| 1991 | 24,700 | 2,482 | 14 |
| 1990 | 23,440 | 2,356 | 23 |
| 1989 | 21,500 | 2,250 | 16 |
| 1988 | 20,680 | 2,124 | 11 |
| 1987 | 20,100 | 1,984 | 25 |
| 1986 | 20,610 | 1,781 | 18 |
| 1985 | 18,980 | 1,591 | 18 |
| 1984 | 18,690 | 1,405 | 21 |
| 1983 | 19,310 | 1,209 | 5 |
| 1982 | 21,010 | 1,050 | 2 |
| 1981 | 22,520 | 856 | 1 |
| 1980 | 23,040 | 691 | N/A |
| 1979 | 21,460 | 593 | 2 |
| 1978 | 19,560 | 482 | N/A |
| 1977 | 19,120 | 423 | 1 |
| 1976 | 18,780 | 420 | N/A |
| 1975 | 20,510 | 488 | N/A |
| 1974 | 20,710 | 244 | N/A |
| 1973 | 19,640 | 134 | N/A |
| 1972 | 18,670 | 334 | N/A |
| Total executions | | | 500 |

*Source:* Pastore and Maguire (2000).

executed from 1977 through 2000, 56 percent were white, 35 percent were African American, and 7 percent were Hispanic (Death Penalty Information Center). In the previous section we saw racial breakdowns by total population and murder/manslaughters. Certainly, the percentage of African Americans on death row or executed far exceeds their percentage of total population.

Thus one of the arguments made against the death penalty is that it has been applied inequitably. Research has shown that it is not the race of the accused that is the factor, but the race of the victim, as measured by the frequency with which the death penalty is imposed (General Accounting Office 1990; Kennedy 1997; Radelet and Vandiver 1987). In 1987, however, while

Table 7.11

**Prisoners Executed by Selected States, 1977–1999**

|  | Number executed | % of U.S. total |
|---|---|---|
| Texas | 197 | 33.1 |
| Virginia | 73 | 12.2 |
| Florida | 44 | 7.4 |
| Missouri | 41 | 6.9 |
| Louisiana | 25 | 4.2 |
| South Carolina | 24 | 4.0 |
| Georgia | 23 | 3.9 |
| Arkansas | 21 | 3.5 |
| Arizona | 19 | 3.2 |
| Oklahoma | 19 | 3.2 |
| North Carolina | 15 | 2.5 |
| Illinois | 12 | 2.0 |
| Delaware | 10 | 1.7 |
| Total of these states | 523 | 87.8 |

*Source:* Duggan (1999).

acknowledging the racial disparity, the Supreme Court held that the race of the defendant could not be used as an automatic basis for appeal against the death sentence: discrimination would have to be proved (***McCleskey v. Kemp* [1987]**) (Kennedy 1997). An attempt in Congress to reverse the Supreme Court ruling and to take racial disparities into effect (the Racial Justice Act) was removed from the 1994 Violent Crime Control and Law Enforcement Act to get support for the bill from conservatives and moderates (Seelye 1994).

There are two major defenses of the death penalty. First is the contention that there are some crimes that are so heinous, so wicked, that those who commit them have forfeited their humanity (Berns and Bessette 1998). A second defense is deterrence, which, combined with the incapacitation defense (executed killers will not kill again), suggests that lives will be saved by continuing to use the death penalty. The National Center for Policy Analysis (a conservative think tank) cites a study showing that eighteen lives are saved for each execution of a convicted murderer (National Center for Policy Analysis 1987). Reynolds (2000), defending Texas's use of the death penalty, points out that the murder rate in the state plummeted after the death penalty was more vigorously carried out.

Part of the problem that advocates of the death penalty see is that the time between imposition of sentence and carrying out of the sentence is much too long. The Supreme Court has recently cut back on death row appeals, which have been the major reason for the time lag.

The traditional argument against the death penalty includes the racial disparities mentioned above. Such disparities, both among and within states, suggest an element of unfairness. There are racial disparities at the federal level as well (Boner and Lacey 2000a), and in the fall of 2000, President Clinton ordered a six-month stay on a pending federal execution (there had not been a federal execution since the early 1960s until two in 2001) (Boner and Lacey 2000b). Why should one person be executed (say, an African American) but another be imprisoned for the same crime (say, a white)? There are some, such as the ACLU, Amnesty International, and Human Rights Watch, who argue against capital punishment on a moral basis: simply that it is wrong to kill, even with state sanction.

One argument against the death penalty reasserted itself in the late 1990s. This is the fear that a person who has been executed may later be found to have been innocent. A life cannot be given back. The resurgence of this line of thought is grounded in the relatively recent use of DNA testing, which has resulted in the release of more than sixty inmates on death row (Oppel 2000). The DNA tests showed that these convicted persons could not have committed the crime.[20] While those who have been released are certainly fortunate, they have also suffered a great deal by their time on death row, which can be ten years or more (Rimer 2000).

The most comprehensive study of mistakes in death penalty convictions was a 2000 study for the Justice Project (Liebman et al. 2000; see also Butterfield 2000a). The major findings of the report were the following: There was reversible error in almost 70 percent of cases that were fully reviewed; 90 percent of death sentences were overturned at the state level; the two major reasons for errors were incompetence of defense counsel[21] and suppression of evidence by police and prosecutors; and in 7 percent of the cases overturned, the accused was found innocent at retrial, while in 82 percent of the cases, the accused was given a lighter sentence.

Of course, the report did not go without its critics. James Q. Wilson (2000), for example, looked at the data in the study and found the study does not say anything about those who were executed. That is, the study does not claim, but implies, that innocent people were actually executed. Wilson further points out that there are considerable reviews of death penalty cases and that errors are eventually caught.

Perhaps most interesting in this debate is the work of David Protess, a journalism professor at Northwestern University. He had his journalism class investigate death penalty cases, and, as a result, some cases have been reversed (Brant 1999). Equally as interesting was the moratorium on executions imposed by the executive order of Illinois governor George Ryan. A Republican and a supporter of the death penalty, Ryan issued the moratorium when he found out that more people on death row had been released (thirteen) because of some sort of error in the case than had been executed (twelve) since 1977. Much of this outcome was due to the efforts of Protess's class (Broder 2000; Cannon 2000).

Indeed, the conservative case against the death penalty, as stated by Cannon (2000) in *National Review*, is that government makes mistakes:

> In other words, if ideology and experience lead one to the conclusion that government is by nature inefficient and inept, then why should it be astonishing that the actions of one branch of government—the judicial branch—are so routinely wrong?

Cannon argues that DNA evidence helps release some innocent people from death row. He asks about those cases in which DNA is not available. He also wonders how many innocent people were executed before DNA evidence was available.

Wilson (2000), a supporter of the death penalty, offers several policies that would help reduce error but still keep the death penalty. First would be a requirement that state and federal courts consider DNA testing, including for indigents who cannot afford the expense. Second, states should make sure that indigent defendants are provided with capable counsel. Third, states should have an alternative punishment for first-degree murder cases: imprisonment without the possibility of parole. Then judges and jurors could consider that alternative. Fifth, Wilson endorses a proposal by the American Law Institute that would allow a judge to impose the life-without-parole alternative, even if the jury recommends the death penalty, if the judge believes that there is still some doubt about the guilt of the defendant. These proposals might provide a fairer way of deciding whether the death penalty should be imposed in a particular case.

The public has traditionally supported the death penalty, though that support has declined in recent years with the new attack on capital punishment (Farrell 2000). Of course, the extremes in this debate will remain. Both sides, the pro– and anti–capital punishment sides, see a moral issue here. The pro-side wants to retain it because of its deterrence and incapacitation effect and also because it does express society's outrage at certain acts of violence. The anti–death penalty side believes that capital punishment is inherently immoral. The politics of the death penalty, here as in many other policy areas, lie somewhere in the middle.

## Case Study: The War over the War on Drugs

> We believe that the use of the "drug war" metaphor is quite appropriate both in terms of domestic and foreign policies. Wars incite public opinion and action and focus attitudes on a problem. They require mobilization and the marshaling of assets and funds, and strengthen political will toward the elimination of a common threat. Some criticize the drug war mentality as exerting unnecessary violence on a medical problem. Police who face the violence of crack houses and methamphetamine labs understand that we are facing a war. DEA agents in South America and policy makers and judges in countries like Colombia understand that we are waging a war as well. (Voth and Levitsky 2000)

> It would be hard to think of an area of U.S. social policy that has failed more completely than the war on drugs. Since 1981, the federal drug budget has soared from

about $1.5 billion a year to more than $17 billion. The United States has sent spy plans over the Caribbean, built a paramilitary base in Peru, financed coca-eradication programs in Bolivia, and set up giant radar-bearing balloons on the Mexican border. From the South Bronx and South-Central Los Angeles to Fort Wayne, Indiana, and Yakima, Washington, narcotics agents have conducted stings, infiltrated drug gangs, hired confidential informants, and busted drug dealers. In 1996, more than 1.5 million people were arrested for drug offenses. The nation's state and federal prisons, which in 1980 housed fewer than 30,000 drug offenders, today harbor nearly 300,000. Despite it all, cocaine is cheaper than ever before, and heroin is being sold at purity levels six times those of the early 1980s. And the abuse of these drugs remains rampant. In 1996, the number of cocaine-related visits to hospital emergency rooms topped 144,000—an all-time high. (Massing 1998, p. 9)

## Problem Identification and Agenda Building

American drug use has gone through a series of cycles. Some drugs become popular and widely used, and then there is a reaction to that drug. The drug becomes illegal and its use plummets (Musto 1973). The current idea of a war on drugs has its origins in the Nixon administration (though with a different emphasis than later efforts) and picked up steam in the Reagan administration. First Lady Nancy Reagan made the antidrug campaign a personal project, using the tool of persuasion, or in this case **moral suasion,** with the "**Just Say No**" campaign.

It was triggered by some well-publicized incidents, such as comedian Richard Pryor's nearly killing himself "freebasing" cocaine, the death of actor John Belushi from a drug overdose, and other celebrities' trials with cocaine (Massing 1998). A new form of cocaine called "crack"—which is cheaper, easier to handle, and more addictive than the powder form—made its appearance in the country and especially the urban ghettoes in 1986. Here the triggering events were the deaths of two prominent athletes from a crack cocaine overdose, Len Bias, the number-one draft pick of the NBA's Boston Celtics, and Don Rogers, a defensive back of the Cleveland Browns.[22] There were also stories about women using crack cocaine while pregnant, resulting in what were called "crack babies." These stories had good media play but were largely inaccurate (Twohey 1999). As we saw previously, the most recent increase in the crime rate, especially in the homicide rate, is at least partially attributable to the introduction of crack cocaine in the cities.[23]

Let us look at some of the data related to the war on drugs. Figure 7.1 shows the trend in illegal drug use from 1979 to 1999 (as measured by drug used in the past thirty days). Drug use among the oldest group, the thirty-five-and-older group, was relatively stable over this twenty-year period. For the next oldest group, the twenty-six-to-thirty-four-year-olds, the drug use rises until the mid-1980s and then declines, with a little blip around 1992. For the eighteen-to-twenty-five-year-olds, there is a consistent decline and then an increase beginning in the mid-1990s. For the youngest group, the twelve-to-seventeen-year-olds, there is a mild decline yearly until the 1990s and then a mild increase. Note the

Figure 7.1    **Illicit Drug Use by Age**

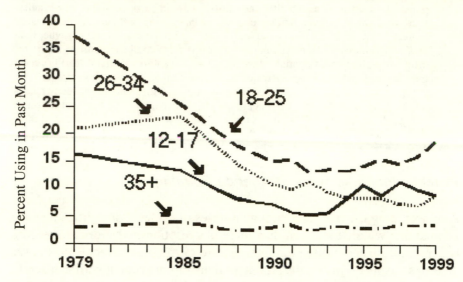

*Source:* Substance Abuse and Mental Health Services Administration (2000).

percent of users by 1999: less than 5 percent among the oldest group and about 20 percent among the eighteen-to-twenty-five-year-olds.

The most frequently used illicit drug is marijuana. Looking at the high school class of 1999, an estimated 23.1 percent of the graduating class had used marijuana within the last thirty days of the survey. The next highest level is for stimulants, at 4.5 percent of the graduating class—1.1 percent of the class used crack and 2.5 percent used some other type of cocaine. By contrast, 51 percent of the class reported using alcohol and 34.6 percent reported smoking cigarettes[24] (Pastore and Maguire 2000).

Table 7.12 presents data about drugs among young adults (defined as about eighteen to twenty-eight years old). As opposed to the data in Figure 7.1 or in the previous paragraph, Table 7.12 looks at the percent of people in the age groups using drugs in the past year. We see the same trend, with use of the substances declining through the early 1990s and then increasing, though not necessarily to the 1986 levels. Alcohol and tobacco are the most used substances.

The data also tell us something about drug use by racial group. Table 7.13 presents the data. Note that a higher percentage of whites than of African Americans has used cocaine (the column includes crack cocaine), but that a higher percentage of African Americans used crack cocaine (more than twice the percentage) compared with whites.

The data also show that people are more likely to engage in criminal behaviors if they use illegal drugs or drink on a regular basis. For example, only 8.4 percent of the eighteen-and-older group engaged in any criminal behavior in 1998. But 21.2 percent of those who used illegal drugs and 26.2 percent of regular drinkers did. The percentages are much higher for the twelve-to-seventeen age group (Pastore and Maguire 2000).

Another way to get a handle on drug use and drug problems in the United States is to look at drug-abuse-related hospital emergency department visits. The major source of data here is the Drug Abuse Warning Network. Table 7.14 presents the data. Apparent first is the continued rise in such episodes. Second, for the most part, the largest percentage increases in emergency room episodes were among the thirty-five-and-older group, with the next largest percentage increases among the twelve-to-seventeen-year-olds. Third, the number of episodes is higher among whites than among African Americans, though this result varies by type of drug. Indeed, the proportion of white episodes to African-American episodes increased over the time period. Heroin and morphine use shows about the same numbers; marijuana and methamphetamine use is higher among whites, especially meth. Cocaine use is higher among African Americans, though the ratio between the two groups has declined.

The data also tell us about the criminal justice system and the war on drugs. First, we can look at arrests for possession versus sale/manufacturing of illegal drugs (Pastore and Maguire 2000). In 1998, 79 percent of drug arrests were for possession, 21 percent for sale and manufacture. The highest percentage of sale/manufacturing arrests was in 1992: 33 percent. For heroin/cocaine, which accounted for 37 percent of all drug arrests in 1998, almost 30 percent were for sale/manufacturing, more than 70 percent for possession. For marijuana, which accounted for 44 percent of drug arrests, a little more than 11 percent were for sale/manufacturing and almost 89 percent for possession.

Related to the drug arrests are drug seizures. The U.S. Customs Service has made over a thousand seizures of heroin, about 2,300 seizures of cocaine, and over 12,000 seizures of marijuana each year during the 1991–1989 period (Pastore and Maguire 2000). The U.S. Drug Enforcement Administration (DEA) made over 2,000 seizures of illegal laboratories, almost all of them for meth labs (Pastore and Maguire).

We can also look at drug use of those who have been arrested. African-American arrestees show a higher percentage of drug use than white arrestees. This is especially true for cocaine, but also appears to be the case for marijuana. In federal court, the bulk of offenders sentenced under the U.S. Sentencing Guidelines were for trafficking. Of the total cases in 1998, 24.2 percent were white, 32.7 percent were African American, and 41 percent were Hispanic. African Americans predominated in crack cocaine, whites in powdered cocaine. Whites predominated in meth and Hispanics in heroin and powdered cocaine. According to the advocacy group Human Rights Watch, African Americans are more likely to be imprisoned than whites for drug use, even though whites used drugs at a much higher rate than blacks (Holmes 2000).

Finally, we can look at the prison system. At the federal level, 16.3 percent of federal prisoners were sentenced for drug offenses in 1970. By 1998, that

Table 7.12

**Reported Drug, Alcohol, and Cigarette Use in Last Twelve Months Among Young Adults, 1986–1999** (percent who used in last twelve months)

|  | 1986 | 1987 | 1988 | 1989 | 1990 | 1991 |
|---|---|---|---|---|---|---|
| Marijuana | 36.5 | 34.8 | 31.8 | 29.0 | 26.1 | 23.8 |
| Hallucinogens | 4.5 | 4.0 | 3.9 | 3.6 | 4.1 | 4.5 |
| Crack cocaine | 3.2 | 3.1 | 3.1 | 2.5 | 1.6 | 1.2 |
| Other cocaine | NA | 13.6 | 11.9 | 10.3 | 8.1 | 5.4 |
| Heroin | 0.2 | 0.2 | 0.2 | 0.2 | 0.1 | 0.1 |
| Stimulants | 10.6 | 8.7 | 7.3 | 5.8 | 5.2 | 4.3 |
| Methamphetamine | NA | NA | NA | NA | 0.4 | 0.3 |
| Alcohol | 88.6 | 89.4 | 88.6 | 88.1 | 87.4 | 86.9 |
| Cigarettes | 40.1 | 40.3 | 37.7 | 38.0 | 37.1 | 37.7 |

*Source:* Pastore and Maguire (2000).

number had increased to 58.9 percent. In 1997, 32.6 percent of state prisoners and 22.4 percent of federal prisoners reported using drugs at the time of their offense. And 69 percent of all state prisoners and 57.3 percent of all federal prisoners said they were regular drug users.

## Policy Formulation

There are a number of types of policies aimed at the drug problem in the United States. They can be categorized as demand- and supply-side policies.

Demand-side drug policies seek to reduce the use of illegal drugs and the collateral impact of drug use. One way is to use persuasion or information. The "Just Say No" campaign of Nancy Reagan is one example. This policy tool uses media advertising to try to convince the most vulnerable of potential users, young people, to stay off drugs. A similar policy tool is the Drug Abuse Resistance Education **(DARE)** program run at the local level. Funded and administered by local police agencies, the DARE program involves sessions between a police officer and students. Originally, this was done at a particular grade level (usually sixth grade), but it has been extended and continued.

A different type of demand-side policy tool involves the criminal justice system. Arresting, trying, and imprisoning drug users does two things. First, it takes those people off the streets. Second, it, hopefully, provides a deterrent effect for users to consider quitting.

A third possibility, which can be done in conjunction with the criminal justice system, is **treatment**, a policy endorsed by Barry McCaffrey, the former head of the White House Office of National Drug Control (Wren 1999). This could involve the use of means such as **drug courts**. The problem, as we saw above, was that the war on drugs is largely responsible for the increase in our

| 1992 | 1993 | 1994 | 1995 | 1996 | 1997 | 1998 | 1999 |
|------|------|------|------|------|------|------|------|
| 25.2 | 25.1 | 25.5 | 26.5 | 27.0 | 26.8 | 27.4 | 27.6 |
| 5.0  | 4.5  | 4.8  | 5.6  | 5.6  | 5.9  | 5.2  | 5.4  |
| 1.4  | 1.3  | 1.1  | 1.1  | 1.1  | 1.0  | 1.1  | 1.4  |
| 5.1  | 3.9  | 3.6  | 3.9  | 3.8  | 4.3  | 4.5  | 4.8  |
| 0.2  | 0.2  | 0.1  | 0.4  | 0.4  | 0.3  | 0.4  | 0.4  |
| 4.1  | 4.0  | 4.5  | 4.6  | 4.2  | 4.6  | 4.5  | 4.7  |
| 0.4  | 0.8  | 0.9  | 1.2  | 0.9  | 0.9  | 1.1  | 0.9  |
| 86.2 | 85.3 | 83.7 | 84.7 | 84.0 | 84.3 | 84.0 | 84.1 |
| 37.9 | 37.8 | 38.3 | 38.8 | 40.3 | 41.8 | 41.6 | 41.1 |

prison population and is clogging the nation's courts. A drug court is a commu-nity-based alternative to imprisonment. A person selected for a drug court closely interacts with a judge who monitors the person's treatment. The idea behind the drug court is that if the person successfully completes the required program, he or she is not sentenced. As of 1997, there were some 200 drug courts in the United States (Drug Court Standards Committee 1997). The 1994 Violent Crime Control and Law Enforcement Act provided grants for drug courts.

Drug courts have met with mixed success. The General Accounting Of-fice (GAO) reports that the drug courts it studied in 1997 had completion rates that varied from 8 to 95 percent and retention rates that varied from 31 to 100 percent (retention rates include those who have completed the pro-gram, as well as those currently in it). The GAO report indicated that more and better follow-up of participants was needed to evaluate the program (General Accounting Office 1997).

Related to the idea of treatment is assistance for addicts, a policy that origi-nated at the federal level with the Nixon administration (Massing 1998). The idea here is twofold. First, providing methadone as an alternative to heroin reduces crime, because the user does not have to steal to support his or her habit. Second, a needle-exchange program (supplying the method of using heroin) would cut down on new AIDS cases (Van Sant 1999). While there is much to be said for such a program, methadone maintenance programs vary in their effectiveness (General Accounting Office 2000). The state of Arizona has also begun a program, mandated by voters, for drug offenders to enter treat-ment rather than go to prison. The program seems to be working (Egan 1999).

The idea behind supply-side drug policies is to reduce the amount of drugs that are available to users. One way, similar to a demand-side strategy, is to arrest those who engage in trafficking. A considerable amount of our drug

Table 7.13

**Estimated and Most Recent Use of Cocaine and Crack by Race, 1998**
(percent use)

| | Cocaine | | | Crack | | |
|---|---|---|---|---|---|---|
| | Ever used | Within past year | Within past 30 days | Ever used | Within past year | Within past 30 days |
| White | 11.4 | 1.7 | 0.7 | 1.8 | 0.3 | 0.1 |
| Black | 8.5 | 1.9 | 1.3 | 4.2 | 1.3 | 0.9 |
| Hispanic | 8.9 | 2.3 | 1.3 | 1.9 | 0.7 | 0.3 |
| Total | 10.6 | 1.7 | 0.8 | 2.0 | 0.4 | 0.2 |

*Source:* Pastore and Maguire (2000).

Table 7.14

**Estimated Number of Emergency Room Drug Episodes, 1992–1999**

| | 1992 | 1993 | 1994 | 1995 | 1996 | 1997 | 1998 | 1999 |
|---|---|---|---|---|---|---|---|---|
| ER drug episodes | 433,493 | 460,910 | 518,521 | 513,633 | 514,347 | 527,058 | 542,544 | 554,932 |
| Age breakdown | | | | | | | | |
| 6–11 | 2,288 | 2,704 | 4,447 | 2,884 | 2,034 | 3,447 | 2,365 | 1,995 |
| 12–17 | 46,822 | 50,039 | 60,472 | 60,722 | 63,949 | 61,437 | 59,086 | 52,783 |
| 18–25 | 96,307 | 98,276 | 112,262 | 103,708 | 98,625 | 104,647 | 103,438 | 109,580 |
| 26–34 | 133,506 | 138,634 | 151,195 | 144,003 | 139,634 | 138,897 | 138,483 | 131,256 |
| 35+ | 154,570 | 171,257 | 190,145 | 202,316 | 210,105 | 218,630 | 239,172 | 259,318 |
| White | 235,643 | 245,243 | 279,312 | 277,637 | 274,057 | 284,242 | 295,447 | 310,072 |
| Black | 122,880 | 126,929 | 141,171 | 139,389 | 135,332 | 134,896 | 136,481 | 132,983 |
| Hispanic | 42,174 | 48,233 | 50,438 | 47,360 | 55,032 | 52,707 | 57,162 | 56,891 |
| Inside central city | 158,892 | 162,210 | 170,269 | 171,372 | 171,926 | 163,581 | 165,660 | 162,466 |
| Outside central city | 70,445 | 74,542 | 82,063 | 81,587 | 81,766 | 81,096 | 81,860 | 79,212 |

*Source:* Substance Abuse and Mental Health Services Administration (1999).

supply comes from outside the United States. To stem this tide, two policies have been implemented. One is **interdiction**, intercepting drug shipments. This involves the border patrol, the Coast Guard and Navy, and so forth. While there is much interdiction, and the numbers keep rising each year, its success is limited. More and more drugs enter the United States.

A related policy is to go to the source of the supply—countries such as Colombia, Mexico, and Peru—and destroy the crops. This approach usually involves American aid and assistance to foreign countries. Like many other drug policies, this one is very controversial. For example, the U.S. effort in conjunction with the government of Colombia has been criticized. Insurgency groups plague Colombia, and it has become difficult to tell whether U.S. funds are being used to stem the flow of drugs or put down the rebellion (Dudley 2000). Corruption in those countries has also been a problem. Nevertheless, it is clear that, in the absence of an interdiction policy, the problem of drug entry into the United States would certainly be worse.

One other drug policy should to be mentioned, one that has gained momentum in recent years. This policy involves what was called in chapter 1 the government issue. Recall that the government issue raises the question of whether government should be involved. In this case, the question has been raised as to whether states or the federal government should relax their drug policy. Doing so would involve either **decriminalization** of one or more drugs or the stronger position of **legalization** of one or more currently illegal drugs. At the end of this case, we will address this policy.

### Adoption and Budgeting

The bulk of American antidrug policy has involved using the criminal justice system, though it was not always that way. At various points in American history, state policy at times was fairly permissive. For example, Alaska legalized drugs in 1985. New York, in the 1970s, passed one of the nation's severest antidrug policies, known as the Rockefeller laws, which called for very lengthy sentences for dealers. The 1990s' antidrug crackdown in New York City under Mayor Rudolph Giuliani followed in this mode.

At the federal level, for the most part, the punitive strategy has been used. In the early days, the Nixon administration focused on treatment for heroin addicts as a way of reducing crime (Massing 1998), but eventually it, too, moved toward a more punitive strategy. In 1973, the Drug Enforcement Administration was created within the Justice Department, and it has been the major drug agency for the federal government. The Reagan administration, beginning in 1982, focused heavily on interdiction and punishment as the major strategy. The "Just Say No" campaign of Nancy Reagan, which began in 1986, was a demand-side strategy. Also in 1986, Congress passed a significant piece of antidrug legislation, the **Anti-Drug Abuse Act**. The act called for mandatory minimum sentences for drug offenses. Massing (1998, p. 184) describes these mandatory minimums, which remain to this day:

> Anyone caught with one or more kilograms of heroin, or five or more kilograms of cocaine, was to serve at least ten years in prison. Specifically targeting crack, Congress voted to impose a mandatory minimum sentence of five years for the sale of just five grams of the drug; triggering the same penalty for [powdered cocaine] would require five hundred grams—a 100–1 disparity that would take on strong symbolic value in the years to come.

Table 7.15

**Federal Drug Funding by Goal**

| Goal | In million $ | % of total |
|---|---|---|
| Reduce youth drug use | 2,028.8 | 11.5 |
| Reduce drug-related crime | 7,574.5 | 42.8 |
| Reduce health and social consequences | 3,300.6 | 18.6 |
| Shield air, land, and sea frontiers | 2,724.9 | 15.4 |
| Reduce sources of supply | 2,082.5 | 11.8 |
| Total | 17,711.3 | |

*Source:* Office of National Drug Control Policy (2000).

The Reagan and first Bush administrations put great emphasis on the war on drugs. The Clinton administration, at least in the early years, placed less emphasis on it (Stewart 1996; Voth and Levitsky 2000). Of course, all states have their own drug laws as well.

One way of understanding priorities, as mentioned in chapter 1, is to look at where we spend our money. The Clinton administration's drug control policy had five goals: reduce youth drug use, reduce drug-related crimes, reduce the health and social costs of drug abuse, defend U.S. borders from drug importation, and reduce foreign sources of drugs. Table 7.15 presents the breakdown of federal spending for these five goals for FY 1999. As can be seen from the table, only about 12 percent of the budget has a demand-side reduction based on something other than punishment.

## Evaluation

An important question is how well the war on drugs is working. There are a number of ways of looking at it. We can look at the number of drug seizures and interdictions over time. We can look at arrests and imprisonment for drug offenses over time. We can look at drug use over time. And there is considerable data available, far beyond what we can look at now.

But some generalities are called for. As we have seen, drug use has declined, especially in the eighteen-to-twenty-five-year-old group. But we also know that there have been recent increases. It is also fair to say that the policies have some impact. For example, in the absence of the interdiction policy, more drugs would freely enter the United States. Putting more people in prison or under some kind of correctional supervision cuts down on some use.

There is some data that suggests the persuasion message is not working well. Research known as the "Monitoring the Future" study asks eighth-, tenth-, and twelfth-graders whether they believe there is great risk from trying drugs once or twice, and from occasionally or regularly using illegal drugs. In general, eighth-graders see a great risk at a higher percentage than do tenth-graders, who in turn see a great risk at a higher percentage than twelfth-graders. As students get older, the perception of risk decreases (perhaps with increasing familiarity with drugs). More dismaying for those who want to reduce drug usage is that the numbers declined pretty much across the board from 1991 through 1999 (see Office of National Drug Control Policy 2000, Table 6). The message is certainly not getting through.

Another way to look at the war on drugs relates to the previous section on minorities. Though minority drug use is, overall, not much different from drug use by whites, minorities are arrested, convicted, and imprisoned at a much higher rate. This disparity is partially due to crack, especially from the middle 1980s to the middle 1990s. Crack markets were out on the street and that was where much of the violence was. Crackdowns (no pun intended) on drug use thus focused on minority communities.

These and other factors have led to a new development or stage in the policy process, the move toward decriminalization/legalization.

### Policy Succession: Legalizing Drugs?

There is a strong movement to legalize or at least decriminalize drugs in the United States. The arguments against the war on drugs come from many different directions. Some have argued that it impacts minority communities in a very disruptive way. A second line of reasoning comes from the liberal end of the spectrum.

The liberal argument is that the war on drugs has led to an erosion of the country's civil liberties. For example, Ira Glasser, the executive director of the American Civil Liberties Union, testified before Congress in 1999 that the war on drugs has led to "the violation of a wide range of constitutional rights so severe that it has led one Supreme Court justice to speak of a 'drug exception' to the Constitution" (Glasser 1999, p. 1). Boyd and Hitt (1999) list a number of Bill of Rights protections that have been reduced because of the war on drugs. These rights include free speech, freedom of assembly, and of the Fourth Amendment prohibition against unreasonable searches and seizures. As a counterpoint, in November 2000 the U.S. Supreme Court upheld a federal circuit court opinion that random drug roadblocks were unconstitutional.

Conservatives have also attacked the war on drugs, especially libertarians. Deroy Murdock (2000) of the Cato Institute describes the war on drugs in especially harsh language:

> Since the days of "Just Say No," this domestic quagmire has lasted longer than the Vietnam War. It has killed, detained and bullied innocent citizens and non-violent offenders in a futile campaign to vacuum every last cannabis seed from America's streets. This fool's errand isn't cheap. Between 1990 and 1999 alone, federal anti-drug

law-enforcement activities have cost taxpayers $81 billion. States and cities have spent even more. Meanwhile, low-cost drugs have become even more plentiful.

Bertram et al. (1996) argue that the war on drugs is fatally flawed at virtually every point. For example, despite interdiction efforts, the price of illegal drugs has declined.

Of course, not all agree that the war on drugs has been a failure. Drug Watch International (DWI) argues that tough law enforcement has been successful and that it has led to less crime, less use, and lower addiction rates. DWI finds that as imprisonment for drug use or trafficking increased, crime and addiction rates fell. Further, DWI argues that, if anything, we are still not tough enough on drug users and traffickers.

A number of arguments are made in favor of decriminalization/legalization. One argument is that because the drug war has done so much harm, particularly to minority communities, harm reduction is the best way to go. Instead of criminalizing behavior, treat it as a public health problem. A related argument here is that crime and addiction will decrease with a cutback in the war on drugs.

A second argument is that some currently illegal drugs have medicinal properties. In particular, marijuana appears to reduce the symptoms of cancer, AIDS, and glaucoma.

A third argument is that legalizing drugs would prove to be beneficial for government finances. The war on drugs would be ended and the $20 billion spent at the federal level and more at the state and local level would be saved. Then if we taxed the sale of newly legalized drugs, it would produce revenue, just as tobacco and alcohol products do.

A fourth argument points to alcohol prohibition during the 1920s and early 1930s as a marked failure. Similarly, the war on drugs, a drug prohibition, has failed.

A fifth argument is that some countries, such as the Netherlands, have decriminalized marijuana, the most widely used drug, and have seen few problems.

The final argument, and a powerful one, is that legal drugs such as tobacco and alcohol are much worse than the illegal ones.

Of course, for every argument in favor of decriminalization/legalization, there is a counterargument.[25] The first argument has to do with harm reduction. Here the argument was that much crime is committed because drugs are illegal and that enforcement is hurting minority communities in particular. Any evidence along these lines is mixed. Certainly some crimes would decrease or disappear. In particular, those crimes involving trafficking and use would, by definition, no longer be criminal activities. But one area where more criminal activity might occur is with domestic violence. Much domestic violence (physical and sexual) of spouses and children is affected by substance abuse, both alcohol and drugs. If drugs were more widely available, such abuse might actually increase. There is also the possibility, backed by some evidence, that episodes of driving under the influence would increase with greater availability of drugs (Maginnis 1996). If drugs were widely available, addiction would likely increase as more people used them.

Some drugs are inherently dangerous, not just to the user but to families and communities. Perhaps the best example of this is methamphetamine. This drug, also known as speed, was popular in the 1960s and regained popularity in the 1990s. Recipes for making meth are widely available and use ingredients that can be found in neighborhood stores. However, the manufacturing of meth produces a very dangerous environment, one that is literally toxic and explosive. Thus its dangers are not limited to the user.

The harm reduction argument for decriminalization points to the devastation that the war on drugs has had on minority communities. This harm comes from two sources. First, a considerable portion of resources for the war on drugs has been used to target minority communities, partly because of the open-market trafficking that occurs there. But the war on drugs has also caused devastation because of the sentencing guidelines, especially at the federal level, which treat crack cocaine much more harshly than powder cocaine. In 1995, the U.S. Sentencing Commission recommended reducing the disparity in mandatory sentences between crack and powder cocaine. Both the Clinton administration and Congress refused to make changes, and under the George W. Bush administration, such a change remains unlikely.

The second argument in favor of decriminalization is that some drugs, particularly marijuana, have beneficial medicinal properties. In particular, it appears that marijuana relieves pain for those with cancer, AIDS, and glaucoma (Joy et al. 1999). Here the evidence is mixed. Much more research needs to be done, and it may be possible to isolate the chemicals within marijuana that ease pain and restore appetite. In any event, a number of states have passed laws or initiatives allowing the use of marijuana for medical purposes (see below). In 2001, the U.S. Supreme Court heard oral arguments on the medical benefits of marijuana (Greenhouse 2001).

The third argument is the economic-benefit one. We will save money, advocates of decriminalization/legalization argue, because we will spend less on imprisonment, interdiction, and so forth. Further, if marijuana or other drugs were legalized, they would be subject to sales taxes and thus provide revenue for government. The model here is alcohol and tobacco.

The problem with this argument can be seen with the tobacco and alcohol models. The use of tobacco and alcohol produces economic costs that outweigh any benefits from sales taxes. Consider, just as one example, the number of people suffering from tobacco-related illnesses and the costs associated with them. Or consider deaths and injuries due to alcohol-related traffic accidents.

The fourth argument is that the war on drugs has been a failure just as

Prohibition was in the 1920s. Maginnis (1996) argues that Prohibition was, in fact, successful, though not perfect. Alcohol abuse was lower and suicides and arrests involving alcohol were lower. When Prohibition was lifted, those rates went up.

The fifth argument against the drug war is that other countries have decriminalized or legalized drugs with success. England and Holland are two examples cited. There are, however, problems, especially in the Dutch case. Marijuana is legal in Holland, and the police rarely enforce laws against harder drugs. However, the property crime rate has increased significantly, as has the addiction rate.[26]

The final argument is that marijuana and other drugs are no more dangerous than alcohol and tobacco. This is an inaccurate statement all around. The harms from alcohol and tobacco are more serious and obvious because they are legal. Legalizing other drugs would show them to be more harmful than alcohol and tobacco. Cocaine is much more addictive than alcohol or tobacco, meth even more so. The consequences of using meth, especially, are readily apparent. Typical consequences include sleeplessness, withdrawal from home and work environment, and child neglect.

Despite all the arguments against decriminalization/legalization, such policies have been adopted at the state level.

### Changes in State Policies

As mentioned in chapter 1, the United States has a federal system. This means, to repeat, that states are, to a large extent, free actors. On a number of policies, they may not follow federal priorities. That is becoming truer with decriminalization.

In the 1970s, following two reports during the Nixon administration, eleven states (Alaska, California, Colorado, Maine, Minnesota, Mississippi, Nebraska, New York, North Carolina, Ohio, Oregon) decriminalized marijuana (Stroup 1999).

In recent years, one mechanism for policy adoption has predominated in the decriminalization debate—direct democracy. A number of states, through initiative elections, have approved some form of decriminalization. Since 1996, voters in nine states—Alaska, Arizona, California, Colorado, Maine, Nevada, Oregon, and Washington—approved the use of marijuana for medical purposes. In 2000, Hawaii became the first state to approve a medical marijuana law by legislation. The New Mexico and New Hampshire governors also favor decriminalization.

As there are groups that oppose decriminalization, there are groups and people who favor it. The major interest group in favor is the National Organization for Reform of Marijuana Laws (NORML). Billionaire George Soros and the Lindesmith Center have funded a number of these voter initiatives (Baker 1999).

The federal government has opposed medical marijuana laws. In 2000, a federal appeals court approved the distribution of marijuana for medical purposes in Oakland, CA. However, the U.S. Supreme Court blocked the appellate court ruling because it went against the federal Controlled Substances Act ("Supreme Court Blocks Medical Marijuana Ruling" 2000).

The controversy over medical marijuana, decriminalization, and the war on drugs is likely to continue.

## Conclusion: Solutions to the Crime Problem?

> Prisons have become our nation's substitute for effective public policies on crime, drugs, mental illness, housing, poverty, and employment of the hardest to employ. In a reasonable culture we would not say we had won the war against disease just because we had moved a lot of sick people from their homes to hospital wards. And in a reasonable culture we would not say we had won the war against crime just because we had moved a lot of criminals from the community into prison cells.
>
> The good news is that we are at a point in our history when we actually have the wherewithal—both the knowledge and the material resources—to launch an honest and effective attack on the violent crime that still afflicts us, in ways that are both enduring and community-wise. Since the late 1960s and based on scientific evaluations, we have learned a great deal about what doesn't work and about what does work to ensure domestic tranquility *at the same time* that we establish justice. America has the scientific information and the money to replicate what works at a scale equal to the dimensions of the problem. (Milton S. Eisenhower Foundation 2000)

Although the crime problem is exceedingly complex, some conclusions can be drawn. First, we have seen a significant drop in crime rates since the early 1990s, including among young people. This is a tremendous success for which the country should take much satisfaction. There are a number of factors that account for the decline: increased imprisonment, the end of the crack cocaine wars, the booming economy, to name just three. At the same time, as the Milton S. Eisenhower Foundation (2000) reported, crime was higher in the late 1990s than it was thirty years earlier (see also Vise and Adams 1999).

Yet there is some evidence, just as the economy slowed down in 2000 and 2001, that the reductions in crime rates has slowed down. The FBI Uniform Crime Report for the January-June 2000 period shows an overall decrease of only 0.3 percent compared to 9.5 percent for the similar period in 1999. Further, while the murder rate continued to decline, though again not as quickly as in previous years, the murder rate in a number of our cities actually increased (Butterfield 2000c; Federal Bureau of Investigation 2000). Some categories of crime, such as aggravated assault and motor vehicle theft, increased. At this point, it is difficult to tell whether the trend is changing, but it is cause for concern.

A second conclusion is that because much crime is committed by young males, the size of that group has an important effect on the amount of crime. Given demographic projections, another crime increase could occur at the beginning of this century (Gladwell 1994; Wilson 1994).

Third, some of the features of the political system and the policy process affect the ability to reduce crime. Intergovernmental relations and variations among states in crime rates, types of crime, and types of punishments imposed (e.g., the death penalty) mean that there is no uniform response to crime. For example, some states have "three strikes" laws, while others do not. Fragmentation means that even on the local level, where the battle against crime is primarily fought, there are problems of coordination. Implementation creates barriers to solutions.

Fourth, ideological differences about the causes of crime influence appropriate strategies. From the conservative perspective, suitable remedies are to make crime look less economically beneficial and to focus on the certainty and severity of punishment. This approach would mean devoting more resources to crime prevention and detection—primarily detection. Harsher sentences are also recommended, accompanied by fewer civil liberty protections for the accused. In fact, some of the conservative views imply that not much can be done about the crime problem, because of the size of the population most likely to commit crimes (Wilson 1994).

The liberal view concentrates on the correlates of crime—age, sex, income, and race— and seeks broader solutions that focus on employment and education. This view would make alternatives to crime more attractive. But the costs of such a strategy would certainly be at least as much as building more prisons.

A modest anticrime strategy would employ a combination of conservative and liberal perspectives (Gurr 1989). Punishing crime, as Wilson and Herrnstein (1985) argue, expresses society's moral outrage, even if it does not reach all those who commit crimes. Certainly stricter enforcement of the law and harsher sentences will have some impact. Indeed, one can argue that this is the strategy largely followed in the United States. By the end of 2000, nearly 2 million people were in prison. But there are important questions raised about the impact of imprisonment, particularly on minority communities. Further, we ought to be concerned not just about the communities but what happens when the people in prison are eventually released to return to those communities. This problem, known as **prisoner reentry**, is one that has not been well thought out and could lead to an increase in the crime rate if preventive strategies are not followed (see Cose 2000; Petersilia 2000).

But there are alternatives to imprisonment. For example, some communities employ neighborhood justice programs, which include mediation by private organizations, churches, and families. Such programs include community-based corrections and community development, in the sense of developing community unity (Scheingold 1984). Intensive probation and community service (Currie 1986) are also alternatives that should be investigated, particularly concerning juvenile offenders. If entry into the criminal lifestyle can be stopped, perhaps much can be done to reduce crime among the most vulnerable group, young males. Some policies focus on a community prevention strategy involving the neighborhood, schools, and families, such as the preventive programs in the 1994 crime bill. Further, some communities have instituted curfews for juveniles to prevent groups of kids from hanging out on the streets (Wilson 1994).

A related aspect is to question who we put in prison and why (Currie 1998). To the extent possible, diversion programs should be used. This method seems particularly important for the casual user of drugs. Rehabilitation and treatment programs, which marked some of the early years of the drug wars (Massing 1998), ought to be better funded. There are programs that work, many of which do not involve government, though government funding may be necessary (Schorr 1997). Prisons should be reserved for recidivists and those for whom treatment programs clearly fail. The drive for decriminalization/legalization is gathering strength, at the state level at least, and will likely remain controversial for some time. It is not clear that decriminalization is an appropriate policy, but the use of currently illicit drugs to help the ill, if done under reasonably controlled conditions, may be appropriate.

One strategy seems to overlap conservative and liberal perspectives. Wilson and Herrnstein (1985), Currie (1986, 1998), Wright (1985), and Bennett et al. (1996) agree that internalization of social mores, conscience, and ethics through formal and informal controls is the best solution to crime.[27] Bennett et al. (1996) contend that the crime problem, and their book focuses especially on juvenile crime, is largely one of what they call **moral poverty**, the inability to judge right from wrong and to feel empathy for those who suffer from criminal actions. They point out that if children have exposure to some adult (parent, coach, teacher, etc.) who will spend some time with them and help them learn good moral values, the likelihood of committing crime goes down substantially. Studies have shown that such mentoring, say through programs like Big Brothers/Big Sisters, can have this effect with as little as twelve hours of contact per month (McLean et al. 1998).

James Wilson and Richard Herrnstein argue that families (good families, not abusive ones) are the best agents for this internalization. Their description of how schools might affect this is very similar to their analysis of how families internalize conscience and social control.

> A desirable ethos—one that contributes to lessened delinquency and higher achievement—involves a teaching style that emphasizes the value of schoolwork, rewards good performance and utilizes fair but firm disciplinary procedures. Good teachers are free with their praise while insistent on their rules. (Wilson and Herrnstein 1985, p. 282)

Currie echoes these remarks:

> The best deterrent to crime is the creation and maintenance of stable communities in which people may reasonably expect that good behavior will lead to esteemed and rewarding social roles. (Currie 1986, pp. 57–58)

## Key Concepts

Anti-Drug Abuse Act (1986)

Brady Bill

conservative perspective

crime index

Drug Abuse Resistance
Education (DARE)

decriminalization

demography

deterrence

direct services

"driving while black" (DWB)

drug courts

equity

fragmentation

freedom

*Furman v. Georgia* (1972)

*Gregg v. Georgia* (1976)

Gun Control Act (1968)

incapacitation

incentive

interdiction

"Just Say No"

legalization

liberal perspective

*McCleskey v. Kemp* (1987)

McClure-Volkmer Act (1986)

moral poverty

moral suasion

National Crime Victimization
Survey (NCVS)

negative inducements

order

persuasion

plea bargaining

positive inducements

prisoner reentry

racial profiling

recidivists

retribution

security

treatment

Uniform Crime Reports (UCR)

victimization surveys

## Reflections

1. The first question in criminal justice policy is, why do people commit crimes? This chapter offers two possible ideological explanations for the causes of crime. One is the conservative perspective, which suggests that one looks to individuals to answer the question. This perspective focuses on psychological and biological explanations. The other perspective is the liberal one, which suggests that one should also look at the societal level for answers. Therefore, liberals look at poverty, broken homes, and poor education as causes of crime. Which of these two perspectives do you think is more accurate? Why? Can the two perspectives be combined in a productive manner? How?

2. Violent crime has decreased in recent years. Why do you think that is the case? What changes in society may have led to this decrease? Which of the different strategies discussed in the chapter do you think influenced the crime rates downward? Crime rates, though down, are still higher than we would like. How should society address this continuing problem?

3. One of the most emotional criminal justice issues is the death penalty. Public opinion polls show strong, though somewhat decreasing, support for the death penalty. What about you? Do you support or oppose the death penalty? Why? Does the recent emphasis on DNA testing change your view of the death penalty?

4. A growing number of people and groups are supporting the decriminalization or legalization of at least some drugs. Where do you stand on this issue? What do you think are the strongest arguments in favor and against decriminalization/legalization?

## Notes

1. For a critique of criminal justice statistics, see Wilson and Herrnstein (1985).

2. There is an argument that corporate crime, which includes white-collar crime, is at least as prevalent, or perhaps more so, as street crime. For a brief discussion of corporate crime (i.e., "crime in the suites"), see "There Is More Crime in the Suites than Crime in the Streets" (1999).

3. A Department of Justice study of 20,000 federal and state prisoners suggests a slightly different picture of offenders. Over 60 percent of prisoners have completed high school, and a appreciable portion have attended college. Most federal prisoners are white as are almost half of state prisoners. A good portion of prisoners were raised by two parents (58 percent of federal prisoners and 43 percent of state prisoners). Most prisoners had full-time jobs prior to their arrest (56 percent of state prisoners and 65 percent of federal prisoners), though the jobs did not pay well. On all these statistics, federal prisoners are more affluent and educated than state prisoners. See Morin (1994).

4. For comments on DiIulio's article, see the fall 1994 issue of *The Public Interest*.

5. James Q. Wilson, a conservative, argues, as we have seen, that criminal behavior does have individual roots. However, he also argues (1994) that one important aspect of the problem is the "concentration in disorderly neighborhoods of people at risk of failing" (p. 34). The concentration is due to the movement of middle-class families out of poor neighborhoods, discrimination, and politics.

6. This argument anticipates the controversial 1994 book by Herrnstein and Charles Murray,

*The Bell Curve*, which is discussed in chapter 9.

7. Wilson's more recent book takes a complementary view of human nature. If *Crime and Human Nature* examines bad behavior, *The Moral Sense* (1993) examines why most people are likely to engage in good behavior.

8. For an overview of the federal role in this area, including policies and agencies, see "The Federal Role in Crime Control" 1994.

9. The data in Table 7.4 reflect a census of the number of prisoners in state and federal facilities as of December of the census year (1990 and 1999 in the case of the table). However, more people will have spent some time in the system during a part of the year, but those people are not reflected in the data. Therefore, the data and table actually *underestimate* the number of prisoners in any given year.

10. This is the argument made by John Lott (2000) in his defense of concealed weapons laws. This topic will be discussed below.

11. For a discussion of focusing on high-crime locations within cities, see Harries 1999.

12. Some local sheriffs, backed by the National Rifle Association, have challenged the constitutionality of the background check in the Brady Bill, on the grounds that it violates the Tenth Amendment. The issue in the challenge is whether the federal government has the "authority to request local officials to carry out federal mandates" (Thomas 1994).

13. The previous information came from the Handgun Control Inc. website (www.handguncontrol.org/stateleg).

14. For a description of Boston's effort and a comparison with New York City's, see Berrien and Winship (1999).

15. For a very strong, unpublished critique of Lott's work, see Lambert 2000.

16. For a balanced treatment of the intersection of race and crime in the United States, see Kennedy (1997).

17. The disparity in perspectives between whites and blacks undoubtedly reflects differences in experience. We will address this issue of perspectives in more detail in chapter 9.

18. Two large city police departments have addressed this issue of minority hiring with somewhat different results. The New York City Police Department made an effort to increase minority hiring. The result was more Hispanics and more African-American women, but not more African-American men. The Boston Police Department made a concerted effort to increase minority hiring. The result was a significant increase in minority hiring, including African-American men, and the drastic reduction of youth homicides mentioned above. See Chivers (2001a, 2001b).

19. There were no executions from 1968 to 1976.

20. One should also consider that prior to the 1960s, some executions, including non-legal executions, were designed to keep blacks in their place (Kennedy 1997). Some, perhaps many, hangings, including one that occurred in the author's hometown of Springfield, MO, in the early part of the twentieth century, were certainly of innocent people. See Lederer (1986).

21. For an analysis of the incompetence of counsel in Texas death penalty cases, see Duggan (2000).

22. It turned out that Bias died using powder, rather than crack, cocaine. The facts of the story were not nearly as important as its impact and timing.

23. In 1996, the *San Jose Mercury News* published a series of articles alleging or implying that the Central Intelligence Agency and its contra allies introduced crack to California inner cities to provide funds for the effort by the contras to overthrow the Sandinista government in Nicaragua. The flooding of crack into the inner cities led not only to the crack epidemic and the increase in violence, but also to money that could be used to purchase the guns that showed up in the inner cities. Investigations by the U.S. Department of Justice and news organizations indicated that while there may have been a contra connection, the CIA was probably not involved. See, for example, Department of Justice (1997).

24. As an aside, the data show that 29.4 percent of the class of 1987 smoked. The lowest figure was with the class of 1992, with 27.8 percent smoking. Since 1992, the percent of those smoking rose to a high of 36.5 percent in 1997, down to 1999's 34.6 percent. This result does not bode well for campaigns based on persuasion. There is a similar trend for alcohol use, though the 1999 figure is substantially below the 1992 figure of 66.4 percent.

25. In the interests of full disclosure, I mention that my wife, Cynthia, a career prosecutor at the local level, has spent much time prosecuting drug cases.

26. My wife and I visited Holland in 1996, and we can confirm the story about high property-crime rates. We were told, for example, by our Amsterdam canal tour guide that there are no new bicycles in Amsterdam because they are stolen to pay for drugs. Further, because of Amsterdam's liberal policy on drugs (and sex), it attracts people from around the world looking for a good time.

27. A sign at a local church neatly captures this view: "Discipline yourself so that others won't have to." See also Wilson (1993).

# 8  Education: The Promise of America

*To believe in education is to believe in the future, to believe in what may be accomplished through the disciplined use of intelligence, allied with coopera-tion and good will. If it seems naively American to put so much stock in schools, colleges, universities, and the endless prospect of self-improvement and social improvement, it is an admirable, and perhaps even a noble, flaw.*
(Ravitch 1983, p. 330)

*Our nation is at risk. . . . The educational foundations of our society are presently being eroded by a rising tide of mediocrity that threatens our very future as a Nation and a people. . . .*

*If an unfriendly foreign power had attempted to impose on America the mediocre educational performance that exists today, we might have viewed it as an act of war. As it stands, we have allowed this to happen to ourselves. . . . We have, in effect, been committing an act of unthinking, unilateral educational disarmament.* (National Commission on Excellence in Education 1983, p. 5)

The two quotes opening this chapter set the stage for the discussion of public policy concerning education in the United States. American schools have been asked to do many things, often beyond the simple, though difficult, task of educating our young. Jefferson envisioned education as the bulwark of de-mocracy. Immigrant groups viewed education as a means of upward mobility. Others saw it as a way of achieving the promise of an equitable and racially integrated society. Some hoped the schools would help foster traditional so-cial values. The schools have been used to help improve the health of disad-vantaged children. In the 1950s, education was viewed as the basis for national security. In the twenty-first century, it is considered the foundation for eco-nomic competitiveness.

This chapter examines two themes related to education policy. A major portion of the chapter is concerned with educational reform. The second theme is that of equality and integration. If we understand reform as meaning change, then the 1980s can be characterized by change in educational policy, though how deep that change has been and how successful it will be remains debatable. The 1990s saw educational change move toward a somewhat greater focus at the national level. Education performance was a central issue of the 2000 presidential elections, and it promises to continue to have this important place in the early years of this century.

# Problem Identification

## Policy Goals

The goals of education as public policy are efficiency, equity, security, and freedom.[1] **Efficiency** is a policy goal in several senses. First, one can raise questions as to how well the educational system is meeting its primary task, teaching the young. If children are not learning what they are supposed to, people need to inquire why and what changes must be made to remedy the situation. A second dimension of efficiency relates to the overall economy. As the nation moves forward in the twenty-first century, it will need an educated workforce; if new workers have poor reading skills, poor work habits, and so forth, then the business sector will have to train workers.

**Equity** also has several dimensions. First, the educational system has been seen as a means of upward mobility in and of itself, and through special programs such as Head Start. Indeed, there is a strong relationship between education and income (though it is not clear what the direction of the relationship is; perhaps students from middle- and high-income families do better in school). The schools have also been seen as a means of overcoming racial segregation in society. By bringing the races together in the schools, it was believed, not only would minorities do better and get better educational facilities, but racial antagonism would decline. One can also look at some of the educational reforms and see to what extent they reduce differential achievement among groups. One of the challenging problems of educational policy has been how to meet the goals of excellence (related to efficiency) and equity. The two worthy goals are not necessarily contradictory in theory; in practice, emphasis has shifted between the two (C. Brown 1985).

The third goal is **security**. Educational change in the 1980s focused partly on achieving certain levels of competency in various subjects. The notion of minimal levels is similar to minimal levels of income or health care examined in earlier chapters. Further, the assumption of the security goal is that minimal levels are necessary for a student to have any chance at economic security after graduation.

The final goal of education policy is **liberty**. Again, this goal has several dimensions. At one level, freedom underlies the move toward school choice. At another level, freedom refers to what goes on in the classroom, from what texts are used to how subjects are taught (e.g., creationism versus evolution) to whether prayer or moments of silence are allowed.

## Policy Tools

Several tools are available to meet these educational goals. First, and most obvious, is the **direct provision of services**. Education in the United States is largely a public enterprise, though a little over 11 percent of elementary and secondary school students attended private schools in 1999–2000 (National Center for Education Statistics 2000b). Associated with education (public and private, though there are considerably fewer for private education) are all kinds of rules. The rules specify qualifications for teaching, what subjects will be taught, generally what school a child must attend, who might be eligible for special services, what graduation requirements are, and so forth.

**Incentives** can also play a role in education policy. The idea behind school choice is that schools will respond to the demands of consumers (parents) or fail. Incentives have also become important in the accountability and testing movements, where principals and teachers either are rewarded if their students do well on standardized achievement tests or are fired (in the case of principals) or required to demonstrate competency (in the case of teachers) (Sacks 1999).

A final policy tool that has marked education debates is **powers**. In particular, the debate over public versus private education, vouchers, and choice programs within public education is directed at changing power relationships within the educational policy system. Some argue that the monopoly over school selection and the large state and local bureaucracies (with their rules) are an inherent part of administrative structures and make it unlikely that schools will make changes needed to meet the challenges the United States faces in the twenty-first century.

## Education and Government

> Public school policy making is embedded in a complex societal matrix. (Kirst 1986, p. 341)

> There's an old saying that education is a local activity, a state responsibility, and a national concern. (Kearns 1988, p. 570)

As with crime, educational policy is primarily a function of state and local governments. Nearly 93 percent of public school financing is by state and local governments (split about equally between states and schools). The states have the primary responsibility for education but delegate implementation to local school districts. There are nearly 15,000 school systems in the United States that vary widely in size, from the New York City school system with over 1 million students to rural districts of only a few hundred (National Center for Education Statistics 2000b).[2]

States set overall policy guidelines, for example, on teacher qualifications and graduation requirements. They also provide a substantial portion of school funding. Since the mid-1970s, the states' share of education funding has grown, one indicator of the growing state role in education. In 1960, local school districts provided about 56 percent of school funding and states about 36 percent (the federal government provided the remainder). Most of the school funding was based on property taxes. Because of the combination of inequities in school financing (some districts are wealthier than others) and the tax revolt of the 1970s epitomized by Proposition 13 in California (1978),[3] the states assumed a larger role. By 1985, the local share had dropped to less than 47 percent and the state share was just over 47 percent (National Center for Education Statistics 1991).

The federal government has played a minor, though not unimportant, role in setting policy (rules) and funding schools (incentives). Education policy has occasionally been set by the federal courts, such as in school desegregation.

The national government assists the schools financially through the 1965 **Elementary and Secondary Education Act (ESEA)**. By 1980, the federal government provided almost 10 percent of school financing. The U.S. Department of Education (DOE) was created in 1980 to fulfill a campaign promise President Carter made to the National Education Association (NEA). DOE's existence symbolized a growing federal role in education. The Reagan administration, philosophically opposed to a strong federal presence in education (Reagan promised in his 1980 campaign that he would abolish the Department of Education), reduced federal funding to less than 7 percent of total school spending (about a 30 percent reduction). Apart from these actions, the federal government has been instrumental in starting compensatory education programs such as Head Start and other programs aimed at disadvantaged students, such as free and reduced school lunch programs and the Title 1 program of increased spending for schools with large percentages of disadvantaged students.

Begun during the 1960s as part of the War on Poverty program, the idea behind **Head Start** is to take children from poor families and neighborhoods and work with them to get them ready for school. The Head Start programs provided not only educational services but also health and nutrition services. The program also sought to involve the parents.[4]

Head Start began as a short summer program. Initial evaluations were negative and the program began year-round sessions. The general consensus was that Head Start children did better than similarly situated children who were not in the program, at least through about the third grade. Thereafter, differences between the two groups disappeared. With changes, programs such as Head Start do seem to have a positive impact over a long period of time (Celis 1993; see also Vinovksis 1999 for a somewhat more pessimistic view of Head Start and Title I).

While there are some problems of quality control with Head Start (DeParle

1993), the program remains popular. Some changes are needed; both the first Bush and Clinton administrations promised to fully fund Head Start (Zigler and Muenchow 1992). One important recommendation that Zigler and Muenchow make is to extend Head Start, both forward and backward. They suggest including infants and toddlers and follow-up programs once the children begin school (Zigler and Muenchow 1992, pp. 211–245). Indeed, the expansion to younger children began in 1995 ("Infants, Tots Will Soon Get a Boost with Head Start" 1994) and the program has received very good evaluations ("HHS: Early Head Start Shows Significant Results" 2001).

Zigler and Muenchow also recommend linking Head Start with the Title I program. Title I, the largest of the federal government programs, has also come in for some criticism (Celis 1992). The program worked by tutoring poor children for a twenty-five-minute period during school hours. The Commission on Title 1 recommended that, rather than having a separate program such as the tutoring, the funds could be better used to enhance the school district programs (Vinovksis 1999).

## Private Schools

The United States also has a fairly sizable private school system, with about 11 percent of all students in private schools. Table 8.1 presents information about private schools. The largest of the private school systems are the Catholic schools, with almost 50 percent of private school children in 1997–98. Other private schools are non-Catholic church affiliated (about 35 percent of private school students) and nonchurch schools (about 16 percent of private school students) (Broughman and Colaciello 1999). Some schools, especially in the South, were established as segregation academies in reaction to the 1954 *Brown* decision.

Private schools became an important factor in attempts by the federal government to assist public schools. The private schools, particularly the Catholic ones, insisted that they should be eligible for any federal assistance that public schools receive. One issue this argument raised was whether the federal government could support church-affiliated private schools without violating the First Amendment prohibition against establishment of religion. The other issue was how to treat segregation academies. Until those two problems were resolved, any attempt to extend federal aid to primary and secondary schools would fail.

The stalemate was broken on two fronts. First, the 1964 Civil Rights Act prohibited federal funding of institutions that discriminated against minorities. Second, the perspective on federal assistance was changed. Rather than granting the aid to *schools*, some of which were public and some private, aid would go to *students* for their secular education, wherever they went to school. With this compromise, Congress passed the Elementary and Secondary Education Act in 1965.

Private schools raise the issue of equity, in two senses. First, private schools relieve some of the burden of overcrowding in public schools, and so school systems are spending less than they otherwise would. Second, parents who send

Table 8.1

## Enrollment in Private Elementary and Secondary Schools, 1998–1999

| Selected characteristics | School | | Students | |
|---|---|---|---|---|
| | Number | % | Number | % |
| Total | 27,402 | 100.0 | 5,079,119 | 100.0 |
| Private school type | | | | |
| Catholic | 8,182 | 29.9 | 2,514,699 | 49.5 |
| Parochial | 4,778 | 17.4 | 1,345,956 | 26.5 |
| Diocesan | 2,556 | 9.3 | 829,250 | 16.3 |
| Private | 848 | 3.1 | 339,494 | 6.7 |
| Other religious | 13,195 | 48.2 | 1,764,447 | 34.8 |
| Conservative Christian | 4,978 | 18.2 | 737,013 | 14.5 |
| Affiliated | 3,287 | 12.0 | 551,517 | 10.9 |
| Unaffiliated | 4,929 | 18.0 | 475,917 | 9.4 |
| Nonsectarian | 6,025 | 22.0 | 796,972 | 15.7 |
| Regular | 2,705 | 9.9 | 553,371 | 10.9 |
| Special emphasis | 2,070 | 7.6 | 158,627 | 3.1 |
| Special education | 1,250 | 4.6 | 84,975 | 1.7 |
| School level | | | | |
| Elementary | 16,623 | 60.7 | 2,824,844 | 55.7 |
| Secondary | 2,487 | 9.1 | 798,339 | 15.7 |
| Combined | 8,292 | 30.3 | 1,452,937 | 28.6 |
| Program emphasis | | | | |
| Regular elementary/secondary | 22,363 | 81.6 | 4,684,016 | 92.3 |
| Montessori | 1,144 | 4.2 | 69,611 | 1.4 |
| Special program emphasis | 589 | 2.2 | 100,149 | 2.0 |
| Special education | 1,387 | 5.1 | 93,498 | 1.8 |
| Early childhood | 160 | 0.6 | 7,898 | 0.2 |
| Alternative | 1,745 | 6.4 | 118,790 | 2.3 |
| Size | | | | |
| Less than 150 | 15,573 | 56.8 | 918,907 | 18.1 |
| 150–299 | 6,656 | 24.3 | 1,439,334 | 28.4 |
| 300–499 | 3,125 | 11.4 | 1,197,240 | 23.6 |
| 500–749 | 1,339 | 4.9 | 800,437 | 15.8 |
| 750 or more | 711 | 2.6 | 720,201 | 14.2 |
| Region | | | | |
| Northeast | 6,325 | 23.1 | 1,287,045 | 25.4 |
| Midwest | 7,426 | 27.1 | 1,345,553 | 26.5 |
| South | 8,111 | 29.6 | 1,510,340 | 29.8 |
| West | 5,542 | 20.2 | 933,182 | 18.4 |
| Community type | | | | |
| Central city | 10,902 | 39.8 | 2,472,859 | 48.7 |
| Urban fringe/large town | 10,263 | 37.5 | 2,018,085 | 39.8 |
| Rural/small town | 6,236 | 22.8 | 585,175 | 11.5 |

*Source:* Broughman and Colaciello (1999), p. 5.

their children to private schools not only pay private school tuition, but also fund the public schools through property and sales taxes. Thus, one could argue that some financial relief for those parents should be forthcoming. Tuition tax credits, where part of private school tuition could be deducted from taxes (usually state, but possibly federal taxes as well), were proposed as an appropriate solution. Minnesota's tuition tax credit law was upheld by the U.S. Supreme Court in 1983.[5] Opponents of tuition tax credits argued that such credits would undermine the financial support for public education. Some people have proposed greater reliance on private schools because of the perceived failures of public education in the United States. The major issue here is vouchers, and there have been several government bodies that have sought to use them (see below).

## How Have We Done?

Education policy has gone through several periods of change.[6] In the early years of the nation, education was limited to the upper classes; the lower classes would have only a few years of education. In the 1830s, the "common school" movement opened the way for much of the populace to receive an education. Even then, by 1940, only half the country had graduated from high school; by 1950, almost 60 percent of the population had a high school degree (Bierlein 1993).

A major traumatic event for the United States was the launching of the Sputnik spacecraft by the Soviet Union in 1957. The United States's technological lead over the Soviet Union had seemingly disappeared, and education was seen as the primary means for regaining the edge. The problem—as it was identified by a 1958 report titled "The Pursuit of Excellence: Education and the Future of America"—was a serious deficiency in math and science teaching. Schools were using social promotions (promoting students on the basis of attendance and age) rather than competency or subject mastery to move students to higher grades. The curriculum was in serious need of upgrading graduation requirements to four years of English and social studies, three years of science and math, and three years of foreign language (Hechinger 1983).[7]

The concerns expressed about the state of American education can be seen in both earlier and later times. Indeed, the tendency to trash the quality of public education in the United States is a long-rooted one. Berliner and Biddle (1995, p. 145) provide several examples of school bashing.

> To illustrate, a 1900 article in *Gunton's Magazine* told us, "The mental nourishment we spoon-feed our children is not only minced, but "peptonized" so that their brains digest it without effort and without benefit, and the result is the anemic intelligence of the average American schoolchild." . . . Again, in 1909, the *Atlantic Monthly* criticized the schools for: (a) not teaching enough facts, (b) not teaching thinking skills, and (c) not preparing young people for jobs.

Criticisms of the public schools continued into the 1980s and 1990s (and 2000s). For example, the second Bush administration presented legislation to

Congress in 2001 to provide extra funding for schools but also threatened to take away federal funding for schools that did not demonstrate improvement over three years.

Is there any basis for this continued concern about our nation's education? To find out, the best source of data is the **National Assessment of Education Progress (NAEP)**. This test, which is also described as the "nation's report card," is given periodically to a national sample of students in fourth, eighth, and twelfth grades in writing, science, mathematics, reading, geography, civics, and the arts. Some of the tests are quite new. The civics test was first given in 1998. Others, such as the reading and math tests, go back to the 1970s. Because teachers cannot teach to the test (see below and Sacks 1999), it is a better gauge of student performance than virtually any other available test, including the SAT (Berliner and Biddle 1995; Sacks 1999). Further, the NAEP allows comparisons of different groups (gender and ethnic/racial).

One last point in understanding the results of the NAEP: For each subject category, the scores are rated by complexity of skills. For the math test, the lowest set of skills (the 150 level) includes simple addition and subtraction, including two-digit subtraction. The highest-level (350) students can do multi-step problem solving and algebra. For the reading test, the lowest-level skills include the ability to follow a brief set of written instructions and pick out words that describe an object. At the highest skill level, students can, for example, restructure ideas contained in complex texts, such as science or literature. For each grade and subject, there is a number indicating achievement and range indicating expected proficiency for that grade.

We first look at the overall trend for the three age groups (nine, thirteen, seventeen) for the 1969–1999 period in reading, math, and science (Campbell et al. 2000). These are the three areas that are of most concern to parents, educators, and policy makers as indicators of how well our children and our schools are doing. Table 8.2 presents the data. The possible scores range from 100 to 400.

First note that overall the numbers do not show much change; the 1999 numbers are not much different from the other numbers.[8] A second thing to notice is that there have been changes. For example, Table 8.2 shows a dip in math and science scores at almost all levels, from the earliest test to 1982. This is consistent with data from the SAT as well (Berliner and Biddle 1995). After 1982 there is a modest rise in the test scores. The math scores all show higher scores in 1999 than in 1973; the science scores are lower than in the early 1970s but higher than the 1982 trough. The decline in scores is one reason that educational reform became an important policy issue in the early 1980s.

Another way of assessing student performance is to look at the percentage of students at a particular age performing at or above a particular performance level. For example, we would be interested in knowing the percentage of students performing at the highest level. As might be expected, the higher the skill level, the smaller the percentage of students performing at that grade

Table 8.2

**Trends in Average Scale Scores\* for the Nation in Reading, Mathematics, and Science**

|  | Reading | | | Mathematics | | | Science | | |
|---|---|---|---|---|---|---|---|---|---|
|  | Age 17 | Age 13 | Age 9 | Age 17 | Age 13 | Age 9 | Age 17 | Age 13 | Age 9 |
| 1999 | 288 | 259 | 212 | 308 | 276 | 232 | 295 | 256 | 229 |
| 1996 | 288 | 258 | 212 | 307 | 274 | 231 | 296 | 256 | 230 |
| 1994 | 288 | 258 | 211 | 306 | 274 | 231 | 294 | 257 | 231 |
| 1992 | 290 | 260 | 211 | 307 | 373 | 230 | 294 | 258 | 231 |
| 1990 | 290 | 257 | 209 | 305 | 270 | 230 | 290 | 255 | 229 |
| 1988 | 290 | 257 | 212 | — | — | — | — | — | — |
| 1986 | — | — | — | 302 | 269 | 222 | 288 | 251 | 224 |
| 1984 | 289 | 257 | 211 | — | — | — | — | — | — |
| 1982 | — | — | — | 298 | 269 | 219 | 283 | 250 | 221 |
| 1980 | 285 | 258 | 215 | — | — | — | — | — | — |
| 1978 | — | — | — | 300 | 264 | 219 | — | — | — |
| 1977 | — | — | — | — | — | — | 290 | 247 | 220 |
| 1975 | 286 | 256 | 210 | — | — | — | — | — | — |
| 1973† | — | — | — | 304 | 266 | 219 | 296 | 250 | 220 |
| 1971 | 285 | 255 | 208 | — | — | — | — | — | — |
| 1970† | — | — | — | — | — | — | — | 255 | 225 |
| 1969† | — | — | — | — | — | — | 305 | — | — |

*Source:* Campbell, Hombo, and Mazzeo (2000), p. xi.
*Notes:* \*Highest possible score = 400.
          †Extrapolated data.

level. In the case of reading, there has been virtually no change in the performance of seventeen-year-olds and nine-year-olds at the highest level. In math, nine-year-olds and thirteen-years-olds saw significant increases, and seventeen-year-olds saw significant increases at the two lower levels. Overall, the most significant increases have been in mathematics (Campbell et al. 2000).

We can look at the data presented so far and assert different conclusions. One conclusion, stated above, is that there has been improvement in all three areas. One could also argue that the overall level of performance ought to be higher, particularly at the higher-level skills.

## The Educational Achievement Gap

The NAEP data also allow us to investigate one of the most important areas in education, gaps in achievement between whites and minorities. Tables 8.3 and 8.4 present the data in a summary form. The two tables present the results for reading, math, and science for the three age groups. But rather than show the scores for each, they show the differences over time between average test

Table 8.3

**Trends in Differences Between White and Black Students' Average Scores**
(white minus black)

|  | Reading | | | Mathematics | | | Science | | |
|---|---|---|---|---|---|---|---|---|---|
|  | Age 17 | Age 13 | Age 9 | Age 17 | Age 13 | Age 9 | Age 17 | Age 13 | Age 9 |
| 1999 | 31 | 29 | 35 | 31 | 32 | 28 | 52 | 39 | 41 |
| 1996 | 29 | 32 | 29 | 27 | 29 | 25 | 47 | 40 | 37 |
| 1994 | 30 | 31 | 33 | 27 | 29 | 25 | 49 | 43 | 39 |
| 1992 | 37 | 29 | 33 | 26 | 29 | 27 | 48 | 43 | 39 |
| 1990 | 29 | 21 | 35 | 21 | 27 | 27 | 48 | 38 | 41 |
| 1988 | 20 | 18 | 29 | — | — | — | — | — | — |
| 1986 | — | — | — | 29 | 24 | 25 | 45 | 38 | 36 |
| 1984 | 31 | 26 | 32 | — | — | — | — | — | — |
| 1982 | — | — | — | 32 | 34 | 29 | 58 | 40 | 42 |
| 1980 | 50 | 32 | 32 | — | — | — | — | — | — |
| 1978 | — | — | — | 38 | 42 | 32 | — | — | — |
| 1977 | — | — | — | — | — | — | 57 | 48 | 55 |
| 1975 | 52 | 36 | 35 | — | — | — | — | — | — |
| 1973 | — | — | — | 40 | 46 | 35 | 54 | 53 | 55 |
| 1971 | 53 | 39 | 44 | — | — | — | — | — | — |
| 1970 | — | — | — | — | — | — | — | 49 | 57 |
| 1969 | — | — | — | — | — | — | 54 | — | — |

*Source:* Campbell, Hombo, and Mazzeo (2000), p. 39.

scores of white and African-American children (Table 8.3) and white and Hispanic children (Table 8.4).

We can, first of all, observe that the gap in school achievement between whites and minorities does exist. It parallels gaps in tests such as the SATs (Vars and Bowen 1998). This persistent gap has been at the heart of debates over programs such as affirmative action in higher education (see chapter 9) and compensatory education programs. Christopher Jencks and Meredith Phillips (1998, pp. 3–4) argue the importance of closing this gap:

> In a country as racially polarized as the United States, no single change taken in isolation could possibly eliminate the entire legacy of slavery and Jim Crow or usher in an era of full racial equality. But if racial equality is America's goal, reducing the black-white test score gap would probably do more to promote this goal than any other strategy that commands broad political support. Reducing the test score gap is probably both necessary and sufficient for substantially reducing racial inequality in educational attainment and earnings. Changes in education and earnings would in turn help reduce racial differences in crime, health, and family structure, although we do not know how large these effects would be.

A second observation, related to the Jencks-Phillips quote, is that the gap

Table 8.4

**Trends in Differences Between White and Hispanic Students' Average Scores**
(white minus Hispanic)

|      | Reading | | | Mathematics | | | Science | | |
|------|---------|---------|--------|---------|---------|--------|---------|---------|--------|
|      | Age 17 | Age 13 | Age 9 | Age 17 | Age 13 | Age 9 | Age 17 | Age 13 | Age 9 |
| 1999 | 24 | 23 | 28 | 22 | 24 | 26 | 30 | 39 | 34 |
| 1996 | 30 | 28 | 25 | 21 | 25 | 22 | 38 | 34 | 32 |
| 1994 | 33 | 30 | 32 | 22 | 25 | 27 | 45 | 34 | 39 |
| 1992 | 26 | 27 | 26 | 20 | 20 | 23 | 34 | 30 | 34 |
| 1990 | 22 | 24 | 28 | 26 | 22 | 21 | 39 | 32 | 31 |
| 1988 | 24 | 21 | 24 | — | — | — | — | — | — |
| 1986 | — | — | — | 24 | 19 | 21 | 38 | 33 | 32 |
| 1984 | 27 | 23 | 30 | — | — | — | — | — | — |
| 1982 | — | — | — | 27 | 22 | 20 | 44 | 32 | 40 |
| 1980 | 31 | 27 | 31 | — | — | — | — | — | — |
| 1978 | — | — | — | 30 | 34 | 21 | — | — | — |
| 1977 | — | — | — | — | — | — | 35 | 43 | 38 |
| 1975 | 41 | 30 | 34 | — | — | — | — | — | — |
| 1973 | — | — | — | 33 | 35 | 23 | — | — | — |

*Source:* Campbell, Hombo, and Mazzeo (2000), p. 40.

has largely shrunk over the years. For example, Table 8.3 shows that the black-white gap has declined twenty-two points in reading and nine points in math for seventeen-year-olds. Having said that, the data (Tables 8.3 and 8.4) also show a mixed picture. The gap reached its lowest point in the 1988–1990 period and then either became stagnant or increased slightly. Results from the 2000 tests show an increase in the gap in reading, even among higher-income African Americans (Zernike 2000a).

The NAEP also present data (not shown here) that look at some factors that might be related to student achievement. For example, taking pre-algebra and algebra classes is related to doing better on the math test. More students are taking those advanced classes (Campbell et al. 2000). The NAEP report notes that while students in general are taking more of the advanced math classes, a higher percentage of whites are taking them than African Americans or Hispanics. One of the more interesting, though not surprising, findings is that students who spend a lot of time watching television do poorer on the tests. Reading, the availability of reading material, and the availability and use of computers are also positively related to doing better on the tests.

Laurence Steinberg et al. (1996) argue that an important reason for the gap between white and minority students (and overall educational achievement) is what they call **student engagement**. They define student engagement as the extent to which students are actively involved, committed, and participate in the educational experience. Steinberg et al. find that the most significant factor in explaining student engagement is race/ethnicity. Asian-American students are more engaged than whites, who are followed by African-American and Hispanic students. Further, and to reinforce their point, the more Asian-American students become Americanized, the poorer their achievement, more like whites than other Asians.

For African Americans, Steinberg and his colleagues write, doing well is "acting white" (Cooke and Ludwig 1998). Further, Asian Americans and whites are more likely to view success as a result of hard work, whereas African-American students are more likely to see success as a result of luck. Further, students' peer groups reinforce these attitudes and beliefs. Steinberg and his colleagues' point is that school reform is unlikely to change these belief systems.

Steinberg and colleagues offer a set of recommendations to deal with the engagement problem. These include doing away with remedial college classes, national standards, increased emphasis on achievement, and so forth.

A different set of recommendations, but one that follows from the Steinberg et al. analysis, is based on a finding that Asian-American students tended to study in groups and African-American students studied by themselves. Bringing students together in study groups, where the importance of good school achievement was reinforced, raised the level of achievement among African-American students (Rothstein 2001).

David Evans (2001) offers a different perspective on how to address this problem. He notes that African-American children look up to sports figures, particularly those with compelling stories. Evans refers in particular to golfer Tiger Woods and tennis stars Venus and Serena Williams. These and others are making lots of money. So Evans suggests that there be monetary rewards ("positive incentives" in our terminology) for students who achieve well. He notes that this is already done for some, through merit scholarships and so forth. Good students also get, he notes, discounts on their automobile insurance. "Similarly, local individuals or groups might consider giving a few hundred dollars to minority students who make the honor roll or improve their grades significantly" (Evans 2001, p. 11).

Psychologist Claude Steele offers another perspective on the black-white test gap (Steele and Aronson 1998; Steele 1999). Steele and his colleagues conducted a series of studies to test the hypothesis that stereotypes of African-American students as underachievers lead to poor test performance (Steele and his colleagues have done similar tests comparing males and females on math achievement tests and whites and Asians on achievement tests in general). Steele's results support the hypothesis.

The Center on Education Policy and the American Youth Policy Forum did an analysis of NAEP test scores and other data (Center on Education Policy n.d., *Do You Know . . .* ) and found that there had been considerable improvement all along the line since 1982. There were fewer drops among all racial and ethnic groups in 1997 as compared to 1972 and 1983. Much higher percentages of students were taking the core curriculum of the type recommended by the NCEE. Students were taking the more challenging math and science courses. The report notes the increase in math scores and the decrease in the gap between whites and Hispanics and African Americans. The same is true for science scores. More students are taking advanced placement exams, especially minority students. The report also notes that more teachers have the desired background than are generally given credit for. For example, two-thirds of high school teachers have a degree in their subject rather than in education. More students are going on to college, especially minorities.

The point: As with international comparisons (see next page), there is a considerable amount of good news about American education. There is certainly room for improvement, but it is not as bad as it has been made to seem.

Some of the literature suggests that the real concern should be students in inner-city, minority-dominant, high-poverty schools. A study by the Education Trust (1999) finds that there are many high-poverty schools that do better than expected. The study found that the schools exceeding expectations had one or more of the following characteristics:

- Use state standards extensively to design curriculum and instruction, assess student work, and evaluate teachers.
- Increase instructional time in reading and math in order to help students meet standards.
- Devote a larger proportion of funds to support professional development focused on changing instructional practice.
- Implement comprehensive systems to monitor individual student progress and provide extra support to students as soon as it's needed.
- Focus their efforts to involve parents on helping students meet standards.
- Have state or district accountability systems in place that have real consequences for adults in the schools. (Education Trust 1999, pp. 2–3)

A more recent report on 2000 fourth-grade NAEP reading scores has raised some alarms. While average reading scores remained flat in the 1992–2000 period, there was a significant increase in the gap between the highest achievers, whose scores increased over this time period, and the lowest achievers, whose scores declined (Zernike 2001b; Donahue et al. 2001). There were considerable differences between the lowest and the highest achievers:

> According to a survey accompanying the test, the low scorers were mostly male black or Hispanic students in urban neighborhoods who were classified as poor under federal guidelines. They were likely to have changed schools within the last two years. Thirty-four percent watched more than six hours of television every day, and 57 percent said they had "friends who make fun of people who try hard in school." The best readers, by contrast, were mostly female and white. About half were in suburban schools, and 87 percent had attended the same school for at least two years. Just 6 percent watched more than six hours of television daily, and 7 percent had friends who made fun of those who work hard. (Zernike 2001b)

Table 8.5

**Trends in Differences Between Private- and Public-School Students' Average Scores** (private minus public)

|      | Reading | | | Mathematics | | | Science | | |
|------|---------|---------|---------|---------|---------|---------|---------|---------|---------|
|      | Age 17  | Age 13  | Age 9   | Age 17  | Age 13  | Age 9   | Age 17  | Age 13  | Age 9   |
| 1999 | 21      | 19      | 16      | 14      | 14      | 11      | 18      | 15      | 11      |
| 1996 | 7       | 17      | 17      | 10      | 13      | 9       | 9       | 14      | 10      |
| 1994 | 20      | 20      | 14      | 15      | 12      | 16      | 18      | 13      | 13      |
| 1992 | 22      | 19      | 14      | 15      | 11      | 14      | 20      | 8       | 11      |
| 1990 | 22      | 15      | 20      | 14      | 11      | 9       | 19      | 15      | 9       |
| 1988 | 11      | 12      | 13      | 19      | —       | —       | —       | —       | —       |
| 1986 | —       | —       | —       | —       | 7       | 10      | 34      | 12      | 10      |
| 1984 | ,16     | 16      | 14      | —       | —       | —       | —       | —       | —       |
| 1982 | —       | —       | —       | 14      | 14      | 15      | 10      | 15      | 11      |
| 1980 | 15      | 14      | 13      | —       | —       | —       | —       | —       | —       |
| 1978 | —       | —       | —       | 14      | 16      | 13      | —       | —       | —       |
| 1977 | —       | —       | —       | —       | —       | —       | 20      | 23      | 17      |

*Source:* Campbell, Hombo, and Mazzeo (2000), p. 55.

Overall, nearly 40 percent of students could not perform at the most basic level, and 67 percent of students did not perform at a proficient level (Zernike 2001b; Donahue et al. 2001).

## Public- Versus Private-School Student Achievement

There is one other set of data relevant to public policy concerns: differences in achievement between students in public and private schools. Table 8.5 presents the data. The most obvious observation is that private school students achieve higher test scores across the board, by age group and subject. A second observation is that the gap in performance of the sets of students has, with the exception of science, stayed about the same. In the case of science, public school students have made significant gains, while private school students' scores have remained about the same.

There is a third, important observation that can be drawn. Both public-and private-school students could perform at higher levels.

## International Comparisons

Another set of data that has been used to assess how well our schools are doing and how well our students are learning is the **TIMSS** test. TIMSS is the acronym for the **Third International Mathematics and Science Study**, which compares students from a number of countries. There have been two TIMSS tests. The first, conducted in 1995, looked at math and science for students in forty-two countries and three grades (fourth, eighth, and twelfth) roughly the equivalent of the NAEP, though not all countries participated in all tests (the United States did). A follow-up study was conducted in 1999, known as the TIMSS-R (for repeat), which looked at science and math achievement of eighth-grade students from thirty-eight countries. So how did our students do compared to students in other countries? In short, the answer is not very well.

> At the fourth grade, United States students were above the international average in both science and mathematics. In the eighth grade, U.S. students scored above the international average in science and below the international average in mathematics. At the end of secondary schooling (twelfth grade in the U.S.), U.S. performance was among the lowest in both science and mathematics, including among our most advanced students. (National Center for Education Statistics 1999, p. 1)

Four years later, the TIMSS-R study was conducted. The preliminary findings from the report were not very encouraging:

- In 1999, U.S. eighth-graders exceeded the international average in mathematics and science among the 38 participating nations.
- Between 1995 and 1999, there was no change in eighth-grade mathematics or science achievement in the United States. Among the 22 other nations, there was no change in mathematics achievement for 18 nations, and no change in science achievement for 17 nations.
- There was an increase in mathematics achievement among U.S. eighth-grade black students between 1995 and 1999. There was no change in science achievement for this group of students over the same period. U.S. eighth-grade white and Hispanic students showed no change in their mathematics or science achievement over the 4 years. . . .
- The relative performance of the United States in mathematics and science was lower for eighth-graders in 1999 than it was for the cohort of fourth-graders 4 years earlier in 1995 (National Center for Education Statistics 2000a, p. 11).

Furthermore, only 9 percent of U.S. students scored in the top 10 percent in math; only 15 percent did so in science. Countries whose students averaged better than U.S. students and who had much larger percentages of their students in the top 10 percent included Singapore, South Korea, Taiwan, Japan, Hungary, and Russia.

Data from TIMSS-R support some of the differences we saw in the NAEP data. White students, on average, perform better on the tests than do African-American or Hispanic students. Students from private schools outperformed those from public schools.

Analysis of the data also showed that American students, compared to international students, were more likely to be taught mathematics by a teacher who had majored in math education than by a teacher who had majored in math. The same was true for physics, though not the other sciences. Further, American students spent less time on homework or studying these subjects outside of school than international students did.

It may well be, however, that the TIMSS-R results are not quite as bad as they seem. David Berliner (2001) makes the important point that the TIMSS-R presents averages and thus masks the wide range in scores of American students:

> Let's take Illinois as an example. Along Lake Michigan, north of Chicago, are 20 public school districts serving predominantly wealthy suburban families. They gained permission to compete in TIMSS as a separate nation. Statistically, these public school students are on a par with the top scorers internationally in mathematics and science. Improving public schools where students are doing this well would be difficult. And this kind of spectacular performance is overlooked by those who claim that our schools are not working—the result of looking only at average U.S. achievement.

Berliner then turns to school districts such as East St. Louis, IL, where the schools perform miserably on such tests (see also Kozol 1991 on the East St. Louis school district). Putting the two sets of school districts together for an average disguises both America's successes and its failures. Berliner says the same thing is true in comparing states. Some states had TIMSS scores that were among the best of the nations participating in the tests, while others were at or near the bottom. He also points out that white students in science and math were near the top among the participating nations while African-American and Hispanic students were near the bottom. So, Berliner asks, who is failing, American students or American schools?

Another consideration is that education in the United States is not like that in other countries. In particular, the Japanese place considerable pressure on their students to perform, with students often receiving tutoring outside of class. The result is that their instructional time, counting the tutoring, is considerably greater than in the United States. On the other hand, there seems to be a growing backlash in Japan to ease off the pressure, and a changed curriculum with more free time is due out in 2002 (Magnier 2001).

Further, Berliner notes that some of the differences between the United States and the highest-score nations were quite small—sometimes the difference was four more items correct out of forty-eight. In the math field, where the differences were greater, considerably fewer American math teachers (41 percent) held math degrees compared to other nations (71 percent). Berliner states that what district a student lives in affects the quality of education. Suburban schools (he uses Phoenix, AZ, as an example) will not hire teachers without certification. In the more impoverished rural and inner-city school districts, the percentage of teachers holding a subject degree is less than 50 percent, and many teachers have emergency certifications.

From a theoretical view, this "problems stream" in educational policy depends upon numbers as symbols (Stone 1997). Numbers are critical because they seem precise and objective. They are also used to establish norms. In the case of educational policy, the decline in a series of numbers is an indicator that a problem exists. International achievement comparisons (TIMSS) further this sense that something is wrong. But not everyone accepts the tests as appropriate measures of achievement. Some have interpreted the test results as showing that schools are doing better than we give them credit for. These defenders of public education also argue that many of the tests used to assess school achievement are themselves flawed (see Berliner and Biddle 1995; Rothstein 1998; Sacks 1999). Rothstein (1998), for example, while arguing that the NAEP tests are reasonably reliable and have shown stability over the years, says they have been less useful for deciding whether students are achieving at appropriate or proficient levels. Additionally, the TIMSS score differences can be partly explained by the fact that fewer American students than foreign students took calculus in high school. In any event, test scores on these and other types of tests created an impetus for education reform.

## Agenda Building and Policy Adoption

### The Policy Stream

Of course, problem recognition and policy solutions go hand in hand. A number of reports, six in 1983 alone, pointed to a crisis in education. The most dramatic of these reports was the **National Commission on Excellence in Education (NCEE)**, commissioned by then-Secretary of Education Terrence Bell. (It is this report that provided one of the quotes that opened this chapter.)[9] The reports had various sponsors, indicating the breadth of concern over declines in achievement and international competitiveness: the U.S. Department of Education, the College Board, the Economic Growth Commission of the States, the Higher Education Forum (a business group), the Carnegie Foundation for the Advancement of Teaching, the Twentieth Century Fund (now the Century Foundation), and the National Association of Secondary School Principals/National Association of Independent Schools.

The reports on education conform to what Stone (1997) calls the decline story: Things used to be good, but now they have gotten worse. Something must be done, or a disaster will follow. In 1957 (after Sputnik), the fear was that the United States would fall behind in the space race. In 1983, the fear was that the United States would fall behind other countries in economic competitiveness.[10] With this in mind, the NCEE report is presented here as the prototype of the education reports.

The NCEE report, *A Nation at Risk*, employed highly dramatic language, declaring that the United States had undergone a "virtual unilateral educational disarmament." The commission was concerned about the international competitive situation, but also talked about education as a bulwark of democracy and a necessity for realizing one's abilities. The goal the commission set forth was the "Learning Society." In the report's words:

> At the heart of such a society is the commitment to a set of values and to a system of education that affords all members the opportunity to stretch their minds' capacity, learning more as the world itself changes. Such a society has as its foundation the idea that education is important not only because of what it contributes to one's career goals but also because of the value it adds to the general quality of one's life. Also at the heart of the Learning Society are education opportunities extending far beyond the traditional institutions of learning, our schools and colleges. They extend into homes and workplaces; into libraries, art galleries, museums, and science centers; indeed into every place where the individual can develop and mature in work and life. In our view, formal schooling in youth is the essential foundation for learning throughout one's life. . . .
>
> In contrast to the ideal of the Learning Society, however, we find that for too many people education means doing the minimum work necessary for the moment, then coasting through life on what may have been learned in its first quarter. But this should not surprise us because we tend to express our educational standards and expectations largely in terms of "minimum requirements." And where there should be a coherent continuum of learning, we have none, but instead an often incoherent, outdated patchwork quilt. (National Commission on Excellence in Education 1983, pp. 13–14)

What caused this "rising tide of mediocrity"? The National Commission identified four major areas—content, expectations, time, and teaching—and compared the patterns in 1964–69 to 1976–1981. It found that the content of the high school curriculum had become homogenized and diluted; more students taking a general track (42 percent in 1979 compared to 12 percent in 1964) and fewer students taking foreign languages, social sciences, and advanced math. As for expectations, the commission found that the amount of homework given students had declined significantly. Students in other countries spent more time on academic subjects, and more students were required to take them than in the United States. Minimum competency requirements became ceilings, or maximum competency requirements. Too many high school students were given too much freedom to take electives. Not enough teachers were involved in writing texts, and the texts that were written were not sufficiently challenging. Not enough money was spent on texts.

The NCEE report noted that students in other industrialized countries spent more days and longer days in school than did students in the United States. The average American school provided only about twenty-two hours of academic instruction a week and did a poor job of teaching study skills. Students in other Western industrialized countries performed at higher levels than American students. Finally, the commission looked at teaching and found that too many people entering the teaching profession were drawn from the bottom quarter of high school and college students. Further, education school curriculums were too heavily based on methods and too little on subject mastery. Salaries of teachers were very low and teachers often had little input in textbook selection. There were shortages of teachers in critical areas such as math, the sciences, and foreign languages. Further, many new teachers were unqualified in these subjects.

Based on these findings, the commission made a series of recommendations. Again, their recommendations paralleled those of the other studies and set the agenda for many of the changes made at the state level (though some had been implemented prior to the commission's report).

The first series of recommendations focused on content. The commission suggested stiffening high school graduation requirements based on what it called "The New Basics" (National Commission 1983, p. 24): [11]

- Four years of English
- Three years of mathematics
- Three years of science
- Three years of social studies
- One-half year of computer science

It also recommended foreign language study beginning in elementary school with an additional two years in high school for college-bound students.

The next series of recommendations concerned standards and expectations. The fundamental recommendation was the raising of standards and expectations. Grades, the commission wrote, should reflect academic performance. Entrance to colleges and universities should be based on specific courses (those recommended previously), performance in those courses, and tests of standardized achievement.

The third set of suggestions centered on time, recommending that "significantly more time be devoted to learning the New Basics. This will require more effective use of the existing school day, a longer school day, or a lengthier school year" (National Commission 1983, p. 26). The recommendations included more homework, the teaching of study skills, and a reduction of teachers' administrative burden. [12]

The fourth area of recommendations focused on teaching. Teachers should meet high educational standards—be competent as teachers and in a specific academic discipline. Salaries for teachers should be increased and "be professionally competitive, market-sensitive, and performance-based" (National Commission 1983, p. 30). Decisions concerning evaluation and compensation of teachers should be based on a merit system. Further, teachers should be given eleven-month contracts for professional development and specialized work with students, and career ladders should be created for teachers, from beginning instructor to master teacher. Nonschool personnel resources should be used to help in the critical shortage areas of math and science.

The final set of recommendations concerned leadership and fiscal support. The major leadership roles are to be played by school principals and district superintendents. By leadership, the commission meant persuasion, setting goals, and developing consensus for reform among the school board and local community. State and local officials have primary responsibility for financing and governing the schools.

The commission considered the role of the federal government in school reform. First, the federal government, along with the other levels, should help meet the needs of special students, including gifted, minority, and handicapped children. Second, the federal government has additional responsibilities that the other levels could not meet: protecting constitutional rights, data collection, support of research, and graduate training. Finally, the federal government has the major responsibility to identify the national interest in education, and also to help fund and support that interest.

The reports, particularly NCEE's, did not go uncriticized. For example, the NCEE report focused heavily on the comparatively poor performance of American students. But as Lawrence Stedman and Marshall Smith (1985; also see Henig 1994) note, the international comparisons were weak. First, they were based on 1964–1971 data; by the time the NCEE report came out, the statistics were at least thirteen years old. Further, the comparisons were unfair. In other countries, those tested were selected students in academic (college-bound) programs, whereas in the United States both college- and non-college-bound students were tested. When the top 5 to 10 percent of students in various countries were tested, American students tested at comparable levels.

The comparison between students tested in the 1964–69 and 1975–1981 periods also was unreasonable. The earlier study looked at twenty-seven high schools outside the South and the largest urban areas; the latter study was a national household sample. Thus, as Stedman and Smith point out: "There is no longitudinal study of a given set of high schools on which the Commission's claims rest" (1985, p. 87; on this point, see Rothstein 1998, chapter 3).

Stedman and Smith criticize some of the policy recommendations. For example, they indicate that most of the content (curriculum) recommendations are uninspiring in the sense that they are quite similar to current curriculum goals. The commission's recommendations also ignore how subjects are taught, the dropout problem, the needs of the poor, and problems of implementation. One estimate was that the NCEE proposals—improved teacher salaries, merit pay, new curriculum material, longer day and year—would cost an additional $14 billion at a time when the federal government was reducing its contribution. But there was much good about the reports, Stedman and Smith write: a problem does exist and the reports were relatively egalitarian (better learning for all students).

### The Politics Stream

Several events coalesced under the politics stream to enable education reform to occur. One—and it is notable in many of the reports of this time—is the declining international economic status of the United States, particularly as compared to Japan and other newly industrial Asian countries, such as Taiwan, Singapore, and South Korea. Educational achievement and the rigor of U.S. schools seemingly paled in comparison with other countries.

There was also a new federal administration. The Reagan administration was conservative, critical of past educational policies (including the progressive educational movement, busing, and bilingual education) and opposed to the growing presence of the federal government in educational policy. Under this administration, school reform, despite the National Commission's recommendations, would largely be a state and local effort, with the federal government identifying the national interest and urging change. The federal government, particularly the Department of Education, could be used (as Theodore Roosevelt might have put it) as a "bully pulpit." For example, in 1986, the U.S. Department of Education issued a report on the best teaching methods. These included the use of phonics in reading, increasing the amount of homework, frequent assessment of student progress, and the early learning of foreign languages. The report also described the characteristics of effective schools: "strong instructional leadership, a safe and orderly climate, school-wide emphasis on basic skills, high teacher expectations for student achievement and continuous assessment of student progress" (Fiske 1986).

Another part of the politics stream concerned the states. Through increased funding and the accountability movement (which advocated holding schools accountable for educational outcomes), the states developed into the most significant players in educational policy. At the same time, the federal government's diminishing involvement in domestic policy during the Reagan administration created a policy vacuum in which the states could operate.

Finally, Chester Finn (1985, p. 75) argued that the national mood, a populist revolt if you will, was the impetus for the reform movement:

> This is an educational reform movement that draws its force neither from the federal government nor from the profession. It is very nearly a populist movement, led primarily by self-interested parents and employers and by elected officials responding to overt and implicit signals from the voting, tax-paying public.

## Adoption

The 1980s saw considerable adoption of educational reform, though some of it predates the "awakening" of the educational crisis in 1983. Thus, as one close observer of the educational scene asked (Pipho 1986), did the reports cause the activity or reflect it? The answer is, some of both.

Adoption of school reform programs came at the request of the nation's governors. From 1982 to 1986, "forty-three states raised high school graduation requirements, thirty-seven states assessed student achievement, thirty states raised teacher certification requirements (many included teacher competency tests)" (Parker 1987, p. 32; see also U.S. Department of Education 1985). Many of the changes were in the form of omnibus (i.e., massive) reform bills, and many of them were in southern states where educational achievement and school financing traditionally have been low.

One of the earliest reform bills came in December 1982 in Mississippi. The goal was to make the state economically attractive and competitive. According to Chris Pipho (1986), the governor made 82 speeches and his staff made another 532 speeches from June to December 1982, urging passage of the reform bill. But perhaps the most comprehensive change came in Texas (Cooper 1985), where Governor Mark White moved to fulfill his campaign pledge to raise teachers' salaries. When the Texas legislature refused, the governor established a special blue ribbon committee to study educational issues, headed by billionaire H. Ross Perot (the third-party candidate for president in 1992 and 1996). Perot attacked the schools, made speeches around the state, held hearings, and lobbied the legislature. The result was a new bill in 1984, basically a revised version of the committee report.

The Texas law addressed five areas of education: teachers, students, elementary education, financing, and administration.[13] The law called for higher minimum teacher salaries, career ladders, and competency testing. The legislation required a minimum grade point average of 70 (2.0, or "C" in some systems), tutoring for students who fall below the average, a limit on the number of allowable absences and on extracurricular activities, skills testing for lower grades, and a high school exit exam. The act provided for half-day prekindergartens and reduction in class sizes. The law requested new taxes for education and an increase in per-student basic education allotments. Finally, a new state board was created, as was a legislative board to oversee implementation (Cooper 1985).

School reform movements, including that passed by Texas, went through two stages in the 1980s (Hoffman 1986). The first stage of reform, 1982 to 1985, focused on the easy changes that would cost little money, such as curricular reform and student and teacher competency tests. The second stage, after 1985, dealt with the more difficult and expensive issues such as increased salaries and merit pay.

Not everyone was pleased with the new state laws in Texas and elsewhere. In 1979, Arthur Wise observed that the American classroom was becoming bureaucratized by legislation, regulation, and centralization. He described this new classroom as "a world characterized by standardized testing, not educational standards; by teacher-proof curricula, not curriculum reform; by standardized teaching, not professional discretion; and by management-by-the-numbers, not instructional leadership" (Wise 1988, p. 328; see also Wise 1979). Educational policy goals changed from equal opportunity to minimal competency (what he called "adequacy"). Between 1963 and 1974, state legislatures passed some seventy-six laws concerned with achievement adequacy. Adequacy was combined with "accountability" for educational achievement.[14] Local school district objectives were to conform to state objectives. The result was "legislated learning" and the use of a variety of scientific management techniques to achieve those goals. Wise saw the 1980s reforms as potentially exacerbating that trend, with distrust of educators and boards of education leading to further state control, especially by the "education" governors (including Mark White in Texas, Christopher Bond in Missouri, and Bill Clinton in Arkansas).

## Implementation

Many of the school reform proposals were adopted. It is in implementation, however, that school reform policies would either fail or succeed. Although governors were the leaders of the school reform, they have limited power over educational school systems. Apart from the approximately 15,000 school districts, there are also some 97,000 school board members (Hoffman 1986) who control how the money will be spent. In fact, they have their own organization, the National School Boards Association, which might not appreciate a stronger state role. Education is a policy area that is fraught with interest groups. Even if the impetus for reform came from outside the educational system, it is those inside who would have to carry it out.

Teachers were both the main implementers (street-level bureaucrats to use Lipsky's [1980] terminology) and major targets of those calling for changes, and they have been partially faulted for achievement failures. Because teachers were (and still are) targets of reformers and other critics of education, teachers associations and unions such as the National Education Association and the American Federation of Teachers were ambivalent about reform. Certainly, teachers and their organizations supported increased pay, but they hesitated over merit pay. Teaching has never been a high-prestige occupation in the United States, and teachers felt that they have been victims. Thus implementation had to focus on the issues of money and working with and not against teachers. A 1988 survey of teachers indicated the success of some of the reform efforts in terms of higher test scores. But the survey also demonstrated the alienation that reform was causing. Teachers felt that they were not really a part of the changes (Daniels 1988). These feelings of alienation reinforce Wise's (1988) analysis of reform as another example of legislated learning. Teachers are implementers of but not participants in change.

## Evaluation

How well did educational reform that began in the 1980s succeed? Certainly there has been improvement. Academic standards were tightened, especially in the South. States increased their spending per pupil by an average of 17.2 percent from 1983 to 1986 (Reinhold 1987). Test scores rose and more students took more math and science courses. In some states, such as Florida, there was an increase in the number of students going to college and some improvement in SAT scores.

On the other hand, reform had different effects in different parts of the country and among different sectors of the population. While much of the reform focused on the South, because of the very low standards and requirements of southern schools, states in the West and East have moved more cautiously. States also have faced fiscal restraint problems. Reform is not cheap, and certain elements, such as merit pay, were dropped in places. The equity goal does not seem to have been furthered by reform. According to former secretary of education Terrence Bell:

> The school reform movement has benefitted about 70 percent of our students but has had no significant impact on the other 30 percent. . . .
> The 30 percent are the low-income minority students, and we are still not effectively educating them. . . . But that should not obscure the fact we are stimulating our better students. That needed to be done. (Quoted in Reinhold 1987)

A 1989 report issued by the Educational Testing Service as part of the National Assessment of Educational Progress summarized the findings of NAEP tests from 1969 to 1986.

> These data suggest a remarkable consistency across recent assessments of student achievement in various academic subjects. By and large, students are learning the basics, and Black and Hispanic students are closing the historical gap in performance with their White peers. Yet despite these signs of progress, it remains true that only some of the nation's students can perform moderately difficult tasks and woefully few can perform more difficult ones. . . . Most of the gains in average proficiency represent improvements in basic skills and knowledge rather than higher-level applications. (Applebee et al. 1989)

A 1995 study of the impact of education reform was encouraging (Smith 1995). Based on a comparison of students in the early 1980s versus the early 1990s, much change and progress was made. Most states had adopted the recommendations of the NCEE, and more students were taking the required number of credits in the core subjects (English, science, social studies, and math). For example, only 13 percent of high school students were meeting this standard in 1982; ten years later 47 percent were. A higher percentage of students were taking foreign languages than ten years earlier. Proficiency scores in math and science rose over the ten-year period, though they were about the same in reading. Achievement of both advanced- and lower-ability students either improved or remained about the same. The report noted:

> Mathematics and science proficiencies (as measured by the NAEP) have increased for the lowest performing students: in 1992, the 10th percentile for 17-year-olds (the score that 10 percent of students score below) was 11 points higher in mathematics and 12 points higher in science than in 1982. (Smith 1995, p. 7)

There were fewer students in high school remedial mathematics classes, although colleges and universities did add more such courses. There were also fewer dropouts in 1990 than in 1980.

Albert Shanker (1995) put these findings into perspective. Much work still needed to be done. Many of the improvements occurred in the ranks of lower achievers rather than the higher achievers (see also Herrnstein and Murray 1994, pp. 417–445). Achievement at all levels was low compared to students in other countries. But Shanker concluded that there have been improvements that should be recognized.[15] A strong defender of the public school system (Shanker was the president of the American Federation of Teachers), he tied the findings of this report to other proposed, more structural educational changes:

> Nevertheless, it is also a mistake not to acknowledge the progress we have made. Setting higher standards works. When we expect more of students, they rise to our expectations. Requiring that students take more rigorous courses is not as sexy as some currently popular school reform schemes—like vouchers or putting public schools under private management or letting each school do its own thing. But there is no track record on any of these reforms. Requiring that students take demanding courses is something that works. It works in the successful school systems of other industrialized countries and it is working here. Let's build on it. (Shanker 1995)

## Evaluation Through Ideology

Reform can also be evaluated through ideological perspectives. Again, the three basic values of order, liberty, and equality play a role. Fred Pincus (1985) distinguishes between two kinds of conservatism in educational policy: New Right conservatism and centrist conservatism. To that can be added liberal ideology. According to Pincus, the "liberal consensus" was the hallmark of the 1960s, and its emphasis was on equality. It relied heavily on the federal government to end racial discrimination and to promote educational opportunities for women, minorities, and others.

The liberal view, with its emphasis on equality, is represented by those who examined the educational reform reports of the 1980s and found them wanting. For example, Cynthia Brown (1985) argued that although the excellence movement (or school reform) did not necessarily restrict concerns about equality, the states had not yet addressed the issue.

> How will increased graduation standards and greater use of competency tests and elimination of social promotions do anything but increase the already growing high school dropout rate, *unless* accompanied by well-thought-through and well-financed remedial assistance programs. Such remedial programs are often missing from new state education programs. (C. Brown 1985, p. 299)

Pincus (1985) asserted that the conservative response to the liberal consensus built up in the 1970s and blossomed in the 1980s. This reaction had very different conceptions about the schools, the role of the federal government in the schools, and the likely success of reform.

Centrist conservatives perceive two problems with educational policy. One is the demand for social experiments, and the other is the excessive promotion of educational equality, particularly by the federal government (see, e.g.,

Ravitch 1983, 2000). To the centrist conservatives, schools have three missions: (1) to promote economic growth, with coordination at the federal level; (2) to preserve a common culture based on a set of common values,[16] and (3) to promote educational equity—schools as a means of upward mobility. The educational reform movement, based on excellence, fits within this agenda, and the centrist conservatives were some of its strongest supporters.

New Right conservatives see the major problem as "overcentralized decision-making caused by increased federal control. This has allowed the schools to become 'monopolized' by powerful 'vested interests'—teachers' unions, educational associations, and federal bureaucrats" (Pincus 1985, p. 331). It follows that appropriate policies to counteract that emphasis would eliminate federal funding and provide for financial assistance to those who send their children to private school. This perspective leads to the debate over private reforms, choice, and market incentives in education as an alternative to reform.

## Equality and Education Policy

### Desegregating the Schools

A long-standing problem in education policy has been one of equality.[17] As we have already seen and will consider some more below, educational achievement differs by race and income. To a certain extent, those differences are related to differences in inputs to education, that is, the quality of the educational system. To understand this problem, we need to go back to the nineteenth century.

After the Civil War, the United States passed three amendments to the Constitution. The Thirteenth Amendment ended slavery. The Fifteenth Amendment gave the former slaves the right to vote. The Fourteenth Amendment, the amendment of concern here, reads in part "No State shall . . . deny to any person within its jurisdiction the equal protection of the laws." Reconstruction provided the newly freed slaves liberties they could only have dreamed about. However, there was a backlash in the South, and the disputed presidential election in 1876 led to the end of Reconstruction. Over the next thirty years or so, the South enacted legislation (known as Jim Crow laws) that systematically took away the rights of African Americans and created a system of **segregation**, separation of the races. Additionally, violence intimidated African Americans from exercising their new rights.

Perhaps the most famous U.S. Supreme Court case interpreting the meaning of the Civil War amendments and segregation in the South was the 1896 case *Plessy v. Ferguson* (**1896**). The case itself involved segregation on railroad passenger cars. The Court ruled that separation of the races was constitutional as long as the facilities were equal; the famous phrase from this case was, therefore, **separate but equal**. Southern legislatures enacted separation laws, creating legal or de jure segregation. Shortly after *Plessy*, the Court applied the "separate but equal" doctrine to schools.

The fact of the matter, of course, was that the southern states (and indeed other states such as Kansas and Missouri) had no intention of creating equal facilities. Black schools were inferior in every aspect: per pupil spending was lower, outdated textbooks were used, and many students were forced to attend a school miles away from their neighborhood school.

The National Association for the Advancement of Colored People (NAACP) adopted a judicial strategy to force the courts to agree that separate but equal was unconstitutional. In a 1938 case out of Missouri, the U.S. Supreme Court found that the state had to admit a black student to the University of Missouri Law School rather than pay the costs for the student to go out of state. Some years later, the Court held that a makeshift law school could not substitute for the University of Texas Law School. In an Oklahoma case, the Court ruled that the University of Oklahoma could not have segregated classrooms that were obviously unequal.

Led by Thurgood Marshall (later the first African American to be appointed to the U.S. Supreme Court), head of its Legal Defense Fund, the NAACP was still looking for a case where the separate facilities would be more or less equal to test the legacy of *Plessy*. Further, the Truman administration was supportive of civil rights.[18] The cases came in 1952 from four states (Kansas, Delaware, South Carolina, and Virgina) and the District of Columbia. In 1954, the cases were reheard under the banner of ***Brown v. Board of Education of Topeka, Kansas* (1954).** The new chief justice of the Supreme Court, appointed by President Eisenhower, was Earl Warren.

The plaintiffs agreed that the black schools in Topeka were, in fact, pretty equal in facilities. However, they still maintained that legal segregation was wrong and urged the overturning of *Plessy*. The evidence presented to the Court and used in the decision was as controversial as the decision itself.

The plaintiffs presented studies from, among others, an African-American psychologist, Dr. Kenneth Clark, showing that legal segregation had a detrimental effect upon the psychological makeup of black children. Clark's studies went something like this:

Dr. Clark and his researchers would hold out two dolls, one black, one white, in front of an African-American child. The researcher would then ask the child which one he or she was. The child picked the black one. The researcher would then ask the child which doll was better, the white or the black. The child would pick the white doll. Finally, the researcher would ask which the child would rather be, the white or the black doll. The child picked the white doll.

The Court, by an 8–0 vote, ruled that separate was inherently unequal and thus violated the equal protection clause of the Fourteenth Amendment. Its opinion cited studies by Clark and others. The decision met with a mixed response. Missouri, Kansas, Delaware, and the District of Columbia abolished de jure segregation. However, the eleven states of the old Confederacy denounced the result and swore not to obey the Supreme Court decision. The state of Virginia led the way. Its political leaders promised massive resistance to the order. Private schools (segregation academies) were established, funded by the state. Prince Edward County, VA, simply closed its public schools for some three years. Another method for avoiding desegregation was "freedom of choice," which ostensibly let students attend the school of their choice. Effectively it meant that little desegregation would occur (Henig 1994).

In 1955, the Supreme Court issued another decision, known as *Brown II*. It summoned the parties to the original *Brown* case and then said desegregation should take place "with all deliberate speed." This was a recognition that the Court could not carry out its order.

Although two civil rights laws were enacted in the 1950s (1957 and 1960), they were fairly mild, a first step, and did not affect schools in the South. An important event took place in Little Rock, AR, when four African-American children tried to enter Central High School. Arkansas governor Orville Faubus was strongly opposed to school desegregation. He ordered the state National Guard to Central High School, ostensibly to protect the African-American children but actually to keep them out. President Eisenhower, no friend of the civil rights movement and opposed to the 1954 *Brown* decision (though he did not say so until years after he left office), was reluctant to get involved. But given the explosive situation, the president took action. He nationalized the Arkansas National Guard and sent in U.S. Army troops as well. They then accompanied the children to school and kept order (Williams 1987; see also Branch 1988).

The breakthrough in school desegregation came in two pieces of congressional legislation, the **Civil Rights Act (1964)** and the **Elementary and Secondary Education Act (ESEA) (1965)**. The Civil Rights Act[19] stated that funds from the federal government could be withheld from programs that discriminated. At the time, however, the federal government provided little money to public elementary and secondary schools. But the Elementary and Secondary Education Act, enacted the next year, did provide funds. The Justice Department began demanding enforcement of the Civil Rights Act now that it had something that could be withheld.

The Civil Rights Act of 1964 also required that the Civil Rights Commission (established by the 1957 legislation) investigate differences in educational outcomes. The result was the report *Equality of Educational Opportunity*. The purpose of the report was to see whether there were differences in educational achievement between whites and minorities (there were, and still are), and, if so, what accounted for those differences. From the standpoint of this text, the major conclusion was that inputs to schools, such as the quality of the teachers, their pay, quality of the physical facilities, newness of texts, and so forth, did not explain differential achievement. What counted most was, first, the family and environmental background of the student, and then the family and environmental background of other students in the school.[20] On the face of it, the report seemed to support the argument for integration: African-American students did better in integrated schools than in racially segregated schools.[21]

In 1969, the U.S. Supreme Court, now with Warren Burger as its chief justice, ruled, again unanimously, that the time for delay in desegregation should end immediately. Two years later, in *Swann v. Charlotte-Mecklenburg County Schools* (**1971**), the Court ruled that busing was an appropriate tool for desegregation. The Court decisions applied to schools in the South. Southern schools met the requirements by forming countywide school districts that allowed busing within the district. Effectively, the South had desegregated its schools in the 1970s.

The North was another matter. Northern school districts tend to be smaller, based on city rather than county lines. In 1974, the Supreme Court ruled that busing could not take place across school districts. The suburbs of the large central cities, such as Detroit (the locus of the 1974 decision), were thus exempt from busing. Further, efforts at **integration** of the public schools in the North (changing the mix of students), which began in the 1960s, met considerable resistance. Boston was perhaps the extreme case, to the point where a federal district court judge effectively ran the Boston school system for years in the 1970s.

In the North and elsewhere, some desegregation was voluntary rather than mandatory. An alternative to busing was the use of **magnet schools**, or schools with special features that would attract white students (Henig 1994; Rossell 1990). Both busing and magnet schools could be employed on a mandatory or voluntary basis. The important difference is that magnet schools do not require forced reassignment of students as do busing plans. The Kansas City, MO, magnet school program was one that was implemented under federal court order.

Schools in the North were segregated, but not because of deliberate state policy.[22] Schools were, and are, segregated in the North because of housing patterns. This is **de facto segregation**, segregation in fact but not in law. Segregated housing, sometimes assisted by law and banking and housing practices, leads to segregated schools under the neighborhood school system.

By the 1970s, there was considerable community opposition to busing in the North. During the 1980s, because of both community opposition, especially outside the South, and the philosophical opposition of the Reagan administration, busing for desegregation or integration purposes came to an end. The St. Louis and Kansas City, MO, school systems were two of the last school systems to be under court-ordered integration. That effort ended in the late 1990s, though even in 2000, court decisions on occasion reflected the problems of segregation in the public schools (Browne 2000; Zernike 2000c). By 1999, desegregation was declared to be "dead" (Twohey 1999).

## Evaluating the Impact of Desegregation Efforts

The major impact of the *Brown* decision was moral: "that racial segregation was immoral and unconstitutional." It provided a principled foundation for the civil rights movement as it shifted into its activist phase (Dellinger 1994, p. 23; see also chapter 9).

Several observations can be made about the impact of efforts to desegregate the public schools. First, the legal system of racial segregation was dismantled.

> According to federal statistics, in 1968 about 77 percent of black students attended schools that were over half minority; by 1988 the black enrollment in predominantly minority schools had declined to 63 percent. Further, in 1968 a majority of black students—about 64 percent—attended schools that were over 90 percent minority; in 1988 that figure had shrunk to 32 percent. (Armor 1992, p. 71)[23]

This was the great achievement of *Brown*. Segregation still remains, especially in the North, due largely to segregation in housing patterns (Celis 1994).

*Brown* also raised the issue of equal opportunity, and here the impact of *Brown* is more questionable (Lehmann 1994). Achievement of black students has gone up, indeed the gap between African-American and white students, though still apparent, has narrowed (National Center for Education Statistics 1991). David Armor (1992) argues that much of the increase in black achievement and closing of the black/white achievement gap from 1970 to 1990 is partly due to compensatory education programs (such as Title I of the Elementary and Secondary Education Act) and to changes in the socioeconomic status of African Americans. Specifically, Armor notes that the increased education (beyond high school) of African-American parents explains about 42 percent of the decreased achievement gap.[24] Armor argues that the data suggest that very little of the black achievement change is due to desegregation.[25]

But there were also negative effects of school desegregation and integration. The major one was **white flight**, the movement of white families out of central cities and out of public schools. As Christine Rossell's (1990) careful study shows, white flight began before efforts at desegregation (whether mandatory or voluntary, busing or magnet schools). But mandatory busing programs did accelerate the problem. The result is that in large central cities, a majority of the public school population is minority. Efforts to create racial balance would inevitably fail. A further problem is that even when schools were desegregated, classrooms were often racially segregated through achievement grouping and so forth. Between white flight and classroom separation, schools have become resegregated. The courts have ruled that busing in these cases could not take place. The result of all this is that desegregation of the public schools is greatest in the South and segregation of the public schools is greatest in the North (DeWitt 1992; Lehmann 1994).

In some places, such as the city of Atlanta and a number of states, students were not integrated, but money was. That is, these cities and states attempted to equalize school funding between rich and poor (or suburban and urban) school districts. This was often done under court order (Traub 1994).

Not everyone agrees that desegregation of students has been ineffective or negative. Several studies have shown positive effects of desegregation. According to this research, students in desegregated schools were more likely to go to college than students in segregated schools. The percentage of students from low-income areas in a school also had an impact on how impoverished students performed on achievement tests. Those in schools with a smaller percentage of low-income students did better than those in schools with higher levels of low-income students. Low-income Hispanic students in San Francisco did better in middle-class schools than their counterparts in largely minority schools (Traub 1994).

> There's a striking conservative conclusion to be drawn from the irreproachably liberal Orfield's[26] claim: It is values and culture, not resources, that determine academic outcomes, and middle-class children bring with them to school values that produce success—self-discipline, a faith in institutions and their rules, and above all, an expectation of success itself. Poor kids, by contrast, often reach school with the cognitive problems that come from having poorly educated or disengaged or preoccupied parents as well as with the assumptions appropriate to their experience. It wasn't only that Don Carso's students hadn't been to the mall or seen a river; they lived in a world in which middle-class success was virtually unimaginable. (Traub 1994, p. 44)

James Traub (1994) recommended that inner cities and their suburbs work together. In the case of Hartford, CT, he suggested sending Hartford students out to the suburban schools (but in low concentrations), combined with magnet schools to attract the middle class to Hartford schools. He called this system "one-way desegregation" because it would be mostly the minorities that would move rather than the white, suburban majority. Apart from the educational benefits it would provide the children, Traub argued that under such a system the suburbs would then feel a sense of common destiny with and collective responsibility for the central city, rather than try to isolate themselves.

One problem with such a solution is that all of the burden is on African Americans to be bused. An alternative that is being examined in cities such as Detroit and Milwaukee, are all-black schools (sometimes just all-black male schools) with full funding and an emphasis on achievement and esteem. This raises the possibility of voluntary resegregation of society.

## The Federal Government and Educational Reform

The federal government has long supported education in a variety of ways. The Center on Education Policy (*A Brief History*) notes that there are four reasons the national government has played a role: supporting democracy, ensuring equality of opportunity, national defense, and improving the nation's productivity. These include things such as the *Brown* decision discussed above, support for the establishment of state universities (the land grant program), school lunch programs, funding for special education, and pressure to improve academic standards. The center concludes that the federal government has played a vital role that needs to continue. One could argue that the Bush plan, proposed in January 2001 (see below), fits in very nicely with this history.

More specifically for our purposes, the federal government has supported school reform in several ways. First, the NCEE was appointed by the federal government. The Department of Education has conducted studies to help states and school districts understand what reforms are effective. Further, the federal government has supported, to greater or lesser degrees, school choice and voucher programs. The Reagan administration favored vouchers and tuition tax credits, and proposed legislation for both in 1983—an unusual proposal for the Reagan administration. First, vouchers and tax credits would exacerbate the federal budget deficit, one by decreasing revenue (tuition tax credits), the other by increasing spending (vouchers). More importantly, the proposal would have represented a massive incursion of the federal government in an area historically dominated by the states. Thus, the whole idea of the "new federalism" would have been reversed.[27]

The first Bush administration went further, in terms of both choice and reform. First of all, the administration proposed a $500 million voucher program (called the "G.I. Bill for Children") that would give 500,000 parents $1,000 for a child to attend a private school (Chira 1991a). Further, the president and the nation's governors agreed on six national goals for the nation's schools and a voluntary system of national testing (Chira 1991b). Congress did not pass the voucher proposal, but the six national goals remained.

The Clinton administration continued the direction of the Bush administration, but with a more assertive federal role. While school choice remained a part of the program, it was a much less significant part than in the Bush administration; the voucher proposal was dropped. The Clinton administration also pushed a new type of school, the charter school, that came on to the American scene beginning in the early 1990s (see below). The goals were incorporated (and expanded) into legislation, the *Goals 2000: Educate America Act*, in 1994. The national education goals, as stated in the legislation were:

- By the year 2000, all children in America will start school ready to learn.
- By the year 2000, the high school graduation rate will increase to at least 90 percent.
- By the year 2000, all students will leave grades four, eight, and twelve having demonstrated competency over challenging subject matter including English, mathematics, science, foreign languages, civics and government, economics, arts, history, and geography, and every school in America will ensure that all students learn to use their minds well, so they may be prepared for responsible citizenship, further learning, and productive employment in our nation's modern economy.
- By the year 2000, United States students will be first in the world in mathematics and science achievement.
- By the year 2000, every adult American will be literate and will possess the knowledge and skills necessary to compete in a global economy and exercise the rights and responsibilities of citizenship.

- By the year 2000, every school in the United States will be free of drugs, violence, and the unauthorized presence of firearms and alcohol and will offer a disciplined environment conducive to learning.
- By the year 2000, the Nation's teaching force will have access to programs for the continued improvement of their professional skills and the opportunity to acquire the knowledge and skills needed to instruct and prepare all American students for the next century.
- By the year 2000, every school will promote partnerships that will increase parental involvement and participation in promoting the social, emotional, and academic growth of children. ("Goals 2000: Educate America Act" 1994)

How well have we achieved the goals set forth by the Bush and Clinton administrations? The National Education Goals Panel was established in 1990 to monitor progress. The panel included eight governors, two members each from the U.S. Senate and House, two members of the administration, and four state legislators. The 1999 report of the panel showed mixed results. Mathematics showed improvement, while reading scores showed improvement only for grade eight (the panel used the NAEP tests as its indicator). The discipline goals, such as drug use and class disruption, showed some setbacks. The project was given some credit as a force behind educational reform, and some states, such as Texas, showed substantial improvements (Wilgoren 1999). The greatest successes were in areas such as increases in the percentage of students going on to college, especially among minorities, and health status indicators (increase in child immunizations) (Wilgoren 1999).

Richard Rothstein (1999) was quite critical of both the goals and recent reports on the achievements of the goals. He argued that there were three problems with Goals 2000. Some goals, he asserted, were simply ridiculous. Other goals were never given the appropriate resources. Still other goals will take well over a decade to achieve.

An example of what Rothstein called a ridiculous, even irresponsible, goal is that U.S. students be first in the world in math and science. He noted that Japanese and Korean students have a very vigorous curriculum but also cram for tests, which are much more important in their countries than in the United States Rothstein suggests that a lower ranking or increases in absolute scores (not relative to other countries) would be more appropriate. A goal that Rothstein approves of is making sure that children are ready to learn when they start school. However, this goal, as with the adult literacy goal, has never been adequately financed.

Rothstein comments, relative to the plan proposed by President George W. Bush in 2000 and 2001, that each state should set its own standards. Efforts to develop national tests and national standards were very controversial and failed.

# Case Study: The Question of Choice

## Arguments for Choice

In the mid-1980s, an alternative to the educational reform movement was proposed. This was **education choice**, the idea that parents would have the right to choose the school their children attended. Choice proposals took two forms, one limited to choice within the public-school sector and the more expanded version that would include private schools. Choice plans are attractive and offer a number of advantages.

> Proponents argue that choice programs will force schools to answer for their failures and distinguish themselves from other schools by emphasizing a rigorous academic curriculum—including, for example, performing arts or some other specialty. Others make the equity argument: Open enrollment plans give to low-income families the same power that always has been held by affluent families who could afford tuition at a private school or an out-of-district school. (Vobejda 1989, p. 33)

Choice proposals are based on economic reasoning. Economist Milton Friedman, in *Capitalism and Freedom* (1962), maintained that the major problem with public education is its monopoly status. Most people do not have a choice of where to send their children. Whereas most would like to send their children to the neighborhood school, busing for desegregation or integration denied some of them that opportunity. (Of course, African Americans were also denied the right to send their children to the neighborhood school when southern school districts were segregated.) Because public schools are a monopoly and involve government's use of coercion, freedom is limited. Further, because of their monopoly status, schools have no competition for clients or customers (students); thus, there is no incentive to meet parents' demands to improve the quality or efficiency of education.[28]

Friedman therefore argued for a **voucher system**, which places public and private schools on the same footing.[29] Under such a system, parents would receive a check, really a piece of paper (the voucher), equal to the average per-pupil expenditures on education in the district or state. The parent would then be free to enroll the student in the school of his or her choice, and the school submits the vouchers to the state or district for reimbursement. The total amount from voucher reimbursement would then constitute the school's budget for that school. If a parent was dissatisfied with the school, the child could enroll in another school the next year. Thus the system would respond to parent (or consumer) desires and would force schools to compete for students. Those schools that did not satisfy demand (did a poor job of education, or did not provide the kind of values education desired) would either change or go out of business. The monopoly power of public schools would thus be eliminated; competition would force schools to change (for a more detailed argument for vouchers and private schools, see Friedman 1995).

Some advocates of choice had a much more antagonistic view of public schools. Recall that conservative ideology in education included a strain called New Right conservatism (Pincus 1985). Peter Brimelow (1985) gives an excellent example of this line of thought, particularly with his assertion that

> The public school system is the American version of Soviet agriculture, beyond help as currently organized because its incentive structure is all wrong. Symptoms include: the persistent tendency, already noted, to treat capital as a free good and all possible uses of it as equal; constant mismatching of supply and demand, so that a shortage like the current dearth of science teachers is inevitably followed by a glut; prices administered without regard to incentives, so that all teachers must be paid on the same scales; an absence of internal checks and balances to prevent wholesale imposition of officially favored enthusiasms. . . . (Brimelow 1985, pp. 351–352)[30]

Continuing this line of thought, Brimelow declares education a "curious and anomalous experiment with socialism" (1985, p. 353) that is not found in the U.S. Constitution.[31] He also asserts that public education for all, and especially high school education, is relatively new.

So far, we have examined two arguments in favor of choice and greater reliance on private schools. One argument is based on economic reasoning, using the market analogy (Henig 1994) as a means of changing the educational system. The other argument, the ideological one, is based on distaste for public education.

There is a third argument that can and has been made for choice. If the schools that parents choose do better than schools that students are assigned to, all other things being equal, then this would be very strong support for some version of choice. Most of this line of reasoning can be seen in comparing public and private schools.

## Public- and Private-School Achievement Compared

The basis for exploring public-private school differences was the study that appeared in the early 1980s called "High School and Beyond" for the National Center for Education Statistics (NCES). One report, called *High School Achievement*, appeared in 1982 (Coleman et al. 1982; see also Coleman 1981). This report will be referred to as the Coleman report, after the principal researcher, James S. Coleman.

Recall that the 1966 study *Equality of Educational Opportunity* report (also headed by Coleman) found that school characteristics made little difference in educational achievement; therefore, spending more money on education would seem to have little effect. Schools did not matter, at least as much as was thought. The 1982 Coleman report, however, indicated that differences in characteristics of schools did lead to differences in student achievements; schools did matter!

The Coleman report addressed three important questions:

First, do students in private schools achieve better—get higher test scores—than students in public schools? After testing sophomores and seniors, dividing schools into public, Catholic, and other private categories, the "High School and Beyond" study found that Catholic students scored highest, followed by other private school students, and finally public school students. This finding was consistent even when controlling for background characteristics of students.[32]

Second, what are the differences between public and private schools? First, public schools are larger than private schools. Secular (nonreligious) private schools have lower teacher-pupil ratios than either public or Catholic schools. Discipline in private schools is stricter (regarding dress codes, attendance, property damage, and so on), more effective, and fairer than in public schools. More homework is assigned in private than in public schools. There is also a narrower curriculum in the private schools, which stresses academics, whereas public schools have vocational, technical, and general as well as academic curricula. A considerably higher proportion of students in private schools (70 percent) are in academic programs than is true for public school students (34 percent).

Further, students in private schools are more likely to take the advanced courses suggested by the National Commission on Excellence in Education and other reports (as we have seen, the percentage of public school students taking these courses has increased dramatically). Students in public schools take fewer semesters of academic subjects than students in private schools, and the percentage of students taking academic subjects is less than in the private schools. Staff in private schools are paid less than in public (and also are not unionized), and private schools are more likely to use volunteers and individuals who are nontraditionally trained.

Finally, are private schools more segregated than public schools? Private schools are expensive and not taxpayer-financed, and at least some of the private schools were opened to avoid desegregation. Coleman's finding was that on both economic and racial grounds, the answer is no. There is slight economic segregation, though Coleman argues that economic segregation is more likely in the public than private sector. The data indicate that the existence of private schools does not increase racial segregation. Coleman et al. (1982) assert instead that white flight to suburban public schools increases racial segregation in public schools and is more likely to have an impact on segregation in the public schools than does the existence of private schools. Thus, they contend that private schools, and Catholic schools in particular (which tend to be located in inner-city areas), are more likely than public schools to be the "common" school with a mixture of races.[33] The only kind of segregation increased by private schools, which stands to reason, was religious.

What is the significance of the Coleman report for public schools? Some, such as Brimelow (1985), maintain that there should be heavier reliance on private schools and competition. Ravitch draws a more positive conclusion for public schools and the educational reform movement:

> No longer can schools be dismissed as little more than sociological cookie cutters, relegated to handing out credentials in accordance with predetermined social-class

categories. The new Coleman report also gives educators, public and private, a considerable body of evidence demonstrating that school policy affects student achievement and student behavior. More important, the report implies that school officials and education policymakers must reexamine their curricula, their programs, and their policies. (Ravitch 1985, p. 111)

Although one could draw the conclusion that the country ought to shift more toward private schools, Coleman himself did not make that assertion. Schools do make a difference, and certain characteristics of a school, whether private or public, lead to better achievement. These attributes include schools with strong academic demands and equally strong demands on behavior and attendance (Coleman 1981). Coleman maintained, however, that private schools are more likely than public schools to have these traits.

John Chubb and Terry Moe make this structural argument in greater detail (Chubb 1988a, 1988b; Chubb and Moe 1986, 1988, 1990). In a follow-up study to the Coleman report, called the "Administrator and Teacher Survey," Chubb and Moe found that the better performing schools are structured more like teams, with strong school leadership, cooperation and delegation among teachers, and parental involvement. Poorer performing schools were more hierarchical, based on formal rules, relationships, and monitoring. Further, the better schools were more autonomous from outside control: from teachers' unions, local boards of education, and state boards of education. Chubb and Moe distinguish between political control, to which public schools are subject, and market control, to which private schools are subject, as two mechanisms for achieving accountability. Under political control, accountability is ensured by testing students and teachers, and by specified curriculum ("legislated learning"). It is regulatory in nature. Under market control, the demands and satisfaction of clients steer the schools in the desired direction.

What does this have to do with the educational reform movement of the 1980s and the changes mandated by the states? Chubb and Moe asserted that educational reform would fail and even be counterproductive because it did not reflect the structural changes needed in the schools. In other words, the changes were superficial and would have little impact on student achievement. They also pointed out that making the necessary structural changes would be difficult for political reasons: opposition by teachers' organizations because of the reduction of tenure and job security that would accompany the changes, and the loss of jobs and control by administrative officials. To paraphrase (Chubb and Moe 1986, p. 28), they are advocating the heresy of less democratic politics; democracy is the problem.

Larry Cuban (1988) agrees with Chubb and Moe. He contends that the education reforms that have occurred in this century were "first-order" or quality-control reforms, focusing on improving efficiency and effectiveness. The basic structure is fine, but we need to do better. His examples of first-order changes include: "recruiting better teachers and administrators, raising salaries, allocating resources equitably, selecting better textbooks, adding (or de-

leting) content and coursework, scheduling people and activities more efficiently, and introducing new versions of evaluation and training" (p. 342).
These are easy reforms, they accept the structure, and they correspond to
most previous reforms, including those of the 1980s.

Second-order, or design, changes introduce new goals, structures, and roles,
reflecting dissatisfaction with current arrangements. Examples of second-order
reforms are: "the open classroom, a voucher plan, teacher-run schools, and
schools in which the local community has authority to make budgetary and
curricular decisions" (Cuban 1988, p. 342). Magnet schools, open enrollments,
and vouchers are three mechanisms for achieving second-order changes. The
schools would make the important decisions about "policy, organization, and
personnel" (Chubb and Moe 1986, p. 28), with the state role limited to setting
minimum requirements.

Chester Finn (1994) argues that choice is only one of a series of changes
that are needed for genuine reform, though perhaps the most important change.
Other changes he advocates include shifting of power to consumers and civil-
ians (i.e., away from the educational establishment); creation of standards
consisting of demonstrating skills and knowledge and of mechanisms for assessing the meeting of those standards; educational pluralism; and profes-
sionalism (letting individual schools make decisions).

E. J. Dionne (2000) states that the best argument vouchers make is that
parents want to do what is best for their children and will enroll their children
in the best schools they can find. But poor parents do not have the resources to
pay for privates schools on their own. Thus, vouchers can help meet that need.

## Arguments Against Choice

As we have seen, the arguments in favor of choice and greater reliance on private
schools have broad and narrow perspectives. This is also true for arguments against
choice and vouchers. Perhaps the broadest argument is that such a change would
likely cause irreparable harm to the public schools. If students leave the public
schools for private schools, and state money follows the students (as most such
proposals recommend), the public schools will become poorer and be populated
predominantly by students with severe educational problems. The public schools
could never recover from such a change. And, as pointed out above, there have
been improvements in student achievement levels.

The narrower arguments focus on the points made by advocates of choice.
Both the Coleman and Chubb and Moe studies have been subjected to adverse commentary. Arthur Goldberger (1981) critiques the Coleman study
from a methodological perspective. First, Goldberger argues that there is insufficient information to judge the validity of the tests of cognitive outcomes.
The one test that had any description in the report was in mathematics, and it
tested, Goldberger pointed out, lower-level rather than higher-level skills. Thus
the tests do not adequately evaluate high school performance. Second,

Goldberger's analysis indicated that public school students missed an average of only one additional item per test than private school students.

Perhaps the most telling argument is that in the Coleman report, most of the students in the private schools were in academic programs, whereas in the public schools, students—both generally and in the study sample—were in academic, general, and vocational programs. Public school students in academic programs did as well as students in the private sector, so when using comparable groups, there is little difference between the sectors. The assumed advantage of private schools is in the screening process: committed parents, the ability to reject or remove students, and so forth. The problem with public schools, then, if this analysis is correct, is that because they are public they have to admit anyone.

This reasoning is reinforced by an analysis of a 1986 NAEP test of history and literature taken by high school juniors (Ravitch and Finn 1987). As was true in the Coleman report study, students in nonpublic schools did better than students in public schools (although students in other private schools did better than students in Catholic schools, a reverse of the earlier study). However, no group of students did well, and the difference between public and private school students, and especially between academic public school students and private school students, was very small. In a 1988 interview, Finn, then an assistant secretary for education, found the small differences quite troubling (Okun 1988). Given that private school students are more likely to come from higher-income homes and have college-educated parents, the educational achievement advantages of private schools would seem to be quite slim. Shanker (1989a, 1989b) points out that even our best students are not competitive internationally. "In addition to the problems of dropouts and those who are 'at risk' [problems not addressed by either school reform or the private-public debate], we're facing another major problem: We're only producing a very small percentage of students who can really do college-level work" (Shanker 1989b).

The Chubb and Moe study was also the subject of criticism (Henig 1994; Lee and Bryk 1993; Sukstorf et al. 1993). Most of the methodological critiques concern how Chubb and Moe measured their variables. As one example, they measured student performance by the gain in composite test scores between the sophomore and senior years, using a procedure that gave more weight to higher-achieving sophomores' gains even though the raw score gain was less than the lower achievers' gains.[34]

Henig examined Chubb and Moe's argument that it is democratic or political control of schools that is ultimately the problem.

> Making government work is difficult. It especially is difficult to work through democratic procedures that invite and accept as legitimate views from disparate actors with conflicting agendas and incompatible styles. Calls for radically restructuring education through market processes appeal in part because they promise to sidestep

this process. In the grand bazaar of education, families would be free to negotiate their own bargains on their own terms, paying only as much attention as they wish to the hubbub around them.

It is seductive, but misleading, to look for miracle cures that propose painlessly and speedily to solve problems that are rooted in fundamental political tensions. Rather than looking for the idea or the technique that will do the trick, it is necessary for us to hunker down for a long-term commitment to ongoing deliberation, unending adjustment and reconceptualization, and contingent—but nonetheless authoritative—collective action. (Henig 1994, p. 23)

Deborah Stone (1997) discusses the political implications of economically based proposals. She maintains that changing from public to private sectors is constitutional engineering, with the underlying argument that "the content of decisions is shaped by the structure of a process in a seemingly automatic fashion" (p. 289). That is, once the change is made as to how decisions are reached, say from political to economic decision making, the kinds of decisions that result will automatically change. But constitutional arguments are also about reallocating power. For example, Chubb and Moe (1986, 1988; Chubb 1988b) advocate moving power away from teachers' unions and states, and toward parents.

An important consideration with market-reform proposals such as vouchers is that they are not self-executing. Market reformers do not consider implementation problems (Rushefsky 1984). However, were states to go to a choice or voucher plan, the amount of regulation and politics that currently exist in education might be reduced but not eliminated. For example, states would probably require that minimum standards be met, say for graduation or promotion. Thus, minimum competency would still reign and public and private curricula (courses offered) would come to resemble each other. Standards for teachers might also be forthcoming (Fiske 1989). Given the accountability movement of the 1970s, one has to ask why states (especially state legislators) would reduce accountability requirements merely because more choice was introduced to the system. Further, one should inquire about those students that public schools but not private schools are forced to take: the disabled, the recalcitrant, and so forth. If public schools become more like private schools, able to reject difficult or disruptive students, what happens to them? The theoretical niceties of market reform do not face political realities. But Chubb and Moe's study, although providing support for restructuring America's schools around choice, vouchers, and increased reliance on private schools, says nothing about the actual experience with choice (see below).

Another problem with voucher programs, a serious one, is what could be called a "supply" problem (Dionne 2000). The difficulty here is that the private sector is too small to meet the needs of public school students (not counting that private schools are selective in whom they admit and may not participate in voucher programs). Dionne (2000) concludes that vouchers might be a short-term solution to the problem, but that the public schools need to be fixed, a problem that is difficult and costly but needs to be done.

Table 8.6

**Nature and Extent of School Choice Programs in the United States**

| Program | Number (in millions) |
|---|---|
| Total elementary and secondary schoolchildren | 50.0 |
| Schoolchildren privately educated | 6.0 |
|   Tuition-paid private schools | 5.0 |
|   Home schooling | 1.0 |
|   Using publicly funded vouchers for private schools | <0.1 |
|   Using privately funded vouchers for private schools | <0.1 |
| Schoolchildren in public school choice programs | 23.5 |
|   Intradistrict choice programs (specialty, alternative, and magnet schools; choice districts; individual transfers' false addresses) | 5.0 |
|   Interdistrict choice | 0.3 |
|   Charter schools | 0.2 |
|   Choice through choice of residence | 18.0 |
| Total schoolchildren in choice schools | 29.5 |

*Source:* Henig and Sugarman (1999), p. 29. Reprinted with permission.

A final consideration is that there is considerably more choice available to parents than voucher advocates acknowledge, though not all parents have access to choice. Henig and Sugarman (1999) list the types of choices available: choice of residence, choice of public schools within districts, interdistrict choice of school, magnet schools, charter schools, private schools, home schooling, and vouchers. By their estimate, more than half of America's schoolchildren are attending a school of choice (see Table 8.6).

## The Experience with Choice

Apart from the experience with public schools, there is a growing private effort to provide vouchers, particularly for low-income, disadvantaged students (Moe 1999; CEO America at www.childrenfirstamerica.org). The idea began in 1991 in Indianapolis, and as of 1999, there were some forty-one such programs around the country (Moe 1999). By 2001, there were seventy-eight such programs in forty-one states (calculated by author from the childrenfirstamerica website).

The nationwide Children's Scholarship Fund began in 1998, and is a good example of how these private funds operate. In April 1999, it held a nationwide lottery. Some 1 million children from disadvantaged families applied; 40,000 children were randomly selected and awarded scholarships ranging from $600 to $1,700. These amounts were deliberately less than the cost of tuition at private schools. The families were to contribute the difference, making them, as Moe (1999) points out, stakeholders in their children's education. The seventy-eight local programs work in generally the same fashion, though the percentage of tuition covered by the voucher may be higher than with the Children's Scholarship Fund.

Even though these scholarships involved private rather than public funds, not everyone was happy with them. Opponents of school vouchers argue that the private scholarships are a way to get around opposition to public ones. Even if they are not, opponents such as Sandra Feldman of the American Federation of Teachers argue that they hurt public schools anyway. Because public schools receive funding based on enrollment, as students transfer to private schools, their former public schools lose money (Rhodes 1999).

In addition, three states have state tuition tax credit programs (Arizona, Illinois, and Minnesota) and six states have statewide public-supported voucher programs (Arkansas, Florida, New Mexico, Michigan, Vermont, and New Hampshire). By 2000, almost 64,000 children were in voucher programs in thirty-one states, including the private scholarships (Wilgoren 2000a).

Courts have addressed the question of school vouchers. Here the issue overlaps into separation of church and state. Because many private schools are sectarian (religious-based), public money going to those schools in the form of vouchers might cross the line. In general, when courts have been presented with voucher cases, they have ruled against the program. The first such case came in 1999 when a federal appeals court ruled in a Maine case that the state could not subsidize (give vouchers to) families who sent their children to private religious schools. In Ohio, the state Supreme Court ruled against the voucher program, which included both religious and nonreligious schools. A federal appeals court agreed with the Ohio Supreme Court (Wilgoren 2000d). Wisconsin courts have upheld the Milwaukee program, the longest-running voucher program (Flaherty 1999). In 2000, a Florida state judge ruled the voucher program unconstitutional (Wilgoren 2000b). The Florida constitution, amended in 1998, was the basis for the ruling:

> The education of children is a fundamental value of the people of the State of Florida. It is, therefore, a paramount duty of the state to make adequate provision for the education of all children residing within its borders. Adequate provision shall be made by law for a uniform, efficient, safe, secure and high quality system of free public schools that allows students to obtain a high quality education and for the establishment, maintenance and operation of institutions of higher learning and other public education programs that the needs of the people may require. (quoted in Wilgoren 2000b)

Later in 2000, a Florida appellate court reversed the judge's ruling, allowing the statewide program to continue ("Florida Appeals Court" 2000).

Florida was the first, and remains the only, state that has a statewide voucher program. However, it too has run into legal problems. The Florida program, part of a campaign pledge by Governor Jeb Bush, became the model for the program his brother, President George W. Bush, sent to Congress in 2001.

Under the Florida program, each school is given a grade depending on scores on standardized tests. Students in schools receiving a failing grade would be given a voucher to attend a private school. As with President Bush's plan, the Florida plan would provide money to schools to help students in failing schools (Bragg 1999). The plan was supposed to be implemented in four schools and then spread to all the state's public schools.

The program began in August 1999. Two of Florida's public schools had been given failing grades, with fifty-eight students enrolled in four Catholic schools and one secular private school. Those five schools were the only ones to agree to participate in 1999. The others wanted to see how well the program was working or did not want to participate fearing that their academic standards would be lowered ("Florida Begins Voucher Plan for Education" 1999).

Even though the Florida program began small and remains relatively small, where it took effect it did have an impact on affected public schools. Two schools that were given failed grades and lost students made concerted efforts to improve. These included reducing class size, hiring more teachers, focusing the curriculum more on testing, increasing the school year, and implementing after-school tutoring programs. The focus on passing the tests means that the teachers are teaching to the test, the same charge made about Texas schools (see below) (Wilgoren 2000a).

One interesting observation is how few students would take part in the various programs. Only 0.1 percent of schoolchildren would participate. Adding in children in charter schools (see below) would raise the percentage to 0.5 percent (Miller 1999).

Although vouchers are generally identified with conservatives (Milton Friedman is, after all, the father of the school voucher ideas, and both Florida governor Jeb Bush and President George W. Bush support the idea), there is a liberal perspective that supports vouchers. This perspective says that students in suburban schools do better than students in public schools because suburban schools do not have the problems of urban schools, in terms of funding and the social problems found in the inner cities (Miller 1999). Matthew Miller and others propose a bargain: Expand the reach to vouchers to many more students and at the same time spend more money on the public schools to help them do better.[35] From an ideological perspective, Friedman's argument is based on the value of liberty, the liberal argument of Miller is based on equality.

Miller (1999) addresses a supposed advantage of private schools: that their costs of educating children are much less than public school costs. But as Miller points out, private schools do not have all the obligations that public schools have to take on, such as special education and school lunch programs. Richard Rothstein (Rothstein and Miles 1995; Rothstein 1997) points out that much of the increase in public school spending is for special education rather than for regular education. Looking at nine school districts selected to represent the range of public school districts (size, location, etc.), he found that the percentage of a school district's budget spent on regular education decreased from 80 percent in 1967 to 58.5 percent percent in 1991 (Rothstein and Miles 1995) to 56.8 percent in 1996 (Rothstein 1997). Rothstein also adjusts increases in education spending for inflation and finds that the increases are much smaller than is commonly assumed. Real growth in per-pupil spending was 2 percent over the 1967–1991 period (Rothstein and Miles 1995). If one looked only at regulation education spending, it would be closer to what private schools spend.

An interesting aspect is the growing support for school vouchers in the African-American community (Moe 1999; Wilgoren 2000c). When Florida began its program in 1999, the Miami branch of the National Urban League supported it, but the NAACP opposed it (Holmes 1999). The Miami Urban League position is that a good education is a civil right and that if urban schools fail to provide it, then vouchers should be used (Gorman 1999). The NAACP position was that vouchers violated the separation of church and state and hurt public schools. The Miami branch's belief is that inner-city public schools are not serving the African-American community well. The Joint Center for Political and Economic Studies found that nearly half of African Americans supported vouchers while nearly 40 percent opposed them (Holmes 1999).

Apart from the results of tests such as the NAEP and the TIMSS, a comparison of public- and private-school students in New York City was made in 1999. The results of New York State tests did show that private school students did better than public school students, and the gap was wider for New York City students than for the state as a whole: 33 percent of New York City public school students passed the test as compared to 44 percent of private school students. However, once students with behavioral or learning problems were excluded, the public school students were more comparable to private school students: the New York City gap decreased to eight points and statewide to just five points. Chester Finn, a strong advocate of vouchers and charter schools, conceded, as he and Diane Ravitch had done before, that private school students were not doing very well (Hartocollis 1999).

So what is the evidence on how well voucher students are doing compared to students who stay in the public schools? The answer is decidedly a mixed one. There is insufficient information to make definitive judgments for two reasons. First, the number of students participating in the voucher programs is, as we have seen, quite small (less than 1 percent). Second, there has not been a lengthy experience with voucher programs (Miller 2000). Nevertheless, there are some data, and there are heated debates over how well the voucher experiment has worked.

A study of three cities released in 2000 found that African-American students who participated in the private voucher program did better on math and reading tests than public school students. One of the authors of the study, and a strong advocate of voucher and choice programs, argued that the results of the study showed that voucher programs may help to reduce the black-white achievement gap (Wyatt 2000; see also Safire 2000).

The study of private voucher students did not go unchallenged. Two weeks after the release of the report, one of the participating research groups, Mathematic Inc., stated that the reports exaggerated the results. In New York City, one of the three cities studied, there were no differences between voucher and public school African-American students. Another problem with the study was that there were, in fact, differences between students and their families who used the vouchers and those who did not. Those who used the vouchers came from families with more education and higher income. Additionally, there was a high dropout rate among the participants that was not accounted for (Zernike 2000b; Rothstein 2000b).

A study of the Cleveland program found very mixed results. There were some small increases in scores for the voucher children, but overall the differences were very minor. A common finding of studies looking at voucher programs is that the parents are satisfied with the education their children are getting. Of course, as with the three cities study mentioned above, the Cleveland evaluations have been challenged on a variety of grounds, including the bias of the researchers (Cohen 1999). It should also be pointed out that the Cleveland voucher program was in existence for a very short period of time before it was shut down by the courts.

Similar comments can be made about evaluations of the **Milwaukee Parental Choice Program** (**MPCP**), the oldest of the school voucher programs. The program, pushed through the Wisconsin legislature by an African-American representative, provided for $2,500 scholarships to selected low-income students. Originally, the program was limited by state law to private, secular schools. Few schools agreed to participate. In 1997, the legislature opened the program to more students and allowed sectarian private schools to participate (Carnoy 2001; Witte 2000). Much controversy brews over how well the MPCP has worked in terms of student achievement. Some studies suggest that there have been small gains for voucher students while other studies have found that there were no gains (Henig 1999). Methodological issues abound (Carnoy 2001; Rouse 1998; Witte 2000). One problem that Carnoy (2001) points to is that private school students are not required to take state achievement tests. This is a major consideration in programs requiring testing such as the one proposed by President George W. Bush (Fletcher 2001). Unless this changes, it is unlikely that we will have a good answer to this question.

There is another argument made in support of voucher programs. This argument is based on the idea that public schools are basically a monopoly and thus do not face competition (Chubb and Moe 1990; Witte 2000). The introduction of competition via vouchers, where schools could potentially lose students and the state funds that accompany them, should, voucher advocates argue, lead to changes by the public schools. That is what Rees (1999) found. For example, the oldest of choice programs is in New York City's East Harlem School District No. 4. The choice program led to increases in reading and math scores in the district and an increase in white students in the district. Jay

Greene (2001) found a similar experience with the Florida voucher program (the A-Plus Accountability and School Choice Program). The evaluation, a joint project of the Manhattan Institute and research institutes at Florida State University and Harvard University, found that schools that had been given a failing grade, and thus were susceptible to losing students through the vouchers, experienced greater increases in their state achievement test scores than other public schools. Greene points out that the state assessment tests scores are strongly related to test scores on a nationally normed test.

## Vouchers from an Equality Perspective

As Witte (2000) points out, there is a value or ideological basis to views toward private school voucher programs. Traditionally, those who support vouchers (conservatives and libertarians) did so on the basis of the value of liberty/freedom. Choice gives parents the freedom to choose where they want their children to be educated and gives educators freedom from stifling bureaucracies. Liberals and populists, more likely to be opposed to vouchers, rely implicitly on the value of equality. They argue that the widespread use of private school vouchers as advocated by Milton Friedman would lead to the demise of public education. Because poor families would not be able to afford to go to private schools (and some elite private schools require tuition well above any proposed plan), the result would be a sorting out of students by race/ethnic group and by class.

But there is the possibility that a middle ground could be found. For example, some conservatives now view equity as an important issue in public education. Here the argument is not just that low-income and minority children are trapped in terrible public schools, though that argument is made. These conservatives also argue that there are considerable inequities in the financing of schools, because a major, if not the major, source of funding for public schools is the local property tax (Keegan 2000) On the other hand, some liberal social scientists supported vouchers as a way of helping students in urban schools. Joseph Viteritti (1999) strongly supports a targeted voucher program, such as the Milwaukee and Florida programs, that limit the vouchers to students from schools that have poor educational achievement outcomes.

## Alternatives to Vouchers

There are alternatives to vouchers. One is smaller class size. Another, which Rothstein (2000a) mentions, is to send students to suburban, middle-class schools where there are "small classes, attractive campuses, highly trained teachers and student bodies where high expectations rub off and become the norm." Rothstein says that voucher advocates are correct in saying that poor children need to go to middle-class schools. But school vouchers will leave too many behind. Instead, he recommends housing vouchers so that poor children can leave their impoverished neighborhoods for the suburbs. A small federal program in 1994 moved some two thousand families from five cities to the suburbs. Rothstein writes that while there have been no studies of academic achievement of students in these families, the families have experienced better health and gotten better jobs, and the teenagers do not commit as many crimes as those in the cities they left.

## Vouchers and Initiative Elections

Vouchers have been the subject of some initiative elections as a form of policy adoption (see chapter 1). One of the early, and most extreme, voucher proposals came in 1993 in California. Albert Shanker, no friend of vouchers, describes the California proposal if the initiative had passed:

> Here's how the new law would work. Each of the 550,000 students already in private schools would be eligible for a voucher worth half the average per-pupil expenditure for a public school student, which is now $5,200. This $2,600 per private school student would come out of the funding now allocated for public education. But that's not all. The law also says that the public school budget must be reduced by *another* $2,600 for every student already in private schools who redeems a voucher; that's called "savings." Let's say only 500,000 private school kids redeem vouchers. At $5,200 per private school student, this means that before a single student transferred out of a public school, public schools would lose $2.6 billion, or 10 percent of the current state education budget.
>
> The hit public schools would take if students moved to private schools is even more devastating. For every *public* school student who transfers to a private school, the public school not only loses the $5,200 average expenditure for that student, but the public education budget must be reduced another $2,600 for the voucher plus another $2,600 for "savings" for a total of $10,400. In other words, every time one student transfers to a private school, the public schools would lose funding for two students. How's that for a way of helping public schools? (Shanker 1993)

Further, the proposal would have allowed anyone to start a school if he or she could bring in twenty-five students; the school would get taxpayer dollars and there would be little oversight. Given the extreme nature of the voucher proposal, it should not have been a surprise that the initiative was decisively defeated, 70–30 percent (Lieberman 1994).

Two well-funded initiatives (Wilgoren 2000e), much more modest than the 1993 California one, nevertheless met a similar fate in the 2000 elections. Thanks to the opposition of teachers unions and other leaders, the two initiatives went down to stinging defeat (Broder 2000). Eight other voucher initiatives suffered similar defeats in previous years (Wilgoren 2000e). Vouchers have become so politically volatile that George W. Bush, the successful Republican candidate for president in 2000, stopped using the phrase during the campaign (Wilgoren 2000e). And when President Bush presented the plan (see below) to Congress in 2001, opposition to vouchers was strong enough that they were not likely to survive the congressional process (Brownstein 2001; Schemo 2001). Nearly thirty states have delayed, postponed, or balked at voucher programs (Wilgoren 2000e).

## Charter Schools

The newest and one of the fastest growing forms of choice is the **charter school**. A charter school is a public school but with some characteristics that distinguish it from both regular public schools and private schools. Voucher proposals would send public school funds, via student enrollees, to private schools. But charter schools are public schools receiving public funds. Charter schools are sanctioned by each state that has a charter law. But they are independent from many of the constraints of regular public schools. Let us look at this in some detail.

Charter schools can be set up by different groups: teachers, the private sector (private firms), parents, community organizations, a school district. The sponsors of charters can be, again depending on the state, a school district, the state itself, or a university (Finn et al. 2000).

Charter schools are granted a charter, essentially an agreement or contract, by the state to undertake educational functions, generally including serving a specific population. Unlike private schools, charter schools cannot charge tuition, and they must accept those who wish to attend (Finn et al. 2000). Also, unlike private schools, charter schools are accountable to the sponsoring institution for producing the results (Finn et al. 2000; see also Center for Education Reform, n.d., "Frequently Asked Questions about Charter Schools").

But charter schools also share some characteristics with private schools, making them a hybrid breed of school. The most important characteristic is that they are independent of many of the requirements of regular schools. That is, once they have been granted the charter, they do not have to meet requirements on curriculum, hiring and firing, calendar, budgeting, and so forth (Finn et al. 2000; see also Center for Education Reform, n.d., "Frequently Asked Questions about Charter Schools").

Charter schools first began in Minnesota in 1991, and by 1997 there were some 700 charter schools with almost 200,000 students attending them. More than half of those students attended charter schools in the three states (California, Michigan, and Arizona) with the most liberal charter school laws (Henig and Sugarman 1999). By 2000, thirty-seven states plus the District of Columbia had charter school laws, with more than 500,000 students attending them (Center for Education Reform, n.d., "Charter School Highlights and Statistics").

As indicated, states vary dramatically on their charter school laws. The Washington-based Center for Education Reform rates states on their charter school laws. The states rated "A" are Arizona, Michigan, Minnesota, the District of Columbia, Delaware, Massachusetts, Texas, California, and Florida. Mississippi is given an "F," and states given a "D" include New Mexico, Hawaii, Wyoming, Arkansas, and Kansas. The liberal or strong laws are ones that allow charter schools to flourish by making them easy to start and providing significant autonomy. Differences in strength of charter school laws are related to the politics of the particular state, such as presence or absence of strong teachers unions (teachers unions support restrictive charter laws) and which party controls the state government (chief executive and legislature). Republicans, in general, have been more supportive of charters than Democrats (Hassel 1999). The Clinton administration was a strong supporter of charter schools; during its tenure the federal government provided funds for startup costs for charters ("Charter Schools Increasing, Report Says" 2000).

One interesting aspect is that not all charter schools succeed. Some have been abysmal failures involving fraud. According to the Center for Education Reform, since 1992 eighty-six charter schools had failed (for various reasons), a 4 percent rate, and another twenty-six were consolidated into public school districts. Another fifty applications for charter schools were never realized. Charter school advocates (such as the Center for Education Reform and Finn et al. 2000) argue that these failures indicate the success of the charter school movement, rather than its collapse. While students may be at a loss if a charter school fails at the beginning or during a school year, the failures winnow out the difficult or incompetent operators. Charter school advocates say that there is failure in the public schools as well, but they continue to operate.

Finally, charter school advocates suggest that studies of charter schools, much more abundant than studies of voucher programs, are invariably positive. Although, again, there are insufficient data on student achievement, the Center for Education Reform argues that charter schools have positive or ripple effects on public schools, that they are accountable and innovative.

Of course, not all the news on charters is good and there is opposition to them. For example, a Michigan State University study said that while charter schools in that state did take on many of the most needy children, they also tended to take students who were the least expensive to educate. This means, to quote Tamar Lewin (1999):

> In Michigan, the state pays schools the same amount, almost $6,000, for each student enrolled. But because younger students are cheaper to educate than teen-agers who need laboratories, athletic equipment, extensive libraries and specialized teachers, most of those who have opened charter schools have chosen to open elementary schools. The study also found that three-quarters of the charter schools offered no special education services, and even the few that did enroll special-needs students provided them with fewer and less costly services than nearby public schools. The report points out that when charters enroll low-cost students and exclude high-cost students, they increase the average costs for public school districts that must still provide the more expensive services.

Another criticism is that some people who choose to send their children to charter schools do so to avoid racial integration or are looking for schools that offer particular religious instruction (see comments of Nicholas C. Biddle in *Talk of the Nation* [2000].

A third criticism is that liberal or strong charter school laws are considered lax, leading to poor results. For example, two studies found that charter school students were getting considerably lower scores on the Texas achievement tests than students in the public schools and that the failure rate among charter schools was much higher in Texas than in the nation overall. The reasons for this result included inexperienced management, inexperienced teachers, and poor curriculum design (Cooper 2000). As a result, a Texas legislative committee recommended a freeze on the number of charter schools in the state ("Freeze Charter Schools, Texas Panel Suggests" 2000).

A further problem is one of accountability. Charter schools are supposed to meet the requirements set forth in their charter and then be evaluated in five years. One question that arises is whether students in charter schools show improvement in test scores. The answer, as with public schools and voucher schools, is mixed. Further, while a number of charter schools have not had their charter renewed—eighty-six by 2000—most were because of financial problems and not academic failure (Zernike 2001a).

## Conclusion

As the case study indicates, there is a lot of ferment and movement for change occurring in America's educational system. Some people have recommended more reliance on competition, new school structures (e.g., charter schools) and private schools, aided by voucher programs. The research on voucher programs, heavily laden by ideological perspectives, has shown mixed results. There does seem to be some competitive effect and parents of children in voucher programs appear to be satisfied with their children's schooling. Much of the rhetoric in education has consisted of bashing the public schools.

Yet there is evidence that even in disadvantaged public schools, children can learn, and better than expected (Education Trust 1999). There is also fascinating data about the impact of class size, especially in the early grades, on educational achievement (U.S. Department of Education 1999).

Two major studies, one in Tennessee and the other in Wisconsin, have documented the very positive impact of small class size on achievement, not just in those early grades (kindergarten through third grade) but continuing through the end of high school.

The most prominent of the studies was the **Tennessee STAR (Student/ Teacher Achievement Ratio)** program. This was an experiment that was conducted from 1985 to 1987. Seven thousand children in grades K-3 were randomly assigned to one of three class sizes: 13–17, 22–25, and 22–25, with a teaching assistant. Students in the 13–17-size classes achieved better than students in the larger class and the differences were maintained throughout high school even though the students returned to regular-size classes after third grade. Bob Chase writes:

> Five years later, STAR found that children who'd been in smaller classes continued to outperform others in reading, math, and science, even though they, too, were now

in larger classes. By eighth grade, in fact, kids who'd attended the smaller classes in K-3 were at least one full year ahead of their peers academically. This is huge.

Today, students in the study have begun donning their caps and gowns for their high school graduations. And yet, some *14 years later*, those from the smaller K-3 classes continue to reap benefits. A greater percentage are graduating from high school than students from the larger classes. Their dropout rate is lower and their GPAs higher. A greater number are ranked within the top 25 percent of their class and have taken the SAT or ACT exams.

Most impressive are the strides made by minority students. The initial STAR project showed that, while students of all backgrounds benefit from smaller classes, those who gain the most academically are poor, minority, inner-city, and rural children. Now STAR has found that, when class sizes are reduced, the gap that usually exists between black and white students taking college entrance exams is cut by more than half as well. (Chase 1999, emphasis in original)[36]

Chase and others (Feldman 1999 and Molnar and Achilles 2000) point out that not only were minority students helped greatly by the smaller class size but the gains were greater than those reported for voucher programs.

Wisconsin has a program, **Student Achievement Guarantee in Education (SAGE** ), that has reported similar results, with K-3 grades (Molnar et al. 2000). The SAGE program, with a student–teacher ratio of 51–1, exists in eighty schools, and the Wisconsin legislature has allocated funds to expand it to 400 schools (Wisconsin Education Association Council 2000). Evaluation of class size reductions in California also shows positive results, though noting problems in implementation (Stecher and Bohrnstedt 2000).

An important problem associated with reducing class size is the shortage of teachers, especially highly qualified teachers. In 1998, Congress provided funds for hiring new teachers in support of class reduction (U.S. Department of Education 1999). This move was part of the Clinton administration initiative to help hire 100,000 teachers, analogous to the 1994 program to hire 100,000 new police officers. Like everything else about education (and other policy areas), the research on the effects of class size have not gone unchallenged (see Economic Policy Institute 2000 for a discussion of this debate).

Education was a prominent policy issue during the 2000 presidential campaign. Keeping to his promise and building on the experience in Texas and Florida, in January 2001, President George W. Bush presented his education proposals to Congress that he wanted incorporated into the reauthorization of the Elementary and Secondary Education Act. Entitled *No Child Left Behind*,[37] the proposal focused dramatically on poor children (Wilgoren 2001). The proposal would require states to annually test their children in grades three through eight using state assessment tests. Additionally, a sample of students in grades four and eight would be given the NAEP tests as a way of assessing the difficulty or ease and reliability of the state assessment tests. This is apparent in the light of an analysis of 1999 NAEP scores. For example, the state achievement tests in Texas showed a narrowing of the gap between whites and minorities and between the high and low achievers. However, the NAEP test results for Texas students showed no such decrease in the gap (Zernike 2001c).[38] States would develop rewards and sanctions based on school performance on the assessment tests. The proposal calls for focusing on reading in the early grades. States would be given more freedom in how they use Title I funds, and choice will be promoted: charter schools, information for parents, and so forth. Funds will be made available for schools that have problems.

Accountability and assessment are the heart of the Bush proposal. Schools that fail—do not show improvement by the third year after the program begins—would lose a portion of their Title I funds. Those funds would then be used for vouchers (equal to about $1,400) that students from those schools could use to enroll in private schools (Bush 2001).

The voucher portion was the most controversial part of the Bush proposal. One of the more important portions, but less publicized, was a provision for a $5,000 tuition tax credit that would be available to those who sent their children to private schools. This would not be limited to poor children from failing schools (Schemo 2001). The tax credit would come in the form of an education savings account, where families could put up to $5,000 a year in the account to pay for school-related expenses (Bush 2001; Schemo 2001).[39]

President Bush's plan faces some obstacles, both of passage and implementation. For example, while states have increased their use of standardized testing for purposes of assessment, promotion, and graduation, only fifteen states (as of February 2001) tested students in all those grades, and even then there is variety in the quality of the tests. Developing tests for those grades will take time and money (Olson 2001).

Others have argued that the increased emphasis on testing (Sacks 1999) will have the effect of harming minority and poor students. A study of Texas and its use of the Texas Assessment of Academic Skills (TAAS), touted by George W. Bush during his campaign, resulted in higher dropout rates among African-American and Hispanic students. Further, the claim is made that the increased emphasis on standardized testing leads to teaching to the test and neglecting other curriculum elements (Orfield and Wald 2000; Sacks 1999).

Perceptions and expectations are also important. In 1980, Eugene Lang, a successful businessman, was giving the graduation speech at his old elementary school in the East Harlem area of New York. It was now a virtually all-black school. He tore up the speech and vowed that he would pay the college costs for that graduation class if the students would stay in high school. He and others followed up his pledge by continuing to work with students who were about to drop out. Over 90 percent of the students graduated and went to college because someone believed in them and cared. Other businessmen have followed this adopt-a-school program (E. Brown 1985; Salholz 1986; Schorr 1988).

A popular film in 1988, *Stand and Deliver*, based on the true experiences of Jaime Escalante, reinforces this message of hope and belief. Escalante, a math teacher in a poor Los Angeles high school, taught advanced-placement calculus to a group of lower-income Hispanic students. They all took the advanced placement test and passed. The Education Testing Service, which administered the test, thought the students must have cheated and had them retake the test, which they again passed. The "trick" was that the teacher believed that his students could do the work, and the students believed in themselves.

> Our children *will* meet our expectations. What would happen if we really believed it? If the people who run schools believed it? If teachers everywhere believed it?
> We are truly disadvantaged if we allow the message of "Stand and Deliver" to go unheard. (Solovy and Brieschkeis 1988)

---

## Key Concepts

*A Nation at Risk*

*Brown v. Board of Education of Topeka, Kansas* (1954)

charter school

Civil Rights Act (1964)

de facto segregation

direct provision of services

educational choice

efficiency

Elementary and Secondary Education Act (ESEA) (1965)

*Equality of Educational Opportunity*

equity

*Goals 2000: Educate America Act* (1994)

Head Start

incentives

integration

liberty

magnet schools

Milwaukee Parental Choice Program (MPCP)

National Assessment of Education Progress (NAEP)

National Commission on Excellence in Education (NCEE)

*No Child Left Behind*

*Plessy v. Ferguson* (1896)

powers

security

segregation

separate but equal

Student Achievement Guarantee in Education (SAGE)

student engagement

*Swann v. Charlotte-Mecklenburg County Schools* (1971)

Tennessee STAR (Student/Teacher Achievement Ratio)

Third International Mathematics and Science Study (TIMSS)

voucher system

white flight

## Reflections

1. A major theme of the chapter is that one of the most important specific goals of education policy is school achievement. Do you agree with this emphasis? Do you think this is the appropriate emphasis for public policy? What other specific policy goals do you think are important?

2. The reform movement had its impetus in declines in educational achievement, as judged by a variety of tests. Do you think educational achievement has declined? If so, why do you think those declines occurred? Were they due to changes in the student population, teaching, or curricula? Some have argued that the declines are more perceptual than real. Where do you stand on this? What do you think about international comparisons that show American students, at best, in the middle of other nations in terms of achievement?

3. Some of you may have gone to a private elementary or secondary school. How would you compare them to public schools? Which of the arguments about the advantages of private schools do you think is the strongest? Which is the weakest? Why? Do you think we should rely more on private schools to educate our children? Do you think we should enact a tuition tax credit or voucher plan? Why or why not? A number of states are allowing choice among public schools. Do you think this is a good idea? Why or why not? Do you think charter schools are a good idea?

4. President Bush has proposed a policy, directed at schools with low-achieving students, that would include more assistance, state assessment tests, and vouchers for students if the schools do not show improvement. How well do you think this policy, if adopted, would work?

5. What changes would you like to see in our public schools? What reforms or proposals do you think have the best chance of achieving those changes?

## Notes

1. Louann Bierlein (1993) argues that the major goals of education policy are equity, liberty, efficiency, and excellence.

2. Prior to school consolidation, there were more than 50,000 school districts.

3. Proposition 13 was a property-tax-cutting proposal approved by California voters in 1978.

4. For an extensive discussion of Head Start, see Zigler and Muenchow (1992).

5. The law allows all parents to deduct part of the cost of education from taxes, seemingly

neutral between public and private schools though actually favoring private school students (Hoffman 1985).

6. For a brief history of the development of education in the United States, see Bierlein (1993).

7. A similar phenomenon was seen in health care, where a 1935 report on problems of meeting the cost of health care could be written today with little change.

8. There is a statistically significant difference in many of the earlier numbers and the 1999 results. Looking at the table, one would likely guess that not much change has taken place. The reason the modest changes are statistically significant is that the sample size is very large, around 17,000 for each test.

9. The following paragraphs rely primarily on the National Commission report. Others issued before and after make essentially the same points, but the NCEE report was the most influential.

10. Obviously, in neither case did this happen. The United States clearly outstripped the Soviet Union and Russia scientifically. The great Asian miracle feared in the 1980s turned to stagnation in the 1990s as the United States grew faster than virtually all other nations.

11. The recommendations are similar to the 1958 report mentioned above.

12. Ironically, the school reform movement and the requirements of testing created additional burdens for teachers.

13. Note the resemblance between the Texas law and the National Commission recommendations.

14. By accountability, using an example from Florida legislation, Wise meant the "establishment of skills for each grade and the use of tests based on specific theories of testing" (Wise 1979, p. 15).

15. This notion of recognizing that things have gotten better permeates this book. It is, indeed, one of the themes of this book.

16. Allan Bloom's *The Closing of the American Mind* (1987) makes this point about higher education.

17. The issue of civil rights and equality is discussed more fully in chapter 9.

18. President Harry Truman desegregated the armed forces in 1948. Further, the Democratic national platform in 1948 had a strong civil rights plank. This led to a walkout by southern Democrats, who formed the Dixiecrat Party with South Carolina's Strom Thurmond as its presidential candidate.

19. The Civil Rights Act is discussed more fully in chapter 9.

20. There have been critiques of this study. The best of these is by William Ryan (1971). For example, the report found that differences in per-pupil spending had little power to explain differences in achievement. Ryan argued, however, that the sociologist that chaired the study, James S. Coleman, did not really test the relationship but controlled for it. That is, per-pupil expenditures in Grosse Pointe, MI, were considerably higher than in East Detroit. The differences were so high that they would overwhelm all other relationships. So the researchers compared wealthy district to wealthy district and poor district to poor district, but not wealthy and poor districts. The relationship was never tested. Later scholars did confirm the general results of the Coleman findings (Ravitch 1985).

21. The finding that minority students achieved better when they were in integrated schools and that white student achievement did not suffer seemed to support busing to integrate the schools. In 1975, Coleman wrote a paper stating that he never recommended busing and that busing was probably causing "white flight." For a discussion of the controversy over Coleman's white flight study, see Glazer (1984).

22. The one exception to this was in Boston, where it appeared that the school system was deliberately keeping the races separate. That was the rationale for the federal court takeover of the school system.

23. According to another report, almost 70 percent of blacks in 1994 attended schools with largely minority enrollment, contrasted with 78 percent in 1968. See Celis (1994).

24. There was only a small increase in this measure among whites. Further, Armor (1992) argues that, given the absolute increase in black achievement as measured by the NAEP studies, one could argue that the school systems are not doing such a bad job and that school reform might not be so critical as it seems. He further makes the point that perhaps some of the problems with the education system are due to changing dynamics of white families. See the chapter on welfare policy.

25. However, students in integrated schools still performed better than students in segregated schools, and students in both settings showed improved performance.

26. Gary Orfield conducted the study of Hispanics in San Francisco.

27. One has to ask, however, whether the proposals were more than symbolic politics to show conservatives that the administration's heart was in the right place.

28. Friedman overstates the monopoly argument in several ways. First, private schools have provided an outlet for parents who are dissatisfied with some aspect of the public school system. "White flight" to avoid busing by moving to the suburbs was another possibility. Both are examples of what Albert Hirschman (1970) calls the "exit" option. If you do not like a service or a product, you leave. Finally, many school bond issues have failed because of distrust or dislike of the school system. This is what Hirschman calls the "voice" option. It, too, sends a signal to the school system.

29. Similar market reform proposals were presented in the health care, poverty, and environmental chapters. The similarity in structure and analysis of these proposals is not coincidental.

30. For a more contemporary version of this perspective, see Zihala (2001).

31. Brimelow refers to the U.S. Constitution, and, of course, he is correct. However, the responsibility for education is found in all state constitutions.

32. According to the Congressional Budget Office (1986), there were parallel declines in achievement in public and private schools, but because testing of private school students was limited, the decline in private schools was less well documented.

33. Black inner-city students in the Catholic schools do better on achievement tests than do such students in the public schools. Defenders of the public schools argue that parents who send their children to Catholic schools are better motivated. Further, Catholic schools can expel troublesome students. See Chira (1991c).

34. The rationale for doing this is that there was less room for improvement on the tests for the high achievers than for low achievers. Let's say that there was a fifteen-item test in a particular area. The high achievers averaged eleven items correct versus five correct items for the low achievers. Two years later, the high achievers averaged thirteen items correct versus ten items correct for the low achievers. The actual gain in raw scores is greater for the low achievers than for the high achievers. But Chubb and Moe contend that because there was less room for improvement, they should be credited with greater gains. The controversy (see the debate in Rasell and Rothstein 1993) is partly over the validity of such choices.

35. President George W. Bush's proposal and the Florida proposal have similar provisions.

36. It should be noted that Chase is the president of the National Education Association, which has opposed vouchers and is, obviously, a strong supporter of public schools.

37. "No Child Left Behind" is the motto of the Children's Defense Fund.

38. This may substantiate the claim that teachers in Texas focused on the state assessment test, which accounts for the improvements seen.

39. Generally speaking, liberals, Democrats, and the education establishment tend to oppose vouchers because they fear it will lead to the abandonment or at least the underfunding of public education. However, there is evidence that conservatives, including Christian conservatives, and Republicans also oppose vouchers, though not for the same reasons. Suburban voters do not want vouchers to undermine their schools, and conservative Christians do not want government intrusion that often accompanies government funding (a problem they also have with President George W. Bush's faith-based initiative). Tax credits, because they do not threaten anything, are more popular among this group. See Wildman (2001).

# 9 Equality: The Second American Revolution

*The equal-results model of social regulation, when applied to civil rights policy, has clashed with the vision of a color-blind Constitution. As a consequence, American society is polarized, with both blocs—the supporters of equal individual opportunity and of equal group results—claiming moral grievance and social injustice.* (Graham 1992, p. 63)

*Now the Star-bellied Sneetches*
*Had stars upon thars.*
*The plain-bellied Sneetches*
*Had none upon thars.*

(Dr. Seuss 1961, p. 3)

The delightful children's story *The Sneetches*, tells of a group of creatures, the Sneetches, some of whom were born with a star on their bellies and some who were not. Those with the stars thought they were better than those without them. As a result, the plain-bellied Sneetches were excluded from various activities, such as beach parties, with the star-bellied Sneetches. Then Sylvester McMonkey McBean came up with a machine that could put stars on bellies, for which he charged a few dollars. The plain-bellied Sneetches, oppressed for years, willingly gave McBean the money and had stars put on their bellies.

The old star-belly Sneetches were horrified because there was no longer any way to tell who was better than whom. McBean then came up to them and, for a few more dollars, offered to take the stars off. They accepted the offer, now declaring that plain-bellied Sneetches were better. McBean continued to go from group to group, offering to take stars off or put them back on, raising his fees each time. There ensued a mad dash of all the Sneetches, in and out of McBean's machine. Finally, the Sneetches' money was all gone and no one knew which group they belonged to. McBean left the beach, smiling and shaking his head, saying: "No, you can't teach a Sneetch."

But the story ends happily. The Sneetches, wiser if poorer, realize that it does not matter whether or not a Sneetch has a star; a Sneetch is a Sneetch.

Dr. Seuss's story did not use either the term "civil rights" or the term "equality." But it did capture, as the civil rights movement was beginning to gain momentum, much of the essentials of the idea of equality.

The United States has always been ambivalent about equality. Our fundamental documents have embodied this contradiction in viewpoints. The Declaration of Independence contains the powerful statement that "We hold these Truths to be self-evident, that all Men are created equal. . . ." At the same time, the paragraph denouncing the slave trade was removed in order to obtain agreement from the southern colonies on independence.[1] In addition, the writers of the Declaration knew that there were differences between people.

The 1787 version of the U.S. Constitution recognized, again because of the necessity of compromise, the existence of both slavery and the slave trade.[2] One can argue that our original founding documents, while asserting liberty, passed over equality.

The change in our understanding of the nation's founding came in 1863. In his dedication at Gettysburg, President Abraham Lincoln placed emphasis on equality: "Fourscore and seven years ago, our forefathers brought forth on this continent, a new nation, conceived in Liberty, and dedicated to the proposition that all men are created equal." As Garry Wills (1992) tells the story, Lincoln's speech had a transforming effect on how we understand the nation's founding:

> Lincoln is here not only to sweeten the air of Gettysburg, but to clear the infected atmosphere of American history itself, tainted with official sins and inherited guilt. He would cleanse the Constitution—not, as William Lloyd Garrison had, by burning an instrument that countenanced slavery. He altered the document from within, by appeal from its letter to the spirit, subtly changing the recalcitrant stuff of that legal compromise, bringing it to its own indictment. By implicitly doing this, he performed one of the most daring acts of open-air sleight-of-hand ever witnessed by the unsuspecting. Everyone in that vast throng of thousands was having his or her intellectual pocket picked. The crowd departed with a new thing in its ideological luggage, that new constitution Lincoln had substituted for the one they brought with them. They walked off, from those curving graves on the hillside, under a changed sky, into a different America. Lincoln had revolutionized the Revolution, giving people a new past to live with that would change their future indefinitely. (Wills 1992, p. 38)

The post–Civil War Amendments to the Constitution (the **Thirteenth Amendment**, the **Fourteenth Amendment,** and the **Fifteenth Amendment**) were, in a sense, a second American revolution, embodying the values of equality. But as Gunnar Myrdal (1944) observed, American rhetoric and values clashed with American practice. Eventually, he predicted, the practice would conform to the values and the rhetoric. And, to a certain extent, Myrdal's prediction and Lincoln's transformation have occurred. But only to a certain extent.

## Problem Identification: Equality Defined

**Equality** means to treat things or people the same. Sometimes it means treating people in similar circumstances the same and treating people in different circumstances differently. Equality as a policy area is synonymous with **civil rights**, which provides for equal protection of the laws (Cummings and Wise 1985). Additionally, equality or civil rights often refers to the group rather than to the individual. This emphasis on group rights, a defining characteristic of this policy area, leads to much of its controversy. Finally, equality was identified in chapter 1 as one of the three major core values of political ideology. We distinguished between three meanings of equality. In this section, those meanings will be elaborated upon. Table 9.1 presents a timetable of major government actions affecting equality.

## Political Equality

The first of these three meanings of equality is **political equality**. In the United States, political equality has usually been related to voting—the most basic act of democracy. The first major thrust toward political equality came in the 1820s, when the property qualification for voting was eliminated by the states. That is, one no longer had to own property to have the right to vote.

The second step toward political equality came with the Fifteenth Amendment, which gave the former slaves the right to vote. Section 1 of the amendment states that "The right of citizens of the United States to vote shall not be denied or abridged by the United States or by any State on account of race, color, or previous condition of servitude." One would have thought that this would have settled the issue. However, following the end of Reconstruction (after the controversial election of 1876), the southern states passed legislation, such as the poll tax and literacy tests, that made it next to impossible for African Americans to vote. Additionally, the use of terror through such organizations as the Ku Klux Klan convinced even the most courageous of African Americans that voting was a dangerous enterprise.

The next movement toward political equality focused on women. Women had won the right to vote in many of the western states, but not in the eastern states. The suffrage movement culminated in the **Nineteenth Amendment** in 1920, giving women the right to vote.

As the twentieth century wore on, much of the progress toward political equality for African Americans came through the courts. The Supreme Court decided, for example, that the white primary was illegal.[3] As a result of the civil rights movement of the 1950s and 1960s, the **Voting Rights Act (1965)** was passed. The act suspended literacy tests and other barriers if African-American registration was below a certain percentage. It called for federal registrars to go to those states and voting districts and register black voters; it also provided for penalties for interfering with those trying to vote. The Voting Rights Act had a powerful impact. It led to a significant increase in African-American voters and to an enormous increase in the number of black elected officials (though not at the highest levels; see Sack 2001). The Voting Rights Act has been extended through the year 2007, and problems remain, though the impact cannot be denied.

In terms of voting rights, the most recent change was the passage in 1971 of the **Twenty-Sixth Amendment**, which gave eighteen-year-olds the right to vote. This was during the Vietnam War, when many of our eighteen-, nineteen-, and twenty-year-olds were asked to go to a foreign country and possibly lose their life. On the other hand, they had no participation in decisions that might lead to that outcome.

An interesting application of voting rights and the equal protection of the laws clause of the Fourteenth Amendment came in 2000. In the highly disputed election of 2000, the U.S. Supreme Court, by a 5–4 decision in *Bush v. Gore*, declined the request of the Democratic presidential candidate, Vice President Al Gore, to allow recounts in some Florida counties. The majority's decision was that because there was no standard for judging voter intent, different standards would be used in different Florida counties (Sullivan 2000). Further, a number of African Americans charged that they were denied the right to vote or that they had to go through state police checkpoints and show more identification than whites (Martin 2000; see also Guinier 2001). The next few years will likely see debates over voter equality and voting technology.

A second meaning of political equality refers to **representation**. This first became an issue at the state level when it was noted that rural districts with small populations had the same number of representatives in state legislatures as urban districts with much larger populations. While each vote in an electoral district had a very small impact on the final outcome, the vote of a rural resident was worth considerably more than that of the urban resident. In 1962, in *Baker v. Carr*, the Supreme Court held that state legislative districts had to be equalized in size. This was the "one man, one vote" decision. Since that time, state districts have been reapportioned after every census to roughly equalize their size.

But it has also been noted that while the voting rights of African Americans have been assured, their representation has not.[4] Table 9.2 presents data comparing demographic groups to the total population. As can be seen, women and minorities are underrepresented, based on their proportion in the total population, in both the U.S. House and Senate. The number of women in the Senate was at an all-time high after the 2000 elections.

One can see many of the problems of equality surrounding the issue of representation. The increase in the number of African-American members of the House of Representatives was possible because southern states, complying with the Voting Rights Act, carved out new congressional districts creating majority African-American districts. The intended result, increased African-American representation, was realized. However, in 1993, the Su-

Table 9.1

## Major Governmental Actions in Civil Rights History

| Year | Event |
|------|-------|
| 1865 | Thirteenth Amendment ends slavery. |
| 1868 | Fourteenth Amendment extends due process and equal protection of the laws to the states. |
| 1870 | Fifteenth Amendment gives former slaves the right to vote. |
| 1896 | *Plessy v. Ferguson:* Court holds that "separate but equal" facilities for blacks and whites are constitutional. |
| 1920 | Nineteenth Amendment gives women the right to vote. |
| 1954 | *Brown v. Board of Education of Topeka, Kansas:* U.S. Supreme Court orders end to de jure segregation in schools. |
| 1957 | Federal troops sent to desegregate Little Rock, AR, high school. |
|      | Civil Rights Act creates Civil Rights Commission. |
| 1960 | Civil Rights Act. |
| 1961 | President Kennedy issues executive order prohibiting discrimination in federally funded programs and calling for efforts to hire minorities. |
| 1962 | Executive order requiring end of housing discrimination. |
| 1963 | Equal Pay Act. |
| 1964 | Civil Rights Act. |
|      | Twenty-fourth Amendment ends poll tax. |
|      | Urban Mass Transportation Act requires access by handicapped and elderly to systems receiving federal funds. |
| 1965 | Voting Rights Act. |
|      | Executive order requiring affirmative action on federal contracts. |
| 1968 | Open Housing Act forbids discrimination in rental or sales. |
|      | Architectural Barriers Act requires handicap access to buildings constructed with the assistance of federal funds. |
| 1971 | *Swann v. Charlotte–Mecklenburg County Schools:* U.S. Supreme Court approves use of busing to end segregation in schools. |
|      | Twenty-sixth Amendment lowers the voting age to eighteen. |
|      | *Griggs v. Duke Power Company:* U.S. Supreme Court rules that employers must demonstrate that specific job qualifications are related to business necessity. |
| 1972 | Equal Rights Amendment approved by Congress and sent to states for ratification. |
|      | Title IX of the Equal Educational Opportunities Act. |
|      | Civil Rights Act extends prohibition of discrimination to states and local governments. |
| 1973 | Vocational Rehabilitation Act prohibits discrimination against handicapped people who are "otherwise qualified." |
| 1975 | Education of All Handicapped Children Act. |
|      | Developmental Disabilities Assistance and Bill of Rights Act. |
| 1977 | Public Works Employment Act provides for minority set-asides. |
| 1978 | *Bakke v. Board of Regents of the University of California:* U.S. Supreme Court rules that race cannot be used as the sole criterion for admission to colleges. |
| 1979 | *United Steelworkers v. Weber:* U.S. Supreme Court approves voluntary affirmative action plan. |

1980    *Fullilove v. Klutznick:* U.S. Supreme Court approves minority set-asides in contracting.

1982    Voting Rights Act extension.

        Equal Rights Amendment fails by three states to be ratified before time limit.

1984    *Memphis Fire Department v. Stotts:* U.S. Supreme Court says that whites cannot be laid off before blacks who have less seniority.

        *Grove City College v. Bell:* U.S. Supreme Court limits use of antidiscrimination laws to specific programs receiving federal assistance.

1986    *Wygant v. Jackson Board of Education:* U.S. Supreme Court endorses affirmative action but also protects whites from layoffs based on race.

1988    Civil Rights Restoration Act overturns *Grove City College* decision.

        Fair Housing Act extends protections to families and the handicapped.

1989    *Richmond v. Croson:* U.S. Supreme Court declares minority preference programs as suspect.

        *Wards Cove v. Atonio:* U.S. Supreme Court holds that those charging discrimination must prove intent.

1990    Americans with Disabilities Act.

1991    Civil Rights Act overturns 1989 Supreme Court decisions.

1992    *Freeman v. Pitts:* U.S. Supreme Court eases desegregation requirements.

        *Presley v. Etowah County Commission:* U.S. Supreme Court ends need for federal preclearance when election districts are changed.

1993    *Shaw v. Reno:* U.S. Supreme Court rules that unusually shaped legislative districts based solely on race are unconstitutional unless they are narrowly tailored and serve a compelling state interest.

1995    University of California regents ban affirmative action programs on university's campuses.

        *Miller v. Johnson:* U.S. Supreme Court rules that the majority African-American district in Georgia is unconstitutional and agrees to hear similar cases from Texas and North Carolina.

        *Adarand Construction v. Pena:* U.S. Supreme Court rules that affirmative action and racial preference programs are unconstitutional unless narrowly tailored and serve a compelling state interest.

        Clinton administration issues affirmative action guidelines for federal agencies to follow in the wake of the *Adarand* decision.

1996    California voters approve California Civil Rights Initiative ending affirmative action in that state.

        *Hopwood v. Texas:* U.S. appeals court rules that race can never be a factor in college admissions decisions. U.S. Supreme Court declines to hear appeal, and decision applies to the three states of the appellate court's jurisdiction.

1997    President Clinton issues executive order establishing initiative on race.

        Voters in Houston, TX, defeat anti-affirmative action initiative.

1998    *Piscataway* case settled out of court.

        Voters in state of Washington approve initiative ending affirmative action programs.

2000    Florida governor Jeb Bush issues executive order banning affirmative action programs. State adopts a "top 20 percent admissions" program, following the lead of Texas and California.

Table 9.2

**Representation of Women and Minorities in Congress, 2001**

|  | House | % of body | Senate | % of body | % of population |
|---|---|---|---|---|---|
| Women | 59 | 13.6 | 13 | 13 | 51.1 |
| African American | 36 | 8.3 | 0 | 0 | 12.8 |
| Hispanic | 19 | 4.4 | 0 | 0 | 11.9 |
| Asians and Pacific Islander | 4 | 0.9 | 2 | 2 | 4.1 |
| American Indian | 1 | 0.2 | 1 | 1 | 0.9 |

*Sources:* Hirschfeld (2001); U.S. Census Bureau (2000).

preme Court started inquiring into the redistricting, noting that the new districts were oddly shaped. They ruled in 1993, in ***Shaw v. Reno***, that these oddly shaped districts may have violated the voting rights of white voters (Greenhouse 1993). The Court seemed to have held that such districts would balkanize or fragment the electorate. But as Randall Kennedy (1993) points out in the case of North Carolina, no African American had been elected to Congress until after the 1990 redistricting. Even with the redistricting, ten of North Carolina's representatives were white. The U.S. Supreme Court has continued to look askance at congressional districts designed for reasons of racial equality. The redistricting that will come subsequent to the 2000 census will also consider, in some ways, the racial/ethnic breakdown of the country (Edsall 2001).

One way to increase African-American representation without resorting to creative drawing of legislative districts might be to experiment with some of the ideas of Lani Guinier. Guinier, a law professor at the University of Pennsylvania, was President Clinton's first choice to be assistant U.S. attorney general for civil rights. Her nomination was derailed because of controversy concerning her views. Her opponents labeled her a "quota queen." But Guinier's ideas were misrepresented and have merit.

Guinier (1994) makes two important points concerning political equality. First, she opposes legislative districts carved out especially for African Americans. On the other hand, she sees the majority-rule system as tyrannical, tracing the idea back to the writing of James Madison. What she recommends, instead of the winner-take-all system, is a more cooperative system, where the majority works with the minority. The task is to create a system in which minority preferences can be taken into consideration, especially in a heterogeneous country such as the United States.

Guinier's solution is **cumulative voting**, which would allow voters, in whatever context, to cast more than one vote in an election, with each voter getting the same number of votes (thus supporting the one-man-one-vote criterion). Guinier uses the example of a high school prom where students were allowed to vote on ten songs that would be played during the dance. Because African Americans were a small minority of the senior class, their choices most likely would not have been selected. As a result, two racially separate proms were held.

Under cumulative voting, each student would be able to cast ten votes. However, the student could decide how to allocate the ten votes. The student could vote for ten different songs, or cast ten votes for one song. This cumulative voting would express the intensity of feeling for a song—or candidate—and would also give more weight to minority viewpoints. Thus the threshold for winning would be lowered, and minorities would be represented. Additionally, cumulative voting might encourage cross-racial coalitions. In any event, cumulative voting would force minority interests to be represented. Guinier points out that corporations often use cumulative voting, and the Reagan and Bush administrations approved of such plans to protect minority rights under the Voting Rights Act.

## Equality of Opportunity

The second major meaning of equality is **equality of opportunity**. At its simplest, equality of opportunity means lack of discrimination, as in equal opportunity laws and regulations. More basically, it refers to allowing people an opportunity to achieve to the limits of their capability, regardless of race, sex, and so on. In some cases, equality of opportunity might require devoting extra resources to a group or a person. It is here that equal opportunity begins to meld into the third and most controversial form of equality (discussed below).

Equality of opportunity was the original, fundamental basis for the civil rights movement.[5] The effort to desegregate the schools, detailed in chapter 8, was based on the notion that separate school systems, mandated by law in the southern states, led to inequalities in education and therefore in the opportunity for African Americans to succeed in life. *Brown v. Board of Education of Topeka, Kansas* (**1954**) stated that separate was inherently unequal. Similarly, the **Equal Pay Act (1963)** mandated that women be paid the same as men for doing the same jobs.

The embodiment of the move toward equality of opportunity, from a legal standpoint, was the **Civil Rights Act (1964)**. Passed in the wake of the March on Washington in 1963 and the assassination of President Kennedy, the Civil Rights Act contained several major provisions. Title II forbids discrimination in public accommodations, such as motels, movie theaters, and restaurants. Title VI provides that federal funds could be canceled in educational institutions receiving federal assistance that did not comply with federal antidiscrimination policy. Title VII forbids employment or union discrimination by the federal government or the private sector by reason of race, national origin, religion, or sex.[6]

Among other moves toward equality of opportunity were two efforts, one unsuccessful, the other successful. The unsuccessful effort was the **Equal Rights Amendment (ERA)**. To understand its origins, we need to go back to the creation of the United States.

As noted above, the Declaration of Independence powerfully stated that "all Men are created equal." In the narrow interpretation of "men," women were excluded. Abigail Adams exhorted her husband, John, who was attending the Continental Congress considering separation from England, to "remember the ladies" (Andrews 1995; Simon and Danziger 1991). At the time of the Declaration, women had few legal rights.

The first stage in the development of the women's movement came during the first half of the nineteenth century. While women were pushing for their own equality, they also became part of the abolitionist movement to end slavery, though not always accepted in that movement. However, the Fourteenth Amendment, although giving rights to the former slaves, made no mention of gender.

After the Civil War, the focus of the women's movement became winning the right to vote. Suffragists were eventually successful, as mentioned above, when the Nineteenth Amendment was ratified in 1920. It was hoped that by winning the vote and full political participation, women would soon gain other rights. However, the suffrage amendment did little to change the status of women.

Apart from working for specific changes in laws affecting women (such as divorce), a major concern was obtaining passage of an equal rights amendment. Such an amendment was first suggested in 1937 and made its appearance in Congress in 1938, but was not approved for state ratification until 1972, even though the Democratic and Republican national party platforms supported it.

The amendment, paralleling the wording of the Fourteenth Amendment, read as follows: "Equality of rights under the law shall not be abridged by the United States or by any State on account of sex." The amendment was originally given a seven-year time limit and then another three years.

Why was such an amendment necessary? After all, as we have seen, the Civil Rights Act of 1964 included sex as one of the grounds against which one could not discriminate. However, the courts have not treated sex-based discrimination the same as race-based discrimination. Race is a "suspect classification" in that only a compelling state interest is required for any potentially discriminatory policy or statute. This is based on the inclusion of race in the Fourteenth Amendment. However, the courts have held that sex is not automatically a suspect classification. That is, there might be lesser reason for making gender distinctions. The ERA would have made gender a suspect classification.

Given the widespread support for the ERA, rapid ratification by the necessary two-thirds of the state legislatures was seen as a foregone conclusion.

However, the ERA soon ran into a groundswell of opposition, much of it from other women. Some women felt that there needed to be some protections for women, at least until full equality was achieved. Other women felt that the ERA, and the women's groups that supported it, such as the National Organization of Women, were downgrading the role of mother and homemaker. It was working women, some thought, who were behind the move toward equality. Others saw the ERA as removing distinctions that should remain. For example, questions were raised as to whether women would be subject to the military draft if the draft were reinstated. Would restrooms have to become unisex restrooms? Conservatives saw the ERA and the women's movement as being behind the breakdown of the traditional family and the increase in divorce. For whatever reason, the ERA failed ratification by three states.[7]

The more successful, and latest, addition to civil rights and equality was on behalf of handicapped or disabled persons.[8] During the 1970s and 1980s, legislation gave more rights to the disabled. This culminated in the 1990 **Americans with Disabilities Act** (**ADA**), probably the most far-reaching civil rights act since the 1964 Civil Rights Act.[9] The Americans with Disabilities Act contains three major provisions: Title I prohibits discrimination in employment against an otherwise qualified person on account of disabilities. Title II prohibits discrimination against the disabled in the provision of public services. Title III prohibits discrimination against the disabled in public accommodations (Berkowitz 1994).[10]

In the mid- and late 1990s, the ADA came under attack as the Republican-controlled Congress sought to narrow the scope of the program. They argued that the act was poorly written, has produced many unjustified lawsuits, and covers too many Americans. Part of the review of the ADA was driven by the desire to cut the budget, part driven by a feeling that there has been too much emphasis on rights and entitlements (Moore 1995). In early 2001, the U.S. Supreme Court held that state employees had no right to sue states in federal court for violations of the ADA (Rosenbaum 2001).

## Equality of Outcome

Although great strides had been made toward equality of opportunity, inequalities remained. As Charles Hamilton (1992) points out, once the Civil Rights Act of 1964 and the Voting Rights Act of 1965 were passed, the move toward equality became less focused on government action and more on institutional and societal factors. Thus, the movement toward equality shifted from a de jure or legal perspective to a de facto or societal perspective.

Equal treatment did little for those who had suffered from discrimination in the past. Perhaps what was needed were efforts that favored an oppressed group to help equality become a reality. This was the rationale behind the third form of equality, **equality of outcome** or results. The reasoning behind equality of outcome was articulated by President Lyndon Johnson in 1965:

Table 9.3

**Demographic Characteristics of the United States** (in thousands of people)

| | Projected 2000 | % of population | Projected 2010 | % of population | Projected 2025 | % of population | Projected 2050 | % of population |
|---|---|---|---|---|---|---|---|---|
| Total population | 276,059 | | 299,862 | | 337,815 | | 403,687 | |
| Men | 134,979 | 48.9 | 146,679 | 48.9 | 165,009 | 48.8 | 197,047 | 48.8 |
| Women | 141,080 | 51.1 | 153,183 | 51.1 | 172,806 | 51.2 | 206,640 | 51.2 |
| White | 226,861 | 82.2 | 241,770 | 80.6 | 265,306 | 78.5 | 302,453 | 74.9 |
| African American | 35,470 | 12.8 | 39,982 | 13.3 | 56,862 | 16.8 | 59,239 | 14.7 |
| American Indian | 2,448 | 0.9 | 2,821 | 0.9 | 4,207 | 1.2 | 4,405 | 1.1 |
| Asian and Pacific Islander | 11,279 | 4.1 | 15,289 | 5.1 | 34,309 | 10.2 | 37,589 | 9.3 |
| Hispanic* | 32,832 | 11.9 | 43,688 | 14.6 | 90,343 | 26.7 | 98,229 | 24.3 |

*Source:* U.S. Census Bureau (2000).
*Note:* *Hispanic includes white and African-American Hispanics.

> But freedom is not enough. You do not wipe away the scars of centuries by saying: Now you are free to go where you want, do as you desire, choose the leaders you please.
>
> You do not take a person who for years has been hobbled by chains and liberate him, bring him up to the starting line of a race and then say, "You are free to compete with all the others," and still justly believe you have been completely fair. (Johnson 1965)

Such a view provides the basis for what might be called **compensatory justice**, compensating a group for past discrimination. Compensatory justice encompasses policies such as affirmative action. It is also the most controversial type of equality.

## A Statistical Portrait of America: Now and in the Future

Equality issues concern women, minorities (racial and ethnic), disabled persons, and sexual-lifestyle issues. Table 9.3 presents some data about the U.S. population in 2000 and projections. As the projections show, the white population will decline from approximately 82.8 percent of the population to an estimated 74.9 percent of the population by 2050. While the proportion of African Americans and Asians will continue to increase, the projections show the fastest increase will be among Hispanics. Indeed, data from the 2000 census show that Hispanics now comprise about the same percentage of the population as African Americans (Sachs 2001). The United States is becoming more diversified, with California leading the way toward a more diversified, multicultural population (Kaplan 1998).

One consideration in talking about equality in the United States, especially race, is knowing exactly what race means and what it signifies. In one sense, race refers to biological/genetic factors that produce differences in skin color. Yet, to a large extent, race is really a **social construct** (Thornton 2001). That is, its meaning is one that is defined socially rather than biologically. This is a point made by Dinesh D'Souza (1995) in his book *The End of Racism*. D'Souza points out that at times we have considered Italians, Irish, and Jews as members of different races. In the United States, the tradition has been to use the **one-drop rule** (D'Souza 1995; Malcomson 2000): a person who had any Negro or black ancestor would be considered an African American and therefore of a second-class status.[11] An indication of the hold that the notion of race has had in the United States is that in 2000 Alabama became the last state to end the ban against interracial marriage, voting to end the ban in the November 2000 elections. Even then, 40 percent of Alabama voters wanted to retain the law (Hansen 2001; see also Sollors 2000).

Some have argued that there are significant genetic differences between the races and these genetic differences are largely responsible for differences in life outcomes, including school achievement, income and wealth, family structure, and criminal behavior or lack of criminal behavior. The strongest statement along these lines was Richard Herrnstein and Charles Murray's *The Bell Curve* (1994).

To briefly summarize the argument of *The Bell Curve*, Herrnstein and Murray, using statistical techniques, find that differences in intelligence, as measured by IQ, are strongly related to differences in life outcomes, exceeding differences in socioeconomic status (SES). Their review of the literature suggests that differences in intelligence are genetically based. They first establish this linkage in the white population that they studied. Having made their argument about the genetic basis for intelligence and the linkage between intelligence and life outcomes, they turn to racial differences. They find differences in average intelligence among the races, with Asian Americans having the highest, whites in the middle, and African Americans the lowest. They repeat their analysis relating intelligence to life outcomes, now adding race to the data. And, sure enough, they find differences in these life outcomes and relate them to genetics.

*The Bell Curve* set off a firestorm of debate. Murray and others (Herrnstein died shortly after the book was published) defended the research, while others accused Murray and Herrnstein of racism and bad social science.[12]

Brent Staples (1994a) writes:

> Despite the impression that there is something new in "The Bell Curve," its authors, Charles Murray and Richard Herrnstein, have merely reasserted the long-unproven claim that IQ is mainly inherited. The language is calmer, the statistical gimmicks slicker, but the truth remains the same: There exist no plausible data to make the case. Belief to the contrary rests mainly on brutal preconceptions about poverty, but also on a basic confusion between pseudo-science and the real thing.

E. D. Hirsch (1994) points out that IQ tests given to recruits in the United States during World War I showed that blacks from states with good educational systems had higher average IQ scores than whites from states with poor educational systems. Thus, schooling seems to have some effect.

Similar comments can be made about Head Start. Early studies of Head Start seemed to show a ten-point improvement in IQ. However, the difference between Head Start participants and similarly situated nonparticipants essentially vanished by the third grade (Herrnstein and Murray 1994). One could conclude, pessimistically, that Head Start therefore does not work, because the differences disappear. One might also conclude, more optimistically, that programs such as Head Start do have an impact, but that impact is diluted when the children leave the Head Start environment and start school. Perhaps if the enriched environment were maintained, IQ gains would be retained. Douglas Massey and Nancy Denton (1993) argue that racial segregation magnifies the impact of poverty by confining blacks to impoverished areas. Further, they assert that such segregation was deliberate and assisted by government policies.

There is considerable evidence that preschool programs can make lasting differences (Passell 1994). Just one example: In a preschool experiment discussed by Herrnstein and Murray, the IQ difference between the experimental and control groups was 11 points (the experimental group had the higher score). The difference did fade away. However, a follow-up study of the children through the age of nineteen found that those in the experimental group were more likely than those in the control group to do better on many of the measures that Herrnstein and Murray employ. They missed school less than the control group, were more likely to graduate from high school, had fewer arrests, and the women in the experimental group had about 50 percent fewer children as teenagers than women from the control group. A higher percentage of the experimental group students were employed and fewer were on welfare (Passell 1994). Again, Herrnstein and Murray rely on a very narrow view of the effects of preschool and similar kinds of interventions.

George Melloan (1994), a sympathetic reviewer of *The Bell Curve*, points out that each individual is the product of thousands of genes passed down through the ages. Even if IQ had a genetic basis, it is only a small part of an individual's genetic makeup. Viewing differences, such as the ability to earn a living, as a function of IQ scores is oversimplified.

There are other criticisms that can be made of *The Bell Curve*. E. J. Dionne (1994) points out that Herrnstein and Murray's estimate of 40 percent (the low estimate) or 60 percent (their middle estimate) of the portion of intelligence that is genetically based leaves considerable room for environmental factors. Tom Morganthau (1994) finds an important contradiction in the book. Herrnstein and Murray assert that IQ cannot be raised. Yet, average IQ scores have in fact risen about fifteen points over the last half century. The authors still insist that average IQ scores are going down. It is, in a sense, having it both ways.

There is also some evidence that intelligence can be taught, or students can at least be taught to do better on intelligence tests. The Washington, DC, public school system undertook a program to improve the performance of their students on achievement tests, such as the National Merit Scholarship test. Based on a program begun at Xavier College in New Orleans, the results suggested that intelligence, at least as measured on tests, may not be as immutable as Herrnstein and Murray suggest (Cose 1995).

Although there is evidence for the Herrnstein-Murray thesis (Cowley 1994; Scarr 1994–1995), Charles Lane (1994) argues that a sizable portion of their evidence is tainted by misinterpretation and reliance on a body of literature with racist intent. Much of their analysis is correlational rather than causal. Their results show that high IQ is associated with better social and economic outcomes and low IQ with poorer outcomes. The implication might be made that low IQ leads to poor outcomes, but Herrnstein and Murray do not say so.

Even if they are correct about the importance of IQ and its genetic basis, that genetic basis is only a blueprint. How that blueprint is actuated depends on other environmental factors, such as prenatal care. Jim Holt (1994) points out that moving a child from a deprived home to a better one can raise IQ by as much as twenty points.

The most interesting questioning of *The Bell Curve* by a sympathetic observer (Besharov 1994) says that the interventions mentioned by Herrnstein and Murray, such as Head Start, are only a small number of possible interventions. Douglas Besharov lists and discusses the following important questions that are unanswered by *The Bell Curve*:

- What if IQ is affected by the mother's behavior during pregnancy?
- What if the first years of life are crucial?
- What if preschool interventions could make a real change in a child's learning environment?
- What if good schools raise scores?
- What if neighborhoods dampen the desire of children to perform well?
- What if a child's entire neighborhood environment is improved dramatically?
- What if racial differences in IQ are the result of over 200 years of slavery and more than 100 more years of discrimination and oppression? (Besharov 1994)

For each of the questions, which look at environmental factors, Besharov offers suggestions of changes that might reduce inequalities. For example, the second question refers to the importance of child rearing in the first years of life. The middle-class child-rearing style lends itself to cognitive development, the lower-class stunts such development. Thus, as more African-American families become middle class, one would expect advances in cognitive development. Besharov notes that the shift could take several generations, and the movement of African-American families into the middle class is a recent phenomenon.

Similarly, the last question, the effects of slavery and discrimination, refers to the development of "stored human capital that has built up over generations" (Besharov 1994). If the legacy of slavery and discrimination is strong (Patterson 1998), the latter of which only legally ended in the mid-1960s, then programs such as affirmative action and "carefully targeted education" could give a boost to the present generation and help subsequent generations move toward equality. The debate over IQ, over inequality, over the causes of inequality has not yet been settled.

*The Bell Curve* adds to the agony of debate over inequalities in society. Those who hold views about the racial inferiority of minorities are bound to have them reinforced (though they would be troubled by the higher average IQ scores of Asian Americans; see Steele 1999). Perhaps the best perspective on *The Bell Curve* is the following:

> Juan Williams made the excellent point that many black people already perceive that society considers them second-class citizens; so the people who should really be upset by this book are less-than-intelligent white people. (Brooks 1994)

What do the new scientific developments in human genetics tell us about these issues? First, there is some evidence linking genetics to IQ. The particular gene, which appears to be more common in children with very high IQs, has a small but discernible effect on IQ. It is very likely, however, that other genes also play a role in intelligence, and there is still the interaction of genetic makeup and environment (Wade 1998).

More recent developments address the question of the validity of the concept of race, mentioned above. In 2000, scientists working on the Human Genome Project announced that they had mapped out the genetic makeup of humans. One of the important findings is that the "races" are considerably more similar genetically than had been previously thought. Only about 0.1 percent of our genetic makeup reflects external differences such as skin color. As Dr. J. Craig Venter, who directed the commercial team analyzing the human genome, said: "Race is a social concept, not a scientific one" (quoted in Angier 2000; see also Olson 2001).

The idea of race raises a whole host of issues. To name just one, let us go back to the one-drop idea. If a person is of mixed race, say a white and an African-American parent, what is the race of the child? This could be called the "Tiger Woods problem." Tiger Woods, the highly successful professional golfer, is of Caucasian, Native American, African-American, and Asian backgrounds. What is his race (Leland and Beals 1997)? Interracial marriages have increased in the United States, particularly among Asian/Pacific Islanders and whites, considerably less so between African Americans and whites.

For the first time, the 2000 census allowed respondents to check more than one racial category.

In one sense, this recognizes the changes taking place in America (see, e.g., Perlmann 1997). On the other hand, there is the fear that this might dilute the number of African Americans in the United States. Because of this, many of mixed race planned to check only one box, for blacks (Schemo 2000).

So should we drop the discussion of race, as D'Souza (1995) recommends. Are the distinctions made of race indicative of racism itself? In one sense, that would mark a great improvement and a move toward, in Dr. Martin Luther King's words, judging people on the basis of their character (who we are) rather than their skin color (what we are). On the other hand, we still judge people on the basis of skin color or ethnicity (see below), and there are considerable attitudinal differences between whites and African Americans. We have not yet reached the color-blind society. And American history is colored by a concern or obsession over race issues.

> Americans are now relatively free to decide who they are, in racial terms, when filling out a census. But that is one of the few times when they are free to do so. Race is a social, not private, reality. And the census should not be misused to make racial policies, which have much more to do with how we act toward each other than what we think about ourselves. (Thornton 2001)

## The Civil Rights Movement

Race relations in the United States have always been difficult. The Civil War was fought to determine the nature of the union, but the ultimate cause was slavery. Should slavery be extended to new states and territories? Should slavery be ended? Could former slaves have the rights of citizenship (the Supreme Court said no in the *Dred Scott* decision). After the Civil War, African Americans were kept in near servitude through legal segregation (the Jim Crow laws) and violence. The beginnings of the civil rights movement in the first half of the twentieth century were focused on a legal strategy designed to end de jure segregation in the south.[13] Philip Klinkner and Roger Smith (1999) assert that most of the progress toward racial equality over the years has occurred during times of stress, such as World War II and the Cold War.

In the 1950s and 1960s, the civil rights movement shifted strategy, moving toward more social action and protest. The bus boycott in Montgomery, AL, brought the Rev. Dr. Martin Luther King Jr. to the forefront of this effort. Freedom rides, the March on Washington, demonstrations met with violence in Birmingham, the murders of Medgar Evers and others all were publicized by the nation's media, especially television. The protests, confined to the South, contained an important moral quality. Shelby Steele (1990, pp. 17–18) describes the power of the civil rights movement:

> I think the civil rights movement in its early and middle years offered the best way out of America's racial impasse: in this society, race must not be a source of advantage or disadvantage for anyone. This is fundamentally a *moral* position, one that seeks to breach the corrupt union of race and power with principles of fairness and

human equality: if all men are created equal, then racial difference cannot sanction power. The civil rights movement was conceived for no other reason than to redress that corrupt union, and its guiding insight was that only a moral power based on enduring principles of justice, equality, and freedom could offset the lower impulse in man to exploit race as a means of power. Three hundred years of suffering had driven the point home, and in Montgomery, Little Rock, and Selma, racial power was the enemy and moral power the weapon.

The protestors were advocating the rights seemingly guaranteed to them in the Constitution. They were met with violence, particularly when Birmingham, AL, sheriff "Bull" Connor ordered hoses turned on African-American children marching in the downtown area. Eventually the movement would be successful in ending de jure segregation.[14]

However, several things happened that changed the way whites and African Americans looked at the push for equality and social justice. First, the civil rights movement was successful. The Civil Rights Act of 1964 and the Voting Rights Act of 1965 (and their enforcement) were the culmination of the movement. But although legalized segregation ended, inequality remained. The civil rights movement raised expectations within the African-American community of changes that in practice would take a long time. The frustration sometimes erupted into violence.

Beginning in 1964 through about 1969, inner cities were the site of summertime violence. Often the riots were precipitated by what appeared to be police brutality against African Americans. Major riots occurred in Harlem, Los Angeles, and Newark, NJ. This led to cries for "law and order," seen first in the 1968 presidential campaign of Richard Nixon. In the wake of the urban riots, President Johnson formed a commission headed by Illinois governor Otto Kerner to study the causes and prevention of violence. The Kerner Commission issued a report with the chilling opening statement that "Our nation is moving toward two societies, one black, one white, separate and unequal" (quoted in Hacker 1992, p. ix). The race and rights issue was one factor in transforming American politics and moving the two parties more ideologically apart (Carmines and Stimson 1989; Edsall and Edsall 1992).

At the same time, the civil rights movement began to change. First, it started targeting de facto segregation in the North. For example, Martin Luther King Jr. led a march in the Chicago suburb of Cicero to desegregate housing. Busing, a tool mandated by the courts to desegregate southern schools, began to be used in the North. New leaders, such as H. Rap Brown and Stokely Carmichael, began to advocate black power and appeared threatening to whites. The change from equality of opportunity to equality of results, embodied in affirmative action plans, was also more difficult to justify.[15]

Charles Hamilton (1992) makes an important historical distinction between ethnic groups and African Americans to explain some of the different perspectives of whites and African Americans. Ethnic immigration to the United States had three important characteristics that were not seen in the African-

American experience. First, they came by choice. Second, the move was seen as improving their economic, political, and social status. Finally, although there was discrimination against ethnic groups, the dehumanization that distinguished African Americans under slavery and later under segregation was not present for most ethnic groups. Thus ethnic groups were more likely to look toward the private sector for advancement and to express gratitude for the new country. African Americans, on the other hand, because of their unique historical situation, were more likely to speak in the language of rights and much more likely to be confined to segregated neighborhoods than any other ethnic group (Massey and Denton 1993).

Television and the movies presented to the nation various views of African Americans and their relationships with whites. The upwardly mobile African-American community was represented by the *Bill Cosby Show*, five children and their parents—a doctor and a lawyer. African-American–white relations were seen in movies such as *Grand Canyon* with its more positive view, and *Jungle Fever* with its more negative view (and chilling depiction of what the crack epidemic was doing to the African-American community).[16] Movies such as *Boyz in the Hood* and *South Central,* which depict life in inner-city communities, ultimately have positive messages,[17] but the problems of the underclass were shown in devastating detail.

## Narrowing the Gap

Seymour Lipset (1992) argues that African Americans, Hispanics, and women and have made substantial progress in terms of employment and income, but many leaders of these groups refuse to admit it. Stephan and Abigail Thernstrom (1997), and Shelby Steele (1998) make similar arguments. The reason is that admitting progress lessens the critical nature of the problem. Lipset notes that poverty among African Americans, although still much higher than white poverty (see chapter 4), has decreased significantly. There are more African Americans in the middle class than in the lower class (and the underclass is quite small). A majority of African Americans live in stable families. Even the increase in the African-American illegitimacy rate is attributed, ironically, to improvements in black socioeconomic status. Middle-class, married African Americans are having fewer children, so even if the number of illegitimate African-American children stayed the same, the rate would rise.

Similar statements can be made about women. In 1960, women earned, on the average, about 60 percent as much as men. This was still true in 1980. By 1990, women made substantial gains relative to men and were earning almost 78 percent of what men were earning (Mishel et al. 2001).

For college-educated women, the figures are more encouraging. College-educated white females make about 89 percent of earnings of college-educated white males. College-educated African-American women make, on the average, a little more than college-educated African-American men. College-educated African-American men earn, on the average, about 89 percent of what college-educated white men earn (Roberts 1994).

## Race Relations as a Wedge Issue

Although there has been considerable progress in the black community, that progress has been uneven. There is a thriving black middle class (though even here there are problems, see below) at the same time that inner-city African Americans suffer; the inequalities within the African-American community mirror the inequalities in the country as a whole (Harrison and Gorham 1992; see also Mishel et al. 2001).

That the problems have not gone away can be seen in three events in the late 1980s and early 1990s.[18] The presidential campaign of 1988 was, in a sense, a rerun of the 1968 campaign. The Republican candidate, Vice President George H. W. Bush, argued that his Democratic opponent, Massachusetts governor Michael Dukakis, was soft on crime. An independent committee supporting the Bush effort ran a series of ads that were known as the "Willie Horton" ads. Horton was "a convicted murderer who had jumped furlough and gone on to rape a Maryland woman and assault her fiance. The convict was black, the couple white" (Jamieson 1992, p. 17). The ad was televised over and over again. The Bush campaign, while never explicitly mentioning the Willie Horton incident or ad, ran a commercial attacking Dukakis on the furlough program, showing prisoners being let out through a revolving door (Jamieson 1992).[19]

In 1992 two incidents demonstrated how tenuous racial relations were in the United States. Senator Jesse Helms (R-NC) was campaigning for reelection against Harvey Gantt, an African-American. Polls showed Gantt running a strong race, at one point ahead of Helms. Helms then began to run a commercial attacking affirmative action. The ad pictured a white male throwing away a job rejection letter. The text of the ad read:

> You needed that job, and you were the best qualified. But they had to give it to a minority because of a racial quota. Is that really fair? Harvey Gantt says it is. Gantt supports Ted Kennedy's racial quota law that makes the color of your skin more important than your qualifications. You'll vote on this issue next Tuesday. For racial quotas: Harvey Gantt. Against racial quotas: Jesse Helms. (Jamieson 1992, p. 97)

The other 1992 incident was in Los Angeles. An African-American man, Rodney King, was driving his car erratically when police began to pursue him. He led them on a high-speed chase. When the police officers caught him, they began to beat him with their nightsticks. The incident was captured on videotape, which was broadcast nationwide. The police were brought to trial on assault charges. Despite the evidence of the videotape (as well as testimony from one of the officers), the police officers were acquitted. The trial was held in a white suburb (because of the pretrial publicity) and all the jurors were white. (Two of the officers were later convicted in federal court of violating King's civil rights). The reaction to the acquittal, including from President Bush, was one of disbelief (Morin 1992). The reaction in the South Central section of Los Angeles was riot, the worst riot in the country's history: "more than 55 dead, at least 2,383 injuries (228 critical), property damage of $785 million, more than 12,5000 rioters, killers and muggers in custody. More than 20,000 out of jobs" (Omincinski 1992). When some of the rioters began attacking whites, at one point taking a white from his truck and beating him, the public and political leaders became unsympathetic.[20]

The local African-American community reaction was that the trial of the police officers proved that African Americans would not be treated fairly in the courts. Whites pointed to the riots and disorder that followed the acquittal. Within the African-American community, those who have been successful, who have attained middle-class status, often view things differently than whites (Carter 1991; Cose 1993).

A more contemporaneous example of race as a political issue, and closer to the author's home, began in 1999 and continued into 2001. Ronnie White was appointed as the first African-American member of the Missouri Supreme Court by Missouri's Democratic governor Mel Carnahan. President Clinton nominated Justice White to a federal judgeship in 1999. Support for White in the U.S. Senate, which has the power of confirmation over federal judicial appointments, seemed to be strong. Missouri's senior senator, Republican Christopher Bond, originally supported White's nomination.

However, Missouri's junior senator, John Ashcroft, opposed the nomination, asserting on the floor of the Senate (but not during the committee hearings) that Justice White was soft on crime because the justice had opposed a particular death penalty verdict. Ashcroft was able to convince Bond and other Republican senators to oppose White's nomination, and it was defeated in 2000. The African-American community in Missouri, particularly in St. Louis and Kansas City, charged that Ashcroft's opposition to White was based on race, and that White had supported the majority of death penalty cases. They vowed to remember the Ronnie White affair.

The story does not end there, however. Ashcroft had to run for reelection in 2000. His opponent was Mel Carnahan, and the White affair was part of the campaign. Carnahan died in a plane crash in mid-October 2000, but his name was kept on the ballot. Partly because of the sympathy for the dead governor (and his wife, Jean, who would be named to the position if Carnahan won) and partly because of the concerted effort by African Americans to oppose Ashcroft, the senator lost his reelection bid.

But the story does not even end there. President George W. Bush then nominated Ashcroft to be the attorney general of the United States. Again, Ashcroft's opposition to White was brought up. This time, White was given an opportunity to respond to Ashcroft's charges, and he defended his record. Ashcroft was approved by the Senate, though forty-two Democrats opposed him (largely because of his politically conservative views). Ashcroft subsequently met with African-American members of Congress to try to rebuild relations (Alvarez 2001; Lewis 2001).[21]

## Attitudes About Race

African Americans have a more encompassing view of race and American culture than whites. They "see racism as an ongoing and pervasive condition of American life, while whites tend to think of racism as individual actions or attitudes of bigotry that are the exceptions" (Duke 1992). Whites resent what they see as preferential treatment of African Americans (and women and other minorities) and fear the violence associated with young African-American males (Hacker 1992; Sack and Elder 2000; Shipler 1997). Recall the Jesse Jackson quote from chapter 7:

> There is nothing more painful to me at this stage in my life than to walk down the street and hear footsteps and start thinking about robbery—then look around and see somebody white and feel relieved. (quoted in Cole 1999, p. 40)

Race was brought to the nation's attention again when, in the fall of 1994, a young white mother, Susan Smith, said that an African-American male had stolen her car and taken her two children, ages three years and fourteen months. A few days later, she confessed that she had in fact killed the boys by sending the car into a pond. While the police in Union County, SC, were suspicious of the story (Adler 1994), the fact that Smith made up the story and accused a young black male of the abduction shows how sensitive race relations are. Nor was this the first time that whites had accused blacks of crimes to shift suspicion from themselves:

> Consider the 1989 case in Boston in which Charles Stuart, a white man, told the police that a black man had shot and killed Mr. Stuart's pregnant wife. After the investigation turned toward Mr. Stuart, he took his own life. And what about the white woman in Philadelphia who accused three black men of killing her children when she herself had killed them? Last August [1994] a white Los Angeles man killed his wife and blamed a black man. (Ross 1994)

Although overt discrimination has considerably diminished, it has not entirely disappeared. This was demonstrated by the behavior of Denny's restaurants. A multistate franchise, the restaurants did not want to serve African Americans, especially African-American males. Restaurant staff would refuse to seat them or, if they were seated, would take a very long time to serve them (Levinson 1993). This practice came to a head when a Denny's restaurant employee seated six white males and would not seat six African-American males. What the restaurant did not know was that all twelve were members of the U.S. Secret Service! ("Secret Service" 1993). Denny's ordered a change in its policy, sold some of its franchises to minority owners, and paid $54 million in a bias suit (Labaton 1994). Asian Americans also faced some of the same problems with the restaurant chain ("Denny's Seeks to Be Dropped from Bias Suit" 1999).

**Racial profiling**, discussed in chapter 7, is another manifestation of discrimination (see, e.g., Taylor 1999a). Steven Holmes (1999), an African-American male reporter with the *New York Times*, tells of how he was stopped by a white Washington, DC, police officer on a fictitious pretext. This, naturally, made him angry:

> The incident left me frustrated and irate. (At the time I was in my mid-40's but often could pass for someone much younger.) I thought: I'm a middle-class black man who works hard, pays his taxes, keeps out of trouble and tries to treat people with dignity and respect. Why should I be an object of suspicion? I railed at the injustice of it all. Yet, as my anger cooled, I asked myself a harder question: Hadn't I done the same thing myself? (Holmes 1999)

Holmes had worked as a taxi driver during his college years. A couple of times he had been held up by African-American males. It made him hesitant to pick up young African-American males wearing sneakers. Remembering this made him wonder:

> As I contemplated this, my anger spread to many targets: the police officer who had confronted me, and the young black hoodlums whose criminal behavior had made the officer suspicious of all African-American men in the first place. And I resented the country's history of racism, which helped to insure that the presence of a black person in a leafy, affluent neighborhood of Washington was still a rare sight. The nexus of race, crime and stereotyping raises difficult questions that are often ignored. Even as crime rates tumble, young black men still commit a disproportionate share of serious offenses, a fact that is driven home in metropolitan areas by television's seemingly incessant airing of crime news. And whether the fear stems from real experience or media-driven perceptions, people—police and civilian, white and black—play the odds all the time when it comes to how they view and respond to young black men. (Holmes 1999)

A version of racial profiling might be called **retail racism**. A chain of children's stores was accused of treating African-American customers differently from white customers. Store clerks were told to keep a careful eye on them, not to offer them credit cards or tell them about sales, and so forth (Goldberg 2000).

One of the more interesting perspectives is that of the African-American middle class. Here we have a group that is economically comfortable, most likely living in the suburbs, and yet discontented. Such discontent is analyzed by Ellis Cose in his 1993 book, *The Rage of a Privileged Class* (see also Hochschild 1993). At the opening of the book, Cose says that middle-class African Americans repeatedly expressed the following anguished feelings:

> I have done everything I was supposed to do. I have stayed out of trouble with the law, gone to the right schools, and worked myself nearly to death. *What more do*

*they want?* Why in God's name won't they accept me as a full human being? Why am I pigeonholed in a "black job"? Why am I constantly treated as if I were a drug addict, a thief, or a thug? Why am I not allowed to aspire to the same things every white person in America takes as a birthright? Why, when I most want to be seen, am I suddenly rendered invisible? (Cose 1993, p. 1)

Cose cites a study of racial attitudes in Los Angeles about the time of the trial of the four police officers accused of beating Rodney King. Prior to the acquittal and the riot, the findings were that African Americans with incomes of $50,000 or more expressed *greater* feelings of alienation than African Americans with lower incomes. After the riot, the alienation among the higher-income group rose.

Cose's book explains the silent rage that characterizes middle-class African Americans. The everyday slights and the assumption that race overpowers status are the problems. Two cases illustrate what Cose is talking about.

Isabel Wilkerson was the Chicago bureau chief of the *New York Times*. She tells of a time that she was late for an appointment and was running through an airport to catch a rental car company bus. As she was getting on the bus, she was approached by two men who identified themselves as agents of the Drug Enforcement Agency and climbed on the bus with her and sat there. She realized that they thought she was a drug courier because she was running and was African American. Wilkerson relates another story of having to convince a secretary that she was the *Times* reporter with the appointment to interview the company executive. She had to demonstrate to the secretary her educational and professional credentials.

The other case demonstrates what is sometimes called the "black tax," the premium paid for being black. In this example, a *Time* magazine reporter was being transferred. *Time* has a policy of buying employees' homes in such circumstances for 105 percent of appraised value. An appraiser valued the house at lower than its expected worth. The reporter then had his white secretary come into the house and replace his family pictures with hers. The next appraisal came in at 15 percent over the first appraisal (see also Massey and Denton 1993).

There are other examples of these stereotyped reactions to middle-class African Americans: not being invited to join country clubs, automatic assumptions that all African Americans must be lower-class (and potentially violent if young and male), the view that any successful African American must have gotten the position because of affirmative action, the view that a law partner who is African American is *the* African-American law partner. These everyday slights are what Cose sees as the cause of middle-class rage, the lack of acceptance. Whites, however, do not see racism as pervading society because, as stated earlier, whites see racism as overt prejudice. Cose has it right when he concludes his book:

The racial gap, as this book has tried to make clear, can only be closed by recognizing it, and by recognizing why it exists. That will not come to pass as long as we insist on dividing people into different camps and then swearing that differences don't count or that repeated blows to the soul shouldn't be taken seriously. For the truth is that the often hurtful and seemingly trivial encounters of daily existence are in the end what most of life is. (Cose 1993, pp. 192–193)

The differences in experiences between whites and African Americans show up in public opinion polls and voting behaviors. In the 2000 presidential elections, about 90 percent of African Americans voted for the Democratic candidate, Al Gore, the highest level of Democratic voting among any demographic group. According to a 1999 Gallup poll, whites are much more likely to favorably view police than are African Americans. African Americans are much more likely than whites to believe that racial profiling is widespread (Gallup Poll n.d.). According to an analysis of a *New York Times* poll conducted in 2000, whites and African Americans seem to live on different planets. "Blacks were roughly four times more likely than whites to say they thought blacks were treated less fairly in the workplace, in neighborhood shops, in shopping malls and in restaurants, theaters, bars and other entertainment venues" (Sack and Elder 2000). One area of agreement was that about the same percentage of African Americans and whites perceived hostility toward each other.

On the other hand, Shelby Steele (1990) argues that much of hidden black middle-class rage is largely the result of that middle class maintaining a "victim-focused black identity" (p. 109). This is a line of reasoning that Steele and others have argued as well. In a later book (1998), Steele asserts that African Americans suffer from a victimization complex that keeps them from succeeding. John McWhorter (2000) refers to this phenomenon among African Americans as "self-sabotage" (see also Will 2001).

## Case Study: Affirmative Action

### Policy Adoption

**Affirmative action** is a policy that tries to expand the number of previously excluded groups in hiring and promotion in jobs and in admission to colleges and universities. It first came to prominence in 1961, when President Kennedy issued an executive order prohibiting discrimination against minorities in federally funded programs and ordering agencies to hire more minorities. In 1965 and 1967, President Johnson issued executive orders requiring federal agencies to take positive steps or affirmative action to get more minorities hired in federally funded projects. The Equal Employment Opportunity Commission and the Office of Federal Contracts Compliance were to monitor the progress. A 1971 executive order by President Nixon continued the effort.

Affirmative action can take several different forms (Fullinwider 1997). One form would be simply to expand the pool of applicants for hiring or for admission to a university program. A second type of affirmative action might follow a rule that says if two applicants have equal credentials, select the minority or woman. A third type might allow hiring, promotion, or admission to minorities or women even if they were not as qualified as other candidates, that is, have lower college test scores. The final type of affirmative action is based on targets and quotas. A **target** is a goal—for example, to achieve a certain percentage of minority hiring. A **quota** reserves a certain number of positions for minorities or women.[22]

Although affirmative action has its origins in executive orders by Presidents Kennedy and Johnson, the use of quotas, goals, and timetables originates with the Nixon administration. The Nixon administration, under the Philadelphia Plan, ordered quotas for building trades, an order that was then extended to the private sector as a whole and to colleges and universities (Lipset 1992). Quotas, as Lipset notes, were never popular among the American public, even among African Americans.

### Arguments in Favor of Affirmative Action

There are a number of rationales or justifications for affirmative action (see, e.g., Bergman 1996). First, affirmative action was designed, as President Johnson's quote above makes clear, to compensate for past injustices that kept deprived groups behind. A second motive is that discrimination still exists; it is not just a thing of the past (Bergman 1996). Christopher Edley (1996) points to the existence of continued inequality along racial lines as important evidence of the need to maintain affirmative action. Some examples support this case. For decades, American General Insurance charged African Americans higher premiums than they did whites for their life insurance policies (Treaster 2000). The Federal Housing Authority (FHA), part of the U.S. Department of Housing and Urban Development (HUD), aided real estate brokers in steering minorities to predominantly minority neighborhoods (Dedman 1998; see also Kilborn 1999). Some companies, such as Texaco, practiced racial and sexual discrimination (Bryant 1997). Top positions in corporations remain closed to minorities, especially minority women (Abelson 1999).

Though there are some networks that feature African Americans (particularly the UPN network), the major broadcast networks are much less likely to feature them. No minorities were featured in any of the networks' new shows in 1999 (Farhi 1999). Less than 1 percent of the writers and editors listed on the mastheads of major magazines are minority. Similarly, an article in the February 2001 issue of *Vanity Fair* discussing the top fifty pundits[23] included not a single African American (Nobile 2001). The problem that these examples indicate is that without some type of special effort or incentive, minorities are not included. The result is, in Nobile's (2001) words, "a segregated society shored up by a series of agreements among the gentlemen."

Then there are the hate crimes. Perhaps the worst was the murder of James Byrd Jr. in Texas. Byrd was returning home from a family meeting when several young white men grabbed him, tied him by the feet to the back of their vehicle, and drove for several miles dragging him behind to his death (Chua-Eoan 1998).

A related reason that some have argued is that although overt discrimination or racism/sexism has been banned, institutional racism/sexism remains. **Institutional racism** is race-neutral (or gender-neutral) practices that result in racial or gender disparities. For example, seniority rules favor promotion or retention of those with the most time on the job, most likely whites (and males). A similar example is the rule of "last hired, first fired," which disproportionately affects African Americans. The use of personal connections in getting jobs also disfavors minorities and women. Job qualifications, such as standardized tests and requirements not directly related to jobs, are a final instance of institutionalized racism. It is these barriers that affirmative action is designed to overcome (Ezorsky 1991).

One of the strongest arguments in favor of affirmative action is the study conducted by Bowen and Bok (1998). They argue that affirmative action programs have worked and have led to the growth of the African-American middle class (they make a similar assertion about Hispanics). They also note that the African-American middle class is much smaller than the white middle class and that diversity in admissions and hiring serves important societal purposes. They provide data showing that there is a gap in SAT scores between whites and African Americans but that the gap has been decreasing and more African Americans are scoring higher on that admissions test. They then point out that, not taking race into account, race-neutral admission policies would result in fewer African Americans' being accepted into the nation's elite colleges and universities (the focus of their study). Their analysis suggests that many of the charges made against affirmative action (see below) just did not hold true: white students appreciated diversity, African-American students did not feel demoralized, and so forth. The African-American students went on to have productive careers and earn high incomes and were civic-minded citizens.

### Arguments Against Affirmative Action

The arguments against affirmative action also take several directions. Perhaps the most fundamental point is that it contradicts the vital American value of individualism. Affirmative action, the equality issue itself, is based on the notion of group rights (remember the story of "The Sneetches"). Those who make this argument (e.g., D'Souza 1995; Steele 1990) like to point to Dr. Martin Luther King Jr.'s vision of a race-neutral America and his famous statement in the "I Have a Dream" speech during the 1993 March on Washington when he proclaimed: "I have a dream that my four little children will one day live in a nation where they will not be judged by the color of their skin but by the content of their character" (King 1963). Those who hold on to this view argue that the civil rights movement divides people and stigmatizes or victimizes those who would supposedly benefit from programs such as affirmative action (Steele 1998).

A second argument against affirmative action is that it is itself a form of discrimination. Some have labeled affirmative action as reverse discrimination or affirmative discrimination (Glazer 1975). It maintains the civil rights group basis of policy by discriminating against whites (particularly against white males) (Canady 1998). A third related point is that affirmative action, in its quota incarnation, crosses the merit principle that the best should be picked for the job or the position. We will return to this argument below.

As we moved toward the stricter forms of affirmative action, toward goals and quotas, the policy becomes more controversial. Expanding the pool of applicants does not raise any red flags, but admitting or hiring people with lower qualifications and excluding some with higher qualifications have caused heated disputes. The debate over quotas affected American politics and political parties.[24] Graham (1992) makes the same point:

> The main intended results [of the new structure of social regulation] were dramatic: the destruction of legal segregation in the South and a sharp acceleration in the drive for equal rights for women. The unanticipated result, however, was a social cleavage that fractured the American consensus on the meaning of justice itself. (Graham 1992, p. 51)

One can see some of the problems in a case out of New Jersey, *Piscataway v. Taxman*. The Piscataway Board of Education had to lay off some teachers in 1989. One of the decisions was between a black woman, Debra Williams, and a white woman, Sharon Taxman. The two women were considered to have the same qualifications. The Board chose to keep Ms. Williams and fired Ms. Taxman on diversity grounds. Ms. Taxman filed a complaint with the Equal Employment Opportunity Commission, and in 1991 the Bush administration sued the Board for racial discrimination. Ms. Taxman joined the lawsuit. In 1993 she was rehired. The case wound its way through the courts, with both a federal district court judge and the U.S. Third Circuit Court of Appeals upholding Ms. Taxman. The case was clearly headed toward the U.S. Supreme Court. In 1994, the Clinton administration Justice Department changed direction and argued that diversity could be grounds for action in voluntary affirmative action programs. Civil rights groups did not want the case to go to the Court, partly because the Court had been handing down anti-affirmative action cases and partly because they felt this was a particularly bad case. The Board and several civil rights groups offered Ms. Taxman a settlement in 1997, which she accepted. The Third Circuit's decision stands, stating that diversity alone could not be a rationale for making decisions based on race. The court, as well as the U.S. Supreme Court, asserted that only specific instances of discrimination could be grounds for such decisions (Bearak 1997; Cohen 1997; Greenhouse 1997; Holmes 1997; and Sullivan 1997).

There is a fourth, interesting argument, against affirmative action. This is one made by African Americans, usually but not always with a conservative bent (such as economist Thomas Sowell). Affirmative action, so this line of reasoning goes, stigmatizes not just those who directly benefited from the program, but all African Americans. If a professional or graduate school has an affirmative action program, then minorities who are admitted under such a program are regarded as inferior, because their grades or test scores were not sufficient for normal admittance. Further, other members of that minority group may be seen in the same way, even if they did meet original admission criteria and were not admitted under preferential treatment (Carter 1991).

One interesting point in the debate over affirmative action and quotas is the place of the Civil Rights Act of 1964. The act, as mentioned above, banned racial discrimination. The sponsors of the bill stated that any attempts at racial preference, such as quota programs, would violate Title VII of the Act (Canady 1998; Fullinwider 1997; Graham 1992; Reynolds 1992).

Shelby Steele (1990) argues that what African Americans need is a twofold focus. Middle-class African-American children need fairness and opportunity, a chance to show what they can do unhindered by racial stereotypes. Lower-class African Americans need "a better shot at development—better elementary and secondary schools, job training, safer neighborhoods, better financial assistance for college, and so on" (Steele 1990, p. 125).

In a later piece, following the Republican takeover of Congress after the 1994 elections, Steele argued that liberalism had the opportunity to help African Americans in a way that bolstered social virtues:

> Suppose liberals had rolled up their sleeves and insisted that minorities achieve academically at the same level as others, and then helped them to do so? Suppose they had said to those who had been oppressed that now—through a commitment to rigor and principle—you will develop an excellence that makes your equality manifest? What if liberalism had made minority schools as academically rigorous as the best suburban schools? And suppose it was an article of the liberal faith that making excuses for minority underachievement only extended their oppression? (Steele 1995, pp. 41–42)

### Impact of Affirmative Action

Affirmative action appears to have benefited the middle class of the protected categories (women and minorities) more than the group as a whole, more than the lower class, and women more than African Americans (particularly in higher education) (Kahlenberg 1996; Orlans 1992; Samuelson 1997). Hugh Graham (1992) points out that most of the economic gains for African Americans occurred from 1964 to 1975, when discrimination was legally banned. Since 1975, minority gains, relative to whites, have slowed (see also Thernstrom and Thernstrom 1997). Further, there appears to be a growing class inequality within the black community. Middle-class African Americans, especially those with two wage earners (or two-parent families), have done well or at least maintained their economic status (Thernstrom and Thernstrom 1997). Those with only one wage earner have fallen behind (Harrison and Gorham 1992).[25]

## Moving Away from Affirmative Action

As we have seen, the push for the quotas version of affirmative action began in the early 1970s. However, the late 1970s saw the beginning of the move away from affirmative action beginning with **Bakke v. Board of Regents of the University of California (1978)**. In a series of 5–4 decisions, the Supreme Court held that race could not be used as the sole criterion for admissions (in this case to medical school), although it could be one of the criteria. The *Weber* and *Fullilove* cases seemed to sustain some form of affirmative action. The Court upheld voluntary affirmative action plans in the *Weber* case and minority set-asides in the *Fullilove* case.

In the 1980s, affirmative action took a beating. The Reagan administration opposed even voluntary affirmative action plans (as it did with voluntary school busing programs). In the mid-1980s, the Court prohibited whites from being laid off to protect the newly hired African Americans. In *Grove City v. Bell*, the Court held that only those programs that directly received federal assistance were subject to affirmative action scrutiny. Prior to that decision, any educational institution accepting federal funds, even if they were only guaranteed student loans, were subject to federal oversight on the grounds of discrimination. The *Grove City* decision limited the scope of federal action. The 1988 Civil Rights Restoration Act overturned *Grove City*, allowing the prior practice of institutional-wide scrutiny to be reinstated.

In 1989, the Court held that minority set-aside programs were inherently suspect, thus effectively ending Philadelphia Plan–type programs. Other decisions that year made it much harder to bring discrimination suits. The Court ruled that intent to discriminate must be shown, a much more difficult standard than just showing statistical discrepancies.[26] The 1991 Civil Rights Act overturned the 1989 decisions. However, the Bush administration was able to obtain a ruling that prohibited the 1991 act from being used retroactively in cases prior to its enactment.

In a 1994 case, a federal appeals court ruled that a minority-only scholarship program was discriminatory (the ruling applied to only a few states). This echoed a ruling by the Department of Education during the Bush administration that minority-only scholarships programs were unconstitutional (they were later restored by the Clinton administration), but the U.S. Supreme Court upheld the ruling in 1995 (Holmes 1995a). If the country is to assist minorities in getting ahead, in some way other than athletic scholarships (which are more exploitation by high schools and colleges than a genuine means of upward mobility, see Staples 1994b), then such scholarships are absolutely necessary. They are a small percentage of the total number of academic scholarships that are available. Yet they do bump up against the reverse discrimination argument.

The pace of change in policy over affirmative action could be seen in 1995 and 1996. In 1995, the regents of the University of California system voted to end affirmative action programs. The next year, voters approved the **California Civil Rights Initiative (CCRI)**, which stated:

> The state shall not discriminate against, or grant preferential treatment to any individual or group on the basis of race, sex, color, ethnicity, or national origin in the operation of public employment, public education, or public contracting. (California Secretary of State, http://vote96.ss.ca.gov/Vote96/html/BP/209text.htm)

A similar measure passed in 1998 in Washington State, but failed in the city of Houston. Part of the reason for the differing results is that affirmative action can be described differently to the public. The Houston issue asked where affirmative action should be banned. In California and Washington State, the emphasis was on preferences (Stanfield 1997; Verhovek 1997a). According to public opinion polls, the public supports diversity in education and the workforce, though it rejects preferences. The public also appears to support special efforts to help minorities and the poor (see, e.g., Verhovek 1997b; also Schneider 1998).

In 1996, a federal circuit court, in *Hopwood v. Texas*, ruled that race could not be a factor in admissions decisions. Recall that the U.S. Supreme Court ruled in *Bakke* that race could be a factor. Now the appeals court effectively overturned the *Bakke* decision. Because the Supreme Court declined to hear an appeal from the circuit court, the decision stands, but only in Texas, Louisiana, and Mississippi, the Fifth Circuit Court's jurisdiction. The immediate impact of the Texas and California decisions was a significant decline in minority admissions and enrollment, though there has been some rebound in those numbers (Applebome 1997b; Stanfield, 1997).

In 1995, Republicans in Congress proposed the Equal Opportunity Act, which would ban affirmative action programs in the federal government. The U.S. Supreme Court ruled 5–4 in *Adarand Contractors v. Pena* that affirmative action programs must meet a very high standard before they will be accepted. Such programs "must be subject to the most searching judicial inquiry and can survive only if they are 'narrowly tailored' to accomplish a 'compelling governmental interest'" (Greenhouse 1995).

In 1995, the Clinton administration ordered a review of affirmative action programs within the federal government. The review examined programs in a variety of areas, such as education, contracts, and the military. The review also contained a history of affirmative action and arguments in favor of the program. In response to *Adarand*, the administration issued guidelines to conform with the U.S. Supreme Court ruling. As one example, the guidelines said that affirmative action programs must be accompanied by specific instances of discrimination (Holmes 1995b).

Later decisions saw some shifts back toward affirmative action. For example, the court in the *Hopwood* case has ruled that Cheryl Hopwood, who sued because of her rejection by the University of Texas Law School, would have been rejected even under a race-neutral admissions policy. It further lifted its injunction that race could never be used in admissions decisions. The *Hopwood* case remains in the courts. In two other important cases regarding admissions to colleges and universities, federal courts in Michigan and the state of Washington accepted the argument that diversity was an important policy goal that would add to the educational experiences of minority and white students, though the Michigan case was still being litigated in spring 2001 (Springer 2001; Steinberg 2000; Wilgoren 2001).

There was an attempt by Ward Connerly's group to have a ballot initiative on affirmative action in Florida in 2000 (Bragg 1999a). However, Florida's governor, Jeb Bush, the brother of the Republican candidate for president in 2000, did not want the initiative on the ballot (Bragg 1999b). Reacting to the California and Texas cases, Governor Jeb Bush pushed a program called "One Florida," similar to what the California and Texas university systems enacted (Bragg 2000).

Legislatures in California and Texas adopted plans to maintain or increase minority enrollment in the university system. California adopted a 4 percent plan. Students taking an academic curriculum, who graduate in the top 4 percent of their class, would be automatically admitted to the university system regardless of test scores, though not necessarily to the more elite schools. Texas adopted a 10 percent plan (Gorman 1999). The admission point in the One Florida plan is 20 percent (Bragg 2000). The One Florida plan also calls for funds to improve the quality of education minority students are receiving (Taylor 1999c). Despite that, the Bush executive order to end affirmative action met with considerable opposition among minorities (Kilborn 2000).

The percentage solution plans in California, Texas, and Florida are not without criticism. There are differences in the quality of high schools, and students from weaker high schools, though in the appropriate percentage of their graduating class, might not be sufficiently well prepared to compete in college. It might provide an incentive for students to raise their grade point average by taking easier courses. Well-qualified minority students at high-quality high schools might not make the percentage cutoff (Gorman 1999).

There is another element to these kinds of plans in the wake of *Hopwood* and the CCRI. Minority high schools in California are much less likely to offer advanced placement courses than predominantly white schools. Because the more prestigious universities in California give extra credit in their admissions decisions to advanced placement courses, this places minority students at a disadvantage ("The New Affirmative Action Fight" 1999). Ward Connerly, one of the opponents of racial preferences, supported a lawsuit against the state complaining about this practice (Staples 1999).

We should also look at the experience since the elimination of affirmative action in California, Texas, and Florida. In California, especially in the elite law and business schools, enrollment of minorities dropped, though there was little change in other components of the University of California system (Bronner 1998). On the other hand, there was also an increase in the number of minority applications to the system (Honan 1998). In 1998 and 1999, minority enroll-ment at the University of Texas rebounded to its previous level as the 10 percent plan was implemented (see "The Diversity Project in Texas" 1999). In 2000, minority enrollment at the Florida university also increased (Bragg 2000).

The decline in enrollment at the University of California system has led a small number of critics of affirmative action to reassess their views (Holmes 1998). For example, Nathan Glazer, whose 1975 book was a strong critique of affirmative action, has changed his mind (Glazer 1997; see also Taub 1998).

> I believe the main reasons we have to continue racial preferences for blacks are, first, because this country has a special obligation to blacks that has not been fully discharged, and second, because strict application of the principle of qualification would send a message of despair to many blacks, a message that the nation is indifferent to their difficulties and problems. (quoted in Holmes 1998)

## Policy Alternatives

One set of policies that those opposed to affirmative action have proposed is to focus not on race, but on need or class (Kahlenberg 1996). For example, Texas state legislators considered admissions standards based on income, giv-ing preference or reserving spaces for low-income disadvantaged students regardless of race or ethnicity. As one Texas legislator put it, "It is inappropri-ate that a wealthy minority child be given a preference over an impoverished Anglo" (Zachary 1997).[27] One problem with the need-based preference is that test scores would still be used to determine which disadvantaged students get admitted under such a program, and whites outperform African American and Hispanic students even at the low-income levels. Thus, one result of such a plan might be to reduce the number of minority students (Zachary 1997). In any event, the 10 percent Texas plan did not include a need-based system.

A problem with need-based systems is that they focus only on the more common indicators of need, such as income, education, and occupation. Ri-chard Kahlenberg (1998) argues that three other measures of need ought to be considered: living in areas of concentrated poverty, wealth, and racial dis-crimination. Using these factors would increase the proportion of African Americans and Hispanics in the California system (using the University of California at Los Angeles as an example).

Lani Guinier (1997) has a different take on affirmative action and test scores. Guinier observes that minority enrollment in California and Texas universi-ties had declined and notes that Cheryl Hopwood grew up poor and went to less well known colleges in Texas. Thus, she lost points because of the lack of prestige of where she went to school. Guinier then argues that test scores, such as the LSAT required for admission to law schools such as the Univer-sity of Texas Law School that Hopwood had applied to, are overemphasized. Students from wealthier families score higher than students from poorer fami-lies. She argues that is because the wealthier families send their children to better schools, can afford coaching for tests, have more books in the home, and have traveled more. In other words, tests such as the SAT and LSAT do not so much test the merit of students as the merits of their backgrounds. Guinier further states that the "drive to succeed" is probably a better predictor of success, especially after school, than test scores. Her recommendation is to have colleges and universities set minimum test scores and then accept students via a lottery. Staying with her idea of cumulative voting, she also recommends that students who have overcome disadvantages or have something special to offer the school, students with excellent grades, and so forth, could be entered more than once to enhance their possibility of selection.

Guinier's and others' attack on the SAT (see, e.g., Sacks 1999) may be gaining support. In 1997, a task force at the University of California at Berkeley recommended that the university stop using the SAT for admission decisions (Garcia 1997). In 2001, the president of the University of California system proposed doing just that (Cloud 2001; Schemo 2001).

Robert Worth (1998) argues that the quota version of affirmative action has led to racial animosity, has diminished support for programs to help the poor, and has not helped African Americans or Hispanics, particularly poor ones. He uses the U.S. Army as an example of an institution that has extended equal opportunity to minorities without using quotas (although see Suro and Fletcher 1999 for a different view). As described by Worth, the Army expands the pool of applicants and then aggressively works with them so that they can be competitive. Students who go through this program enter West Point. Their SAT scores improved by over 100 points, they have better grade-point averages, fewer are dropouts, and so forth. He then turns to actions taken by University of California schools in the wake of the 1995 board of regents decision to end affirmative action programs. The schools, and Worth uses the University of California at San Diego (UCSD) as his major example, began an aggressive outreach program. There is evidence that the effort works, and the curriculum being used has been adopted by a large number of schools around the country (Rothstein 2001). In 1998, the University of Wisconsin adopted a plan, called Plan 2008, designed to increase the number of minorities in the university system over the next ten years. Elements of the plan included the kind of outreach program mentioned above, increasing the number of minority faculty and using private scholarships for disadvantaged and minority student high achievers (Selingo 1998). Of course, outreach programs and accepting college and university students based on need are very expensive and this would limit their application (Applebome 1997a; Worth 1998).

## Conclusion

The issue of equality is one that has troubled the country since the colonial period. **Prejudice** (the dislike of someone because of membership in a group) is not limited to the United States, but it does run up against important American ideals and values. Some would say that prejudice, racism, and sexism are an integral part of the United States (see, e.g., Bell 1987, 1992) and that they still remain a problem. Others, such as Thernstrom and Thernstrom (1997), argue that African Americans have made considerable progress, much of it before the advent of affirmative action.[28] What needs to be done is for African Americans to escape from victimology (Steele 1998; McWhorter 2000). There is evidence that prejudice is declining. Although inequality from a class or economic standpoint is increasing (see chapter 2), gaps between minorities and whites in income and education have narrowed. Things have improved in the United States; this has been one of the themes of this book. Much remains to be done, yet we have also come far.

The country also needs to understand the implications of demographic changes occurring in the United States. Consider the following quote:

> Already 1 American in 4 defines himself or herself as Hispanic or nonwhite. If current trends in immigration and birth rates persist, the Hispanic population will have further increased an estimated 21%, the Asian presence about 22%, blacks almost 12% and whites a little more than 2% when the 20th century ends. . . . By 2056, when someone born today [1990] will be 66 years old, the "average" U.S. resident, as defined by Census statistics, will trace his or her descent to Africa, Asia, the Hispanic world, the Pacific Islands, Arabia—almost anywhere but white Europe. (Henry 1990, p. 28)

To that we can add that women already comprise more than half the population. Will it make sense to talk about minorities at that point? Does it make sense to do so now? Such changes, and the implications for political power and economic resources, have underlined debates over things such as affirmative action, immigration reform, and bilingual education.

Perhaps the best way to handle problems of inequality is to allow for fairness (which may mean programs such as Head Start) and to replace looking at each other as a member of a group with looking at each other as a unique individual. Martin Luther King Jr. told us decades ago that we should learn to judge others not on the basis of their race, ethnic group, religious group, and so forth, but "on the content of their character" (Williams 1987, p. 205). It is a goal that has not yet been achieved, but it is a goal worthy of our aspirations.

## Key Concepts

*Adarand Contractors v. Pena* (1995)

affirmative action

Americans with Disabilities Act (ADA) (1990)

*Baker v. Carr* (1962)

*Bakke v. Board of Regents of the University of California* (1978)

*Brown v. Board of Education of Topeka, Kansas* (1954)

California Civil Rights Initiative (CCRI)

civil rights

Civil Rights Act (1964)

compensatory justice

cumulative voting

Equal Pay Act (1963)

Equal Rights Amendment (ERA)

equality

equality of opportunity

equality of outcome

Fifteenth Amendment

Fourteenth Amendment

Hopwood v. Texas (1996)

institutional racism

Nineteenth Amendment

one-drop rule

political equality

prejudice

quota

racial profiling

representation

retail racism

Shaw v. Reno (1993)

social construct

target

Thirteenth Amendment

Twenty-Sixth Amendment

Voting Rights Act (1965)

---

## Reflections

1. The subject of this chapter is equality, one of the three political values discussed in chapter 1. Where do you stand on the idea of equality versus freedom or order? Given the history of the United States, what priority do you think equality has had as compared to freedom or order? Why?

2. One of the most controversial issues of equality is affirmative action. It is based on the idea of compensatory justice, to make up for past wrongs done to groups and for institutional barriers that remain for those groups. Do you think affirmative action is an appropriate remedy for past wrongs? Do you agree with the argument that affirmative action is itself a form of discrimination? How would you reconcile these two conflicting ideas? Do you agree with policies established in California, Texas, and Florida to guarantee college admissions to students at the top of their high school graduating class?

3. One group not mentioned in this chapter is gays. Gay rights has been as

charged an issue as any considered in this entire text. President Clinton sought, only partially successfully, to legitimize gays in the military. A number of states and local governments have had gay rights ordinances or initiatives while others have had anti-gay rights ordinances and initiatives. Why do you think gay rights has been so controversial? Some have argued that gay rights should be considered as another kind of civil right, similar to those advocated in the civil rights movement. Do you agree with this position? Why or why not?

4. According to the 2000 census, the United States is becoming more diversified and Hispanics will soon be the largest minority group. What do you think will the impact of these demographic changes? In what ways might they affect public policy?

## Notes

1. The agreement was necessitated by the rule adopted by the Continental Congress in Philadelphia that the revolution had to be unanimously agreed upon. The movie *1776* presents a dramatic and moving depiction of these events.

2. Slavery is recognized in Article I, Section 2, the "three-fifths compromise," which referred to three-fifths of "other persons" in calculating representation for the House of Representatives and for taxation. Those "other persons" were the slaves. Article I, Section 9 says that the slave trade shall not be prohibited prior to 1808. Again, the Constitution uses euphemistic language, referring to "The Migration or Importation of such Persons as any of the States now existing shall think proper to admit."

3. The white primary, one of the pieces of legislation introduced in southern states in the 1890s and 1900s, forbade blacks from voting in primary elections. Because Democrats won virtually all the general elections during this time, the primary vote was the only meaningful one.

4. On the importance of proportional representation of African Americans, see Bell (1987).

5. For a history of the civil rights movement, with a focus on the period from 1954 to 1965, see Branch (1988) and Williams (1987).

6. Sex was added on the floor of the House of Representatives by a Virginia congressman hoping that it would cause the bill to lose support.

7. There have been some attempts to get three more state legislatures to ratify the ERA even though the deadline has passed. After all, the most recent amendment to be ratified, the Twenty-Seventh, was originally proposed in 1789 as part of the original Bill of Rights. It was not ratified until 1992, 203 years later! On the other hand, several state legislatures that ratified the ERA have considered rescinding their ratification.

8. For a history of the disability movement, and the lessons drawn from that movement, see McGuire 1994 and Shapiro 1994.

9. For a history of the disability rights movement, see Berkowitz (1994).

10. For a discussion of the implementation and likely success of the Americans with Disabilities Act, see Johnson and Baldwin (1993) and Bishop and Jones (1993).

11. This is similar to the rule of thumb used in Nazi Germany to determine who was Jewish and therefore should be exterminated. A person was considered a Jew if at least one grandparent was Jewish.

12. See, for example, Fischer et al. (1996), Jacoby and Glauberman (1995), and Kincheloe et al. (1997).

13. For a history of the civil rights movement, see Klinkner and Smith (1999).

14. The acclaimed television series *I'll Fly Away* dramatized through two families, one white, one black, the changes the civil rights movement was beginning to bring in the South and how difficult that change was.

15. The changes in the civil rights movement and the national reaction to it can be seen in the Public Broadcasting System series *Eyes on the Prize*. The original series documented racial

oppression and the marches and demonstrations. Part II focused on the riots and urban marches. There is a much more positive tone to the first series than to the second.

16. There is a scene in *Jungle Fever* that hauntingly parallels one in *Gone with the Wind*. In the latter movie, Scarlett O'Hara, living in Atlanta as Sherman's northern army is making its inexorable march to the city, is trying to find a doctor to help her friend's childbirth delivery. She comes across a gruesome scene of wounded and dying Confederate soldiers out in the street with the doctor and nurses able to do very little. The camera fades to a panorama and one sees, without a shot being fired, the devastation of war.

In *Jungle Fever*, the character played by Wesley Snipes is looking for his crack-addicted brother (played by Samuel L. Jackson), trying to retrieve a television set the brother stole from their parents. He goes to a crack hotel and confronts his brother, who tells him that he sold it to pay for more drugs. As Snipes leaves, the camera fades to a panorama of the addicted, those injured and dying in the drug wars.

17. In *Boyz in the Hood*, the young male character is saved from inner-city life because he was raised by his father. Others in the neighborhood had no father and were not so lucky. In *South Central*, the main character goes to jail and meets an inmate who straightens him out. He then rescues his son from a boyhood friend.

18. For an argument by a moderate Republican that the Republican Party, which had historically supported African Americans, had politically abandoned African Americans, see Sanders 2001.

19. The furlough program was actually enacted under Dukakis's Republican predecessor. Nor, of course, did Dukakis personally approve of Horton's furlough. Further, Horton's first name was William. Only in the ads was he known as "Willie."

20. It should be pointed out that the white truck driver was saved because nearby African American residents came to his rescue.

21. There seems little doubt that Ashcroft did, indeed, misstate White's record (Taylor 1999b, 2001). For an interesting story of why Ashcroft was wrong about White, see Boehlert (2001).

22. For a discussion of the different forms affirmative action can take, see Ezorsky (1991).

23. A pundit is a person who is asked his or her expert opinion about public affairs.

24. For a discussion on how racial quotas affected American politics, see Carmines and Stimson (1989) and Edsall and Edsall (1992).

25. Gertrude Ezorsky (1991) argues that affirmative action programs have helped African Americans move into more blue-collar jobs as well.

26. This is similar to death penalty cases, where the U.S. Supreme Court held that the presence of statistical discrepancies was insufficient grounds for overturning death penalties. Actual racial discrimination needed to be demonstrated.

27. In a special 1996 *Firing Line* debate over affirmative action, the team supporting the end of race-based preferences supported class-based preferences.

28. For a critique of Thernstrom and Thernstrom (1997), see Loury (1997). For a sympathetic though critical biographical snapshot of the Thernstroms, see Shatz (2001).

# 10 At the Dawn of the Twenty-First Century

*Consider how policy typically gets made. Experts squabble, interest groups
lobby, and staff members horse-trade. Then politicians, who may or may not
know all of the ins and outs of what they're doing, work out an awkward
compromise that keeps a majority of their constituencies barely content.*
(Solomon 2001)

Difficult policy challenges and exciting opportunities are facing the United
States and those who lead this country at the beginning of the twenty-first
century. There is pessimism and cynicism about the ability of government at
any level to solve problems and deliver services. That cynicism grew out of
the perceived failures of the Great Society of the 1960s and the inability to
resolve the economic problems of the 1970s. It led to the tax revolt epitomized by Proposition 13 in California and the election of Ronald Reagan in
1980. Government, Reagan said during his 1981 inaugural address, was not
the solution; it was the problem. The answer was therefore less government.
The elections of 1994 seem to fit this cynical view that government cannot do
anything.

In capturing Congress for the first time in a generation, Republicans made a
number of promises. Some of the changes called for under the Contract with
America have come about. Welfare policy, disliked by almost all, was changed
in a comprehensive fashion. Perhaps most surprising of all was the disappearance of the federal budget deficits and their replacement by budget surpluses.
The Clinton administration, as well as the Republican-controlled Congress,
contributed to many of the policy changes that occurred in the 1990s and set the
context for policy making in the twenty-first century. Cynicism and pessimism
still abound, but as has been shown throughout the book, a certain amount of
optimism is warranted. Government programs can work. Difficult policy problems can be alleviated. The highly disputatious election of 2000 put government in the hands of the Republicans, at least temporarily.[1] The second Bush
administration faces, as does any administration, challenges and opportunities.

One of the lessons of this book is how much public policy is influenced by the way it is made (the policy process), by features of the political system, and by ideology. Policy identification and formulation are critical in structuring the rest of the policy process. Identification, in particular, is affected by differing ideological perspectives. Policy adoption may produce unanticipated consequences (Gillon 2000; Solomon 2001). Adoption is difficult to trace when it interacts with federalism. Incrementalism is a characteristic of adoption. Because of the presence of so many groups (pluralism) and intellectual limitations, there is compromise, bargaining, and small adjustments. Thus, even policies rightfully billed as overhauls, such as the Republican agenda outlined above, leave much of the present system in place. But over time, small adjustments can add up to significant change (health policy is a good example). Those who understand these features can work within the system and move it in desired directions.

This closing chapter has three purposes. First, it summarizes the major themes of the book. Second, it looks at significant policy changes and challenges that affect the United States. Finally, the chapter offers reasons to view the future optimistically.

## Themes

### The Government Issue

One theme that recurs throughout this book is the government issue. The government issue has three related dimensions. First, should government get involved? There are some policy areas where government involvement is critical and undisputed. Criminal justice and defense policies are perhaps the best examples of this. If government's most important function is the maintenance of order, then there is little question that government should be involved. Even in the foreign policy area, there are questions raised about how assertive a foreign policy the United States should have (see below). Most also accept government's role in the education of their children. About 90 percent of elementary and secondary schoolchildren attend public schools. However, the other 10 percent obviously do not, and some have argued that the private sector does better at educating the young than the public sector.

Other policy areas require a rationale for government's involvement. In health and environmental policy, that rationale is the failure of private markets to consider those who are poor and/or uninsured or are not easily incorporated into private decision making (e.g., negative externalities). Even where there is a justification for governmental action, market alternatives are offered as a better or more efficient means of achieving public ends. In most policy areas, therefore, the question of whether government should be involved underlies policy debates.

The second dimension of the government issue emanates from the first. If it is agreed that government should be involved in a particular issue, which level of government should it be? In some areas, the consensus is strong. Education is a state responsibility, administered by local school districts, though even here the Bush administration is proposing a more assertive federal role (see below). In other policy areas, the question is not so easily resolved. Thus federalism and intergovernmental relations are an inherent part of many policy debates. President Reagan's "new federalism," in both its proposed and de facto forms, was an attempt to shift domestic policy responsibility onto the states. And, indeed, much of this has happened.

The third dimension of the government issue is the nature of its involvement. Consider, again, environmental policy. Although the United States relies primarily on regulation, there are alternative government methods that might be used. For example, market reform proposals such as the effluent tax would retain government's responsibility, but allow private decision makers to react to economic incentives rather than to directives or mandates. Within the regulatory approach, environmental agencies might set standards but let industry decide how to meet them. In the criminal justice area, a broad perspective would look at societal-level concerns, such as the existence of an urban "underclass," for the causes of crime and try to treat them. The narrower view, which focuses on the individual's deviant behavior, would concentrate on law enforcement and punishment.

### Federalism

In virtually every public policy area, the states have become major actors. While the federal government was unable to pass a comprehensive health insurance bill during the first two years of the Clinton administration, states have acted. Even when the federal government made significant changes, the states played a major role in implementation. Welfare reform is a case in point. Educational reform was primarily a state initiative, though with increasing federal involvement. States even led the way in welfare reform, with several states cutting off additional AFDC payments for additional children. Of course, the states and local governments already had an important role in administering federal programs.

## Public Opinion

One of the most significant findings of this book is the important role of public opinion in public policy making. It was argued in chapter 1 that policy adoption normally requires agreement among two of the three following groups: the chief executive, legislature, and the public. Public opinion initially supported President Clinton's Health Security Act, but over time developed concerns about the proposal (aided by interest group attempts to influence public opinion).

Another interesting example of public opinion concerns affirmative action (chapter 9). As we saw, although there has been a considerable flurry of activity over the issue from the mid-1990s on, the public view is more complex, perhaps, than the policy system or policy leaders realize. The public opposes quotas, targets, and other preferential programs that seek equality of outcome. However, the public strongly favors compensatory programs, such as Head Start, and efforts to expand the pool of applicants to include more minorities and women ("Affirmative Action: The Public Reaction" 1995). Such a view supports the concept of equality, but the debate over affirmative action has been simplified down to quotas.

There are other ways that public opinion influences public policy. While public opinion is seldom well informed (see the discussion in chapter 1), it does set boundaries or restrictions that limit policy makers' options. Within those boundaries, policy makers are reasonably free to choose.

Additionally, the public's views toward government affects policy making. As we saw in the first chapter, the public does not think highly of government, especially at the federal level. Trust and efficacy measures are substantially lower than in the 1990s; pessimism and cynicism, perhaps fueled by the media, are up. But the public's views can be safely characterized as ambivalent: While the public does not like government in general, it does like many of the things that government does. The trick for policy makers, and those who seek to influence them, is how to gauge, and perhaps manipulate, public opinion to support particular policy proposals.

## Divided Government

Another important concept that has affected the making of public policy in the United States is divided government. Divided government (where one party controls Congress and the other the presidency) has been the rule since the end of World War II. The normal institutional jealousies between the president and Congress are exacerbated by partisan differences. Some had hoped that with a Democratic president and Congress in 1993, much of the bickering would end and needed policy changes could be made. But Bill Clinton won the presidency in 1992 with only 43 percent of the vote, and the course for him in 1993–94 was difficult. The big deficit reduction act in 1993 was passed with virtually no Republican support. Trade bills, such as the North American Free Trade Agreement, saw much opposition among the Democrats and won approval only with the support of Republicans. While much was accomplished, health care reform, which lacked solid Democratic support, typified, perhaps unfairly, the problems of the Clinton administration.

When the Republicans regained control of Congress following the 1994 elections, divided government was resurrected with a vengeance. Republicans threatened many programs dear to the heart of Democrats. Whereas President Clinton did not cast a veto in his first two years of office, he cast a number beginning in 1995. The conflict between the Republican majority and the Democratic president was so strong and so bitter that it led to two government shutdowns.

Clinton won reelection in 1996 and Republican majorities in Congress grew slimmer. The bitterness of the 1995–96 session was enhanced in 1999, when scandals, the probing of the independent prosecutor, and policy conflict resulted in President Clinton's impeachment by the House of Representatives, though the Senate did not convict.

Despite the continued divided government and the partisan and personal acrimony, there were a number of accomplishments: welfare was reformed, budget deficits turned into budget surpluses, significant changes were made to Medicare, the economy experienced its longest expansion, and U.S. intervention was productive in Northern Ireland, the Balkans, and the Middle East (though the troubles in those three places have not ended).

The very interesting 2000 elections create a different situation. George W. Bush won the presidency, though he lost the popular vote (and Democrats think he probably lost Florida as well). Republican majorities in Congress grew slimmer, with the Senate a tie. Nevertheless, the Republicans entered the twenty-first century in control of the presidency and Congress (and the Supreme Court) until Vermont Senator Jim Jeffords defected from the Republican Party, turning control of the Senate over to the Democrats. The Bush administration promises very different policy priorities than the Clinton administration. While we did have (briefly) a unified, rather than a divided, government, a working majority, particularly in the Senate, does not exist. The 2002 elections may produce political changes that have policy implications.

## Challenges and Opportunities

In addition to recurring themes, individual chapters suggest challenges and opportunities that will face policy makers in the twenty-first century.

### The Economy

As 2001 began, the status of the American economy was decidedly mixed. Budget deficits had for decades provided the context for economic policy making. While America still has a substantial public debt, surpluses have replaced deficits. If one can believe ten-year budget projections, the surpluses could very well continue at least through 2010. That is the good news. The bad news is that beginning in the second half of 2000, the economy as a whole and the stock market in particular weakened. Economic growth slowed dramatically and the markets declined. Recession was on everyone's lips. Perhaps by the time you read this book, we will be in a full-blown recession. Maybe the economy will move back to its expansion track.

An important question is what to do with the surplus. One could save the surplus and therefore pay down the debt. We could give back some or all of the surplus through tax relief. President Bush's tax cut passed in 2001, costing at least $1.35 trillion over ten years. We could use it to reinforce programs such as Social Security and Medicare. We could spend some of the funds on new programs, say, to cover those without health insurance or Medicare recipients without prescription drug coverage.

Social Security was (and is) the focus of much discussion. There is disagreement about elements of the policy problem and proposed solutions. Some think that Social Security is a bad deal, a bad investment, especially for the young. Some think (often the same as the previous group) that Social Security will become bankrupt as the large baby-boomer generation retires. Others do not see the problem, but believe the program is basically sound. Some want to tinker with the program while others support significant change. Some would like to scrap the program and replace it with a fully privatized system. President Bush favors partial privatization. The decline in the stock market in 2000 and 2001 makes privatization look a bit riskier.

### Foreign and Defense Policy

If U.S. foreign and defense policy had a theme or underlying framework in the post–World War II era, it may be summed up as containment of communism. From Harry Truman to the elder George Bush, containment characterized America's relationships with her allies, with Eastern Bloc nations, and with Third and Fourth World countries. The triumph of the Persian Gulf War in 1991 set the stage for American dominance.

The end of the Cold War changed many of our assumptions. With the absence, at least to this point, of an enemy that directly threatens national security, we are unsure about our role in the world. The pre–World War II isolationism that typified American foreign policy, hidden during the Cold War, has reappeared. Ethnic conflicts, the clash of civilizations, as Samuel Huntington (1993a) would put it, exist in many parts of the world. What is the United States to do when it sees a Bosnia, a Somalia, or a Rwanda? The answer is not yet clear, though some, such as Richard Haass (1997a), have suggested possible roles. Haass's "reluctant sheriff" concept looks promising.

The Clinton administration was ambivalent here. While candidate Clinton was critical of the elder Bush's hands-off policy in the Balkans, President Clinton was also somewhat reluctant to get involved at first. The failed mission in Somalia created a hesitancy that took several years to shed. The lack of U.S. intervention in Rwanda is largely attributable to the failure in Somalia.

But that changed in the mid- and late-1990s. U.S. and NATO forces intervened in Bosnia and later in Kosovo. The administration also was actively engaged in trying to resolve conflicts in the Middle East and Northern Ireland.

The George W. Bush administration is likely to have a much different foreign policy. It promises to be much less interventionist, much less likely to use humanitarian problems as the rationale for engagement. Realism and national self-interest are the likely watchwords.*

Further, in 2001, the Bush administration began a review of our defense capability and needs. That review is likely to provide direction for U.S. defense policy over the next several years. The administration is also committed to some kind of missile defense.

## Welfare and Poverty Policy

The 1996 Personal Responsibility and Work Opportunities Reconciliation Act dramatically reformed the nation's welfare programs. Gone is the federal entitlement to cash assistance. Gone is the categorical grant program Aid to Families with Dependent Children. They are replaced by work requirements, family caps, and time limitations on welfare. The welfare rolls have dramatically declined, partly because of welfare reform, partly because of action by states that predate welfare reform, and partly by the growing economy of the late 1990s.

But issues remain. How are those off welfare faring? What do we do with those who cannot get off welfare when their time limit is up? What happens if the economy goes into a recession?

Welfare reform is due for reauthorization in 2002, and there are studies to answer some of those questions. It seems clear that the changes wrought by welfare reform, changes that are anything but incremental, are here to stay. Tinkering with the program is the most likely outcome.

## Health Policy

The failure of the Clinton Health Security Act to be passed was another in a long history of failures in enacting national health insurance in the United States. At the same time, fundamental change has occurred in this area, known as the managed care revolution. Most people with employment-based health insurance, a majority of Medicaid recipients, and about 13 percent of Medicare recipients are covered under some kind of managed care arrangement (Dudley and Luft 2001; Patel and Rushefsky 1999).

There are a number of health care policy issues facing policy makers in the twenty-first century. One set focuses on what was mentioned above: managed care. There has been a backlash to the imposition of managed care (a form of rationing) that has led many of the states and the federal government to pass or consider legislation providing for patient rights. The strongest part of the various pieces of legislation, seen in only a handful of states, is the right to sue a health plan for lack of service.

---

*The September 11, 2001, terrorist attacks on the United States changed American foreign policy. The "war on terrorism" led the Bush administration to seek international cooperation, work with the United Nations, engage in nation-building in Afghanistan, and seek a solution to the Israeli-Palestinian problem. Of course, all of this can be justified on the basis of national self-interest.

Medicare is the focus of other policy issues. It faces some of the same problems as Social Security: the demographic reality of an aging population as the baby-boomer generation begins to retire around 2010. The solvency of the Part A trust fund is the center of concern here. Going in a different direction are attempts to expand and modernize Medicare, particularly by adding some kind of prescription medication benefit. Underlying all these issues are the costs of Medicare.

The costs of Medicaid to the states is also a concern. While managed care has alleviated some of the cost problems, there is continued pressure on state budgets from the program (Enos 2001).

Much of the pressure on Medicare, Medicaid, and private plans comes from the increase in spending for prescription medication. In 1999, overall health spending rose just a bit over 6 percent; spending for prescription drugs increased by just over 18 percent (Enos 2001). There is little sign that there will be any abatement in prescription drug costs, and it will continue to create problems for policy makers.

There is one other problem in health care that we need to mention, the uninsured. Nearly 40 million Americans lack health insurance. The literature is clear that those without health insurance make less use of the health care system and tend to have their health problems less well treated than those with health insurance (Patel and Rushefsky 1999). This issue was little discussed during the 2000 presidential elections and is not currently high on the policy agenda. Managed care, by eliminating cross-subsidies and trying to squeeze costs as much as it can, has exacerbated the problem. There are some proposals, such as tax credits, for dealing with the issue. But it seems to lack a sense of urgency.

### Environmental Policy

Except for certain periods, such as the late 1960s to early 1970s, concern about the environment has never been foremost. Public opinion polls show consistent support for strong environmental protection, even at the expense of other goals, but it has never been a critical issue. Nevertheless, the underlying support is there for environmental protection.

The environmental problems of the twenty-first century are complex indeed. Some are global in nature. The major one is global climate warming or the greenhouse effect. While there appears to be mounting evidence of global warming (see the discussion in Lemonick 2001), that evidence is controversial and subject to challenge. Further, meeting the challenge of global warming would be expensive. But perhaps not meeting that challenge will be costly as well, except the costs lie in the future. In any event, it does not appear that the United States will support the Kyoto Protocols or the 2001 amendments.

There are also environmental policy problems of a less global nature. Evaluating environmental threats and ordering action priorities are the two major challenges here. For example, how much evidence is needed to confirm (or disaffirm) an environmental threat? This is the risk-control issue discussed in chapter 6. Environmental controversies begin at this most basic level of knowledge: How safe is safe enough? What is the risk? Which are the more serious environmental problems and which can be placed on the back burner? Nevertheless, our environment, particularly our air and water, is cleaner than it was thirty years ago.

## Criminal Justice

This has been one of the major success stories of government policy. For whatever reason, crime rates have declined, though they began to level in 2000. Perhaps it was because we were putting more people in prison. Perhaps it was because we put more police out there. Perhaps it was the economy. Perhaps it was a decline in the crack cocaine wars. We have done better, but crimes rates are still high and policy problems remain.

One major policy issue is the war on drugs. Clearly drug use and the attempt to stem it are related to the amount of crime and the number of people in prison. Some have argued that the war on drugs, like Prohibition in the 1920s, is a failure and ought to be ended. Drugs, these advocates argue, should be legalized or decriminalized, particularly marijuana, which may have useful medicinal properties. Others argue that the costs of drug addiction would outweigh any gains from legalization.

A second criminal justice issue is the reexamination of the death penalty. Based on the use of DNA evidence, a number of people on death row have been freed. It has led one state, Illinois, to suspend the death penalty until new procedures can be developed to make sure innocent people are not condemned to the ultimate sanction. Perhaps enforcing life imprisonment without the possibility of parole will help resolve this issue.

Finally, there are issues in this area surrounding equality. Minorities, primarily Hispanics and African Americans, are disproportionately represented in the criminal justice system. This can even have an impact on elections, as the 2000 election in Florida showed (Lantigua 2001). Further, problems with the police and minorities, particularly relating to racial profiling, remain (see, e.g., Clines 2001).

## Education

Education has been the subject of much policy interest. Some think that, based on national and international exams, many of our schools are failing. Proposed solutions include better teaching training and more testing (accountability). Others seek more fundamental reforms.

Those seeking major reforms look to inject competition into the public school system. The fastest-growing option is charter schools. Milwaukee has a voucher program that is now nearly a decade old, and Florida has started a statewide voucher program. There are also private voucher programs. Controversy rages over vouchers, in particular whether they weaken the public schools and whether they result in better student achievement.

George W. Bush, as candidate and president, has straddled both incremental and fundamental sides. He proposes additional federal money for education, more flexibility for the states in using that money, and stringent testing. If poor schools, which get the bulk of federal funds, do not show improvement, the president would like to use the federal funds (Title I) for vouchers.

One policy that has gained support is smaller class size. Gains in student achievement and other outcomes stemming from this change, according to some of the literature, outweigh those from voucher programs or charter schools.

### Equality

Perhaps the most difficult issue for the United States to come to grips with is race. It has marked this nation since its founding (in the Declaration of Independence, the Constitution, Jim Crow, the civil rights movement, and so on) and affected its politics. There is absolutely no question that minorities, especially African Americans, are better off since the heyday of the civil rights movement.

Yet race continues to haunt us. This perhaps nowhere more true than in the debate over affirmative action. Legislative, executive, judicial, and electoral challenges suggest that affirmative action as a policy is fading. Affirmative action is, in many ways, a divisive policy. It sometimes tries to end discrimination (which continues to exist in the United States) by discriminating, by looking at group differences. While we have always considered ethnic group differences, few policies have been so institutionalized as affirmative action (Jim Crow laws being a major exception). Some African Americans oppose affirmative action on the grounds that it is harmful to them.

But the public is of two minds on this issue. Quotas and targets are opposed, but compensatory help for minorities is strongly supported. The great task here is to transform affirmative action into a policy that all groups can support and do so without raising ethnic and racial conflict. That is no easy task.

Finally, findings from the 2000 census reinforce the need to look at equality issues. Hispanics are now tied with African Americans for the largest minority and will soon overtake them. Diversity in the United States is increasing. In many (though not all) places, segregation is decreasing (Cohen and Cohn 2001; Glaeser and Vigdor 2001).

## Some Concluding Thoughts

This survey of American public policy shows both failures and successes. It also shows considerable change and a degree of responsiveness to public opinion. Government at all levels, but especially at the federal level, is considerably larger than it was 200 or 100 or even 30 years ago. This growth has come about because of demands for new services, and technological, economic, and demographic changes.

America's historical roots suggest a skepticism and fear of government, yet a belief that government is a necessity. The Founding Fathers wrought a system that balanced the need for order with the need for restraint—the two work hand in hand. Thus, the inability to make rapid, massive policy shifts reflects a carefully crafted design that would set one branch of government against the other. The result has sometimes been stalemate, frequently frustration (Kelman 1987), but also continuing order in the face of change and challenge.

There are reasons for the cynicism and skepticism about government's ability to act. Some conservatively based ideologies fear government coercion and seek to limit it wherever possible. Others look at the challenges to be faced and express dismay that they cannot be resolved. The problems that government must address are difficult and complex; perhaps this is one reason the private sector does not consider these kinds of problems. The U.S. political system is based on compromise and negotiation, and few participants are completely satisfied with the outcome. Further, because of the nation's democratic, liberal nature, government tools for influencing others are limited. Mussolini, it was said, made the trains run on time; Amtrak does not. Would you prefer the former to the latter?

Yet we should not completely accept this cynical and skeptical view. Things have been accomplished. The budget deficits have, at least for a while, disappeared. Our welfare system has been reformed. Our environment is cleaner. Crime rates are down. Teen pregnancy rates are down. Discrimination has lessened, though by no means disappeared. Some of these have occurred because we engaged in a policy of tough love. Robert Samuelson (2000) argues that the lesson of tough love policies is "if you demand more of people—if you make them more responsible for their own behavior—you will get more from them. Their lives will improve." That is one path for public policy.

One of the themes of this book has been a spirit of optimism. A hopeful view of public policy, cautioned by appropriate realities and a willingness to meet challenges and opportunities, is fully warranted.

> Seen over the broad span of historic time and place, American society works pretty well. We have been spared secret police knocking at our doors; we have enjoyed extended economic prosperity; there has been no widespread starvation. We have absorbed multitudes of the wretched of the earth, succeeded in assuring most people a decent old age, and saved a surprising amount of the natural beauty of the American continent. Compared with our achievements, our problems and shortcomings seem trivial. Although we should not give government all the credit for this, we should not deny it *any* credit either. (Kelman 1987, p. 286; emphasis in the original)

> But what the good news unequivocally tells us is that it is never too late to change the world. In that sense, there is a bright thread running through all these examples: intractable or "impossible" dilemmas can be solved. Our efforts matter; when we attempt reform, we can be crowned with success. It is not coincidence that the aspects of life that have gotten better are those that people have dedicated themselves to improving. America can still become what it wants to be. We do not have to

accept what we see out the window; rather, we can make the view one of our choosing. (Easterbrook 1999, p. 25)

## Reflections

1. In chapter 1, the policy process and the structural features of the political system that affect it were examined. Now that you have read the eight policy chapters, which of these features do you think has the strongest impact on policy making? Are there any features that you would change? Which ones? Why? What changes in the political features would you make?

2. Now that you have gone through these chapters, which phases of the policy process do you think are the most important? It is argued in chapter 1 that problem identification is vital. Do you agree with that emphasis? Is budgeting or implementation as important or more important than the earlier stages of the policy process?

3. In this closing chapter are brief descriptions of major policy challenges and opportunities facing our leaders in the twenty-first century. Which of these challenges do you think are the more important ones? Why? Are there any other challenges that you see as vital? Which ones?

4. This chapter attempts to present a "cautiously optimistic" view of government in America. Do you think such optimism is warranted? Are there grounds for being more optimistic? Or is this text, perhaps, not pessimistic or skeptical enough?

5. Finally, consider again the government issue. Based on the chapters and other reading and research you may have done, do you think there is too much government involvement in your life? If so, in which areas? Are there some policy issues that you think call for more government action? Which ones?

## Notes

1. Writing a book that is reasonably current is a risky business, because things can change. For example, between the first and second editions of this book, the Soviet Union disappeared and the Cold War ended. As a result of the 2000 elections, Republicans controlled the presidency, the House, and the Senate. Then Senator Jeffords's decision to leave the Republican Party and become an independent turned control of the Senate over to the Democrats. Divided government had returned, placing in jeopardy some of President George W. Bush's policy proposals. The 2002 elections could return control of the Senate to the Republicans, or the Democrats could regain control over both houses.

\* \* \*

The terrorists attacks against the United States on September 11, 2001, changed politics and public policy. A strong majority of the American public trusted government and thought the country was moving in the right direction. A spirit of national unity appeared among our leaders. President Bush declared a war on terrorism. But the country was also moving into a recession, and a number of public policy issues were taken off the policy agenda. Finally, the era of budget surplus, only a few years old, seemed to come to an end.

# References

## Preface and Chapter 1

Advisory Commission on Intergovernmental Relations. 1984. *Regulatory Federalism: Policy, Process, Impact and Reform*. Washington, DC: Advisory Commission on Intergovernmental Relations.

Anderson, James E. 1997. *Public Policymaking*. 3d ed. Boston: Houghton Mifflin.

Apple, R.W., Jr. 1986. "A Lesson from Schultz." *New York Times* (December 12).

———. 1995. "Risky Course for Clinton." *New York Times* (February 1).

*Baker v. Carr*, 369 US 186 (1962).

Baumgartner, Frank R., and Bryan R. Jones. 1993. *Agendas and Instability in American Politics*. Chicago: University of Chicago Press.

Berry, Jeffrey M. 1997. *The Interest Group Society*. 3d ed. New York: Longman.

Blendon, Robert J., John M. Benson, Mollyann Brodie, Mario Brossard, Drew E. Altman, and Richard Morin. 1997. "What Do Americans Know About Entitlements?" *Health Affairs* 16, no. 5 (September/October): 111–116.

Bowman, Ann O'M., and Richard C. Kearney. 1986. *The Resurgence of the States*. Englewood Cliffs, NJ: Prentice-Hall.

Brewer, Garry D., and Peter DeLeon. 1983. *The Foundations of Policy Analysis*. Pacific Grove, CA: Brooks/Cole.

Broder, David S. 1989. "No-Hands Government." *Washington Post* (January 8).

Brown, Lawrence D. 1994. "Politics, Money, and Health Care Reform." *Health Affairs* 13, no. 2 (Spring): 175–184.

Brownstein, Ronald. 1999a. "Millennium Mark Is a Good Time to Fix Our Anachronistic Systems." *Los Angeles Times* (July 5).

———. 1999b. "Good Times Allow U.S. to Tackle Its Woes—If Politicians Don't Fumble." *Los Angeles Times* (July 12).

Burns, James MacGregor, J.W. Peltason, Thomas E. Cronin, and David B. Magleby. 1998. *Government by the People*. 17th ed. Upper Saddle River, NJ: Prentice Hall.

Cantril, Albert H., and Susan Davis Cantril. 1999. *Reading Mixed Signals: Ambivalence in American Public Opinion About Government*. Washington, DC: Woodrow Wilson Center Press.

Cappella, Joseph N., and Kathleen Hall Jamieson. 1997. *Spiral of Cynicism: The Press and the Public Good*. New York: Oxford University Press.

Cobb, Roger, Jennie Keith-Ross, and Marc Howard Ross. 1976. "Agenda Building as a Comparative Political Process." *American Political Science Review* 70, no. 1 (March): 126–138.

Cohen, Richard E. 1993. "Some Unity!" *National Journal* 25, no. 39 (September 25): 2290–2294.

———. 2000. "A History of Election-Year Lawmaking." *National Journal* 32, no. 4 January 22): 224–225.

Corwin, Edwin S. 1940. *The President: Office and Powers*. New York: New York University Press.

Council on Excellence in Government. 1999. *America Unplugged: Citizens and Their Government*. www.excelgov.org/excel/unplugged.htm.

Craig, Stephen C. 1993. *The Malevolent Leaders: Popular Discontent in America*. Boulder: Westview Press.

Cushman, John H., Jr. 1995. "G.O.P.'s Plan for Environment Is Facing a Big Test in Congress." *New York Times* (July 17).

Cutler, Lloyd N. 1987. "The Cost of Divided Government." *New York Times* (November 22).

Dahl, Robert A. 1967. *Pluralist Democracy in the United States: Conflict and Consent*. Chicago: Rand McNally.

DeLeon, Peter. 1999. "The Stages Approach to the Policy Process: What Has It Done? Where Is It Going?" In *Theories of the Policy Process*, ed. Paul A. Sabatier. Boulder: Westview Press, pp. 19–32.

Dery, David. 1984. *Problem Definition in Policy Analysis*. Lawrence: University of Kansas Press.

Dietz, Thomas, and Robert W. Rycroft. 1988. *The Risk Professionals*. New York: Russell Sage Foundation.

"Does More Money Make Better Schools?" 1999. *Springfield News-Leader* (November 5).

Domhoff, G. William. 1983. *Who Rules America Now? A View for the '80s*. Englewood Cliffs, NJ: Prentice-Hall.

Dye, Thomas R. 1983. *Who's Running America? The Reagan Years*. 3d ed. Englewood Cliffs, NJ: Prentice-Hall.

Easterbrook, Gregg. 1995. *A Moment in Time: The Coming Age of Environmental Optimism*. New York: Penguin Books.

———. 1999. "America the O.K." *New Republic* 4381–4382 (January 4 and 11): 19–25.

Easton, David. 1965. *A Systems Analysis of Political Life*. Chicago: University of Chicago Press.

Eckholm, Erik. 1993. "On 'Managed Competition': Primer on Health-Care Idea." *New York Times* (May 1).

Edelman, Murray. 1964. *The Symbolic Use of Politics*. Urbana: University of Illinois Press.

Edwards, George C., III, Martin P. Wattenberg, and Robert L. Lineberry. 1996. *Government in America: People, Politics, and Policy*. 7th ed. New York: HarperCollins.

Egan, Timothy. 1999. "Violence by Youths: Looking for Answers." *New York Times* (April 22).

Enthoven, Alain C. 1980. *Health Plan: The Only Practical Solution to the Soaring Cost of Medical Care*. Reading, MA: Addison-Wesley.

Enthoven, Alain C., and Richard Kronick. 1992. "Will Managed Competition Work? Better Care at Lower Cost?" *New York Times* (January 25).

Etzioni, Amitai. 1993. *The Spirit of Community: The Reinvention of American Society*. New York: Touchstone Books.

———. 1996. *The New Golden Rule: Community and Morality in a Democratic Society*. New York: Basic Books.

Eyestone, Robert. 1978. *From Social Issues to Public Policy*. New York: Wiley.

Feldman, Sandra. 1999. "A STAR Story." *New York Times* (June 6).

Freudenheim, Milt. 1994. "H.M.O.'s Offering a Choice Are Gaining in Popularity." *New York Times* (February 7).

Frymer, Paul. 1994. "Ideological Consensus within Divided Party Government." *Political Science Quarterly* 109, no. 2 (Summer): 287–311.

General Accounting Office. 1994. *Multiple Employment Training Programs: Conflicting Requirements Hamper Delivery of Services*. Washington, DC: GAO.

Geraghty, Jim. 2000. "Attitudes in America Part Two: Changing Priorities." Policy.com (July 8).

Gilens, Martin. 1999. "With Friends Like These." www.TomPaine.com/features/1999/10/19/index.html.

Gillespie, Ed, and Bob Schellas, eds. 1994. *The Contract with America: The Bold Plan by Rep. Newt Gingrich, Rep. Dick Armey, and the House Republicans to Change the Nation*. New York: Times Books.

Ginsberg, Benjamin, Theodore J. Lowi, and Margaret Weir. 1999. *We the People: An Introduction to American Politics*. 2d ed. New York: Norton.

Glaser, William A. 1993. "Universal Health Insurance That Really Works: Foreign Lessons for the United States." *Journal of Health Politics, Policy and Law* 18, no. 3 (Fall): 695–722.

Glathar, Jill, and Mark E. Rushefsky. 1999. "Reconsidering Ideology." Paper presented at the annual meeting of the Western Political Science Association, Seattle, WA, 1999.

Graig, Laurence A. 1999. *Health of Nations: An International Perspective on U.S. Health Care Reform*. 3d. ed. Washington, DC: CQ Press.

Greenhouse, Linda. 1999. "The Justices Decide Who's in Charge." *New York Times* (June 27).

Gugliotta, Guy. 1999. "A Balkanized Congress." *Washington Post National Weekly Edition* 16, no. 29 (May 17): 14.

Hall, Thad E., and Laurence J. O'Toole. 2000. "Structures for Policy Implementation: An Analysis of National Legislation, 1965–1966 and 1993–1994." *Administration & Society* 31, no. 6 (January): 667–686.

Hayes, Michael T. 1992. *Incrementalism and Public Policy*. New York: Longman.

Heclo, Hugh. 1978. "Issue Networks and the Executive Establishment." In *The New American Political System*, ed. Anthony King. Washington, DC: American Enterprise Institute, pp. 87–124.

Herson, Lawrence J.R. 1984. *The Politics of Ideas: Political Theory and American Public Policy*. Pacific Grove, CA: Brooks/Cole.

Hoadley, John F. 1986. "Easy Riders: Gramm-Rudman-Hollings and the Legislative Fast Track." *PS* 19, no. 1 (Winter): 30–36.

Jacobs, Lawrence R., and Robert Shapiro. 1997. "The Myth of Pandering and Public Opinion During Clinton's First Term." Mimeograph.

———. 2000. *Politicians Don't Pander: Political Manipulation and the Loss of Democratic Responsiveness*. Chicago: University of Chicago Press.

Janda, Kenneth, Jeffrey M. Berry, and Jerry Goldman. 1995. *The Challenge of Democracy: Government in America*. 4th ed. Boston: Houghton Mifflin.

Jones, Charles O. 1984. *An Introduction to the Study of Public Policy*. 3d ed. Pacific Grove, CA: Brooks/Cole.

———. 1994. *The Presidency in a Separated System*. Washington, DC: Brookings Institution.

Karp, David. 1996/1997. "Americans as Communitarians: An Empirical Study." *The Responsive Community: Rights and Responsibilities* 7, no. 1 (Winter): 42–51.

Kerbel, Matthew Robert. 1995. *Remote & Controlled: Media Politics in a Cynical Age*. Boulder: Westview Press.

King, Anthony. 1997. *Running Scared: Why America's Politicians Campaign Too Much and Govern Too Little*. New York: Free Press.

Kingdon, John W. 1984. *Agendas, Alternatives, and Public Policies*. Boston: Little, Brown.

Kurtz, Howard. 1996. *Hot Air: All Talk, All the Time*. New York: Times Books.

Landau, Martin. 1978. "Redundancy, Rationality and the Problem of Duplication and Overlap." Reprinted in *Current Issues in Public Administration*, ed. Frederick S. Lane. New York: St. Martin's, pp. 234–249.

LeLoup, Lance T., and Steven A. Shull. 1999. *The President and Congress: Collaboration and Conflict in National Policymaking*. Boston: Allyn and Bacon.

Levit, Katharine, Cathy Cowan, Helen Lazenby, Arthur Sensenig, Patricia McDonnell, Jean Stiller, Anne Martin, and the Health Accounts Team. 2000. "Health Spending in 1998: Signals of Change." *Health Affairs* 19, no. 1 (January/February): 124–132.

Lichter, S. Robert, Linda S. Lichter, and Dan Amundson. 1999. *Images of Government in TV Entertainment*. Washington, DC: Center for Media and Public Affairs.

Lindblom, Charles E. 1959. "The Science of Muddling Through." *Public Administration Review* 14, no. 2 (Spring): 79–88.

Lindblom, Charles E., and Edward J. Woodhouse. 1993. *The Policy-Making Process*. 3d ed. Englewood Cliffs, NJ: Prentice-Hall.

Lipsky, Michael. 1969. *Protest in City Politics: Rent Strikes, Housing, and the Power of the Poor*. Chicago: Rand McNally.

Maddox, William S., and Stuart A. Lilie. 1984. *Beyond Liberal and Conservative: Reassessing the Political Spectrum*. Washington, DC: Cato Institute.

Mayhew, David R. 1991. *Divided We Govern: Party Control, Lawmaking, and Investigations, 1946–1990*. New Haven, CT: Yale University Press.

Mazmanian, Daniel A., and Paul A. Sabatier. 1983. *Implementation and Public Policy*. Glenview, IL: Scott, Foresman.

McKey, Ruth Hubbell, Smith, Allen N., and Aitken, Sherrie S. 1985. *The Impact of Head Start on Children, Families and Communities*. Department of Health and Human Services. Washington, DC: Government Printing Office.

Menner, Laura Bauer. 2001. "Authorities Cast Blame Over Crime." *Springfield News-Leader* (March 11).

Michels, Robert. [1916] 1962. *Political Parties: A Sociological Study of the Oligarchical Tendencies of Modern Democracy*. New York: Free Press.

Mills, C. Wright. 1956. *The Power Elite*. New York: Oxford University Press.

Monroe, Alan D. 1979. "Consistency Between Public Preferences and National Policy Decisions." *American Politics Quarterly* 7, no. 1 (January): 3–19.

Morin, Richard. 1999. "Have People Lost Their Voice?" *Washington Post National Weekly Edition* 16, no. 35 (June 28): 34.

Morin, Richard, and John M. Berry. 1996. "Economic Anxieties." *Washington Post National Weekly Edition* 14, no. 1 (November 4–10): 6–7.

Moore, Thomas H. 1993. "Health Care Around the Globe." *Congressional Quarterly* 51, special supplement (September 25): 34.

Murray, Charles. 1984. *Losing Ground: American Social Policy, 1950–1980*. New York: Basic Books.

———. 1993. "The Coming White Underclass." *Wall Street Journal* (October 29).

Nathan, Richard P. 1983. *The Administrative Presidency*. New York: Wiley.

Neustadt, Richard E. 1960. *President Power: The Politics of Leadership*. New York: Wiley.

Nivola, Pietro S. 2000. "Last Rites for States Rights?" *Brookings Reform Watch* no. 1 (June).

Nye, Joseph S., Jr., Philip D. Zelikow, and David C. King. 1997. *Why People Don't Trust Government*. Cambridge: Harvard University Press.

Office of Management and Budget. 1999. *Historical Tables, Budget of the U.S. Government, FY 2000*. Washington, DC: Executive Office of the President.

Olson, Mancur. 1982. *The Rise and Decline of Nations*. New Haven, CT: Yale University Press.

Page, Benjamin, and Robert Shapiro. 1992. *The Rational Public: Fifty Years of Trends in Americans' Policy Preferences*. Chicago: University of Chicago Press.

Palazzolo, Daniel J. 1999. *Done Deal: The Politics of the 1997 Budget Agreement*. New York: Chatham House.

Patel, Kant, and Mark E. Rushefsky. 1999. *Health Care Politics and Policy in America*. 2d ed. Armonk, NY: M.E. Sharpe.

"Patients, Therapists Reel from Medicare Reform." 1999. *Springfield News-Leader* (November 28).

Patterson, Thomas E. 1994. *Out of Order*. New York: Vintage Books.

Patton, Michael Q. 1978. *Utilization-Focused Evaluation*. Newbury Park, CA: Sage.

Pear, Robert. 1999. "Study Links Medicaid Drop to Welfare Changes." *New York Times* (May 14).

Perl, Peter. 2000. "Poisoned Package." *Washington Post* (January 16).

Peterson, Peter G. 1993. *Facing Up: How to Rescue the Economy from Crushing Debt & Restore the American Dream*. New York: Simon & Schuster.

Polsby, Nelson A. 1980. *Community Power and Political Theory*. 2d ed. New Haven, CT: Yale University Press.

Posner, Michael. 2000. "Blocking the Presidential Power Play." *National Journal* 32, no. 1 (January 1): 48–49.

Pressman, Jeffrey, and Aaron Wildavsky. 1984. *Implementation*. 3d ed. Berkeley: University of California Press.

Public Agenda. 1999. *On Thin Ice: How Advocates and Opponents Could Misread the Public's View on Vouchers and Charter Schools*. New York: Public Agenda. www.publicagenda.org.

Qiao, Yuhua. 1999. *Interstate Fiscal Disparities in America: A Study of Trends and Causes*. New York: Garland.

Quade, E.S. 1982. *Analysis for Public Decisions*. 2d ed. New York: North-Holland.

Rauch, Jonathan. 1999. *Government's End: Why Washington Stopped Working*. New York: PublicAffairs.

Reinhold, Robert. 1993. "A Health-Care Theory Hatched in Fireside Chats." *New York Times* (February 10).

Ripley, Randall B., and Grace A. Franklin. 1984. *Congress, the Bureaucracy, and Public Policy*. 3d ed. Pacific Grove, CA: Brooks/Cole.

Rivlin, Alice M. 1992. *Reviving the American Dream: The Economy, the States and the Federal Government*. Washington, DC: Brookings Institution.

Rochefort, David A., and Roger W. Cobb. 1994. "Problem Definition: An Emerging Perspective." In *The Politics of Problem Definition*, ed. David A. Rochefort and Roger W. Cobb. Lawrence: University of Kansas Press, pp. 1–31.

Rubin, Irene S. 1999. *The Politics of Public Budgeting: Getting and Spending, Borrowing and Balancing*. 4th ed. Chatham, NJ: Chatham House.

Rushefsky, Mark E., and Kant Patel. 1998. *Politics, Power & Policy Making: The Case of Health Care Reform in the 1990s*. Armonk, NY: M.E. Sharpe.

Sabatier, Paul A. 1999. "The Need for Better Theories." In *Theories of the Policy Process*, ed. Paul A. Sabatier. Boulder: Westview Press, pp. 3–17.

Sabatier, Paul A., and Hank Jenkins-Smith. 1999. "The Advocacy Coalition Framework: An Assessment." In *Theories of the Policy Process*, ed. Paul A. Sabatier. Boulder: Westview Press, pp. 117–166.

Sabato, Larry J. 1991. *The Feeding Frenzy: How Attack Journalism Has Transformed American Politics*. New York: Free Press.

Samuelson, Robert J. 1993. "The Debate Misled the Public." *Newsweek* 122, no. 7 (August 16): 23.

———. 1995. *The Good Life and Its Discontents: The American Dream in the Age of Entitlements 1945–1995*. New York: Times Books.

Scheuer, Jeffrey. 1999. *The Sound Bite Society: Television and the American Mind*. New York: Four Walls Eight Windows.

Schneider, Anne Larason, and Helen Ingram. 1997. *Policy Design for Democracy*. Lawrence: University of Kansas Press.

Schneider, William. 1986. "A Year of Continuity." *National Journal* 18 (May 17): 1162–1167.

———. 1988. "No Political Consensus on the Deficit." *National Journal* 20, no. 9 (February 27): 570.

———. 1989. "A Test for Government by Commission." *National Journal* 21, no. 4 (January 14): 106.

Schroedel, Jean Reith, and Daniel R. Jordan. 1998. "Senate Voting and Social Construction of Target Populations: A Study of AIDS Policy Making, 1987–1992." *Journal of Health Politics, Policy and Law* 23, no. 1 (February): 107–132.

Schulman, Paul R. 1975. "Nonincremental Policy Making: Notes Toward an Alternate Paradigm." *American Political Science Review* 69, no. 4 (December): 1354–1370.

Schwarz, John E. 1988. *America's Hidden Success: A Reassessment of Public Policy from Kennedy to Reagan*. New York: Norton.

Sharkansky, Ira. 1970. "Environment, Policy, Output and Impact: Problems of Theory and Method in the Analysis of Public Policy." In *Policy Analysis in Political Science*, ed. Ira Sharkansky. Chicago: Markham, pp. 61–69.

Simon, Herbert A. 1985. "Human Nature in Politics: The Dialogue of Psychology with Political Science." *American Political Science Review* 79 (June): 293–304.

Smith, Hedrick. 1988. *The Power Game: How Washington Works*. New York: Ballantine Books.

"States Illegally Denying Medicaid, Audit Finds." 1999. *Springfield News-Leader* (December 15).

Stoesz, David. 1996. *Small Change: Domestic Policy Under the Clinton Presidency*. White Plains, NY: Longman.

Stokey, Edith, and Richard Zeckhauser. 1978. *A Primer for Policy Analysis*. New York: Norton.

Stone, Deborah. 1997. *Policy Paradox: The Art of Political Decision Making*. New York: Norton.

Sullivan, Andrew. 1999. "The Assault on Good News." *New York Times Magazine* (November 7): 38–40.

Sung, Ellen. 2000. "Testing Gene Therapy." Policy.com (February 7). www.policy.com/news/dbrief/.

Thernstrom, Stephan, and Abigail Thernstrom. 1997. *America in Black and White: One Nation, Indivisible*. New York: Simon & Schuster.

Tiefer, Charles. 1994. *The Semi-Sovereign Presidency: The Bush Administration's Strategy for Governing Without Congress*. Boulder: Westview Press.

Tolchin, Susan J. 1996. *The Angry American: How Voter Rage Is Changing the Nation*. Boulder: Westview Press.

Toner, Robin. 1994. "Gold Rush Fever Grips Capital as Health Care Struggle Begins." *New York Times* (March 13).

True, James L. 2000. "Avalanches and Incrementalism: Making Policy and Budgets in the United States." *American Review of Public Administration* 30, no. 1 (March): 3–18.

True, James L., Bryan D. Jones, and Frank R. Baumgartner. 1999. "Punctuated-Equilibrium Theory: Explaining Stability and Change in American Policymaking." In *Theories of the Policy Process*, ed. Paul A. Sabatier. Boulder: Westview Press, pp. 97–115.

*United States v. Lopez, Alfonso* 512 US 1286 (1994).

Van Horn, Carl E., Donald C. Baumer, and William T. Gormley Jr. 1992. *Politics and Public Policy*. 2d ed. Washington, DC: CQ Press.

Weaver, R. Kent. 1988. *Automatic Government: The Politics of Indexation*. Washington, DC: Brookings Institution.

Weimer, David L., and Aidan R. Vining. 1992. *Policy Analysis: Concepts and Practice*. 2d ed. Englewood Cliffs, NJ: Prentice Hall.

Weiss, Carol. 1972. *Evaluation Research*. Englewood Cliffs, NJ: Prentice-Hall.

Weitz, Tracy A. 1993. "Executive Regulation of Abortion During the Reagan-Bush Years." MPA Thesis, Southwest Missouri State University.

Wells, Donald T., and Chris R. Hamilton. 1996. *The Policy Puzzle: Finding Solutions in the Diverse American System*. Upper Saddle River, NJ: Prentice-Hall.

West, Darrell M., and Burdett A. Loomis. 1999. *The Sound of Money: How Political Interests Get What They Want*. New York: Norton.

White, John Kenneth. 1990. *The New Politics of Old Values*. 2d ed. Hanover, NH: University Press of New England.

White, Joseph. 1995. *Competing Solutions: American Health Care Proposals and International Experience*. Washington, DC: Brookings Institution.

Whitman, David. 1998. *The Optimism Gap: The I'm OK—They're Not Syndrome and the Myth of American Decline*. New York: Walker.

Wildavsky, Aaron. 1988. *The New Politics of the Budgetary Process*. Glenview, IL: Scott, Foresman.

Williams, Walter, and John W. Evans. 1976. "The Politics of Evaluation: The Case of Head Start." In *Cases in Public Policy-Making*, ed. James E. Anderson. New York: Praeger, pp. 292–309.

Wills, Garry. 1999. *A Necessary Evil: A History of American Distrust of Government*. New York: Simon & Schuster.

Wines, Michael. 1992. "Bush Announces Health Plan, Filling Gap in Re-election Bid." *New York Times* (February 7).

Woll, Peter. 1977. *American Bureaucracy*. 2d ed. New York: Norton.

Zahariadis, Nikolaos. 1999. "Ambiguity, Times, and Multiple Streams." In *Theories of the Policy Process*, ed. Paul A. Sabatier. Boulder: Westview Press, pp. 73–93.

Zernike, Kate. 2001. "Antidrug Program Says It Will Adopt a New Strategy." *New York Times* (February 15).

# Chapter 2

Aaron, Henry J., Alan S. Blinder, Alicia H. Munnell, and Peter R. Orszag. 2000. "Governor Bush's Individual Account Proposal: Implications for Retirement Benefits." Issue Brief no. 11, the Social Security Network. New York: Century Foundation. www.tcf.org or www.socsec.org.

Ackerman, Bruce, and Anne Alstott. 1999. *The Stakeholder Society.* New Haven, CT: Yale University Press.

Akhtar, M.A., and Ethan S. Harris. 1992. "The Supply-Side Consequences of U.S. Fiscal Policy in the 1980s." *Federal Reserve Bank of New York Quarterly* 17 (Spring): 1–20.

Baker, Dean, and Mark Weisbrot. 1999. *Social Security: The Phony Crisis.* Chicago: University of Chicago Press.

Bartlett, Bruce R., ed. 1981. *Reaganomics: Supply-Side Economics in Action.* New York: Quill.

Bartlett, Donald L., and James B. Steele. 1992. *America: What Went Wrong?* Kansas City, MO: Andrews and McMeel.

———. 1996. *America: Who Stole the Dream?* Kansas City, MO: Andrews and McMeel.

Bartlett, Robert V. 1984. "The Budgetary Process and Environmental Policy." In *Environmental Policy in the 1980s: Reagan's New Agenda,* ed. Norman J. Vig and Michael E. Kraft. Washington, DC: CQ Press, pp. 121–141.

Bartley, Robert L. 1992. *The Seven Fat Years (and How To Do It Again).* New York: Free Press.

Bernstein, Jared. 2001. "Slow Economy Threatens Earnings of Low-Wage Workers, Risks Increase in Inequality." Washington, DC: Economic Policy Institute.

Berry, John M. 1995. "A Challenge to the Inflation Yardstick." *Washington Post National Weekly Edition* 12 (January 23–29): 18.

Board of Trustees. 2000. *The 2000 Annual Report of the Board of Trustees of the Federal Old Age and Survivors Insurance and Disability Insurance Trust Funds.* Washington, DC: Social Security Administration. www.ssa.gov.

Bosworth, Barry. 1984. "Lowering the Deficits and Interest Rates." In *Economic Choices 1984,* ed. Alice R. Rivlin. Washington, DC: Brookings Institution, pp. 19–43.

Broder, David S. 2000. "Of Janitors and Billionaires." *Washington Post National Weekly Edition* 17, no. 26 (April 24): 4.

Bruni, Frank. 1999. "Federal Seers. Telling Nation's Fiscal Fortune." *New York Times* (July 5).

Bureau of Economic Analysis. 2000. "Gross Domestic Product: Fourth Quarter (Advanced)." Washington, DC: Department of Commerce (January 28). www.bea.doc.gov/newsrel/gdp499a.htm.

Bureau of Labor Statistics. 2001. "Labor Statistics from the Current Population Survey." U.S. Department of Labor. http://stats.bls.gov/cpsaatab.htm#empstat.

Burtless, Gary. 1999. "Growing American Inequality: Sources and Remedies." *Brookings Review* 17, no. 1 (Winter): 31–36.

———. 2000. "Social Security Privatization and Financial Market Risk." Washington, DC: Center on Social and Economic Dynamics, Brookings Institution. Working paper no. 10 (February).

Calleo, David P. 1982. *The Imperious Economy.* Cambridge: Harvard University Press.

Cannon, Carl M. 2000. "The '89s vs. the '90s." *National Journal* 32, no. 16 (April 15): 1186–1194.

Center on Budget and Policy Priorities. 2000. "What the Trustees' Report Indicates About the Financial Status of Social Security." Washington, DC (March 30). www.cbpp.org/3–30–00socsec-rep.htm.

Century Foundation, n.d. "Broken English: The United Kingdom's Troubled Experiment with Personal Pensions." www.tcf.org.

———. n.d. "Chile's Experience with Social Security Privatization: A Model for the United States or a Danger Sign?" www.tcf.org.

———. n.d. "10 Myths About Social Security." www.tcf.org.

Chapa, Jorge. 2000. "Including Latinos in Broadly Shared Prosperity." In *Back to Shared Prosperity: The Growing Inequality of Wealth and Income in America*, ed. Ray Marshall. Armonk, NY: M.E. Sharpe, pp. 103–109.

Clark, Timothy B. 1987. "Respected Naysayer." *National Journal* 19 (March 7): 540–545.

Common Cause. 2000. "Lining Their Own Pockets: Wall Street's Campaign to Privatize Social Security." www.tompaine.com (May 30).

Concord Coalition. 1998. "The Surplus Mirage." *New York Times* (January 25).

Congressional Quarterly. 1984. *Congressional Quarterly Almanac 1984*. Washington, DC: CQ Press.

Council of Economic Advisers. 2000. *Economic Report of the President*. Washington, DC: Government Printing Office.

———. 2001. *Economic Report of the President*. Washington, DC: Government Printing Office.

Cox, W. Michael, and Richard Alm. 1999. *Myths of Rich & Poor*. New York: Basic Books.

———. 2000. "Why Decry the Wealth Gap?" *New York Times* (January 24).

Crook, Clive. 2000. "Why Does the Economy Always Vote Democratic in November?" *National Journal* 32, no. 11 (March 11): 764–765.

Danziger, Sheldon, and Peter Gottschalk. 1995. *American Unequal*. Cambridge: Harvard University Press.

Danziger, Sheldon, and Deborah Reed. 1995. "Winners and Losers: The Era of Inequality." *Brookings Review* 17, no. 4 (Fall): 14–17.

Degen, Robert A. 1987. *The American Monetary System: A Concise Survey of Its Evolution Since 1896*. Lexington, MA: DC Heath.

Eisner, Robert. 1986. *How Real Is the Federal Deficit?* New York: Free Press.

———. 1994. *The Misunderstood Economy: What Counts and How to Count It*. Boston: Harvard Business School Press.

Eizenstat, Stuart. 1999. "The U.S. Perspective on Globalization." Washington, DC: Overseas Development Council. www.odc.org/commnetary/vpaper99.html.

Elkin, Sam, and Robert Greenstein. 1999. "Much of the Projected Non-Social Security Surplus is a Mirage." Washington, DC: Center on Budget and Policy Priorities. www.cbpp.org (July 2).

Feldstein, Martin. 2000a. "The Case for Privatization." *Foreign Affairs* 76, no. 4 (July/August): 24–38.

———. 2000b. "Bush's Low-Risk Pension Reforms." *New York Times* (May 22).

Financial Markets Center. 2000. "Interest Rates and Election Cycles: The Fed's 1999–2000 Tightening Is Exceptional." Philomont, VA: Financial Markets Center. News release found at their website: www.fmcenter.org.

Fischer, Stanley, ed. 1980. *Rational Expectations and Economic Policy*. Chicago: University of Chicago Press.

Frank, Robert H., and Philip J. Cook. 1995. *The Winner-Take-All Society: How More and More Americans Compete for Ever Fewer and Bigger Prizes, Encouraging Economic Waste, Income Inequality and an Impoverished Cultural Life*. New York: Free Press.

Friedman, Thomas L. 1994a. "U.S. Enters Currency Market to Prop Up Tumbling Dollar." *New York Times* (April 4).

———. 1994b. "16 Nations Aid U.S. in Backing Value of the Dollar." *New York Times* (May 5).

Galbraith, James K. 1998. *Created Unequal: The Crisis in American Pay*. New York: Free Press.

Geraghty, Jim. 2000. "Does Washington Have a Cheating Heart?" Policy.com daily briefing (February 28).

Greenfield, Meg. 1996. "Back to Class War?" *Newsweek* 127, no. 7 (February 12): 84.

Greenstein, Robert. 2001. "Following the Money: The Administration's Budget Priorities." Washington, DC: Center on Budget and Policy Priorities.

Greider, William. 1981. "The Education of David Stockman." *Atlantic Monthly* 247, no. 12 (December): 27–54.

———. 1987. *Secrets of the Temple: How the Federal Reserve Runs the Country*. New York: Simon & Schuster.

Hager, George, and Eric Pianin. 1999. *Mirage: Why Neither Democrats Nor Republicans Can Balance the Budget, End the Deficit, and Satisfy the Public*. New York: Times Books.

Hager, George, and Alissa J. Rubin. 1995. "Last-Minute Maneuvers Forge a Conference Agreement." *Congressional Quarterly* (June 27): 1814–1819.

Hahm, Sung-Deuk, et al. 1992. "The Influence of the Gramm-Rudman-Hollings Act on Federal Budgetary Outcomes, 1986–1989." *Journal of Policy Analysis and Management* 11 (Spring): 207–234.

Heilbroner, Robert. 1961. *The Worldly Philosophers*. New York: Time.

Herbert, Bob. 2000. "Do You Feel Lucky?" *New York Times* (May 18).

Hershey, Robert D., Jr. 1992. "U.S. Economy Grew at Rate of 2.7% During 3rd Quarter." *New York Times* (October 27).

Hirsh, Michael. 1997. "Into the Deep." *Newsweek* 130, no. 23 (December 8): 46–48.

Holzer, Harry J. 2000. "The Labor Market for Young African-American Men: Recent Trends, Causes and Implications." In *Back to Shared Prosperity: The Growing Inequality of Wealth and Income in America*, ed. Ray Marshall. Armonk, NY: M.E. Sharpe, pp. 95–102.

Horney, James, and Robert Greenstein. 2000. "What Do the New Baseline Budget Projections Mean?" Washington, DC: Center on Budget and Policy Priorities. (February 2).

Howe, Neil, and Richard Jackson. 2000. "The Truth About Entitlements and the Budget." *Facing Facts Alert* 6, no. 1 (February 14). www.concordcoalition.org/facing_facts/alert_v6_n1.html.

James, Estelle. 1998. "Social Security Reform in Other Nations." *Heritage Lectures*, no. 618 www.heritage.org (June 4).

Jenislawski, Sarah. 2000. "Hastert Proposes Public Debt Elimination by 2015." Policy.com (January 20).

Joint Economic Committee, U.S. Congress. 1981. *Expectations and the Economy: A Volume of Essays*. Washington, DC: Government Printing Office.

Kessler, Glenn. 2000. "The Lightened Federal Tax Load." *Washington Post National Weekly Edition* 17, no. 23 (April 3): 18.

Kosterlitz, Julie. 1999. "A Newer New Deal." *National Journal* 31, nos. 1–2 (January 2 and 9): 12–23.

Kristof, Richard D., and Sheryl WuDunn. 1999. "Of World Markets, None an Island." *New York Times* (February 17).

Krugman, Paul. 1994a. *The Age of Diminished Expectations: U.S. Economic Policy in the 1990s*, rev. ed. Cambridge: MIT Press.

———. 1994b. *Peddling Prosperity: Economic Sense and Nonsense in the Age of Diminished Expectations*. New York: Norton.

———. 2000a. "Trillions and Trillions." *New York Times* (February 2).

———. 2000b. "Death and Taxes." *New York Times* (June 14).

Kudlow, Lawrence. 2000. "Greenspan, Through the Looking Glass." *New York Times* (March 10).

Kuttner, Robert. 2000. "A Few Uses for Our New Budget Surplus." www.epn.org/kuttner/bk980120.htm.

Lav, Iris J. 2000. "Taxes on Middle-Income Families Are Declining." Washington, DC: Center on Budget and Policy Priorities. www.cbpp.org/4-10-00tx.htm (April 10).

Lawrence, Robert Z. 2000. "Inequality in America: the Recent Evidence." *Responsive Community* 10, no. 2 (Spring): 4–10.

Levy, Frank. 2000. *The New Dollars and Dreams: American Incomes and Economic Change*. New York: Russell Sage Foundation.

Makin, John H., and Norman J. Ornstein. 1994. *Debt and Taxes: How America Got into Its Budget Mess and What to Do About It*. New York: Times Books.

Marshall, Ray, ed. 2000. *Back to Shared Prosperity: The Growing Inequality of Wealth and Income in America*. Armonk, NY: M.E. Sharpe.

McMurrer, Daniel P., and Isabel V. Sawhill. 2000. "The Effects of Economic Growth and Inequality on Opportunity." In *Back to Shared Prosperity: The Growing Inequality of*

*Wealth and Income in America*, ed. Ray Marshall. Armonk, NY: M.E. Sharpe, pp. 64–68.

Meyer, Laurence H., ed. 1981. *The Supply-Side Effects of Economic Policy*. St. Louis: Center for the Study of American Business, Washington University.

Mishel, Lawrence. 1995. "Rising Tides, Sinking Wages." *American Prospect* 23 (Fall): 60–64.

Mishel, Lawrence, Jared Bernstein, and John Schmitt. 1999. *The State of Working America 1998–1999*. Ithaca, NY: Cornell University Press.

———. 2001. *The State of Working America 2000–2001*. Ithaca, NY: Cornell University Press.

Montagne, Renee. 2000. "Examining the Severance Package of Former Mattel CEO Jill Barad, Which is Worth More than $37 Million." *Morning Edition*, National Public Radio (May 3). Lexis-Nexis transcript.

Morris, Charles R. 1993. "It's Not the Economy, Stupid." *Atlantic Monthly* 272, no. 1 (July): 49–62.

Moyers, John. 2000. "Media Criticism: The Duped and the Dupers." www.tompaine.com (May 24).

Moynihan, Daniel Patrick. 1985. "Reagan's Inflate-the-Deficit Game." *New York Times* (July 21).

Nau, Henry R. 1990. *The Myth of America's Decline: Leading the World Economy into the 1990s*. New York: Oxford University Press.

*New York Times*. 1996. *The Downsizing of America*. New York: Times Books.

Office of Management and Budget. 1986. *Historical Tables: Budget of the United States Government, Fiscal Year 1987*. Washington, DC: Government Printing Office.

———. 2000. *Historical Tables: Budget of the United States Government, Fiscal Year 2001*. Washington, DC: Government Printing Office.

Olson, Elizabeth. 2000. "Environmentalists Applaud a W.T.O. Ruling on Asbestos." *New York Times* (July 25).

OMB Watch. 1999. "The Budget Surplus Comes from Cuts in Discretionary Spending." www.ombwatch.org/budget/surplus.html (July 7).

Ornstein, Norman J. 1985. "The Politics of the Deficit." In *Essays in Contemporary Economic Problems, 1985: The Economy in Deficit*, ed. Phillip Cagan. Washington, DC: American Enterprise Institute, pp. 311–333.

Palazzollo, Daniel J. 1999. *Done Deal? The Politics of the 1997 Budget Agreement*. Chatham, NJ: Chatham House.

Papadimitriou, Dimitri B. 2000. Preface in *A Dual Mandate for the Federal Reserve: The Pursuit of Price Stability and Full Employment*, ed. Willem Thorbecke. Blithewood, Annandale-on-the-Hudson, NY: Jerome Levy Economics Institute of Bard College, pp. 5–6.

Passell, Peter. 1996. "The Rich Are Getting Richer, Etc., and It's Likely to Remain that Way." *New York Times* (March 28).

Pearlstein, Steven. 1995a. "The Rich Get Richer and. . ." *Washington Post National Weekly Edition* 12, no. 32. (June 12–18): 6–7.

———. 1995b. "The Winners Are Taking All." *Washington Post National Weekly Edition* 13, no. 6 (December 11–17): 6–10.

———. 1999. "WTO Negotiators' Reach Far Exceeded Grasp of Complexities." *Washington Post* (December 5).

Peterson, Peter G. 1993. *Facing Up: How to Rescue the Economy from Crushing Debt & Restore the American Dream*. New York: Simon & Schuster.

———. 1996. *Will America Grow Up Before It Grows Old? How the Coming Social Security Crisis Threatens You, Your Family, and Your Country*. New York: Random House.

Powell, Bill. 1997. "The Globe Shudders." *Newsweek* 130, no. 19 (November 10): 30–34.

Ramo, Joshua Cooper. 1999. "The Three Marketers." *Time* 153, no. 6 (February 15): 34–42.

Rashid, Salim. 1986. "Historical Notes on the Origins of Supply-Side Economics and Its Ethical Roots: Say's Law, Smith's Law, or Moral Law?" *Quarterly Review of Economics and Business* 26, no. 4 (Winter): 222–234.

Rauch, Jonathan. 1985. "Stockman at OMB." *National Journal* 17, no. 21 (May 25): 1212–1217.

———. 1986. "Deficit Reduction Deadlock." *National Journal* 18, no. 1 (January 4): 15–20.

———. 1993. "Stage Two." *National Journal* 25 (August 7): 1962–1966.

———. 1999. *Government's End: Why Washington Stopped Working*. New York: PublicAffairs.

Redburn, Tom. 2001. "Down Goes the Market? Is the Surplus Next?" *New York Times* (March 11).

Reich, Robert B. 1999. "Making Room on the Up Elevator." *Washington Post National Weekly Edition* 16, no. 30 (May 24): 23.

———. 2000. "Working Principles." *American Prospect* 11, no. 15 (June 19–July 3): 21–23.

Rich, Spencer. 2000. "Again, a Boon for Boomers." *National Journal* 32, no. 18 (April 29): 1350–1354.

Robinson, James, III. 1994. "Inflation Overkill." *Foreign Affairs* 73, no. 5 (September/ October): 2–7.

Rodriguez, L. Jacobo. 1999. "Chile's Current Pension System at 18: Its Current State and Future Challenges." *The Cato Project on Social Security Privatization* 17 (July 30): 1–23.

Rogers, Joel, and Ruy Teixeira. 2000. "America's Forgotten Majority." *Atlantic Monthly* 285, no. 6 (June): 66–75.

Rowe, James L., Jr. 1999. "In the Money: What Goes on Behind the Doors of the Federal Reserve." *Washington Post* (February 10).

Rubin, Irene S. 1990. *The Politics of Public Budgeting: Getting and Spending, Borrowing and Balancing*. Chatham, NJ: Chatham House.

Samuelson, Robert J. 1994a. "Maestro of the Business Cycle?" *Newsweek* 124, no. 11 (August 29): 29.

———. 1994b. "Economic Amnesia." *Newsweek* 124 (September 12): 52.

———. 1995. *The Good Life and Its Discontents: The American Dream in the Age of Entitlements 1945–1995*. New York: Times Books.

———. 1998. "The Surplus: An Accident." *Newsweek* 131, no. 7 (January 16): 44.

———. 1999. "The Seduction of Surpluses." *Newsweek* 134, no. 2 (July 12): 74.

———. 2000a. "Social Insecurity." *Washington Post* (May 31).

———. 2000b. "What Greenspan Doesn't Know. . ." *Newsweek* 135, no. 18 (May 1): 78.

Sanger, David E. 2000. "Rounding Out a Clear Clinton Legacy." *New York Times* (May 25).

Sawicky, Max B. 2000. "Budget Surplus? What to Do with the Surplus." tap.epn.org/ sawicky/sa980112.html.

Schick, Allen. 2000. "A Surplus, If We Can Keep It." *Brookings Review* 18, no. 1 (Winter): 36–39.

Schwarz, John E. 1988. *America's Hidden Success: A Reassessment of Public Policy from Kennedy to Reagan*, rev. ed. New York: Norton.

———. 1998. "The Hidden Side of the Clinton Economy." *Atlantic Monthly* 282, no. 4 (October): 18–21.

Scott, Robert E. 1999. "NAFTA's Pain Deepens: Job Destruction Accelerates in 1999 with Losses in Every State." Washington, DC: Economic Policy Institute, November.

———. 2000. "Trade Picture: NAFTA Imports Lead Growth in U.S. Trade Deficit." Washington, DC: Economic Policy Institute, February 18.

Seelye, Katharine Q. 2000. "Gore to Announce $200 Billion Plan to Aid Retirement." *New York Times* (June 19).

Shaikh, Anwar M. 2000. "Explaining the U.S. Trade Deficit." Jerome Levy Economics Institute. www.levy.org.

Shapiro, Isaac, and Robert Greenstein. 1999. "The Widening Income Gulf." Washington, DC: Center for Budget and Policy Priorities. www.cbpp.org/9-4-99tax-rep.htm (September 4).

Silk, Leonard. 1984. *Economics in the Real World: How Political Decisions Affect the Economy*. New York: Simon & Schuster.

Skidmore, Max J. 1999. *Social Security and Its Enemies: The Case for America's Most Efficient Insurance Program*. Boulder: Westview Press.

Skocpol, Theda. 1995. *Social Policy in the United States: Future Possibilities in Historical Perspective*. Princeton, NJ: Princeton University Press.

———. 2000. *The Missing Middle: Working Families and the Future of American Social Policy*. New York: Norton.

Social Security Administration 2000a. "Fast Facts." www.ssa.gov/statistics/ics/fast-facts/ 2000.

———. 2000b. "Social Security History." www.ssa.gov/history6.html.

Spelman, William. 2000. "Crime and Prosperity: Neighborhood Explanations for Change in Crime Rates." In *Back to Shared Prosperity: The Growing Inequality of Wealth and Income in America*, ed. Ray Marshall. Armonk, NY: M.E. Sharpe, pp. 110–118.

Starobin, Paul. 1991. "The Fed's Image." *National Journal* 23 (May 18): 1161–1166.

———. 1993. "The Fed Tapes." *National Journal* 25 (December 18): 1984–2989.

———. 1994. "Bankers' Dozen." *National Journal* 26 (November 11): 2772–2777.

Stevenson, Richard W. 2000. "Benefits and Drawbacks to Bush and Gore Proposals for Overhauling Social Security." *New York Times* (May 19).

Stockman, David. 1987. *The Triumph of Politics: The Inside Story of the Reagan Revolution.* New York: Avon.

Tanner, Michael. 2000. "Saving Social Security Is Not Enough." *Social Security Privatization* 20 (May 25): 1–10. www.Cato.org.

Thorbecke, Willem. 2000. *A Dual Mandate for the Federal Reserve: The Pursuit of Price Stability and Full Employment.* Blithewood, Annandale-on-the-Hudson, NY: Jerome Levy Economics Institute of Bard College.

Thurow, Lester C. 1983. *Dangerous Currents: The State of Economics.* New York: Random House.

Uchitelle, Louis. 1994a. "A Matter of Timing." *New York Times* (August 18).

———. 1994b. "Industry Leaders Warn Against Rise in Interest Rates." *New York Times* (September 25).

———. 1994c. "Who's for More Inflation and Who Isn't." *New York Times* (October 2).

———. 2000. "U.S. Productivity Rose at 5% Rate in 2nd Half of '99." *New York Times* (February 9).

U.S. Census Bureau. 2000. *Statistical Abstract of the United States.* Washington, DC: Government Printing Office.

Wanniski, Jude. 1978. *The Way the World Works.* New York: Touchstone Press.

Weaver, Kent. 1988. *Automatic Government*: The Politics of Indexation. Washington, DC: Brookings Institution.

Weiner, Tim. 1999. "House Spenders Look for Bookkeeping Magic." *New York Times* (July 27).

Weinstein, Michael M. 2000. "America's Rags-to-Riches Myth." *New York Times* (February 18).

———. 1999. "A Wrong Turn on the Road to Social Security." *New York Times* (May 6).

Weisbrot, Mark. 2000a. "Does Alan Greenspan Deserve an A?" www.TomPaine.com/news (January 10).

———. 2000b. "Precarious Economy: Two Bubbles Are at the Heart of Our Prosperity." www.tompaine.com (June 14).

Weisman, Jonathan. 2000. "A Texas Alternative to Social Security." *SunSpot.* www.sunspot.net (May 17).

Wildavsky, Aaron B. 1988. *The New Politics of the Budgetary Process.* Glenview, IL: Scott, Foresman.

Will, George. 1996. "Healthy Inequality." *Newsweek* 121, no. 18 (October 28): 92.

Wilson, William Julius. 1999. *The Bridge Over the Racial Divide: Rising Inequality and Coalition Politics.* Berkeley: University of California Press.

———. 2000. "Jobless Ghettos: The Social Implications of the Disappearance of Work in Segregated Neighborhoods." In *Back to Shared Prosperity: The Growing Inequality of Wealth and Income in America*, ed. Ray Marshall. Armonk, NY: M.E. Sharpe, pp. 85–94.

Wolff, Edward N. 1995. *Top Heavy: A Study of the Increasing Inequality of Wealth in America.* New York: Twentieth Century Fund Press.

———. 1998. "Recent Trends in the Size Distribution of Household Wealth." *Journal of Economic Perspectives* 12, no. 3 (Summer): 131–150.

———. 2000. "Recent Trends in the Distribution of Household Wealth." In *Back to Shared Prosperity: The Growing Inequality of Wealth and Income in America*, ed. Ray Marshall. Armonk, NY: M.E. Sharpe, p. 63.

Woodward, Bob. 1994. *The Agenda: Inside the Clinton White House*. New York: Simon & Schuster.

———. 2000. *Maestro: Greenspan's Fed and the American Boom*. New York: Simon & Schuster.

Woolley, John T. 1984. *Monetary Politics: The Federal Reserve and the Politics of Monetary Policy*. Cambridge: Cambridge University Press.

# Chapter 3

Allison, Graham T., Jr. 1989. "Success Is Within Reach." *New York Times* (February 19).

Alter, Jonathan. 1994. "When the World Shrugs." *Newsweek* 123 (April 25): 34.

Ambrose, Stephen E. 1985. *Rise of Globalism: American Foreign Policy Since 1938*. 4th ed. New York: Penguin.

Amuzegar, Jahangir. 1997. "Adjusting to Sanctions." *Foreign Affairs* 76, no. 3 (May/June): 31–41.

Aslund, Anders. 1994. "Russia's Success Story." *Foreign Affairs* 73, no. 5 (September/ October): 58–71.

Banerjee, Neela. 1994. "Russia Combines War and Peace to Reclaim Parts of Its Old Empire." *Wall Street Journal* (September 2).

Baucom, Donald R. n.d. "Ballistic Missile Defense: A Brief History." Ballistic Missile Defense Organization. www.acq.osd.mil/bmdo/bmdolink/html/origins.html.

Beschloss, Michael R., and Strobe Talbott. 1993. *At the Highest Levels: The Inside Story of the End of the Cold War*. Boston: Little, Brown.

Boyd, Charles G. 1998. "Making Bosnia Work." *Foreign Affairs* 77, no. 1 (January/ February): 42–67.

Broad, William J. 2000. "Antimissile Testing Is Rigged to Hide a Flaw, Critics Say." *New York Times* (June 9).

Brown, Justin. 2000. "Holding Africa at Arm's Length." *Christian Science Monitor* (February 22).

Brzezinski, Zbigniew. 1994. "Getting Real on Central Europe." *New York Times* (June 28).

Burk, James. 1999. "Public Support for Peacekeeping in Lebanon and Somalia: Assessing the Casualties Hypothesis." *Political Science Quarterly* 114, no. 1 (Spring): 53–78.

Center for Strategic and Budgetary Assessment. n.d. N-1 "Bottom-Up Review." www.csbaonline.org.

Clad, James, and Michael Rabjohns. 2000. "Rethinking India." intellectualcapital.com (March 9).

Clarke, Jonathan 1993. "The Conceptual Poverty of U.S. Foreign Policy." *Atlantic Monthly* 272, no. 3 (September): 54–66.

Cleveland, Harlan. 1986. "Coherence and Consultation: The President as Manager of American Foreign Policy." *Public Administration Review* 46, no. 2 (March–April): 97–104.

Cohen, Eliot A. 1994. "What to Do About National Defense." *Commentary* 98 (November): 21–32.

Cohen, Steven P. 1998. "Nuclear Weapons and Conflict in South Asia." Paper presented to the Harvard/MIT Transnational Security Project Seminar (November 23). www.brook.edu/views/articles/cohenS/1998TSP.htm.

Commission to Assess the Ballistic Missile Threat to the United States. 1998. www.highfrontier.org/report.htm.

Congressional Budget Office. 2000. *Budgetary and Technical Implications of the Administration's Plan for National Missile Defense*. Washington, DC: CBO (April).

Cordesman, Anthony H. 1999. "The Lessons and Non-Lessons of the Air and Missile Campaign in Kosovo." Washington, DC: Center for Strategic and International Studies. www.csis.org.

Corwin, Edwin S. 1940. *The President: Office and Powers*. New York: New York University Press.

Crabb, Cecil V., Jr., and Pat M. Holt. 1984. *Invitation to Struggle: Congress, the President and Foreign Policy*. Washington, DC: CQ Press.

Crocker, Chester A. 1995. "The Lesson of Somalia: Not Everything Went Wrong." *Foreign Affairs* 74, no. 4 (May–June): 2–8.

Crossette, Barbara. 1999. "Rwanda Genocide Seen as Worsened by U.N. Inaction." *New York Times* (December 17).

Cushman, John H., Jr. 1994. "President Orders Pentagon Action to Aid Rwandans." *New York Times* (July 23).

Daalder, Ivo H., and Michael B.G. Froman. 1999. "Dayton's Incomplete Peace." *Foreign Affairs* 78, no. 6 (November/December): 106–113.

Daalder, Ivo H., and Michael E. O'Hanlon. 1999. "Unlearning the Lessons of Kosovo." *Foreign Policy,* no. 116 (Fall). www.foreignpolicy.com.

Darnton, John. 1994. "Africa Tries Democracy, Finding Hope and Peril." *New York Times* (June 21).

Department of Defense. 1997. *The Report of the Quadrennial Defense Review.* www.defenselink.mil/pubs/qdr/toc.html.

Dixon, William J. 1994. "Democracy and the Peaceful Settlement of International Conflict." *American Political Science Review* 88, no. 1 (March): 14–32.

Dobbs, Michael. 1999. "The Pitfalls of Pendulum Diplomacy." *Washington Post National Weekly Edition* 16, no. 30 (May 24): 22.

Dreyfuss, Robert. 2000. "The Phantom Menace." *Mother Jones* 25, no. 5 (September/ October): 40–45, 88–91.

Elliott, Michael. 1999. "Getting to the Table." *Newsweek* 133, no. 24 (June 14): 30–34.

Erlanger, Steven. 1995. "Pressure on NATO to Expand." *New York Times* (February 9).

Fatton, Robert, Jr. 1990. "Liberal Democracy in Africa." *Political Science Quarterly* 105, no. 3 (Fall): 455–471.

Fischer, Beth A. 1997. "Toeing the Hardline? The Reagan Administration and the Ending of the Cold War." *Political Science Quarterly* 112, no. 3 (Fall): 477–496.

Fisher, Ian. 1999. "Hutu and Tutsi Ask: Is a Unified Rwanda Possible?" *New York Times* (April 6).

Fitzgerald, Frances. 2000. *Way Out There in the Blue: Reagan, Star Wars and the End of the Cold War.* New York: Simon & Schuster.

Flatin, Paul. 2000. "Sanctions Policy Under Fire." www.policy.com (April 19).

"Framework for Peace: Agreement Between Israel and the P.L.O." 1994. *New York Times* (May 5).

Gaddis, John Lewis. 1992. *The United States and the End of the Cold War: Implications, Reconsiderations, Provocations.* New York: Oxford University Press.

Gardner, Richard N. 2000. "The One Percent Solution." *Foreign Affairs* 79, no. 4 (July/ August): 2–11.

Gellman, Barton. 1999a. "Is This 'Immaculate Coercion'?" *Washington Post National Weekly Edition* 16, no. 23 (April 5): 6–7.

———. 1999b. "The Path to Crisis: How the United States and Allies Went to War." *Washington Post* (April 18).

Gill, Bates. 1999. "Limited Engagement." *Foreign Affairs* 78, no. 4 (July/August): 65–76.

Gillespie, Ed, and Bob Schellhas. 1994. *Contract with America.* New York: Times Books.

"Global Hot Spots: Congo." 2000. Policy.com.

"Global Hot Spots: Korea." 2000. Policy.com.

Goldberg, Jonathan. 2000. "A Continent Bleeds." *National Review Online* (May 3). www.nationalreview.com/goldberg/goldbergprint050300.html.

Gompert, David. 1994. "How to Defeat Serbia." *Foreign Affairs* 73 (July/August): 30–47.

Gordon, Michael R. 1992. "Limits of U.S. Role." *New York Times* (August 11).

———. 1994. "U.S. and Bosnia: How a Policy Changed." *New York Times* (December 4).

Gordon, Michael R., and Bernard E. Trainor. 1994. "How Iraq Escaped to Threaten Kuwait Again." *New York Times* (October 23).

Gourevitch, Philip. 1998. *We Wish to Inform You That Tomorrow We Will Be Killed with Our Families.* New York: Farrar Straus Giroux.

Greenberger, Robert S. 1995–1996. "Dateline Capitol Hill: The New Majority's Foreign Policy." *Foreign Policy* 101 (Winter): 159–169.

Greenhouse, Steven. 1994. "A G.O.P. House Leader Presses Attack on Clinton Foreign Policy." *New York Times* (December 9).

Gurr, Ted Robert. 2000. "Ethnic Warfare on the Wane." *Foreign Affairs* 79, no. 3 (May/June): 52–64.

Haass, Richard N. 1995. "Paradigm Lost." *Foreign Affairs* 74, no. 1 (January/February): 43–58.

———. 1997a. *The Reluctant Sheriff: The United States After the Cold War*. New York: Council on Foreign Relations.

———. 1997b. "Sanctioning Madness." *Foreign Affairs* 76, no. 6 (November/December): 74–85.

———. 1999a. "What to Do with American Primacy." *Foreign Affairs* 78, no. 5 (September/October): 37–49.

———. 1999b. *Intervention: The Use of American Military Force in the Post-Cold War World*. Rev. ed. Washington, DC: Brookings Institution.

Haberman, Clyde. 1994. "Israel and Jordan Sign a Peace Accord." *New York Times* (October 27).

Hagen, William W. 1999. "The Balkans' Lethal Nationalisms." *Foreign Affairs* 78, no. 4 (July/August): 52–64.

Harden, Blaine. 1999. "Waging War on the Serbs: Old Problem, New Lesson." *New York Times* (June 6).

Harden, Blaine, and John M. Broder. 1999. "Clinton's Aims: Win the War, Keep the U.S. Voters Content." *New York Times* (May 22).

Harris, John F. 1999. "And if Airstrikes Weren't Enough. . . ?" *Washington Post National Weekly Edition* 16, no. 23 (April 5): 9.

Hartmann, Frederick H., and Robert L. Wendzel. 1994. *America's Foreign Policy in a Changing World*. New York: HarperCollins.

Hendrickson, David C. 1992. "The Renovation of America's Foreign Policy." *Foreign Affairs* 71, no. 2 (Spring): 48–96.

Hickey, Dennis Van Vranken. 1999. "The United States and Cross-Strait Rivalry: Strategic Partnership and Strategic Ambiguity." New York: Atlantic Council of the United States.

Hildreth, Steven A. 1992. "Evaluation of U.S. Army Assessment of Patriot Antitactical Missile Effectiveness in the War Against Iraq." Testimony prepared for the House Government Operations Subcommittee on Legislation and National Security, April 7, 1992.

Hirsh, Michael. 1999. "The Fall Guy." *Foreign Affairs* 78, no. 6 (November/December): 2–8.

Hoagland, Jim. 2000. "The Concorde and the Kursk." *Washington Post National Weekly Edition* 17, no. 44 (August 28): 5.

Hoge, James F., Jr. 1994. "Media Pervasiveness." *Foreign Affairs* 73, no. 4 (July/August): 136–144.

Hufbauer, Gary. 1998. "Foreign Policy on the Cheap." *Washington Post National Weekly Edition* 15, nos. 38–39 (July20–27): 22–23.

Huntington, Samuel P. 1993a. "The Clash of Civilizations?" *Foreign Affairs* 72, no. 6 (Summer): 22–49.

———. 1993b . "If Not Civilizations, What?" *Foreign Affairs* 72 (November/December): 186–194.

———. 1996. *The Clash of Civilizations and the Remaking of World Order*. New York: Simon & Schuster.

Ibrahim, Youssef M. 1992. "The Arab World Comes to the End of Illusions." *New York Times* (January 5).

International Labour Office. 2000. *HIV/AIDS: A Threat to Decent Work Productivity and Development*. Geneva, Switzerland (June 8).

Ivanov, Igor. 2000. "The Missile-Defense Mistake." *Foreign Affairs* 79, no. 5 (September/October): 15–20.

Isenberg, David. 1994. "The Pentagon's Fraudulent Bottom-Up Review." Policy Analysis No. 206, Cato Institute. www.cato.org/pubs/pas/pa-206.html.

———. 1998. "The Quadrennial Defense Review: Reiterating the Tired Status Quo." Policy Analysis No. 317, Cato Institute. www.cato.org/pubs/pas/pa-317.pdf.

Jehl, Douglas. 1994. "Jordan and Israel Join in Pact Aimed at Broad Mideast Peace." *New York Times* (July 26).

Kaplan, Robert D. 2000. "The Lawless Frontier." *Atlantic Monthly* 286, no. 3 (September): 66–80.

Kifner, John. 1999. "How Serb Forces Purged One Million Albanians." *New York Times* (May 29).

Kissinger, Henry A. 1999. "New World Disorder." *Newsweek* 133, no. 22 (May 31): 41–43.

Kitfield, James. 1999a. "A War of Limits." *National Journal* 31, no. 30 (July 24): 2154–2161.

———. 1999b. "Not-So-Sacred Borders." *National Journal* 31, no. 47–48 (November 20): 3386–3387.

———. 2000. "The Ultimate Bomb Shelter." *National Journal* 32, no. 28 (July 8): 2212–2221.

Kopecky, Ladislar. 1994. "Velvet Revolution Five Years Later." *Forum for Applied Research and Public Policy* 9 (Fall): 24–26.

Korb, Lawrence J. n.d. "Why a Cold War Budget Without a Cold War?" New York: Business Leaders for Sensible Priorities. www.businessleaders.org/blsp/home_flash_yes.htm.

———. 2000. "Defense." Council on Foreign Relations Campaign 2000 briefing paper. www.foreignpolicy2000.org/library/issuebriefs/IBDefense.html.

"Kosovo: The Jerusalem of Serbia." 1999. *Washington Post.* www.washingtonpost.com.

Krugman, Paul. 1994. "The Myth of Asia's Miracle." *Foreign Affairs* 73, no. 6 (November/December): 62–78.

Kull, Steven. 1995–1996. "What the Public Knows That Washington Doesn't." *Foreign Policy* 101 (Winter): 102–129.

Kuperman, Alan J. 2000. "Rwanda in Retrospect." *Foreign Affairs* 79, no. 1 (January/February): 94–118.

Kurth, James. 1994. "The *Real* Clash." *National Interest* 37 (Fall): 3–15.

Ladd, Everett C. 1987. *The American Polity: The People and Their Government.* New York: Norton.

Lindsay, James M. 2000. "The New Apathy." *Foreign Affairs* 79, no. 5 (September/October): 2–8.

Lipsitz, Lewis. 1986. *American Democracy.* New York: St. Martin's.

Mansfield, Edward, and Jack Snyder. 1995. "Democratization and War." *Foreign Affairs* 74, no. 3 (May/June): 79–96.

Marquis, Christopher. 2000. "U.S. Declares 'Rogue Nations' Are Now 'States of Concern.'" *New York Times* (June 20).

Miller, Judith. 1999. "Sovereignty Isn't So Sacred Anymore." *New York Times* (April 18).

Myers, Steven Lee. 2000a. "Signs of Iraqi Buildup Bedevil U.S. Administration." *New York Times* (February 1).

———. 2000b. "Army Weighs an Expanded Role for National Guard Combat Units." *New York Times* (August 4).

———. 2000c. "Military Reserves Are Falling Short in Finding Recruits." *New York Times* (August 28).

Myers, Steven Lee, and James Dao. 2001. "Bush Plans Modest Increase for the Pentagon, Aides Say." *New York Times* (February 1).

Neustadt, Richard E., and Ernest R. May. 1986. *Thinking in Time: The Uses of History for Decision Makers.* New York: Free Press.

Nye, Joseph S., Jr. 1992. "What New World Order?" *Foreign Affairs* 71, no. 3 (Summer): 83–96.

———. 1999. "Redefining the National Interest." *Foreign Affairs* 78, no. 4 (July/August): 22–35.

Odom, William E. 1999. "A Conditional Surrender." *New York Times* (June 6).

Office of Management and Budget. 2000. *Historical Tables: Budget of the United States Government, Fiscal Year 2001.* Washington, DC: Government Printing Office.

O'Hanlon, Michael. 1999. "Star Wars Strikes Back." *Foreign Affairs* 78, no. 6 (November/December): 68–82.

Omicinski, John. 1992. "Balkan Ethnic Hatred Goes Back 600 Years." *Springfield News-Leader* (August 9).

Perlez, Jane. 2000. "U.S. Missile Plan Could Hurt Security Ties, European Says." *New York Times* (May 2).

Pomfret, John, and David B. Ottaway. 1996. "Keeping the Pipeline Well-Armed." *Washington Post National Weekly Edition* 13, no. 29 (May 20–26): 14.

Powell, Colin L. 1992/1993. "U.S. Forces: Challenges Ahead." *Foreign Affairs* 71 (Winter): 32–45.

Power, Stephanie. 2001. "Bystanders to Genocide." *The Atlantic* 288, no. 2 (September): 84–108.

Rice, Condoleezza. 2000. "Promoting the National Interest." *Foreign Affairs* 79, no. 1 (January/February): 45–62.

Richburg, Keith B. 1994. "Full Circle in Somalia." *Washington Post National Weekly Edition* 12 (December 12–18): 17.

Roberts, Brad, Robert A. Manning, and Ronald N. Montaperto. 2000. "China: The Forgotten Nuclear Power." *Foreign Affairs* 79, no. 4 (July/August): 53–63.

Rodman, Peter W. 1999. "The Fallout from Kosovo." *Foreign Affairs* 78, no. 4 (July/August): 45–51.

Rohde, David. 2000. "Kosovo Seething." *Foreign Affairs* 79, no. 3 (May June): 65–79.

Rubenstein, Alvin Z. 1991. "New World Order or Hollow Victory?" *Foreign Affairs* 70 (Fall): 53–65.

Rubenstein, Richard E., and Jarle Crocker. 1994. "Challenging Huntington." *Foreign Policy* 96 (Fall): 113–128.

Ruggie, John Gerard. 1994. "Third Try at World Order? America and Multilateralism after the Cold War." *Political Science Quarterly* 109 (Fall): 553–570.

Ryan, Randolph. 1998. "Saying Goodbye to the Exit Strategy." *Washington Post National Weekly Edition* 15, no. 10 (January 5): 21–22.

Sadowski, Yahya. 1998. "Ethnic Conflict." *Foreign Policy* (Summer): 12–23.

Safire, William. 1999. "Lessons of Kosovo." *New York Times* (June 7).

Sanger, David E. 2000. "All Pumped Up and Nowhere to Go." *New York Times* (July 9).

———. 2001. "Bush Tells Seoul Talks with North Korea Won't Resume Now." *New York Times* (March 8).

Schmidt, William E. 1994. "Once Chosen Tribal Elites Now Suffer Consequences." *New York Times* (April 17).

Schmitt, Eric. 1998. "U.S. Backs Off Sanctions, Seeing Poor Effect Abroad." *New York Times* (July 31).

Schneider, William. 1989. "Assessing the Post-Cold War World." *National Journal* 21, no. 25 (June 24): 1670.

Sciolino, Elaine. 1994a. "For West, Rwanda Is Not Worth the Political Candle." *New York Times* (April 15).

———. 1994b. "Israel and Jordan Agree to Call Off a State of War That Has Endured 46 Years." *New York Times* (July 25).

———. 1995a. "New Dole Bills Seeking to Steer Foreign Policy." *New York Times* (January 5).

———. 1995b. "G.O.P. Senators Take Aim at Foreign Policy and U.N." *New York Times* (January 27).

———. 2000. "Surprise Failure of an Interceptor Dooms Missile Test." *New York Times* (July 9).

Sciolino, Elaine, and Ethan Bronner. 1999. "How a President, Distracted by Scandal, Entered Balkan War." *New York Times* (April 18).

Sciolino, Elaine, and Steven Lee Myers. 2000. "A U.S. Study Reopens Division Over Nuclear Missile Threat." *New York Times* (July 5).

Scobell, Andrew. 2000. "Show of Force: Chinese Soldiers, Statesmen, and the 1995–1996 Taiwan Strait Crisis." *Political Science Quarterly* 115, no. 2 (Summer): 227–246.

Shuster, Mike. 2000. "U.S. Missile Defense System Plan Creates Concerns by Other Countries." *Morning Edition*, National Public Radio (July 12).

Singer, Max, and Wildavsky, Aaron. 1993. *The Real World Order: Zones of Peace/Zones of Turmoil*. Chatham, NJ: Chatham House.

Sloan, Elinor C. 1998. *Bosnia and the New Collective Security*. Westport, CT: Praeger.

Sloyan, Patrick J. 1994. "The Secret Path to a Bloodbath." *Washington Post National Weekly Edition* 11 (April 18–24): 24–25.

Smith, Craig S. 2000. "Russia and China Unite in Criticism of U.S. Antimissile Plan." *New York Times* (July 19).

Smith, R. Jeffrey. 1994. "Spooked by the Shadow of Somalia." *Washington Post National Weekly Edition* 11 (September 12–18): 16.

————. 1998. "Giving the Possibility of Peace a Chance." *Washington Post National Weekly Edition* 15, no. 10 (January 5): 16.

Smith, R. Jeffrey, and William Drozdiak (1999). "Serbs' Offensive Was Meticulously Planned." *Washington Post* (April 11).

Smyrl, Marc E. 1988. *Conflict or Codetermination? Congress, the President, and the Power to Make War.* Cambridge, MA: Ballinger.

Solomon, Burt. 1999. "Isolationism Be Damned." *National Journal* 31, no, 16 (April 17): 1006–1008.

Sorenson, Theodore C. 1992. "America's First Post-Cold War President." *Foreign Affairs* 71, no. 4 (Fall): 13–30.

Spanier, John, and Joseph Nogee, eds. 1981. *Congress, the Presidency and American Foreign Policy.* New York: Pergamon Press.

Spanier, John, and Eric M. Uslaner. 1994. *American Foreign Policy Making and the Democratic Dilemmas.* 6th ed. New York: Holt, Rinehart, and Winston.

Spencer, Jack, and Joe Dougherty. 2000. *The Quickest Way to Global Missile Defense: First From the Sea.* Heritage Foundation Backgrounder No. 1384, July 13. www.heritage.org/library/backgrounder/bg1384.html.

Stedman, Stephen John. 1992–1993. "The New Interventionists." *Foreign Affairs* 72, no. 1 (Winter): 1–16.

Stremlau, John. 2000. "Ending Africa's Wars." *Foreign Affairs* 79, no. 4 (July/August): 117–132.

Sullivan, Scott. 1992. "Memo to U.S: Europe Matters." *Newsweek* 120 (November 30): 48.

Suro, Robert. 2000. "Clinton Defers Missile Defense." *Washington Post* (September 2).

Suro, Robert, and Thomas E. Ricks. 2000. "More Doubts Are Raised on Missile Shield." *Washington Post* (June 18).

Thomas, Jo. 1994. "Aid for Rwandans Begins at Refuge in Zaire." *New York Times* (July 22).

Underwood, Geoffrey S. 2000. "A History of National Missile Defense." Policy.com (June 16).

U.S. Census Bureau. 1999. *Statistical Abstract of the United States 1999.* Washington, DC: Government Printing Office.

Vickers, Michael, and Steven Kosiak. 1997. *The Quadrennial Defense Review—An Assessment.* Washington, DC: Center for Strategic and Budgetary Analysis. www.csbaonline.org.

Von Clausewitz, Karl. [1833] 1976. *On War.* Princeton, NJ: Princeton University Press.

Wheatcroft, Geoffrey. 1999. "A Land of Reluctant Warriors." *New York Times* (April 14).

Whitney, Craig R., and Eric Schmitt. 1999. "NATO Had Signs Its Strategy Would Fail Kosovars." *New York Times* (April 1).

Wildavsky, Aaron. 1975. "The Two Presidencies." In *Perspectives on the Presidency,* ed. Aaron Wildavsky. Boston: Little, Brown, pp. 448–461.

Will, George F. 1993. "America's Inoculation by Somalia." *Newsweek* 122 (September 6): 62.

Woodward, Bob. 1991. *The Commanders.* New York: Simon & Schuster.

————. 1994. *The Agenda: Inside the Clinton White House.* New York: Simon & Schuster.

Yankelovich, Daniel. 1992. "Foreign Policy After the Election." *Foreign Affairs* 71 (Winter): 1–12.

Zoellick, Robert. 2000. "A Republican Foreign Policy." *Foreign Affairs* 79, no. 1 (January/February): 63–78.

# Chapter 4

Administration for Children and Families. 1999. "Temporary Assistance for Needy Families Program (TANF); Final Rule." *Code of Federal Regulations* 45 CFR 260 et al., pp. 17719–17931. www.acf.dhhs.gov/programs/ofa/finalru.htm.

————. 2000. "Change in TANF Caseloads Since Enactment of New Welfare Reform Law." www.acf.dhhs.gov/news/stats/aug-dec.htm.

Alan Guttmacher Institute. 1999. "Teen Sex and Pregnancy." www.agi-usa.org/pubs/fb_teen_sex.html.

Allen, Katherine, and Maria Kirby. 2000. "Unfinished Business: Why Cities Matter to Welfare Reform." Washington, DC: Brookings Institution, Center on Urban and Metropolitan Policy.

Alter, Jonathan, and Pat Wingert. 1995. "The Return of Shame." *Newsweek* 125 (February 6): 21–25.

Anderson, Martin. 1978. *Welfare: The Political Economy of Welfare Reform in the United States*. Stanford, CA, Hoover Institution.

Baumann, David. 1999. "Government on Autopilot." *National Journal* 31, no. 11 (March 13): 688–692.

Bawden, D. Lee, and John L. Palmer. 1984. "Social Policy: Challenging the Welfare State." In *The Reagan Record: An Assessment of America's Changing Domestic Priorities*, ed. John Palmer and Isabel Sawhill. Cambridge, MA: Ballinger, pp. 117–215.

Beeghley, Leonard. 1983. *Living Poorly in America*. New York: Praeger.

Bell, Stephen. 1999. "New Federalism and Research: Rearranging Old Methods to Study New Social Policies in the States." Washington, DC: Urban Institute.

Bell, Stephen, and Toby Douglas. 2000. "Making Sure of Where We Started: State Employment and Training Systems for Welfare Recipients on the Eve of Federal Reform." Washington, DC: Urban Institute.

Bennett, William J. 1999. *The Index of Leading Cultural Indicators: American Society at the End of the Twentieth Century*. Updated and expanded. New York: Broadway Books.

Berkowitz, Edward D. 1991. *America's Welfare State: From Roosevelt to Reagan*. Baltimore: Johns Hopkins University Press.

Bernstein, Nina. 2000. "Studies Dispute 2 Assumptions About Welfare Overhaul." *New York Times* (December 12).

Butler, Stuart, and Anna Kondratas. 1987. *Out of the Poverty Trap: A Conservative Strategy for Welfare Reform*. New York: Free Press.

Cammisa, Anne Marie. 1998. *From Rhetoric to Reform? Welfare Policy in American Politics*. Boulder: Westview Press.

Chira, Susan. 1994. "Novel Idea in Welfare Plan: Helping Children by Helping Their Fathers." *New York Times* (March 30).

Clines, Francis X. 1996. "Clinton Signs Bill Cutting Welfare; States in New Role." *New York Times* (August 23).

Collins, Susan D. 2000. "Washington's New Poor Law: Welfare 'Reform's' Legacy and *Real* Welfare Reform." National Jobs for all Coalition (September) www.njfac.org/us23.htm.

Congressional Budget Office. 1987. *Work-Related Programs for Welfare Recipients*. Washington, DC: CBO.

Corbett, Thomas. 1993. "Child Poverty and Welfare Reform." *Focus* 15, no. 4 (Spring): 1–17.

Coughlin, Richard, ed. 1989. *Reforming Welfare: Lessons, Limits, and Choices*. Albuquerque: University of New Mexico Press.

Council of Economic Advisers. 1999. *The Effects of Welfare Policy and the Economic Expansion on Welfare Caseloads: An Update*. www.whitehouse.gov/WH/EOP/CEA/html/welfare/nontechv3.html.

Danziger, Sheldon H., ed. 1999. *Economic Conditions and Welfare Reform*. Kalamazoo, MI: W.E. Upjohn Institute for Employment Research.

Danziger, Sheldon, and Daniel Weinberg, eds. 1987. *Fighting Poverty: What Works and What Doesn't*. Cambridge: Harvard University Press.

Dalaker, Joseph, and Bernadette D. Proctor. 2000. "Poverty in the United States 1999." Washington, DC: Bureau of the Census.

Davis, Karen, and Cathy Schoen. 1978. *Health and the War on Poverty: A Ten-Year Appraisal*. Washington, DC: Brookings Institution.

DeLong, J. Bradford. 2000. "Changes in the Earned-Income Tax Credit Are a Success in the Effort to Fix Welfare, but There's Room for Improvement." *New York Times* (May 4).

DeParle, Jason. 1991. "California Plan to Cut Welfare May Prompt Others to Follow." *New York Times* (December 18).

———. 1993. "Wisconsin Pledges to Exit U.S. System of Public Welfare." *New York Times* (December 14).

———. 1994a. "New Strategy for Financing Welfare Plan." *New York Times* (April 21).

———. 1994b. "Scrap Welfare? Surprisingly, the Notion Is Now a Cause." *New York Times* (April 22).

————. 1994c. "Clinton to Propose a Strategy to Curb Youth Pregnancies." *New York Times* (June 10).

————. 1994d. "The Clinton Welfare Bill Begins Trek in Congress." *New York Times* (July 15).

————. 1996. "Mugged by Reality." *New York Times Magazine* (December 8).

————. 1997. "Cutting Welfare Rolls but Raising Questions." *New York Times* (May 5).

————. 1998. "Shrinking Welfare Rolls Leave Record High Share of Minorities." *New York Times* (July 27).

————. 1999a. "The Silence of the Liberals." *The Washington Monthly* 31, no. 4 (April): 12–22.

————. 1999b. "States Struggle to Use Windfall Born of Shifts in Welfare Law." *New York Times* (August 29).

"The Depths of the Food Stamp Cuts in the Final Welfare Bill." 1996. Washington, DC: Center on Budget and Policy Priorities (August 12).

Dionne, E.J., Jr. 1996. "Resigning on Principle. . ." *Washington Post* (September 17).

————. 1998. "Some Good News About Teen Pregnancy." *Washington Post National Weekly Edition* 15, no. 28 (May 11): 27.

————. 1999. "A Ladder for the Poor." *Washington Post National Weekly Edition* 16, no. 33 (June 14): 27.

Dolbeare, Kenneth M., and Russell M. Lidman. 1985. "Ideology and Policy Research: The Case of Murray's *Losing Ground*." *Policy Studies Review* 4 (May): 587–594.

Dye, Thomas R. 1987. *Understanding Public Policy.* 6th ed. Englewood Cliffs, NJ: Prentice-Hall.

Edelman, Peter. 1997. "The Worst Thing Bill Clinton Has Done." *Atlantic* 279, no. 3 (March): 43–58.

Edsall, Thomas Byrne, and Mary D. Edsall. 1991. *Chain Reaction: The Impact of Race, Rights, and Taxes on American Politics.* New York: Basic Books.

Ellwood, David T. 1989. "The Origins of 'Dependency': Choices, Confidence, or Culture?" *Focus* 12, no. 1 (Spring/Summer): 6–13.

Etzioni, Amitai. 1996. *The New Golden Rule: Community and Morality in a Democratic Society.* New York: Basic Books.

FamiliesUSA. 1999. "The Unintended Consequences of Welfare Reform." Washington, DC: FamiliesUSA.

Freedman, Stephen, Daniel Friedlander, Gayle Hamilton, JoAnn Rock, Marissa Mitchell, Jodi Nudelman, Amanda Schweder, and Laura Storto. 2000. *National Evaluation of Welfare-to-Work Strategies; Executive Summary.* New York: Manpower Demonstration Research Corporation. www.mdrc.org/Reports2000/NEWWS-11Prog/ NEWWS-11ProgExSum.htm.

Friedman, Milton, with Rose D. Friedman. 1962. *Capitalism and Freedom.* Chicago: University of Chicago Press.

Gallagher, L. Jerome, Megan Gallagher, Kevin Perese, Susan Schreiber, and Keith Watson. 1998. "One Year After Federal Welfare Reform: A Description of State Temporary Assistance for Needy Families (TANF) Decisions as of October 1997." Washington, DC: Urban Institute.

Galbraith, John Kenneth. 1957. *The Affluent Society.* Boston: Houghton Mifflin.

Garrett, Bowen, and John Holahan. 2000. "Welfare Leavers, Medicaid Coverage, and Private Health Insurance." Washington, DC: Urban Institute.

General Accounting Office. 1994. *Federal Aid: Revising Poverty Statistics Affects Fairness of Allocation Formulas.* Washington, DC: GAO.

Gilder, George. 1981. *Wealth and Poverty.* New York: Basic Books.

Gilens, Martin. 1999. *Why Americans Hate Welfare: Race, Media, and the Politics of Antipoverty Policy.* Chicago: University of Chicago Press.

Gillespie, Ed, and Bob Schellhas, eds. 1994. *The Contract with America: The Bold Plan by Rep. Newt Gingrich, Rep. Dick Armey and the House Republicans to Change the Nation.* New York: Times Books.

Greenberg, Mark. 1997. "Welfare-to Work Grants and Other TANF-Related Provisions in the Balanced Budget Act of 1997." Washington, DC: Center for Law and Social Policy (August).

Greenberg, Mark, and Steve Savner. 1996. "The Temporary Assistance for Needy Families Block Grant." Washington, DC: Center for Law and Social Policy (August).

Harpham, Edward J., and Richard K. Scotch. 1989. "Ideology and Welfare Reform in the 1980s." In *Reforming Welfare: Lessons, Limits, and Choices*, ed. Richard Coughlin. Albuquerque: University of New Mexico Press, pp. 43–60.

Harrington, Michael. 1962. *The Other America: Poverty in the United States*. New York: Penguin.

Health Care Financing Administration. National Health Expenditures Tables. U.S. Department of Health and Human Services. www.hcfa.gov/stats/nhe-oact/tables.

Ierley, Merritt. 1984. *With Charity for All: Welfare and Society, Ancient Times to the Present*. New York: Praeger.

Katz, Michael B. 1989. *The Undeserving Poor: From the War on Poverty to the War on Welfare*. New York: Pantheon Books.

Kerwin, Cornelius M. 1994. *Rulemaking: How Government Agencies Write Law and Make Policy*. Washington, DC: CQ Press.

King, Wayne. 1992. "U.S. Approves New Jersey's Plans to Overhaul Its Welfare System." *New York Times* (July 21).

Knox, Virginia, Cynthia Miller, and Lisa A. Gennatian. 2000. *Reforming Welfare and Rewarding Work: A Summary of the Final Report of the Minnesota Family Investment Program*. New York: Manpower Development Research Corporation. www.mdrc.org/Reports2000/MFIP/MFIP-ExSum-Final.htm.

Kosterlitz, Julie. 1985. "Working for Welfare." *National Journal* 17 (October 26): 2418–2422.
———. 1992. "Reworking Welfare." *National Journal* 24 (September 26): 2189–2192.

Kuttner, Robert. 1984. "A Flawed Case for Scrapping What's Left of the Great Society; Review of *Losing Ground: American Social Policy, 1950–1980*." *Washington Post National Weekly Edition* 1 (December 4): 34–35.

Lewin, Tamar. 2000. "Cut Down on Out-of-Wedlock Births, Win Cash." *New York Times* (September 24).

Lipsky, Michael. 1980. *Street-Level Bureaucracy: Dilemmas of the Individual in Public Services*. New York: Russell Sage Foundation.

Loprest, Pamela. 1999. "How Families That Left Welfare Are Doing: A National Picture." Washington, DC: Urban Institute.

Loprest, Pamela, and Sheila R. Zedlewski. 1999. "Current and Former Welfare Recipients: How Do They Differ?" Washington, DC: Urban Institute.

Marmor, Theodore R., Jerry L. Mashaw, and Philip L. Harvey. 1990. *America's Misunderstood Welfare State: Persistent Myths, Enduring Realities*. New York: Basic Books.

McLanahan, Sara S. 1994. "The Consequences of Single Motherhood." *American Prospect* 18 (Summer): 48–58.

McLanahan, Sara, and Irwin Garfinkel. 1994. "Welfare Is No Incentive." *New York Times* (July 29).

Meckler, Laura. 2001. "Debate Renewed Over Welfare Changes." Associated Press (February 1).

Moynihan, Daniel P. 1973. *The Politics of a Guaranteed Income: The Nixon Administration and the Family Assistance Plan*. New York: Vintage Books.

Murray, Charles. 1984. *Losing Ground: American Social Policy 1950–1980*. New York: Basic Books.
———. 1992. "Stop Favoring Unwed Mothers." *New York Times* (January 16).
———. 1993. "The Coming White Underclass." *Wall Street Journal* (October 29).
———. 1994. "Does Welfare Bring More Babies?" *Public Interest* 115 (Spring): 17–30.

National Center for Health Statistics. 2000. *Health, United States, 2000*. Centers for Disease Control and Prevention, U.S. Department of Health and Human Services. www.cdc.gov/nchs/products/pubs/pubd/hus/hus.htm.

Nightingale, Demetra Smith, and Kathleen Brennan. 1998. The Welfare-to-Work Grant Program: A New Link in the Welfare Reform Chain. Washington, DC: The Urban Institute.

Nightingale, Demetra Smith, and Kelly S. Mikelson. 2000. An Overview of Research Related to Wisconsin Works (W-2). Washington, DC: Urban Institute.

"No Such Thing as Typical American Family Anymore." 1994. *Springfield News-Leader* (August 10).

Office of Management and Budget. 2000. *Historical Tables: Budget of the United States Government, Fiscal Year 2001.* Washington, DC: Government Printing Office.

Palazzolo, Daniel. J. 1999. *Done Deal? The Politics of the 1997 Budget Agreement.* Chatham, NJ: Chatham House.

Parrott, Sharon. 1998. *Welfare Recipients Who Find Jobs: What Do We Know About Their Employment and Earnings.* Washington, DC: Center on Budget and Policy Priorities.

Patel, Kant, and Mark E. Rushefsky. 1995. *Health Care Politics and Policy in the United States.* Armonk, NY: M.E. Sharpe.

———. 1999. *Health Care Politics and Policy in America.* 2d ed. Armonk, NY: M.E. Sharpe.

Pear, Robert. 1984. "Many Who Lost Aid Work More But Stay Poor, Study Concludes." *New York Times* (March 31).

———. 1993. "Poverty in U.S. Grew Faster Than Population Last Year." *New York Times* (October 5).

———. 2000. "Changes in Welfare Bring Improvements for Families." *New York Times* (June 1).

Peterson, Peter G. 1993. *Facing Up: How to Rescue the Economy from Crushing Debt & Restore the American Dream.* New York: Simon & Schuster.

Piven, Frances Fox, and Richard A. Cloward. 1971. *Regulating the Poor: The Functions of Public Welfare.* New York: Vintage Books.

Rank, Mark Robert. 1994. *Living on the Edge: The Realities of Welfare in America.* New York: Columbia University Press.

Rich, Spencer. 1988. "Falling Through the Reagan Safety Net." *Washington Post National Weekly Edition* 6 (December 26): 6–7.

Savner, Steve. 1996. A Brief Summary of Key Provisions of the Temporary Assistance for Needy Families Block Grant of H.R. 3734. Washington, DC: FamiliesUSA.

Schmalz, Jeffrey. 1988. "Belying Popular Stereotypes, Many of Homeless Have Jobs." *New York Times* (December 19).

Schneider, Anne Larason, and Helen Ingram. 1997. *Policy Design for Democracy.* Lawrence: University of Kansas Press.

Schwarz, John E., and Thomas J. Volgy. 1992. *The Forgotten Americans: Thirty Million Working Poor in the Land of Opportunity.* New York: Norton.

Skolnick, Arlene, and Stacy Rosencrantz. 1994. "The New Crusade for the Old Family." *American Prospect* 18 (Summer): 59–65.

Sottile, Noell, ed. 1988. *Current American Government.* Washington, DC: CQ Press.

Stanfield, Rochelle L. 1992. "Valuing the Family." *National Journal* 24 (July 4): 1562–1566.

Starr, Paul. 1986. "Health Care for the Poor: The Past Twenty Years." In *Fighting Poverty: What Works and What Doesn't,* ed. Sheldon Danziger and Daniel Weinberg. Cambridge: Harvard University Press, pp. 106–132.

Stevens, William K. 1988. "Welfare Bill: Historic Scope but a Gradual Impact." *New York Times* (October 2).

Stockman, David A. 1987. *The Triumph of Politics: The Inside Story of the Reagan Revolution.* New York: Avon Books.

Stoesz, David. 1996. *Small Change: Domestic Policy Under the Clinton Presidency.* New York: Longman.

Stolberg, Sheryl Gay. 1999. "U.S. Birth Rate at New Low as Teen-Age Pregnancy Falls." *New York Times* (April 29).

Stone, Deborah A. 1994. "Making the Poor Count." *American Prospect* 17 (Spring): 83–88.

———. 1997. *Policy Paradox: The Art of Political Decision Making.* New York: Norton.

"Study Says Budget Made 557,000 Poor." 1984. *New York Times* (July 26).

Swarns, Rachel L. 1998. "Hispanic Mothers Lagging as Others Escape Welfare." *New York Times* (September 15).

Taylor, Paul. 1991. " 'A Meaner, Harsher Nation.'" *Washington Post National Weekly Edition* 9 (December 29–January 5): 32.

Toy, Vivian S. 1998. "Tough Welfare Rules Used as Way to Cut Welfare Rolls." *New York Times* (April 15).

Trutko, John, Nancy Pindus, Burt S. Barnow, and Demetra Smith Nightingale. 1999. "Early

Implementation of the Welfare-to-Work Grants Program." Washington, DC: Urban Institute.

U.S. Census Bureau. 1999. *Statistical Abstract of the United States 1999*. Washington, DC: Government Printing Office.

———. 2000. "Poverty Thresholds in 1999, by Size of Family and Number of Related Children Under 18 Years." www.census.gov/hhes/poverty/threshld/thresh99.html.

U.S. House of Representatives Committee on Ways and Means. 1998. *The 1998 Green Book Overview of Entitlement Programs*. aspe.hhs.gov/98gb/intro.htm.

Ventura, Stephanie J., T.J. Matthews, and Sally C. Curtin. 1998. "Declines in Teenage Birth Rates, 1991–1997: National and State Patterns." *National Vital Statistics Reports* 47, no. 12 (December).

Vobejda, Barbara, and Judith Havemann. 1997. "Welfare Clients Already Work, Off the Books." *Washington Post* (November 3).

———. 1998a. "Losing Welfare as a Punishment." *Washington Post National Weekly Edition* 15, no. 22 (March 30): 29.

———. 1998b. "Social Policy vs. Human Nature." *Washington Post National Weekly Edition* 14, no. 23 (April 7): 30–31.

———. 1998c. "Sidestepping the Dole." *Washington Post National Weekly Edition* 15, no. 44 (August 31): 29.

Waldman, Steven. 1994. "Taking on the Welfare Dads." *Newsweek* 123 (June 20): 34–38.

Wingert, Pat. 1998. "The Battle Over Falling Birthrates." *Newsweek* 131, no. 19 (May 11): 40.

White, Theodore H. 1962. *The Making of the President 1960*. New York: Atheneum.

Whitehead, Barbara D. 1993. "Dan Quayle Was Right." *Atlantic Monthly* 271 (April): 47–84.

"Whites Leaving Welfare Faster." 1999. *Springfield News-Leader* (March 30).

Whitman, David, and Dorian Friedman. 1994. "The White Underclass." *U.S. News & World Report* 117 (October 17): 40–53.

Zedlewski, Sheila R. 1999. "Work Activity and Obstacles to Work Among TANF Recipients." Washington, DC: Urban Institute.

Zedlewski, Sheila R., and Sarah Brauner. 1999. "Declines in Food Stamp Participation: Is There a Connection?" Washington, DC: The Urban Institute.

# Chapter 5

Anders, George. 1996. *Health Against Wealth: HMOs and the Breakdown of Medical Trust*. Boston: Houghton Mifflin.

Barry, Patricia. 2000. "Hard Pills to Swallow." *AARP Bulletin* 41, no. 10 (November): 1, 3, 22–26.

Berk, Marc L., and Alan C. Monheit. 2001. "The Concentration of Health Care Expenditures, Revisited." *Health Affairs* 20, no. 2: 9–18.

Board of Trustees. 2001. *2001 Annual Report Of the Board of Trustees of the Federal Hospital Insurance Trust Fund*. Washington, DC.

Bodenheimer, Thomas. 2000. "Selective Chaos." *Health Affairs* 19, no. 4 (July/August): 200–205.

Branigin, William. 1998. "Paying More Than Their Fair Share." *Washington Post National Weekly Edition* 16, no. 6 (December 7): 34.

Brown, E. Richard. 1979. *Rockefeller Medicine Men: Medicine and Capitalism in America*. Berkeley: University of California Press.

Brown, Lawrence D. 1983. *Politics and Health Care Organizations: HMOs as Federal Policy*. Washington, DC: Brookings Institution.

———. 1986. "Introduction to a Decade of Transition." *Journal of Health Politics, Policy and Law* 11, no. 4 (Winter): 569–583.

Century Foundation. 2000. *The Basics: Medicare Reform, 1999 Edition*. www.tcf.org/Publications/Basics/new_medicare/Introduction.asp.

Christensen, Sandra, and Judith Wagner. 2000. "The Costs of a Medicare Prescription Drug Benefit." *Health Affairs* 19, no. 2 (March /April): 212–218.

"Clinton Seeks New Rules to Expand Patient Rights." 1999. *New York Times* (November 5).

Congressional Budget Office. 1997. *Trends in Spending by the Private Sector.* Washington, DC: CBO.

Duggan, Paul, and Susan Levine. 2000. "Health Care Costs Will Pinch Employers; Insurance Squeeze Also to Hit Workers." *Washington Post* (September 26).

Enthoven, Alain C. 1980. *Health Plan: The Only Practical Solution to the Soaring Cost of Medical Care.* Reading, MA: Addison-Wesley.

Falkson, Joseph L. 1980. *HMO's and the Politics of Health Service Reform.* Chicago: American Hospital Association and Robert J. Brady Company.

FamiliesUSA. 1998. *Hit and Miss: State Managed Care Laws.* Washington, DC: FamiliesUSA.

———. 1999a. "The Breaux-Thomas Proposal: What Will It Mean for Medicare Beneficiaries." Washington, DC: FamiliesUSA. www.familiesusa.org/btprop.htm.

———. 1999b. "State Managed Care Protections." Washington, DC: FamiliesUSA. www.familiesusa.org/hitmisup.htm.

———. 2000a. *Go Directly to Work, Do Not Collect Health Insurance: Low-Income Parents Lose Medicaid.* Washington, DC: FamiliesUSA.

———. 2000b. *Cost Overdoses: Growth in Drug Spending for the Elderly, 1992–2010.* Washington, DC: FamiliesUSA.

———. 2001. "Bush Budget Speeds Medicare Insolvency by 15 Years." Washington, DC: FamiliesUSA.

Feder, Judith, Harriet L. Komisar, and Marlene Niefield. 2000. "Long-Term Care in the United States: An Overview." *Health Affairs* 19, no. 3 (May/June): 40–56.

Feldstein, Martin. 1977. "The High Cost of Hospitals—and What to Do About It." *Public Interest* 43: 40–54.

Findlay, Steven, and Joel Miller. 1999. *Down a Dangerous Path: The Erosion of Health Insurance Coverage in the United States.* Washington, DC: National Coalition for Health Care.

Fossett, James W. 1994. "Cost Containment and Rate Setting." In *Making Health Reform Work: The View from the States,* ed. John J. DiIulio, Jr. and Richard P. Nathan. Washington, DC: Brookings Institution, pp. 60–84.

Freudenheim, Milt. 1994. "H.M.O.'s Offering a Choice Are Gaining in Popularity." *New York Times* (February 7, 1994).

Friedman, Joel, and Iris J. Lav. 2000. "Health Insurance Deduction of Little Help to the Uninsured." Washington, DC: Center for Budget and Policy Priorities.

Frogue, James. 2000. "A Guide to Tax Credits for the Uninsured." Backgrounder #1365. Washington, DC: Heritage Foundation.

Gabel, Jon R., et al. 2000. "Job-Based Health Insurance in 2000: Premiums Rise Sharply While Coverage Grows." *Health Affairs* 19, no. 5 (September/October): 144–151.

General Accounting Office. 1999. *Medicaid Enrollment: Amid Declines, State Efforts to Ensure Coverage After Welfare Reform Vary.* Report # HEHS-99–163. Washington, DC: GAO.

———. 2000. *Medicare+Choice: Plan Withdrawals Indicate Difficulty of Providing Choice While Achieving Savings.* Report # HEHS-00–183. Washington, DC: GAO.

Ginzberg, Eli. 1977. *The Limits of Health Reform: The Search for Realism.* New York: Basic Books.

Gluck, Michael E. 2000. "A Side-by-Side Comparison of Selected Medicare Prescription Drug Coverage Proposals." Kaiser Family Foundation. www.kff.org/content/2000/1601/sidebyside.pdf.

Goldstein, Amy. 1999. "Is the Remedy to Retreat?" *Washington Post National Weekly Edition* 16, no. 29 (May 17): 19.

———. 2001a. "When a Helping Hand Isn't Enough." *Washington Post National Weekly Edition* 18, no. 18 (February 26–March 4): 8–9.

———. 2001b. "The Price Isn't Always Right." *Washington Post National Weekly Edition* 18, no. 19 (March 5–11): 8–9.

Graig, Laurene. 1999. *Health of Nations: An International Perspective on U.S. Health Care Reform.* 3d ed. Washington, DC: CQ Press.

Greenhouse, Linda. 2000. "H.M.O.'s Win Critical Ruling on Liability for Doctors' Acts." *New York Times* (June 12).

Gruber, Jonathan, and Larry Levitt. 2000. "Tax Subsidies for Health Insurance: Costs and Benefits." *Health Affairs* 19, no. 1 (January/February): 72–85.

Guyer, Jocelyn, and Cindy Mann. 1998. "Taking the Next Step: States Can Now Expand Health Coverage to Low-Income Working Parents Through Medicaid." Washington, DC: Center for Budget and Policy Priorities.

Health Care Financing Administration. 1998. *1998 Data Compendium.* Baltimore: Health Care Financing Administration, Office of Strategic Planning.

———. 2000. *The State Children's Health Insurance Program: Preliminary Highlights of Implementation and Expansion.* www.hcfa.gov/init/wh0700.pdf.

———. n.d. "National Summary of Medicaid Managed Care Programs and Enrollment." www.hcfa.gov/medicaid/trends99.htm.

———. Website. www.hcfa.gov/stats.

Health Leadership Council. 2001. "Statement of the Health Leadership Council on the 2001 Medicare Trustees Report." Washington, DC: Health Leadership Council.

Heffler, Stephen, et al. 2001. "Health Spending Growth up in 1999: Faster Growth Expected in the Future." *Health Affairs* 20, no. 2 (March/April): 193–203.

Helerman, Kelly. 2000. "Low-Cost Clinics Sought to Avert Crisis." *Springfield News-Leader* (November 1).

Holahan, John, and Johnny Kim. 2000. "Why Does the Number of Uninsured Americans Continue to Grow?" *Health Affairs* 19, no. 4 (July/August): 188–196.

Johnson, Haynes, and David S. Broder. 1996. *The System: The American Way of Politics at the Breaking Point.* Boston: Little, Brown.

Kahn, Charles N., III, and Ronald F. Pollack. 2001. "Building a Consensus for Expanding Health Coverage." *Health Affairs* 20, no. 1 (January/February): 40–48.

Kaiser Commission on Medicaid and the Uninsured. 2000. *CHIP Program Enrollment: December 1998 to December 1999.* Washington, DC: Kaiser Commission on Medicaid and the Uninsured.

Kaiser Family Foundation. 1999. "Medicare Managed Care." www.kff.org/content/archive/2052/MedicareManaged.pdf.

Kaiser Family Foundation and Health Education and Research Trust. 2000. *Employee Health Benefits: 2000 Annual Survey.* Menlo Park, CA and Chicago, IL: Kaiser Family Foundation and Health Education and Research Trust.

Kramon, Glenn. 1987. "Overpayments on H.M.O.s." *New York Times* (October 20).

Krause, Elliott A. 1977. *Power & Illness: The Political Sociology of Health and Medical Care.* New York: Elsevier.

Ku, Leighton, and Matthew Broaddus. 2000. "The Importance of Family-Based Insurance Expansions: New Research Findings About State Health Reforms." Washington, DC: Center for Budget and Policy Priorities.

Laschober, Mary A., et al. 1999. "Medicare HMO Withdrawals: What Happens to Beneficiaries?" *Health Affairs* 18, no. 6 (November/December): 150–157.

Levit, Katherine, et al. 2000. "Health Spending in 1998: Signals of Change." *Health Affairs* 19, no. 1 (January/February): 124–132.

Leyerle, Betty. 1994. *The Private Regulation of American Health Care.* Armonk, NY: M.E. Sharpe.

Luft, Harold S. 1981. *Health Maintenance Organizations: Dimensions of Performance.* New York: Wiley.

Marmor, Theodore R. 2000. *The Politics of Medicare.* 2d ed. New York: Aldine de Gruyter.

———, ed. 1983. *Political Analysis and American Medical Care.* Cambridge, England: Cambridge University Press.

Marmor, Theodore R., Donald A. Wittman, and Thomas C. Heagy. 1983. "The Politics of Medical Inflation." In *Political Analysis and American Medical Care*, ed. Theodore Marmor. Cambridge, England: Cambridge University Press, pp. 61–75.

McClellan, Mark, Ian D. Spatz, and Stacie Carney. 2000. "Designing a Medicare Prescription Drug Benefit: Issues, Obstacles and Opportunities." *Health Affairs* 19, no. 2 (March/April): 26–41.

MedicareWatch. 1999. "President Clinton's Medicare Prescription Drug Benefit: Issues and Choices." Issue Brief No. 1 (September). Washington, DC: Century Foundation.

Miller, Joel E. 2000. *Deja Vu All Over Again: The Soaring Cost of Private Health Insurance and Its Impact on Consumers and Employers.* Washington, DC: National Coalition on Health Care.

Mills, Robert J. 2000. "Health Insurance Coverage 1999." Washington. DC: U.S. Census Bureau.

Moffit, Robert E., Richard Teske, and Stephen Moses. 2000. "How to Cope with the Coming Crisis in Long-Term Care." *Heritage Lectures*, no. 658 (April 27). Washington, DC: Heritage Foundation.

Moon, Marilyn. 1996. *Medicare Now and in the Future.* 2d ed. Washington, DC: Urban Institute.

Mooney, Brian C. 2000. "On Question 5, Money Isn't Everything." *Boston Globe* (November 1).

National Center for Health Statistics. 2000. *Health, United States 2000.* Washington, DC: National Center for Health Statistics, U.S. Department of Health and Human Services. www.cdc.gov/nchs/products/pubs/pubd/hus/hus.htm.

Patel, Kant, and Mark E. Rushefsky. 1999. *Health Care Politics and Policy in America.* 2d ed. Armonk, NY: M.E. Sharpe.

Pear, Robert. 1999a. "Medicare Panel, Sharply Divided, Submits No Plan." *New York Times* (March 17).

———. 1999b. "Many States Slow to Use Children's Insurance Fund." *New York Times* (May 9).

———. 1999c. "Insurers Ask Government to Extend Health Plans." *New York Times* (May 23).

———. 1999d. "Drug Makers Fault the Details of Clinton Medicare Proposal." *New York Times* (July 16).

———. 1999e. "Annual Spending on Medicare Dips for the First Time." *New York Times* (November 14).

———. 2000a. "Medicare Spending for Care at Home Plunges by 45%." *New York Times* (April 18).

———. 2000b. "Democrats Say Bush Exaggerated State Spending on Health Care for Uninsured." *New York Times* (October 16).

———. 2000c. "G.O.P. Chiefs Push Medicare Bill That Clinton Threatens to Veto." *New York Times* (October 20).

———. 2001. "Bush Outlines His Principles for Protecting Patient Rights." *New York Times* (February 7).

Penner, Rudolph G., Isabel V. Sawhill, and Timothy Taylor. 2000. *Updating America's Social Contract: Economic Growth and Opportunity in the New Century.* New York: Norton.

Phillips, Martha. n.d. *A Primer on Medicare.* Washington, DC: Concord Coalition.

Polzer, Karl. 1999. "HIPAA as a Regulatory Mode: Early Experiences and Future Prospects." Issue Brief #735. Washington, DC: National Health Policy Forum.

"President Clinton Endorses Consumer Bill of Rights and Calls for Immediate Action to Implement." 1997. hippo.findlaw.com/hmo.html.

Redman, Eric. 1973. *The Dance of Legislation.* New York: Simon & Schuster.

Relative Risk Reduction Strategies Committee. 1990. *Reducing Risk: Setting Priorities and Strategies for Environmental Protection.* Washington, DC: Environmental Protection Agency.

"Republicans Backing Tax Break for Care of Elderly Relatives." 1999. *New York Times* (July 7).

Revkin, Andrew C. 2001. "178 Nations Reach A Climate Accord." *New York Times* (July 23).

Rice, Thomas, Katherine Desmond, and Jon Gabel. 1990. "Medicare Catastrophic Coverage Act: A Post-Mortem." *Health Affairs* 9, no. 3 (Fall): 75–87.

Rimer, Sara. 1999. "Caring for Elderly Kin Is Costly, Study Finds." *New York Times* (November 27).

Rushefsky, Mark E., and Kant Patel. 1998. *Politics, Power & Policy Making: The Case of Health Care Reform in the 1990s.* Armonk, NY: M.E. Sharpe.

Schroeder, Steven A. 2001. "Prospects for Expanding Health Insurance Coverage." *New England Journal of Medicine* 344, no. 11 (March 15). www.nejm.org/content/2001/0344/0011/0847.asp.

Serafini, Marilyn Werber. 1997. "Brave New World." *National Journal* 29, no. 33 (August 16): 1636–1639.

———. 1998. "Now, the Hard Part." *National Journal* 30, no. 47 (November 21): 2774–2780.

———. 1999. "The Other Drug War." *National Journal* 31, no. 17 (April 24): 1104–1108.

Singer, Sara J. 2000. "What's Not to Like About HMOs." *Health Affairs* 19, no. 4 (July/August): 206–209.

Skocpol, Theda. 1996. *Boomerang: Clinton's Health Security Effort and the Turn Against Government in U.S. Politics.* New York: Norton.

Sloan, Frank A. 1983. "Rate Regulation as a Strategy for Hospital Cost Control: Evidence from the Last Decade." *Milbank Memorial Fund Quarterly: Health and Society* 61 (Spring): 195–221.

Starr, Paul. 1982. *The Social Transformation of American Medicine.* New York: Basic Books.

Stearns, Sally C., and Rebecca T. Slifkin. 1997. "The Structure and Experience of State Risk Pools: 1988–1994." *Medicare Care Research and Review* 54, no. 2 (June): 233–248.

Steinberg, Earl P., et al. 2000. "Beyond Survey-Data: A Claims-Based Analysis of Drug Use and Spending by the Elderly." *Health Affairs* 19, no. 2 (March/April): 198–211.

Steinhauer, Jennifer. 2000. "States Prove Unpredictable in Aiding Uninsured Children." *New York Times* (September 28).

Stone, Deborah. 1997. *Policy Paradox : The Art of Political Decision Making.* New York: Norton.

Study Panel on Medicare's Larger Social Role. 1999. *Medicare and the American Social Contract.* Washington, DC: National Academy of Social Insurance. www.nasi.org/Medicare/largerpt.htm.

Sullivan, Kip. 2000. "On the 'Efficiency' of Managed Care Plans." *Health Affairs* 19, no. 4 (July/August): 139–148.

Thompson, Frank J. 1981. *Health Policy and the Bureaucracy: Politics and Implementation.* Cambridge: MIT Press.

Toner, Robin. 1999. "Clinton Lays Out Plan to Overhaul Medicare System." *New York Times* (June 30).

Urban Institute. 1999. *Can Competition Improve Medicare? A Look at Premium Support.* Washington, DC: The Urban Institute. www.urban.org/health/Medicare_comp.html.

U.S. Census Bureau. 1994. *Statistical Abstract of the United States 1994.* Washington, DC: Government Printing Office.

———. 1999. *Statistical Abstract of the United States 1999.* Washington, DC: Government Printing Office.

Volpp, Kevin G., and Bruce Siegel. 1993. "New Jersey: Long-Term Experience with All-Payer Rate Setting." *Health Affairs* 12, no. 2 (Summer): 59–65.

Walsh, Mary Williams. 2000. "Factory Workers Fight the Squeeze on Health Benefits." *New York Times* (October 25).

Wiener, Joshua M., and David G. Stevenson. 1998. "State Policy on Long-Term Care for the Elderly." *Health Affairs* 17, no. 3 (May/June): 81–100.

Wilkes, Michael S., Robert A. Bell, and Richard L. Kravitz. 2000. "Direct-to-Consumer Prescription Drugs: Trends, Impact, and Implications." *Health Affairs* 19, no. 2 (March/April): 110–128.

Wilson, James Q., ed. 1980. *The Politics of Regulation.* New York: Basic Books.

Wolf, Charles, Jr. 1979. "A Theory of Non-Market Failures." *The Public Interest*, no. 55: 114–133.

# Chapter 6

Alvarez, Lizette. 2000. "Senate Approves $7.8 Billion Plan to Aid Everglades." *New York Times* (September 26).

Anderson, Robert C., and Alan Carlin. 1997. *The United States Experience with Economic Incentives in Environmental Pollution Control Policy.* Washington, DC: Environmental Law Institute.

Anderson, Terry L., and Donald R. Leal. 1991. *Free Market Environmentalism*. San Francisco: Pacific Research Institute for Public Policy.

Andrews, Richard N.L. 2000. "Risk-Based Decisionmaking." In *Environmental Policy*, ed. Norman J. Vig and Michael E. Kraft. 4th ed. Washington, DC: CQ Press, pp. 210–231.

Arrandale, Tom. 1993. "When the Poor Cry NIMBY." *Governing* 6, no. 12 (September): 36–41.

———. 1994a. "A Guide to Environmental Mandates." *Governing* 7, no. 4 (March): 73–85.

———. 1994b. "Environmental Regulation and the Private-Property Line." *Governing* 7, no. 8 (June): 82.

———. 1997. "The Price of Portability." *Governing* 11, no. 12 (December). Lexis-Nexis.

Ashford, Nicholas A., C. William Ryan, and Charles C. Caldart. 1983. "A Hard Look at Federal Regulation of Formaldehyde: A Departure from Reasoned Decisionmaking." *Harvard Environmental Law Review* 7: 297–370.

Bartsch, Charles, and Elizabeth Collaton. 1997. *Brownfields: Cleaning and Reusing Contaminated Properties*. Westport, CT: Praeger.

Belsky, Martin H. 1984. "Environmental Policy Law in the 1980's: Shifting Back the Burden of Proof." *Ecology Law Quarterly* 12, no. 1: 1–88.

Berke, Richard L. 1993. "Clinton Supports Two Major Steps for Environment." *New York Times* (April 22).

Blodgett, Jon E. 1997. *Environmental Protection: How Much It Costs and Who Pays*. Washington, DC: Congressional Research Service.

Bosso, Christopher J. 1987. *Pesticides & Politics: The Life Cycle of a Public Issue*. Pittsburgh: University of Pittsburgh Press.

———. 1994. "After the Movement: Environmental Activism in the 1990s." In *Environmental Policy in the 1990s*, ed. Norman J. Vig and Michael E. Kraft. 2d ed. Washington, DC: CQ Press, pp. 31–50.

———. 2000. "Environmental Groups and the New Political Landscape." In *Environmental Policy*, ed. Norman J. Vig and Michael E. Kraft. 4th ed. Washington, DC: CQ Press, pp. 55–76.

Brown, Lester R., and Alan Durning, eds. 1989. *State of the World 1989*. Washington, DC: Worldwatch Institute.

Browne, Malcolm W. 1989. "In Protecting the Atmosphere, Choices Are Costly and Complex." *New York Times* (March 7).

Bruni, Frank. 2000. "Bush Plans to Ease Rules for Use of Polluted Land." *New York Times* (April 4).

Bryner, Gary C. 1993. *Blue Skies, Green Politics: The Clean Air Act of 1990*. Washington, DC: CQ Press.

Burnett, H. Sterling. 1999. "The Collapsing Scientific Cornerstone of Global Warming Theory." Issue Brief #299. Dallas: National Center for Policy Analysis.

Bullard, Robert D., ed. 1994. *Unequal Protection: Environmental Justice & Communities of Color*. San Francisco: Sierra Club Books.

Burtraw, Dallas. 2000. "Innovation Under the Tradable Sulfur Dioxide Emissions Permits Program in the U.S. Electricity Sector." Washington, DC: Resources for the Future.

Carson, Nancy, and Don Munton. 2000. "Flaws in the Conventional Wisdom on Acid Deposition." *Environment* 42, no. 2 (March) 33–35.

Carson, Rachel. 1962. *Silent Spring*. Boston: Houghton Mifflin.

Caulfield, Henry P. 1989. "The Conservation and Environmental Movements: An Historical Analysis." In *Environmental Politics and Policy: Theories and Evidence*, ed. James P. Lester. Durham, NC: Duke University Press, pp. 13–56.

Clinton, Bill, and Al Gore. 1995. "Reinventing Environmental Regulation." ww.npr.gov/library/rsreport/251a.html#overview. March 16, 1995.

Cohen, Richard E. 1992. *Washington at Work: Back Rooms and Clean Air*. New York: Macmillan.

Commoner, Barry. 1971. *The Closing Circle: Nature, Man and Technology*. New York: Knopf.

Conservation Foundation. 1987. *State of the Environment: A View Toward the Nineties*. Washington, DC: Conservation Foundation.

Cushman, John H., Jr. 1994a. "E.P.A. Critics Get Boost in Congress." *New York Times* (February 7).

―――. 1994b. "Few Environmental Laws Emerge from 103d Congress." *New York Times* (October 3).

―――. 1994c. "Congress Forgoes Its Bid to Speed Cleanup of Dumps." *New York Times* (October 6).

―――. 1995. "Backed by Business, Republicans Take Steps to Overhaul Environmental Regulations." *New York Times* (February 10).

Davies, J. Clarence, Sam Gusman, and Frances Irwin. 1979. *Determining Unreasonable Risk Under the Toxic Substances Control Act*. Washington, DC: Conservation Foundation.

Davis, Charles E. 1993. *The Politics of Hazardous Waste*. Englewood Cliffs, NJ: Prentice Hall.

Davis, Charles E., and James P. Lester. 1989. "Federalism and Environmental Policy." In *Environmental Policy and Politics: Theories and Evidence*, ed. James P. Lester. Durham, NC: Duke University Press, pp. 57–84.

Davis, Charles E., and David J. Webber. 1995. "Approaches to Regulating Environmental Protection." *Public Policy Analysis and Management* (1990 Research Annual), ed. Stuart S. Nagel. Greenwich, CT: JAI Press, pp. 243–269.

Department of Energy. 1987. *Energy Security: A Report to the President of the United States*. Washington, DC: Department of Energy.

Doniger, David D. 1988. "Politics of the Ozone Layer." *Issues in Science and Technology* 4, no. 2 (Spring): 86–92.

Downey, Kristen. 1992. "This Land Is Your Land? Maybe." *Washington Post National Weekly Edition* 9 (February 24–March 1): 32–33.

Dunlap, Riley E. 1989. "Public Opinion and Environmental Policy." In *Environmental Politics and Policy: Theories and Evidence*, eds. James P. Lester. Durham, NC: Duke University Press, pp. 87–134.

―――. 1992. "Trends in Public Opinion Toward Environmental Issues: 1965–1990." In *American Environmentalism: The U.S. Environmental Movement, 1970–1990*, ed. Riley E. Dunlap and Angela G. Mertig. Philadelphia: Taylor and Francis, pp. 89–116.

Dunlap, Riley E., and Angela G. Mertig, eds. 1992. *American Environmentalism: The U.S. Environmental Movement, 1970–1990*. Philadelphia: Taylor and Francis.

Easterbrook, Gregg. 1995. *A Moment on the Earth: The Coming Age of Environmental Optimism*. New York: Viking Press.

―――. 1999. "America the O.K." *New Republic* 4381–4382 (January 4 and 11): 19–25.

Eckersley, Robyn. 1992. *Environmentalism and Political Theory: Toward an Ecocentric Approach*. Albany: State University of New York Press.

Efron, Edith. 1984. *The Apocalyptics: Cancer and the Big Lie*. New York: Simon & Schuster.

Energy Information Administration. 1999. "Russian Environmental Issues." Washington, DC: Department of Energy. www.eia.doe.gov/cabs/russenv.html.

Environmental Protection Agency. 1987. *Unfinished Business: A Comparative Assessment of Environmental Problems*. Washington, DC: Environmental Protection Agency.

―――. 1999a. *Progress Report on the EPA Acid Rain Program*. Washington, DC: Environmental Protection Agency.

―――. 1999b. *U.S. Emissions Inventory—1999*. Washington, DC: Environmental Protection Agency. www.epa.gov/globalwarming/publications/emissions/us1999/index.html.

Epstein, Samuel S. 1978. *The Politics of Cancer*. San Francisco: Sierra Club Books.

Field, Barry C. 1994. *Environmental Economics: An Introduction*. New York: McGraw-HIL

Fischhoff, Baruch, Sarah Lichenstein, Paul Slovic, Stephen L. Derby, and Ralph L. Keeney. 1981. *Acceptable Risk*. Cambridge, England: Cambridge University Press.

Framework Convention on Climate Change. 1998. *Summary Compilation of Annual Greenhouse Gas Emissions from Annex I Parties*. Buenos Aires, Argentina: Convention of the Parties.

Funke, Odelia. 1994. "National Security and the Environment." In *Environmental Policy in the 1990s*, ed. Norman J. Vig and Michael E. Kraft. 2d ed. Washington, DC: CQ Press, pp. 323–345.

Gelbspan, Ross. 2000. "Taking Charge: Time to Act on Climate Change." www.tompaine.com (October 12).

General Accounting Office. 1980. *Environmental Protection: Agenda for the 1980s.* Washington, DC: GAO.

———. 1987. *Air Pollution: States Assigned a Major Role in EPA's Air Toxics Strategy.* Washington, DC: GAO.

———. 1993. *Air Pollution: Impact of White House Entities on Two Clean Air Rules.* Washington, DC: GAO.

———. 1999. *Environmental Protection Agencies Have Made Progress in Implementing the Federal Brownfield Partnership Initiative.* Washington, DC: GAO.

Gillespie, Ed, and Bob Schellhas, eds. 1994. *The Contract with America: The Bold Plan by Rep. Newt Gingrich, Rep. Dick Armey and the House Republicans to Change the Nation.* New York: Times Books.

Gist, Ginger L. 1998. "National Environmental Health Association Position on Endocrine Disrupters." *Journal of Environmental Health* 60, no. 6 (January–February): 1–5.

Glick, Daniel. 1993. "Barbarians Inside the Gate." *Newsweek* 122, no. 18 (November 1): 32.

Goldstein, Amy, and Eric Pianin. 2001. "Hill Pressure Fueled Bush's Emissions Shift." *Washington Post* (March 15).

Graham, Frank, Jr. 1970. *Since Silent Spring.* Boston: Houghton Mifflin.

Greenhouse, Linda. 1994. "High Court Limits the Public Power on Private Land." *New York Times* (June 25).

Hamilton, James T., and W. Kip Viscusi. 1999. *Calculating Risks? The Spatial and Political Dimensions of Hazardous Waste Policy.* Cambridge: MIT Press.

Hardin, Garrett. 1968. "The Tragedy of the Commons." *Science* 162, no. 3859 (December 13): 1243–1248.

Hempel, Lamont C. 2000. "Climate Policy on the Installment Plan." In *Environmental Policy*, ed. Norman J. Vig and Michael E. Kraft. 4th ed. Washington, DC: CQ Press, pp. 281–302.

Ingram, Helen M., and Dean E. Mann. 1989. "Interest Groups and Environmental Policy." In *Environmental Politics and Policy: Theories and Evidence*, ed. James P. Lester. Durham, NC: Duke University Press, pp. 135–157.

Jehl, Douglas. 2000. "Clinton Approves Rules to Curb Emissions of Big Rigs and Buses." *New York Times* (December 21).

———. 2001. "U.S. Offers Further Delay to Forest Rules." *New York Times* (March 16).

John, DeWitt. 1994. *Civic Environmentalism: Alternatives to Regulation in States and Communities.* Washington, DC: CQ Press.

Kennedy, Robert F., Jr., and Dennis Rivera. 1992. "Pollution's Chief Victims: The Poor." *New York Times* (August 15).

Kerr, Richard A. 1998. "Acid Rain Control: Success on the Cheap." *Science* 282, no. 5391 (November 6): 1024–1027.

Kingdon, John W. 1984. *Agendas, Alternatives, and Public Policy.* Boston: Little, Brown.

Kolata, Gina. 1999. "Study Inconclusive on Chemicals' Effects." *New York Times* (August 4).

Konisky, David M. 1999. *Comparative Risk Projects: A Methodology for Cross-Project Analysis of Human Health Risk Rankings.* Washington, DC: Resources for the Future.

Kraft, Michael E. 1988. "Analyzing Technology Risks in the Federal Regulatory Agencies." In *Technology and Politics*, ed. Michael E. Kraft and Norman J. Vig. Durham, NC: Duke University Press, pp. 189–207.

———. 2000. "Environmental Policy in Congress: From Consensus to Gridlock." In *Environmental Policy*, ed. Norman J. Vig and Michael E. Kraft. 4th ed. Washington, DC: CQ Press, pp. 121–144.

Kraft, Michael E., and Norman J. Vig. 2000. "Environmental Policy from the 1970s to 2000: An Overview." In *Environmental Policy*, ed. Norman J. Vig and Michael E. Kraft. 4th ed. Washington, DC: CQ Press, pp. 1–31.

Kraft, Michael E., and Norman J. Vig, eds. 1988. *Technology and Politics.* Durham, NC: Duke University Press.

Kriz, Margaret. 1993a. "Their Turn." *National Journal* 25, no. 7 (February 13): 388–391.

———. 1993b. "Lukewarm." *National Journal* 25, no. 33 (August 14): 2038–2031.

————. 1994a. "What's the Point of Finger-Pointing?" *National Journal* 26, no. 19 (May 7): 1097.

————. 1994b. "A Scheme for Cutting Through the Blather." *National Journal* 26, no. 27 (July 2): 1578–1579.

————. 1994c. "The Conquered Coalition." *National Journal* 26 (December 23): 2824–2829.

Lemons, John, ed. 1996. *Scientific Uncertainty and Environmental Problem Solving.* Cambridge, MA: Blackwell Science.

Lester, James P. 1986. "New Federalism and Environmental Policy." *Publius* 16, no. 4 (Winter): 149–165.

————. 1994. "A New Federalism? Environmental Policy in the States." In *Environmental Policy in the 1990s*, ed. Norman J. Vig and Michael E. Kraft. 2d ed. Washington, DC: CQ Press, pp. 51–68.

————. ed. 1989. *Environmental Politics and Policy: Theories and Evidence.* Durham, NC: Duke University Press.

Lewis, Anthony. 1995. "Is Reality Dawning." *New York Times* (July 31).

Lieberman, Ben. 1994. *The High Cost of Cool: The Economic Impact of the CFC Phaseout in the United States.* Washington, DC: Competitive Enterprise Institute.

Lotspeich, Richard. 1998. "Comparative Environmental Policy: Market-Type Instruments in Industrialized Capitalist Nations." *Policy Studies Journal* 26, no. 1 (Spring): 85–104.

Marquis, Christopher. 2001. "Whitman Backs Clinton Rules Designed to Cut Diesel Pollution." *New York Times* (March 1).

Marzulla, Nancie G. 1995. "The Magic of Property Rights." Washington, DC: National Wilderness Institute. www.nwi.org/ResourceArticles/MagicProperty.html.

Mazmanian, Daniel, and David Morell. 1992. *Beyond Superfailure: America's Toxic Policy for the 1990s.* Boulder: Westview Press.

McCloskey, Michael. 1992. "Twenty Years of Change in the Environmental Movement: An Insider's View." In *American Environmentalism: The U.S. Environmental Movement, 1970–1990*, ed. Riley E. Dunlap and Angela G. Mertig. Philadelphia: Taylor and Francis, pp. 51–62.

McKibben, Bill. 1995. "Not So Fast." *New York Times Magazine* (July 23): 23–24.

McNeil, Mary. 1981. *Environment and Health.* Washington, DC: CQ Press.

McSpadden, Lettie. 2000. "Environmental Policy in the Courts." In *Environmental Policy*, ed. Norman J. Vig and Michael E. Kraft. 4th ed. Washington, DC: CQ Press, pp. 145–164.

Michaels, Patrick J. 1998a. "Long Hot Year: Latest Science Debunks Global Warming Hysteria." Washington, DC: Cato Institute.

————. 1998b. "The Consequences of Kyoto." Washington, DC: Cato Institute.

Miller, G. Tyler, Jr. 1985. *Living in the Environment.* 4th ed. Belmont, CA: Wadsworth.

————. 1994. *Living in the Environment.* 8th ed. Belmont, CA: Wadsworth.

Mitchell, Robert Cameron. 1984. "Public Opinion and Environmental Politics in the 1970s and 1980s." *Environmental Policy in the 1980s: Reagan's New Agenda*, ed. Norman Vig and Michael Kraft. Washington, DC: CQ Press, pp. 51–74.

Mitchell, Robert Cameron, Angela G. Mertig, and Riley E. Dunlap. 1992. "Twenty Years of Environmental Mobilization: Trends Among National Environmental Organizations." In *American Environmentalism: The U.S. Environmental Movement, 1970–1990*, ed. Riley E. Dunlap and Angela G. Mertig. Philadelphia: Taylor and Francis, pp. 11–26.

Monastersky, R. 1999. "A Sign of Healing Appears in Stratosphere." *Science News* 156, nos. 25 and 26 (December 18): 391.

Montague, Peter. 2000. "The Precautionary Principle." tompaine.com (April 25).

Munton, Don. 1998. "Dispelling the Myths of the Acid Rain Story." *Environment* 46, no. 6 (July/August): 1–12.

Nagel, Stuart S., ed. 1995. *Public Policy Analysis and Management* (1995 Research Annual). Greenwich, CT: JAI Press.

Nathan, Richard P. 1983. *The Administrative Presidency.* New York: Wiley.

Office of Air Quality Planning and Standards. 1997. *National Air Quality and Emissions Trends Report 1997.* Washington, DC: Environmental Protection Agency. www.epa.gov/airprogm/oar/aqtrnd97/toc.html.

Office of Solid Waste. n.d. "Treat, Store and Dispose of Waste." Washington, DC: Environmental Protection Agency. www.epa.gov/epaoswer/osw/tsd.htm.

Office of Wastewater Management. 1998. *Water Pollution Control: 25 Years of Progress and Challenges for the New Millennium*. Washington, DC: Environmental Protection Agency. www.epa.gov/owm/25prog.pdf.

Olson, Erik D. 1984. "The Quiet Shift of Power: Office of Management & Budget Supervision of Environmental Protection Agency Rulemaking Under Executive Order 12,291." *Virginia Journal of Natural Resources Law* 4 (Fall): 1–80a.

Ophuls, William. 1977. *Ecology and the Politics of Scarcity*. San Francisco: Freeman.

Ophuls, William, and A. Stephen Boyan, Jr. 1992. *Ecology and the Politics of Scarcity Revisited: The Unraveling of the American Dream*. New York: Freeman.

Paehlke, Robert C. 2000. "Environmental Values and Public Policy." In *Environmental Policy*, ed. Norman J. Vig and Michael E. Kraft. 4th ed. Washington, DC: CQ Press, pp. 77–97.

Peirce, Neal R. 1994. "The Dawn of 'Civic Environmentalism.'" *National Journal* 26, no. 2 (January 15): 136.

Portney, Paul R. 1988. "Reforming Environmental Regulation: Three Modest Proposals." *Issues in Science and Technology* 4, no. 4 (Winter): 74–81.

———. 1990. *Public Policies for Environmental Protection*. Washington, DC: Resources for the Future.

———. 1995. "Chain-Saw Surgery: Beware of the Killer Clauses Inside the GOP's 'Contract.'" *Washington Post* (January 15).

President's Council on Sustainable Development. 1999. *Towards a Sustainable America: Advancing Prosperity, Opportunity, and a Healthy Environment for the 21st Century*. Washington, DC: President's Council on Sustainable Development.

Probst, Katherine N. 1995. "The Strengths and Weaknesses of the Current Superfund Law." Testimony before the U.S. Senate Subcommittee on Superfund, Waste Control and Risk Assessment, Committee on Environment and Public Works (March 10). www.rff.org/testimony/remarks/superfund.htm.

Rabe, Barry G. 2000. "Power to the States: The Promise and Pitfalls." In *Environmental Policy*, ed. Norman J. Vig and Michael E. Kraft. Washington, DC: CQ Press, pp. 32–54.

Raven, Peter H. 1995. "Book Review: *A Moment on the Earth: The Coming Age of Environmental Optimism*." *Amicus Journal* 17, no. 1 (Spring): 42–45.

Relative Risk Reduction Strategies Committee. 1990. *Reducing Risk: Setting Priorities and Strategies for Environmental Protection*. Washington, DC: Environmental Protection Agency.

Revkin, Andrew C. 2000a. "Record Ozone Hole Refuels Debate on Climate." *New York Times* (October 10).

———. 2000b. "A Shift in Stance on Global Warming Theory." *New York Times* (October 26).

———. 2000c. "Talks Go Down to the Wire on a Global Warming Pact." *New York Times* (November 25).

———. 2000d. "U.S. Move Improves Chance for Global Warming Treaty." *New York Times* (November 20).

———. 2000e. "7 Companies Agree to Cut Gas Emissions." *New York Times* (October 18).

———. 2001. "178 Nations Reach a Climate Accord." *New York Times* (July 23).

Ringquist, Evan J. 1993. *Environmental Protection at the State Level: Policies and Progress in Controlling Pollution*. Armonk, NY: M.E. Sharpe.

Roan, Sharon L. 1989. *Ozone Crisis: The 15 Year Evolution of a Sudden Global Emergency*. New York: Wiley.

Roberts, Leslie. 1999. "Acid Rain: Forgotten, Not Gone." *U.S. News & World Report* 127, no. 17 (November 1): 70.

Rosenbaum, Walter A. 1977. *The Politics of Environmental Concern*. 2d ed. New York: Praeger.

———. 1985. *Environmental Politics and Policy*. Washington, DC: CQ Press.

———. 1994. "The Clenched Fist and the Open Hand: Into the 1990s at EPA." In *Environmental Policy in the 1990s*, ed. Norman J. Vig and Michael E. Kraft. Washington, DC: CQ Press, pp. 121–143.

———. 1998. *Environmental Politics and Policy*. 4th ed. Washington, DC: CQ Press.

————. 2000. "Escaping the 'Battered Agency Syndrome': EPA's Gamble with Regulatory Reinvention." In *Environmental Policy*, ed. Norman J. Vig and Michael E. Kraft. 4th ed. Washington, DC: CQ Press, pp. 165–189.

Rushefsky, Mark E. 1986. *Making Cancer Policy*. Albany, NY: State University Press of New York.

Samuelson, Paul A. 1964. *Economics: An Introductory Analysis*. 6th ed. New York: McGraw-Hill.

Schneider, Keith. 1992a. "Campaign Concerns Prompt White House to Drop Waste Plan." *New York Times* (September 30).

————. 1992b. "When the Bad Guy Is Seen as the One in the Green Hat." *New York Times* (February 16).

————. 1993. "Unbending Regulations Incite Move to Alter Pollution Laws." *New York Times* (November 29).

Shabecoff, Philip. 1988. "Most Authoritative Study Yet Shows Declining Ozone Layer." *New York Times* (March 16).

Shanahan, John. 1992. "A Guide to Global Warming Theory." Backgrounder #896. Washington, DC: American Enterprise Institute.

Shea, Cynthia Pollock. 1989. "Protecting the Ozone Layer." In *State of the World 1989*, ed. Lester R. Brown and Alan Durning. Washington, DC: Worldwatch Institute, pp. 77–96.

Siebert, Horst. 1981. *Economics of the Environment*. Lexington, MA: D.C. Heath.

Singer, S. Fred. 1996. "My Adventures in the Ozone Layer." www.heartland.org/earthday96/ozone.htm.

Smeloff, Ed, and Fred Branfman. 1998. "Kyoto, Global Warming and the 21st Century: 'Global Warming Center' Perspective." Pace University School of Law. www.law.pace.edu/env/energy/perspective1.html.

Smith, Zachary A. 2000. *The Environmental Policy Paradox*. 3d ed. Upper Saddle River, NJ: Prentice Hall.

Soroos, Marvin. 1994. "From Stockholm to Rio: The Evolution of Global Environmental Governance." In *Environmental Policy in the 1990s*, ed. Norman J. Vig and Michael E. Kraft. 2d ed. Washington, DC: CQ Press, pp. 299–321.

Stavins, Robert N. 1989. "Harnessing Market Forces to Protect the Environment." *Environment* 31, no. 1 (January–February): 4–7, 28–35.

Stockman, David. 1980. "The Stockman Manifesto." *Washington Post* (December 14).

Stone, Deborah A. 1997. *Policy Paradox*. New York: Norton.

Tiefer, Charles. 1994. *The Semi-Sovereign Presidency: The Bush Administration's Strategy for Governing Without Congress*. Boulder: Westview Press.

Ungar, Sheldon. 1998. "Bringing the Issue Back In: Comparing the Marketability of the Ozone Hole and Global Warming." *Social Problems* 45, no. 4 (November): 510–523.

U.S. Census Bureau. 1994. *Statistical Abstract of the United States 1994*. Washington, DC: Government Printing Office.

————. 1999. *Statistical Abstract of the United States 1999*. www.census.gov/prod/99pubs/99statab/sec09.pdf.

Verjheid, Martine. 2000. "Health Effects of Residence Near Hazardous Waste Landfill Sites: A Review of Epidemiological Literature." *Environmental Health Perspectives* 108, Supplement 1 (March): 101–112.

Victor, David. 2000. "Kyoto Is Dead: An Upbeat Requiem." *Grist*, www.gristmagazine.com (January 17).

Vig, Norman J. 2000. "Presidential Leadership and the Environment: From Reagan to Clinton." In *Environmental Policy*, ed. Norman J. Vig and Michael E. Kraft. Washington, DC: CQ Press, pp. 98–120.

Vig, Norman J., and Michael E. Kraft, eds. 1984. *Environmental Policy in the 1980s: Reagan's New Agenda*. Washington, DC: CQ Press.

————. 1994. *Environmental Policy in the 1990s*. 2d ed. Washington, DC: CQ Press.

————. 2000. *Environmental Policy*. 4th ed. Washington, DC: CQ Press.

Wald, Matthew L. 2000. "Clinton Seeks to Regulate Common Gas to Clean Air." *New York Times* (November 12).

Whelan, Elizabeth. 1985. *Toxic Terror: The Truth About the Cancer Scare*. Ottawa, IL: Jameson Books.

Whitaker, John C. 1976. *Striking a Balance: Environment and Natural Resources Policy in the Nixon-Ford Years*. Washington, DC: American Enterprise Institute.

Whitman, David. 1998. *The Optimism Gap: The I'm OK—They're Not Syndrome and the Myth of American Decline*. New York: Walker Press.

Whittington, Dale, and W. Norton Grubb. 1984. "Economic Analysis in Regulatory Decisions: The Implications of Executive Order 12291." *Science, Technology & Human Values* 9, no. 4 (Winter): 63–71.

Wilson, James, and J.W. Anderson. 1997. "What the Science Says: How We Use It and Abuse It to Make Health and Environmental Policy." Washington, DC: Resources for the Future. www.rff.org/resources_articles/files/science.htm.

Wolf, Charles, Jr. 1979. "A Theory of Non-Market Failures." *Public Interest* 55: 114–123.

World Meteorological Association. 1998. *Scientific Assessment of Ozone Depletion: 1998. An Executive Summary*. Washington, DC: National Oceanographic and Atmospheric Administration.

# Chapter 7

"Abortion Has Cut Crime, Controversial Study Suggests." 1999. *Atlanta Journal and Constitution* (August 9).

Baker, Russ. 1999. "George Soros' Long Strange Trip." *Nation* (September 20). www.past.thenation.com/cgi-bin/framizer.cgi?url'past.thenation.com/issue/990920/0920baker.shtml.

Beck, Allen J. 2000. "Prisoners in 1999." Washington, DC: Bureau of Justice Statistics.

Bennett, William J., John J. DiIulio, Jr., and John P. Walters. 1996. *Body Count: Moral Poverty . . . and How to Win America's War Against Crime and Drugs*. New York: Simon & Schuster.

Berns, Walter, and Joseph Bessette. 1998. "Why the Death Penalty Is Fair." *Wall Street Journal* (January 9).

Berrien, Jennifer, and Christopher Winship. 1999. "Lessons Learned from Boston's Police-Community Collaboration." *Federal Probation* 58, no. 2 (December): 25–32.

Bertram, Eva, Morris Blachman, Kenneth Sharpe, and Peter Andreas. 1996. *Drug War Politics: The Price of Denial*. Berkeley: University of California Press.

Blumstein, Alfred. 2000. "Disaggregating the Violence Trends." In *The Crime Drop in America*, ed. Alfred Blumstein and Joel Wallman. New York: Cambridge University Press, pp. 13–44.

Blumstein, Alfred, and Joel Wallman, eds. 2000. *The Crime Drop in America*. New York: Cambridge University Press.

Boner, Raymond, and Marc Lacey. 2000a. "Clinton Again Delays Execution of a Murderer." *New York Times* (December 7).

———. 2000b. "Pervasive Disparities Found in the Federal Death Penalty." *New York Times* (September 12).

Boyd, Graham, and Jack Hitt. 1999. "This Is Your Bill of Rights, on Drugs." *Harper's* 299, no. 1795 (December): 57–62.

Brant, Martha. 1999. "Last Chance Class." *Newsweek* 133, no. 22 (May 31): 32–35.

Broder, David S. 2000. "When the Sentence Is Death." *Washington Post* (May 14).

Bureau of Justice Statistics. 1983. *Report to the Nation on Crime and Justice: The Data*. Washington, DC: Department of Justice.

———. 2000. "Homicide Trends in the United States." www.ojp.usdoj.gov/bjs/.

Butterfield, Fox. 1999. "Gun Flow to Criminals Laid to Tiny Fraction of Dealers." *New York Times* (July 1).

———. 2000a. "Death Sentences Being Overturned in 2 of 3 Appeals." *New York Times* (June 12).

———. 2000b. "Often, Parole Is One Stop on the Way Back to Prison." *New York Times* (November 29).

———. 2000c. "Data Hint Crime Plunge May Be Leveling Off." *New York Times* (December 20).

Cannon, Carl M. 2000. "The Problem with the Chair: A Conservative Case Against Capital Punishment." *National Review* (June 19). www.nationalreview.com/19jun00/cannon061900.html.

Celis, William, III. 1994. "Schools Getting Tough on Guns in the Classroom." *New York Times* (August 31).

Centers for Disease Control and Prevention. 1997. "Rates of Homicide, Suicide, and Firearm-Related Deaths Among Children—26 Industrialized Countries." *Journal of the American Medical Association (JAMA)* 277, no. 9 (March 5): 704–705.

Chivers, C.J. 2001a. "Alienation Is a Partner for Black Officers." *New York Times* (April 3).
———. 2001b. "From Court Order to Reality: A Diverse Boston Police Force." *New York Times* (April 4).

Cohen, Richard. 1993. "Common Ground on Crime." *Washington Post* (December 21).

Cole, David. 1999. *No Equal Justice: Race and Class in the American Criminal Justice System.* New York: New Press.

"Cops Terrify President's Top Black Aides." 2000. *Jet* 98, no. 19 (October 16): 4–7.

Cose, Ellis. 1994. "Breaking the 'Code of Silence.'" *Newsweek* 123, no. 2 (January 10): 22–23.
———. 2000. "The Prison Paradox." *Newsweek* 136, no. 20 (November 13): 40–49.

"Crime Drop Linked to More Police." 1998. National Center for Policy Analysis. www.ncpa.org.

Currie, Elliott. 1986. *Confronting Crime: An American Challenge.* New York: Pantheon.
———. 1998. *Crime and Punishment in America: Why the Solutions to America's Most Stubborn Social Crisis Have Not Worked—and What Will.* New York: Metropolitan Books.

Death Penalty Information Center. www.deathpenaltyinfo.org.

Department of Justice. 1997. *The CIA-Contra-Crack Cocaine Controversy: A Review of the Justice Department's Investigations and Prosecutions.* Washington, DC: Department of Justice/Office of Inspector General.

DiIulio, John J., Jr. 1994a. "The Black Crime Gap." *Wall Street Journal* (July 11).
———. 1994b. "The Question of Black Crime." *Public Interest,* no. 117 (Fall): 3–32.

Donziger, Stephen R., ed. 1996. *The Real War on Crime: The Report of the National Criminal Justice Commission.* New York: HarperPerennial.

Drug Court Standards Committee. 1997. *Defining Drug Courts: The Key Components.* Alexandria, VA: National Association of Drug Court Professionals. www.ojp.usdoj.gov/dcpo/Define/dfdpdf.pdf.

Drug Watch International. n.d. "The Success of Tough Drug Enforcement." www.drugwatch.org/Documents?BP1.html.

Dudley, Steven. 2000. "The Columbia Quagmire." *American Prospect* 11, no. 7 (July 31). www.prospect.org/archives/V11–17/dudley-s.html.

Duggan, Paul. 1999. "To Kill or Not to Kill." *Washington Post National Weekly Edition* 17, nos. 18–19 (December 20–27): 31–33.
———. 2000. "George W. Bush: The Record in Texas; Attorneys' Ineptitude Doesn't Halt Executions." *Washington Post* (May 12).

Easterbrook, Greg. 1999. "America the O.K." *New Republic,* nos. 4381–4382 (January 4 & 11): 19–25.

Ebinger, Nick. 2000. "*IC* Insider: Of Abortion and Crime." www.intellectualcapital.com/issues/issues366/item9116.asp. (April 20).

Eck, John E., and Edward R. Maguire. 2000. "Have Changes in Policing Reduced Violent Crime?" In *The Crime Drop in America,* ed. Alfred Blumstein and Joel Wallman. New York: Cambridge University Press, pp. 205–265.

Eckholm, Erik. 1995. "Studies Find Death Penalty Often Tied to Victim's Race." *New York Times* (February 24).

Egan, Timothy. 1999. "In States' Anti-Drug Fight, A Renewal for Treatment." *New York Times* (June 10).

Farrell, John Aloysius. 2000. "Majority for Death Penalty Slips in Poll." *Boston Globe* (September 15).

Federal Bureau of Investigation. 2000. *Uniform Crime Reports, January–June 2000.* Washington, DC: FBI, U.S. Department of Investigation.

"The Federal Role in Crime Control." 1994. *Congressional Digest* 73 (June–July): 161–192.

Flynn, Kevin. 1999. "State Cites Racial Inequality in New York Police Searches." *New York Times* (December 1).

Fox, James Alan. 2000. "Demographics and U.S. Homicide." In *The Crime Drop in America*, ed. Alfred Blumstein and Joel Wallman. New York: Cambridge University Press, pp. 288–317.

Gainsborough, Jenni, and Marc Mauer. 2000. "Diminishing Returns: Crime and Incarceration in the 1990s." Washington, DC: Sentencing Project.

Gallup Poll. 1999. "Racial Profiling Is Seen as Widespread, Particularly Among Young Black Men." (December 9). www.gallup.com//poll/releases/pr991209.asp.

General Accounting Office. 1990. *Death Penalty Sentencing: Research Indicates Pattern of Racial Disparities*. Washington, DC: GAO.

———. 1997. *Drug Courts: Overview of Growth, Characteristics, and Results*. Washington, DC: GAO.

———. 2000. "Methadone Maintenance—Some Treatment Programs Are Not Effective; Greater Federal Oversight Needed." Washington, DC: GAO.

Gifford, Lea, Devon B. Adams, and Gene Lauver. 2000. "Background Checks for Firearm Transfers, 1999." Washington, DC: Bureau of Justice Statistics.

Gilder, George. 1986. *Men and Marriage*. Gretna, LA: Pelican Publishers.

Gladstone, Brooke. 1999. "Practice of Racial Profiling as It Relates to Law Enforcement Situations as Well as Everyday Incidents." *Talk of the Nation*, National Public Radio (November 30). Transcript from Lexis/Nexis.

Gladwell, Malcolm. 1994. "Baby Boom's Urban Cradle Braces for Future Rocked by Crime." *Washington Post* (May 26).

Glasser, Ira. 1999. Testimony before the Criminal Justice Drug Policy and Human Resources Subcommittee of the House Government Reform Committee, June 16th. 106th Congress, 1st session. www.aclu.org/congress/1061699a.html.

Greenhouse, Linda. 2001. "Supreme Court Hears U.S. Argue Against Marijuana as a Medical Necessity." *New York Times* (March 29).

Grogger, Jeff. 2000. "An Economic Model of Recent Trends in Violence." In *The Crime Drop in America*, ed. Alfred Blumstein and Joel Wallman. New York: Cambridge University Press, pp. 266–287.

Gurr, Ted Robert. 1989. "Drowning in a Crime Wave." *New York Times* (April 13).

Harries, Keith. 1999. *Mapping Crime: Principle and Practice*. Washington, DC: National Institute of Justice.

Harris, David A. 1999. "Driving While Black: Racial Profiling on our Nation's Highways." Washington, DC: American Civil Liberties Union. www.aclu.org/profiling/report/index.html.

Henig, Jeffrey R. 1985. *Public Policy & Federalism: Issues in State & Local Politics*. New York: St. Martin's Press.

Herbert, Bob. 1993. "Blacks Killing Blacks." *New York Times* (October 20).

———. 1999a. "Hounding the Innocent." *New York Times* (June 13).

———. 1999b. "Attention Must Be Paid." *New York Times* (September 30).

———. 1999c. "Breathing While Black." *New York Times* (November 4).

Herrnstein, Richard J., and Charles Murray. 1994. *The Bell Curve: Intelligence and Class Structure in American Life*. New York: Free Press.

Holmes, Steven A. 1999a. "Black and Middle Class." *New York Times* (April 25).

———. 1999b. "Clinton Orders Investigation on Possible Racial Profiling." *New York Times* (June 10).

———. 2000. "Race Analysis Cites Disparity in Sentencing for Narcotics." *New York Times* (June 8).

"In the Line of Fire." 1999. *Newsweek* (August 23), pp. 20–25.

Institute for Legislative Action. 1999. "Fact Sheet: The 'Brady Handgun Violence Prevention Act' Does Not Live Up to its Name." Washington, DC: National Rifle Association (July 28).

———. 2000a. "Fact Sheet: Licensing and Registration." Washington, DC: National Rifle Association (April 9).

———. 2000b. "Fact Sheet: The Second Amendment & the United States Supreme Court."

Washington, DC: National Rifle Association (May 4).

Jacob, Herbert. 1984. *The Frustration of Policy: Responses to Crime by American Cities*. Boston: Little, Brown.

Jacoby, Jeff. 2000. "Death Penalty Is Necessary." *Boston Globe* (June 8).

Johnson, Bruce D., Andrew Golub, and Eloise Dunlap. 2000. "Drugs and Violence in Inner-City New York." In *The Crime Drop in America*, ed. Alfred Blumstein and Joel Wallman. New York: Cambridge University Press, pp. 164–206.

Joy, Janet E., Stanley J. Watson, Jr., and John A. Benson, Jr., eds. 1999. *Marijuana and Medicine: Assessing the Science Base*. Washington, DC: Institute of Medicine.

Justice Research and Statistics Association. 2000. *Crime and Justice Atlas*. Washington, DC, Justice Research and Statistics Association. www.jrsainfo.org/programs/crimeatlas.html.

Kennedy, Randall. 1997. *Race, Crime, and the Law*. New York: Pantheon Books.

Kocieniewski, David. 2000. "U.S. Wrote Outline for Race Profiling, New Jersey Argues." *New York Times* (November 29).

Lambert, Tim. 2000. "Do More Guns Cause Less Crime?" Unpublished paper available at www.cse.unsw.edu.au/~Lambert?guns/Lott.

Lederer, Katherine. 1986. *Many Thousands Gone: Springfield's Lost Black History*.

Lewis, John. 1995. "Crimes as a Cause of Poverty." *Atlantic Monthly* 276, no. 1 (July): 49.

Liebman, James S., Jeffrey Fagan, and Valerie West. 2000. "A Broken System: Error Rates in Capital Cases, 1973–1995." www.justice.policy.net/jpreport.

Lott, John R., Jr. 2000. *More Guns, Less Crime: Understanding Crime and Gun Control Laws*. 2d ed. Chicago: University of Chicago Press.

Maginnis, Robert L. 1996. "Legalization of Drugs: The Myths and the Facts." Washington, DC: Family Research Council.

Maguire, Kathleen, Ann L. Pastore, and Timothy J. Flanagan, eds. 1993. *Sourcebook of Criminal Justice Statistics—1992*. U.S. Department of Justice, Bureau of Justice Statistics. Washington, DC: Government Printing Office.

Maier, Mark H. 1991. *The Data Game: Controversies in Social Science and Statistics*. Armonk, NY: M.E. Sharpe.

Massing, Michael. 1998. *The Fix*. Berkeley: University of California Press.

Mauer, Marc, and Tracy Huling, 1995. "Young Black Americans and the Criminal Justice System: Five Years Later." Washington, DC: Sentencing Project.

McCormick, Patrick T. 2000. "Just Punishment and America's Prison Experiment." *Theological Studies* 61, no. 3 (September): 508–532.

McLean, Kathryn Taafe, Diane Colasanto, and Cathy Schoen. 1998. "Mentoring Makes a Difference: Findings from the Commonwealth Fund 1998 Survey of Adults Mentoring Young People." New York: Commonwealth Foundation.

Mead, Lawrence M. 1992. *The New Politics of Poverty: The Nonworking Poor in America*. New York: Basic Books.

Milton S. Eisenhower Foundation. 2000. *To Establish Justice, to Ensure Domestic Tranquility: A Thirty Year Update of the National Commission on the Causes and Prevention of Violence*. Washington, DC: Milton S. Eisenhower Foundation.

Moore, John W. 1988. "Locked In." *National Journal* 20, no. 31 (July 30): 1834.

Morin, Richard. 1994. "Redrawing the Face of Crime." *Washington Post National Weekly Edition* 11 (October 10–16): 50.

———. 1997. "An Airwave of Crime." *Washington Post National Weekly Edition* 14, no. 41 (August 18): 34.

Murdock, Deroy. 2000. "War on Drugs Costs American Lives and Liberties." Washington, DC: Cato Institute. www.cato.org//dailys/04–07–00.html. (April 7).

Murray, Iain. 2000. "Juvenile Murders: Guns Least of It." *Christian Science Monitor* (March 27).

Musto, David F. 1973. *The American Disease: Origins of Narcotic Control*. New Haven, CT: Yale University Press.

National Center for Policy Analysis. 1987. "Capital Punishment Saves Lives." Dallas: National Center for Policy Analysis. www.ncpa.org/ea/eama87a.html.

———. 1999a. "Crime and Punishment in America: 1999." Dallas: National Center for Policy Analysis. www.ncpa.org.

———. 1999b. "Background Checks on Gun Purchasers." Dallas: National Center for Policy Analysis. www.ncpa.org.

Office of Juvenile Justice and Delinquency Prevention. 1999. "Minorities in the Juvenile Justice System." Washington, DC: Department of Justice. www.ncjrs.org/html/ojjdp/9912_1/contents.html.

Office of National Drug Control Policy. 2000. *The National Drug Control Strategy 2000 Annual Report*. Washington, DC: Executive Office of the White House, Office of National Drug Control Policy. www.whitehousedrugpolicy.gov/policy/ndcs00/index.html.

Oppel, Richard A., Jr. 2000. "States Move Toward Easing Obstacles to DNA Testing." *New York Times* (June 10).

"Our View: Involvement in Mankind Foils Crime." 1994. *Springfield News-Leader* (August 21).

Overstreet, Mark. 2000. "Firearm Tracers: The Anti-Gunners' Big Lie." Washington, DC: National Rifle Association, Institute for Legislative Action (February 4).

Pastore, Ann L., and Kathleen Maguire, eds. 2000. *Sourcebook of Criminal Justice Statistics*. www.albany.edu/sourcebook.

Quindlan, Anna. 2000. "The Problem of the Color Line." *Newsweek* 135, no. 11 (March 13): 76.

Petersilia, Joan. 2000. "When Prisoners Return to the Community: Political, Economic, and Social Consequences." *Sentencing & Corrections: Issues for the 21st Century* 9 (November).

Poe-Yamagata, Eileen, and Michael A. Jones. 2000. *And Justice for Some*. Washington, DC: Building Blocks for Youth. www.buildingblocksforyouth.org/justiceforsome/jfs.html.

"Prison Construction—Part 2." 2000. *Corrections Compendium* 25, no. 2 (February): 8–15.

Prothrow-Stith, Deborah. 1998. "Revitalizing Communities: Public Health Strategies for Violence Prevention." In *What Can the Federal Government Do to Decrease Crime and Revitalize Communities*. Washington, DC: National Institute of Justice, pp. 59–63.

Radelet, Michael L., and Margaret Vandiver. 1987. "Race and Capital Punishment: An Overview of the Issues." *Crime and Social Justice* 25: 94–113.

Rennison, Callie Marie. 1999. "Criminal Victimization 1998: Changes 1997–1998 with Trends 1993–1998." Washington, DC: National Crime Victimzation Survey. Bureau of Justice Statistics.

———. 2000. "Criminal Victimization 1999: Changes 1998–1999 with Trends 1993–1999." Washington, DC: National Crime Victimization Survey. Bureau of Justice Statistics.

Reynolds, Morgan O. 1998. "Does Punishment Deter?" Dallas: National Center for Policy Analysis.

———. 2000. "The Death Penalty Is Fair and Effective in Texas." Dallas: National Center for Policy Analysis.

Rimer, Sara. 2000. "Life After Death Row." *New York Times* (December 10).

Scheingold, Stuart A. 1984. *The Politics of Law and Order: Street Crime and Public Policy*. New York: Longman.

Schorr, Lisbeth, with Daniel Schorr. 1988. *Within Our Reach: Breaking the Cycle of Disadvantage*. New York: Doubleday.

Schorr, Lisbeth. 1997. *Common Purpose: Strengthening Families and Neighborhoods to Rebuild America*. New York: Doubleday.

Seelye, Katherine Q. 1994. "Accord Reached on Sweeping Bill to Battle Crime." *New York Times* (July 29).

Senate Committee on the Judiciary. 1999. *Crimes Committed with Firearms: A Report for Parents, Prosecutors, and Policymakers*. Washington, DC: Senate Committee on the Judiciary, 106th Congress, 1st session.

Spelman, William. 2000. "The Limited Importance of Prison Expansion." In *The Crime Drop in America*, ed. Alfred Blumstein and Joel Wallman. New York: Cambridge University Press, pp. 97–129.

Springen, Karen. 1994. "Gun Sweeps and Civil Liberties." *Newsweek* 123, no. 16 (April 18): 18.

Stewart, Kate. 1996. "Giving Back Gained Ground: The Clinton Administration and the War on Drugs." National Policy Analysis Paper #15. Washington, DC: National Center for Public Policy Research. www.nationalcenter.org/ht0725.htm.

Stout, David. 1999. "Customs Service Will Review Drug-Search Process for Bias." *New York Times* (April 9).

Stroup, R. Keith. 1999. Testimony before the Subcommittee on Criminal Justice, Drug Policy, and Human Resources of the House Committee on Government Reform. 106th Congress, 1st session, July 13. www.norml.org/recreational/testimony99.shtml.

Substance Abuse and Mental Health Services Administration. 1999. *Drug Abuse Warning Network: Detailed Emergency Department Tables 1999*. Washington, DC: Department of Health and Human Services.

————. 2000. *1999 National Household Survey on Substance Abuse*. Washington, DC: Department of Health and Human Services.

"Supreme Court Blocks Medical Marijuana Ruling." 2000. *United Press International* (August 30).

Taylor, Jared, and Glayde Whitney. 1999. "Crime and Racial Profiling by U.S. Police: Is There an Empirical Basis?" *Journal of Social, Political and Economic Studies* 24, no. 4 (Winter): 485–509.

Taylor, Stuart, Jr. 2000a. "Racial Profiling: The Liberals Are Right." *National Journal* 31, no. 17 (April 24). Lexis/Nexis.

————. 2000b. "Cabbies, Cops, Pizza Deliveries, and Racial Profiling." *National Journal* 31, no. 25 (June 17). Lexis/Nexis.

"There Is More Crime in the Streets than Crime in the Suites." 1999. *Washington Spectator* 25, no. 18 (October 1): 1–3.

Thomas, Pierre. 1994. "The Brady Law: Sheriffs Challenge Federal Authority." *Washington Post* (September 19).

Twohey, Megan. 1999. "The Crack-Baby Myth." *National Journal* 31, no. 46 (November 13): 3340–3341.

U.S. Department of Justice. n.d. *World Factbook of Criminal Justice Systems*. Washington, DC: Department of Justice, Bureau of Justice Statistics. www.ojp.usdoj.gov/bjs/abstract/wfcj.htm.

Van Sant, Will. 1999. "On Pins and Needles." *National Journal* 31, no. 20 (May 15): 1341–1343.

Violence Policy Center. 1998. "Gun Shows in America: Tupperware Parties for Criminals." executive summary. www.vpc.org/studies/tupstudy.htm.

————. 2000. *Handgun Licensing and Registration: What It Can and Cannot Do*. www.vpc.org/studies/lnrcont.htm.

Vise, David A., and Lorraine Adams. 1999. "From Bad to Worse Than We Thought." *Washington Post National Weekly Edition* 17, no. 7 (December 13): 29.

Voth, Eric A., and Melvyn Levitsky. 2000. "Contemporary Drug Policy." *Northwestern University Journal of International Policy* (January 1). www2.druginfo.org./orgs/dsi/Legalizit/DrugPolicy/LegalizationHar.html.

Walker, Samule, Cassia Spohn, and Miriam DeLone. 1996. *The Color of Justice: Race, Ethnicity and Crime in America*. Belmont, CA: Wadsworth.

Whitman, David. 1998. *The Optimism Gap: The I'm OK—They're Not Syndrome and the Myth of American Decline*. New York: Walker and Company.

Widom, Cathy S., and Michael G. Maxfield. 2001. "An Update on the 'Cycle of Violence.'" *Research in Brief* (February). Washington, DC: Department of Justice, National Institute of Justice.

Wilson, James Q. 1993. *The Moral Sense*. New York: Free Press.

————. 1994. "What to Do About Crime." *Commentary* 98, no. 2 (September): 25–34.

————. 2000. "What Death-Penalty Errors?" *New York Times* (July 10).

Wilson, James Q., and Richard J. Herrnstein. 1985. *Crime and Human Nature*. New York: Simon & Schuster.

Wilson, William Julius. 1980. *The Declining Significance of Race: Blacks and Changing American Institutions*. Chicago: University of Chicago Press.

————. 1987. *The Truly Disadvantaged: The Inner City, the Underclass, and Public Policy*. Chicago: University of Chicago Press.

Wintemute, Garen. 2000. "Guns and Gun Violence." In *The Crime Drop in America*, ed. Alfred Blumstein and Joel Wallman. New York: Cambridge University Press, pp. 45–96.

Witkin, Gordon. 1998. "The Crime Bust." *U.S. News Online* (May 25). www.usnews.com/usnews/issue980525/25crim.htm.

Wren, Christopher S. 1999. "Nation's Top Drug Official Proposes Shift in Policy." *New York Times* (December 9).

Wright, Kevin N. 1985. *The Great American Crime Myth*. Westport, CT: Greenwood Press.

Zimring, Franklin, and Gordon Hawkins. 1997. "Concealed Handguns: The Counterfeit Deterrent." *Responsive Community* 7, no. 2 (Spring): 46–60.

# Chapter 8

Applebee, Arthur N., Judith A. Langer, and Ina V. S. Mullis. 1989. *Crossroads in American Education: A Summary of Findings*. Princeton, NJ: Educational Testing Service.

Armor, David J. 1992. "Why Is Black Educational Achievement Rising?" *Public Interest* 108 (Summer): 65–80.

Berliner, David C. 2001. "Our Schools vs. Theirs: Averages That Hide the True Extremes." *Washington Post* (January 28).

Berliner, David C., and Bruce J. Biddle. 1995. *The Manufactured Crisis: Myths, Fraud and the Attack on America's Schools*. Reading, MA: Addison Wesley.

Bierlein, Louann A. 1993. *Controversial Issues in Educational Policy*. Newbury Park, CA: Sage.

Bloom, Allan D. 1987. *The Closing of the American Mind*. New York: Simon & Schuster.

Bragg, Rick. 1999. "Florida to Allow Student Vouchers." *New York Times* (April 28).

Branch, Taylor. 1988. *Parting the Waters: America in the King Years 1954–1963*. New York: Touchstone.

Brimelow, Peter. 1985. "Competition for Public Schools." In *The Great School Debate: Which Way for American Education?* ed. Beatrice Gross and Ronald Gross. New York: Simon & Schuster, pp. 345–353.

Broder, David S. 2000. "Vouchers Failing an Election Test." *Washington Post* (October 31).

Broughman, Stephen P., and Lenore A. Colaciello. 1999. *Private School Universe Survey, 1997–1998*. Washington, DC: Department of Education.

Brown, Cynthia G. 1985. "Is 'Excellence' a Threat to Equality?" In *The Great School Debate: Which Way for American Education?* ed. Beatrice Gross and Ronald Gross. New York: Simon & Schuster, pp. 298–301.

Brown, Ezra. 1985. "I Will Keep My Promise." *Time* 126 (November 25): 96.

Browne, J. Zamgba. 2000. "NAACP Secures School Desegregation Victory." *Amsterdam News* (December 14).

Brownstein, Ron. 2001. "Voucher Deal Takes Shape with Proposal by Democrats." *Los Angeles Times* (February 7).

Bush, George W. 2001. *No Child Left Behind*. Washington, DC: Office of the Presidency.

Campbell, Jay R., Catherine M. Hombo, and John Mazzeo. 2000. *NAEP 1999 Trends in Academic Progress: Three Decades of Student Performance*. Washington, DC: Department of Education, Office of Education Research and Improvement, National Center for Education Statistics.

Carnoy, Martin. 2001. "Do School Vouchers Improve Student Performance?" *American Prospect* 12, no. 1 (January 1): 42–45.

Celis, William, III. 1992. "School Program for Poor Is Failing, a Panel Says." *New York Times* (December 11).

———. 1993. "Study Suggests Head Start Helps Beyond School." *New York Times* (April 20).

———. 1994. "40 Years After Brown, Segregation Persists." *New York Times* (May 18).

Center for Education Reform. n.d. "Charter School Highlights and Statistics." Washington, DC. www.edreform.com/pubs/chglance.htm.

———. n.d. "Frequently Asked Questions about Charter Schools." Washington, DC. www.edreform.com/school_reform_faq/charter_schools.htm.

Center on Education Policy. n.d. *A Brief History of the Federal Role in Education: Why It Began & Why It's Still Needed*. Washington, DC: Center on Education Policy.

———. n.d. *Do You Know . . . The Good News About American Education?* Washington, DC: Center on Education Policy.

"Charter Schools Increasing, Report Says." 2000. *Springfield News-Leader* (February 12).

Chase, Bob. 1999. "Smaller Is Better." *Washington Post National Weekly Edition* 16, no. 30 (May 24): 20.

Chira, Susan. 1991a. "Bush Presses Bill Allowing Parents to Choose Schools." *New York Times* (April 19).

———. 1991b. "Educators Draw Outline for Nationwide Testing." *New York Times* (August 7).

———. 1991c. "Where Children Learn How to Learn: Inner-City Pupils in Catholic Schools." *New York Times* (November 20).

Chubb, John E. 1988a. "Why the Current Wave of School Reform Will Fail." *Public Interest* 90 (Winter): 28–49.

———. 1988b. "To Revive Schools, Dump Bureaucrats." *New York Times* (December 9).

Chubb, John E., and Terry M. Moe. 1986. "No School Is an Island: Politics, Markets, and Education." *Brookings Review* 4, no. 4 (Fall): 21–28.

———. 1988. "Politics, Markets, and the Organization of Schools." *American Political Science Review* 82, no. 4 (December): 1065–1087.

———. 1990. *Politics, Markets & America's Schools*. Washington, DC: Brookings Institution.

Cohen, Adam. 1999. "A First Report Card on Vouchers." *Time* 153, no. 16 (April 26): 36–38.

Coleman, James. 1981. "Private Schools, Public Schools, and the Public Interest." *Public Interest*, no. 64 (Summer): 19–30.

Coleman, James S., Thomas Hoffer, and Sally Kilgore. 1982. *High School Achievement: Public, Catholic, and Private Schools Compared*. New York: Basic Books.

Congressional Budget Office. 1986. *Trends in Educational Achievement*. Washington, DC: CBO.

Cooke, Phillip J., and Jens Ludwig. 1998. "The Burden of 'Acting White': Do Black Adolescents Disparage Academic Achievement?" In *The Black-White Test Score Gap*, ed. Christopher Jencks and Meredith Phillips. Washington, DC: Brookings Institution, pp. 375–400.

Cooper, Ann. 1985. "In the Real World of Education Reform, Vigilance May Be the Key to Success." *National Journal* 17 (March 2): 460–466.

Cooper, Kenneth J. 2000. "For Texas Charter Schools, Shaky Grades." *Washington Post* (October 15).

Cuban, Larry. 1988. "A Fundamental Puzzle of School Reform." *Phi Delta Kappan* 69, no. 1 (January): 341–344.

Daniels, Lee A. 1988. "Study Shows Teachers Still Feel Left Out on Policy." *New York Times* (September 14).

Dellinger, Walter. 1994. "A Southern White Recalls a Moral Revolution." *Washington Post* (May 15).

DeParle, Jason. 1993. "Sharp Criticism for Head Start, Even by Friends." *New York Times* (March 19).

DeWitt, Karen. 1992. "The Nation's Schools Learn a 4th R: Resegregation." *New York Times* (January 19).

Dionne, E.J., Jr. 2000. "Vouchers Guilt Trip." *Washington Post* (March 1).

Donahue, Patricia L., Robert J. Finnegan, Anthony D. Lutkus, Nancy L. Allen, and Jay R. Campbell. 2001. *Fourth-Grade Reading 2000*. Washington, DC: National Center for Education Statistics, U.S. Department of Education.

Economic Policy Institute. 2000. *The Class Size Policy Debate*. Washington, DC: Economic Policy Institute.

Education Trust. 1999. *Dispelling the Myth: High Poverty Schools Exceeding Expectations*. Washington, DC: Education Trust.

Evans, David L. 2001. "Paying Kids to Study? It's Not a Crazy Idea." *Newsweek* 137, no. 6 (February 5): 11.

Feldman, Sandra. 1999. "A STAR Story." *New York Times* (June 6).

Finn, Chester E., Jr. 1985. "The Drive for Excellence: Moving Towards a Public Consensus." In *The Great School Debate: Which Way for American Education?* ed. Beatrice Gross and Ronald Gross. New York: Simon & Schuster, pp. 74–82.

———. 1994. "What to Do about Education: The Schools." *Commentary* 98, no. 10 (October): 30–37.

Finn, Chester E., Jr., Bruno V. Manno, and Gregg Vanourek. 2000. *Charter Schools in Action: Renewing Public Education*. Princeton, NJ: Princeton University Press.

Fiske, Edward B. 1986. "U.S. Education Department Study Reports Best Ways to Teach." *New York Times* (March 1).

———. 1989. "From Bush on Down, a Greater Federal Role in Education Is Sought." *New York Times* (June 22).

Flaherty, Julie. 1999. "Court Upholds Denial of Vouchers to Families at Parochial Schools." *New York Times* (June 1).

Fletcher, Martin A. 2001. "Milwaukee Will Vouch for Vouchers; Parochial, Private Schools Draw Pupils—and Questions About Success." *Washington Post* (March 20).

"Florida Appeals Court Rules in Favor of Voucher Program." 2000. *New York Times* (October 4).

"Florida Begins Voucher Plan for Education." 1999. *New York Times* (August 17).

"Freeze Charter Schools, Texas Panel Suggests." 2000. *Springfield News-Leader* (December 29).

Friedman, Milton, with the assistance of Rose D. Friedman. 1962. *Capitalism and Freedom*. Chicago: University of Chicago Press.

Friedman, Milton. 1995. "Public Schools: Make Them Private." *Washington Post* (February 19).

Glazer, Nathan, ed. 1984. *The Public Interest on Education*. Cambridge, MA: Abt Associates.

Goldberger, Arthur S. 1981. "Coleman Goes Private (in Public)." Mimeo.

Gorman, Siobhan. 1999. "Desperate Measures." *National Journal* 31, nos. 51–52 (December 18): 3598–3603.

"Goals 2000: Educate America Act." 1994. 103d Congress, 2d session.

Greene, Jay P. 2001. *An Evaluation of the Florida A-Plus Accountability and School Choice Program*. New York: Manhattan Institute.

Gross, Beatrice, and Roland Gross, eds. 1985. *The Great School Debate: Which Way for American Education?* New York: Simon & Schuster.

Hartocollis, Anemona. 1999. "Putting Private Education to the Test." *New York Times* (July 11).

Hassel, Bryan C. 1999. *The Charter School Challenge: Avoiding the Pitfalls, Fulfilling the Promise*. Washington, DC: Brookings Institution.

Hechinger, Fred M. 1983. "A Call from the Past for Excellence." *New York Times* (July 19).

Henig, Jeffrey R. 1994. *Rethinking School Choice: Limits of the Market Metaphor*. Princeton, NJ: Princeton University Press.

———. 1999. "School Choice Outcomes." In *School Choice and Social Controversy: Politics, Policy, and Law*, ed. Stephen D. Sugarman and Frank R. Kemerer. Washington, DC: Brookings Institution, pp. 68–107.

Henig, Jeffrey R., and Stephen D. Sugarman. 1999. "The Nature and Extent of School Choice." In *School Choice and Social Controversy*, ed. Stephen D. Sugarman and Frank R. Kemerer. Washington, DC: Brookings Institution, pp. 13–35.

Herrnstein, Richard J., and Charles Murray. 1994. *The Bell Curve: Intelligence and Class Structure in American Life*. New York: Free Press.

"HHS: Early Head Start Shows Significant Results for Low Income Children, Parents." 2001. U.S. Newswire.

Hirschman, Albert O. 1970. *Exit, Voice, and Loyalty: Responses to the Decline in Firms, Organizations, and State*. Cambridge: Harvard University Press.

Hoffman, Ellen. 1985. "Debate over 'Choice.'" *National Journal* 17 (October 13): 2369–2372.

———. 1986. "Reform's Second Wave." *National Journal* 18, no. 37 (September 13): 2165–2169.

Holmes, Steven A. 1999. "Black Groups in Florida Split Over School Voucher Plan." *New York Times* (May 30).

"Infants, Tots Will Soon Get a Boost with Head Start." 1994. *Springfield News-Leader* (November 11).

Jencks, Christopher, and Meredith Phillips, eds. 1998. *The Black-White Test Score Gap*. Washington, DC: Brookings Institution.

Kearns, David T. 1988. "An Education Recovery Plan for America." *Phi Delta Kappan* 69, no. 8 (April): 565–570.

Keegan, Lisa Graham. 2000. "Equity and Accountability in Public Education." *Annals of the American Academy of Political and Social Science* 572 (November): 101–105.

Kirst, Michael W. 1986. "Sustaining the Momentum of State Education Reform: The Link Between Assessment and Financial Support." *Phi Delta Kappan* 67, no. 5 (January): 341–345.

Kozol, Jonathan. 1991. *Savage Inequalities: Children in America's Schools*. New York: Crown.

Lee, Valerie, and Anthony S. Bryk. 1993. "Science or Policy Argument: A Review of the Quantitative Evidence in Chubb and Moe's *Politics, Markets, and America's Schools*." In *School Choice: Examining the Evidence*, ed. Edith Rasell and Richard Rothstein. Washington, DC: Economic Policy Institute, pp. 185–208.

Lehmann, Nicholas. 1994. "Brown, Now." *New York Times* (May 18).

Lewin, Tamar. 1999. "In Michigan, School Choice Weeds Out Costlier Students." *New York Times* (October 26).

Lieberman, Myron. 1994. "The School Choice Fiasco." *Public Interest* 114 (Winter): 17–34.

Lipsky, Michael. 1980. *Street-Level Bureaucracy: Dilemmas of the Individual in Public Service*. New York: Russell Sage Foundation.

Magnier, Mark. 2001. "Japan Wants Its Students to Learn—for the Joy of It." *Los Angeles Times* (February 9).

Miller, Matthew. 1999. "A Bold Proposal to Fix City Schools." *Atlantic Monthly* 284, no. 1 (July): 15–31.

———. 2000. "Private School Vouchers: Introduction." *Annals of the American Academy of Political and Social Science* 572 (November): 91–97.

Moe, Terry M. 1999. "A Look at . . . School Vouchers." *Washington Post* (May 9).

Molnar, Alex, and Charles Achilles. 2000. "Voucher and Class-Size Research." *Education Week* 20, no. 8 (October 25): 64. www.edweek.com/ew/ewstory.cfm?slug'08molnar.h20& keywords'Molnar.

Molnar, Alex, Philip Smith, and John Zahork. 2000. *1999–2000 Evaluation Results of the Student Guarantee in Education (SAGE) Program*. Milwaukee, WI: Sage Evaluation Team, School of Education, University of Wisconsin-Milwaukee.

National Center for Education Statistics. 1991. *Trends in Academic Progress*. Washington, DC: Government Printing Office.

———. 1999. *Highlights from TIMSS: The Third International Mathematics and Science Study*. Washington, DC: Department of Education.

———. 2000a. *Pursuing Excellence: Comparisons of International Eighth-Grade Mathematics and Science Achievement from a U.S. Perspective, 1995 and 1999*. Washington, DC: Department of Education.

———. 2000b. *Digest of Education Statistics 1999*. Washington, DC: Government Printing Office. http://nces.ed.gov.

National Commission on Excellence in Education. 1983. *A Nation at Risk: The Imperative of Educational Reform*. Washington, DC: Government Printing Office.

Okun, Stacey. 1988. "Private Schools' Thin Edge." *New York Times* (April 10).

Olson, Lynn. 2001. "Few States Are Now in Line with Bush Testing Plan." *Education Week* (January 31).

Orfield, Gary, and Johanna Wald. 2000. "Testing, Testing." *The New Republic* (June 5). past.thenation.com/issue/00605/0605orfield.shtml.

Parker, Franklin. 1987. "School Reform: Recent Influences." *Phi Kappa Phi Journal* 67, no. 3 (Summer): 32–33.

Pincus, Fred L. 1985. "From Equity to Excellence: The Rebirth of Educational Conservatism." In *The Great School Debate: Which Way for American Education?* ed. Beatrice Gross and Ronald Gross. New York: Simon & Schuster, pp. 329–344.

Pipho, Chris. 1986. "States Move Reform Closer to Reality." *Phi Delta Kappan* 68, no. 4 (December): K1–K8.

Rasell, Edith, and Richard Rothstein, eds. 1993. *School Choice: Examining the Evidence*. Washington, DC: Economic Policy Institute.

Ravitch, Diane. 1983. *The Troubled Crusade: American Education 1945–1980*. New York: Basic Books.

———. 1985. *The Schools We Deserve*. New York: Basic Books.

———. 2000. *Left Back: A Century of Failed School Reforms*. New York: Simon & Schuster.

Ravitch, Diane, and Chester E. Finn, Jr. 1987. *What Do Our 17-Year-Olds Know: A Report on the First National Assessment of History and Literature*. New York: Harper & Row.

Rees, Nina Shokraii. 1999. "Public School Benefits of Private School Vouchers." *Policy Review* 93 (January/February): 16–19.

Reinhold, Robert. 1987. "School Reform: 4 Years of Tumult, Mixed Results." *New York Times* (August 10).

Rhodes, Steve. 1999. "The Luck of the Draw." *Newsweek* 133, no. 17 (April 26): 41.

Rossell, Christine H. 1990. *The Carrot or the Stick for School Desegregation Policy: Magnet Schools or Forced Busing*. Philadelphia: Temple University Press.

Rothstein, Richard. 1997. *Where's the Money Going? Changes in the Level and Composition of Education Spending, 1991–1996*. Washington, DC: Economic Policy Institute.

———. 1998. *The Way We Were? The Myths and Realities of America's Student Achievement*. New York: Century Foundation Press.

———. 1999. " 'Goals 2000' Score: Failure 8, U.S. 0." *New York Times* (December 22).

———. 2000a. "Better than a Voucher, a Ticket to the Suburbs." *New York Times* (October 18).

———. 2000b. "Judging Vouchers' Merits Proves to Be Difficult Task." *New York Times* (December 13).

———. 2001. "Where 'Scaffolding' Is Raised, So Are Some Sights." *New York Times* (February 28).

Rothstein, Richard, and Karen Hawley Miles. 1995. *Where's the Money Gone? Changes in the Level and Composition of Education Spending*. Washington, DC: Economic Policy Institute.

Rouse, Cecilia Elena. 1998. "Private School Vouchers and Student Achievement: An Evaluation of the Milwaukee Parental Choice Program." *Quarterly Journal of Economics* 113, no. 2 (May): 553–602.

Rushefsky, Mark E. 1984. "Implementation and Market Reform." In *Public Policy Implementation*, ed. George C. Edwards III. Greenwich, CT: JAI Press, pp. 195–226.

Ryan, William F. 1971. *Blaming the Victim*. New York: Pantheon Books.

Sacks, Peter. 1999. *Standardized Minds: The High Price of America's Testing Culture and What We Can Do to Change It*. Cambridge, MA: Perseus Books.

Safire, William. 2000. "Vouchers Help Blacks." *New York Times* (August 31).

Salholz, Eloise. 1986. "Hearts, Minds and Money: The Private Sector Rallies to Keep Kids in School." *Newsweek* 108, no. 9 (September 1): 89.

Schemo, Diana Jean. 2001. "Focus on Tax Break as Support Wanes on School Vouchers." *New York Times* (February 1).

Schorr, Lisbeth B., with Daniel Schorr. 1988. *Within Our Reach: Breaking the Cycle of Disadvantage*. New York: Doubleday.

Shanker, Albert. 1989a. "Our Successful Students . . . Are Not Very Successful." *New York Times* (April 16).

———. 1989b. "Why Are We So Far Behind." *New York Times* (April 23).

———. 1993. "California Vouchers." *New York Times* (August 22).

———. 1995. "A Reform That Works." *New York Times* (July 16).

Smith, Thomas M. 1995. "High School Students Ten Years After 'A Nation at Risk.' " Abstracted from *The Condition of Education 1994*. Washington, DC: Department of Education, Office of Educational Research and Improvement.

Solovy, Dolores Kohl, and Patricia Brieschkeis. 1988. "Yes, Kids Can Stand and Deliver." *New York Times* (May 28).

Stecher, Brian M., and George W. Bohrnstedt, eds. 2000. *Class Size Reduction in California: The 1998–1999 Evaluation Findings*. Sacramento, CA: California Department of Education.

Stedman, Lawrence C., and Marshall S. Smith. 1985. " 'Weak Arguments, Poor Data, Simplistic Recommendations': Putting the Reports under the Microscope." In *The Great School Debate: Which Way for American Education?* ed. Beatrice Gross and Ronald Gross. New York: Simon & Schuster, pp. 83–105.

Steele, Claude M. 1999. "Thin Ice: 'Stereotype Threat' and Black College Students." *Atlantic Monthly* 284, no. 2 (August): 44–54.

Steele, Claude, and Joshua Aronson. 1998. "Stereotype Threat and Test Performance in

Academically Successful African Americans." In *The Black-White Test Score Gap*, ed. Christopher Jencks and Meredith Phillips. Washington, DC: Brookings Institution, pp. 401–427.

Steinberg, Laurence, B. Bradford Brown, and Sanford M. Dornbusch. 1996. *Beyond the Classroom: Why School Reform Has Failed and What Parents Need to Do*. New York: Simon & Schuster.

Stone, Deborah. 1997. *Policy Paradox: The Art of Political Decision Making*. New York: Norton.

Sugarman, Stephen D., and Frank R. Kemerer, eds. 1999. *School Choice and Social Controversy: Politics, Policy, and Law*. Washington, DC: Brookings Institution.

Sukstorf, Marla E., Amy Stuart Wells, and Robert L. Crain. 1993. "A Re-examination of Chubb and Moe's *Politics, Markets, and America's Schools*." In *School Choice: Examining the Evidence*, ed. Edith Rasell and Richard Rothstein. Washington, DC: Economic Policy Institute, pp. 209–218.

*Talk of the Nation*. 2000. "Controversy over Public School Quality and Arguments for and Against Vouchers and Charter Schools." National Public Radio (October 26).

Traub, James. 1994. "Can Separate Be Equal?" *Harper's* 288, no. 1729 (June): 36–47.

Twohey, Megan. 1999. "Desegregation Is Dead." *National Journal* 31, no. 38 (September 18): 2614–2619.

U.S. Department of Education. 1985. "Responses to the Reports from the States, the Schools, and Others." In *The Great School Debate: Which Way for American Education?* ed. Beatrice Gross and Ronald Gross. New York: Simon & Schuster, pp. 391–399.

———. 1999. *Class-Size Reduction Program: Guidance for Fiscal Year 2000*. Washington, DC: Department of Education.

Vars, Frederick E., and William G. Bowen. 1998. "Scholastic Aptitude Test Scores, Race, and Academic Performance in Selective Colleges and Universities." In *The Black-White Test Score Gap*, ed. Christopher Jencks and Meredith Phillips. Washington, DC: Brookings Institution, pp. 457–479.

Vinovksis, Maris A. 1999. "Do Federal Compensatory Education Programs Really Work? A Brief Historical Analysis of Title I and Head Start." *American Journal of Education* 107, no. 3 (May): 187–200.

Viteritti, Joseph P. 1999. *Choosing Equality: School Choice, the Constitution and Civil Society*. Washington, DC: Brookings Institution.

Vobejda, Barbara. 1989. "Public Schools Go to Market, Giving Parents More Choices." *Washington Post* (January 2).

Whitman, David. 1998. *The Optimism Gap: The I'm OK—They're Not Syndrome and the Myth of American Decline*. New York: Walker.

Wildman, Sarah. 2001. "Credit Is Due: Who Says Conservatives Like Vouchers?" *New Republic* 4, no. 493 (February 26): 15–16.

Wilgoren, Jodi. 1999. "Credit Given to Failed Education Goals." *New York Times* (December 3).

———. 2000a. "2 Florida Schools Become Test Ground for Vouchers." *New York Times* (March 14).

———. 2000b. "School Vouchers Are Ruled Unconstitutional in Florida." *New York Times* (March 15).

———. 2000c. "Young Blacks Turn to School Vouchers as Civil Rights Issue." *New York Times* (October 9).

———. 2000d. "A Ruling Voids Use of Vouchers in Ohio Schools." *New York Times* (December 12).

———. 2000e. "School Vouchers: A Rose by Other Name?" *New York Times* (December 20).

———. 2001. "Plan by Bush for Education Focuses on Poor." *New York Times* (January 23).

Williams, Juan. 1987. *Eyes on the Prize: America's Civil Rights Years, 1954–1965*. New York: Viking.

Wisconsin Education Association Council. 2000. "SAGE Report Links Smaller Classes to Higher Achievement." www.weac.org/sage/news/sagereport.htm.

Wise, Arthur E. 1979. *Legislated Learning: The Bureaucratization of the American Classroom*. Berkeley: University of California Press.

———. 1988. "Legislated Learning Revisited." *Phi Delta Kappan* 69 (January): 328–333.

Witte, John F. 2000. *The Market Approach to Education: An Analysis of America's First Voucher Program*. Princeton, NJ: Princeton University Press.

Wyatt, Edward. 2000. "Study Finds Higher Test Scores Among Blacks with Vouchers." *New York Times* (August 29).

Zernike, Kate. 2000a. "Gap Widens Again on Tests Given to Blacks and Whites." *New York Times* (August 25).

———. 2000b. "New Doubt Is Cast on Study That Back Voucher Efforts." *New York Times* (September 15).

———. 2000c. "Judge Affirms Bias Ruling in Yonkers School Lawsuit." *New York Times* (December 1).

———. 2001a. "A Second Look: Charting the Charter Schools." *New York Times* (March 25).

———. 2001b. "Gap Between Best and Worst Widens on U.S. Reading Test." *New York Times* (April 7).

———. 2001c. "Test Results from States Reveal Gaps in Learning." *New York Times* (April 9).

Zigler, Edward, and Susan W. Muenchow. 1992. *Head Start: The Inside Story of America's Most Successful Educational Experiment*. New York: Basic Books.

Zihala, Maryann. 2001. "Some Competition Would Help Ensure Quality of Schools." *Springfield News-Leader* (January 31).

# Chapter 9

Abelson, Ree. 1999. "Women Minorities Not Getting to the Top." *New York Times* (July 14).

Adler, Jerry. 1994. "Innocents Lost." *Newsweek* 124, no. 20 (November 14): 26–30.

Alvarez, Lizette. 2001. "Ashcroft Meets with Black Lawmakers Who Opposed His Nomination." *New York Times* (March 1).

Andrews, Pat. 1995. *Voices of Diversity: Perspectives on American Political Ideals and Institutions*. Guilford, CT: Dushkin.

Angier, Natalie. 2000. "Do Races Differ? Not Really, DNA Shows?" *New York Times* (August 22).

Applebome, Peter. 1997a. "Seeking New Approaches for Diversity." *New York Times* (April 23).

———. 1997b. "Affirmative Action Bar Transforms Law School." *New York Times* (July 2).

Bearak, Barry. 1997. "Settlement Ends High Court Cases on Preferences." *New York Times* (November 22).

Bell, Derrick 1987. *And We Are Not Saved: The Elusive Quest for Racial Justice*. New York: Basic Books.

———. 1992. *Faces at the Bottom of the Well: The Permanence of Racism*. New York: Basic Books.

Bergman, Barbara R. 1996. *In Defense of Affirmative Action*. New York: Basic Books.

Berkowitz, Edward D. 1994. "A Historical Preface to the Americans with Disabilities Act." *Journal of Policy History* 6, no. 1: 98–119.

Besharov, Douglas J. 1994. "Do We Have to Give Up? No, We Know How to Get Smart About IQ." *Washington Post* (October 23).

Bishop, Peter C., and Augustus J. Jones Jr. 1993. "Implementing the Americans with Disabilities Act of 1990: Assessing the Variables of Success." *Public Administration Review* 53, no. 2 (March/April): 121–128.

Boehlert, Eric. 2001. "Why Won't Rush Limbaugh Denounce Ronnie White." Salon.com. www.salon.com/politics/feature/2001/01/17/rush/index.html.

Bowen, William G., and Derek Bok. 1998. *The Shape of the River: Long-Term Consequences of Considering Race in College and University Admissions*. Princeton: NJ: Princeton University Press.

Bragg, Rick. 1999a. "Fighting an Uphill Battle." *New York Times* (June 6).

———. 1999b. "Florida Plan Would Ban Admissions Based on Race." *New York Times* (November 11).

———. 2000. "Minority Enrollment Rises in Florida College System." *New York Times* (August 30).

Branch, Taylor. 1988. *Parting the Waters: America in the King Years, 1954–1963*. New York: Simon & Schuster.

Bronner, Ethan. 1998. "Some Minority Admissions Drop in California." *New York Times* (January 14).

Brooks, David. 1994. "Dark Gray Matter: How IQ Trumps Everything Else." *Wall Street Journal* (October 20).

Bryant, Adam. 1997. "How Much Has Texaco Changed?" *New York Times* (November 2).

Canady, Charles T. 1998. "America's Struggle for Racial Equality." *Policy Review* 87 (January/February): 42–47.

Carmines, Edward G., and James A. Stimson. 1989. *Issue Evolution: Race and the Transformation of American Politics*. Princeton, NJ: Princeton University Press.

Carter, Stephen L. 1991. *Reflections of an Affirmative Action Baby*. New York: Basic Books.

Chua-Eoan, Howard. 1998. "Beneath the Surface." *Time* 151, no. 24 (June 22): 34–35.

Cloud, John. 2001. "Should SATs Matter?" *Time* 157, no. 10 (March 10): 62–70.

Cohen, Richard. 1997. "Affirmative for Whom?" *Washington Post National Weekly Edition* 14, no. 45 (September 15): 27.

Cole, David. 1999. *No Equal Justice: Race and Class in the American Criminal Justice System*. New York: New Press.

Cose, Ellis. 1993. *The Rage of a Privileged Class*. New York: HarperCollins.

———. 1995. "Teaching Kids to Be Smart." *Newsweek* 126, no. 8 (August 21): 58–60.

Cowley, Geoffrey. 1994. "Testing the Science of Intelligence." *Newsweek* 124, no. 17 (October 24): 56–60.

Cummings, Milton C., Jr., and David Wise. 1985. *Democracy Under Pressure: An Introduction to the American Political System*. New York: Harcourt Brace Jovanovich.

Dedman, Bill. 1998. "Home Loans Discriminate, Study Shows." *New York Times* (May 13).

"Denny's Seeks to Be Dropped from Bias Suit." 1999. *New York Times* (October 10).

Dionne, E.J, Jr. 1994. "Race and IQ: Stale Notions." *Washington Post* (October 18).

"The Diversity Project in Texas." 1999. *New York Times* (November 27).

D'Souza, Dinesh. 1995. *The End of Racism: Principles for a Multiracial Society*. New York: Free Press.

Duke, Lynn. 1992. "You See Color-Blindness, I See Discrimination." *Washington Post National Weekly Edition* 9 (June 15–21): 33.

Edley, Christopher, Jr. 1996. *Not All Black and White: Affirmative Action and American Values*. New York: Hill and Wang.

Edsall, Thomas B. 2001. "Parties Play Voting Rights Reversal." *Washington Post* (February 25).

Edsall, Thomas B., with Mary D. Edsall. 1992. *Chain Reaction: The Impact of Race, Rights, and Taxes on American Politics*. New York: Norton.

Ezorsky, Gertrude. 1991. *Racism and Justice: The Case for Affirmative Action*. Ithaca, NY: Cornell University Press.

Farhi, Paul. 1999. "In Networks' New Programs, a Startling Lack of Racial Diversity." *Washington Post* (July 13).

Fischer, Claude S., Michael Hout, Martin Sanchez Jankowski, Samuel R. Lucas, Ann Swidler, and Kim Voss. 1996. *Inequality by Design: Cracking the Bell Curve Myth*. Princeton, NJ: Princeton University Press.

Fullinwider, Robert K. 1997. "Civil Rights and Racial Preferences: A Legal History of Affirmative Action." *Philosophy & Public Policy* 17, nos. 1 and 2 (Winter/Spring): 9–20.

Gallup Poll. n.d. "Race Relations." www.gallup.com/poll/indicators/indrace.asp.

Garcia, Eugene E. 1997. "Where's the Merit in the S.A.T.?" *New York Times* (December 26).

Glazer, Nathan. 1975. *Affirmative Discrimination*. New York: Basic Books.

———. 1997. *We Are All Multiculturalists Now*. Cambridge: Harvard University Press.

Goldberg, Carey. 2000. "Accused of Discrimination, Clothing Chain Settles Case." *New York Times* (December 22).

Gorman, Siobhan. 1999. "The 4 Percent Solution." *National Journal* 31, no. 12 (March 20): 774–775.

Graham, Hugh Davis. 1992. "The Origins of Affirmative Action: Civil Rights and the Regulatory State." *Annals of the American Academy of Political and Social Science* 523 (September): 50–62.

Greenhouse, Linda. 1993. "Justices Plan to Delve Anew into Race and Voting Rights." *New York Times* (July 11).

————. 1995. "By 5–4, Justices Cast Doubts on U.S. Programs That Give Preferences Based on Race." *New York Times* (June 13).

————. 1997. "Tactical Retreat." *New York Times* (November 22).

Guinier, Lani. 1994. *The Tyranny of the Majority: Fundamental Fairness in Representative Democracy.* New York: Free Press.

————. 1997. "The Real Bias in Higher Education." *New York Times* (June 24).

————. 2001. "What We Must Overcome." *American Prospect* 12, no. 5 (March 12–26). www.prospect.org/print/V12/5/guinier-l.html.

Hacker, Andrew. 1992. *Two Nations: Black and White, Separate, Hostile, Unequal.* New York: Charles Scribner's Sons.

Hamilton, Charles V. 1992. "Affirmative Action and the Clash of Experiential Realities." *The Annals of the American Academy of Political and Social Science* 523 (September): 10–18.

Hansen, Suzy. 2001. "Mixing It Up." Salon.com. www.salon.com/books/int/2001/03/08/sollors. (March 8).

Harrison, Bennett, and Lucy Gorham. 1992. "Growing Inequality in Black Wages in the 1980s and the Emergence of an African-American Middle Class." *Journal of Policy Analysis and Management* 11 (Spring): 235–253.

Henry, William A., III. 1990. "Beyond the Melting Pot." *Time* 135 (April 9): 28–31.

Herbert, Bob. 1997. "The Wrong Case." *New York Times* (October 5).

Herrnstein, Richard J., and Charles Murray. 1994. *The Bell Curve: Intelligence and Class Structure in American Life.* New York: The Free Press.

Hirsch, E.D., Jr. 1994. "Good Genes, Bad Schools." *New York Times* (October 29).

Hirschfeld, Julia R. 2001. "Congress of Relative Newcomers Poses Challenge to Bush, Leadership." *CQ Weekly Report* 59, no. 3 (January 20): 178–182.

Holmes, Steven A. 1995a. "Minority Scholarship Plans Are Dealt Setback by Court." *New York Times* (May 23).

————. 1995b. "U.S. Issues New, Strict Tests for Affirmative Action Plans." *New York Times* (June 29).

————. 1997. "Rights Groups Folded on Case in Bid for Time." *New York Times* (November 23).

————. 1998. "Re-Rethinking Affirmative Action." *New York Times* (April 5).

————. 1999. "Black and Middle Class: Both a Victim of Racial Profiling—And a Practitioner." *New York Times* (April 25).

Holt, Jim. 1994. "Anti-Social Science?" *New York Times* (October 19).

Honan, William H. 1998. "Minority Applications Rise at California, Easing Fears." *New York Times* (January 29).

Hochschild, Jennifer L. 1993. "Middle-Class Blacks and the Ambiguities of Success." In *Prejudice, Politics, and the American Dilemma*, ed. Paul M. Sniderman, et al. Stanford, CA: Stanford University Press, pp. 148–172.

Jacoby, Russell, and Naomi Glauberman, eds. 1995. *The Bell Curve Debate: History, Documents, Opinions.* New York: Times Books.

Jamieson, Kathleen Hall. 1992. *Dirty Politics: Deception, Distraction, and Democracy.* New York: Oxford University Press.

Janofsky, Michael. 1997. "Blacks' Story of Harassment Is Backdrop for New Fines." *New York Times* (November 11).

Johnson, Lyndon B. 1965. "To Fulfill These Rights." Commencement address at Howard University (June 4). www.lbjlib.utexas.edu/johnson/archives.hom/speeches.hom/650604.htm.

Johnson, William G., and Marjorie Baldwin. 1993. "The Americans with Disabilities Act: Will It Make a Difference?" *Policy Studies Journal* 21, no. 4 (Winter): 775–788.

Kahlenberg, Richard D. 1996. *The Remedy: Class, Race, and Affirmative Action.* New York: Basic Books.

————. 1998. "In Search of Fairness: A Better Way." *Washington Monthly* 30, no. 6 (June): 26–30.

Kaplan, Robert D. 1998. "Travels Into America's Future." *Atlantic Monthly* 282, no. 2 (August). www.theatlantic.com/issues/98aug/amfuture.htm.

Kennedy, Randall. 1993. "Still a Pigmentocracy." *New York Times* (July 21).

Kilborn, Peter T. 1999. "Bias Worsens for Minorities Buying Homes." *New York Times* (September 16).

———. 2000. "Jeb Bush Roils Florida on Affirmative Action." *New York Times* (February 4).

Kincheloe, Joe L., Shirley R Steinbert, and Aaron D. Gresson III, eds. 1997. *Measured Lies: The Bell Curve Examined.* New York: St. Martin's Press.

King, Martin Luther, Jr. 1963. "I Have a Dream." Keynote speech given on August 28 at the March on Washington for Jobs and Freedom. Douglass Archives of American Public Address. douglass.speech.nwu.edu/king_b12.htm.

Klinkner, Philip A., and Roger M. Smith. 1999. *The Unsteady March: The Rise and Decline of Racial Equality in America.* Chicago: University of Chicago Press.

Lane, Charles. 1994. "The Tainted Sources of 'The Bell Curve.'" *New York Review of Books* (December 1): 14–19.

Labaton, Stephen. 1994. "Denny's Restaurants to Pay $54 Million in Race Bias Suits." *New York Times* (May 25).

Leland, John, and Gregory Beals. 1997. "In Living Color." *Newsweek* 129, no. 18 (May 5): 58–60.

Levinson, Marc. 1993. "Always Open to Its Customers?" *Newsweek* 122, no. 3 (July 19): 36.

Lewis, Neil A. 2001. "Judge Testifies That Ashcroft Willfully Distorted the Record." *New York Times* (January 18).

Lipset, Seymour Martin. 1992. "Equal Chances Versus Equal Results." *Annals of the American Academy of Political and Social Science* 523 (September): 63–74.

Loury, Glenn C. 1997. "The Conservative Line on Race." *Atlantic Monthly* (November). www.theatlantic.com/issues/97nov/race.htm.

Malcomson, Scott L. 2000. *One Drop of Blood: The American Misadventure of Race.* New York: Farrar Straus Giroux.

Martin, Phillip. 2000. "NAACP Prepares Legal Challenge to the Conduct of Florida's Election." *Morning Edition*, National Public Radio (December 1).

Massey, Douglas S., and Nancy A. Denton. 1993. *American Apartheid: Segregation and the Making of the Underclass.* Cambridge: Harvard University Press.

McGuire, Jean Flatley. 1994. "Organizing from Diversity in the Name of Community: Lessons from the Disability Civil Rights Movement." *Policy Studies Journal* 22, no. 1 (Spring): 112–122.

McWhorter, John H. 2000. *Losing the Race: Self-Sabotage in Black America.* New York: Free Press.

Melloan, George. 1994. "The 'Bell Curve' Sells Genetic Science Short." *Wall Street Journal* (October 31).

Mishel, Lawrence, Jared Bernstein, and John Schmitt. 2001. *The State of Working America 2000–2001.* Ithaca, NY: Cornell University Press.

Morganthau, Tom. 1994. "IQ: Is It Destiny?" *Newsweek* 124, no. 17 (October 24): 52–55.

Moore, Stephen, ed. 1995. *Restoring the Dream: The Bold New Plan by House Republicans.* New York: Times Books.

Morin, Richard. 1992. "Brought Together by Outrage." *Washington Post National Weekly Edition* 9 (May 11–17): 37.

Myrdal, Gunnar. 1944. *An American Dilemma: The Negro Problem and Modern Democracy.* New York: Harper & Row.

"The New Affirmative Action Fight." 1999. *New York Times* (August 9).

Nobile, Philip. 2001. "White Pundit Supremacy." Tompaine.com (March 2). www.tompaine.com/news/2001/03/02/index.html.

Olson, Steve. 2001. "The Genetic Archaeology of Race." *Atlantic Monthly* 287, no. 4: 69–80.

Omincinski, John. 1992. "L.A. Cry: 'Everybody's Wrong.'" *Springfield News-Leader* (May 10).

Orlans, Harold. 1992. "Affirmative Action in Higher Education." *Annals of the American Academy of Political and Social Science* 523 (September): 144–158.

Passell, Peter. 1994. "'Bell Curve' Critics Say Early I.Q. Isn't Destiny." *New York Times* (November 9).

Patterson, Orlando. 1998. *Rituals of Blood: Consequences of Slavery in Two American Centuries.* Washington, DC: Civitas/Counterpoint.

Perlmann, Joel. 1997. "Reflecting the Changing Face of America." Public Policy Brief No. 35A. Annandale-on-Hudson, NY: Jerome Levy Economics Institute of Bard College.

Reynolds, William Bradford. 1992. "Affirmative Action and Its Negative Repercussions." *Annals of the American Academy of Political and Social Science* 523 (September): 38–49.

Roberts, Sam. 1994. "Black Women Graduates Outpace Male Counterparts." *New York Times* (October 31).

Rosenbaum, David E. 2001. "Ruling on Disability Rights Called a Blow by Advocates." *New York Times* (February 22).

Ross, Kevin A. 1994. "Letter: Drowning Case Embitters U.S. Race Relations." *New York Times* (November 11).

Rothstein, Richard. 2001 "Where 'Scaffolding' Is Raised, So Are Some Sights." *New York Times* (February 28).

Sachs, Susan. 2001. "What's in a Name?" *New York Times* (March 11).

Sack, Kevin. 2001. "Pressed Against a 'Race Ceiling.'" *New York Times* (April 5).

Sack, Kevin, and Janet Elder. 2000. "Poll Finds Optimistic Outlook but Enduring Racial Division." *New York Times* (July 11).

Sacks, Peter. 1999. *Standardized Minds: The High Price of America's Testing Culture and What We Can Do to Change It.* Cambridge, MA: Perseus Books.

Samuelson, Robert J. 1997. "Poisonous Symbolism." *Newsweek* 130, no. 4 (July 28): 53.

Sanders, Dennis. 2001. "An African American on Being a Republican." www.moderaterepublican.com/Commentaries.htm#Commentary two. (March 3).

Scarr, Sandra. 1994–1995. "What Is Equality?" *Issues in Science and Technology* 11, no. 2 (Winter): 82–85.

Schemo, Diana Jean. 2000. "Despite Options on Census, Many to Check 'Black' Only." *New York Times* (February 12).

———. 2001. "Head of U. of California System Seeks to End SAT Use in Admissions." *New York Times* (February 17).

Schneider, William. 1998. "The Meanings of Affirmative Action." *New York Times* (January 3): 42.

"Secret Service." 1993. *Time* 141, no. 23 (June 7): 19.

Selingo, Jeffrey. 1998. "Affirmative-Action Plan for the '90s? Wisconsin Tries for Diversity Without Numerical Goals." *Chronicles of Higher Education* 44, no. 35 (May 8): A40–A41.

Seuss, Dr. 1961. *The Sneetches and Other Stories.* New York: Random House.

Shapiro, Joseph. 1994. "Disability Policy and the Media: A Stealth Civil Rights Movement Bypasses the Press and Defies Conventional Wisdom." *Policy Studies Journal* 22, no. 1 (Spring): 123–132.

Shatz, Adam. 2001. "The Thernstroms in Black and White." *American Prospect* (12–26). www.prospect.org/print/V12/5/shatz-a.html.

Shipler, David K. 1997. *A Country of Strangers: Blacks and Whites in America.* New York: Alfred A. Knopf.

Simon, Rita J., and Gloria Danziger. 1991. *Women's Movements in America: Their Successes, Disappointments, and Aspirations.* New York: Praeger.

Sniderman, Paul M., Philip E. Tetlock, and Edward G. Carmines, eds. 1993. *Prejudice, Politics, and the American Dilemma.* Stanford, CA: Stanford University Press.

Sollors, Werner. 2000. *Interracialism: Black-White Intermarriage in American History, Literature, and Law.* New York: Oxford University Press.

Springer, Ann. 2001."An Update on Affirmative Action in Higher Education: A Current Legal Overview." Washington, DC: American Association of University Professors. www.aaup.org/aaintro.htm (January).

Stanfield, Rochelle L. 1997. "Affirmative Inaction." *National Journal* 29, no. 28 (July 12): 1414–1417.

Staples, Brent. 1994a. "The 'Scientific' War on the Poor." *New York Times* (October 28).

———. 1994b. "The Cruelest Game: Review of *The Last Shot* by Darey Frey." *New York Times Book Review* (November 13): 1, 66–67.

———. 1999. "California Schools, After Affirmative Action." *New York Times* (August 23).

Steele, Claude M. 1999. "Thin Ice: 'Stereotype Threat' and Black College Students." *Atlantic Monthly* 284, no. 2 (August): 44–54.

Steele, Shelby. 1990. *The Content of Our Character: A New Vision of Race in America*. New York: HarperCollins.

———. 1995. "How Liberals Lost Their Virtue Over Race." *Newsweek* 125, no. 2 (January 9): 41–42.

———. 1998. *A Dream Deferred: The Second Betrayal of Black Freedom in America*. New York: HarperCollins.

Steinberg, Jacques. 2000. "Defending Affirmative Action with Social Science." *New York Times* (December 17).

Sullivan, Kathleen M. 1997. "Getting Around the Supreme Court." *Washington Post National Weekly Edition* 15, no. 7 (December 15): 21.

———. 2000. "One Nation, One Standard Way to Ballot." *New York Times* (November 15).

Suro, Roberto, and Michael A. Fletcher. 1999. "75 Percent of Military's Minorities See Racism; In Survey, Whites Offer Drastically Different View." *Washington Post* (November 23).

Taub, James. 1998. "Nathan Glazer Changes His Mind, Again." *New York Times Magazine* (June 28): 22–25.

Taylor, Stuart, Jr. 1999a. "Racial Profiling: The Liberals Are Right." *National Journal* 31, no. 17 (April 24): 1084–1085.

———. 1999b. "The Shame of the Ronnie White Vote." *National Journal* 31, no. 42 (October 16): 2949–2950.

———. 1999c. "Seeking Diversity Without Racial Preferences." *National Journal* 31, no. 47 (November 20): 3368–3369.

———. 2001. "A Character Assassin Should Not Be Attorney General." *National Journal* 33, no. 2 (January 13): 78–79.

Thernstrom, Stephan, and Abigail Thernstrom. 1997. *America in Black and White: One Nation, Indivisible*. New York: Simon & Schuster.

Thornton, Russell. 2001. "What the Census Doesn't Count." *New York Times* (March 23).

Treaster, Joseph B. 2000. "Insurer Agrees It Overcharged Black Clients." *New York Times* (June 22).

U.S. Census Bureau. 2000. *Statistical Abstract of the United States 2000*. Washington, DC: Government Printing Office.

Verhovek, Sam Howe. 1997a. "Houston Vote Underlined Complexity of Rights Issue." *New York Times* (November 6).

———. 1997b. "In Poll, Americans Reject Means but Not Ends of Racial Diversity." *New York Times* (December 14).

Wade, Nicholas. 1998. "Gene Linked to High I.Q. Is Reported Found with New Technique." *New York Times* (May 14).

Wilgoren, Jodi, 2001. "Law School Wins Reprieve on Admissions Policy." *New York Times* (April 6).

Will, George F. 2001. "The Ultimate Emancipation." *Newsweek* 132, no. 10 (March 5): 64.

Williams, Juan. 1987. *Eyes on the Prize: America's Civil Rights Years, 1954–1965*. New York: Viking.

Wills, Garry. 1992. *Lincoln at Gettysburg: The Words That Remade America*. New York: Simon & Schuster.

Worth, Robert. 1998. "Beyond Racial Preferences." *The Washington Monthly* 30, no. 3 (March): 28–33.

Zachary, G. Pascal. 1997. "Needs, as a Substitute for Race Preferences, Is Just as Hot an Issue." *Wall Street Journal* (April 10).

# Chapter 10

"Affirmative Action: The Public Reaction." 1995. *USA Today* (March 24).

Clines, Francis X. 2001. "Blacks in Cincinnati Hear Echoes Amid the Violence." *New York Times* (April 14).

Cohen, Sarah, and D'Vera Cohn. 2001. "Racial Integration's Shifting Patterns." *Washington Post* (April 1).

Dudley, R. Adams, and Harold S. Luft. 2001. "Managed Care in Transition." *New England Journal of Medicine* 344 no. 14 (April 5): 1087–1092.

Easterbrook, Gregg. 1999. "America the O.K." *New Republic* 4381–4382 (January 4 and 11): 19–24.

Enos, Gary. 2001. "Heading for a Hemorrhage." *Governing* 14, no. 7 (April): 43–45.

Glaeser, Edward L., and Jacob L. Vigdor. 2001. *Racial Segregation in the 2000 Census: Promising News*. Washington, DC: Center on Urban and Metropolitan Policy, Brookings Institution.

Gillon, Steven M. 2000. *That's Not What We Meant to Do: Reform and Its Unintended Consequences in Twentieth-Century America*. New York: Norton.

Haass, Richard N. 1997a. *The Reluctant Sheriff: The United States After the Cold War*. New York: Council on Foreign Relations.

Huntington, Samuel P. 1993a. "The Clash of Civilizations?" *Foreign Affairs* 72, no. 6 (Summer): 22–49.

Kelman, Steven. 1987. *Making Public Policy: A Hopeful View of American Government*. New York: Basic Books.

Lantigua, John. 2001. "How the GOP Gamed the System in Florida." *Nation* 272, no. 17 (April 30). www.thenation.com.

Lemonick, Michael D. 2001. "Life in the Greenhouse." *Time* 157, no. 14 (April 9): 24–29.

Patel, Kant, and Mark E. Rushefsky. 1999. *Health Care Politics and Policy in America*. Armonk, NY: M.E. Sharpe.

Samuelson, Robert J. 2000. "The Lessons of Tough Love." *Newsweek* (September 4).

Solomon, Burt. 2001. "Oops!" *National Journal* 33, no. 11 (March 17): 770–777.

# Index

**Mark E. Rushefsky** (PhD, SUNY/Binghamton) is a professor of Political Science at Southwest Missouri State University. *Public Policy in the United States: At the Dawn of the Twenty-First Century*, 3rd ed., draws from his more than twenty-five years teaching public policy courses and his experiences as a caseworker in the New York City Department of Social Services. He is also a member of the Springfield Police Civilian Advisory Board.

Dr. Rushefsky has written extensively in a variety of public policy areas, such as health, energy, and the environment. His works include the critically acclaimed *Making Cancer Policy* (1986), *Health Care Politics and Policy in America*, 2nd ed. (1999) (with Kant Patel), and *Politics, Power and Policy Making: The Case of Health Care Reform in the 1990s* (1998) (with Kant Patel).

Dr. Rushefsky has been married for thirty-two years (to the same person!). His wife, Cynthia, is a career prosecutor, serving in her current position in the Greene County Prosecutor's Office since 1986. He and his wife have two daughters.